HIGH COURT
CASE SUMMARIES

Editor in Chief **Dana L. Blatt, J.D., Esq.**

Managing Editor **Marie H. Stedman**

Written By **Alex Vinnitsky, J.D., Esq.**
Annette L. Anderson, J.D., Esq.
Sunil Gupta, J.D., Esq.
John M. Huberty, J.D., Esq.
Jennifer Weinzierl, J.D., Esq.
Daniel R. Dinger, J.D., Esq.
Susannah J. May, J.D., Esq.
Phillip J. Valdivia, J.D., Esq.
Jennifer L. McDonough, J.D., Esq.

Memory Graphics By **Norman Vance**

Cover Illustration and Page Design By **Terri Asher**

Chief Administrator **Richard A. Strober**

Keyed to Kadish and Schulhoffer's Casebook on Criminal Law, 7th Edition

Published By **WEST GROUP**
610 Opperman Drive
Eagan, MN
55123

Copyright © 2001 West Group
       610 Opperman Drive
       P.O. Box 64526
       St. Paul, MN 55164-0526

ISBN 0-314-25820-5

Printed in the United States of America

1st reprint 2003

A Message from Dana L. Blatt, J.D., Editor In Chief
High Court Case Summaries

As Editor in Chief of High Court Case Summaries, I am pleased to be associated with West and its tradition of providing the highest quality law student study aids such as Nutshells, Hornbooks, the Black Letter Series, and Sum and Substance products. I am also pleased that West, as the new publisher of High Court Case Summaries, will continue its tradition of providing students with the best quality student briefs available today. When you use these High Court Case Summaries, you will know that you have the advantage of using the best-written and most comprehensive student briefs available, with the most thorough analyses. Law students cannot afford to waste a minute of their time. That's why you need High Court Case Summaries. You'll find that with High Court you not only save time, but also have the competitive edge with our exclusive features such as memory graphics, "party lines," overview outlines, and case vocabulary. The following two pages will introduce you to the format of a High Court Brief.

Dana L. Blatt, J.D., Editor In Chief

FORMAT FOR A HIGH COURT BRIEF

THE HEADNOTE

Like a headline in a newspaper, the headnote provides you with a brief statement highlighting the importance of the case to the course.

"PARTY" LINE

A quick memory aid. For instantaneous recollection of the names of the parties and their relationship to each other.

MEMORY GRAPHIC

"A picture is worth a thousand words." Our professional cartoonists have created an entertaining "picture of the facts." To assist you in remembering what a particular case is about, simply glance at the picture.

INSTANT FACTS

Another great memory aid. A quick scan of a single sentence will instantly remind you of all of the facts of the case.

BLACK LETTER RULE

This section contains the single most important rule of the case (determined by reference to the chapter of the casebook where the case can be found). Read together with instant facts, you have a perfect mini brief.

CASE VOCABULARY

Every new or unusual legal, Latin or English word found in the original case is briefly defined in this section. This timesaver eliminates constant references to separate dictionaries.

PROCEDURAL BASIS

In a single sentence we summarize what happened, procedurally, to cause the case to be on appeal.

FACTS

"Just the facts ma'am..." Our facts are clearer and easier to understand than the original case. In fact, you can have a complete understanding of the original case without ever having to read it. Just read our brief.

ISSUE

Utilizing our I.R.A.C. format (Issue, Rule, Application, Conclusion), we put it all in focus by simply stating the single most important question of every case.

DECISION AND RATIONALE

We know you need to understand the rationale of every case to learn the law. In a clear, concise, and meticulous fashion we lay it all out for you. We do the work of separating what is important from what is not. Yet, we provide you with a thorough summary of every essential element of every case. Every concurrence and dissent is summarized as well.

ANALYSIS

We provide you with an extensive analysis of every single case. Here you will learn what you want to know about every case. What is the history or background of the litigation? What do authorities say about the opinion? How does it fit in with the course? How does each case compare with others in the casebook? Is it a majority or minority opinion? What is the importance of the case and why did the casebook author choose to include it as a major opinion in the casebook? What types of things will the professor be asking about the case? What will be said about the opinion in class? Will people criticize or applaud it? What would you want to say about the case if called upon in class to brief it? In other words, what are the "secret" essential things that one must know and understand about each case in order to do well in the course? We answer these and many other questions for you. Nobody else comes close to giving you the in-depth analysis that we give!

A Great All-Around Study Aid!

Henningsen v. Bloomfield Motors, Inc.

(Auto Purchaser) v. (Auto Dealer)

32 N.J. 358, 161 A.2d 69 (N.J. 1960)

M E M O R Y G R A P H I C

Instant Facts

An automobile purchaser sued the dealer and manufacturer for breach of an implied warranty of merchantability, although the express contractual terms of the sale disclaimed all implied warranties.

Black Letter Rule

A contract of adhesion does not trump statutory implied warranties of merchantability.

Case Vocabulary

CAVEAT EMPTOR: Let the buyer beware.

CONTRACT OF ADHESION: A contract between parties of unequal bargaining position, where the buyer must "take it or leave it."

IMPLIED WARRANTY OF MERCHANTABILITY: A warranty that means that the thing sold must be reasonably fit for the general purpose for which it is manufactured and sold.

Procedural Basis: Certification to New Jersey Supreme Court of appeal of judgment awarding damages for breach of implied warranty.

Facts: Mr. Henningsen purchased a car from Bloomfield Motors Inc. (D), a retail dealer. The car had been manufactured by Chrysler Corporation (D). Mr. Henningsen gave the car to his wife for Christmas. Mrs. Henningsen (P) was badly injured a few days later when the steering gear failed and the car turned right into a wall. When he purchased the car, Mr. Henningsen signed a contract without reading the fine print. The fine print contained a "warranty" clause which disclaimed all implied warranties and which granted an express warranty for all defects within 90 days or 4000 miles, whichever came first. Mrs. Henningsen (P) sued Bloomfield (D) and Chrysler (D). The trial court dismissed her negligence counts but ruled for Mrs. Henningsen (P) based on the implied warranty of merchantability. Bloomfield (D) and Chrysler (D) appealed.

Issue: Does a contract of adhesion trump statutory implied warranties of merchantability?

Decision and Rationale: (Francis, J.) No. A contract of adhesion does not trump statutory implied warranties of merchantability. In order to ameliorate the harsh effects of the doctrine of caveat emptor, most states have imposed an implied warranty of merchantability on all sales transactions. This warranty simply means that the thing sold must be reasonably fit for the general purpose for which it is manufactured and sold. The warranty extends to all foreseeable users of the product, not merely those in privity of contract with the seller. In order to avoid the implied warranty obligations, many manufacturers, including Chrysler (D) and all other automobile manufacturers, include an express warranty provision which disclaims all statutory implied warranties. We must determine what effect to give this express warranty. Under traditional principles of freedom of contract, the law allows parties to contract away obligations. However, in the auto sales context, the fine-print disclaimer of implied warranties is a contract of adhesion. It is a standardized form contract, and the purchaser has no opportunity to bargain for different terms. He must "take it or leave it," and he cannot shop around to different dealers because all of them use the same standard contract. Because the purchaser and seller occupy grossly inequal bargaining positions, we feel that justice must trump the principle of freedom of contract. Chrysler's (D) attempted disclaimer of an implied warranty of merchantability is so inimical to the public good as to compel an adjudication of its invalidity. Affirmed.

Analysis:

This well-written opinion presents an excellent exegesis of several areas of law, ranging from products liability to various contract principles. The opinion notes several conflicting interests and principles which the court must weigh. First, the traditional principle of caveat emptor faces the modern doctrine of implied warranties of merchantability. The court has little difficulty in holding that modern commercial transactions require protection for purchasers. An implied warranty of merchantability is imposed in all auto sales transactions in order to protect the buyer. Second, the requirement of privity of contract is weighed against an implied warranty. The court notes that, in modern sales transactions, a warranty safeguards all consumers of a product, not merely those in direct contractual privity with the seller. Third, the principle of freedom of contract is weighed against this implied warranty. Freedom of contract is one of the fundamental tenets of the law. Parties should be free to contract for any provisions, and generally parties are bound by the terms of their contract. However, an important exception exists when a contract is one of adhesion. Contracts of adhesion typically involve terms in fine print, written by a powerful seller to limit liabilities or impose responsibilities upon an unsuspecting buyer. No bargaining occurs for these terms, and indeed the buyer is in no position to bargain. If the buyer attempts to change the terms of the contract, the seller simply will not complete the transaction. In order for a contract to be considered "adhesive" or "unconscionable," the buyer usually has nowhere else to go. As in the case at bar, all sellers of a particular type of goods may include similar terms in their adhesive contracts. Weighing all of these factors, a court may rule that the express contractual terms are invalid, notwithstanding the principle of freedom of contract. The arguments for and against this approach are easy to see. On one hand, a buyer should not be allowed to benefit from his failure to read the terms of a contract or to attempt to change some unwanted terms. On the other hand, social justice requires that the buyer be protected from an all-powerful seller, especially where the buyer has no other option but to accept the contract as written. All in all, public policy, and not traditional law, shapes this court's opinion.

Table of Contents

Alphabetical Table of Cases

Alphabetical Table of Cases

Chapter 1

The case of *Nix v. Whiteside*, a 1986 Supreme Court case found in this chapter, deals with the murder of one Calvin Love by the defendant, Emanuel Whiteside. Another case detailed in this chapter, the 1930 New York Court of Appeals case of *People v. Zackowitz*, addressed the 1929 murder of Frank Coppola at the hands of Joseph Zackowitz. While both Whiteside and Zackowitz were eventually sent to prison for their crimes, a number of steps had to be followed first. More specifically, their guilt had to be established through the proper channels.

Our criminal justice system involves three distinct groups, each separate though not independent of the other two: the police, the courts (divided into prosecutors, defense attorneys, and judges), and corrections (the prison system). The first two—the police and the courts—are directly involved in the establishment of guilt in a particular case. The case of *Whiteside* is an instructive example.

Whiteside killed Calvin Love with a knife by way of stabbing him in the chest. Soon after Love was killed, the first step of establishing Whiteside's guilt began as police investigated the death. Concluding that Whiteside was the killer, the police then had to arrest Whiteside and take him into custody. At that point the guilt was not established, however. The arrest was certainly followed by an arraignment in front of a judge, a hearing on probable cause, and, in Whiteside's case, a trial in front of a jury. In Whiteside's case, an attorney was hired to defend him at the trial, and the government had its own attorney whose job it was to prove that Whiteside committed the crime.

In most criminal trials, like Whiteside's, certain procedures are followed. In the usual case, the government is given the first opportunity to establish the defendant's guilt, which they must do "beyond a reasonable doubt." Following the presentation of the government's case, it then becomes the defendant's opportunity to either disprove the elements of the crime charged, or to prove an affirmative defense. In Whiteside's case, the defense attempted to prove self-defense. As a part of establishing guilt or innocence at trial, witnesses are called and evidence brought forth. Following the presentation of the evidence by both sides, the jury then deliberates on the case before them, applies the law given to them by the judge (or hopefully they do), and then makes a decision as to guilt or innocence. In Whiteside's case, the jury opted for guilty.

The above is the basic outline of the process in which guilt is established in a particular criminal action. In all cases, the Constitution requires that these (or similar) steps be taken before a person can be punished for a crime. In other words, before a person can be punished for a crime, his or her guilt must be established.

Chapter 1

NOTE: THE PURPOSE OF THIS OUTLINE IS TO ORGANIZE THE CASES SO THAT ONE CAN QUICKLY UNDERSTAND THE RELEVANCE OF EACH CASE TO THE COURSE. NO ATTEMPT IS MADE IN THIS OVERVIEW TO ADDRESS EVERY CONCEPT THAT MUST BE STUDIED. BE SURE TO READ THE ENTIRE CASEBOOK AND/OR OTHER MATERIALS TO GAIN A FULL UNDERSTANDING OF ALL CONCEPTS.

I.   The Structure of our Criminal Justice System
  A.   Criminal Justice Agencies and Officials: The American criminal justice system involves 3 distinct groups, each separate though not independent: police, courts (prosecutors, defense attorneys, and judges), and corrections (the prison system).
    1.   Police: Police officers arrest suspects, but also have the discretion to not arrest.
    2.   Prosecutors: Prosecutors must technically present evidence against the defendant before a judge (at a "preliminary hearing") and before a grand jury before the defendant may be "indicted" (charged), but indictment is virtually assured. Practically, prosecutors decide whether to press or drop cases, decide the charge to be proven at trial, and arrange plea bargains.
    3.   Judiciary
      a.   Magistrates: Magistrate judges are empowered to hold preliminary hearings, to determine whether there is sufficient evidence to hold and charge the accused, but in practice, magistrates usually allow trial with minimal scrutiny.
      b.   Judges: Judges try cases, supervise plea bargains, and sentence convicts. Judges are either elected or appointed.
      c.   Lower Courts: Urban lower courts try "misdemeanors" and "petty offenses," (crimes punishable by under 6 months' imprisonment) and process felony cases' first stages.
    4.   Corrections: Corrections officials imprison convicts, and supervise probation and parole.
  B.   Criminal Justice Procedures
    1.   The basic criminal justice procedures employed in establishing the guilt of a particular defendant, include: the commission and investigation of a crime; arrest of a suspect and determination of whether or not to press charges; a hearing for probable cause; a plea or trial; and sentencing.
    2.   Initial Stages
      a.   Investigation: Crimes are investigated by police detectives. Often, their only clue is a personal identification of the criminal by witnesses or victims. Police may arrest on "probable cause."
      b.   Diversion: Of those arrested, half are released by police, prosecutors, or magistrates, because it appears they are innocent, or there is insufficient evidence to indict/prosecute.
      c.   Pretrial Release
        (1)   Magistrates may release arrestees until trial.
        (2)   Traditionally, released defendants must post a cash "bond," recoverable when (and if) they return for trial.
        (3)   Defendants who cannot afford bond often obtain the money from bail-bond agencies, at a 10% fee.
        (4)   However, pretrial release may be denied on a finding that "no condition [of release]... will reasonably assure the [defendant's] appearance ... and the safety of [others] and the community." *Bail Reform Act of 1984 (18 U.S.C. §§1341-1350); United States v. Salerno* (S.Ct. 1987).
      d.   Guilty Plea: Most defendants plead guilty, after negotiations with prosecutors and/or magistrates.
      e.   Trial: Few cases go to trial; these usually

involve difficult issues.

    f.   Sentencing: Sentencing is done by judges, often by informal standards.

C.   Flow of Cases: Practically, the criminal justice system is decentralized, and overloaded with cases. Participants often have loose discretion in deciding which cases to prosecute, and which to abandon.

II.   The Process of Proof

A.   Overview of Criminal Trial Procedure: Criminal trials generally follow a formally-prescribed procedure where each side, in turn, presents evidence of the defendant's guilt/innocence to the jury.

    1.   Credibility: Guilt or innocence usually turns on factual disputes, and especially on witnesses' credibility, rather than on legal issues. Unfortunately, fact-finders -- the judge or jury -- may be highly biased in evaluating credibility.

    2.   Plea Negotiation: 90% of convictions are obtained by negotiated guilty pleas. Negotiations are usually based on the case's merits.

    3.   Formal Trial Procedure

        a.   Jury Selection

            (1)   Trial begins with jury selection.

            (2)   A "venire" (panel of prospective jurors) enters the courtroom.

            (3)   The judge describes the case and identifies the parties; jurors who are involved personally are excused.

            (4)   Then, the judge or lawyers conduct "voire dire" (witness questioning), to identify bias.

            (5)   The questioner may excuse jurors "for cause" (i.e., bias), or without cause by exercising a limited number of "peremptory challenges."

        b.   Presentation: Next, the case is presented to the jury.

            (1)   The "indictment" (criminal charge) is read.

            (2)   Then, the prosecutor makes an opening statement, outlining the facts to be proven.

            (3)   Then, defense counsel makes an opening statement, presenting the defense.

            (4)   Opening statements are not evidence, merely talk.

        c.   Prosecution's Witnesses: Next, the prosecution calls its witnesses.

            (1)   The defense may object to certain witness statements.

            (2)   The judge must rule on which testimony is admissible, under evidence rules.

        d.   Directed Verdict

            (1)   Criminal defendants are presumed innocent until proven guilty "beyond a reasonable doubt."

            (2)   After the prosecution presents its evidence, the defense may move for a "directed verdict" or "judgement of acquittal," contending the prosecution has not proven guilt beyond reasonable doubt.

            (3)   If this motion is waived or denied, the defense must offer its evidence.

        e.   Defense Witnesses: Next, the defense offers its evidence.

            (1)   The prosecution may then present evidence rebutting the defense's, and the defense may rebut the prosecution's.

            (2)   When both sides "rest" (finish presenting evidence), both sides may make closing arguments.

        f.   Jury Instructions: After all evidence is presented, the judge instructs the jury, sometimes summarizing the evidence, and always giving detailed instructions on the law, to guide the jury's decision.

        g.   Jury Deliberation

            (1)   Finally, the jury "retires" to deliberate and reach a verdict, by substantial majority or (usually) unanimous vote.

            (2)   If the jury cannot agree by the required vote ("hung jury"), the judge must declare a "mistrial," and the prosecutor may retry the case, at his

discretion.

h. Sentencing: If the defendant is convicted, the judge sentences him.

i. Appeal: Guilty verdicts may be appealed upon showing of error.

B. Presenting Evidence

1. Order of Proof: At trial, each side presents evidence of the defendant's guilt or innocence.

   a. Generally, the prosecution goes first, presenting evidence supporting its "case-in-chief."

   b. Then, the defense presents evidence rebutting the prosecution or proving "affirmative defenses."

   c. Then, the prosecution may call/recall witnesses to "rebut" (refute previously-offered evidence).

   d. Then, the defense is allowed "rejoinder" (chance to prove truth of allegations the prosecution attempted to rebut).

   e. Each witness is "directly examined" by one side, then "cross examined" by the other, then "re-directed" (questioned) by the first, then "re-crossed" by the other.

2. Evidence Admissibility: Rules of evidence -- the *Federal Rules of Evidence* (*FRE*) or state evidence rules -- determine what evidence may be presented at trial.

   a. Relevance: For evidence to be "admissible" (used to establish guilt/innocence), it must be "relevant." *Federal Rule of Evidence* (*FRE*) *402*. Evidence is relevant when it is both "probative" (tends to make an alleged fact more/less probable) and "material" (supports/refutes an element of the charge). *FRE 401*.

   b. Privilege: Some relevant evidence is inadmissible because "privileged" under evidentiary rules, usually to protect certain witness interests.

   (1) Privilege Against Self-Incrimination:

      (a) Especially important is the *Fifth Amendment* privilege against self-incrimination, under which no crimi-nal defendant "shall ... be compelled in any criminal case to be a witness against himself."

      (b) Supreme Court caselaw holds this to mean the prosecution cannot require defendants to testify, cannot suggest the refusal to testify connotes guilt, and cannot make defendants disclose incriminating facts.

   c. Prejudice: Evidence will not be admitted if it has more "prejudicial effect" than probative value. Evidence is "prejudicial" if it will affect the outcome of a criminal trial in some way that is deemed improper. *FRE 403*.

   d. Character Evidence: Prosecutors cannot present evidence of defendants' bad "character" (e.g., general malicious tendencies, proclivity for violence/criminality, etc.) unless the defendant makes character an issue. *FRE 404* (evidence of past wrongdoing inadmissible to prove propensity for wrongdoing); *People v. Zackowitz* (N.Y. 1930) (prosecution cannot offer evidence defendant possessed guns to suggest "vicious" propensities); *Michelson v. United States* (S.Ct. 1948).

   e. Other Crimes: Evidence of the defendant's past crimes is inadmissible to suggest he committed the charged crime. However, such evidence may be admissible for purposes other than suggesting the defendant acted in conformity with (bad) character or past misdeeds, as follows. *FRE 404(b)*; *Zackowitz*.

   (1) Signature Exception: If the defendant previously committed crimes so distinctive and similar to the charged crime, such evidence is admissible to prove the defendant committed the charged crime. *Rex v. Smith* (U.K. 1915) (may admit evidence that husband previously drowned 2 ex-wives to prove he drowned third). Even if the defendant

was previously *acquitted*, prosecutors may still offer evidence to suggest he committed those crimes. *Dowling v. United States* (S.Ct. 1990).

(2) Sex Offense Exception: If the defendant is accused of criminal sex assaults/offenses, evidence he committed other sex assaults/crimes is admissible if relevant and not unduly prejudicial. *FRE 413(a)* (sex offenses); *FRE 414(a)* (child molestation); *Violent Crime Control and Law Enforcement Act of 1994.*

(3) Impeachment Exception: If the defendant chooses to testify, the prosecution may cross-examine him about, and present evidence of, his past crimes, for the purpose of impeaching his testimony/credibility.

3. Jury Instructions' Effectiveness: When other-crimes evidence is introduced to impeach, the jury instruction will typically be that previous convictions may be considered only in assessing the defendant's credibility, but not his guilt of the charged crime. However, it is unlikely that juries follow this instruction.

C. Burden of Proof "Beyond a Reasonable Doubt"

1. In criminal trials, the prosecution bears the "burden of proof," meaning it must bring forth enough evidence to convince the jury that the defendant committed the crime charged.

2. The prosecution must prove, "beyond a reasonable doubt," that the defendant committed *each element* of the crime charged. *In re Winship* (S.Ct. 1970) (required by *Due Process Clause*). "Beyond reasonable doubt" is traditionally accepted to mean the jurors must have an "abiding conviction" or "moral certainty" the defendant committed the crime. *See, e.g., Cal. Penal Code §1096; Commonwealth v. Webster* (Mass. 1850).

3. Allocating the Proof Burden

   a. There are 2 proof burdens: the "burden of production" (duty to introduce enough evidence of a fact to put it into issue) and the "burden of persuasion" (burden of convincing the jury the fact alleged is true).

      (1) Typically, the prosecution bears both.

      (2) However, some defenses are "affirmative defenses," meaning the defendant bears the burden of proving it applicable. (e.g., defendant claiming insanity as a defense to prosecution must prove it; the prosecution need not disprove it).

   b. States may not place upon defendants the initial burden of proving their *innocence*.

      (1) However, when the defendant pleads innocence based on an affirmative defense, states may lawfully require the defendant to bear the burden of proving the affirmative defense's elements, rather than requiring the prosecution to disprove them. *Patterson v. New York* (S.Ct. 1977) (killer claiming defense of emotional disturbance has burden of proving it).

4. Presumptions: Sometimes, the law provides "presumptions," meaning that if one fact is present, another related fact is assumed to also be present. (E.g., if a defendant intentionally shot someone in the head, it is presumed he intended to kill, unless he proves otherwise.)

   a. Rebuttability: Some ("permissive") presumptions may be "rebutted" (disproved by preponderant evidence); other ("mandatory" or "conclusive") presumptions are irrebuttable.

   b. Permissive Inferences: Sometimes, when a fact is proven, the jury is instructed that it *may* (but need not) presume a related fact.

   c. Constitutional Limitations: Under Supreme Court caselaw, it is unconstitutional to impose a *conclusive* (irrebuttable) presumption of any required element of a crime. *See Patterson; County Court v. Allen* (S.Ct. 1979).

D. The Jury's Role: In criminal trials, the jury acts as fact-finder, while the judge decides questions of law.

   1. Right to Jury Trial: The *Fourteenth Amendment* guarantees a right of jury trial in all *criminal* cases which, were they to be tried in a federal court, would come within the *Sixth Amendment*'s guarantee (speedy and impartial jury trial for criminal prosecutions). *Duncan v. Louisiana* (S.Ct. 1968) (defendant charged with battery cannot be convicted without jury trial). "Petty offenses," punishable by under 6 months' imprisonment, do not require jury trial. *Baldwin v. New York* (S.Ct. 1970).

   2. Composition: Juries are usually composed of 12 jurors, but larger/smaller juries are not unconstitutional. *Rochin v. California* (S.Ct. 1970) (6-member jury is constitutional).

   3. Voting: Many states require that, to convict, the jury must be unanimous. However, unanimity is not required constitutionally. *Apodaca v. Oregon* (S.Ct. 1972) (unanimity not required; conviction is allowed on votes of 11-1 and 10-2).

   4. Discretion:
      a. The jury has significant discretion to determine whether a defendant should be found guilty or innocent. In federal and most state courts, the jury has the power of "nullification," under which it may disregard the law and evidence to acquit a defendant.

      b. But while juries have this power, which is irreversible, the judge may instruct the jury that it is required to follow the instructions of the court on all matters of law, and need not tell juries they have nullification power. *United States v. Dougherty* (D.C. Cir. 1972).

      c. However, jury nullification is unpopular with many judges, and many later cases permit various tactics limiting it, without denying it completely.

   5. Sentencing Information: Nearly all courts hold juries need not be told of the severity of the punishment should they convict. *Shannon v. United States* (S.Ct. 1994).

E. The Attorney's Role

   1. Attorneys are required to act in a manner loyal to their client. They must also zealously advocate their client's position. Finally, they must keep confidential any communications between themselves and their client, except to prevent crimes. *ABA Model Rules of Professional Conduct Rule 1.6.*

   2. However, an attorney may not assist a client in presenting false evidence, committing perjury, or in otherwise violating the law. *Nix v. Whiteside* (S.Ct. 1986) (defendant's lawyer's refusal to allow perjured testimony is not "ineffective assistance of counsel"); *Code of Professional Responsibility Disciplinary Rule 7-102; ABA Model Rules of Professional Conduct Rule 3.3.*

People v. Zackowitz

(State of New York) v. (Murderer)
254 N.Y. 192, 172 N.E. 466 (1930)

M E M O R Y   G R A P H I C

Instant Facts

Evidence that Zackowitz (D) had guns in his apartment was introduced into evidence.

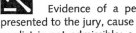

Black Letter Rule

Evidence of a person's character that will, if presented to the jury, cause them to reach an improper verdict is not admissible; a prosecutor cannot present evidence of a defendant's bad character unless the defendant makes character an issue.

Case Vocabulary

PREJUDICIAL EVIDENCE: Evidence is considered prejudicial if it is likely to affect the result of a trial in an improper way. For example, if the evidence arouses the jury to undue anger toward one side, it is prejudicial.
SPHYGMOGRAPH: An instrument used for recording the movements of the pulse.

Procedural Basis: Certification to the New York Court of Appeals of an appeal of a state trial judge's decision to allow a prosecutor to present irrelevant character evidence to the jury in a murder trial.

Facts: On November 10, 1929, Zackowitz (D) and his wife attended a dance where he became quite drunk. While walking home, the two encountered a group of young men on the side of the road, trying to fix a car. While Zackowitz (D) stopped to pick up a newspaper, one of the young men propositioned Zackowitz's wife, which caused her great distress. When Zackowitz (D) found out what had happened, he threatened the young men, claiming that "if they did not get out of there in five minutes, he would come back and bump them all off." After convincing his wife to tell him more of what happened, and becoming angrier in the process, Zackowitz (D) returned to the scene with a pistol in his pocket. Words and blows followed, and Frank Coppola, one of the young men, was shot and killed. At trial, the prosecutor showed the jury a number of weapons that Zackowitz (D) kept in his apartment, none of which had been used to perpetrate the crime. The prosecution also put forth evidence of Zackowitz's (D) "vicious and dangerous propensities." Zackowitz (D) was convicted of the crime and appealed.

Issue: As a part of its case-in-chief, can the prosecution in a criminal case put forth evidence of a defendant's poor character?

Decision and Rationale: (Cardozo, J.) No. At the trial, the vital question was Zackowitz's (D) state of mind at the time of the homicide—whether he killed with premeditation or in the heat of the moment. In such a case, the jury has the duty of getting into the mind of the defendant, to decide what exactly he was thinking. Doing so is difficult enough without a blurring of the issues by evidence illegally admitted and carrying with it in its admission an appeal to prejudice and passion. Such evidence was admitted here. From the beginning of the trial, the People (P) began the endeavor to load Zackowitz (D) down with the burden of an evil character. He was put before the jury as a man of murderous disposition, and to that end the People (P) were allowed to prove that at the time of the encounter, he had in his apartment a radio box, three pistols, and a teargas gun, none of which were involved in the crime. The purpose of this irrelevant evidence was to persuade the jury that Zackowitz (D) was a man of vicious and dangerous propensities, who because of these propensities was more likely to kill with deliberate and premeditated design than a man of irreproachable life and amiable manners. If a murderous propensity may be proved against a defendant as one of the tokens of his guilt, a rule of criminal evidence, long believed to be of fundamental importance for the protection of the innocent, must first be declared away. For long has it been the rule that character is never an issue in a criminal prosecution unless the defendant chooses to make it one. The natural and inevitable tendency of the tribunal—whether judge or jury—is to give excessive weight to the vicious record of crime thus exhibited, and either to allow it to bear too strongly on the present charge, or to take the proof of it as justifying a condemnation irrespective of guilt of the present charge. The endeavor was to generate an atmosphere of professional criminality, and that is unfair. Reversed.

Dissent: (Pound, J.) The real question here is whether the matter relied on has such a connection with the crime charged as to be admissible on any ground. If Zackowitz (D) had been arrested at the time of the killing and these weapons had been found on his person, the People (P) would not have been barred from proving that fact, and the further fact that they were nearby in his apartment should not preclude the proof as bearing on the entire deed of which the act charged forms a part. Defendant was presented to the jury as a man having dangerous weapons in his possession, making a selection therefrom and going forth to put into execution his threats to kill; not as a man of a dangerous disposition in general, but as one who, having an opportunity to select a weapon to carry out his threats, proceeded to do so.

Analysis:

The basic rule of *Zackowitz*—that evidence of other crimes or actions brought forth to show bad character may not be introduced to a finder of fact to demonstrate that because of malicious propensities a defendant is more likely to have committed the charged offense—is embodied in federal statutory law as well as in case law. Today, Federal Rules of Evidence 403 and 404 embody this principle. In *Michelson v. United States*, the Supreme Court articulated the reasons behind the rule: "The inquiry is not rejected because character is irrelevant; on the contrary it is said to weigh too much with the jury and to so overpersuade them as to prejudice one with a bad general record and deny him a fair opportunity to defend against a particular charge." Thus, the purpose of the rule is to protect a criminal defendant from evidence that is likely to arouse the undue hostility of the jury and affect the result of the trial in some improper way. In sum, the purpose is to provide the defendant with a fair trial on the merits of the case before the court, not any other case. Further, the rule serves to keep the focus of the trial on the crime charged. If the prosecution were free to delve into myriad crimes, or the defendant to focus great attention on explaining away past actions, the focus of the jury may well leave the place that it should be—the trial, and crime, at hand. Finally, the rule serves to protect a defendant who has already paid his debt to society from being convicted for the charged crime based on past evidence; it allows certain past crimes to remain in the past.

Patterson v. New York

(Jealous Estranged Husband) v. (State)
(1977) 432 U.S. 197

M E M O R Y   G R A P H I C

Instant Facts

The Supreme Court upheld the second-degree murder conviction (of an estranged husband who killed his (soon-to-be) ex-wife's boyfriend) stating that it did not violate due process for defendant to have to affirmatively show he acted under extreme emotional disturbance [which the jury didn't buy].

Black Letter Rule

A state may require a defendant to bear the burden of proving to a jury that he should not be found guilty of the crime charged because he has a valid affirmative defense.

Case Vocabulary

AFFIRMATIVE DEFENSE: A legal defense that, when proved, relieves the accused from the responsibility for his otherwise criminal conduct.

MITIGATING CIRCUMSTANCES: The extenuating circumstances which surround illegal conduct which may lessen the severity of the punishment.

Procedural Basis: The Supreme Court upheld New York Court of Appeals judgment finding state statute constitutional and convicting defendant.

Facts: Patterson (D) was estranged from his wife (Roberta) after a short and unstable marriage. Roberta resumed a relationship with John Northrup (Northrup) to whom she was at one time engaged. Patterson (D) borrowed a rifle, went to his father-in-law's house, and through a window saw Roberta (partially undressed) and Northrup together. He entered the house and shot Northrup in the head twice which [of course] killed him. Patterson (D) was charged with second degree murder. There are two elements to New York's (P) statute, 1.) Intent to cause the death of another person, and 2.) Causing the death of such person or of a third person. New York (P) also has a manslaughter statute under which "a person is guilty of manslaughter if he intentionally kills another person under circumstances which do no constitute murder because he acts under the influence of extreme emotional disturbance for which there was a reasonable explanation or excuse." Extreme emotional disturbance is an affirmative defense in New York. Although Patterson (D) confessed to the killing, at trial he raised this defense. The jury was instructed that if it found beyond a reasonable doubt Patterson (D) intentionally killed Northrup but that Patterson (D) had demonstrated by a preponderance of the evidence that he had acted under the influence of extreme emotional disturbance, it had to find Patterson (D) guilty of manslaughter instead of murder. The jury found Patterson (D) guilty of second degree murder. On appeal Patterson (D) argued that New York's (P) statute unconstitutionally shifted the burden of proof. The Court of Appeals did not find the statute unconstitutional and upheld the conviction as did the Supreme Court.

Issue: Does it violate a defendant's 14th amendment due process rights if a state requires him to bear the burden of proof regarding an affirmative defense?

Decision and Rationale: (White) No. Patterson (D) argues that New York's statute is the same kind of statute that we recently found to be unconstitutional because it improperly placed the burden of proof upon a defendant to disprove an element of the crime charged. In *Mullaney v. Wilbur*, the charge was murder under a Maine statute which included an element of malice aforethought, whether express or implied. Maine's manslaughter statute provided a lesser punishment for "whoever unlawfully kills a human being in the heat of passion, on sudden provocation, without express or implied malice aforethought . . . ." In *Mullaney*, the jury was instructed that malice could be implied from "any deliberate, cruel act committed by one person against another suddenly or without a considerable provocation," in which event an intentional killing was murder unless by a preponderance of the evidence it was shown that the act was committed "in the heat of passion, on sudden provocation." We held that Maine's statute unconstitutionally shifted the burden of proof from the prosecution to the defendant in that it required the defendant to prove that the killing had occurred in the heat of passion on sudden provocation. While we did hold that under the due process clause the prosecution had the burden of proving *each element* of the crime charged beyond a reasonable doubt, we did not find and do not now find, that the prosecution has the burden of proving the nonexistence of all available affirmative defenses. The case here differs from *Mullaney*. In *Mullaney*, the statutory *presumption* was of malice aforethought. Maine's statute required the defendant to prove that he acted without malice. A defendant is not required to disprove any of the elements that constitute the crime for which he is charged. New York's (P) statute does not shift the burden of proving an essential element of the crime charged. New York's (P) statue only requires that the prosecution show that Patterson (D) intended to kill another person, and did kill such person. There is no malice aforethought element. If an intentional killing is shown it is murder. The affirmative defense of extreme emotional disturbance does not negate any of the elements of the crime. It is a separate issue regarding mitigating circumstances. It is the defendant's burden to demonstrate any mitigating circumstances. Just because New York (P) recognizes mitigating circumstances it is not constitutionally required to prove their nonexistence in each case in which the fact is put in issue. The New York Court of Appeals is affirmed.

Dissent: (Powell) The effect of Maine's unconstitutional statute is no different from the effect of New York's (P) statute. The Court is upholding New York's (P) law which requires the defendant to prove extreme emotional disturbance. The Court struck down Maine's law because the defendant was required to show that he acted in the heat of passion, in order to negate the element of malice. We held that this shifting of the burden of proof was unconstitutional. The Court states that because the burden showing extreme emotional disturbance is written as an affirmative defense, it passes constitutional scrutiny. We struck down the statute in *Mullaney* because it required a defendant to disprove an element of the crime charged. Maine's statute was invalid, the Court reasoned, because it defined murder as the unlawful killing of a human being with malice aforethought, either express or implied. Malice, the Court reiterates, in the sense of the absence of provocation, was part of the definition of the crime. The fact of malice was presumed unless the defendant persuaded the jury otherwise by showing that he acted in the heat of passion. Under New York's (P) statute, there is no mention of the element of, or the fact of malice. The absence of malice is written into its statute entitled as an affirmative defense. The defendant is required to show by preponderance of the evidence that he acted under extreme emotional disturbance. The burden in *Mullaney*, which we found unconstitutional, is the same burden here and should be found unconstitutional. The unstated presumption in New York's (P) law is the same presumption we held unconstitutional in Maine's law. Historically, the prosecution bore the burden of proving factors that made a substantial difference in punishment or stigma attached to the defendant's actions. Heat of passion (of which extreme emotional disturbance is a direct descendent) was an important element distinguishing both punishment and stigma. The presence or absence of extreme emotional disturbance makes a critical difference in being convicted of murder or manslaughter. The prosecution should bear the burden in order to gain a conviction. A legislature's ability to "write around" the requisite elements should not provide constitutional protection to this statute.

Analysis:

Is the presumption in the statute(s) as written and enforced that a defendant is guilty unless he can prove otherwise, or is it that he is innocent until proven guilty? If a statute states, "a person who causes the death of another human being is guilty of murder *unless* he can show that he did not kill with malice aforethought or that he acted in self-defense," it reads as if a person is guilty unless proven innocent. If a defendant claims that he acted in self-defense in killing another person, should the prosecution, in order to get a conviction, have to prove (beyond a reasonable doubt) the defendant did not act in self-defense, or should the defendant have to prove by a lesser standard (preponderance of the evidence) that he acted in self-defense? According to the reasoning in *Patterson*, it depends on how the statute is written. If written "guilty unless defendant can prove otherwise," it is unconstitutional. However, if just the basic elements are set forth in defining the crime ("a person who causes the death of another human being is guilty of murder"), and the rest of the sentence is written separately ("a person is only guilty of manslaughter, not murder, if he can show that he acted in self-defense") and entitled an affirmative defense, the court states it is constitutionally permissible under the due process clause. There are different burdens of proof in a criminal trial. There is the burden of production, e.g., when the prosecution must have enough evidence to bring the charges in the first place, or a defendant claims he acted in self-defense. If the court finds enough evidence to support the claim, it is allowed to be argued in front of a jury. The next issue is who bears the burden of persuasion, that is, who bears the burden of proving the issue to the jury. The burden of persuasion is what is at issue in Patterson.

Duncan v. Louisiana

(Convicted Criminal) v. (State of Louisiana)
391 U.S. 145 (1968)

M E M O R Y   G R A P H I C

Instant Facts

A man convicted of simple battery appealed his conviction on the ground that the State of Louisiana (P) did not provide him with a jury trial.

Black Letter Rule

Because trial by jury in criminal cases is fundamental to the American scheme of justice, the Fourteenth Amendment guarantees a right of jury trial in all state criminal cases which—were they to be tried in a federal court—would come within the Sixth Amendment's guarantee.

Case Vocabulary

PETTY OFFENSE: A crime of minor or no significance, as opposed to a serious crime or felony.
SIXTH AMENDMENT GUARANTEE: The guarantee, contained in the Sixth Amendment, that in every criminal prosecution a defendant shall be provided a speedy trial in front of an impartial jury.

Procedural Basis: Certification to the United States Supreme Court of a Louisiana Supreme Court decision not to review a criminal conviction appealed on the ground that the convicted party did not receive a trial by jury.

Facts: While driving along one day in October of 1966, Duncan (D), a black man, saw two of his cousins on the side of the road speaking with four white boys. Knowing that the cousins, recent transfers to a previously all-white high school, had experienced some negative racial bias at school, Duncan (D) pulled over and encouraged his cousins to end the encounter. As he and the cousins were getting back into the car, Duncan either slapped or merely touched one of the white boys on the elbow (depending on who was asked). He was subsequently tried for simple battery in Louisiana (P) state court. Under Louisiana (P) law, simple battery was punishable by two years' imprisonment and a $300.00 fine. Duncan (D) sought a jury trial, but was denied that right as Louisiana (P) gave jury trials only in cases in which capital punishment or imprisonment at hard labor might have been imposed. Duncan (D) was convicted and sentenced to 60 days in jail and a fine of $150.00. He appealed the conviction, arguing that the denial of a jury trial violated his rights guaranteed by the United States Constitution.

Issue: Can a state deny a criminal defendant a jury trial in state court where one would be guaranteed in federal court?

Decision and Rationale: (White, J.) No. Because we believe that trial by jury in criminal cases is fundamental to the American scheme of justice, we hold that the 14th Amendment guarantees a right of jury trial in all state criminal cases which—were they to be tried in a federal court—would come within the Sixth Amendment's guarantee. Since we consider the appeal before us to be such a case, we hold that the Constitution was violated when Duncan's (D) demand for jury trial was refused. The guarantees of jury trial in the Federal and State Constitutions reflect a profound judgment about the way in which law should be enforced and justice administered. A right to jury trial is granted to criminal defendants in order to prevent oppression and arbitrary action by the Government. Providing an accused with the right to be tried by a jury of his peers gave him an inestimable safeguard against the corrupt or overzealous prosecutor and against the compliant, biased, or eccentric judge. Beyond this, the jury trial provisions in the Federal and State Constitutions reflect a fundamental decision about the exercise of official power—a reluctance to entrust plenary power over the life and liberty of a citizen to one judge or to a group of judges. The deep commitment of the Nation to the right of jury trial in serious criminal cases as a defense against arbitrary law enforcement qualifies for protection under the Due Process Clause of the 14th Amendment, and must therefore be respected by the States. We are aware of the long debate as to the wisdom of permitting untrained laymen to determine the facts in civil and criminal cases. Yet the most recent and exhaustive study of the jury in criminal cases concluded that juries do understand the evidence and come to sound conclusions in most of the cases presented to them and that when juries differ with the result at which the judge would have arrived, it is usually because they are serving some of the very purposes for which they were created and for which they are now employed. Louisiana (P) urges that holding that the 14th Amendment assures a right to jury trial will cast doubt on the integrity of every trial conducted without a jury. This simply is not true. Louisiana (P) also argues that even if it must grant jury trials in serious criminal cases, the conviction before us is valid because it was not a serious case, but a simple battery. We are not persuaded. It is doubtless true that there is a category of petty crimes or offenses which is not subject to the Sixth Amendment jury trial requirement here applied to the States. We need not, however, here settle the exact location of the line between petty offenses and serious crimes. It is sufficient to say that a crime punishable by two years in prison (as this one was) is a serious crime and not a petty offense. Reversed.

Dissent: (Harlan, J.) There is a wide range of views on the desirability of a trial by jury, and on the ways to make it most effective; there is also considerable variation from State to State in use of jury trials. We should not force the federal view of a jury trial on any state.

Analysis:

In the area of criminal procedure and constitutional law, *Duncan* is a very significant case. Its significance stems from the fact that, in *Duncan*, the United States Supreme Court, through the 14th Amendment, extended to the states the obligation and constitutional duty to provide jury trials in all criminal prosecutions other than petty offenses. Prior to this decision, the right to a jury trial in a criminal case was considered to be a right that could only be invoked in federal court—state courts were not required to provide this right. That all changed with *Duncan*, and now states must provide jury trials in non-petty offense trials. Thus, this decision vastly changed the landscape of criminal law. A significant educational aspect of *Duncan* lies in Justice White's explanation of the importance and usefulness of jury trials in American jurisprudence. Among the reasons given in support of the importance of the right to a jury trial Justice White included the prevention of oppression and arbitrary action by the government, a safeguard against corrupt or overzealous prosecutors, and protection against biased or eccentric judges. Further, the jury trial right reflects a reluctance to entrust plenary powers over the life and liberty of citizens to one judge. Thus, this case teaches that the jury trial is not simply a tradition of history employed for no better reason than we have always used it, but it is a critical and fundamental part of American jurisprudence based on important views of the role and power of government.

United States v. Dougherty

(Federal Government) v. (Criminal Defendant)
473 F.2d 1113 (1972)

M E M O R Y   G R A P H I C

Instant Facts

Seven criminal defendants appealed a judge's decision not to instruct the jury that it was free to disregard the law and the evidence and acquit them.

Black Letter Rule

While juries have an unreviewable and unreversible power to acquit a defendant in disregard of the instructions on the law given by the trial judge, there is no doubt that the judge may instruct the jury that they are required to follow the instructions of the court on all matters of law.

Case Vocabulary

CHICANE: Trickery or cheating.
IGNOBLE PURPOSES: Mean, ignorant, or base purposes.
JURY NULLIFICATION: The power of a jury in a criminal trial to disregard the law and the evidence and enter an acquittal for a defendant who might have been found guilty.
SEDITIOUS LIBEL: No longer prosecuted as a criminal offense, seditious libel was libel published with an intention to incite persons to acts of sedition (overthrow of the government or resistance to lawful authority).

Procedural Basis: Certification to the D.C. Circuit Court of Appeals of an appeal of a district court conviction of seven joint defendants.

Facts: Dougherty (D) and eight others were arrested for their unconsented entry into the Washington office of the Dow Chemical Company, and their destruction of certain property therein. After a six-day trial in which seven of the so-called "D.C. Nine" were each convicted of two counts of malicious destruction, all seven defendants, including Dougherty (D), appealed their conviction on the ground that the trial judge erroneously refused to instruct the jury of its right to acquit the defendants without regard to the law and the evidence. The judge also refused to permit Dougherty (D) and the others to argue that issue to the jury.

Issue: Must a trial judge inform the jury that they can, at their discretion, completely disregard the law and the evidence and acquit a defendant in a criminal trial?

Decision and Rationale: (Leventhal, J.) No. There has evolved in the Anglo-American system an undoubted jury prerogative-in-fact, derived from its power to bring in a general verdict of not guilty in a criminal case, that is not reversible by the court. The pages of history shine on instances of jury exercise of its prerogative to disregard uncontradicted evidence and instructions of the judge, such as the 18th century acquittal of Peter Zenger of seditious libel. But while juries have an unreviewable and unreversible power to acquit a defendant in disregard of the instructions on the law given by the trial judge, there is no doubt that the judge may instruct the jury that they are required to follow the instructions of the court on all matters of law. This is because under a republic the protection of citizens lay not in recognizing the right of each jury to make its own law, but in following democratic processes for changing the law. The right of jury nullification is put forward in the name of liberty and democracy, but its explicit avowal risks the ultimate logic of anarchy. The jury knows well enough that its prerogative is not limited to the choices articulated in the formal instructions of the court, and so when the legal system relegates the information of the jury's prerogative to an essentially informal input, it is not being duplicitous, chargeable with chicane and intent to deceive. The limitation to informal input is, rather, a governor to avoid excess. We cannot gainsay that occasionally jurors uninstructed as to the prerogative may feel themselves compelled to the point of rigidity. The danger of the excess rigidity may now occasionally exist, but it is not as great as the danger of removing the boundaries of constraint provided by the announced rules. Moreover, to compel a juror to assume the burdens of mini-legislator or judge, as is implicit in the doctrine of nullification, is to put untoward strains on the jury system. To tell him expressly of a nullification prerogative is to inform him, in effect, that it is he who fashions the rule that condemns. That is an overwhelming responsibility, an extreme burden for the juror's psyche. And it is not inappropriate to add that a juror called upon for an involuntary public service is entitled to the protection when he takes action that he knows is right, but also knows is unpopular, that he can fairly put it to friends and neighbors that he was merely following the instructions of the court. Affirmed.

Concurrence and Dissent: (Bazelon, J.) The majority concedes that the power of nullification is a necessary counter to case-hardened judges and arbitrary prosecutors, and that the exercise of the power may enhance the overall normative effect of the rule of law. The sticking point, however, is whether or not the jury should be told of its power to nullify. Here the judge not only denied an instruction on the power, but also barred defense counsel from raising the issue before the jury. I see no justification for, and considerable harm in, this lack of candor. The justification lies in a fear that occasionally noble doctrine will, if acknowledged, often be put to ignoble and abusive purposes. The Court assumes that these abuses are most likely to occur if the doctrine is formally described to the jury, but it seems to me that the opposite is true. Awareness is preferable to ignorance, and I simply do not understand the justification for relying on a haphazard process of informal communication of the power to the jury. If the jury should know of its power to disregard the law, then the power should be explicitly described by instruction of the court or argument of counsel.

Analysis:

As this case demonstrates, the law still recognizes the doctrine of jury nullification, which is that a jury can, in its discretion, wholly disregard the law and all evidence and acquit a defendant even when, under the proper law and according to the evidence, they should not do so. What the majority further demonstrates, however, is that courts have no duty to tell the jury about its power of nullification. The majority opinion sets forth a number of justifications for its holding, but perhaps more important is the impact of the holding on criminal jury trials. In sum, that impact is that a defendant has no right to tell the jury of their power of nullification, or to ask the jury directly to invoke that power on his or her behalf. Use of the nullification power is something that either side simply cannot bring up in front of the jury. *Dougherty* is the majority rule as most states follow the rule announced in this decision and reject any contention that the judge must instruct the jury of their nullification power. Three states do not accept the *Dougherty* rule. The federal courts follow *Dougherty* as well.

Nix v. Whiteside

(Not Stated) v. (Convicted Murderer)
475 U.S. 157 (1986)

M E M O R Y   G R A P H I C

Instant Facts
A convicted murderer petitioned for a writ of habeas corpus on grounds of ineffective assistance of counsel.

Black Letter Rule
Whatever the scope of a constitutional right to testify, it is elementary that such a right does not extend to testifying falsely.

Procedural Basis: Certification to the United States Supreme Court of an Eighth Circuit Court of Appeals decision granting a writ of habeas corpus on the ground that there had been problems with effective assistance of counsel.

Facts: Whiteside (P) and two friends went to the apartment of one Calvin Love in order to purchase marijuana. While they were there an argument ensued. According to Whiteside (P), Love, having threatened to get a gun, reached under his pillow at one point and began moving toward Whiteside (P). Whiteside (P) stabbed Love in the chest, killing him. Whiteside (P) was charged with murder. At the time Whiteside's (P) attorney, Robinson, first interviewed him, Whiteside (P) claimed that he stabbed Love as he "was pulling a pistol from underneath the pillow on the bed." Upon further questioning, however, Whiteside (P) admitted that he never saw a gun, but that he believed that Love did have one. No one else saw a gun either. Robinson advised Whiteside (P) that the existence of a gun was not necessary to establish his claim of self defense, and that only a reasonable belief that the victim had a gun was necessary. About a week before trial, during the preparation of direct examination, Whiteside (P) told Robinson, for the first time, that he had seen something "metallic" in Love's hand. When asked about it, Whiteside (P) expressed his feeling that, in order to get off, he would have to say that there was a gun: "If I don't say I saw a gun I'm dead." Robinson told Whiteside (P) that to so testify would be perjury, and that it was not necessary to establish the defense. On Whiteside's (P) insisting that he would testify that he saw something "metallic," Robinson told him "we could not allow him to [testify falsely] because that would be perjury, and as officers of the court we would be suborning perjury if we allowed him to do it." Robinson also told Whiteside (P) that if there was any false testimony, he would have to advise the court that Whiteside (P) was, in his view, committing perjury. Whiteside (P) never testified that he had seen a gun, but only that he thought that one was in the house. He was convicted of second-degree murder, and moved for a new trial on the ground that he had been deprived a fair trial by not being able to testify as to seeing something "metallic." The Supreme Court of Iowa affirmed the conviction, concluding that Robinson's actions had been appropriate. Whiteside (P) then petitioned for a writ of habeas corpus in the federal courts.

Issue: Does a criminal defendant have a right to testify falsely on the stand?

Decision and Rationale: (Burger, J.) No. In *Strickland v. Washington* [establishing a standard for effective representation] we held that to obtain relief on a claim of ineffective assistance of counsel under the Sixth Amendment, the movant must establish both serious attorney error and prejudice. To show such error, it must be established that "counsel made errors so serious that counsel was not functioning as 'counsel' guaranteed by the Sixth Amendment." To show prejudice, it must be established that the claimed lapses in counsel's performance rendered the trial so unfair as to undermine confidence in the outcome of the trial. In *Strickland* we recognized counsel's duty of loyalty and his overarching duty to advocate the defendant's cause. Plainly, that duty is limited to legitimate, lawful conduct compatible with the very nature of a trial as a search for truth. Although counsel must take all reasonable lawful means to attain the objectives of the client, counsel is precluded from taking steps or in any way assisting the client in presenting false evidence or otherwise violating the law. This principle is recognized by the American Bar Association, the Model Code of Professional Responsibility, and the Model Rules of Professional conduct. Both the Model Code and the Model Rules adopt the specific exception from the attorney-client privilege for disclosure of perjury that a client intends to commit or has committed; both do not merely authorize disclosure, but require it. This is because perjury is as much a crime as tampering with witnesses or jurors by way of promises and threats, and undermines the administration of justice. It is universally agreed that at a minimum the attorney's first duty when confronted with a proposal for perjurious testimony is to attempt to dissuade the client from the unlawful course of conduct. Withdrawal from representation is also an appropriate response. The suggestion that "a lawyer must believe his client not judge him" in no sense means a lawyer can honorably be a party to or in any way give aid to presenting known perjury. In this case, Robinson's representation involved no failure to adhere to reasonable professional standards that would in any sense make out a deprivation of the Sixth Amendment right to counsel. Nothing he did in any way undermined Whiteside's (P) claim that he believed the witness was reaching for a gun. He divulged no client communication until compelled to do so in response to Whiteside's (P) post-trial challenge to the quality of his performance. We see this as a case in which the attorney successfully dissuaded the client from committing the crime of perjury. Whatever the scope of a constitutional right to testify, it is elementary that such a right does not extend to testifying falsely. Robinson's admonitions to Whiteside can in no sense be said to have forced respondent into an impermissible choice, for there was no permissible choice to testify falsely. Similarly, we can discern no breach of professional duty in Robinson's admonition that he would disclose Whiteside's (P) perjury to the court. An attorney's duty of confidentiality does not extent to a client's announced plans to engage in future criminal conduct. Since there has been no breach of any recognized professional duty, it follows that there can be no deprivation of the right to assistance of counsel under the *Strickland* standard. Reversed.

Concurrence: (Brennan, J.) This Court has no constitutional authority to establish rules of ethical conduct for lawyers practicing in the state courts. The Court's essay regarding what constitutes the correct response to a criminal client's suggestion that he will perjure himself is pure discourse without force of law. Lawyers, judges, bar associations, students and others should understand that the problem has not now been "decided."

Concurrence: (Blackmun, J.) The only federal issue in this case is whether Robinson's behavior deprived Whiteside (P) of the effective assistance of counsel, not whether his actions conformed to a particular code of legal ethics. Whether an attorney's response to what he sees as a client's plan to commit perjury violates a defendant's Sixth Amendment right depends on many factors, and the complex interaction of factors, which is likely to vary from case to case, makes inappropriate a blanket rule that defense attorneys must reveal anticipated perjury. Except in the rarest of cases, attorneys who adopt the role of the judge or jury to determine the facts pose a danger of depriving their clients of the zealous and loyal advocacy required by the Constitution. I am therefore troubled by the Court's implicit adoption of a set of standards of professional responsibility for attorneys in state criminal proceedings. This Court's responsibility is only to ensure that the restrictions a State enacts do not infringe a defendant's constitutional rights, and no more.

Concurrence: (Stevens, J.) Beneath the surface of this case there are areas of uncertainty that cannot be resolved today. A lawyer's certainty that a change in his client's recollection is evidence of intended perjury should be tempered by the realization that, after reflection, the most honest witness may recall, or seriously believe he recalls, details that were previously overlooked. Further, one can be convinced, as I am, that this lawyer's actions were a proper way to provide his client with effective representation without confronting the more difficult questions of what a lawyer must, should, or may do after his client has given testimony that the lawyer does not believe.

Analysis:

This case reveals much about the process of proof and the role of counsel in that process. First, *Nix* reminds us that attorneys are constrained in their actions by rules, written and unwritten, of ethics and ethical conduct. In fact, *Nix* teaches, attorneys are sometimes required to adhere to ethical standards even when doing so is injurious to their client. One such situation, as demonstrated by this case and the model code and rules mentioned therein, occurs when a client intends to commit perjury. *Nix* stands for the proposition that, when a client so intends to lie to the court, his or her attorney has a duty to make sure that the lying or presentation of false proof does not occur. *Nix* also stands for the proposition that rules of ethics are not a nice guideline that attorneys should follow when convenient, but they are to be given serious attention and adherence. A second lesson that *Nix* brings to the forefront deals with the issue of false proof. As the opinion states, there is no constitutional right to present false proof to a jury. This is significant in that it demonstrates that the process of proof must involve only the truth—the process of proof used in criminal trials requires both sides to deal with true facts, and not made-up falsehoods. *Nix*, then, means that attorneys cannot simply make up any plausible story or defense to protect their client from prosecution; defense attorneys do not have free reign to bring in any evidence, true or false, whatsoever. This concept protects juries, or at least is intended to protect juries, from having to sift through made-up falsehoods in reaching a decision on the merits of the case. It further stresses the idea that a criminal trial is, as the majority states, a quest for the truth that should not be marred by lies or trickery. Finally, it is important to note that the commentary to Rule 3.3 of the ABA Model Rules of Professional Conduct describes three proposed resolutions for the dilemma that arises in cases of intended perjury: (1) Allow the defendant to testify by means of a narrative that does not involve questions by the attorney that will solicit perjury; (2) Excuse defense attorneys from the duty to reveal a client's perjury or intended perjury; and (3) Require the attorney to disclose the defendant's perjury or intended perjury only when necessary to resolve the problems caused by the perjury. None of these solutions have been widely-accepted, however, and the view set forth in *Nix* stands as the majority view in such cases.

Chapter 2

Why does society punish convicted criminal offenders? How do you justify the imposition of imprisonment or the death penalty? The primary theories for justifying the punishment of convicted criminal offenders proffered by legal scholars, lawmakers, judges, and attorneys are retribution, deterrence, reform or rehabilitation, and incapacitation. After you become familiar with these theories, you may discover that you were unaware of some of the deep-seated beliefs you use to justify punishing convicted criminal offenders.

For a retributivist, the moral culpability of criminal offenders justifies their punishment. This culpability is a necessary and sufficient condition for punishment. Furthermore, the moral culpability of criminal offenders creates a societal duty to punish them.

The deterrence theory rejects retribution as a justification for punishment. Its objective is to deter the commission of future crimes. The general deterrent approach attempts to deter potential offenders in the general community from committing future criminal offenses. The specific deterrent approach attempts to deter convicted criminal offenders from committing future criminal offenses.

The reform approach focuses on the personality of the criminal offender and the external circumstances affecting his past and future conduct. In essence, this approach attempts to prevent or reduce criminality by attacking or controlling the disease of crime.

The objective of incapacitation is crime prevention. To achieve this objective, collective incapacitation strategies promote imposing identical sentences on all criminal offenders convicted for a designated offense (e.g., burglary or robbery). Selective incapacitation strategies promote individualized sentences based on predictions that particular convicted criminal offenders are likely to commit future serious crimes at a high rate if not incarcerated.

A theory is one thing. The implementation of that theory is another. The institutions that share the authority to impose punishment are the legislature, prosecutor, judge, and parole or correctional authorities. A crucial aspect of this authority is the exercise of discretion.

Another very important consideration when attempting to ascertain an objective or reasonable justification for punishment is the relationship between morality and the criminal law. Should the criminal law become a tool of religious or other groups to promote their moral agendas, or is morality an indispensable component of criminal law? These are difficult questions to answer; nonetheless, society must answer them in a satisfactory manner if it desires to declare that its criminal laws support and uphold justice.

Chapter 2

NOTE: THE PURPOSE OF THIS OUTLINE IS TO ORGANIZE THE CASES SO THAT ONE CAN QUICKLY UNDERSTAND THE RELEVANCE OF EACH CASE TO THE COURSE. NO ATTEMPT IS MADE IN THIS OVERVIEW TO ADDRESS EVERY CONCEPT THAT MUST BE STUDIED. BE SURE TO READ THE ENTIRE CASEBOOK AND/OR OTHER MATERIALS TO GAIN A FULL UNDERSTANDING OF ALL CONCEPTS.

I.   What is Punishment?

  A.   When sentencing a defendant, courts have a number of different forms of punishment from which to choose. These include: death, imprisonment, fine, probation, home detention, labor, and community service.

    1.   Which type of punishment a judge will impose depends on the crime committed, the criminal's background, the rules and statutes under which the judge must work, and any number of other factors.

    2.   Imprisonment generally involves more than the loss of freedom of movement. It entails a deprivation of material possessions, intimate relationships, and in some cases personal security.

  B.   Society often imposes other less formal types of punishment on convicted criminals. These include social stigma, barriers to employment, and the risk of enhanced punishment for future criminal offenses.

  C.   Providing for the punishment of criminals is often a difficult task. Prison violence, overcrowding, insufficient funds, and myriad other problems often cause headaches for those charged with overseeing our prison systems.

II.   Society's Justifications for Punishment

  A.   Introduction: The Purpose of Punishment

    1.   There are two primary types of justifications for punishment. The first is retribution, which involves punishing an offender for past behavior. The second type is more utilitarian, and involves punishment as a means of producing future benefits.

      a.   The utilitarian goals include prevention of future criminal behavior, rehabilitation of the prisoner, and incapacitation.

    2.   Many state criminal codes, as well as the Model Penal Code, set forth one or more of these theories of justification as underlying the purpose of criminal punishment in their respective jurisdictions.

      a.   For example, New York Penal Law § 1.05 states that the purposes of that state's penal law include the prevention of crime through deterrence, the rehabilitation of convicted defendants, and the confinement of convicted defendants in the interests of public safety.

  B.   Retribution

    1.   Many different views exist on the theory of retribution as a justification for punishment:

      a.   The state has a right to punish criminals. This includes the right, in some cases, to inflict pain on criminals. Courts do not merely impose punishment to promote the good of society or the criminal offender. Courts inflict punishment because the offenders have committed crimes. *Immanuel Kant, The Philosophy of Law*.

      b.   It is morally correct to hate criminals, and the criminal law proceeds upon this principle. The criminal law confirms, justifies, and expresses the public's hatred of criminals by inflicting them with punishment. *A History of the Criminal Law of England*.

      c.   Society expresses its disgust for wrongful conduct by punishing criminal offenders. The goal of punishment is something more than a deterrence of crime or a reformation of a criminal offender. The ultimate justification of any punishment is society's denunciation of a crime. *Royal Commission on Capital Punishment, Minutes of Evidence*.

      d.   Punishment is a way of showing disapproval of a person's actions. It is a way of demonstrating a vindictive and hostile resentment towards a criminal; it is legitimized vengefulness. *Doing and Deserving*.

      e.   For a retributivist, a criminal offender's moral culpability justifies his or her punishment. This culpability is a necessary and sufficient condition for punishment. Furthermore, it creates a societal duty to punish the offender, who deserves what he or she gets. *The Moral Worth of Retribution*.

f. Punishment serves to maintain society's cohesion with all of its vitality. It also heals the wounds that criminals inflict upon society. It acts upon and serves the sentiments of upright people. *The Division of Law in Society*.

2. There are also a number of views on the morality of punishment as a means of exacting retribution:

a. The criminal law promulgates rules that prohibit violence and deception.

   (1) Compliance with the rules benefits society as it results in non-interference by others with what each person values (e.g., life, liberty, and the pursuit of happiness). The price of the benefit is the burden of compliance. A person who takes advantage of the benefits but renounces their accompanying burdens acquires an unfair advantage.

   (2) Therefore, punishment provides assurances that those who follow the rules are not assuming burdens others are not prepared to assume. It prevents an unequal distribution of benefits and burdens by inducing compliance with the law.

   (3) Further, it restores the equilibrium of benefits and burdens by extracting the unfair advantage a criminal offender gained when he renounced his burdens by committing a criminal offense. *On Guilt and Innocence*.

b. Punishment should not be inflicted where it is groundless, inefficacious, unprofitable, and needless. *An Introduction to the Principles of Morals and Legislation*.

c. Criminality derives from need and deprivation on the part of disadvantaged members of society and from motives of greed and selfishness that a capitalistic society promulgates. In other words, criminality is both directly and indirectly economically based.

   (1) If a retributive theory of punishment is grounded on justice, is it just to punish people who act out of the motives that a capitalistic society encourages?

   (2) It is naive to hold that people in a capitalistic society comprehend criminal laws as a mechanism for allocating benefits in society.

   (3) Perhaps the only true solution to this dilemma is a radical approach that restructures society in a manner that enables potential criminals to obtain autonomy and the benefits of society. Without this restructuring, it is difficult to hold that society has a moral right to punish criminal offenders. *Jeffrie Murphy, Marxism and Retribution*.

d. Retributive punishment is a means of repaying with harm a criminal offender who caused harm. Morality does not appear to justify this approach to punishment.

   (1) First, the fact that a person suffers the harm of punishment does not mean that he has repaid a debt to society.

   (2) Second, it is inconceivable that punishment serves as an annulment of a criminal offense or in some mysterious way removes its effects from society.

   (3) Third, the idea that punishment conforms with the notion of fair play may be appealing, but in that way it is deceptive.

   (4) Problems arise when one attempts to determine the amount of punishment necessary to level the playing field. The enormity of these problems become clear when one must consider the criminal conduct in relation to the unfair benefit that the criminal offender supposedly gained. Lacking the support of moral ideas, retributive attitudes appear to be sentiments that have emerged and sustained through biological and sociological processes. *Retribution: A Test Case for Ethical Objectivity*.

e. The principle of retribution justifies punishment because a criminal offender deserves punishment.

   (1) The principle of utilitarianism justifies punishment because it achieves a net social gain. Utilitarian principles hold that punishment is deserving if and only if it achieves a net social gain and is given to criminals who deserve it.

(2)　However, this theory is open to criticism because one can construct examples in which society might incarcerate individuals who are known to be dangerous, but who have not committed a criminal offense, because the incarceration can produce a net social gain (e.g., crime prevention).

(3)　Another criticism is that utilitarianism permits a person who committed a grave criminal offense to escape any punishment when there exists sufficient evidence to prove that the person will not commit any future criminal offense. This is because in such a case punishment does not yield a net social gain (e.g., rehabilitation).

(4)　These deficiencies of utilitarianism can indirectly lead a person to discover, to his surprise, that he is a retributivist. *Law and Psychiatry*.

C.　Deterrence (Prevention of Future Crime)
　1.　Introduction to Deterrence
　　a.　The focus of the deterrence theory is the idea that punishment will deter the commission of future crimes.
　　b.　Deterrence theorists distinguish between two types of deterrence: general deterrence and specific deterrence.
　　　(1)　Punishment acts as a general deterrent to criminal behavior when it deters potential offenders in the general community from committing future crimes.
　　　(2)　Punishment acts as a specific deterrent when it deters convicted offenders from committing future crimes.
　　　(3)　The theory of general deterrence and the desire to avoid depreciating the seriousness of an offense support the imposition of imprisonment on one unlikely to commit any crimes in the future (i.e., in a situation in which specific deterrence is not an issue). *United States v. Bergman*.
　　c.　The deterrence theory rejects retribution as a justification for punishment.
　2.　Deterrence Through a Threat of Imprisonment
　　a.　Some people feel that a threat of lengthy imprisonment will have a deterrent effect on people contemplating the commission of a crime. This theory presupposes that criminals will engage in a cost-benefit analysis before

committing a crime.
　　b.　Others, however, disagree.
　　　(1)　Some of those who disagree feel that the threat of severe punishment may deter prosecutors, judges, and others from seeking such a severe punishment for a particular defendant. *James Q. Wilson, Thinking About Crime*.
　　　(2)　Others subscribe to the theory that the majority of criminals are beyond feeling and do not have the ability to weigh the benefits and costs of certain criminal behavior, meaning they will not be deterred by the potentially severe punishment. *James Gilligan, Violence*.
　　　(3)　Still others argue that a severe punishment for a particular crime will cause those who commit the crime to freely engage in more criminal behavior because they are already going to be in prison for life (or a long period of time) anyway.
　　c.　Some commentators feel that an increase in the prosecution of a particular crime will have a greater deterrent effect than an increase in the punishment for that same crime. *Johannes Andenaes, The General Preventative Effects of Punishment*.
　3.　Deterrence Through Social Stigma and Expressive Condemnation
　　a.　Most people will agree that a criminal conviction carries with it a certain negative stigma. There is some disagreement, however, about the value of that stigma in the sense of stigma as a deterrent.
　　　(1)　Some people feel that the negative stigma that accompanies a criminal conviction is a valuable deterrent against future crime. *Dan M. Kahan, What do Alternative Sanctions Mean?*
　　　(2)　Others, however, will argue that severe negative stigma will either cause a criminal to associate himself with those who do not see such a stigma (e.g., other criminals) or will cause him or her to react violently when the stigma arises. *Toni M. Massaro, Shame, Culture, and American Criminal Law; James Gilligan, Violence*.
　　b.　Some commentators have condemned the formal use of shaming sanctions for criminal

offenders because they are not the type of measured punishment that courts generally affix. *James Q. Whitman, What is Wrong with Inflicting Shame Sanctions?*

4. Moral Influences

a. Punishment sometimes serves to strengthen people's moral inhibitions against committing crimes. Punishment may also stimulate habitual law-abiding conduct. *Johannes Andenaes, General Prevention – Illusion or Reality?*; *Louis Seidman, Soldiers, Martyrs, and Criminals: Utilitarian Theory and the Problem of Crime Control.*

b. In some cases, the criminal law even serves as a source of moral authority, as people defer to the criminal law when there is some ambiguity as to the wrongfulness of certain conduct. *Paul H. Robinson & John M. Darley, The Utility of Desert.*

D. Reform and Rehabilitation

1. The theory of punishment as a form of rehabilitation focuses on the idea that the criminal mind can be changed in such a way that recidivism will be curtailed. The goal of reform is to strengthen the criminal offender's disposition and capacity to conform his conduct to the law.

2. Reform methods include the inducement of repentance, the recognition of moral guilt, the greater awareness of the character and demands of society, education, training, and psychological treatment.

3. There are at least two different theories or aims of rehabilitation. The first seeks to rehabilitate criminals so that they are safe to return to the streets. The second seeks to rehabilitate criminal offenders so that they can lead flourishing and successful lives. *Law and Psychiatry.*

4. The principles of reforming criminal offenders and protecting the public from them encompass the goals of rehabilitation, incapacitation, specific deterrence, general deterrence, and retribution. *State v. Chaney.*

5. Experts disagree on whether the rehabilitation function of punishment actually works, and if it does, what it is that brings success.

E. Incapacitation

1. The objective of incapacitation is crime prevention in the sense that a criminal who is incapaci-

tated (e.g., behind bars) cannot commit additional crimes.

2. Experts disagree about the effectiveness of incarceration in regard to incapacitation, or the prevention of crime. Some argue that by keeping criminals in prison for longer periods of time, significant numbers of crimes are prevented. *John J. Dilulio, Prisons are a Bargain, by any Measure.*

a. Others, however, disagree with the cited statistics. *John J. Donahue & Peter Seligman, Allocating Resources Among Prisons and Social Programs in the Battle against Crime.*

3. There are two types of incapacitation strategies: collective incapacitation and selective incapacitation.

a. Collective incapacitation strategies focus on imposing an identical sentence on all criminal offenders convicted for a designated offense.

b. Selective incapacitation strategies focus on individualized sentences, sometimes differing for similar crimes, based on predictions about a particular criminal offender's likelihood of committing future crimes.

(1) The theory of selective incapacitation presents ethical considerations because it relies on predictions about criminal offenders' future criminality.

(2) Critics of selective incapacitation argue that it is unfair to punish individuals for crimes they have not and may not commit. They also argue that predictive methods are subject to error. *Jacqueline Cohen, Incapacitating Criminals: Recent Research Findings.*

4. Courts have held that general deterrence and incapacitation are appropriate sentencing considerations when sentencing a career criminal. *United States v. Jackson.*

F. The Allocation of Sentencing Authority

1. Traditionally, sentencing judges have authority to determine the punishment that offenders receive; however, this authority is not absolute. The institutions of the legislature, prosecutor, and parole or corrections boards also influence the punishment that criminal offenders receive.

a. The legislature prescribes the range of sentences available for particular criminal offenses.

b. Prosecutors determine what charges will be brought against a defendant. By selecting the charges, the prosecutor influences the sentence that a court will imposes upon conviction.

c. Judges exercise discretion in imposing sentences within the range prescribed by the legislature.

d. Parole or corrections authorities have the power to modify judicial sentences by determining when to release convicted offenders from custody.

2. Some feel that the broad and unstructured sentencing discretion that is inherent in the traditional sentencing system should be done away with.

a. Many of these argue that discretion in sentencing leads to inconsistencies and uncertainties that undermine deterrence and permit undue lenience.

b. Others feel that discretion permits the imposition of vindictively harsh sentences and invidious discrimination among criminal offenders.

c. Still others argue that since judges are human, their life condition on any given day has the potential to influence a sentencing decision. Therefore, a sentencing system that permits substantially limitless discretion is arbitrary, capricious, and antithetical to the rule of law. *Criminal Sentences: Law without Order*.

3. In response to public demands for harsh and consistent punishment, many jurisdictions have implemented determinate sentencing systems. Under such systems, there is a reduction in the possibility for release on parole and a narrower range of sentences that is applicable after conviction.

4. Congress passed the Crime Control Act of 1984 to address sentencing disparities in federal courts. The Act abolished parole and created the United States Sentencing Commission. The commission promulgates guidelines for judges to use in federal sentencing decisions.

a. The Sentencing Guidelines prescribe circumstances in which judicial sentencing discretion may be particularly important. The Guide-

lines also prescribe how judges should exercise their discretion.

b. Under the Guidelines, judges have discretion in granting upward and downward departures based on aggravating and mitigating circumstances. For example, a federal sentencing judge may exercise discretion and grant a downward departure from the applicable sentencing guidelines when a criminal defendant has extraordinary family circumstances. *United States v. Johnson*.

III. What Should be Punished?

A. The criminal law does not impose imprisonment for all conduct considered by society to be improper. Other sanctions such as fines, taxes, civil liability, licensing, and injunctive relief induce compliance with societal norms.

B. Killing another is generally punishable. This includes killing another to avoid starvation, because a proposition that justifies such a killing as anything other than murder is dangerous, immoral, and opposed to all legal principle and analogy. *Regina v. Dudley and Stephens*.

C. Some feel that homosexual conduct should be punished. Others disagree:

1. The United States Constitution does not create a fundamental right to privately engage in sodomy, and states may punish individuals who engage in such conduct. *Bowers v. Hardwick*.

2. It is proper for the criminal law to prohibit public homosexual behavior. However, it is not proper for the law to concern itself with a man's private conduct unless it is so contrary to the public good that the law ought to intervene. There is a realm of private morality and immorality that does not concern the law, unless society equates the sphere of crime with the sphere of sin. *Home Office, Scottish Home Department, Report of the Committee on Homosexual Offenses and Prostitution*.

D. Some feel that it is proper for the law to enforce moral values, and to punish actions that go against those values. Others disagree.

1. The criminal law of England has always concerned itself with moral principles.

a. In a number of crimes, the criminal law functions solely to enforce moral principles. Therefore, there is a feeling that a complete separation of crime from sin would harm the moral law and might be disastrous for the criminal. There is also a feeling that the law can punish immoral activity.

    b. Society has the right to use its laws to protect itself from internal as well as external dangers. Therefore, the suppression of vice is a proper concern for the law.

    c. Nonetheless, the law should not punish conduct that lies within society's limits of tolerance. *The Enforcement of Morals.*

2. The use of the criminal law to achieve conformity with private moral standards affects law enforcement adversely.

    a. Criminal laws that prohibit extra-marital and abnormal sexual intercourse between a man and a woman are rarely enforced. The lack of enforcement contradicts the moral message that the law is to communicate; breeds cynicism and indifference to criminal law processes; and invites discriminatory enforcement.

    b. Laws prohibiting consensual adult homosexuality are ineffective because the private and consensual nature of this conduct precludes achieving substantial deterrence through law enforcement.

    c. Additionally, attempts at enforcement create grave consequences for law enforcement authorities and the community. In essence, enforcement techniques reduce enforcement personnel to peeping toms who enforce the law arbitrarily.

    d. Laws against prostitution create similar problems, and laws against gambling and narcotics spawn organized crime.

      (1) Laws that prohibit vice crimes have minimal effectiveness; yet, they suck enormous amounts of money from public coffers.

      (2) Since their costs outweigh their benefits, it is time to redirect resources allocated to vice crimes to more profitable law enforcement purposes. *The Crisis of Overcriminalization.*

Regina v. Dudley and Stephens

(English Society) v. (Cannibals)
(1884) 14 Q.B.D. 273

M E M O R Y   G R A P H I C

Instant Facts

One of three men faced with starvation kills a teenage boy, and the three men eat his body parts.

Black Letter Rule

The prospect of starvation is not a justification for killing an innocent person for subsistence, and a proposition that justifies such a killing as anything other than murder is dangerous, immoral, and opposed to all legal principle and analogy.

Case Vocabulary

GENERAL DETERRENCE: A principle that supports punishing a criminal offender to deter others from committing crimes by warning them to anticipate similar punishment if they violate the law.

RETRIBUTION: A principle that sanctions punishment because of the offender's moral culpability and therefore he/she deserves the punishment.

Procedural Basis: Request to Queen's Court to determine if murder was justifiable after lower court rendered a special verdict.

Facts: On July 5, 1884, Mr. Dudley (D1), Mr. Stephens (D2), Mr. Parker, and a teenage English boy set out to sea on a yacht. Subsequently, a storm carried the yacht 1600 miles away from the Cape of Good Hope and forced the men and the teenager to abandon the yacht and board an open boat. For three days, the four individuals subsisted upon two 1-pound cans of turnips. On the fourth day, they caught a small turtle. On the twelfth day in the boat, they had completely consumed the remains of the turtle. From the twelfth day to the twentieth day, the men and the teenager were without food. On the twentieth day, Mr. Dudley (D1), with the assent of Mr. Stephens (D2), approached the teenage boy, who was ill, and fatally cut his throat. The three men then consumed the teenager's body parts. Four days after the incident, a vessel rescued the three men. An English court tried Mr. Dudley (D1) and Mr. Stephens (D2) for murder. The jury returned a special verdict and asked the Queen's Court to tell it if the killing of the teenager was murder under the circumstances.

Issue: Does the prospect of starvation justify killing an innocent person for subsistence?

Decision and Rationale: (Coleridge) No. The prospect of starvation is not a justification for killing an innocent person for subsistence, and a proposition that justifies such a killing as anything other than murder is dangerous, immoral, and opposed to all legal principle and analogy. If the extreme necessity of hunger does not justify larceny, how can it justify murder? The issue is whether Mr. Dudley's (D1) and Mr. Stephens's (D2) acts constitute murder. The special verdict states that it is unlikely that the teenager would have survived and that it is likely that he would have died before the men. Whether they were or were not rescued in a timely manner, the killing of the teenager is unnecessary. The present law does not permit a person to save his life by killing, if necessary, an innocent and unoffending individual. Therefore, the temptation that led to the killing at issue is not a necessity under the law. The law and morality are not the same. Immoral conduct may be legal. Notwithstanding, an absolute divorce of law from morality would lead to fatal consequences. To preserve one life is a general duty, but to sacrifice it may be a higher duty. Christianity reminds us of this fact when we reflect on the Great Example we profess to follow. Temptation is not an excuse for murder, nor can compassion for the criminal change the definition of the crime. The facts in the instant case do not support a finding of a justifiable homicide. Mr. Dudley (D1) and Mr. Stephens (D2) are guilty of murder.

Analysis:

Why should England punish Mr. Dudley (D1) and Mr. Stephens (D2)? The principle of retributivism sanctions punishment because the offender's moral culpability makes punishment his just desert. Pursuant to the principle of general deterrence, courts punish criminal offenders to warn other members of society to anticipate similar punishment if they violate the law. A careful reading of this case suggests that the court used a mixed theory to punish Mr. Dudley (D1) and Mr. Stephens (D2). The court states that it is *immoral* to allow the temptation of starvation to justify the killing of an innocent person. This language suggests that Mr. Dudley (D1) and Mr. Stephens (D2) are morally culpable. This culpability supports punishing the two men under the principle of retribution, because their culpability makes punishment their just desert. However, the court also states that it is *dangerous* to allow the temptation of starvation to justify the killing of an innocent person. This language suggests permitting a justification for killing under the circumstance in this case places society on a slippery slope. Individuals could begin to cloak themselves in the law to justify the killing of innocent people. The implication is that the court should punish Mr. Dudley (D1) and Mr. Stephens (D2) to deter others from killing innocent people and attempting to justify their acts. There are retribution extremists and general deterrence extremists. [Sounds like the far right and the far left.] However, the world and the law are not black and white. So maybe the Queen's Court had the right idea when it took a mixed or centrist approach to punishment.

United States v. Bergman

(Federal Government) v. (Wealthy Defrauder)
(1976) 416 F.Supp. 496

M E M O R Y   G R A P H I C

Instant Facts

Wealthy and successful businessman receives a four-month prison term after accepting a plea agreement.

Black Letter Rule

The sentencing considerations of general deterrence and the avoidance of depreciating the seriousness of an offense support the imposition of imprisonment on a wealthy and successful criminal offender who is unlikely to commit any crimes in the future.

Case Vocabulary

COLLECTIVE INCAPACITATION: A principle that supports incarcerating all persons convicted of a particular type of crime in an attempt to lower the crime rate.

SELECTIVE INCAPACITATION: A principle that supports incarcerating particular offenders based on predictions that suggest that they are likely to commit serious offenses at a high rate unless incarcerated.

SPECIFIC DETERRENCE: A principle that supports punishing a criminal offender to deter him from committing future crimes.

Procedural Basis: Sentencing hearing for criminal offender who plead guilty to two federal criminal offenses.

Facts: Mr. Bergman (D) appeared to be a man of high character, attainments, and distinction. He is a doctor of divinity and an ordained rabbi. People around the world recognize him for his works of public philanthropy, private charity, and leadership in educational enterprises. Mr. Bergman (D) has considerable wealth resulting from the ownership of nursing homes, real estate ventures, and substantial investments. The state of New York and the federal government indicted Mr. Bergman (D) following an investigation of fraudulent claims by nursing homes for Medicaid funds. Mr. Bergman (D) entered a plea agreement with the United States District Attorney's Office. Pursuant to the agreement, he plead guilty to conspiracy to defraud the United States Government by wrongfully padding his nursing homes' Medicaid claims for payments and filing a partnership return that was false and fraudulent. During his sentencing hearing, Mr. Bergman's (D) attorney argued that incarcerating Mr. Bergman (D) serves no legal purpose. The district court disagreed and sentenced Mr. Bergman (D) to a term of four months in prison.

Issue: Do the sentencing considerations of general deterrence and the avoidance of depreciating the seriousness of an offense support the imposition of imprisonment on a wealthy and successful criminal offender who is unlikely to commit any crimes in the future?

Decision and Rationale: (Frankel) Yes. The sentencing considerations of general deterrence and the avoidance of depreciating the seriousness of an offense support the imposition of imprisonment on a wealthy and successful criminal offender who is unlikely to commit any crimes in the future. Rehabilitation does not support sentencing Mr. Bergman (D) to a term in prison because prison is punishment. If a court imprisons a person for other valid reasons, then it is appropriate to make rehabilitative resources available to that person. Additionally, the goal of incapacitation is not appropriate in the instant case. There is no need for specific deterrence because Mr. Bergman (D) is not dangerous. Further, it is unlikely that he will commit similar, or any, offense in the future. Notwithstanding, the goal of general deterrence demands a prison sentence in this case. This deterrence will remind individuals that the law's prohibition on crimes of deception is real and imprisonment is the likely consequence for violations of the law. Mr. Bergman (D) invokes Immanuel Kant's axiom that "one man ought never be dealt with merely as a means subservient to the purposes of another" to avoid a prison term. Criminal punishment in the interest of general deterrence is not merely a means subservient to the purposes of others. The enforcement of the law serves each of us. It even serves persons, such as Mr. Bergman (D), whose wealth and privilege is a result of the benefits that the law offers. Additionally, Mr. Bergman (D) argues that there is no evidence that a prison term is a general deterrent to crime. Even though more evidence is desirable, the working hypotheses include a belief that deliberate, purposeful, continuing, non-impulsive, and for profit crimes are among those most likely to be generally deterrable. Further, avoiding the depreciation of the seriousness of Mr. Bergman's (D) offense demands a prison sentence. This court's judgment should proclaim the seriousness of Mr. Bergman's (D) offenses and demonstrate that the courts apply justice equally. Equal justice demands that the court apply the penalty of imprisonment to privileged criminal offenders with the same regularity and vigor as applied to non-privileged offenders. Proclaiming the seriousness of the crimes and demanding equally justice raise the issue of retribution because the infliction of punishment for crime may not be divorced from ideas of blameworthiness, recompense, and proportionality. Firm in his resistance to a sentence of imprisonment, Mr. Bergman (D) suggests that a philanthropic behavioral sanction is more appropriate under the circumstance. However, the seriousness of Mr. Bergman's (D) crimes requires more than a token sentence comprised of his efforts to further philanthropic enterprises. Further, the fact that Mr. Bergman (D) has suffered public humiliation is not a reason to lighten or enhance his sentence. Since this type of non-judicial punishment is not available to lesser-known individuals, it should not be available to Mr. Bergman (D). Therefore, this court sentences Mr. Bergman (D) to a term of four months in prison.

Analysis:

When discussing why it should punish Mr. Bergman (D), The United States District Court for the Southern District of New York rejects rehabilitation as a justification of punishment. It is easy to understand this rejection. A prison sentence deprives a person of his freedom and possessions. This deprivation is punishment in and of itself. Therefore, it is incorrect to sentence a person to prison under the guise of rehabilitation because a prison sentence is punishment. The court correctly states that rehabilitation service may be offered to prison inmates, but these services are secondary to the punishment that results from a prison sentence. Under the principle of incapacitation, the courts sentence criminal offenders to prison terms to remove them from society in an attempt to reduce crime. Collective incapacitation seeks to impose the identical sentence on all persons convicted of a particular type of crime (e.g., burglary or robbery). Selective incapacitation seeks to incarcerate particular offenders based on predictions that suggest that they are likely to commit serious offenses at a high rate if they are not incarcerated. The court rejects selective incapacitation as a justification for sentencing Mr. Bergman (D) to a prison term since it is unlikely that he would commit any offense in the future. In its opinion, the court equates selective incapacitation with specific deterrence, punishing an offender to deter him from committing future crimes. Notwithstanding, the court justifies sentencing Mr. Bergman (D) to a prison term. These justifications are general deterrence and the avoidance of depreciating the seriousness of an offense. Legal scholars, such as Immanuel Kant, have suggested that deterrence is not a justification for imprisonment. Specifically, Immanuel Kant wrote that, " Judicial punishment can never be administered *merely* as a means of promoting another good either with regard to the criminal himself or to civil society, but must in all cases be imposed only because the individual on whom it is inflicted *has committed a crime*." Kant also wrote that, " [O]ne man ought never be dealt with merely as a means subservient to the purpose of another." The district court rejects Kant's logic and states that it is widely recognized that punishment in the interest of general deterrence is not merely a means subservient to the purposes of another because the law serves each member of society. Regarding sentencing Mr. Bergman (D) to avoid the depreciation of the seriousness of the offense, the court emphasizes that crimes of deception are grave. Further, it stresses that courts are to apply justice equally to privileged and non-privileged offenders. The punishment justification of avoiding the depreciation of the seriousness of the offense suggests that the offender is morally culpable and deserves his just desert. The court admits that by necessity retribution plays a role when sentencing Mr. Bergman (D) because the infliction of punishment cannot be divorced from ideas of blameworthiness, recompense and proportionality.

State v. Chaney

(People of Alaska) v. (Rapist and Robber)
(1970) 477 P.2d 441

M E M O R Y   G R A P H I C

Instant Facts

Man convicted of two counts of rape and one count of robbery received a concurrent one-year term of imprisonment for all counts.

Black Letter Rule

The principles of reforming criminal offenders and protecting the public from them encompass the goals of rehabilitation, incapacitation, specific deterrence, general deterrence, and retribution.

Procedural Basis: Appeal from lenient sentencing court order.

Facts: Mr. Chaney (D) and a companion picked up a female. After driving her around in their car, they rapped her four times and robbed her. The jury convicted Mr. Chaney (D) for two counts of forcible rape and one count of robbery. The district attorney recommended that Mr. Chaney (D) serve five years in prison for his rape convictions and receive a five-year term of probation for his robbery conviction. The term of probation would begin after Mr. Chaney (D) completed his prison term. The department of corrections recommended that Mr. Chaney (D) serve a prison term of four years with the possibility of parole for the rape convictions and receive a term of probation for the robbery conviction. The sentencing judge sentenced Mr. Chaney (D) to a concurrent one-year prison term for the three offenses. When imposing its sentence, the court was apologetic for its decision to order incarceration. Additionally, the court commended Mr. Chaney's (D) military record and expressed hope that Mr. Chaney (D) would receive early parole. The People of Alaska appealed the sentencing order.

Issue: Do the principles of reforming criminal offenders and protecting the public from them encompass the goals of rehabilitation, incapacitation, specific deterrence, general deterrence, and retribution?

Decision and Rationale: (Rabinowitz) Yes. The principles of reforming criminal offenders and protecting the public from them encompass the goals of rehabilitation, incapacitation, specific deterrence, general deterrence, and retribution. In Alaska, the principles of reformation and protecting the public are central to penal administration. The principles encompass the goals of rehabilitating criminal offenders to become non-criminal members of society, isolating them so that they cannot commit criminal offenses during their terms of incarceration, deterring them from committing future crimes, deterring other member of society from committing crime, and community condemnation of the criminal offender. This court expresses its disapproval of the trial court's sentencing order because the sentence is too lenient and appears to be void of any consideration of the goals of penal administration. In this matter, the court only expresses an opinion as the law prohibits remanding the case to the trial court with an order to increase Mr. Chaney's (D) sentence. [Darn!!!] Forcible rape and robbery are very serious and dangerous crimes. During trial, Mr. Chaney (D) alleged that the sexual intercourse with the alleged victim was consensual and that he had planned to return the alleged victim's money to her as he had later found it on the floor of the car. Since the trial judge and the jury disbelieved Mr. Chaney's (D) version of the events, it is difficult to understand the one-year concurrent prison sentence. The trial court's conduct and sentence essentially tells Mr. Chaney (D) that he is only technically guilty and minimally blameworthy for his acts. This message minimizes the possibility that Mr. Chaney (D) will comprehend the wrongfulness of his conduct. Further, Mr. Chaney's (D) sentence fails to express society's condemnation of Mr. Chaney's (D) acts. Community condemnation reaffirms societal norms to maintain society's respect for its norms. The trial court's sentence suggests that forcible rape and robbery do not represent serious antisocial conduct that society should condemn.

Analysis:

The Supreme Court of Alaska cites numerous goals of penal administration in Alaska; however, the court chose only to focus on three of these goals. They are specific deterrence, rehabilitation, and retribution. The principle of reformation encompasses the goals of specific deterrence and rehabilitation. The court displays its displeasure for the trial court's lack of consideration of the goal of reformation when it states the trial court's sentence tells Mr. Chaney (D) that he is only technically guilty and minimally blameworthy. This message minimizes the possibility of Mr. Chaney (D) comprehending the wrongfulness of his acts. Essentially, the court finds that the message that the lenient sentence sends to Mr. Chaney (D) is unlikely to be strong enough to deter Mr. Chaney (D) from committing future crimes. If you support the principle of specific deterrence, you may agree with the court's assessment when you consider that Mr. Chaney (D) committed three violent felonies and may receive early parole. There are two types of rehabilitation. One type justifies the punishment of criminal offenders with imprisonment. The idea is the harshness of this punishment will make it safe to return criminal offenders to the street. The focus is on protecting society rather a genuine concern for the criminal offender. The other type of rehabilitation, in addition to seeking to return offenders safely to the streets, attempts to help criminal offenders lead flourishing and successful lives once they return to the streets. In the instant case, the focus of the Supreme Court of Alaska is the first type of rehabilitation. Due to the dangerousness and seriousness of Mr. Chaney's (D) offenses, the court believes that the lenient sentence may not achieve the goals of retribution. Pursuant to the principle of retribution, a criminal's moral culpability justifies his punishment. The principle holds that punishment is the means that society uses to express its denunciation of wrongful conduct. Additionally, to maintain respect for the law, punishment for grave crimes should adequately reflect society's outrage at wrongful conduct. Without using the word "retribution," the court expresses support for this principle when it states that the trial court's sentence fell short of achieving the goal of community condemnation or the reaffirmation of societal norms for the purpose of maintaining respect for those norms.

United States v. Jackson

(U.S. Government) v. (Bank Robber)
(1987) 835 F.2d 1195

M E M O R Y   G R A P H I C

 ## Instant Facts

A trial court sentenced a career criminal to life in prison for bank robbery.

Black Letter Rule

General deterrence and incapacitation are appropriate sentencing considerations when sentencing a career criminal.

 ## Case Vocabulary

POUR ENCOURAGER LES AUTRES: Deterrence.

Procedural Basis: Appeal from life imprisonment sentence.

Facts: Mr. Jackson (D) was serving a prison sentence for two bank robberies when prison authorities released him from prison to participate in a work release program. On the day of his release, Mr. Jackson (D) robbed a bank. The trial court convicted Mr. Jackson (D) for his latest bank robbery. A federal criminal statute mandates that a person who has three previous felony convictions of robbery receive a prison sentence term that is not less than fifteen years. The statute also prohibits suspension of the sentence, the grant of a probationary sentence, and a grant of parole with respect to the sentence. Since Mr. Jackson (D) brandished a firearm when he robbed the bank and had four prior armed bank robbery convictions and an armed robbery conviction, the trail judged sentenced him to life in prison, and Mr. Jackson (D) appealed his sentence.

Issue: Are general deterrence and incapacitation appropriate sentencing considerations when sentencing a career criminal?

Decision and Rationale: (Easterbrook) Yes. General deterrence and incapacitation are appropriate sentencing considerations when sentencing a career criminal. Even though Mr. Jackson (D) acknowledges that the sentencing statute permits any term of imprisonment that is not less than fifteen years, he contents that the statute only allows the imposition of a determinate sentence. Therefore, he further contents that the statute does not authorize a life sentence. Mr. Jackson (D) misinterprets the sentencing statute. When parole is not a sentencing option, a sentencing judge may impose a determinate sentence or a life sentence, because a long determinate sentence term may in effect equate to a life sentence. Mr. Jackson's (D) life imprisonment sentence is permissible because it is within the statutory sentencing range. The instant offense and Mr. Jackson's (D) prior offenses define him as a career criminal. Mr. Jackson's (D) criminal history demonstrates that specific deterrence remedies have not deterred him in his pursuit of criminal activity. The sentencing statute reflects Congresses judgment that career criminals who persist in possessing weapons must receive severe punishment. Therefore, the trial court could consider general deterrence and incapacitation when sentencing Mr. Jackson (D). Sentenced affirmed.

Concurrence: (Posner) The court's judgment is correct, but Mr. Jackson's (D) sentence is too harsh.   Mr. Jackson's (D) criminal history demonstrates that he is a dangerous and hardened criminal; however, the fact remains that he has never inflicted physical injury when committing his criminal offenses. This fact is relevant and vitiates the need to impose a life sentence. The trial judge found that a life sentence was required to prevent Mr. Jackson (D) from committing future crimes. If prison authorities released Mr. Jackson (D) from prison tomorrow, he probably would commit another bank robbery. However, it is unlikely that he would commit a bank robbery thirty or thirty-five years from today because bank robbery is a young man's crime. Therefore, the appropriate sentence appears to be a twenty-year sentence, since twenty years from today, Mr. Jackson (D) would be unlikely rob another bank at that age. To incarcerate him into is seventies or eighties and then presume that he could commit a crime upon his release is too speculative to impose a life sentence. The value of retribution is in question, and incapacitation may simple replace one criminal with another. Therefore, deterrence is the most appropriate ground for punishment. However, whether the last ten or twenty years of Mr. Jackson's (D) life sentence will deter others from committing crime is a matter of speculation. Bank robbery is a losers' game since most bank robbers are prosecuted. Therefore, a civilized society should incarcerate bank robbers until they become harmless rather than incarcerating them for life.

Analysis:

The majority finds that traditional principles of general deterrence and incapacitation are appropriate sentencing considerations when sentencing career criminals. Judge Posner's concurring opinion is somewhat perplexing. Judge Posner begins by rejecting incapacitation as a reason to impose a prison sentence. He believes that while incapacitation removes one criminal from the streets it serves as an invitation for another person to take his place. Yet, he advocates incarcerating criminals for a period of time that would make them harmless to society. That is one of the goals of selective incapacitation.. Selective incapacitation seeks to sentence criminal offenders based on predictions that suggest that they would commit crimes at a high rate if they are not incarcerated. Judge Posner admits that Mr. Jackson (D) is likely to commit another bank robbery if corrections authorities immediately released him from prison, but suggest that he would not commit another bank robbery after serving a determinate sentence of twenty years. In other words, he predicts that Mr. Jackson (D) will commit criminal offenses at a high rate if he is not incarcerated for a period of time. This case, along with the other cases in this chapter, demonstrates that while judges must sentence criminal offenders they appear to lack a true understanding of the justifications for punishment.

United States v. Johnson

(U.S. Government) v. (Thief)
(1992) 964 F.2d 124

M E M O R Y   G R A P H I C

Instant Facts

A single mother convicted of theft and bribery receives six-month sentence of home detention instead of a thirty-three-to forty-one-month federal prison term because of a sentencing judge exercised discretion and granted a downward departure from the applicable sentencing guidelines.

Black Letter Rule

A federal sentencing judge may exercise discretion and grant a downward departure from the applicable sentencing guidelines when a criminal defendant has extraordinary family circumstances.

Procedural Basis: Federal government appeals trial judge's sentencing order.

Facts: In the spring of 1989, Ms. Johnson (D) was a single mother. She had a seventeen-year-old son, two children aged five and six, and a five-month-old infant. Additionally, she was the caregiver for her six-year-old grandchild. During that time, Ms. Johnson (D) worked as a payroll clerk for a V.A. Hospital. While working with the hospital, Ms. Johnson (D) became involved with a scheme to inflate the paychecks of hospital employees. In return for fraudulently increasing the wages for employees that agreed to participate in the scheme, Ms. Johnson (D) received a fifty percent kickback on the inflated wages. Upon discovering the scheme, the United States Government indicted Ms. Johnson (D) and charged her with stealing money from the government and bribery. A jury convicted Ms. Johnson (D) on all counts. Using the U.S. Sentencing Guidelines, the sentencing judge determined Ms. Johnson's (D) sentence. The judge began its sentencing calculation at a base offense level of ten. This level specifies a sentence of six to twelve months of imprisonment. The judge, finding aggravating circumstances, increased the offense level to twenty. This level specifies a sentence of thirty-three to forty-one months of imprisonment. The judge then exercised his discretion to grant a downward offense level departure, reduced Ms. Johnson's (D) offense level to ten, and sentenced her to six months of home detention. The judge granted the downward departure because the special circumstances of defendant's children and grandchild justified the downward departure. The basis of the special circumstances is the fact that the children were totally dependant upon Ms. Johnson (D). The government appealed the sentencing judge's exercise of discretion and the grant of the downward departure.

Issue: Can a federal sentencing judge exercise discretion and grant a downward departure from the applicable sentencing guidelines when a criminal defendant has extraordinary family circumstances?

Decision and Rationale: (Oakes) Yes. A federal sentencing judge may exercise discretion and grant a downward departure from the applicable sentencing guidelines when a criminal defendant has extraordinary family circumstances. The government contends that family circumstances, taken alone, can never justify downward departure. A guidelines policy statement provides that family ties and responsibilities are not ordinarily relevant in determining if a sentence should be outside the applicable guidelines range. However, the Sentencing Reform Act of 1984 expressly gives a sentencing judge the authority to depart from the applicable guideline range if it finds a circumstance not adequately considered during the formulation of the guidelines. The Sentencing Commission when formulating the guidelines considered family ties and responsibilities because disruption to them is inherent when a criminal offender receives a sentence of incarceration. However, extraordinary circumstances, by their very nature, are not capable of adequate consideration and may constitute proper grounds for a downward departure. Ms. Johnson (D) faces more responsibility that an ordinary single parent. She is responsible for the upbringing of her seventeen-year-old son, two young children, her five-month-old infant, and her six-year-old grandchild. Given these facts, a court can find that Ms. Johnson's (D) parental responsibilities are extraordinary. The basis for the sentencing judge's downward departure was not a finding that Ms. Johnson's (D) family circumstances decreased her culpability. Rather, the judge granted the departure because courts are reluctant to inflict extraordinary destruction on dependant family members who rely solely on the defendant for their upbringing. Therefore, the sentencing judge's departure was reasonable. Judgment affirmed.

Analysis:

The Sentencing Reform Act of 1984 provides for the development of guidelines that will further the purposes of criminal punishment. These purposes are deterrence, incapacitation, just punishment, and rehabilitation. In enacting the Sentencing Reform Act, Congress sought to enhance the ability of the criminal justice system to combat crime, through an effective and fair sentencing system. Congress also sought to achieve sentencing uniformity and proportionality in sentencing. To achieve these goals, the act provides for the development of sentencing guidelines. Notwithstanding, Congress recognized that there remains a place for the exercise of discretion by sentencing judges. The mechanism for exercising this discretion is the grant of a downward departure. Since sentencing judges exercise their discretion when granting downward departures, there is a great deal of disparity in downward departures. Some members of the federal bench are more liberal or compassionate than other members. Other members of the bench assume all defendants are guilty and deserve punishment. As arguing for and receiving a downward departure is the name of the game for federal criminal defense attorneys, federal criminal defendants still find themselves at the mercy and the whims of sentencing judges.

Bowers v. Hardwick

(Attorney General of the State of Georgia) v. (Sodomite)
(1986) 478 U.S. 186

M E M O R Y   G R A P H I C

Instant Facts

The Attorney General of Georgia charged a male with violating a statute that prohibits individuals to engage in sodomy.

Black Letter Rule

The United States Constitution does not create a fundamental right to privately engage in sodomy, and states may punish individuals who engage in such conduct.

Procedural Basis: Appeal from United States Court of Appeals ruling that Georgia's sodomy statute violates an individual's fundamental rights.

Facts: A 1984 Georgia statute states that a person commits the offense of sodomy when he performs or submits to any sexual act involving the sex organs of one person and the mouth or anus of another. Violators of this statute receive a one-to twenty-year prison term. The Attorney General of Georgia charged Mr. Hardwick (P), a homosexual, with violating this statute. The trial court dismissed the case because the Attorney General's office failed to state a claim for which the court could grant relief. Mr. Hardwick (P) then brought an action in federal district court and alleged that Georgia's sodomy statute violates the United States Constitution. Later a United States Court of appeals ruled that Georgia's sodomy statute violated Mr. Hardwick's (P) fundamental rights because his homosexual activity is a private and intimate association that the Ninth Amendment and the Due Process Clause of the Fourteenth Amendment protects. The Attorney General of Georgia appealed to the Supreme Court of the United States.

Issue: May states punish individuals who engage in sodomy without violating the individuals' fundamental right to privacy?

Decision and Rationale: (White) Yes. The United States Constitution does not create a fundamental right to privately engage in sodomy, and states may punish individuals who engage in such conduct. Since many states have held, and continue to hold that the act of sodomy is illegal, the issue before this Court is whether the Constitution grants a fundamental right to homosexuals to engage in sodomy. In a prior opinion, this Court stated that fundamental liberties are those liberties that are implicit in the concept of ordered liberty, such that neither liberty nor justice would exist if they were sacrificed. In another opinion, the Court stated that fundamental liberties are those liberties that are deeply rooted in the Nation's history and tradition. Sodomy was an offense at common law, and in 1868, thirty-two of the thirty-seven states had criminal sodomy laws. Furthermore, until 1961, all fifty states prohibited sodomy, and today twenty-four states and the District of Columbia continue this prohibition. Therefore, sodomy performed in private between two consenting adults is neither deeply rooted in the nation's history and tradition nor implicit in the concept of ordered liberty. In short, to engage in private consensual sodomy is not a fundamental right. Notwithstanding that consensual sodomy is not a fundamental right, Mr. Hardwick (P) alleges that Georgia's sodomy statute lacks a rational basis. He contends that the belief of the majority that homosexual sodomy is immoral and unacceptable is not a rational basis for a secular law that prohibits sodomy. Notions of morality are the basis of the law, and Mr. Hardwick (P) even admits that all laws representing moral choices should not be held unconstitutional under the Due Process Clause. Therefore, this Court finds Mr. Hardwick's (P) rational basis argument lacks merit. Judgment reversed.

Concurrence: (Burger) The Constitution does not grant a fundamental right to engage in homosexual sodomy. Throughout the history of Western civilization, states have intervened in matters involving homosexual conduct. Judeo-Christian moral and ethical standards condemn homosexual practices. If this Court holds that homosexual sodomy is a fundamental right, it discards millennia of moral teachings.

Dissent: (Blackmun) The issue in this case is not about a fundamental right to engage in homosexual sodomy. The issue is whether individuals have the right to be let alone. The right to privacy is the correct analytical approach to assess Mr. Hardwick's (P) claim. Under this approach, more is required of the State of Georgia than Christian condemnation, if it is to prosecute individuals for the decisions that they make regarding the most intimate aspects of their lives. The majority's opinion focuses on homosexual activity; however, the language of the statute is broad and lacks such a focus. Homosexual activity is not the issue. The issue is the promise embodied in the Constitution that grants individuals a right to privacy. Sexual intimacy permeates human existence and human relationships. In this diverse nation, there may be many correct manners of conducting those relationships. The Attorney General's claim that the statute protects the health and welfare of the public is without merit because the record is void of any evidence that suggests that individuals that engage in sodomy spread communicable disease, foster criminal activity, or pose a danger to themselves or others. The Attorney General's main contention is the nation and the states have a right to maintain a decent society. Traditional Judeo-Christian values do not justify Georgia's sodomy statute. The fact that some religious groups condemn sodomy does not give a state a license to impose their beliefs on the entire citizenry. Conformity to religious doctrine is not a sufficient justification for secular law. There is a difference in laws that protect public sensibilities and those that enforce private morality. States do not have a license to regulate intimate behavior that occurs in private places simply because that same behavior may be punished when it occurs in public.

Analysis:

If you remove all of the constitutional law rhetoric from this case, you are left with the fundamental problem of what conduct should society punish. In cases such as this one, the enormity of the problem and its consequence become evident. If you live in Georgia and profess to have Judeo-Christian values or simply hate homosexuals, you support sending people who engage in sodomy to prison for one-to-twenty years. How moral is that? Clearly, Judeo-Christian values have played a significant role in the development of the United States. However, a person can condemn murder without adorning his condemnation with moral values. Does society condemn murder and theft crimes because of the moral values that it holds, or does society condemn these crimes to maintain order and minimize the violence which each of us is capable of displaying in certain circumstances? If not unusual, a prison sentence for an intimate sex act is cruel punishment. Is not cruel punishment immoral? Are not the Constitution and the United States form of government designed to protect the minority from the abuses that the majority can inflict? In reality, whether you agree or disagree with this case is irrelevant. However, it is important that you grasp the danger that exists when criminal laws and punishment are used to articulate and vindicate the moral views of certain groups.

Chapter 3

This chapter will introduce you to some of the basic premises underlying Anglo-American substantive criminal law. Many if not all of these basics have been adopted from English common law as developed over the centuries. Notwithstanding the roots of the American legal system, all jurisdictions have seen fit to transform the criminal law into statutory form, although one does hear of a common law crime being committed and prosecuted from time to time. That is, however, an extreme rarity.

One of the most fundamental basic premises in our criminal law is the requirement that there be some act, i.e., actus reus. After all, criminality does not consist of merely having a bad state of mind. Of course, where one has a legal duty, refraining from action, i.e. omission, may be considered criminal. Legal scholars have struggled over this issue for a long time, but there seems to be emerging, if not a consensus just yet, at least a very slight trend to create more legal duties to our fellow human beings.

Another fundamental basic premise is the requirement that the criminal actor have the requisite state of mind, i.e. mens rea. Legal thinkers have reasoned that if the actor does not intend the crime, then he is not legally culpable and no crime has been committed. One must always keep in mind, however, that legislatures are quite fond of enacting criminal statutes that do not require any mens rea. These are termed strict liability offenses and you will learn more about them as you continue in this course.

The third most fundamental basic premise is that the required mental state must concur or jibe with the criminal conduct. It is generally accepted that the actor's mental state must activate the criminal action in order for the two to concur.

You can rest assured that these basic premises, while being fundamental to criminal law, are not the only ones you will need to learn. They are definitely three of the most important though. It also bears mentioning, at least if you haven't already guessed, that they are somewhat more involved than this short perspective may seem to indicate. So keep reading and learning the many interesting concepts included in this chapter. They are extremely important in understanding the American criminal justice system.

Chapter 3

NOTE: THE PURPOSE OF THIS OUTLINE IS TO ORGANIZE THE CASES SO THAT ONE CAN QUICKLY UNDERSTAND THE RELEVANCE OF EACH CASE TO THE COURSE. NO ATTEMPT IS MADE IN THIS OVERVIEW TO ADDRESS EVERY CONCEPT THAT MUST BE STUDIED. BE SURE TO READ THE ENTIRE CASEBOOK AND/OR OTHER MATERIALS TO GAIN A FULL UNDERSTANDING OF ALL CONCEPTS.

I. Three principles limit the distribution of punishment in the criminal law.
   A. Culpability—ensures conduct is criminal before it is punished.
   B. Legality—ensures that people have fair warning of proscribed conduct.
   C. Proportionality—differentiates between serious and minor offenses.

II. Culpability
   A. Actus Reus
      1. Positive actions
         a. A defendant must perform the physical act for each element of a crime requiring an actus reus component. *Martin v. State*.
         b. When an element of a crime is a voluntary act, a lack of consciousness while committing the act is a complete defense. *People v. Newton*.
         c. Under the Model Penal Code, a habitual action done without thought is treated as a voluntary act.
         d. The majority rule is that possession crimes require knowledge of possession. *U.S. v. Anderson*.
         e. Some jurisdictions use a "should have known" standard when it comes to possession. *U.S. v. Garrett*.
         f. Conduct committed while hypnotized is not voluntary under the Model Penal Code.
         g. Somnambulism, i.e., sleep walking, has been held to be a complete defense to a crime requiring a voluntary act. *Norval*

Morris Somnambulistic Homicide: Ghosts, Spiders, and North Koreans.
         h. One who suffers from epilepsy may incur criminal liability for causing harm while having an involuntary epileptic reflex.
      2. Omissions
         a. The common law of the United States does not impose a duty to take affirmative action upon bystanders in emergency situations if they are not responsible for the situation, thus the common law crime of omission is abolished. *Pope v. State*.
         b. While Congress enacted a misprision of felony statute in 1909, the federal courts have required active attempts at concealment of the felony rather than just a failure to report it. *U.S. v. Johnson*.
         c. One of the elements of an omission crime a jury must find to have existed in order to judge a defendant guilty is that there existed a legal duty of care owed to the victim by the defendant. *Jones v. U.S.*
         d. One who in some way prevents another from getting needed aid may be held criminally liable for any harm resulting therefrom. *People v. Oliver*.
         e. Removal of life support from a patient who is unlikely to recover, as opposed to active euthanasia, is an act of omission that, if in accord with the patient's or surrogate's wishes, does not create criminal liability. *Barber v. Superior Court*.
         f. Some countries permit the withdrawal of feeding and drugs from a patient with no hope of recovery, and who will die shortly. This is distinguished from administering a lethal drug, in order to end the patient's life. *Airedale NHS Trust v. Bland*.
         g. Although a person has a constitutionally protected liberty interest in refusing

unwanted medical treatment, a State may require clear and convincing evidence of the patient's consent before ordering the removal of devices provided life sustaining nourishment to a patient in a permanently vegetative state. *Cruzan v. Director, Missouri Dept. of Public Health.*

B. Mens Rea

1. Mens rea can generally be equated with criminal intent, ill will, malice, knowledge, awareness, purpose and so on. Not all crimes require a mens rea.

2. A mens rea requirement of malice can usually be met by showing the act was done with either intent to cause harm or reckless disregard as to whether harm would result; a showing of mere wickedness will not suffice. *Regina v. Cunningham.*

3. One who is engaged in the commission of a felony is not criminally responsible for every result occasioned thereby, unless it is a probable consequence of his act or such that he could have reasonably foreseen or intended it. *Regina v. Faulkner.*

4. Model Penal Code—4 levels of culpability for each material element of an offense.

   a. Purpose—committing an act with the conscious object of performing a proscribed action or to cause the proscribed result.

   b. Knowingly—a state of being aware that the actor's conduct is of the required nature or that the proscribed result is practically certain given the conduct.

   c. Recklessness—a state of being aware of a substantial and unjustifiable risk that the proscribed result will occur.

   d. Negligence—a state of creating a substantial and unjustifiable risk, of which the actor ought to be aware, that the proscribed result will occur.

5. When a criminal statute includes "negligently" as the mens rea element, but does not define it, the required degree of negli-

gence should be that of criminal negligence rather than ordinary civil negligence. *Santillanes v. New Mexico.*

6. Under the Model Penal Code, "negligence" is conduct that is inadvertent. The person was not aware of the danger, but should have been. "Recklessness" exists where the person was aware of the danger, but acted anyway.

7. A statute that has intent to cause death or serious bodily harm as an element of the crime does not require proof of *unconditional* intent to kill or harm; rather mere proof of intent to kill or harm is sufficient even if accompanied by a condition. *Holloway v. United States.*

8. The "knowledge" element of a crime does not require actual positive knowledge, but only requires the defendant to have had an awareness of a high probability of the existence of the fact of which "knowledge" is required. *U.S. v. Jewell.*

C. Mistake of Fact

1. Under the Model Penal Code, a mistake of fact is a defense if it negatives the purpose, belief, recklessness or negligence required to establish a material element of the offense.

   a. Some states have added a qualifying clause providing "only if the mistake is one for which there is a reasonable explanation or excuse."

2. Criminal statutes that do not require the proscribed conduct to be done "knowingly" cannot be defended against by a mistake of fact; they are strict liability. *Regina v. Prince.*

3. A reasonable mistake of fact, that if true would still not make the actor's conduct legal, is not a valid affirmative defense against the crime actually committed. *People v. Olsen.*

D. Strict Liability

1. Some criminal statutes concerning the sale of narcotics do not require proof of scienter; thus the legislative intent establishes

that good faith or ignorance will not constitute a defense. *United States v. Balint.*

2. The Supreme Court upheld a conviction for mislabeling a shipment of drugs where the statute did not require any mens rea. The conduct is penalized though consciousness of wrongdoing may be totally wanting. Such statutes dispense with the conventional requirement for awareness of some wrongdoing. *U.S. v. Dotterweich.*

3. Failure by the legislature to include the mens rea in criminal statutes that is normally required at common law does not mean the crime is strict liability; such statutes will be interpreted to require the mens rea such crimes required at common law. *Morissette v. U.S.*

4. A criminal statute written without a mens rea requirement will be construed in light of the background common law for such crimes to include a mens rea requirement unless there is an explicit indication that the legislature intended there to be no such requirement. *U.S. v. Staples.*

5. Vicarious criminal liability—such as holding the employer criminally responsible for conduct by its employee—violates due process unless the state interest involved outweighs the liberty interest of the offender in light of any possible alternative means of achieving the state interest. *State v. Guminga.*

   a. However, courts generally will uphold vicarious criminal liability convictions if the punishment is a fine as opposed to imprisonment.

6. Though some strict liability offenses do not require any mens rea, they still require a voluntary act by the offender before guilt may be found. *State v. Baker.*

7. There is a middle level of offenses, those where the prosecution is not required to show any required mens rea, but in which the defendant has the option of presenting the affirmative defense that he took all

reasonable care. *Regina v. City of Sault Ste. Marie.* This is not an accepted rule in the United States.

   a. Most scholars oppose absolute liability where the defendant may not exculpate himself by showing that he was free of fault.

E. Mistake of Law

1. An erroneous interpretation of the law, no matter how reasonable, will not excuse a violation of the law. *People v. Marrero.*

2. Under the Model Penal Code

   a. Mistake of law is a defense if it negatives the purpose, belief, recklessness or negligence required to establish a material element of the offense.

   b. Knowledge of the existence, meaning or application of the law determining the elements of an offense is not an element of that offense, unless the definition of the offense or the Code so provides.

3. A mistake of law, whether reasonable or unreasonable, will be a defense to a crime if it negates the specific intent required for conviction. *Cheek v. U.S.*

4. The one exception to the rule that a mistake of law is not a valid defense is the reasonable reliance upon an official, but mistaken or later overruled, statement of the law. *U.S. v. Albertini.*

5. A conviction for violation of a law requiring certain classes of persons to register with authorities requires that such person either have knowledge of the registration requirement or have probable reason to know of the requirement. *Lambert v. California.*

III. Proportionality

A. The Eighth Amendment, which prohibits cruel and unusual punishment, does not contain a provision that requires a criminal punishment to be proportionate to the crime for which one is being punished. *Harmelin v. Michigan.*

1. This case contains a dissent by Justice White that very cogently makes the case for

a proportionality requirement in the Eighth Amendment.

B. Many states have independent proportionality guarantees.

IV. Legality

A. In some countries, one may be prosecuted for a general offense at common law, though there exists no such legal precedent reflecting the actual offense committed, so long as a jury finds the offender guilty. *Shaw v. Director of Public Prosecutions*.

1. *Shaw* represents the ideal that acts done to the public mischief are, as such, punishable by law.

2. The result reached in *Shaw* would be nearly impossible in the U.S. because just about all jurisdictions have eliminated common law crimes in favor of statutes.

B. The construction of a statute that is contrary to legislative intent and applied retroactively violates due process of law. *Keeler v. Superior Court*.

C. An act containing a criminal provision is not unconstitutional because it contains in its definition of the crime an element of degree regarding the actor's conduct as to which estimates may differ. *Nash v. United States*.

D. Vagueness may invalidate a criminal law by:

1. Failing to provide notice to enable the ordinary person to understand what conduct it prohibits and

2. It may authorize or encourage arbitrary and discriminatory police enforcement. *City of Chicago v. Morales*.

E. Years before *City of Chicago v. Morales* was decided, *Papachristou v. City of Jacksonville* was considered the leading case concerning the constitutionality of vagrancy-type laws. The court held the ordinance in question was void due to vagueness because it failed to provide notice that the conduct is illegal, and had the effect of arbitrary law enforcement by the police and prosecutors.

F. The Model Penal Code has formulated its own loitering statute. Courts are divided on whether it meets constitutional muster pursuant to *Papachristou*.

Martin v. State

(Intoxicated Man) v. (People of Alabama)

(1944) 31 Ala. App. 334, 17 So. 2d 427

M E M O R Y   G R A P H I C

Instant Facts

Police officers arrested an intoxicated man at his home, took him onto a highway, and then arrested him for public drunkenness.

Black Letter Rule

A defendant must perform the physical act for each element of a crime that has an actus reus component.

Procedural Basis: Appeal from conviction of being drunk in a public place and engaging in conduct manifesting drunkenness.

Facts: Police officers arrested Mr. Martin (D) at his home and took him onto a public highway. While on the highway, Mr. Martin (D) used loud and profane language in a manner that suggested that he was intoxicated. Mr. Martin (D) was convicted for violating a statute that prohibited appearing in a public place in an intoxicated condition and manifesting that condition with indecent conduct or loud and profane language. Mr. Martin (D) appealed the conviction.

Issue: Must a defendant perform the physical act for each element of a crime that has an actus reus component?

Decision and Rationale: (Simpson) Yes. A defendant must perform the physical act for each element of a crime that has an actus reus component. Mr. Martin (D) was convicted for violating a statute that provides that an individual in an intoxicated condition who appears in a public place where one or more persons are present and manifest his intoxication by boisterous or indecent conduct, or loud and profane language shall be fined upon conviction. On its face, the statute requires voluntary appearance in a public place. The State (P) cannot prove an accusation of public drunkenness by establishing that the arresting officer, while the defendant was in an intoxicated condition, involuntarily and forcibly carried him to a public place. Reversed and rendered.

Analysis:

Alabama's public drunkenness statute has two elements. First, the accused must appear in a public place. Appearance requires a voluntary physical act. Mr. Martin (D) appeared in a public place; however, he did not perform any physical act, voluntary or involuntary, that led to his appearance, since the police officers *took* him onto the public highway. Therefore, the required actus reus for this element does not exist. Second, the accused must manifest his drunken condition at the public place he appeared. Since Mr. Martin (D) voluntarily used loud and profane language while he was on the highway in an intoxicated condition, the required actus reus for this element exists. Notwithstanding, a crime did not occur, because the statute requires a coincidence of voluntarily appearing in public and manifesting an intoxicated condition through certain conduct.

People v. Newton

(State) v. (Black Panther)

8 Cal. App. 3d 359, 87 Cal. Rptr. 394 (CA 1970)

M E M O R Y G R A P H I C

Instant Facts

Newton (D) was accused of committing manslaughter after allegedly shooting and killing a police officer during a struggle with the police.

Black Letter Rule

When a person commits an act that is criminal if done voluntarily, lack of consciousness is a complete defense.

Procedural Basis: Appeal after a jury conviction for voluntary manslaughter.

Facts: Newton's (D) car was stopped by Police Officer John Frey who ordered Newton (D) to get out of his car. An altercation then ensued. The prosecution witnesses testified as follows: that Newton (D) had drawn a gun and, during the struggle for possession of the gun it went off and wounded another police officer, Officer Heanes. As the struggle continued, Officer Heanes fired a shot into Newton's (D) midsection. At some point, Newton (D) wrested the gun from Officer Frey and fired several fatal shots at Frey. Newton (D) then ran away only to appear shortly thereafter at a local hospital where he sought treatment for a gunshot wound in the abdomen. Newton (D) testified as follows: that he carried no gun and that the struggle with Frey started when Frey struck Newton (D) for protesting his arrest. As Frey stumbled backwards he drew his revolver. At this point Newton (D) felt great pain in his stomach and heard an "explosion", then a "volley of shots." Newton (D) then remembers "crawling" or moving somehow, but nothing else until he found himself at the entrance to Kaiser Hospital with no knowledge of how he got there. Newton (D) also testified that he was "unconscious or semiconscious" during this time, and only "semiconscious" at the hospital entrance. Also, that after recalling being at Kaiser Hospital he later "regained consciousness" at another hospital. A defense witness, Dr. Bernard Diamond, M.D., testified that Newton's (D) testimony about being semiconscious or unconscious was "compatible" with the wound he'd received. Specifically, Diamond testified that a gunshot wound that penetrates in a body cavity is "very likely to produce a profound reflex shock reaction..." and that "it is not at all uncommon for a person shot in the abdomen to lose consciousness...." The trial judge failed to give Newton's (D) requested instruction to the jury on the defense of unconsciousness.

Issue: Did the trial judge commit reversible error by failing to instruct the jury on the defense of unconsciousness?

Decision and Rationale: (Rattigan, J.) Yes. Even though the evidence presented is both conflicting and confused as to who shot whom and when, there is support for the inference that Newton (D) was shot first. Given this, and Newton's (D) testimony of his sensations when shot—supported to some degree by Dr. Diamond's testimony—there is some support for the conclusion that Newton (D) was unconscious when Officer Frey was shot. The rule regarding unconsciousness is clear. Where not self-induced—such as voluntary intoxication—unconsciousness is a complete defense to a charge of criminal homicide. "Unconsciousness," as used in this rule does not imply the normal definition of unconsciousness—coma, inertia, incapability of locomotion, etc.—it merely implies that the defendant has physically acted in fact, but was not conscious of those actions. Because Newton (D) presented some evidence of unconsciousness, the trial judge's refusal to give the requested instruction on the subject, and its effect as a complete defense if found to have existed, is prejudicial error. Reversed.

Analysis:

Simply stated, this case stands for the premise that a crime of which a required element is a voluntary act, requires that the actor be conscious of what he is doing. This is because a person who commits criminal acts without knowing is not culpable. After all, three of the goals of the criminal justice system are to (1) punish the guilty mind; (2) deterrence; and (3) to rehabilitate criminals. If a person had no knowledge of committing the criminal act then they simply cannot have a "guilty mind." Furthermore, how can the defendant and others be deterred from crime when they never had the subjective intent to commit a crime in the first place. Finally, what good does it do to rehabilitate a person who was not aware of his actions at the time they were committed. To try and do so would be futile since, presumably, the person is not in the unconscious state during the rehabilitation. Why is it that unconsciousness is not a defense when the person has voluntarily made themselves unconscious of their actions—for instance, when a person is intoxicated? It is not the act of being intoxicated that is illegal, but the act stemming from intoxication. Is it reasonable to say there is a deterrent effect of persuading people not to drink, or to drink in moderation? From a procedural standpoint this case stands for the proposition that the consciousness/unconsciousness determination is for the jury to make after hearing all of the evidence. Having presented some credible evidence that he was unconscious at the time Officer Frey was shot, Newton (D) was entitled to have the jury instructed on the unconsciousness defense. When the court failed to do so, in essence it made the determination, as a matter of law, that Newton (D) was conscious at the time of the shooting.

Pope v. State

(Good Samaritan) v. (State Government)
284 Md. 309, 396 A.2d 1054 (MD 1979)

M E M O R Y   G R A P H I C

Instant Facts

Pope (D) is charged with a crime after having failed to summon the police or stop a mother from committing child abuse that resulted in the death of the child, after Pope (D) had provided the mother and child with lodging in her home.

Black Letter Rule

The common law of the United States does not impose a duty to take affirmative action upon bystanders in emergency situations if they are not responsible for the situation, thus the common law crime of omission is abolished.

Case Vocabulary

MISPRISION OF FELONY: The failure to report a felony by someone not a party to the crime.

Procedural Basis: Appeal from the trial court after a conviction for the common law crime of misprision of felony.

Facts: Pope (D) allowed a Melissa Norris and her three month old infant to stay in Pope's (D) home because the two did not have a place to stay. Norris suffered from a serious mental illness and experienced episodes of violent religious frenzy. During their stay, Pope (D) fed Norris and her infant, and looked after the infant in a variety of ways. One day, Norris experienced one of her episodes and claimed she was God and that Satan had hidden himself in the body of her child. With Pope (D) present, Norris beat, ripped, and tore at the infant, causing the child serious injury. During the prolonged period of this episode, Pope (D) took no action to protect the child, summon the authorities or seek medical assistance. At some point the infant died from the beatings received from Norris. Pope (D) was convicted of felony child abuse under a statute that imposed criminal liability for abuse occurring to a child when the defendant was "…in loco parentis to, or responsible for the supervision of a minor child…AND caused, by being in some manner accountable for, by act of commission or omission, abuse to the child in the form of (a) physical injury or injuries sustained by the child as the result of (i) cruel or inhumane treatment, or (ii) malicious act or acts by such person,…." and also had "the permanent or temporary care or custody or responsibility for the supervision of a minor child…." Pope (D) was also convicted under the common law crime of 'misprision of felony,' because she had unlawfully and willfully conceal[ed] and fail[ed] to disclose a felony to wit: the murder of [the child]…having actual knowledge of the commission of the felony and the identity of the felon, with the intent to obstruct and hinder the due course of justice and to cause the felon to escape unpunished…."

Issue: (1) May criminal liability be imposed for a failure to take affirmative action or intervene when a parent is abusing his or her child? (2) May criminal liability be imposed under the common law rule of omission for failure to intervene or take reasonable affirmative action to prevent a crime, or report it?

Decision and Rationale: (Orth, J) (1) No. Pope's (D) failure to attempt to prevent the abuse committed by the mother and her failure to seek medical attention for the child, although the need was obvious, could be viewed as a cause of the worsening of the child's condition and eventual death. These omissions constitute cruel and inhumane treatment within the meaning of the statute. But Pope (D) can only be guilty if her status was that of a person covered by the statute. It is clear that Pope (D) was neither the child's parent, nor adoptive parent, and that there is no evidence sufficient to show Pope (D) had the "permanent or temporary care or custody" of the child as required by the statute, so as to be in loco parentis to the child. Therefore, the sole question is whether Pope (D) was "responsible for the supervision of" the child. However, the record shows that the child's mother was always present. To impute responsibility for the child under the statute out of the action of taking the mother and child in is simply illogical. Pope (D) had no right to usurp the role of parent and as long as the mother was present, Pope (D) cannot be held responsible for the ultimate well-being of the child. It would be extremely ironic if one who, out of concern for the well-being of a mother and child, took them in could then be held criminally liable for abusing the child she sought to look after. While Pope (D) may have had a moral obligation to intervene, she had no legal obligation to do so and cannot be punished for a failure to meet a moral obligation. We hold that the evidence was insufficient to prove Pope (D) fell within the class of persons to whom the child abuse statute applies. Reversed. (2) No. The Court assumes for the sake of argument that misprision was a crime under the English common law. The question is whether it is a crime today, here in this state. Considering its origin, the broad and indiscriminate width of its scope, and its long non-use that is now incompatible with our general code of laws and jurisprudence. If the legislature feels it appropriate to enact a statute making it a crime to fail to disclose knowledge of criminal acts it is free to do so.

This Court believes that the common law offense is not acceptable by today's standards, and we are not free to fashion a rule by judicial fiat that would be acceptable. We therefore hold that misprision of felony is no longer a chargeable offense in this state. Reversed.

Analysis:

In considering the statutory crime of child abuse the Court relies quite heavily on the fact that Pope (D) had taken Norris and her child into her home, fed them, provided them with lodging and generally took care of them. Are these facts germane to the issue of whether she was guilty of the crime charged? Nowhere in the statute is there an exception for good Samaritans. The Court stated quite simply that it did not believe Pope (D) was in the class of persons covered by the statute because the mother of the child was present at all times—indeed, it was she who committed the abuse. This was enough to reverse without all of the sentimental window dressing about it being ironic that a person with only good intentions should be prosecuted for abuse. Regarding the common law crime of misprision of felony, are there any common law crimes anymore? Does the maintenance of a civilized society require the enactment of a "Good Samaritan" law? There are some states that have enacted such laws (Rhode Island, Vermont and Wisconsin are some). These laws are usually, if not always, predicated on an obligation to take reasonable actions. But how does a person in that situation judge reasonableness and what happens if the Samaritan's actions worsen the situation? In response to the last concern, there is usually a conditional immunity from tort liability as long as the Samaritan took reasonable action.

BEFORE A DEFENDANT MAY BE FOUND GUILTY OF ANY CRIME OF OMISSION THE JURY MUST FIRST FIND THAT THE DEFENDANT OWED A LEGAL DUTY OF CARE TO THE VICTIM

Jones v. United States

(Babysitter) v. (Federal Government)
308 F.2d 307 (D.C. Cir. 1962)

M E M O R Y   G R A P H I C

Instant Facts

Jones (D) was purportedly left in charge of the infant victim who died from neglect.

Black Letter Rule

One of the elements of an omission crime a jury must find to have existed in order to find a defendant guilty is that there was a legal duty of care owed the victim by the defendant.

Case Vocabulary

OMISSION: Failure to fulfill a duty imposed by law.

Procedural Basis: The case arises on appeal to the United States Circuit Court of Appeals after a jury verdict finding the defendant guilty of involuntary manslaughter. Assigned as error by the trial court is its failure to instruct the jury on the requirement of a legal duty of care.

Facts: Jones (D) was found guilty of involuntary manslaughter because of her failure to provide proper care for Anthony Lee Green, an infant child. The infant was placed with Jones (D), who was a family friend. The record shows that Shirley Green, the infant's mother, along with the infant, had lived with Jones (D) for some time, but there is a conflict as to how long. Also unclear in the evidence is whether Jones (D) was paid to take care of the infant. Uncontested medical evidence showed that Jones (D) had ample means to provide food and medical care. At the end of arguments the court failed to instruct that the jury must find, beyond a reasonable doubt that Jones (D) was under a legal duty to provide food and other necessities to the infant.

Issue: Is a court required to instruct a jury that a defendant charged with a crime of omission must first be found, beyond a reasonable doubt, to have owed a legal duty to the victim, such that a failure to give the instruction is reversible error?

Decision and Rationale: (Wright, J) Yes. An element of a crime of omission of a duty owed to one individual by another is that the duty be one imposed by law, not simply a moral duty. Also, the omission must be the immediate and direct cause of the harm to the victim. There are at least four situations in which a failure to act may constitute breach of a legal duty: (1) where a statute imposes a duty to care for another; (2) where one stands in a certain status relationship to another, such as a parent to a child; (3) where one has assumed a contractual duty to care for another; and (4) where one has voluntarily assumed the care of another and so secluded the helpless person so as to prevent others from rendering aid. The prosecution submits that either the third or fourth ground applies here. However, in any of the four there are critical issues of fact that the jury must pass on. Here it is whether Jones (D) had entered into a contract with the child's mother for the care of the infant or, in the alternative, whether Jones (D) assumed the care of the child and secluded him from the care of his mother. With respect to both of these issues the evidence is in direct conflict—Jones (D) insisting that the mother was actually living with her and the infant, while the mother testified that she was living with her parents and was paying Jones (D) to care for the child. Despite this factual conflict, the court failed to even suggest the necessity for finding a legal duty of care. A finding of legal duty is the critical element of the crime and failure to instruct the jury on this requirement is plain error. Reversed and remanded.

Analysis:

How is it that criminal liability may be imposed when a defendant has not committed any affirmative act? The law gets around this dilemma by requiring that there be a legal duty to render aid. This legal duty is usually imposed by some provision of the civil law, such as the law of tort, which imposes a duty to act in the given circumstances. If there is such a law, then it can be said there is a legal duty, even though it is not a criminal law. But the burden of proof for imposing liability under the civil law is usually much less stringent than in the criminal law because the interests at stake are of differing values. Therefore, imposing criminal penalties for violating a duty imposed by the civil law implicates constitutional issues of due process and fundamental fairness. So why is it appropriate to extrapolate a legal duty from tort law to provide for a legal duty in the criminal law?

Barber v. Superior Court

(Physician) v. (Trial Court)
(1983) 147 Cal.App.3d 1066, 195 Cal.Rptr. 484

M E M O R Y   G R A P H I C

Instant Facts

Barber (D), a physician, removed Herbert (a comatose patient with little chance of recovery) from life support at his family's request.

Black Letter Rule

Removal of life support equipment from a comatose patient who is unlikely to recover is not an affirmative act, but an act of omission, that, if in accord with the patient's or surrogate's wishes, does not give rise to criminal liability.

Case Vocabulary

BRAIN DEATH: A condition where the body shows no response to stimuli, shows no bodily function such as breathing or movement, and shows no brain activity.

Procedural Basis: Appeal from reinstatement of complaint for murder and conspiracy to commit murder.

Facts: Shortly after surgery, Clarence Herbert suffered a cardiac arrest. He was revived and placed on life support. After a few days, Barber (D) and other physicians determined that Herbert was in a deep coma from which he would probably not recover. Herbert had severe brain damage, leaving him in a vegetative state, although there remained some brain activity. Barber (D), Herbert's internist, informed Herbert's family of his opinion and chances for recovery. The family drafted a written request to the hospital, stating that they wished to take Herbert off life support. When they took him off, Herbert continued to breathe without the equipment. After two more days, the family ordered the removal of Herbert's intravenous tubes [just what was in Herbert's will?]. Herbert died some time later.

Issue: Does removal of life support from a vegetative, but not brain dead, person constitute murder?

Decision and Rationale: (Compton) No. If Barber (D) lawfully and intentionally killed Herbert, malice is presumed regardless of motive. Euthanasia is neither excusable nor justifiable in California. It is conceded by all that Herbert was not dead by either statutory or historical standards, since there was still minimal brain activity. If Herbert were "brain dead," this prosecution could not have been instituted. We conclude that cessation of "heroic" life support measures is not an affirmative act, but a withdrawal of treatment. Although the treatments are self-propelled to a degree, each pulsation of the respirator or each drop of fluid from the IV device is comparable to a manually administered injection or medication. The authority cited by the Government (P) holds that a murder charge may be supported by the failure to feed a child. This case is easily distinguishable. The parent in that case had a clear duty to feed an otherwise healthy child. Here, faced with a vegetative patient with little chance of recovery, the duty of a physician is markedly different. Where it is not possible to ascertain the choice the patient himself would have made when in such a state, the surrogate [usually the family] ought to be guided by their knowledge of the patient's feelings and desires. If the patient's feelings and desires are not known, the surrogate should be guided by the patient's best interests, and the impact on those closest to the patient. There is evidence that Mr. Herbert did not want to be kept alive by machines. Herbert's wife and children decided that Herbert should receive no further treatment—we find no legal requirement that prior judicial approval was necessary. Writ prohibiting prosecution issued.

Analysis:

The court in *Barber* seems to get around the issue of euthanasia by an act/omission analysis, but some scholars are not convinced by the court's reasoning. Herbert was still alive after the respirator was turned off—what killed Herbert was the denial of food and water. Thus, some commentators argue that the physicians caused Herbert's death, just as if Herbert's wife starved her comatose husband at home. The court brings up the issue of omission and the doctor's duty to the comatose patient, asserting that burdens of treatment outweighed the benefits, so that it was not worth continuing treatment. The family made the decision after consulting with the physicians. Clearly, the physician is faced with a difficult task that presents many moral concerns that must be carefully balanced. Operating in a medical system largely under control by HMO's that must maintain profitability [as an assurance to those who love their HMO, this is asserted as a market fact and not as a condemnation], one hopes that physicians are able to weigh the benefits and burdens without interference, and are able to consult the family having as their sole concern the patient's and family's well-being.

Regina v. Cunningham

(English Government) v. (Thief)

(1957) 41 Crim. App. 155, 2 Q.B. 396, 2 All. Eng. Rep. 412

M E M O R Y   G R A P H I C

 ## Instant Facts

A thief stole a gas meter from the basement of a house, which caused the gas to leak into an adjoining house and partially asphyxiate an elderly woman who lived there.

 ## Black Letter Rule

The mens rea requirement of malice is satisfied by a showing of either intentional or reckless conduct; a showing of wickedness will not suffice.

Case Vocabulary

INTENTIONALLY: A state of mind indicating that a person performed an act purposefully or willfully, and not accidentally.

MALICE: A state of mind showing an evil intent, or one that causes a person to purposely or willfully commit an act with no regard for its effect on others.

RECKLESSNESS: A state of mind indicating a callous disregard for the foreseeable consequences of performing an act.

Procedural Basis: Appeal after a conviction for unlawfully and maliciously poisoning a person.

Facts: Cunningham (D) was engaged to Mrs. Wade's daughter. Mrs. Wade owned a house that had been divided into two individual homes. Mrs. Wade lived on one side with her husband and Cunningham (D) was to live on the other side after his marriage to the Wades' daughter. Cunningham (D) was out of work and needed money, so he went into the basement of the unoccupied portion of the house and stole the gas meter. In a statement to the police, Cunningham (D) admitted that he wrenched the gas meter from the wall, stole the money from within (8 shillings) and discarded the meter. Although there was a shut off valve about 2 feet from the meter, Cunningham (D) did not turn off the gas. As a result, gas leaked through the basement wall and into Mrs. Wade's house, where it partially asphyxiated her while she was sleeping in her bedroom. Cunningham (D) was indicted for violating Section 23 of the Offenses against the Person Act [making it a felony to unlawfully and maliciously administer poison to a person, or cause poison to be administered to a person, so as to endanger the person's life]. The trial judge instructed the jury that the term "malicious" in the statute meant "wicked." The jury convicted Cunningham (D) and he appealed, claiming that the judge erroneously instructed the jury as to the meaning of the word "malicious."

Issue: Will a mens rea requirement of "maliciousness" be satisfied by a finding that the actor acted "wickedly" when he performed the proscribed acts?

Decision and Rationale: (Byrne, J.) No. In order to satisfy the mens rea requirement of maliciousness, the actor must either intentionally set out to cause the harm that resulted, or he must have been reckless with regard to whether the harm would in fact result. If the actor did not intend to bring about the harm, he must at least have been able to foresee that the harm could occur if he persisted in his actions. He would be acting recklessly if he chose to disregard the foreseeable risk of harm and to act anyway. In the instant case, it does not appear that Cunningham (D) intentionally released the gas to poison Mrs. Wade. [The notion is open to debate, however, as Mrs. Wade was his mother-in-law to be, after all.] The trial judge instructed the jury that the statutory concept of "malicious" meant wicked; that is, they could convict if they found that Cunningham (D) was doing something he knew he should not have been doing, something that was wrong. We think that definition was too broad. In the context of this statute, an act is "malicious" if it is done intentionally or recklessly. The jury should have been instructed that Cunningham (D) could have been convicted if he acted "maliciously" in that he intended to cause an injury to Mrs. Wade, or he foresaw that *someone* might be injured by the escaping gas, but recklessly persisted in stealing the meter anyway. Because the jury was erroneously instructed as to the meaning of "malicious," we cannot be sure beyond a reasonable doubt that they found that Cunningham (D) acted with the requisite state of mind. Appeal allowed and conviction quashed.

Analysis:

As this case demonstrates, the concept of mens rea is a tricky one—even for judges. As you have already seen, the concept of mens rea evolved over time from a general notion of moral blameworthiness i.e. being possessed of "evil intent" or an immoral motive, to a more narrowly defined state of mind—often one that is specifically required by the wording of the offense. This case shows that evolution because, quite clearly, the trial court and the appellate court applied two different definitions of mens rea. The trial court followed the "culpability" approach to mens rea, which would support a finding of guilt based on more general immoral or improper motives. In this case, the offense required that an actor "maliciously" cause poison to be administered to a person. The trial court's instruction suggested that Cunningham (D) could be convicted if he acted wickedly; that is, if he was morally blameworthy in a general sense for stealing the gas meter, or if he knew he was doing something wrong. But Cunningham (D) certainly knew he was doing something wrong when he stole the meter. The crucial question becomes whether his knowledge that he was doing something wrong when he stole the meter was enough to constitute the maliciousness that was required to hold him accountable for the much greater offense of endangering a person's life. The appellate court's concern was that the jury may have convicted Cunningham (D) because his act of stealing the meter indicated that he was a "bad" or "immoral" man. Although such a finding may have been sufficient under the "culpability" approach to mens rea, the appellate court clearly found that more was required to constitute the "malice" required by the statute. The appellate court applied the "elemental" approach to mens rea, under which the proper inquiry was whether Cunningham (D) acted intentionally or recklessly to cause the gas to escape and poison someone. It is important to recognize that the appellate court *did not* quash the conviction because the evidence indicated that Cunningham (D) lacked the requisite mens rea. It could be argued that Cunningham (D) foresaw when he wrenched the meter from the pipes that someone might be injured by the gas. The jury might have found that he was reckless by disregarding a very real risk. The appellate court quashed the conviction because, as the jury was instructed, it may have (and probably did) convict Cunningham (D) because his act of stealing the meter was wrong, rather than inquiring as to whether he possessed the necessary level of intent or recklessness mandated by the statute.

Regina v. Faulkner

(Prosecution) v. (Ship Arsonist)
(1877) 13 Cox Crim. Cas. 550

M E M O R Y   G R A P H I C

 ## Instant Facts
Faulkner (D) was convicted of arson in burning ship, even though he only intended to steal rum.

 ## Black Letter Rule
One who is engaged in the commission of a felony is not criminally responsible for every result occasioned thereby, unless it is a probable consequence of his act or such that he could have reasonably foreseen or intended it.

 ## Case Vocabulary

COURT FOR THE CROWN CASES RESERVED: Court composed of judges who considered questions of law after prisoner had been found guilty, and trial judge would "state a case" for the opinion of the court. Abolished in 1907.

MALA IN SE: Morally wrong acts that are wrongs in themselves.

Procedural Basis: Appeal from criminal conviction for violation of malicious damage act.

Facts: Faulkner (D), a sailor sailing the high seas, went to steal some rum on board the ship. [He really needed a drink.] He lit a match near the rum, the rum caught fire destroying the ship, and Faulkner (D) was injured. He was convicted of violating the Malicious Damage Act by maliciously setting fire to the ship (arson). [Faulkner (D) says he only intended to steal, not cause the ship to burn.] The judge instructed the jury that "although the prisoner had no actual intention of burning the vessel, still, if they found he was engaged in stealing the rum, and that the fire took place in the manner above stated, they ought to find him guilty."

Issue: Is one who engages in the commission of a felony criminally responsible for every result occasioned thereby?

Decision and Rationale: (Barry) No. One who is engaged in the commission of a felony is not criminally responsible for every result occasioned thereby, unless it is a probable consequence of his act or such that he could have reasonably foreseen or intended it. It is contended by the Crown [equivalent to The People] that if one commits a felony and in so doing, he accidentally does some collateral act, which if done willfully would be another felony, he is guilty of the latter felony. [In other words, they want to convict Faulkner (D) of arson, not just theft of the rum.] In *Reg v. Pembliton*, it was decided that to constitute an offense under the Malicious Injuries to Property Act, the act done must be in fact intentional and willful, although the intention and will may be proved by the fact that the accused knew that the injury would be the probable result of his unlawful act, and yet acted recklessly of such consequences. In this case, the jury was directed to render a guilty verdict if the firing of the ship, though accidental, was caused by an act done in the course of, or immediately consequent upon, a felonious operation. There was no issue for the jury regarding the prisoner's malice, constructive or otherwise. This direction was erroneous, and the conviction should be quashed.

Concurrence: (Fitzgerald) I concur and note that there was no authority cited for such an extensive proposition asserted by the prosecution and thus, it is not warranted by law.

Analysis:

This case looks at the culpability requirements to establish a criminal conviction for injury to property by way of arson. The evidence was undisputed that Faulkner (D) did not intend to set fire to the ship and destroy it. Rather, he accidentally set the fire during the commission of another crime. The prosecution's theory was that he should be criminally responsible for all conduct resulting from his attempted theft of the rum. The court was unwilling to extend criminal responsibility this far, when there was no consideration by the jury of whether Faulkner (D) was acting with malice. Note that the arson was caused "accidentally," which may be classified as "negligently," which is a different kind of culpability than "recklessness," in that it does not involve a state of awareness. In other words, the person inadvertently creates a risk of which he ought to be aware. Recall in the last case, *Regina v. Faulkner*, the conviction was quashed where the jury was not properly instructed on whether the defendant acted maliciously. Similarly, in this case, the jury should have considered whether Faulkner (D) should have been aware of the risk and whether he acted with malice.

Santillanes v. New Mexico

(Knife Wielder) v. (People)
115 N.M. 215, 849 P.2d 358 (NM 1993)

M E M O R Y   G R A P H I C

Instant Facts
Santillanes (D) was convicted of child abuse for cutting his nephew's neck with a knife during an altercation.

Black Letter Rule
While the legislature is free to impose criminal liability upon whatever standard of culpability it desires, unless specifically stated in the statute, "negligence" shall be interpreted as requiring criminal negligence.

Case Vocabulary

CRIMINAL NEGLIGENCE: Negligence that rises to the level of being an act or omission with reckless disregard of a duty imposed by law, and of the possible consequences caused another person.

Procedural Basis: Appeal taken from a jury conviction for child abuse.

Facts: Santillanes (D) cut his 7-year-old nephew's neck with a knife during an altercation [maybe he should pick on someone his own size]. At the close of all the evidence, Santillanes' (D) counsel submitted jury instructions that included a criminal negligence standard patterned on the definition provided in the Model Penal Code Section 2.02(2)(d) (1985). The trial court refused to give this instruction, opting instead to instruct the jury on a civil negligence standard to wit: "An act, to be 'negligence,' must be one which a reasonably prudent person would foresee as involving an unreasonable risk of injury to himself or to another and which such a person, in the exercise of ordinary care, would not do." Santillanes (D) maintains that felony punishment should attach only to criminal acts, in this case criminal negligence, not to ordinary civil negligence.

Issue: When the legislature, in writing a criminal statute based on negligence, does not define the level of negligence required, may civil negligence be applied?

Decision and Rationale: (Frost, J) No. When the legislature has remained silent on the level of intent required in a criminal statute, we do not assume they intended a no-fault or strict liability crime. Rather, it is well settled that we must presume criminal intent is required unless it is clear the legislature intended to omit the mens rea element. The present issue is when the mens rea has been included in a criminal statute, here the term "negligently," but not defined this term, what degree of negligence is required. We interpret this statute to require criminal negligence instead of ordinary civil negligence. There is reasonable doubt here as to the intended scope of proscribed conduct under the child abuse statute. Therefore, strictly construing the statutory language in favor of lenity, and in the absence of clear legislative intent that ordinary civil negligence is sufficient, we conclude that the criminal negligence standard applies. This is because we construe the intended scope of the statute as aiming to punish conduct that is morally culpable, not merely inadvertent. [The conviction was affirmed anyway, because the Court found on the facts of the case that the erroneous jury instruction was harmless error.]

Analysis:

Notice that the Court quickly goes over one of the canons of statutory interpretation: that all criminal statutes are to be strictly construed, with ties going to the defendant. Why is this so? If a statute is ambiguously written, it does not do an effective job of informing people of what conduct is proper. How can someone be fairly punished under a statute that is not clear as to the conduct it makes illegal? This is an issue of fundamental fairness and due process. One can also make a case that punishing a person under an ambiguous statute may also be an effective enactment of an ex post facto law. Surely if a society is to maintain the legitimacy of its system of laws, it may not hand out punishment in a capricious and arbitrary manner. Hence the requirement of strict construction of criminal statutes and the rule of lenity alluded to by the Court.

Holloway v. United States

(Carjacker) v. (Government)

(1999) 526 U.S. 1

CARJACKING STATUTE:
A Carjacker is Guilty if he has Intent to Kill or Harm a Person.
Conditional or Uncondital Intent?

M E M O R Y G R A P H I C

Instant Facts

Interpretation by the Supreme Court of carjacking statute and whether "conditional" or "unconditional" intent to kill or harm is required.

Black Letter Rule

A statute that has intent to cause death or serious bodily harm as an element of the crime does not require proof of *unconditional* intent to kill or harm; rather mere proof of intent to kill or harm is sufficient even if accompanied by a condition.

Procedural Basis: Appeal to United States Supreme Court regarding interpretation of federal criminal statute.

Facts: Carjacking statute provides, "Whoever, with the intent to cause death or serious bodily harm takes a motor vehicle that has been transported, shipped, or received in interstate or foreign commerce from the person or presence of another by force and violence or by intimidation, or attempts to do so, shall…" be fined or imprisoned or both. The issue is whether the Government must prove that Holloway (D) had an unconditional intent to kill or harm in all events, or whether merely proof of an intent to kill or harm if necessary to effect a carjacking is required.

Issue: Does a statute that has intent to cause death or serious bodily harm as an element of the crime require proof of *unconditional* intent to kill or harm?

Decision and Rationale: (Stevens) No. We hold that a statute that has intent to cause death or serious bodily harm as an element of the crime does not require proof of *unconditional* intent to kill or harm; rather mere proof of intent to kill or harm is sufficient even if accompanied by a condition. Most courts have concluded, as do we, that Congress intended to criminalize the more typical carjacking carried out by means of a deliberate threat of violence, rather than just the rare case in which the defendant has an unconditional intent to use violence regardless of how the driver responds to his threat. Cases and scholarly writing have recognized that the "specific intent" to commit a wrongful act may be conditional. For example, In *People v. Connors*, the court affirmed the conviction for assault with intent to kill of a union organizer who had pointed a gun at a worker and threatened to kill him forthwith if he did not take off his overalls and quit work. The jury was properly instructed that "specific intent to kill" could be found even though that intent was "coupled with a condition" that the defendant would not fire if the victim complied with his demand. [Probably because you can never trust what a criminal says.] Thus, a defendant may not negate a proscribed intent by requiring the victim to comply with a condition the defendant has no right to impose.

Dissent: (Scalia) In customary English usage the word "intent" does not usually connote a purpose that is subject to any conditions precedent except those so remote they are effectively non-existent. Other criminal statutes that contain intent requirements make it clear that the doctrine of conditional intent cannot be applied across-the-board to the criminal code. For example, a statute makes it a crime to possess drugs with intent to distribute them. Possession alone is a lesser crime. Assume a person possesses an illegal drug, but at the time of acquiring it, he tells his wife not to worry about the expense, because, if they had an emergency need for money, he could always resell it. If conditional intent suffices, the person who has never sold drugs and never intended to sell in any normal sense has been guilty of possession with intent to distribute.

Analysis:

This case examines the meaning of "intent" in a crime requiring proof of specific intent. The majority opinion holds that "intent" to commit a crime may be conditional or unconditional. The strong dissent asserts that it is absurd to permit "conditional "intent to constitute a violation of the particular criminal statute. The Model Penal Code follows the majority. It provides, "When a particular purpose is an element of an offense, the element is established although such purpose is conditional, unless the condition negatives the harm or evil sought to be prevented by the law defining the offense." The majority correctly notes that Congress intended the criminal carjacking statute to apply to the typical car-jacking incident, not just the rare case where a carjacker intends to use violence even if the driver peacefully gives over possession of the car to the carjacker. However, the dissent makes a valid point in its example of the drug possessor being convicted for intent to distribute merely because he commented to his wife about a hypothetical future possibility of selling the drug if necessary.

United States v. Jewell

(People) v. (Drug Runner)
532 F.2d 697 (1976)

M E M O R Y   G R A P H I C

Instant Facts

Jewell (D) is being prosecuted for smuggling drugs in a secret compartment of a vehicle, but claims he did not know for sure that the compartment contained drugs.

Black Letter Rule

The "knowledge" element of a crime does not require actual positive knowledge, but only requires the defendant to have had an awareness of a high probability of the existence of the fact of which "knowledge" is required.

Case Vocabulary

WILLFULL BLINDNESS: A criminal defendant's intentional ignorance or avoidance of the knowledge or facts he is required to have known in order to be guilty.

Procedural Basis: Appeal to the federal circuit court of a conviction for the knowing transportation of a controlled substance.

Facts: Jewell (D) was caught entering the United States from Mexico in an automobile containing 110 pounds of marijuana, concealed in a secret compartment. Jewell (D) testified that while he knew the compartment existed, he did not know that it contained marijuana. [That's believable?] At trial there was presented circumstantial evidence from which the jury could infer that Jewell (D) had positive knowledge of the presence of the marijuana. There was also evidence presented that although Jewell (D) knew of the compartment and had knowledge of facts tending to indicate the presence of marijuana, he deliberately avoided positive knowledge of the marijuana in order to avoid criminal liability in the event it was discovered. Jewell (D) tendered an instruction requiring the jury to find that Jewell (D) knew he was in possession of marijuana. This instruction was rejected. Instead, the court instructed the jury that it must find beyond a reasonable doubt that Jewell (D) "knowingly" possessed the marijuana and that "if the defendant was not actually aware that there was marijuana in the vehicle he was driving when he entered the United States his ignorance in that regard was solely and entirely a result of his having made a conscious purpose to disregard the nature of that which was in the vehicle, with a conscious purpose to avoid learning the truth." The jury found Jewell (D) guilty of the charge.

Issue: When a crime requires "knowledge" of an element before a finding of guilty, does the requirement imply actual positive knowledge?

Decision and Rationale: (Browning, J) No. The legal premise of the instructions given by the trial court is firmly supported by leading commentators here and in England. The substantive justification of the rule is that deliberate ignorance and positive knowledge are equally culpable. The textual justification is that in common understanding one "knows" facts of which he is less than absolutely certain. In other words, when one acts with an awareness of the high probability that some fact exists, he is acting "knowingly" with respect to that fact. This principle does not apply, however, when the actor has actual belief the fact does not exist. This rule is meant to keep actors from escaping liability through "wilful blindness" or "connivance," when the actor is aware of the probable existence of a material fact but does not satisfy himself that it does not in fact exist. This required state of mind differs from positive knowledge only so far as necessary to encompass a calculated effort to avoid the sanctions of the statute while violating its substance. A court can properly find wilfulness only where it can be said that the defendant actually knew. When the prosecution proves that the defendant would have known but-for his conscious purpose to avoid learning the truth it has proven "knowledge" as contemplated under the statute. No legitimate interest of an accused is prejudiced by such a standard, and society's interest in a system of criminal law that is enforceable and that imposes sanctions upon all who are equally culpable requires it. Affirmed.

Dissent: (Kennedy, J) The approach adopted in the Model Penal Code section 2.02(7) restricts the English doctrine in important ways. It requires an awareness of a high probability that a fact exists, not merely a reckless disregard, or a suspicion followed by a failure to make further inquiry. It also establishes knowledge as a matter of subjective belief. In light of the Model Penal Code's definition, the "conscious purpose" jury instruction has three flaws. First, it fails to mention the requirement that Jewell (D) have been aware of a high probability that a controlled substance was in the car. It is not culpable to form a "conscious purpose to avoid learning the truth" unless one is aware of facts indicating a high probability of that truth. Thus, a conscious purpose instruction is only proper when coupled with a requirement that one be aware of a high probability of the truth. Second, the instruction did not alert the jury that Jewell (D) could not be convicted if he "actually believed" there was no controlled substance in the car. This failure to emphasize the subjective belief may allow a jury to convict on an objective theory of knowledge—that a reasonable man should have inspected the car and would have discovered what was hidden inside. Third, the instruction states that Jewell (D) could have been convicted even if found ignorant or "not actually aware" that the car contained a controlled substance. This is unacceptable because true ignorance, no matter how unreasonable, cannot provide a basis for criminal liability when the statute requires knowledge.

Analysis:

What is the difference between "knowledge" and "intent"? In some areas of criminal law it might not matter, but in many areas it does. The approach taken by the Model Penal Code is to define separately the mental states of knowledge and intent (or purpose). The Code says that one acts "purposely" when it is the person's "conscious object" to cause the criminal result, while one acts "knowingly" when he is aware that the results are "practically certain." Putting the two together, one acts "purposely" with regard to the nature of his conduct when he has the conscious objective to engage in such conduct, and he acts "knowingly" with regard to the nature of his conduct when he is aware that his conduct is of that nature. As illustrated, the Model Penal Code does have an exception for cases like *Jewell* where the defendant has deliberately avoided actual knowledge in an attempt to skirt the bounds of the law. Remember that the exception is one predicated on a subjective theory of knowledge. Therefore, one may not be convicted because, given the circumstances, he should have known because a reasonable person would have. Why not impose liability for failing to know what a reasonable person would? This happens in civil law all of the time. Are not criminals, by definition, unreasonable people? After all, so-called reasonable people don't go around committing crimes. Criminal liability may not be imposed unless the defendant had the proper state of mind. The focus is the defendant's mind because that is the mind that was at the scene, conscious of and controlling what was happening. If the defendant is not aware of what he is doing or cannot control himself, no matter what a reasonably prudent person would do in the same situation, he is not mentally culpable and therefore not responsible in the eyes of the law.

Regina v. Prince

(Queen) v. (Teen Napper)
L.R. 2 Cr.. Cas. Res. 154 (1875)

M E M O R Y   G R A P H I C

Instant Facts

Prince (D), under the reasonable, but false pretense that she was 18 years old, took a 14-year-old girl without the permission of her parents and was convicted of a misdemeanor.

Black Letter Rule

Criminal statutes that do not require the proscribed conduct to be done "knowingly" cannot be defended against by a mistake of fact, they are strict liability.

Case Vocabulary

MENS REA: The frame of mind, pursuant to a criminal statute, the prosecution must prove the actor had in order to establish guilt.

Procedural Basis: Appeal from a conviction for unlawfully taking a girl under sixteen years old without parental permission.

Facts: Prince (D) was convicted under a criminal statute making it a crime to "unlawfully take or cause to be taken any unmarried girl, being under the age of sixteen years, out of the possession and against the will of her father or mother, or of any person having the lawful care or charge of her, shall be guilty of a misdemeanor...." The jury found that the girl, only fourteen years old, had told Prince (D) that she was eighteen before he took her away. Also, that Prince (D) honestly and reasonably believed the girl was eighteen. Prince (D) appeals, claiming that the statute requires that the person not believe that the girl he takes is over sixteen.

Issue: When a statute does not explicitly require that the proscribed conduct be done with knowledge of the facts making it illegal, will a reasonable mistake of such facts be a valid defense?

Decision and Rationale: (Denman, J) No. Affirmed. [The rationale is not given.]

(Bramwell, J) Nowhere in the statute is there any requirement that the defendant not have a belief that the girl is sixteen years old or greater in order for guilt to lie. For the following reasons this Court is not bound to read such a mens rea requirement into the statute: The act forbidden is wrong in itself; I do not say illegal, but wrong. No argument is necessary to prove this; it is enough to state the case. The legislature has decided that anyone who does this wrong act, does it at the risk of her turning out to be under sixteen. This opinion gives full scope and accord to the doctrine of mens rea. If the taker believes he has the father's permission, though wrongly, he would have no mens rea. In such a case he would not know he was doing the forbidden act. He would not know he was doing an act wrong in itself, whatever was his intention, if done without lawful cause. The same principle holds true in other cases. For instance, the man held liable for striking a police officer in the execution of his duty, though he did not know the man was a police officer. Why? Because the act is wrong in and of itself. It seems to me impossible to say that where a person takes girl out of her father's possession, not knowing whether she is or is not under sixteen, that he is not guilty; and equally impossible when he believes, but erroneously, that she is old enough for him to do a wrong act with safety. I think the conviction should be affirmed.

Concurrence: Upon all the cases I think it is proved that there can be no conviction for crime in England in the absence of a criminal mind or mens rea. I don't doubt that the proper mens rea is present in the case of the person who knowingly does acts which would constitute a crime if the result were as he anticipated, but in which the result may not improbably end by bringing the offense within a more serious class of crime. For example, when a man strikes with the intent to do grievous bodily harm, and kills, the result makes the crime murder. The man has run the risk. The same would be the case where one takes a girl without any belief as to her age, or without caring how young she is. He has run the risk. It is clear that ignorance of the law is not an excuse. It is a different case where one, if the facts were as he believed, would be guilty of no crime at all because in such a case the required mens rea does not exist. I come to the conclusion that a mistake of facts, on reasonable grounds, to the extent the facts were as believed, would make him not guilty.

Analysis:

Consider the reasoning of Judge Bramwell. He bases his holding mostly on the normative consideration that because the act was "wrong," and Prince (D) had to know it was "wrong," the fact he thought she was eighteen does not excuse his conduct. He seems to be saying that because the act in and of itself is morally wrong no criminal intent is required. He fails to support his contention with any type of rational argument, instead he simply says that "no argument is necessary," or seemingly that everyone knows as a matter of common knowledge that the act is wrong and therefore there should be strict liability. Judge Brett draws a more lenient line. He feels that if the facts were as the actor believed them to be there would be no crime, then such a mistake will be a valid defense as long as the mistake is reasonable. However, if the facts as believed by the actor would still make the act a crime, albeit a lesser one, or if the actor has acted with a reckless disregard as to what the facts are, then he has run the risk and his belief, no matter how honest and reasonable, will not excuse him from criminal liability. Notice the requirement that the actor's beliefs as to the facts must be reasonable. This requires a jury to apply an objective standard. If the actor does not have the proper mens rea, no matter how unreasonable his belief, if it were an honest belief, what justifies holding him criminally liable?

People v. Olsen

(State Citizens) v. (Accused Rapist)
36 Cal. 3d 638, 685 P.2d 52 (1984)

M E M O R Y   G R A P H I C

Instant Facts

Olsen (D) was convicted of the statutory rape of a girl under fourteen years old, even though he reasonably thought she was seventeen. He now appeals on the basis that he lacked the required knowledge to make his actions culpable.

Black Letter Rule

A reasonable mistake of fact, that if true would still not make the actor's conduct legal, is not a valid affirmative defense against the crime actually committed.

Case Vocabulary

STRICT LIABILITY: Liability without fault or negligence, based on a violation of an absolute duty.

Procedural Basis: Appeal to the State's highest court after a conviction in the trial court for the statutory rape of a girl less than fourteen years old.

Facts: Olsen (D) was convicted of committing a lewd or lascivious act with a child under fourteen years old. At trial the victim, named Shawn, who was just under fourteen years at the time if the incident testified that she was staying in her family's trailer in their driveway due to the presence of a number of houseguests. That during the third night she'd locked the trailer as directed by her parents and was sleeping when she was awakened by Olsen (D) knocking on the window and asking to be let in. That she ignored his requests and he soon left only to have another person named Garcia come and also knock on the window asking to enter. Once again she did not answer and Garcia left. That she was once again awoken by barking dogs and by Garcia who had a knife by her side and his hand over her mouth. Garcia is then said to have called out to Olsen (D) to enter the trailer. That upon entering the trailer, Garcia told Olsen (D) to have intercourse with the girl which Olsen (D) proceeded to do. That while Olsen (D) was having intercourse with Shawn her father entered the trailer and was stabbed by Garcia as he tried to leave. Shawn also testified that she knew Garcia "pretty well" and that she was very good friends "off and on" with Olsen (D) and that for one three month period she'd spent almost every day at Olsen's (D) house. Also, that at the time of the incident she considered Garcia her boyfriend. Shawn also admitted telling both Garcia and Olsen (D) that she was over sixteen and she also conceded that she looked older than sixteen. Garcia testified that the day before the incident Shawn had invited him to spend the night in the trailer so they could have sex. That he and Shawn had engaged in intercourse about four times that evening and that she'd invited him to come back the next evening at midnight. Garcia continued that the next night, after trying twice unsuccessfully to enter the trailer, he and Olsen (D) were told by Shawn to come back at midnight. That when they did they were greeted at the door by Shawn wearing only panties who told them that she wanted "to make love" with Olsen (D) first. When Shawn's father, Mr. M, entered the trailer, Olsen (D) was on top of Shawn. Garcia denied threatening Shawn with a knife, taking her nightgown off, breaking into her trailer or forcing her to have sex. There was also testimony by Shawn indicating she knew both Garcia and Olsen (D) and had had sexual relations, excluding intercourse, with both in the past. The court found both Garcia and Olsen (D) guilty of violating Penal Code § 288, subd. (a) that makes it a crime to "willfully and lewdly commit any lewd or lascivious act ... upon or with the body ... of a child under the age of 14 years .... Subdivision (a) contains no knowledge requirement regarding the child's age.

Issue: Is a reasonable mistake as to the victim's age a defense to the charge of lewd or lascivious conduct with a child under fourteen years of age?

Decision and Rationale: (Bird, C.J.) No. The language of § 288 is silent as to whether a good faith, reasonable mistake as to the victim's age constitutes a defense to a charge under that statute. This Court previously held, against established precedent, in *People v. Hernandez* that an accused's good faith and reasonable belief that a victim was 18 years or more of age was a defense to a charge of statutory rape. One Court of Appeal has declined to apply this holding to a case where a marijuana dealer made out a reasonable mistake of age defense to a charge of offering or furnishing marijuana to a minor. That court distinguished the case from *Hernandez* by noting that the act of furnishing marijuana is illegal regardless of the age of the recipient and that when the recipient is a minor the crime is viewed as being more serious. A mistake of fact relating only to the gravity of the offense will not shield a deliberate offender from the full consequences of the wrong actually committed. Section 288 was enacted to serve the strong public policy that children of tender years should be protected. Even the *Hernandez* court recognized this consideration when it made clear that it did not contemplate applying the mistake of age defense when the victim was of such tender years. This conclusion is also supported by the legislature's enactment of § 1203.066, subd. (a)(3) which makes people convicted of the crime Olsen (D) has been convicted of eligible for probation if they "honestly and reasonably believed the victim was 14 years old or older." This is a strong indication that the legislature did not intend for a mistake of age to be a defense against such a charge. For the Court to hold that it is a defense would nullify § 1203.066, subd. (a)(3). Other legislative provisions also support our holding. For instance, the legislature has determined that persons who commit sexual offenses on children under 14 should receive a more severe punishment than those who've committed such offenses against children under 18. The legislative purpose of § 288 wouldn't be served by recognizing the defense of reasonable mistake of age. Affirmed.

Concurrence and Dissent:
(Grodin, J) I am convinced that the Court is correct in its holding that the legislature did not want a reasonable mistake of age to be a defense against a charge under § 288, subd. (a). What troubles me is the notion that a person who acted with such belief, and is not otherwise shown to be guilty of any criminal conduct, may not only be convicted but sentenced to prison notwithstanding his eligibility for probation when it appears his belief did not accord with reality. That is cruel and unusual punishment. While our legal institutions include certain "strict liability" crimes, these are mostly confined to "regulatory" or "public welfare" offenses. But even in the regulatory sphere judicial and academic acceptance of liability without fault has not been enthusiastic. With respect to traditional crimes, it is a widely accepted normative principle that conviction should not be had without proof of fault. When a person has acted under a reasonable belief that his actions are in accord with the law, such person is acting in a way which is no different from the way our society would expect a reasonable, careful, and law abiding citizen to act. When this is the case, it seems to me that the imposition of criminal sanctions, particularly imprisonment, simply cannot be tolerated in a civilized society.

Analysis:

The holding of this court seems to be in line with the dissent of Judge Brett in the *Prince* case—that when a actor would not be guilty of any crime had the facts been as he believed them to be, as long as the mistake of fact is reasonable it will constitute a valid defense. California is in the minority in this regard, but there are a substantial number of states that agree and allow a defense of reasonable mistake of age. In footnote 2 of Judge Grodin's opinion he points out that even though the prosecution suggests that Olsen (D) was at least guilty of having sexual intercourse with a female under eighteen years, he was never charged with such a crime let alone convicted, and that it is not clear from the record that Olsen (D) even had intercourse with Shawn. In light of this revelation, how is it that Olsen's (D) reasonable mistake of age defense was not allowed? Perhaps the Court relied on the reasoning of Judge Bramwell in *Prince*, that because the act was morally wrong from the beginning the defendant runs the risk that the facts are not quite as he believed. Maybe the Court is relying on the prosecution's assertion that Olsen (D) is at least guilty of having sex with a person under eighteen years of age. If this is the case then there are some very serious due process considerations implicated. As Judge Grodin has pointed out, Olsen (D) was never proved to have had intercourse with Shawn because intercourse is not a required element under § 288, subd. (a). This means that the prosecution never demonstrated that Olsen (D) would have been guilty even had the facts been as he reasonably believed them to be. In such a situation shouldn't the *Hernandez* rule apply?

UNLESS A STATUTORY OFFENSE IS OF THE PUBLIC WELFARE VARIETY, IT MUST BE PROVEN THAT THE ACTOR HAD THE PROPER MENS REA AS REQUIRED UNDER COMMON LAW DESPITE LEGISLATIVE OMISSION OF SUCH AN ELEMENT

Morissette v. United States

(Junk Dealer) v. (People)
342 U.S. 246 (1952)

M E M O R Y   G R A P H I C

Instant Facts

Morissette (D) ventured onto an Air Force bombing range and retrieved some very old and rusting bomb casings which he then sold as scrap.

Black Letter Rule

Failure by the legislature to include the mens rea in criminal statutes that is normally required at common law does not mean the crime is strict liability; such statutes will be interpreted to require the mens rea of such crimes required at common law.

Case Vocabulary

LARCENY: The unlawful taking of another's personal property with the intent to permanently deprive the person of that property.

Procedural Basis: Certification to the U.S. Supreme Court after the Circuit Court of Appeals affirmed defendant's conviction for "knowingly converting" government property.

Facts: Morissette (D), a junk dealer, openly entered an Air Force practice bombing range where he retrieved spent bomb casings that had been lying about for several years exposed to the weather and rusting away. He then sold them at junk market at an $84 profit. At trial it was adduced that there was no question Morissette (D) knew that what he took and sold were Air Force bomb casings. Morissette's (D) defense was that he honestly believed the casings had been abandoned by the Air Force and that he therefore had not violated anyone's rights by taking them. The trial judge rejected this defense and instructed the jury that the "question on intent is whether or not he intended to take the property." Morissette (D) was convicted of a felony under 18 U.S.C. §641. The Appeals Court held that since the statute did not expressly require criminal intent then Morissette (D) was guilty even if he didn't have such intent.

Issue: If a crime normally required intent under the common law, but as codified does not expressly include an intent requirement, can a criminal defendant be proven guilty without proving intent?

Decision and Rationale: (Jackson, J) No. The requirement of criminal intent is an old and imbedded tradition in law. Crime, as a compound concept, generally constituted only from concurrence of an evil-meaning mind with an evil-doing hand, was congenial to an intense individualism and took deep and early root in American soil. As states codified the common law of crimes, even if their enactments were silent on the subject, their courts assumed that the omission did not signify disapproval of the principle but merely recognized that intent was so inherent in the idea of the offense that it required no statutory affirmation. There have been cases where an intent requirement has been held inapplicable, but these cases dealt with regulatory or "public welfare offenses," crimes which have been deemed to not require intent because they are regarded as offenses against the state's authority. Such offenses impair the efficiency of controls deemed essential to the social order as presently constituted. In this respect, whatever the intent of the violator, the injury is the same, and the consequences are injurious or not according to fortuity. Hence, legislation applicable to such offenses, as a matter of policy, does not specify intent as a necessary element. Even if the accused in such offenses does not will the violation, he is usually in a position to prevent it with the plain and ordinary care that society expects from all. Furthermore, penalties for such offenses are relatively small and a conviction does no grave damage to the violator's reputation. Under such conditions, courts have interpreted such statutes as having dispensed with the intent requirement, though this has not been without some misgiving. However, neither this Court nor any other has undertaken to delineate a precise line or set forth comprehensive criteria for distinguishing between crimes that require a mental element and crimes that do not. We make no attempt to do so here. The question we are faced with is whether to extend the lack of an intent requirement to the offense Morissette (D) stands convicted of. Stealing, larceny, and its variants and equivalents, were among the earliest offenses known to the law that existed before legislation. They are serious crimes with serious consequences, such as prison sentences and grave harm to one's reputation. The state courts of last resort have consistently retained the intent requirement in larceny-type offenses. Congress, therefore, omitted any express description of criminal intent from the enactment before us in light of an unbroken string of judicial interpretation holding intent inherent in this class of offense. Such silence as to mental elements in an Act that merely adopts into the statutory scheme a concept of crime so well defined at common law is far different than the same silence in creating an offense new to general law and for whose definition the courts have no guidance except the Act. The Government has asked us, by a feat of construction, to radically change the weights and balances in the scales of justice. The purpose and obvious effect of doing away with the intent requirement would be to ease the prosecution's path to conviction by stripping the defendant of the benefits derived at common law from the absence of evil purpose. Such a manifest impairment of the immunities of the individual should not be extended to common law crimes on judicial initiative. We hold that the mere omission from §641 of any mention of intent will not be construed as eliminating that element from the crimes denounced by the statute. Reversed.

Analysis:

The Court stated that it was manifestly unwilling to adjust the relative burdens upon the defendant and prosecutor, as imposed at common law, on its own judicial initiative. The plain language of §641 clearly states the conversion must be done "knowingly." It seems that the statute does therefore require some type of mens rea—knowingly. So by holding that the defendant must have had the intent required at common law instead of construing the statute by its plain language, the Court is doing exactly what it said it did not want to do—defining the statute to require intent on its own judicial initiative. The exact words of the statute include one who "knowingly converts to his use..., sells ... any ... thing of value of the United States...." Looking at these words it is obvious that Morissette (D) knowingly converted or sold something. He knew and admitted as much. The key inquiry revolves around the words "thing of value." From whose standpoint is this judged by? Remember the saying "One man's junk is another man's treasure?" If the question of whether the casings had value is being defined from the point of view of the Air Force then the answer is clearly no because they'd abandoned the casings long ago. Under such an interpretation Morissette (D) is obviously not guilty. However, if the question is answered from Morissette's (D) position then it is equally clear that he is guilty, since he would not have even collected the casings if he wasn't anticipating some profit. Under the canon of statutory instruction that says any ambiguities in a criminal statute must be construed in favor of the defendant, Morissette (D) is not guilty. The Court therefore reached the correct answer, but it may have done so in a less direct, and somewhat convoluted way.

United States v. Staples

(People) v. (Gun Owner)
114 S. Ct. 1793 (1994)

M E M O R Y   G R A P H I C

Instant Facts

Staples (D) was convicted of violating the National Firearms Act, a felony, for possessing a machine gun, even though he did not know the gun was capable of firing more than one shot with each activation of the trigger.

Black Letter Rule

A criminal statute written without a mens rea requirement will be construed in light of the background of the common law for such crimes to include a mens rea requirement unless there is an explicit indication that the legislature intended there to be no such requirement.

Procedural Basis: Certification to the U.S. Supreme Court after the Circuit Court of Appeals denied defendant's appeal from a felony conviction for possession of a dangerous weapon.

Facts: Staples (D) was convicted of violating the National Firearms Act (Act) for possessing an unregistered firearm as defined under the Act. The rifle Staples (D) possessed was covered under the Act's definition of a firearm—a weapon capable of automatically firing more than one shot with a single pull of the trigger. Apparently, the rifle had a metal part that kept it from being fired on fully automatic, but this part had been filed down in order to allow fully automatic firing. Staples (D) testified that the rifle had never fired automatically while in his possession and that he didn't know it was capable of doing so. He asked for a jury instruction that the government had to prove that he "knew the gun would fire fully automatically." This instruction was refused and Staples (D) was convicted.

Issue: Should the Act be construed in light of the background common law pertaining to such crimes to require a mens rea when there is no such requirement written into the statute?

Decision and Rationale: (Thomas, J) Yes. Whether the Act requires proof that Staples (D) knew his gun was capable of being fired as a machine gun is a question of statutory construction. The Act is silent concerning the mens rea required for such a violation. However, silence on this point by itself does not necessarily suggest that congress intended to dispense with a conventional mens rea element. On the contrary, we must construe the statute in light of the background rules of the common law, in which the requirement of some mens rea for a crime is firmly embedded. Offenses that require no mens rea are generally disfavored so that there must be some indication of congressional intent, express or implied, in order to dispense with mens rea as an element of a crime. The Government argues that the Act fits in a line of precedent concerning what we have termed "public welfare" or "regulatory" offenses, in which we have understood Congress to impose a form of strict criminal liability through statutes that do not require the defendant to know the facts that make his conduct illegal. In construing such statutes, we have inferred from silence that Congress did not intend to require proof of mens rea. It is true that in such cases we have reasoned that as long as the defendant knows that he is dealing with a dangerous device of a character that places him in responsible relation to a public danger he should be alerted to the probability of strict regulation. In such instances we have assumed that Congress intended to place the burden on the defendant to ascertain at his peril whether his conduct comes within the inhibition of the statute. The Government's position is that all guns, whether covered under the statute or not, are dangerous devices that put gun owners on notice that they must determine at their hazard whether their weapons come within the scope of the Act. In support of this position the Government cites *United States v. Freed*, which involved a prosecution for possession of unregistered grenades under the Act. The defendant knew that what he possessed were grenades, and we concluded that the Act did not require the Government to prove the defendant knew that the grenades were unregistered. However, our analysis in that case rested on the assumption that the defendant knew he was dealing with hand grenades—that is, that he knew he possessed a particularly dangerous type of weapon, possession of which was not entirely "innocent" in and of itself. This is where the case at bar parts ways with *Freed*. There is a long tradition of widespread lawful gun ownership in this country. Such a tradition did not apply to possession of hand grenades in *Freed*. Roughly 50 per cent of American homes contain at least one firearm of some sort, and in the vast majority of states, buying a shotgun or rifle is a simple transaction that would not alert a person to regulation any more than would buying a car. It is unthinkable to us that Congress intended to subject law-abiding, well-intentioned citizens to a possible ten-year term of imprisonment if what they genuinely and reasonably believed was a conventional semiautomatic weapon turns out to have worn down into or been secretly modified to be a fully automatic weapon. As this Court has noted, the purpose and obvious effect of doing away with the requirement of a guilty intent is to ease the prosecution's path to conviction. We are reluctant to impute that purpose to Congress where, as here, it would mean easing the path to convicting persons whose conduct would not even alert them to the probability of strict regulation. The potentially harsh penalty attached to the Act—up to 10 years' imprisonment—confirms our reading of the Act. Punishing a violation as a felony is simply incompatible with the theory of the public welfare offenses. In this view, absent a clear statement from Congress that mens rea is not required, we should not apply the public welfare offense rationale to interpret any statute defining a felony offense as dispensing with mens rea. Reversed and remanded.

Concurrence: (Ginsburg, J) Conviction under the Act, the Government concedes, requires proof that Staples (D) "knowingly" possessed the machine gun. The question before us is not whether knowledge of possession is required, but what level of knowledge suffices: (1) knowledge simply of possession of the object; (2) knowledge, in addition, that the object is a dangerous weapon; (3) knowledge, beyond dangerousness, of the characteristics that render the object subject to regulation, for example, awareness that the weapon is a machine gun. As the Court recognizes, the generally "dangerous" character of all guns did not suffice to give individuals in Staples' (D) situation cause to inquire about the need for registration. Only the third reading suits the purpose of the mens rea requirement—to shield people against punishment for apparently innocent activity.

Analysis:

Look at the two ways Justices Thomas and Ginsburg come to the same conclusion. Are they the same? Justice Thomas begins by looking at the offense in light of the common law and coming to the conclusion that there must be some mens rea requirement. He supports this conclusion at the end of his opinion by looking at the maximum penalty allowed for a conviction under the Act and suggesting that when such serious consequences are involved there must be some form of criminal intent. In between he gets to the heart of the matter when he compares the possession of hand grenades with possession of a normal appearing gun that happens to have been modified to fire in fully automatic mode. What he says in a round about way, but never directly, is that grenades, just by being grenades—devices that are not normally found in homes, or anywhere else besides military installations for that matter—are of such characteristics as to put the possessor on notice that there is a good chance the devices are very closely and strictly regulated. A normal appearing rifle on the other hand does not provide its owner with any type of inherent warning because it is ordinary in appearance and very commonplace in America. Unless he'd been told, the only conceivable way an owner of such a gun could ever know it is fully automatic would be to fire it. Mere possession therefore does not show the owner has any sort of criminal intent. Justice Ginsburg breaks the inquiry down into a very logical sequence of three questions which allow her to very quickly come to her conclusion. The first two are obviously incorrect because there are millions of people in the country who possess objects that are considered dangerous weapons that do not require registration, even though many look almost exactly like Staples' (D) rifle. None of these people are on notice that they need to register their firearms because they are not required to. Justice Ginsburg recognizes that a greater level of mens rea is therefore required. The only alternative is that the defendant be required to know that his particular firearm is of such characteristic that it is covered under the Act.

State v. Guminga

(People) v. (Restaurant Owner)
395 N.W.2d 344 (Minn. S. Ct. 1986)

M E M O R Y   G R A P H I C

Instant Facts

Guminga (D), a restaurant owner, is being charged with vicarious criminal liability for the sale of intoxicating liquor to a minor by one of his employees at the restaurant.

Black Letter Rule

Vicarious criminal liability violates due process unless the state interest involved outweighs the liberty interest of the offender in light of any possible alternative means of achieving the state interest.

Case Vocabulary

VICARIOUS LIABILITY: Holding an employer criminally accountable for another's illegal actions because the employer was in a position to control or prevent the illegal actions of the violator, even though the employer was not directly at fault. Similar to the doctrine of respondeat superior in tort law.

Procedural Basis: Certification of a question of law to the State Supreme Court by the Court of Appeals, after the trial court had ruled that vicarious liability does not violate due process.

Facts: Guminga (D) owned a restaurant at which intoxicating beverages were sold. One day, two undercover investigators entered the restaurant with a 17-year-old woman. All three ordered alcoholic beverages. The minor had never been in the restaurant before and the waitress did not ask the minor her age or request any identification. When the waitress returned with the drinks the minor paid for all three. Once the officers confirmed the drinks contained alcohol they arrested the waitress for serving intoxicating liquor to a minor in violation of Minn. Stat. §340.73 (1984). The owner of the restaurant, defendant Guminga (D), was subsequently charged with violating §340.73 pursuant to Minn. Stat. §340.941 (1984), which imposes vicarious criminal liability on an employer whose employee serves intoxicating liquor to a minor. The state does not contend that Guminga was aware of or ratified the waitress's actions. Guminga (D) moved to dismiss the charges on the ground that §340.941 violates the Due Process Clauses of the federal and state constitutions. The trial court denied this motion. The court of appeals asked the State Supreme Court to take jurisdiction over the question.

Issue: Does holding an employer vicariously criminally liable for an employee's sale of alcohol to a minor violate the Due Process Clause of either federal or state constitutions?

Decision and Rationale: (Yetka, J) Yes. We find that the statute in question does violate the due process clauses of the Minnesota and the United States Constitutions and thus answer the certified question in the affirmative. Under Minnesota law, a defendant who commits a gross misdemeanor, the level of crime Guminga (D) is charged with, may be sentenced to "imprisonment for not more than one year or to payment of a fine of not more than $3,000 or both." In addition, a defendant convicted under §340.941 may, at the discretion of the licensing authority, have his license suspended, revoked or be unable to obtain a new license. Even if Guminga (D) were to ultimately not receive any prison sentence, a gross misdemeanor conviction will affect his criminal history score were he to be convicted of a felony in the future. A due process analysis of a statute involves a balancing of the public interest protected against the intrusion on personal liberty while taking into account any alternative means by which to achieve the same end. §340.941 serves the public interest by providing additional deterrence to violation of the liquor laws. The private interests affected, however, include liberty, damage to reputation and other future disabilities arising from criminal prosecution for an act that Guminga (D) did not commit or ratify. Such an intrusion upon personal liberty is not justified by the public interest protected, especially when there are alternative means by which to achieve the same end, such as civil fines or license suspension, which do not entail the legal and social ramifications of a criminal conviction. The dissent argues that vicarious liability is necessary as a deterrent so that owners will impress upon their employees the importance of not selling alcohol to minors. But we believe it is deterrent enough that the employee who does sell to a minor can be charged under the statute and that the business is subject to fines or suspension or revocation of license. We find that, in Minnesota, no one can be convicted of a crime punishable by imprisonment for an act he did not commit, did not have knowledge of, or give expressed or implied consent to the commission thereof. The certified question is thus answered in the affirmative.

Dissent: (Kelley, J) The strong public interest in prohibiting the sale of liquor to minors justifies the imposition of vicarious liability on the bar owner/employer for illegal sales to minors made by an employee. The majority has failed to give proper weight to the clearly expressed, longstanding public policy of this state as reflected in §340.941. Such has been the law in this state since 1905. Without the deterrent of possible personal criminal responsibility and a sentence, the legislature could have rationally determined that liquor establishment owners will be less likely to impress upon employees the need to require identification of age before serving liquor. The gravity of the problems associated with minors who consume alcoholic beverages justifies the importance by the legislature of harsher punishment on those who help contribute to those problems. The state has the right to impose limited criminal vicarious liability on bar proprietors as a reasonable exchange for the state-granted privilege of a liquor license.

Analysis:

What are the relative merits and drawbacks of vicarious criminal liability? Such provisions make it much easier to hold an employer responsible for the missteps of employees because proving that the employer knew or authorized the employee's conduct can be extremely difficult. By making such elements irrelevant, the legislature has relieved the prosecutors of such time consuming burdens. Maybe lawmakers have enacted such laws with the expectation that prosecutors will only go after those who most probably did know of or authorized the employee's conduct. Also, vicarious liability may tend to cause employers to be more careful in choosing who to hire and how to supervise employees. But the imposition of criminal liability without fault runs counter to the traditions of the American legal system. In the case of public welfare offenses the problem is greatly reduced because those offenses generally are not considered of a "criminal" nature and usually entail only a small fine. In most jurisdictions though, imposition of vicarious criminal liability brings with it the possibility of serious consequences, including imprisonment. One possible solution is to place on the defendant the burden of proving he took reasonable steps to prevent the crime by his employees and then allow the jury to decide if the steps were in fact reasonable. This would help reduce the danger of an employer being held liable even after taking all reasonable actions, something that most vicarious liability statutes do not make room for. It might be very difficult for a prosecutor to prove that an employer knows his employee has violated the law.

State v. Baker

(People) v. (Driver)
571 P.2d 65 (Kans. Ct. App. 1977)

M E M O R Y   G R A P H I C

Instant Facts

Baker (D) was convicted of speeding, a strict liability offense, after his proffer of evidence indicating that the cruise control device on his automobile had caused the vehicle to speed out of control was suppressed upon the prosecution's motion as being irrelevant.

Black Letter Rule

Though some offenses be strict liability and do not require any mens rea, they still require a voluntary act by the offender before guilt may be found.

Facts: Baker (D) was convicted of driving in excess of the posted speed limit, a strict liability offense. Before trial the state moved to suppress evidence offered by Baker (D) that: (1) Defendant's cruise control stuck in the "accelerate" position causing the car to accelerate beyond the posted speed limit; (2) The defendant attempted to deactivate the cruise control by hitting the off button, and the coast button and tapping the breaks; (3) These actions were not immediately successful in deactivating the cruise control; (4) Subsequent to the date of the incident, Baker (D) had the defective cruise control repaired. The trial court sustained the motion, thus stopping Baker (D) from introducing the proffered evidence at trial. Baker (D) was fined $10 plus costs, but both were suspended pending this appeal based on Baker's (D) assertion that the offense requires a voluntary act which was not proved in his case.

Issue: Does a strict liability offense require a voluntary act by the defendant in order for guilt to lie?

Decision and Rationale: (Spencer, J) Yes. Baker (D) readily concedes that a violation of the speeding statute is an absolute liability offense and there is no requirement that a defendant be proven to have had any intent to break the law. Further, he agrees that any evidence of the defective cruise control would be inadmissible if introduced merely to negate an intent or culpable state of mind on the part of the motorist. However, Baker (D) contends that the evidence was offered to show that his speeding was not a voluntary act and, therefore, there was no criminal liability. We do not doubt that if Baker (D) were able to establish that his speeding was the result of an unforeseen occurrence, which was not caused by him and which he could not prevent, that such would constitute a valid defense to the charge. But the evidence that was proffered suggests a malfunction of a device attached to the vehicle, over which he had or should have had absolute control. Baker (D) has not suggested that the operation of the vehicle on the day of the offense was anything but a voluntary act on his part, nor that anyone else activated the cruise control, which may have caused his excessive speed. There are cases where equipment malfunction has been held to be a valid defense to a strict liability offense when there could not be shown an overt voluntary act by the defendant. In the New York case *People v. Shaughnessy*, a passenger in a vehicle that drove onto another's private property was found not guilty of trespassing because he was just a passenger and the state failed to show an overt voluntary act or omission by the defendant. In *State v. Kremer*, a Minnesota case, the Court held that a defendant could not be guilty of running a red stop light when the evidence showed that the defendant's breaks had failed with no prior warning because, again, there was no voluntary act. Same result in *State v. Weller*, where a Connecticut court found no voluntary act when a man's throttle malfunctioned with no prior warning. In our view though, unexpected break failure and unexpected malfunction of a vehicle's throttle mechanism, both being essential components to the operation of the vehicle, differ significantly from the malfunction of a cruise control device to which the driver has voluntarily delegated partial control of that automobile. It must be said that the defendant assumed the full operation of his motor vehicle and when he did so and activated the cruise control attached to that automobile, he clearly was the agent in causing the act of speeding. Judgment Affirmed.

Analysis:

Are you as confused as this writer is regarding the way Judge Spencer has "distinguished" the *Kremer* and *Weller* cases from the instant case? It seems as if the Court is punishing Baker (D) for relying on a technical gadget to control his speed. The only way this is not the case is if the Court knows of some facts tending to show that Baker (D) had some forewarning that his cruise control was prone to malfunction. If it does, it or the editors have chosen to keep those facts hidden. The cruise control on a car is a device that people have come to trust and rely on nearly as much as breaks or a throttle. The only thing that distinguishes a cruise control from these other devices is the fact that it was considered somewhat of a luxury and less trustworthy in 1977. But surely a consumer should be free to use all the innovations of the modern age without being held liable when they fail. By concentrating on whether the drivers had any warning that their cars would malfunction the Court is entertaining a tort form of proximate causation in deciding whether there was a voluntary act. The person whose breaks fail has made an overt voluntary act by pressing his break pedal just as positively as the person who pushes the cruise control button. If there is no evidence indicating that there was a problem or probability of malfunction such that a reasonably prudent person wouldn't hesitate to use these devices, how can there be a voluntary act with one and not with another?

Regina v. City of Sault Ste. Marie

(People) v. (Municipality)
85 D.L.R.3d 161 (S. Ct. Canada 1978)

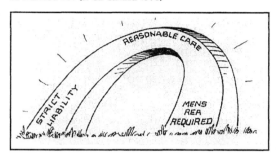

M E M O R Y   G R A P H I C

Instant Facts

Not stated. The case does not go into the facts of any specific offense, but merely discusses the relative merits of strict liability offenses, offenses requiring mens rea, and another choice between the two extremes—those where the defendant has the option of presenting the affirmative defense of reasonable care.

Black Letter Rule

There is a middle level of offenses, those where the prosecution is not required to show any required mens rea, but in which the defendant has the option of presenting the affirmative defense that he took all reasonable care.

 ### Case Vocabulary

MORAL TURPITUDE: Actions that are dishonest, immoral, or unjust.

Procedural Basis: This information is not presented.

Facts: Not stated.

Issue: Is the fact the defendant exercised all reasonable care a valid affirmative defense to some offenses that do not require any mens rea in order that guilt shall be found?

Decision and Rationale: (Dickson, J) Yes. There are various and several arguments advanced to justify absolute liability in public welfare offenses. Two predominate. First, it is argued that the protection of social interests requires a high standard of care and that absolute liability will cause people to pay more attention to such standards if they know ignorance or mistake will not excuse a failure to adhere to them. The second main argument is based on administrative efficiency. Because of the difficulty of proving mental culpability and the high number of such petty cases that jam judicial calendars, proof of fault is just too great a burden in time and money to place upon the prosecution and may result in most violators escaping without consequence. It is therefore contended that absolute liability is the most efficient and effective way of ensuring compliance with minor regulatory legislation and the social ends to be achieved are of such importance as to override the unfortunate by-product of punishing those who may be free of moral turpitude. Further justifications are that slight penalties are usually imposed and that conviction for breach of a public welfare offense carries no stigma as a conviction of a criminal offense does. Arguments of greater force are advanced against absolute liability though. Strongest is that it violates fundamental principles of penal liability. It also rests on assumptions that have not been and may be impossible to prove. There is no showing that a higher standard of care results from absolute liability. The argument that no stigma attaches does not pass muster either. For the accused will have suffered loss of time, legal costs, exposure to the criminal process, and possibly, the opprobrium of conviction. It is not sufficient to say that the public interest is engaged, and, therefore, liability may be imposed without fault. In serious crimes, the public interest is even more involved and mens rea must still be proven. The administrative argument also has little force. The unfortunate tendency in the past has been to view the choice as between two stark alternatives. However, there is an impressive and increasing stream of authority that holds that where an offense does not require full mens rea, it is nevertheless a good defense for the defendant to prove that he was not negligent. The burden of proving that all reasonable care was taken is upon the defendant, as he is the only one who will generally have the means of proof. Such burden-shifting may seem a bit unfair, but when viewed with the alternative—absolute liability—surely fairness is not an issue. While the prosecution must prove beyond a reasonable doubt that the defendant committed the proscribed act, the defendant need only prove on the balance of probabilities that he took all reasonable care. This Court therefore declares that there is room for another category of offenses rather than the two that have heretofore been recognized. Between those offenses requiring proof of mens rea and those that are of absolute liability lie a third category—those offenses in which there is no necessity for the prosecution to prove the existence of mens rea; the doing of the prohibited act is prima facie proof of the offense, leaving it open to the defendant to avoid liability by proving that he took all reasonable care. Which category an offense falls into would depend upon the wording in the statute. Offenses which are criminal in the true sense would fall in the first category, or that which requires proof of mens rea. Public welfare offenses would fall into the middle category normally, unless the statute includes such words as "wilfully," "with intent," "knowingly," or "intentionally," in which case the offense would fall into the first category. Offenses of absolute liability would be those in respect of which the

Legislature had made clear that guilt would follow proof merely of the proscribed act. The over-all regulatory pattern of the Legislature, the subject-matter of the legislation, the importance of the penalty, and the precision of the language used will be primary considerations in determining whether the offense falls into the third category.

Analysis:

This case extends and somewhat clears up what the Court in *Baker* hinted at regarding the voluntary act question. Now we have a court that has clearly set forth a tort-like causation standard, that of the reasonably prudent person. As stated in the opinion, proving criminal intent is a very difficult, time consuming and resource consuming venture. Forcing the state to carry such a burden in all public welfare offense cases would be taxing to say the least and could result in many more people getting off without suffering the consequences. Instead of forcing the prosecution to prove intent, the model posited by Judge Dickson basically forces the defendant to prove he did not have the requisite criminal intent, or conversely, that he took all reasonable care to avoid violating the law and ended up doing so despite these efforts. Such a scheme would cost very little in the form of time and expense and would not be prone to let more people off the hook. There are very few people who claim lack of intent or voluntary act when it comes to public welfare offenses because first, the penalties are so small, and second, because very few actually have a valid defense that they can actually prove at trial. Adoption of such a burden shifting scheme would therefore result in little if any increase in costs, but would give those who truly are innocent of any criminal intent a chance at a fair hearing—something that would tend to increase people's faith in the fundamental fairness of the law.

People v. Marrero

(Government) v. (Federal Corrections Officer)

(1987) 69 N.Y.2d 382, 515 N.Y.S.2d 212, 507 N.E.2d 1068

M E M O R Y   G R A P H I C

Instant Facts

Marrero (D), a federal corrections officer, was convicted for violating a statute which he believed gave him the right to carry a gun.

Black Letter Rule

An erroneous interpretation of the law does not excuse violation of the law, even where the interpretation is reasonable.

Case Vocabulary

ACTING IN RELIANCE: Actions based on trust in another person's words or actions.

MISTAKE OF LAW: An incorrect interpretation of the legal effect of a given law or set of facts.

Procedural Basis: Appeal after conviction for unlawful possession of a pistol.

Facts: Marrero (D), a federal corrections officer, was convicted of unlawful possession of a pistol under a statute containing an exemption for "peace officers." The statutory definition of "peace officers" included "correction officers of any state correction facility or of any penal correctional institution." The trial court dismissed the charge, but the Appellate Division ruled by a 3-2 vote that only state and not federal officers were covered by the provision. At the ensuing criminal trial, the court refused to instruct the jury that it should acquit Marrero (D) if he reasonably believed himself to be a peace officer under the statutory definition. Marrero (D) claimed that he relied on interpretations of fellow officers and teachers, as well as the language of the statute itself, in forming his belief that he could carry a pistol.

Issue: Does misinterpretation of a statute excuse its violation, where the statute does not have a mens rea requirement?

Decision and Rationale: (Bellacosa) No. A mistake of law does not excuse the commission of prohibited acts. Contrasted with kidnapping, which allows a showing of good-faith belief in the legality of the conduct to negate intent, a weapons statute violation imposes criminal liability regardless of intent. The mistake of law defense is available to defendants who have relied on an "official statement" of the law, either expressed in a statute or by a public servant or agency charged with administering, enforcing, or interpreting the law. Marrero (D) claims that his conduct was based on an official statement of the law contained in the statute itself. In view of the ambiguous wording, Marrero (D) argues that his "reasonable" interpretation falls under this exception. However, allowing Marrero (D) this exception would make mistake of law a generally applied or available defense, rather than an unusual exception. The Government (P) analogizes New York's *official statement* defense to the Model Penal Code. The Model Penal Code provides that the *official statement* defense only applies when the accused acts in reliance on a statute that actually authorizes his conduct. If the *official statement* of the law is afterward determined to be invalid or erroneous, the *official statement* defense protects those who mistakenly acted in reliance. Reviewing the legislative history, it is evident that the legislature intended the New York official statement defense statute to be similarly construed. Marrero's (D) conduct was never authorized by statute; he only thought that it was. If Marrero's (D) arguments were accepted, the exception would swallow the rule. Mistakes of law would be encouraged. Wrong-minded individuals would use the defense to avoid conviction. To avoid these consequences, the conviction is affirmed.

Dissent: (Hancock) In interpreting a statute, a court should look first to the particular words of the statute in question. Here, there is but one natural and obvious meaning: If a defendant founded his interpretation on an official interpretation of the statute, he should have a defense. The precise phrase from the Model Penal Code limiting the defense to reliance on a statute "afterward determined to be invalid or erroneous" was omitted from New York's penal code. How can the legislature be assumed to have enacted the very language that it specifically rejected? Also, the majority suggests that the Legislature intended the defense to be available solely in acts involving mala in se offenses, such as kidnapping. On the contrary, it is with mala prohibita (regulatory) offenses that reasons of policy and fairness call for a relaxation of the rule limiting the mistake of law defense.

Analysis:

The majority is concerned that if Marrero (D) is acquitted, people might get the message that the law is subjective, that the law is whatever the individual believes it to be. Marrero (D) does not argue, however, that he should be able to interpret the statute however he likes, but that the statute is so ambiguous that his interpretation is completely reasonable, and that a reasonable interpretation should be covered under the defense. The majority possibly exaggerates the effect an acquittal would have. For most statutes, the window of "reasonable" interpretation is fairly narrow, and judges and juries could be trusted to spot the occasional "unreasonable" interpretation. A positive effect of allowing a broader mistake of law defense would be that, where a law allows a wide array of reasonable interpretations, legislators might make a better effort to ensure that legislation is clear and understandable. Also, individualists might be pleased with an interpretation of the mistake of law defense that does not sacrifice the individual for the sake of society at large.

Cheek v. United States

(Delinquent Taxpayer) v. (Government)
(1991) 498 U.S. 192, 111 S. Ct. 604, 112 L.Ed.2d 617

M E M O R Y   G R A P H I C

Instant Facts

A pilot who had previously filed tax returns stopped filing them because he became influenced by a group who believed that the income tax system was unconstitutional. The IRS charged him with willful tax evasion.

Black Letter Rule

A mistake of law, either reasonable or unreasonable, will be a defense to a crime if it negates the specific intent required for conviction.

Procedural Basis: Appeal to United States Supreme Court of conviction for tax evasion.

Facts: Cheek (D) was a pilot for American Airlines. He duly filed his tax returns through the year 1979, but thereafter ceased to file his returns. Beginning in 1980, he began claiming excessive withholding deductions—eventually claiming 60 [not a typo!] allowances on his W-2—and also claimed he was exempt from federal income taxes. Cheek (D) did so because he had become associated with and influenced by a group that believed that the federal income tax system was unconstitutional. He was charged with tax evasion under a statute that provided, "any person who willfully attempts . . . to evade or defeat any tax imposed by this title . . . shall be guilty of a felony." Evidence was presented at trial that Cheek (D) was involved in a number of civil lawsuits challenging the constitutionality of the federal income tax between 1982 and 1986. At each of those trials, Cheek (D) and the other plaintiffs were told that their claims were frivolous or had been repeatedly rejected by the courts. At trial, Cheek (D) represented himself and testified that because he had been attending seminars and listening to lectures sponsored by this anti-tax group he believed that the federal income tax laws were invalid. He also believed that his wages were not income under the federal statute. Cheek (D) presented evidence of a letter from an attorney stating that the Sixteenth Amendment did not authorize a tax on wages as income—only profits and gain. [It's probably safe to assume that this attorney is no longer practicing.] His defense was that he sincerely believed that the tax laws were being unconstitutionally applied and that his failure to file income tax returns was therefore lawful. He argued that, based on his belief that he was acting lawfully, he did not possess the willfulness necessary to convict him of tax evasion. The trial court instructed the jury that if it found that Cheek (D) "honestly and reasonably believed he was not required to pay income taxes" then he could be acquitted. When the jury could not make this decision, the trial judge further instructed them that an honest but unreasonable belief is not a defense and does not negate willfulness. The jury convicted Cheek (D). His argument on appeal was that the judge erred by instructing the jury that only a reasonable mistake about the law negated willfulness.

Issue: Is a mistake of law that relates to the specific intent of a crime a defense to criminal prosecution?

Decision and Rationale: (White, J.) Yes. The general rule is that a mistake of law is no excuse. A limited exception applies when a mistake of law negates the specific mental state required for conviction. The statute makes it a criminal violation to willfully evade federal income tax obligations. Because of the extreme complexity of the modern tax code, our cases have repeatedly interpreted the term "willfully" to mean a voluntary, intentional violation of a *known legal duty*. In order for a mistake of law to negate willfulness, then, the mistake must relate to whether the accused *knows* of a legal duty. If, because of the complexity of the tax laws, an individual does not know of a legal duty, the mistake affords him a defense because it negates the requirement that he voluntarily and intentionally violate a known legal duty. We do not agree with the Court of Appeals that such a mistake must be reasonable. Even an unreasonable mistake would negate a finding that the individual knew of a legal duty. In this case, if the jury believed Cheek's (D) assertion that he did not think the federal tax code treated wages as income, then it could find that he did not know he had a legal duty to pay income taxes on his wages. His mistaken belief as to his duty to pay taxes on his wages would negate any finding that he intentionally violated a known legal duty. With respect to Cheek's (D) constitutional claims, however, the general rule that mistake is no defense applies. Unlike his belief about wages, Cheek's (D) constitutional claims do not arise from a mistaken belief derived from the complexity of the tax code. Instead, his claims indicate that he was intimately familiar with the applicable provisions of the federal income tax code. Cheek (D) claims mistake in that he believed that the tax laws were unconstitutional as applied to him. In other words, he was aware that the law imposed upon him a duty to pay taxes, but mistakenly believed that the law itself was unconstitutional. Because of his mistaken belief as to constitutionality, Cheek (D) voluntarily and intentionally did not pay his taxes. We believe that Cheek's (D) views about the constitutionality of the tax code in general would not preclude a finding that he willfully attempted to evade the tax laws. The District Judge did not err by instructing the jury not to consider Cheek's views about constitutionality. Remanded for a new trial.

Dissent: (Blackmun, J.) It is simply unbelievable to me that in this day and age an individual could try to defend the fact that he did not file a tax return by claiming that he mistakenly believed that his wages were not income. Our cases have defined "willfulness" with respect to the tax code as a voluntary and intentional violation of a known legal duty. Cheek (D) undoubtedly knew he had a legal duty to pay taxes on his income. He should not have been allowed to assert his "mistaken" belief that his wages were not income as a defense to "willfulness."

Analysis:

This is a difficult case to follow. The Court begins by acknowledging that the term "willfulness" in the tax code has a particularized meaning. The common law rule is that ignorance of the law or a mistake of the law is no defense. Because the tax code has grown so complex, though, the courts have had to soften the common law rule with respect to tax offenses. The government is not interested in punishing those individuals who genuinely did not know they were subject to a particular provision of the code. Instead, the government seeks to punish those who know they have a legal duty to pay taxes but purposefully and intentionally do not do so. Thus, the courts have interpreted the statutory requirement of "willfulness" in the tax code as meaning the individual voluntarily and intentionally violated a known legal duty. It is because of this definition of willfulness that the Court finds that the lower courts erred by instructing the jury that only a reasonable mistake on Cheek's (D) part would constitute a defense. Cheek (D) was essentially claiming that he did not know of his statutory duty to pay taxes on his wages. As is the case with a mistake of fact, when a crime is a specific intent offense and a mistake negates the existence of the specific intent, the accused is entitled to a defense. As applied to this case, if Cheek (D) mistakenly believed his wages were not income, he would not have known he had a legal duty to pay income taxes on his wages. If he did not know he had a legal duty under the tax code, he could not have voluntarily and intentionally set out to violate that duty. It does not matter whether his belief was objectively unreasonable. If the jury believed his claim, then he was entitled to an acquittal. The same is not necessarily true of his claim of mistake as to the constitutionality of the tax laws. There, Cheek (D) did not claim he was unaware of his statutory duty. Instead, the gravamen of his claim was that he knew he had a duty to pay taxes but mistakenly thought that the law itself was unconstitutional. Therefore, his mistake claim had nothing to do with negating the mental element of the crime—it was simply a mistake as to whether the law was applicable. In other words, Cheek (D) mistakenly thought the law did not apply to him. This is the kind of mistake that fits squarely within the common law rule that a mistake of law does not excuse its violation.

MISTAKE OF LAW IS NEVER A VALID DEFENSE UNLESS THE MISTAKE RESULTS FROM THE DEFENDANT'S REASONABLE RELIANCE UPON AN OFFICIAL—BUT MISTAKEN OR LATER OVERRULED—STATEMENT OF THE LAW

United States v. Albertini

(People) v. (Protester)
830 F.2d 985 (9th Cir. 1987)

M E M O R Y G R A P H I C

Instant Facts

After the Ninth Circuit Court of Appeals reversed his conviction for unauthorized demonstration on a military base, but before the Supreme Court granted certiorari and again reversed, Albertini (D) was arrested a second time on the same charge and seeks to use his reliance on the Ninth Circuit's reversal as a defense to the second prosecution.

Black Letter Rule

The one exception to the rule that a mistake of law is not a valid defense is the reasonable reliance upon an official, but mistaken or later overruled, statement of the law.

Case Vocabulary

MISTAKE OF LAW: When a false conclusion is made regarding the legal effects of certain known facts.

Procedural Basis: Appeal to the Ninth Circuit Court of Appeals after conviction in the District Court.

Facts: Albertini (D) had engaged in a peace demonstration on a Hawaii naval base after being barred from entering the installation by its commander. His entry constituted a violation of 18 U.S.C. §1832, and he was convicted of the offense. On appeal, the Ninth Circuit reversed the conviction in *Albertini I*, on the ground that the First Amendment protected Albertini's (D) right to demonstrate at the base. After the reversal Albertini (D) demonstrated several more times, in defiance of another order barring him from entering the installation, and was again prosecuted. About this time, the government petitioned for certiorari on *Albertini I*, but the Supreme Court did not grant certiorari until after the second group of demonstrations. The Supreme Court eventually did reverse the Ninth Circuit's decision in *Albertini I* and held that the First Amendment did not protect Albertini's (D) right to demonstrate on the installation in the face of an order barring him. The government then pressed its prosecution on for the second group of demonstrations and obtained a conviction. Albertini (D) appeals, arguing that due process precludes the retroactive application of the Supreme Court's decision reversing *Albertini I* (which had upheld the legality of his conduct).

Issue: Is the fact that a person's activities were conducted in reasonable reliance on an official and current statement of the law saying such activity is lawful a valid defense when it is later decided by a higher authority that the statement of law in question was wrong?

Decision and Rationale: (Goodwin, J) Yes. The government maintains that this Court could not create a window of opportunity to engage in challenged conduct while the Supreme Court review was still possible. Albertini (D) says that once he received a favorable ruling from this Court, and at least before the petition for certiorari was granted, he was acting within his adjudicated legal rights and had a due process right to rely upon the judgment of this Court. The Constitution provides that neither Congress nor any state shall pass an ex post facto law. This means that people cannot be prosecuted under laws that were not on the books when the offense was actually committed. Even though the rule against ex post facto laws applies to the legislature and not the courts, the principle on which it is based is fundamental to our concept of constitutional liberty. In effect, Albertini (D) obtained a declaratory judgment from this Court that his actions were lawful. Albertini (D) should be able to rely on such a declaration pursuant to the Due Process Clause until the Court's opinion is reversed, or at least until the Supreme Court has granted certiorari. The government argues that mistake of law is never a defense. There is an exception to the mistake of law doctrine, however, in circumstances where the mistake results from the defendant's reasonable reliance upon an official—but mistaken or overruled—statement of the law. To hold persons criminally liable for activities conducted in such reliance would be an act of intolerable injustice. As delineated by section 2.04 of the Model Penal Code, the doctrine may in some instances protect a defendant's reasonable reliance on official advisory opinions. Albertini (D) acted during a window of time when he reasonably believed his acts were protected under *Albertini I*. He cannot be convicted for acting in reliance on that opinion at least until the Supreme Court has granted certiorari. Reversed.

Analysis:

A reasonable mistake of fact can be a valid defense to a crime if no crime would have been committed had the facts, believed to be true, actually were true. Why aren't mistakes of law treated the same way? After all, if the actor reasonably believes that his actions are not illegal then there can be no intent to commit a criminal act. One of the answers to this question is that if mistake of law were a valid defense, presumably, individuals would deliberately keep themselves in a state of ignorance with regard to the law and then try and use their ignorance as a defense.

Then there would be the problem of proving that defendants knew what the law was. This would become an element of proof for every criminal act—did the actor know his actions were unlawful? (This is not to be confused with the inquiry of whether the actor knew what he was doing was wrong.) Also, there are so many new laws and changes to existing laws that are promulgated every year that it would be virtually impossible to keep up. It is much easier from an administrative standpoint to not allow the mistake of law defense. Moreover, lack of such a defense makes for a safer environment that allows society to operate and flourish much more smoothly.

Lambert v. California

(Convicted Felon) v. (People)

355 U.S. 225 (1957)

M E M O R Y   G R A P H I C

Instant Facts

Lambert (D) was prosecuted for failing to comply with a Los Angeles municipal ordinance requiring all convicted felons to register if staying for more than five days.

Black Letter Rule

A conviction for violation of a law requiring certain classes of persons to register with authorities requires that such person either have knowledge of the registration requirement or have probable reason to know of the requirement.

Case Vocabulary

FEASANCE: The executing or commission of some act or condition.

Procedural Basis: Certification to the U.S. Supreme Court from an appeal on due process grounds after conviction for failure to comply with the city's felon registration law.

Facts: Section 52.39 of the Los Angeles Municipal Code prohibits any person ever convicted of a felony to be or remain in Los Angeles for more than five days without registering with the Chief of Police. Section 52.43(b) makes the failure to register a continuing offense, with each day's failure constituting a separate offense. Lambert (D) was arrested for suspicion of having committed another offense and was charged with violating the registration law. The jury found Lambert (D) guilty and she was fined $250 and placed on probation for three years.

Issue: May a person be convicted of violating a required registration law without proof that they either actually knew of the requirement or had probable knowledge of such requirement?

Decision and Rationale: (Douglas, J) No. The registration provision includes no element of willfulness and such an element is not read into the provision by the California courts. For the purposes of this appeal we assume that Lambert (D) had no actual knowledge of the requirement that she register under the ordinance becuase she offered proof of this defense which was refused by the court. The question is whether a registration act of this character violates due process where it is applied to a person who has no actual knowledge of his duty to register, and where no showing is made of the probability of such knowledge. The lawmakers have wide latitude to declare an offense and exclude elements of knowledge from its definition. But here the conduct was wholly passive. It is unlike the commission of acts, or the failure to act under circumstances that should alert the doer of his duty to act. The rule that ignorance of the law will not excuse is deeply ingrained in our law. But due process does place some limits on its exercise. Fundamental to our concept of due process is the requirement of notice. Notice is required in a myriad of situations where a penalty or forfeiture might be suffered for mere failure to act. While recent cases involved only property interests in civil litigation, the principle is equally appropriate where a person is prosecuted in a criminal case. Registration laws are common in this country with many being akin to licensing statutes in that they pertain to the regulation of business activities. But the ordinance under scrutiny here is different. Violation of its provisions requires no activity whatever, mere presence in the city being the test. Furthermore, circumstances that might cause a person to inquire as to the necessity of registration are completely lacking. At most the ordinance is simply a convenient law enforcement technique by which the names and locations of felons is kept up to date. The list is merely a compilation of former convictions already recorded where they occurred. Nevertheless, this registrant on first becoming aware of her duty to register was given no opportunity to comply with the law and avoid its penalty, even though her default was entirely innocent. She thus had no choice but to suffer the serious consequences of the ordinance—conviction with the imposition of heavy criminal penalties. We believe that actual knowledge of the duty to register or proof of the probability of such knowledge and subsequent failure to comply are necessary before a conviction under the ordinance can stand. Reversed.

Dissent: (Frankfurter, J) The present laws of the United States and of the forty-eight States [shows you how old this opinion is] are thick with the command that some things not be done and others be done, although persons convicted under such provisions may have had no awareness of what the law required or that what they did was wrongdoing. Surely there can hardly be a difference as a matter of fairness, of hardship, or of justice, if one may invoke it, between the case of a person wholly innocent of wrongdoing, in the sense that he was not remotely conscious of violating any law, who is imprisoned for five years for conduct relating to narcotics (see *United States v. Balint*, (involving a defendant prosecuted under a narcotics taxing act)), and the case of another person who is placed on probation for three years on condition that she pay $250, for failure, as a local resident, convicted under local law of a felony, to register under a law passed as an exercise of the State's "police power." What the Court does here today is draw a constitutional line between a State's requirement of doing and not-doing. This is a distinction that may have had significance in the evolution of common law notions of liability, but is inadmissible as a line between constitutionality and unconstitutionality. If the generalization that underlies, and alone can justify, this decision were to be given its relevant scope, a whole volume of the United States Reports would be required to document in detail the legislation in this country that would fall or be impaired.

Analysis:

Justice Frankfurter takes pains to try and illustrate his belief that there is no difference between this case and the *Balint* case. In *Balint*, Balint and his partner were prosecuted under a narcotics taxing act, the purpose of which was to keep track of and control the sale of illegal narcotics. Apparently, the two forgot to pay the tax. Justice Frankfurter asserts that Balint did not know he was breaking the law, even so far as knowing he had narcotics in his possession. Even if this is true the *Balint* case is easily distinguishable from the instant case. Balint was obviously guilty of committing some act that was illegal. He had knowledge that dealing in narcotics was against the law and whether he knew or not, failure to pay taxes on the drug is a collateral issue. Lambert (D), on the other hand, was guilty of nothing more than moving to Los Angeles. She had no indication that her conduct in any way implicated any criminal codes. Therein lies the crux of the Court's ruling. Behavior that would seem benign to any normal, rational citizen; that gives no indication of being unlawful so as to put the actor on notice that he may be breaking the law, may not be punished unless the actor has prior notice. Justice Frankfurter's position that volumes of the United States Reports would be required to document the legislation that would fall or be impaired is alarmist at best. The Court's ruling here is narrow enough to avoid that problem, as history has borne out.

THE EIGHTH AMENDMENT OF THE CONSTITUTION DOES NOT GUARANTEE THAT
CRIMINAL PUNISHMENT WILL BE PROPRTIONATE TO THE CRIME COMMITTED

Harmelin v. Michigan

(Drug Possessor) v. (People)
501 U.S. 957 (1991)

M E M O R Y   G R A P H I C

 Instant Facts

Harmelin (D) was convicted of possessing a large amount of cocaine and was sentenced to life in prison without possibility of parole.

Black Letter Rule

The Eighth Amendment does not contain a provision that requires a criminal punishment to be proportionate to the crime being punished for.

Case Vocabulary

A FORTIORI: With even greater force; even more so. [Use of this phrase will greatly impress professors and friends alike.]

Procedural Basis: Certification to the U.S. Supreme Court after all appeals of defendant's drug possession conviction sentence were unsuccessful at the State court levels.

Facts: Harmelin (D) was convicted of possessing 672 grams of cocaine and sentenced to a mandatory life prison term without any possibility of parole. Harmelin (D) appeals his sentence as being unconstitutionally "cruel and unusual" because it is "significantly disproportionate" to the crime he was convicted of.

Issue: Does the Eighth Amendment prohibit criminal punishments that are disproportionate to the crime committed?

Decision and Rationale: (Scalia, J) No. The Eighth Amendment, which applies to the States through the Fourteenth Amendment, provides: "Excessive bail shall not be required, nor excessive fines imposed, nor cruel and unusual punishment inflicted." In *Solem v. Helm*, we set aside a life sentence without possibility of parole, as being disproportionate to the crime committed, handed down pursuant to the South Dakota recidivist statute for successive offenses that included three convictions of third-degree burglary, one of obtaining money by false pretenses, one of grand larceny, one of third-offense driving while intoxicated, and one of writing a "no account" check with intent to defraud. In so doing, the Court held in favor of a general principle of proportionality. However, that 5-4 decision eight years ago was hardly an expression of clear and well-accepted constitutional law. So once again we address the issue in greater detail and come to the conclusion that *Solem* was simply wrong; the Eighth Amendment contains no proportionality guarantee. [Justice Scalia goes on to discuss the history of the English Bill of Rights and its influence on the Eighth Amendment and concludes that the Amendment was adopted to outlaw certain modes of punishment, for example drawing and quartering, and to prevent judges from inventing and imposing unusual penalties not prescribed by law.] While there are relatively clear historical guidelines that enable judges to determine which modes of punishment are cruel and unusual, proportionality does not lend itself to such analysis. The three factors used in *Solem* to make the proportionality determination illustrate the problems. Those factors are: (1) the inherent gravity of the offense, (2) the sentences imposed for similarly grave offenses in the same jurisdiction, and (3) sentences imposed for the same crime in other jurisdictions. Looking at the first factor, the determination of how grave drug possession is depends on how odious and socially threatening one believes drug use to be. It is a clearly subjective question, with a wide array of possible answers with just about all having at least some merit. The members of the Michigan legislature, not this Court, know the situation on the streets of Detroit and are therefore much better equipped to make this type of value judgment with the most accuracy. The second factor fails for the same reason. It is impossible to compare the sentences for "similarly grave" offenses when there is no objective standard of gravity. Judges can only compare what they consider comparable. Also, even if similarly grave crimes could be found, the penalties would not necessarily be comparable, since there are many other valid reasons for a difference. Whether such differences will occur, and to what extent, depends, of course, upon the weight society accords to deterrence and rehabilitation, rather than retribution, as the objective of criminal punishment. Looking at the third factor it is admitted that it can be applied with clarity and ease. The one difficulty though, is that it has no relevance to the Eighth Amendment. The federalist system accords the individual States much autonomy. It goes without saying that one State is entitled to treat with stern disapproval an act that other States punish with the mildest of sanctions. This follows, a fortiori, from the fact that one State may criminalize an act that other States do not criminalize at all. After all, diversity not only in policy, but also in the means of implementing policy, is the very reason for being of our federal system. Notwithstanding the preceding, there is an exception in the use of proportionality review. This is capital punishment. Proportionality review is one of several respects in which we have held that "death is different," and have imposed protections that the Constitution nowhere else provides. We would leave it there, but will not extend it further. Affirmed.

Concurrence: (Kennedy, J) I write this separate opinion because my approach to the Eighth Amendment proportionality analysis differs from Justice Scalia's. No matter whether Justice Scalia or the dissent has the best of the historical argument, stare decisis counsels our adherence to the narrow proportionality principle that has existed in our Eighth Amendment jurisprudence for 80 years. Our prior decisions in this arena have not been clear or consistent in all ways, but they can be reconciled, and require us to uphold Harmelin's (D) sentence. Our decisions recognize that the Cruel and Unusual Punishment Clause encompasses a narrow proportionality principle, and although its most extensive application has been in death penalty cases, it also applies to noncapital sentences. We have in the past upheld sentences of a very long term of years for crimes that may not seem to warrant such penalties. Even in *Solem*, where we invalidated a sentence of life imprisonment without possibility of parole as being "grossly disproportionate" to the crime of recidivism based on seven underlying nonviolent felonies, the dissent observed that in extreme cases it could apply to invalidate a punishment for a term of years. A close analysis of our decisions reveals some common principles that give content to the uses and limits of proportionality review. The first of these is that the fixing of prison terms involves a substantive penological judgment that is properly within the sphere of the legislature, not the courts. Therefore, legislatures should be given substantial deference in determining the limits and punishments for crimes. The second principle is that the Eighth Amendment does not mandate the adoption of any one penological theory. States are free to give whatever weight they desire to the penological goals of retribution, deterrence, incapacitation, and rehabilitation. This freedom will naturally lead to different sentences for the same crimes in different States. The next principle is that proportionality review by federal courts should be informed by objective factors to the maximum possible extent. The most prominent of these objective factors is the type of punishment imposed, with different types ranging from hard labor, to strict isolation, to the death penalty. Now because the death penalty, for instance, differs so much from simply being locked up for a term of years there can be an objective line drawn between the two. This is not the case when trying to distinguish only between different terms of years. There are no objective factors available for making that distinction. This lack of objective standards means that outside the context of capital punishment, successful challenges to the proportionality of particular sentences are exceedingly rare. All of these aforementioned principles inform the final one: the Eighth Amendment does not require strict proportionality between crime and sentence. Rather, it forbids only extreme sentences that are "grossly disproportionate" to the crime. Harmelin's (D) crime is much more grave than that at issue in *Solem*, and therefore falls into a different category. What it boils down to is that the Michigan Legislature, in light of all the information regarding the damage drugs do to society, could reasonably conclude that life imprisonment without possibility of parole is the correct measure, in terms of sentencing, that crimes such as Harmelin's (D) warrant.

Dissent: (White, J) While the language of the Eighth Amendment doesn't refer to proportionality in so many words, it does forbid "excessive" fines, a restraint that suggests that a determination of excessiveness should be based at least in part on whether the fine imposed is disproportionate to the crime committed. It would also be reasonable to conclude that it would be both cruel and unusual to punish overtime parking with life imprisonment, or to impose any punishment that is grossly disproportionate to the offense for which the defendant has been convicted. Later in Justice Scalia's opinion he backtracks by appearing to accept that the Amendment does insist on proportional punishments in a particular class of cases, that is, capital cases. This position fails to explain the Court's several past pronouncements regarding the Amendment's proportionality component. It also fails to explain why the words "cruel and unusual" include a proportionality requirement in some cases but not in others. This Court has recognized that a punishment may violate the Amendment if it is contrary to the evolving standards of decency that mark the progress of a maturing society. This test takes into account not the subjective views of the individual justices, but the objective values of modern American society as a whole in determining what standards have evolved and how. It is this type of objective factor that forms the basis for the tripartite proportionality analysis set forth in *Solem*. Application of the *Solem* factors to the punishment in the instant case reveals that the punishment fails muster under the Eighth Amendment. In applying the first factor—gravity of the offense—it is appropriate to consider the harm caused or threatened to the victim or society. Drugs are a serious societal problem, but to justify such a penalty as that imposed here the offense should be one that will always warrant that punishment. Mere possession of drugs, even in large quantities, does not rise to the level of seriousness that will always warrant, much less mandate, life imprisonment without possibility of parole. Even the State's assertion that the purpose of the drug possession statute is to reach drug dealers is belied by the existence of a separate statute that reaches manufacture, delivery, or possession with intent to do either. Also, this statute applies equally to first-time offenders, such as Harmelin (D), and recidivists. Consequently, the particular concerns reflected in our previous cases, such as *Solem*, are not at issue here. The second prong of the *Solem* analysis reveals that the punishment imposed here is the strictest allowed under Michigan law being that they do not have capital punishment. The other two crimes life imprisonment without parole is reserved for are first degree murder, and the manufacture, distribution, or possession with intent to manufacture or distribute 650 grams or more of narcotics. Other, violent crimes such as second-degree murder, rape, and armed robbery, do not carry such a harsh mandatory sentence. It is therefore clear that Harmelin (D) has been treated in an equal or more harsh manner than criminals who've committed far more serious crimes. The third *Solem* factor compares punishments for the same crime between states. This shows that of the remaining 49 States, only Alabama has a mandatory life sentence without parole for a first time drug offender, and then only when the defendant possessed more than 10 kilograms of cocaine. Thus, it appears that Harmelin (D) was treated more severely than he would have been in any other State. Application of the *Solem* proportionality analysis leaves no doubt that the Michigan statute violates the Eighth Amendment's prohibition against cruel and unusual punishment.

Analysis:

Justice Scalia's opinion represents a classic case of one burying one's head in the sand. He is very cavalier in rejecting the *Solem* proportionality analysis as being impractical and fatally flawed. His criticism that the process involves too much subjective analysis is, at worst, belied by the dissenting opinion, which represents a very cogent analysis using the *Solem* factors. Scalia seems to be willing to simply throw in the towel and boldly say that the Eighth Amendment contains no proportionality guarantee, just before he very quickly backtracks and says that it does have such a guarantee in capital cases. Which is it? Logic dictates that if the Amendment guarantees proportionality in one case, it must do so in all.

IN SOME COUNTRIES ONE MAY BE PROSECUTED AND CONVICTED OF AN OFFENSE NOT PROSCRIBED BY STATUTE AND NOT SPECIFICALLY DEALT WITH IN COMMON LAW PRECEDENT

Shaw v. Director of Public Prosecutions

(Pimp) v. (People)
House of Lords (1962) A.C. 220

M E M O R Y G R A P H I C

Instant Facts

Shaw (D) stands convicted of the common law offence of conspiracy to corrupt public morals even though there is no precedent in the common law that deals specifically with the offense he committed.

Black Letter Rule

One may be prosecuted for a general offense at common law, though there exists no such legal precedent reflecting the actual offense committed, so long as a jury finds the offender guilty.

Case Vocabulary

CONSPIRACY: An agreement, involving at least two people, to commit a crime.

Procedural Basis: Appeal to the House of Lords of a conviction for an offense not covered by statute nor specifically prohibited by any recognized common law precedent.

Facts: The Street Offences Act of 1959 (Act) prohibited prostitutes from soliciting business in the streets meaning they had to find some other means of advertising their services. Because of this, Shaw (D) decided to publish a magazine or booklet called the 'Ladies' Directory' containing the names, addresses and telephone numbers of prostitutes with photos of nude female figures, and in some cases, details that conveyed a willingness by some prostitutes to engage in various perverse practices. Shaw (D) was convicted on an indictment containing the following counts: (1) conspiracy to corrupt public morals, (2) living on the earning of prostitution in violation of the Sexual Offences Act of 1956, and (3) publishing an obscene publication in violation of the Obscene Publications Act of 1959. The first count was not charged pursuant to any criminal statute, but instead under the common law. It specifically charged Shaw (D) with attempting to induce readers of his magazine to resort to the advertisers in the publication for the purposes of fornication and taking part in or witnessing "disgusting immoral acts and exhibitions with intent thereby to debauch and corrupt the morals as well of youth as divers[e] other liege subjects of Our Lady the Queen and to raise and create in their minds inordinate and lustful desires."

Issue: May a person be prosecuted under the common law for an offense that has not been prohibited by a specific statute and that is not prohibited under a specific precedent?

Decision and Rationale: (Viscount Simonds) Yes. Although the counsel for Shaw (D) asserted the opposite, there is such an offense known to the common law, and it was for the jury to decide whether Shaw (D) is guilty of committing the offense. If this were not so, the courts would have failed in their duty as servants and guardians of the common law. This is so even though I am certainly no advocate of judges creating new criminal offenses. Though there may not be an exact precedent for such a conspiracy as this case presents, it must still fall fairly within the general words by which it is described. In the sphere of criminal law I entertain no doubts that there remains in the courts of law a residual power to enforce the supreme and fundamental purpose of the law, to conserve not only the safety and order but also the moral welfare of the State, and that it is their duty to guard it against attacks which may be the more insidious because they are novel and unprepared for. This is necessary because there are still some gaps remaining in the criminal code as there always will remain because no one can foresee every way in which the wickedness of man may disrupt the order of society. Must we wait until parliament finds time to deal with such conduct? I say no. The appeals should, in my opinion, be dismissed.

Concurrence: (Lord Morris of Borth-y-Gest) Some feel that there is a measure of vagueness in a charge of conspiracy to corrupt public morals, and that it presents the risk of prosecutions in order to suppress unpopular or unorthodox views. I entertain no anxiety on these lines. Even if public standards change with the passing of time, current standards are in the keeping of juries who can be trusted to maintain the good sense of the community and to discern attacks upon values that must be preserved. If there were prosecutions that were not genuinely and fairly warranted, juries would be quick to perceive this and would thus stop it before it really starts. I would dismiss the appeal.

Dissent: (Lord Reid) In my opinion there is no such general offense known to the law as conspiracy to corrupt public morals. There are great theoretical objections to any general rule that an agreement by a jury may make punishable that which would not be punishable without such agreement. It should be well established that courts cannot simply create new offenses by individuals. It is surely now the province of the legislature and not the judiciary to create new criminal offenses. When there is sufficient public support Parliament doesn't hesitate to intervene and make new law. However, where Parliament fears to tread it is not for the courts to rush in. I totally disagree that this very general offense even exists. It has always been thought to be of primary importance that our law, and particularly our criminal law, should be certain: that a man should be able to know what conduct is and is not criminal, particularly when heavy penalties are involved. It has been suggested that the words "debauch" and "corrupt" in this indictment ought to be entirely for the jury, so that any conduct of this kind is criminal if, in the end, a jury thinks it so. In other words, you cannot tell what is criminal except by guessing what view a jury will take, and juries' views may change with the passing of time. Normally the meaning of words is left up to the court. If this is not the case then it seems to me that the court has transferred to the jury the whole of its functions as moral censor and the law will be whatever any jury may happen to think it ought to be. This branch of the law will therefore have lost all the certainty that we rightly prize in other branches of our law.

Analysis:

Although this is a recent case, it is not a United States case. This case presents the issue of whether someone may be prosecuted for an offense that, although it may be morally repugnant to the great majority, is not prohibited by any statute and has never been dealt with at common law, i.e. an ex post facto law. It has been said that there are no common law crimes in the United States. All criminal offenses are statutory offenses. The reason for this is notice—notice of what conduct will entail criminal liability is fundamental to a fair system of laws. Otherwise the law could be used as a weapon of oppression against whatever persons or groups may be unpopular. Viscount Simonds seems to advocate prosecution by presenting the facts to the jury and letting them decide if they fit into any broad or general category of proscribed conduct at common law. This would be a true representation of the morality police at work. Lord Reid recognizes the folly of this reasoning when he discusses the proper role of courts in defining what conduct is barred and then letting the jury decide if the conduct in question meets the definition of that conduct. The U.S. Supreme Court, in a line of First Amendment defamation cases starting with *New York Times v. Sullivan*, has recognized that the decisions of juries can be arbitrary and capricious. Allowing juries to decide anew exactly what conduct is illegal will lead to a system of law that is so malleable as to provide individuals with only a faint hint of whether their conduct is proscribed. Couple this with the longstanding rule that ignorance of the law is no excuse and what we would have is a system upon which no one can depend; one that fails to promote a society in which people may thrive and improve upon the human condition. It is pretty doubtful that the law of this case is the rule in this country.

Keeler v. Superior Court

(Murderer of Unborn Fetus) v. (Court Alleged to Lack Jurisdiction Over the Murder Charge)

(1970) 2 Cal. 3d 619, 87 Cal. Rptr. 481, 470 P.2d 617

M E M O R Y   G R A P H I C

Instant Facts

Mr. Keeler (D) allegedly murdered an unborn but viable fetus by kicking his pregnant wife in the stomach.

Black Letter Rule

There is a violation of the Due Process Clause when a court construes a criminal statute contrary to the legislative intent and applies its expanded definition of the statute retroactively to a person's conduct.

Procedural Basis: A writ of prohibition to arrest murder proceedings.

Facts: Mrs. Keeler became pregnant by a man who was not her husband before receiving a divorce from Mr. Keeler (D). After Mr. Keeler (D) learned of the pregnancy, he met Mrs. Keeler while she was driving down a mountain road, blocked the road with his car, and impeded Mrs. Keeler's progress. He then walked over to Mrs. Keeler's car and confronted her about the pregnancy. When Mrs. Keeler did not respond, he assisted her out of her car. Mr. Keeler (D) then looked at Mrs. Keeler's stomach and became extremely upset. He pushed her against the car, shoved his knee into her abdomen, and struck her in the face. The blow to Mrs. Keeler's abdomen caused extensive bruising of the abdomen wall. Medical personnel performed a Caesarian section on Mrs. Keeler. They discovered that the head of the fetus was severely fractured and delivered it stillborn. A pathologist opined that the death was immediate and caused by the skull fracture. He also opined that the injury could have been the result of Mr. Keeler (D) shoving his knee into Mrs. Keeler's stomach. Mrs. Keeler's obstetrician provided evidence that the fetus had developed to a stage of viability prior to its death. The district attorney filed an information that charged Mr. Keeler (D) with murder of the viable but unborn fetus and infliction of traumatic injury and assault upon his wife. Mr. Keeler (D) then filed a writ of prohibition to arrest the murder proceeding against him, and the Supreme Court of California granted review.

Issue: Is there is a violation of the Due Process Clause when a court construes a criminal statute contrary to the legislative intent and applies its expanded definition of the statute retroactively to a person's conduct?

Decision and Rationale: (Mosk) Yes. There is a violation of the Due Process Clause when a court construes a criminal statute contrary to the legislative intent and applies its expanded definition of the statute retroactively to a person's conduct. Section 187 of California's Penal Code defines murder as the unlawful killing of a human being with malice aforethought. The legislature of 1872 enacted section 187. It took the language for this section from an 1850 enactment. An important question is whether the fetus that Mr. Keeler (D) is alleged to have murdered is a human being under California law. The inquiry begins by examining the intent of the 1850 legislature. This court presumes that the legislature was familiar with the common law in 1850. It further presumes that a legislature intends to continue common law rules in statutory form when it uses common law language in its enactments. Pursuant to the common law of 1850, a child must be born alive to support a charge of murder. Additionally, an infant could not be the subject of homicide at common law unless it had been born alive. The legislature of 1850 used common law language to define murder as the unlawful killing of a human being, and the common law at that time required a person to be born alive to support a charge of murder. Therefore, the legislature of 1850 intended that the term *human being* refer to a person that is born alive. We further find that there is nothing in the legislative history that demonstrates the legislature of 1872 had a different intention when in enacted section 187. It is the policy of California to construe a penal statute as favorably to the defendant as its language and the circumstances of its application permit. Since Mr. Keeler (D) is entitled to the benefit of reasonable doubt as to the true interpretation of section 187, we hold, for the aforementioned reasons, that the legislature did not intend to include the killing of an unborn fetus under the purview of section 187. The People of California (P) argue that science now facilitates the survival of a viable fetus born prematurely. They then conclude that this fact supports the finding that the killing of such a fetus is punishable under section 187. Their argument is unpersuasive. First, the authority to define punishable crimes rest entirely with the legislature. While a court may construe a statute according to a fair import of its terms to promote justice, it lacks authority to create offenses by enlarging a statute. The fair import of the terms in section 187 compels this court to reject enlarging the statute by construing its terms to cover an unborn but viable fetus. Second, even if we enlarge the statute to cover an unborn but viable fetus, the enlargement would not be applicable to Mr. Keeler (D) because the Due Process Clause guarantees him fair notice of punishable acts. California case law does not hold that killing an unborn but viable fetus supports a charge of murder, nor does the case law of our sister states. To apply a new definition of section 187 to Mr. Keeler (D) is not fair notice; it is an application without any notice. The Ex Post Facto Clause's prohibition against retroactive penal legislation supports this reasoning. The People's (P) suggested enlargement as applied to Mr. Keeler (D) violates the Due Process Clause. Therefore, this court refuses to engage in such unconstitutional folly.

Dissent: (Burke) The majority incorrectly suggests that it must confine its reasoning to common law concepts and the common law definition of murder. The California Penal Code defines homicide as the unlawful killing of a human being. The interpretation of the term human being need not remain static or fixed in time. The duty of this court is to render a fair and reasonable interpretation of the term in accordance with present conditions to promote justice and carry out the evident purpose of the legislature when enacting section 187.

Human existence is a spectrum that stretches from birth to death. Damaging a corpse is not homicide, because a corpse is not a human being. Nonetheless, medical life revival, restoration, and resuscitation advancements have modified society's understanding of what constitutes a corpse. If the majority would not ignore these advancements nor exonerate a killer of an apparently drowned child simply because the child would have been considered dead in 1850, why does it ignore medical advances that promote the survivability of a fetus? In this case, the issue before the court should have been determined with medical testimony about the survivability of the fetus prior to Mr. Keeler's (D) conduct. The majority states its lack of authority to create new offenses, however, murder is not a new offense. The legislature used the broad term human being and directed the courts to construe the term according to its fair import to promote justice. Do we serve justice by excluding an unborn viable fetus from the definition of a human being given the present conditions of our time? Further, Mr. Keeler (D) knew or should have known that his conduct could cause a homicide. Therefore, contrary to the majority, the potential for a Due Process Clause violation for lack of fair notice that his conduct could constitute a murder does not exist.

Analysis:

Even though most states have abolished common law offenses, this case provides an excellent example of the importance of common law doctrine as it relates to criminal offenses. A dispositive question in this case is whether a viable but unborn fetus is a human being pursuant to California law. As courts are to interpret the law rather than create it, they must determine the intent of their legislatures when construing statutes. Courts use various techniques to ascertain the intent of their legislatures. They include the legislative history of an act and the circumstances surrounding its enactment, earlier statutes on the same subject, the common law as understood at the time of the act's adoption, and interpretation of the same or similar statutes. In this case, the Supreme Court of California primarily used the common law to ascertain the intent of the 1850 and 1872 legislatures. It is interesting to note that the court presumes that the legislatures were familiar with the relevant common law. The court also presumes that common law language in statutory form means that the legislature intended a common law interpretation. These two presumptions are critical as they take the court directly where it wants to go. Armed with these presumptions, the court states that under the common law in 1850 an infant could not be the subject of a homicide unless it had been born alive. [The California Legislature must have known this]. The statute employs common law language. As a result, the case is resolved. This raises two interesting questions. Is a presumption of common law knowledge by a legislature a good one, or is the presumption simply a technique used to make a finding of legislative intent when the a court cannot truly ascertain the intent? Since it is found that a viable fetus is not a human being, the remainder of the opinion is academic. Clearly, a court that speaks eloquently about its limited judicial authority and duty to ascertain legislative intent will not contradict itself with judicial enlargement of a statute. Further, it is reasonable to presume that the Supreme Court of California is not interested in a tongue thrashing by The United States Supreme Court for violating the Due Process Clause. Perhaps this case is of interest because of the secondary implications the ruling has on the issue of the legality of abortion. If the court had ruled that the fetus was a human being, what would this mean for a person seeking an abortion?

AN ORDINANCE IS UNCONSTITUTIONALLY VAGUE WHERE IT GIVES ABSOLUTE DISCRETION TO POLICE OFFICERS TO DETERMINE WHAT ACTIVITIES CONSTITUTE "LOITERING," AND DOES NOT INFORM CITIZENS WHAT "LOITERING" IS OR IS NOT COVERED BY IT

City of Chicago v. Morales

(Anti-Loitering City) v. (Gang Member)
(1999) 527 U.S. 41

M E M O R Y   G R A P H I C

Instant Facts

Chicago's (P) anti-loitering ordinance was challenged as unconstitutionally vague because it failed to give adequate notice of what it prohibited and gave police too much discretion.

Black Letter Rule

Vagueness may invalidate a criminal law where the ordinance 1) fails to provide notice to enable the ordinary person to understand what conduct it prohibits and 2) where it authorizes or encourages arbitrary and discriminatory police enforcement.

Procedural Basis: United States Supreme Court granted certiorari from judgment declaring City's anti-loitering ordinance unconstitutional.

Facts: The Chicago City Council enacted the Gang Congregation Ordinance, which prohibits "criminal street gang members" from "loitering" with one another or with any other person in any public place. The ordinance creates a criminal offense based upon four predicates: 1) the police officer must reasonably believe that at least one of the two or more persons present in a "public place" is a "criminal street gang member;" [Are baggy pants and tank tops the gang member look?] 2) the persons must be "loitering," which the ordinance defines as "remaining in any one place with no apparent purpose;" [taking care of gang business is an "apparent purpose" isn't it?] 3) the officer must then order "all" of the persons to disperse and remove themselves "from the area;" and, 4) a person must disobey the officer's order. If any person, gang member or not, disobeys the officer's order, that person is guilty of violating the ordinance. The Supreme Court of Illinois held that the ordinance violates the Due Process Clause of the Fourteenth Amendment in that it is impermissibly vague on its face and an arbitrary restriction on personal liberties. The United States Supreme Court granted certiorari to determine the constitutionality of the ordinance.

Issue: Can a criminal ordinance be declared invalid if it is vague?

Decision and Rationale: (Stevens) Yes. Vagueness may invalidate a criminal law where the ordinance 1) fails to provide notice to enable the ordinary person to understand what conduct it prohibits and 2) where it authorizes or encourages arbitrary and discriminatory police enforcement. We first note that the ordinance covers a significant amount of additional activity than the intimidating gang members' conduct that interferes with the neighborhood residents' enjoyment of their homes and surrounding areas. Morales (D) contends that the scope of the additional coverage makes the ordinance too vague. With respect to proper notice, the definition of the term "loiter" in the ordinance—"to remain in any one place with no apparent purpose"—does not have a common and accepted meaning. An ordinary citizen standing in a public place with a group of people would not know if he or she had an "apparent purpose." However, since the City (P) obviously did not mean to criminalize each instance a citizen stands in public with a gang member, the vagueness of the ordinance relates to what loitering is covered by it and what is not. The fact that loiterers must first fail to comply with an order to disperse before violating the ordinance is unpersuasive. If the loitering is in fact harmless and innocent, the dispersal order in itself in an unjustified impairment of liberty. In addition, the terms of the dispersal order raise questions concerning how long must the loiterers remain apart, how far apart should they be, if they re-meet later, are they subject to arrest or merely subject to a dispersal order again? [These seem to be valid concerns.] The ordinance also violates the requirement that a legislature establish minimal guidelines to govern law enforcement. The police may order disbursement without first making any inquiry about possible purposes of the loitering. The ordinance gives absolute discretion to police officers to determine what activities constitute loitering. We agree with the Illinois Supreme Court that the ordinance does not provide sufficiently specific limits on the enforcement discretion of the police. The ordinance affords too much discretion to the police and too little notice to citizens who wish to use the public streets. Affirmed.

Concurrence: (O'Connor) Today's holding is of a narrow scope. The City (P) has alternatives. The term "loiter" might be construed to mean "to remain in any one place with no apparent purpose other than to establish control over identifiable areas, to intimidate others from entering those areas, or to conceal illegal activities." This would avoid the vagueness problems.

Dissent: (Thomas) The ordinance does not criminalize loitering per se. Rather, it penalizes the failure to obey a police officer's order to move along. This merely enables police officers to fulfill one of their traditional functions, and does not vest them with too much discretion. With respect to adequate notice, persons of ordinary intelligence are perfectly capable of evaluating how outsiders perceive their conduct, and here it is self-evident that there is a whole range of conduct that anyone with at least a semblance of common sense would know is loitering and that would be covered by the statute.

Analysis:

This case certainly is an example of the difficulty in drafting an anti-loitering ordinance that can withstand constitutional challenge for vagueness. Chicago's ordinance unfortunately failed in two areas—it did not give the citizens adequate notice of what was meant by "loitering" and it gave the police too much discretion in enforcing the law. Justice O'Connor in her concurring opinion gave the City guidance in how the ordinance could have been construed more narrowly, even suggesting a definition of the term "loiter." Justice Thomas in his strongly worded dissent shamed the majority for focusing exclusively on the imagined "rights" of the 2 percent of the people in the City who are causing the problems that keep the other 98 percent in their homes and off the streets and afraid to shop. However, Justice Thomas addresses the "vagueness" argument by saying that common sense dictates what would or would not be covered by the ordinance. This is a weak argument, when contrasted with the majority's examples of what persons should do once a dispersal order has been given. As the majority noted, if the loitering is in fact harmless and innocent, the dispersal order itself is an unjustified impairment of liberty.

Chapter 4

Imagine a scene at a lively college party in a fraternity house. People are mingling and having a good time, the lines around the kegs are three deep, the beer is flowing and the music is pumping. Some people are dancing on the dance floor, some are playing pool or foosball in the game room and some are wandering upstairs to the dorm rooms. Now imagine a girl and a guy who might have met that night, or might have been friends for a time before the party. The girl agrees to go up to the guy's bedroom with several others to watch movies, play games or just to talk. Maybe there is drinking involved and maybe there isn't. But somehow, everyone else leaves and the girl and the guy are alone in the room together. Sometime during the night, an act of sexual intercourse occurs between the girl and the guy.

Is this a picture of rape? Maybe it is and maybe it isn't. We deliberately left out some very important facts—facts that would make you think one way or the other. What if the girl came on to the guy? What if she actively pursued him? On the other hand, what if she passed out and only woke up when they were having sex? What if the girl originally consented, or at least consented to a heavy make-out session, but changed her mind just before intercourse? What if the girl eagerly and actively participated but then felt guilty and ashamed about it in the morning? What if she wound up with an unplanned pregnancy that she couldn't or wouldn't explain to her parents? Lastly, what if the girl flat out refused and the guy forced her to have sex by threatening her life?

As you can see, all of these variables could potentially change your initial reaction to the purposely-vague scenario in the first paragraph. Did she consent or didn't she? Did he force her or didn't he? Should she have resisted or shouldn't she? All these [and more!] are questions that are asked every day by juries and judges in rape trials. About the only thing that is definitively clear about rape is that it is a criminal act. But this particular criminal act has sparked more controversy and led to more statute reform in the past few decades than any other. At the outset, a major problem exists because there is no general consensus as to what rape is [besides the obvious.] Some define rape as a crime of violence; some call it an unwanted sexual intrusion. Whatever the definition, however, it is clear that as attitudes about sex in general have changed throughout the course of the last 40 years, courts and legislatures have attempted to keep up with society's changing values by revamping and refining existing rape laws.

This chapter illustrates many of the divisive issues that pervade the laws surrounding rape and many of the rape law reforms that have come out of the last few decades. As society struggles to redefine traditional roles of men and women, both in and out of the bedroom, the courts are likely to have to respond to changing social mores in the future just as they have had to do so throughout the past 40 years.

Chapter 4

NOTE: THE PURPOSE OF THIS OUTLINE IS TO ORGANIZE THE CASES SO THAT ONE CAN QUICKLY UNDERSTAND THE RELEVANCE OF EACH CASE TO THE COURSE. NO ATTEMPT IS MADE IN THIS OVERVIEW TO ADDRESS EVERY CONCEPT THAT MUST BE STUDIED. BE SURE TO READ THE ENTIRE CASEBOOK AND/OR OTHER MATERIALS TO GAIN A FULL UNDERSTANDING OF ALL CONCEPTS.

I. Introduction
    A. Studies show that incidents of rape are far higher in the United States than official statistics suggest. There is no good estimate of the extent to which rapes go unreported either to official agencies, i.e. the police, or to victimization survey interviewers. Acquaintance rape, date rape and campus rape rates seem to be rising in the past few decades, but there is no evidence of whether this is attributable to more willingness to report such incidents or if it is a true increase in the number of such rapes. *Margaret T. Gordon & Stephanie Riger, The Female Fear: The Social Cost of Rape.*
    B. Attempts to estimate the frequency of rape are highly controversial.
        1. One major study found that 27% of college women had been the victim of rape or attempted rape. A Department of Justice survey indicated a prevalence of about 5600 rapes per 100,000 women, or 2.8%.
        2. Even the low estimates indicate an enormous amount of sexual abuse.
        3. The definition of rape is an important variable among the studies and could account for some of the differences in the findings.
            a. Intertwined with the definition of rape are society's views of normal male-female sexual interactions and the proper role of male aggression or coercion in sexual matters. Society's views about these matters have been in a state of flux over the past four decades.
            b. Some define rape as a crime of violence, but many feminists stress that violence is not the only consideration and that rape should be viewed simply as unwanted sexual intrusion.
        4. The criminal law has struggled to keep up with the many changes that have occurred over the last few decades with respect to rape laws, attitudes about sex, and changing societal values.

II. Statutory Frameworks.
    A. Since the 1950s, statutory definitions of rape have undergone substantial changes.
    B. Until the 1950s, most American statutes adopted Blackstone's 1765 definition of rape: "carnal knowledge of a woman forcibly and against her will."
        1. Many states still adhere to this basic concept. For example, Maryland defines rape as "vaginal intercourse ... by force or threat of force against the will and without the consent of the other person.
    C. State statutes differ in their definitions of rape in terms of the gravity of the facts required to be proved; whether the crime is divided by degree; the punishment authorized; and whether spousal rape is recognized.
        1. California
            a. California no longer requires the victim to be a female.
            b. Actual force or threat of force is not necessary. For example, force is not necessary if the victim is incapable of consenting due to intoxication or unconsciousness, and this is known or should be known to the perpetrator.
            c. California punishes rape by imprisonment for three, six, or eight years.
            d. Spousal rape is recognized under certain situations.
        2. New York divides rape into distinctly graded offenses.
            a. "Sexual misconduct" is when a male has sexual intercourse with a female without her consent. It is punishable by imprisonment for a maximum of one year.
            b. Second degree rape is sexual intercourse with someone to whom the actor is not married who is less than 14 years old. It is punishable by imprisonment for a maximum of seven years.

c. First degree rape is sexual intercourse by a male with a female by forcible compulsion or with a female who is incapable of consent or who is less than 11 years old. It is punishable by imprisonment for a maximum of 25 years.

d. Spousal rape is recognized.

3. Wisconsin rape statutes do not require sexual intercourse. For example, first degree sexual assault is "sexual contact" or sexual intercourse with another person without consent, that causes pregnancy or great bodily harm, or by use or threat of use of a dangerous weapon.

III. Actus Reus (the Criminal Act) in Rape.

A. Most rape statutes have a force requirement.

1. However, there are some exceptions.

a. A victim's reasonable fear of death or serious bodily injury precludes the need to show force on the part of the attacker or resistance on the part of the victim. *State v. Rusk*. The *Rusk* court found that issues of fear, consent, resistance and force are questions of fact.

b. Force is not necessary when the victim is underage, unconscious, or mentally incompetent.

2. As part of the force requirement, many jurisdictions used to require proof of resistance by the victim.

a. The old requirement was that a woman resist to the "utmost." This requirement was based on a basic distrust of women's testimony regarding rape. *People v. Barnes*. Today, all jurisdictions, except Louisiana, have abandoned this requirement.

b. Many jurisdictions still require "reasonable" resistance by the victim, unless resistance would lead to death or serious bodily injury.

c. Some jurisdictions require "earnest" resistance, meaning that resistance that could be expected from a person who genuinely does not want to participate in sexual intercourse.

d. Some jurisdictions have completely abandoned the resistance requirement, recognizing that the absence of resistance is not necessarily probative on the issues of force and nonconsent. *People v. Barnes*.

e. All courts recognize that resistance is unnecessary in at least some circumstances, i.e. when deadly force is used.

f. Many courts excuse the resistance requirement if the woman had a reasonable fear that resisting would lead to death or bodily injury, but the fear must be objectively reasonable.

(1) Studies differ regarding whether women who resist rape are more likely to suffer serious injury. *Michelle Anderson, Reviving Resistance in Rape Law*.

(2) Resistance is not required if resistance would be futile or life-threatening, or if the victim is overcome by superior strength or paralyzed by fear. However, the victim must at least communicate her lack of consent. *People v. Warren*.

g. Some feminist writers are extremely critical of the resistance requirement, viewing it as a male notion of fighting as force or resistance. *Susan Estrich, Real Rape*.

(1) Other rape reform advocates counsel against encouraging rape laws that are too patronizing towards women, claiming that women fought against that kind of patronizing protection in the law for many years. *Vivian Berger, Not So Simple Rape*.

3. Some jurisdictions have eliminated the force requirement and made liability rest upon the victim's lack of consent. *Wisconsin Criminal Code 940.225*.

4. Force is sometimes said to include non-physical threats that induce fear or intimidation.

a. However, many jurisdictions do not accept non-physical threats as evidence of force. *People v. Thompson*; *Commonwealth v. Mlinarich*.

b. Some jurisdictions have created lesser sexual offenses where the victim is compelled to have sexual intercourse by the use of non-physical threats that create fear or misapprehension.

c. Model Penal Code §213.1(2) provides for "gross sexual imposition" when sex is compelled by threat of force or "by any threat that would prevent resistance by a woman of ordinary resolution."

d. Allowing convictions based on non-physical threats, such as sex in exchange for employment or financial support, would impinge on society's values regarding sexual autonomy and would create difficulties in distinguishing between legitimate persuasion and illegitimate coercion. *Stephen J. Schulhofer, Unwanted Sex.*

5. Some jurisdictions have adopted the inherent force standard, which permits a finding of force with only that force necessary to actually accomplish the act of penetration.

   a. This requirement of force is satisfied by the physical act of sexual penetration without the victim's consent. *State in the Interest of M.T.S.*

   b. The inherent force standard is accepted by a minority of jurisdictions.

6. Forcible compulsion has been interpreted in some jurisdictions to mean some degree of physical force beyond that which is necessary to engage in sexual intercourse. This is the "external force" standard and has been adopted by a majority of jurisdictions.

B. Some states criminalize intercourse whenever consent is absent. But proving lack of consent is difficult.

C. Views on consent induced by deception, fraud, trick or strategem.

   1. Most jurisdictions hold that consent induced by fraud or deception is still valid consent. *People v. Evans.* Some courts differentiate between fraud in the factum and fraud in the inducement.

      a. Fraud in the factum is when the victim does not know the nature of the act, e.g., a doctor pretends to be giving a woman a pelvic exam, but actually has sexual intercourse with her. If the victim is not aware of the nature of the act because of fraud in the factum, many courts hold the perpetrator is guilty of rape because the victim did not consent.

      b. Fraud in the inducement occurs when the victim understands the nature of the act but is induced to consent by fraud or deception, e.g., a doctor tells the victim that she must have sexual intercourse with him as part of her treatment. Most courts hold that fraud in the inducement does not vitiate consent because the victim consented to the act of intercourse. *Boro v. Superior Court.*

2. Some jurisdictions have created lesser sexual offenses for cases where the victim was fraudulently induced to consent.

IV. The Defendant's Belief About the Victim's Consent

A. Some courts hold that a defendant's reasonable mistake as to the victim's consent may be a defense to rape. *Commonwealth v. Sherry.*

   1. However, some states, like Massachusetts and Pennsylvania, apply strict liability for defendants in rape cases on the issue of consent. *Commonwealth v. Fischer; Commonwealth v. Ascolillo.*

   2. Most courts do not follow *Fischer* and *Ascolillo*, and hold that a reasonable mistake as to the victim's consent is a defense to rape.

B. Recklessness or Negligence?

   1. Most courts permit a mistake of fact defense if the defendant's error is reasonable, i.e. they apply an objective negligence standard.

      a. It is arguable that convictions are easier to obtain when the issue of consent is decided by the fact finder on an objective, "reasonable man" standard.

      b. There is disagreement about what "reasonable" means in this regard. Some feminists believe there is a gender difference regarding what constitutes a reasonable belief that a woman is consenting.

   2. Some courts require the state to prove the defendant was reckless regarding the victim's consent rather than just negligent. In these jurisdictions, an honest belief, reasonable or unreasonable, that the victim consented prevents a conviction. *Regina v. Morgan; Reynolds v. State.*

V. Reform Efforts.

A. Stephen J. Schulhofer has drafted a proposed model statute that takes into account the problems regarding determining a victim's consent and a defendant's intent. *Stephen J. Schulhofer, Unwanted Sex.*

B. Reform efforts, such as the strict 1975 Michigan statute, have not increased rape convictions. This has been attributed to the criminal justice officials who use cultural norms, rather than the statutory language, to process cases.

VI. The Marital Exemption.

A. At common law, a husband could not be prosecuted for raping his wife. The rationale for the "marital exemption" for rape was that the wife gave her irrevocable consent to sexual intercourse upon entering into the marriage.

1. Most jurisdictions have significantly limited the marital exemption. Indeed, the common law marital exemption has been held unconstitutional. *People v. Liberta.*

   a. About half the states have abolished the exemption entirely or retain it only to exempt husbands from prosecution for statutory rape.

   b. Two states (Kentucky and Oklahoma) still maintain the exemption.

   c. Almost half the states restrict the husband's liability by requiring aggravated force or by treating marital rape as a lesser offense than other rapes.

   d. When a state statute is silent as to whether it contains a marital exemption, several courts have held that the exemption should not be read into the statutes.

   e. Virginia courts have held that a husband cannot avail himself of the marital exemption if the wife has declared a de facto end to the marriage by moving out or by other conduct that tends to show the marriage is over.

2. The Model Penal Code preserves the marital exemption. The drafters justify this view by arguing that marriage implies a generalized consent and that rape prosecutions would intrude upon the intimacies of the marital relationship.

B. Studies show that approximately 10-14% of women who have been married were the victims of a least one completed or attempted rape by their husbands.

VII. Evidentiary Issues.

A. Although at common law accusations of rape did not have to be corroborated, until recently most jurisdictions have required corroboration.

1. Corroboration was justified on the grounds that false charges of rape are more prevalent than other false charges and that rape charges are unusually difficult to defend against.

2. Many jurisdictions sought corroboration of at least some portion of the victim's story so the jury could be convinced beyond a reasonable doubt that the victim was not fabricating the accusations. *United States v. Wiley.*

3. Reform advocates protested adamantly and societal views changed; today, no American state requires corroboration in forcible rape cases.

B. Many jurisdictions used to require special jury instructions in rape cases. The instructions informed the jury that rape charges were easily made and hard to defend against, and therefore, instructed the jury to consider the woman's story with caution.

1. The Model Penal Code, drafted in the 1950's, requires both corroboration and a special jury instruction warning the jury to evaluate the victim's allegations with "special care."

2. Many states have abolished the special jury instruction requirement in rape cases.

C. The efforts of rape reform advocates and changing societal views have led to the adoption of rape shield laws in many states and in the Federal Rules of Evidence. Some of these changes have been initiated by the courts in re-evaluating prior evidentiary rules about the admissibility of evidence regarding the victim's character in rape cases.

1. Evidence of the victim's unchaste character is generally inadmissible in rape cases. *State ex rel. Pope v. Superior Court.* An exception is when the probative value of the evidence exceeds its potential prejudicial effect.

   a. Evidence of the victim's prior sexual history may be considered prejudicial because the jury may place too much weight on it and confuse the issues.

   b. The evidence is also considered prejudicial because it may aggravate the victim's psychological injuries caused by the rape and deter other victims from reporting rapes.

2. An important exception to the inadmissibility of the victim's prior sexual history exists when excluding such evidence violates the defendant's Sixth Amendment right to confront the witnesses against him.

   a. Constitutional concerns trump the rape shield laws. The defendant must be afforded the opportunity to cross-examine the witnesses against him, absent extraordinary circumstances. *State v. Delawder.*

   b. Some courts have held that highly restrictive rape shield laws are unconstitutional.

   c. Other courts have saved such laws by reading into them a catch-all exception for any evidence that is necessary to preserve the defendant's right to a fair trial.

  3. Rape shield laws were originally enacted to protect victims from abusive trial tactics which tended to put the victim on trial rather than the defendant. A number of empirical studies indicate that victims are treated better in the judicial process since the enactment of rape shield laws.

  4. A number of courts have held that the victim's public behavior is admissible even under a rape shield law. The rationale is that testimony regarding the victim's public behavior does not impinge the victim's privacy. *State v. Colbath.*

D. A defendant's prior bad acts are generally inadmissible in rape cases, as in other criminal cases, when they are used to prove a propensity to commit the crime.

  1. Some feminist writers protest the inadmissibility of the defendant's prior history in rape cases. Susan Estrich contends that evidence that a man has abused women in the past is highly probative of rape. *Susan Estrich, Teaching Rape Law.*

E. Evidence laws often limit the defendant's access to the victim's prior history of psychological treatment.

  1. The decision to order a psychiatric evaluation of the victim rests within the sound discretion of the trial judge. *Government of the Virgin Islands v. Scuito.*

  2. The same concerns for the victim's privacy that are espoused in support of limiting admissibility of her prior sexual history can be advanced to support limiting the defendant's ability to force her to have a psychiatric evaluation or to access her psychiatric treatment records.

  3. Some courts have permitted the defendant to access the victim's prior psychiatric treatment records and have allowed those records to be examined at trial. *Commonwealth v. Stockhammer.*

State v. Rusk

(Government) v. (Accused Rapist)
289 Md. 230, 424 A.2d 720 (Md. 1981)

M E M O R Y   G R A P H I C

Instant Facts

A woman drove a man she met at a bar home and, after he took her car keys and she went to his room with him, he allegedly raped her.

Black Letter Rule

A victim's reasonable fear of death or serious bodily injury will preclude the need to show force on the part of the attacker or resistance on the part of the victim.

Case Vocabulary

RESISTANCE: An attempt to withstand the force or exertion that is applied to oneself either by forcible means in turn or by more passive or subtle means.

Procedural Basis: Appeal to the Court of Appeals of Maryland of a conviction for rape and subsequent reversal of the conviction by the Court of Special Appeals.

Facts: A woman named Pat went out for the evening with her friend, Terry. After they attended a high school alumni meeting, the women went to a bar in Fells Point to have a few drinks. Rusk (D) approached the two women, and Terry interrupted her conversation with another to say, briefly, "Hi Eddie." Rusk (D) then began talking to Pat and during the conversation they learned that they had both recently separated from their spouses and each had a child. Rusk (D) asked for a ride home. Pat agreed to give him a ride home because she thought her friend Terry knew him. On the ride home, Pat cautioned Rusk (D) that she was giving him a ride and it meant nothing more. When they arrived at Rusk's home, which was located in an area with which Pat was unfamiliar, Rusk (D) asked Pat to come up to his room. She refused but he reached over and turned the car off and took her keys. Rusk (D) then got out of the car and asked Pat if she would come up to his room now. Pat later testified that she went with him because she was scared. She testified that at that moment Rusk (D) was looking at her strangely and she was afraid he was going to rape her. She accompanied him into the rooming house and into his one-room apartment. Pat sat in a chair beside the bed and Rusk (D) sat on the bed. After they talked for a few minutes Rusk (D) left the room for between 1-5 minutes. Pat made no noise and did not attempt to leave. When Rusk (D) returned, he turned off the light and approached Pat. Pat told him she wanted to leave, but Rusk (D) still had her car keys and said that he wanted her to stay. He pulled her on to the bed and began to undress her. Pat eventually removed the rest of her clothes and Rusk's (D) pants and testified that she did because he told her to do so. Pat testified that at that point she was begging him not to continue and that he put his hands around her throat and began to lightly choke her. She asked Rusk (D) if he would let her go without killing her if she let him do what he wanted. Pat claimed that she was crying at this time. She claimed that Rusk (D) said he would let her go and thereafter she performed oral sex and they had sexual intercourse. Immediately after she asked if she could leave and Rusk (D) said yes. He walked her to her car and asked if he could see her again. She told him that she'd see him in Fells Point and left. After thinking about the incident in her car she decided to report it to the police. Rusk (D) denied placing his hands on Pat's throat and had two friends testify on his behalf that Pat had been with him willingly. He also denied using any force or threats of force to get Pat to have intercourse with him and claimed that she went to his room willingly. Rusk (D) was convicted of rape at trial but his conviction was reversed on direct appeal because the appellate court found that the evidence did not support a finding of force or resistance.

Issue: Will a reasonable fear of death or bodily injury preclude the necessity of showing that an alleged rapist used force or the victim was unable to resist?

Decision and Rationale: (Murphy, C.J.) Yes. The appellate court reversed the conviction because it found that the evidence must support a conclusion either that the victim resisted and was overcome by force or that she was prevented from resisting by threats to her safety. The appellate court concluded that the evidence in this case was insufficient to show either of these factors. In its words, "we have been unable to see any resistance on her part ...and certainly can we see no fear as would overcome her attempt to resist." We recognize that lack of consent is generally established by proof of resistance or failure to resist due to force or threats to the victim's safety. However, the majority of courts have held that the victim's reasonable fear for her life or her safety obviates the need to prove force or resistance. We think that is the correct standard to apply in this case. We disagree with the appellate court that the evidence was insufficient to show this degree of fear in Pat. The appellate court substituted its own interpretation of the evidence for that of the jury's. We think that was a fundamental error. Whether Pat's apprehension of fear was reasonable under the circumstances was a question of fact for the jury to decide. The jury obviously believed Pat and did not believe Rusk (D). The evidence was such that a jury could have believed that Pat was afraid that Rusk (D) would kill her if she did not do what he wanted. Reversed.

Dissent: (Cole, J.) The majority concludes that the jury could have found that Pat's fear was reasonable under the circumstances. I submit that that issue should not have been reached without first deciding whether Rusk's (D) behavior could reasonably have been seen as able to give rise to such a fear. I recognize that courts no longer require a woman to resist to the utmost in a rape case. But it is not enough for a woman to simply say, "I was scared." We cannot convict a man of rape on the basis of that naked statement. A victim's statement that she was scared does not by itself transform consent or mere unwillingness into submission by force. The woman must make it plain that she regards the sexual acts as abhorrent and that they offend her very sense of pride and dignity. And she should resist unless the man has made it clear to her that he will force her if she tries to resist. There is no evidence of such fear in this case as would prevent Pat from resisting. She testified that she did not like the way Rusk (D) looked at her and that he choked her. Yet she was able to talk to him during the alleged choking, and a vague and undescribed look is not enough to show the fear necessary to excuse her lack of resistance. The state (P) failed to prove the required element of force in this case and the judgment of conviction should have been reversed.

Analysis:

The fundamental disagreement between the majority and the dissent is over when resistance is required and to what degree. It is not an issue on which courts have reached a consensus. The element of force or the threat of force is usually required in order to obtain a rape conviction. One way of proving force is for the victim to show that she tried to resist in some manner. Some rape statutes actually require a showing of resistance as an element of the crime. It is true that the old requirement that a woman "resist to the utmost" has been abandoned by all American jurisdictions, but many, if not most courts still require a showing of reasonable resistance. This despite the fact that many studies have shown that it can actually be more dangerous for a victim to resist her attacker than to submit. Many advocates of rape law reform would have the courts recognize the serious issues that surround a requirement of resistance. As a result, some states, like New York, have removed the resistance requirement entirely from their rape statutes. The important thing to recognize is that there is diversion amongst the courts and the statutes with respect to resistance and how it connects with a showing of force.

State in the Interest of M.T.S.

(Government) v. (Juvenile)

129 N.J. 422, 609 A.2d 1266 (1992)

M E M O R Y   G R A P H I C

Instant Facts

A seventeen-year-old is convicted of sexual assault for having intercourse with a fifteen-year-old girl who lived in the same house while she was sleeping.

Black Letter Rule

The requirement of force is satisfied by the physical act of sexual penetration without the victim's consent.

Case Vocabulary

AFFIRMATIVE PERMISSION: An act or words that positively established consent to engage in certain conduct.

RAPE LAW REFORM: Efforts made to change rape laws by advocates who believed that the traditional rape laws were too harshly constructed and placed too much of a burden on women to prove non-consent, resistance and forcible submission.

Procedural Basis: Appeal to the New Jersey Supreme Court of an appellate reversal of a trial court's adjudication of delinquency for having committed a sexual assault.

Facts: Fifteen-year-old C.G. was living with her mother and siblings and several other people, one of whom was seventeen-year-old M.T.S. (D). M.T.S. (D) slept downstairs on the couch while C.G. had her own bedroom on the second floor. Each teenager told very different versions of the incident at trial. The trial court did not credit either fully. C.G. claimed that on the day of the incident M.T.S. (D) told her three or four times that he was going to pay her a surprise visit in her bedroom that night. She claimed that she thought he was joking. She also claimed that M.T.S. had tried to fondle and kiss her on other occasions, but that she had rejected his advances. C.G. testified that she awoke about 1:30 A.M. to find M.T.S. (D) standing in her doorway, but didn't think anything of it. She went to use the bathroom, then returned to her room and fell in to a deep sleep. C.G. claimed that the next thing she remembered was waking up with M.T.S. (D) on top of her. She said her clothes were off and his penis was inside her. She said she slapped M.T.S. (D) in the face and immediately told him to get off of her. M.T.S. (D) complied within a minute. C.G. testified that M.T.S. (D) did not otherwise harm her. She told her mother about the encounter in the morning. M.T.S.(D) claimed that he and C.G. had been kissing and necking for a few days prior to the incident and that they had discussed having sexual intercourse. M.T.S. (D) also claimed that C.G. invited him to make a surprise visit to her room that evening. He claimed that they engaged in petting and kissing and that C.G. willingly engaged in sexual intercourse with him. M.T.S. (D) said that just as they had started to have intercourse, C.G. pulled him off of her and said stop. M.T.S. (D) testified that he stopped immediately. The trial court concluded from their testimony that they had engaged in consensual petting and kissing, but that C.G. had not consented to sexual intercourse. Accordingly, the trial court found that the state (P) had proven second degree sexual assault. Sexual assault was defined by statute to be sexual penetration with another person with the use of physical force or coercion. The appellate court reversed and the state (P) appealed.

Issue: Does the offense of sexual assault require the application of some amount of force in addition to the act of penetration?

Decision and Rationale: (Handler, J.) No. The act of penetration itself is sufficient to satisfy the requirement of force for sexual assault. The statute does not define "physical force" or "coercion." It has been left to the courts to define these terms. The state (P) urges us to define force as any amount of sexual touching that occurs without consent. The Public Defender would have us interpret force as some amount of force over and above the act of non-consensual penetration. In deciding which definition to apply, we examine the recent incidents of rape law reform that have taken place in our state. The legislature has defined sexual assault as penetration brought about by the use of physical force or coercion. Although it did not define these terms, legislative history shows that the legislature's concept of sexual assault was influenced by its understanding of assault and battery law. Any unauthorized and offensive touching of another is a battery. Likewise, any unauthorized sexual contact is a crime under the reformed law of sexual assault. We no longer have a requirement of resistance in this state. If we accepted the Public Defender's definition of force, we would be reintroducing a resistance requirement into the reformed law. We do not believe that the legislature intended that the victim be required to show force in addition to the act of non-consensual sexual penetration. We conclude that the act of sexual penetration itself engaged in without the affirmative permission of the victim constitutes physical force. It is the factfinder's duty to decide whether, in the circumstances of each case, the defendant reasonably believed the alleged victim had given permission to the act of sexual penetration. It must also be recognized that the law does not require the victim to have expressed non-consent or to have denied permission. Reversed.

Analysis:

The court in this case applied what has been characterized as the "intrinsic force" standard. Under such a standard, the force element is satisfied by a showing of the act of sexual penetration itself. Courts that apply this standard require no showing of force greater than that which is necessary to accomplish sexual penetration. The intrinsic force standard is undoubtedly a minority standard. Still and all, it is less ambiguous than other force requirements. The far more common rule is [predictably] called the "extrinsic force" standard. The extrinsic force standard requires a showing of force beyond that which is sufficient to accomplish nonconsensual sexual penetration. There is much more room for disagreement over what constitutes sufficient force to meet the "extrinsic force" standard. That is why you will commonly see discussion within the cases applying the extrinsic force standard about the facts and circumstances of the particular case. In other words, whether such force exists in a particular case, and to what degree, will largely depend on the facts, evidence and circumstances of the case. You can probably see that consent issues become hopelessly intertwined with force issues in extrinsic force cases.

People v. Evans

(State) v. (Lecherous Seducer)
85 Misc. 2d 1088, 379 N.Y.S. 2d 912 (1975)

M E M O R Y   G R A P H I C

Instant Facts

A thirty-seven-year-old bachelor lured a naïve twenty-year-old woman to his apartment by pretending to conduct a psychological experiment and used various strategies to manipulate her into having sex.

Black Letter Rule

A woman's consent to sexual intercourse procured by deception or misrepresentation is still valid consent and will prevent a conviction for rape.

Case Vocabulary

SEDUCTION: A common law civil action available when a man unlawfully persuaded a woman to have sex with him by means of flattery, trickery or false promises, i.e. by falsely promising to marry her. Some jurisdictions criminalized seduction in addition to providing a civil remedy.

Procedural Basis: Bench trial for charges of first degree rape.

Facts: The statute involved defined first degree rape as engaging in sexual intercourse by forcible compulsion, among other things. Forcible compulsion was defined as "physical force that overcomes earnest resistance; or a threat, express or implied, that places a person in fear of immediate death or serious physical injury. . . ." Evans (D) was charged with committing first degree rape. A thirty-seven-year-old bachelor, he met Miss P., a twenty-year-old student, when he went to LaGuardia Airport to meet a flight. Miss P. was naïve and unworldly and Evans (D) struck up a conversation with her, claiming to be a psychologist conducting an interview for a magazine. Evans (D) invited Miss P. to accompany him and a girl named Bridget to a singles bar in Manhattan. Evans (D) claimed it was to conduct an experiment in which he would observe Miss P.'s reactions and the reactions of males to her. Afterward, Miss P. was invited to come up to Evans' (D) apartment, which he explained was used as one of his five offices throughout the city. Two hours after they entered the apartment, Evans (D) began making advances. Miss P. rejected him. Evans (D) then told her that he was disappointed in her because she had failed the experiment and that he was trying to reach her innermost consciousness. He made statements such as "How do you know that I am who I say I am, " and "I could kill you or rape you or hurt you physically." He further stressed that Miss P. was in a strange apartment with a strange man. Evans (D) thereafter changed his tactics and told Miss P. a story about his lost love who had died when she drove her car off of a cliff. Evans (D) said that Miss P. reminded him of his lost love. Miss P. became sympathetic and went to Evans (D) to put her arms around him. He grabbed her at that time, saying "you're mine, you are mine." The two had sexual intercourse, then another act of sexual intercourse approximately one-half hour later. There were instances of oral-genital contact and various other sexual acts throughout the night. Miss P. left Evans' (D) apartment about seven o'clock the next morning. There were no items of torn clothing and Miss P. had no scratches or bruises.

Issue: Is consent to sexual intercourse obtained by artifice or deception valid consent so as to bar a rape conviction?

Decision and Rationale: (Greenfield, J.) Yes. Rape is defined in our Penal Law as engaging in sexual intercourse by forcible compulsion, among other ways not relevant to this case. Forcible compulsion is defined as physical force that overcomes earnest resistance or a threat, express or implied, that places a person in fear of immediate death or serious physical injury. The question in this case is whether the act that occurred between Evans (D) and Miss P. was rape according to our Penal Code. Provided there is actual consent to the act, it is not rape, despite the fact that the consent was obtained by fraud or trickery. Rape requires forcible compulsion. The lesser crime of seduction, recognized in some states, consists of engaging in sexual intercourse after obtaining consent by artifice, deception, flattery, fraud or promise. This state does not recognize either a criminal or civil action for seduction. It is clear from the evidence that Miss P. was intimidated and confused; she may even have been terrified after her experience. But it is equally clear that Evans (D) did not resort to actual physical force. Physical compulsion can consist of threats, however. The instant question is whether Evans' (D) statements of "I could kill you," "I could rape you," and "I could hurt you physically" were sufficient to show threats of the magnitude contemplated by the statute. Evans' (D) words are subject to two different interpretations. The first would be a threat to Miss P.—that she better do what he said or he would hurt her. The second, equally plausible interpretation would be that Evans (D) was chiding Miss P.—in effect, showing her how foolish she had been to go up to the apartment with a strange man. Evans could have been trying to show her the folly of making herself so vulnerable and defenseless. We have to examine his statements not by the effect they had on Miss P. but by Evans' (D) intent in speaking them. That is so because this is a criminal trial and the defendant's intent must be proven beyond a reasonable doubt. Clearly, the intent behind these words is ambiguous. The words spoken are subject to two alternative constructions—one that would support a conviction and one that would not. In these circumstances, it is impossible to say that Evans (D) possessed the requisite intent beyond a reasonable doubt. Although his trickery and other actions were despicable and predatory, they were not criminal.

Analysis:

There is generally no criminal liability when false representations are used to obtain consent to sexual intercourse. At common law, there was a civil action for seduction, which entailed enticing a person to have sex—usually adultery—by the use of flattery, promises, fraud or deception. Some jurisdictions also penalized seduction. In modern times, however, there is generally no civil or criminal liability for seduction or seduction-like conduct. There have been some limited efforts to make sexual intercourse obtained by such methods a lesser crime, but as you've seen from the first portion of this chapter, the vast majority of rape statutes require forcible compulsion or its equivalent. Contrast this "no liability for consent obtained by fraud or deception" with the fact that every criminal code recognizes some form of larceny by trick. Larceny by trick is accomplished when a person knowingly uses a misrepresentation or fraud to obtain personal property. Many rape reform advocates protest the fact that the law recognizes the taking of personal property by fraud or deception as a crime but does not recognize the arguably more serious invasion of obtaining sex by the same means.

Boro v. Superior Court

(Liar) v. (Court)

163 Cal. App.3d 1224, 210 Cal. Rptr. 122 (1985)

M E M O R Y   G R A P H I C

 ## Instant Facts

Boro (D) induced a woman to have sexual intercourse with him by falsely telling her that intercourse with him would treat her alleged fatal disease.

 ## Black Letter Rule

Consent to sexual intercourse induced by fraud is valid consent and prevents a rape conviction.

Case Vocabulary

FRAUD IN THE FACTUM: Fraud regarding the nature of the act undertaken.

FRAUD IN THE INDUCEMENT: Fraud regarding the reason for undertaking a specific act.

WRIT OF PROHIBITION: A writ that prevents a lower court from taking an action beyond its jurisdictional powers. It applies only if the court's duty is clearly fixed and required by law and if to do other than that sought by the petitioner would be a clear violation of official duty.

Procedural Basis: Appeal of trial court's failure to set aside criminal rape charge.

Facts: The victim, Mrs. R, received a phone call from a man identifying himself as "Dr. Stevens." "Dr. Stevens" told Mrs. R that he had the results of her blood test and that she had a dangerous, highly infectious, possibly fatal, disease. "Dr. Stevens" explained that the disease could be treated by a painful surgical procedure costing $9000 and requiring uninsured hospitalization for six weeks. Or, for a mere $4500, Mrs. R could have sexual intercourse with a man who was injected with a serum that would cure the disease. When Mrs. R said she did not have $4500, "Dr. Stevens" reduced the price to $1000. Mrs. R got the money and checked into a hotel. Boro (D) entered the room and had sexual intercourse with her. Boro (D) was charged under Penal Code §261(4) with rape "where a person is at the time unconscious of the nature of the act and this is known to the accused" and under Penal Code §261(2) with rape "accomplished by means of force or fear of immediate and unlawful bodily injury." The trial court dismissed the §261(2) charge, but not the §261(4) charge.

Issue: Is consent to sexual intercourse that is induced by fraud valid consent that prevents a rape conviction?

Decision and Rationale: (Justice's name not stated) Yes. The People (P) argue that §261(4) applies because Mrs. R believed the intercourse was a medical treatment and not an ordinary act of sexual intercourse. Boro (D) argues that Mrs. R was aware of the nature of the act, so her motivation is irrelevant. This situation is similar to that of a person inducing intercourse by pretending to be married to the victim. In that situation, California's legislature passed Penal Code §261(5), adopting the majority view that such consent is fraud in the factum, not in the inducement, and thus vitiates consent. The People (P) cite Penal Code §261.6 which defines "consent" as an act of free will where the person acts freely and voluntarily with knowledge of the nature of the act or transaction. However, if the legislature had wanted to make a situation like the present one vitiate consent, it could have done so. In addition, the People's (P) reading of §261.6 would render §261(5) unnecessary. While we recognize the heartless cruelty of Boro's (P) scheme, we hold that it does not comprise a violation of §261(4). Reversed.

Dissent: (Holmdahl, J.) Although the legislature did not expressly repeal the distinction between fraud in the factum and fraud in the inducement in §261.6, it certainly intended to limit consent to that which is truly free, voluntary, unrestricted, and knowledgeable. I believe there is sufficient basis to prosecute Boro (D) under §261(4).

Analysis:

As was held in *People v. Evans*, the general rule is that there is no criminal liability when a perpetrator makes false representations to obtain consent to sexual intercourse. This case is a twist on the class of cases where a doctor has intercourse with a patient by fraudulently misrepresenting that the intercourse is a necessary medical treatment for a real or fake malady. This typically does not constitute rape. This is considered a case of fraud in the inducement, i.e. the patient knew she was engaging in sexual intercourse but misunderstood a collateral matter. However, when a doctor has intercourse with a patient, but conceals it by portraying the event as a pelvic examination or other treatment involving vaginal penetration, the doctor may be convicted of rape. This is considered fraud in the factum, where the patient is unaware of the basic fact that sexual intercourse was occurring and, thus, could not have consented. Cases that are hard to classify involve those where the victim believes that the perpetrator is the victim's spouse, either because the perpetrator entered the victim's bedroom in the dark, or because the victim was deceived by a sham wedding. Some jurisdictions view these as fraud in the factum or fraud in the inducement. In California, where *Boro* was decided, a statute expressly makes these situations rape. Opinions differ as to whether the fraud in the inducement/fraud in the factum distinction is the proper one for determining whether rape has been committed. Other views look at the materiality of the misrepresentation (if he says he's rich, but he's not, is that rape?) or the totality of the circumstances. Some states have held that fraud in the inducement in certain professional relationships, such as clergy/parishioner, supports a rape prosecution. It is interesting to note that, in response to *Boro*, California enacted a new law making it unlawful to fraudulently induce another person to engage in sexual intercourse with the intent to cause fear. "Fear" is defined as fear of physical injury or death to the victim or to any relative of the victim.

Commonwealth v. Sherry

(State) v. (Doctor)
386 Mass. 682, 437 N.E.2d 224 (1982)

M E M O R Y   G R A P H I C

Instant Facts

Three doctors are convicted of rape after taking a nurse to a house and separately having intercourse with her, despite the doctors' mistake-of-fact as to the nurse's consent.

Black Letter Rule

A defense of mistake-of-fact must be based on a reasonable good faith standard.

Case Vocabulary

MISTAKE-OF-FACT: A reasonable or good faith mistake, concerning the existence of an essential element of a crime.

Procedural Basis: Certification to the Supreme Judicial Court of Massachusetts of a conviction for rape.

Facts: The victim, a registered nurse, and defendants, all doctors, were employed at the same hospital in Boston. On September 5, 1980, Sherry (D1), along with another doctor, was a host at a party for some hospital staff. At this party, the victim had a conversation with Hussain (D2), during which he made sexual advances toward her. Later in the evening, Hussain (D2) and Sherry (D1) pushed her and Lefkowitz (D3) into a bathroom together, shut the door, and turned off the light. They did not open the door until Lefkowitz (D3) asked them to leave her in peace. At various times, the victim danced with both Hussain (D2) and Sherry (D1). Some time later, Hussain (D2) and Sherry (D1) grabbed the victim by her arms and pulled her out of the apartment, as Lefkowitz (D3) said, "We're going up to Rockport." The victim verbally protested but did not physically resist the men because she thought that they were just "horsing around." Nor was she physically restrained as they rode down an elevator with an unknown fifth person, or as they walked through the lobby of the apartment building. The victim testified that once outside, Hussain (D2) carried her over his shoulder to Sherry's car and held her in the front seat as the four drove to Rockport. En route she engaged in superficial conversation with the three defendants. She testified that she was not in fear at this time. When they arrived at Lefkowitz's (D3) home in Rockport, she asked to be taken home. Instead Hussain (D2) carried her into the house. Once in the house, the victim and two of the men smoked marijuana, and all of them toured the house. After being invited by Lefkowitz (D3) to view an antique bureau in a bedroom, all of them entered and the men began to disrobe. Although the victim was frightened and began to verbally protest, the three men proceeded to undress her and maneuver her onto the bed. One of the defendants attempted to have the victim perform fellatio while another attempted intercourse. After the victim told them to stop, two of the defendants left the room temporarily, and each defendant separately had intercourse with the victim in the bedroom. The victim testified, that she felt physically numbed, humiliated, and disgusted and could not fight. After this sequence of events, the victim claimed that she was further sexually harassed and forced to take a bath. Some time later, Lefkowitz (D3) told the victim that they were returning to Boston because Hussain (D2) was on call at the hospital. On their way back, the group stopped to view a beach, eat breakfast, and get gasoline. The victim was taken back to where she left her car and drove herself home. The defendants testified to a similar sequence of events, although details of the episode varied significantly. According to their testimony, Lefkowitz (D3) invited Sherry (D1) to accompany him from the party to a home that his parents owned in Rockport. The victim, upon hearing this, inquired as to whether she could go along. As the three were leaving, Sherry (D1) extended the invitation to Hussain (D2). At no time did the victim indicate her unwillingness to accompany the defendants. Upon arrival in Rockport, the victim wandered into the bedroom where she inquired about the antique bureau. She sat down on the bed and kicked off her shoes, whereupon Sherry (D1) entered the room, dressed only in his underwear. Sherry (D1) helped the victim get undressed, and she proceeded to have intercourse with all three men separately in turn. Each defendant testified that the victim consented to the acts of intercourse. Sherry (D1), Hussain (D2), and Lefkowitz (D3) were convicted of rape without aggravation. Sherry (D1), Hussain (D2), and Lefkowitz (D3) appeal.

Issue: Must a defense of mistake-of-fact as to whether consent was given be based on a reasonable good faith standard?

Decision and Rationale: (Liacos, J.) Yes. Sherry (D1), Hussain (D2), and Lefkowitz (D3) contend that the judge's jury charge was inadequate and the cause of prejudicial error. However the instructions given by the trial judge placed before the jury the essential elements of the crime required to be proved.

The judge instructed the jury that intercourse must be accomplished with force sufficient to overcome the woman's will, or by threats of bodily harm, inferred or expressed, which engendered sufficient fear so that it was reasonable for her not to resist. These instructions correctly stated the elements of proof required for a rape conviction. Sherry (D1), Hussain (D2), and Lefkowitz (D3), appear to have been seeking to raise a defense of good faith mistake on the issue of consent. They would require the jury to "find beyond a reasonable doubt that the accused had actual knowledge of [the victim's] lack of consent." In doing so, they argue that mistake-of-fact negating criminal intent is a defense to the crime of rape. A defense of mistake-of-fact must be based on a reasonable good faith standard. Whether a reasonable good faith mistake-of-fact as to consent is a defense to the crime of rape has never, to our knowledge, been decided in this Commonwealth. We do not reach the issue whether a reasonable and honest mistake to the fact of consent would be a defense, for even if we assume it to be, the defendants did not request a jury instruction based on a reasonable good faith standard. We are aware of no American court of last resort that recognizes mistake-of-fact, without consideration of its reasonableness as a defense, nor do the defendants cite such authority. Affirmed.

Analysis:

This case raises the issue of the mens rea or intent aspect of the crime of rape. Rape is a general-intent offense. Therefore a defendant is guilty of rape if he possessed a morally blameworthy state of mind regarding the female's lack of consent. Thus, as a general rule, a person is not guilty of rape if he entertained a genuine and reasonable belief that the female voluntarily consented to intercourse with him. As you can see, this rule conforms with ordinary common law mistake-of-fact doctrine relating to general-intent offenses. As illustrated by the opinion, the issue of mens rea rarely arises in rape prosecutions. Most likely, the reason for this is because, in traditional rape prosecutions, the element of force required to secure intercourse would effectively invalidate a claim that the perpetrator was mistaken with regards to consent. However, the issue of mens rea is more significant in acquaintance-rape prosecutions, in jurisdictions where the resistance rule has been eliminated, and in jurisdictions where a conviction may be obtained in the absence of force beyond that which is necessary for intercourse. Moreover, the analysis of this issue is the same in rape cases, as it is in other general-intent offenses. All in all, the main purpose of this case is to show the reader that, although the issue of mens rea and the defense of mistake-of-fact is rare in rape cases, it is worth attention.

Commonwealth v. Fischer

(State) v. (Horny College Student)

721 A.2d 1111 (1998)

M E M O R Y   G R A P H I C

Instant Facts

During the second sexual encounter between Fischer (D) and the victim, Fischer (D) believed the victim consented to their rough sex even when the victim was protesting.

Black Letter Rule

A mistake of fact regarding the victim's consent is not a defense to rape.

Case Vocabulary

MENS REA: A criminal intent.

Procedural Basis: Appeal of criminal conviction based on ineffective assistance of counsel.

Facts: Fischer (D) and the victim were college freshman. Several hours before the incident at issue, Fischer (D) and the victim went to Fischer's (D) dorm room and had intimate contact. The victim testified that they just kissed and fondled each other. Fischer (D) testified that they engaged in "rough sex," with the victim acting aggressively, and culminating in the victim performing oral sex on him. They met up again later and went back to Fischer's (D) dorm room. According to the victim, Fischer (D) locked the door and forced his penis into her mouth. She struggled and repeatedly stated that she did not want to engage in sex. She escaped only after striking Fisher (D) in the groin. According to Fischer (D), as he led the victim to his dorm room, the victim stated that it would have to be a "quick one." Fischer (D) acted roughly with her, just as he had in their previous encounter. After Fischer (D) disregarded the victim's protests, telling her that "you know you want it," the victim stated that she honestly did not want it. According to Fischer (D), he then removed himself from the victim's body, but they continued to kiss and fondle each another. Fischer (D) testified that the victim seemed to enjoy the contact, but then abruptly left the room. The jury convicted Fischer (D) of involuntary deviate sexual intercourse, aggravated indecent assault, and related offenses.

Issue: Is a defendant's mistake of fact regarding the victim's consent a defense to rape?

Decision and Rationale: (Beck, J.) No. Even if we were inclined to change the law, we could not do so in the context of an appeal based on ineffective assistance of counsel. Fischer (D) claims his trial counsel was ineffective because counsel did not seek a jury instruction regarding mistake of fact. About 18 years ago, in *Commonwealth v. Williams* [where defendant drove victim to dark place and threatened to kill her if she did not have sex, and victim said "go ahead," mistake of fact instruction not available], we held that it is up to the legislature, not the courts, to decide whether a defendant's mistaken belief about the victim's state of mind should be a defense to rape. Fischer (D) argues that *Williams* can be distinguished on two grounds. First, Fischer (D) argues that *Williams* involved a rape by a stranger rather than an acquaintance. Fischer (D) also argues that the laws with respect to rape and all its permutations have changed significantly in the last decade. Specifically, the legislature has broadened the definition of the "forcible compulsion" element of rape to include intellectual, moral, emotional, and psychological force, not just physical force. Fischer (D) argues that this new definition prompts the need for the mistake of fact instruction because the new definition inextricably links the issue of consent with mens rea. It is true that mistake of fact has long been a fixture in criminal law. We also agree that the rule in *Williams* is inappropriate in a date rape case where the boy does not intend or suspect that his vigorous wooing is intimidating, and the girl mistakenly believes the boy will become violent if thwarted. However, in this case, the victim alleges physical force in a sexual assault. Therefore, *Williams* controls. We recognize that this case differs from *Williams* in that, here, Fischer (D) and the victim knew each other and had engaged in intimate contact just hours before the incident in question. However, we must abide by *Williams'* holding that the law does not require a mistake of fact instruction and that the judiciary has no authority to change the law. Moreover, because this appeal is based on ineffective assistance of counsel, we must determine whether Fischer's (D) prior counsel made a mistake by not asking for an instruction that would have changed the law. We cannot change the law and find counsel ineffective for refusing to predict we would do that. Affirmed.

Analysis:

By not allowing a jury instruction regarding Fischer's (D) mistaken belief that the victim consented, the court adopts a general intent approach to rape. In other words, Fischer (D) had the requisite mens rea if he voluntarily committed a sexual act, e.g., placing his penis in the victim's mouth, whether or not he intended to rape her. Other courts have held that a mistaken belief bars a conviction unless the belief is negligently held. For example, in *People v. Mayberry* [only negligently held mistaken belief regarding consent is a defense], the defendant testified that the woman voluntarily went to his apartment and willingly engaged in intercourse. The woman testified that the defendant used force and threats of force prior to the intercourse. The California Supreme Court held that the defendant was entitled to an instruction on mistake of fact regarding the woman's consent. The Court reasoned that due to the severe penalty imposed, the legislature probably did not intend to exclude the element of wrongful intent from the crime of rape. The Court applied an objective negligence standard, i.e. whether a reasonable person would believe the victim consented. A few courts have held that mistaken belief bars a conviction unless the belief is recklessly held. For example, in the English case, *Regina v. Morgan*, and the Alaska case, *Reynolds v. State*, the courts held that a mistaken belief, whether reasonable or unreasonable, about the woman's consent bars a rape conviction unless the belief is held recklessly. These courts applied a subjective standard regarding the mistaken belief. Another view holds that an instruction on mistake of fact is unnecessary if the defendant testifies that the victim unequivocally consented. For example, in *Tyson v. State*, boxer Mike Tyson testified that "D.W." agreed to accompany him to his hotel room and willingly engaged in intercourse. D.W. testified that she repeatedly objected and tried to fight off Tyson. The court refused to instruct the jury on mistake of fact. The Court of Appeals affirmed, holding that, according to Tyson's testimony, there was no gray area from which Tyson could logically argue that he was mistaken about D.W.'s consent. Another issue raised by this case is how to determine whether the woman does not consent. Is just saying "no" enough? Does the woman have to resist to the utmost? If the woman feels threatened and, thus, submits, should the defendant know she did not consent? In any event, the issues of the defendant's mens rea and his perception of the victim's consent are intertwined.

People v. Liberta

(Government) v. (Wife-Abuser)

64 N.Y.2d 152, 474 N.E.2d 567 (N.Y. 1984).

SEE THE RING? I CAN'T BE GUILTY... I'M MARRIED TO HER!

M E M O R Y G R A P H I C

Instant Facts

A man who was separated from his wife convinced his wife to accompany him and their son back to the man's motel room. The man beat and raped his estranged wife in front of their young son.

Black Letter Rule

The common-law marital exception for rape is unconstitutional.

Case Vocabulary

MARITAL EXEMPTION: At common law, a man could not be convicted of raping his wife because the marital exemption applied to always imply the wife's consent to sexual intercourse with her husband.

Facts: Mario Liberta (D) and Denise Liberta were married in 1978 and had a son shortly thereafter. After the birth of their son, Mario (D) began to beat Denise. Denise sought a protective order against Mario (D) in early 1980. Family court issued a temporary protective order in April, 1980, which required Mario (D) to move out and remain away from the family home. Mario (D) was allowed to see his son once every weekend. In March of 1981, Mario (D) arranged with Denise to pick both she and their son up for a visit. He convinced her to go back to his motel room by assuring her that a friend would be present at all times. Shortly after they arrived, the friend left. Mario (D) attacked Denise, beat her and threatened to kill her, then forced her to have sexual intercourse. In addition, he forced Denise to tell their son to watch what he was doing to her. After Denise left, she went first to her parents house and then to the hospital to be treated for various scratches and bruises on her body. She filed a complaint against Mario (D). Mario (D) was convicted of first degree rape under a statute that had a marital exemption for rape and his conviction was affirmed by the appellate court. He appealed to New York's highest court.

Issue: Does the marital exemption for rape violate equal protection?

Decision and Rationale: (Wachtler, J.) Yes. The relevant statute provides that a man is guilty of rape in the first degree when he engages in sexual intercourse by forcible compulsion with a woman to whom he is not married. "Not married" has been defined most recently by the legislature to include cases where husband and wife are no longer living together pursuant to a court order or decree or a written separation agreement. Accordingly, the statute contains a marital exemption for rape, but the exemption has been somewhat limited in recent years. Under the statute, then, Mario (D) and Denise were "not married" at the time of the attack and the marital exemption as written did not apply to Mario (D). Mario (D) argues, however, that the marital exemption as written is unconstitutional because it violates equal protection by treating him differently than another man similarly situated. Of course, legislatures may constitutionally treat different categories of people differently if there is a rational basis for doing so. At present, over 40 states retain some form of marital exemption for rape. In order to pass constitutional muster in this state, though, there must be some rational basis for treating marital rape differently from nonmarital rape. We cannot find any rational basis for doing so. Those rationales that have been advanced as supporting the difference are out-dated and indefensible. The most common rationale is that there is implied consent because the woman and man are married. We think it is absurd to ever imply consent to the violent and degrading crime of rape. This rationale extends from the days when a married woman was the property of her husband. We no longer consider women chattel or property and therefore, these archaic notions cannot provide a rational basis for retaining the marital exemption. The final argument in favor of retaining the exemption is that it protects marital privacy and encourages reconciliation. We do not accept this argument because we feel that, in a marriage that has degraded to where a husband must resort to forcible rape, there is little left to reconcile. Just as a husband cannot invoke marital privacy to avoid liability for beating or abusing his wife, he should not be able to do so to protect himself from liability for rape. Marital rape is as serious as nonmarital rape. Therefore, we hold that the marital exemption for rape violates the equal protection clauses of both our state and federal constitutions. Having found so, we choose to nullify only the marital exemption portion rather than the entire statute, as Mario (D) would have us do. The effect of our decision is to remove any disparate treatment of married and non-married individuals. The rape statute is equally applicable to all. Because the statute under which Mario (D) was convicted is not being struck down, his conviction is affirmed.

Analysis:

Only 15 states have followed New York's lead and have completely abolished the marital exemption for rape. Most states retain the exemption in some form or another. However, no state retains the marital exemption in its common law, unqualified form. At common law, a married man could never rape his wife because her consent to sexual intercourse was considered given with the marriage and irrevocable by her. Today, most jurisdictions limit the exemption either by allowing prosecution as a lesser offense or by permitting prosecution only when force is used. Despite the fact that most states retain some form of the exemption, there have been studies that indicate that marital rape may be the most prevalent form of rape and may also be the most underreported.

IN A PROSECUTION FOR RAPE THE CORROBORATION REQUIREMENT IS SATISFIED BY INDEPENDENT EVIDENCE THAT SHOWS THE VICTIM'S ALLEGATIONS ARE NOT A FABRICATION

United States v. Wiley

(Government) v. (Accused Rapist)

492 F.2d 547 (D.C. Cir. 1974)

M E M O R Y   G R A P H I C

Instant Facts

The court held that the complainant's testimony had not been corroborated by independent evidence so as to support a rape conviction.

Black Letter Rule

Independent corroboration of at least some of the victim's story is required to support a rape conviction.

Case Vocabulary

CORROBORATION: A requirement that independent evidence exist that strengthens or verifies evidence that has already been presented.

Procedural Basis: Appeal to the United States Court of Appeals for the District of Columbia of a rape conviction.

Facts: In a prosecution for rape, the court held that the victim's testimony had not been corroborated by independent evidence as was then required under D.C. Law. Judge Bazelon wrote a concurring opinion that voiced some of the issues surrounding the corroboration requirement and the arguments for its retention in rape laws.

Issue: Is independent corroboration of at least some portion of the victim's allegations required to support a rape conviction?

Decision and Rationale: (Bazelon, J., concurring.) Yes. There must be independent corroboration sufficient so that a jury could find beyond a reasonable doubt that the victim's story was not a fabrication. There are several justifications that have been advanced for the corroboration requirement. One is that a charge of rape is unusually difficult to defend against. Juries are said to be unusually sympathetic to a woman who alleges rape, which in turn weakens the required presumption of innocence in criminal cases. Of course, there have been no studies that indicate that these arguments are true. In fact, some studies show that juries may be more skeptical of rape accusations than is often supposed. Another is that false charges of rape are more prevalent than false charges of other crimes. It is contended that women sometimes fabricate allegations of rape to explain a pregnancy or because they are ashamed or bitter toward the man. But there are countervailing reasons for a woman not to report a rape. The woman may feel degraded and stigmatized by society, and she may also receive harsh treatment from medical and official personnel. It is for these types of reasons that rape is such an underreported crime. Of course, the corroboration requirement has been historically used to lessen the dangers of prejudice in our society—especially when a white woman accuses a black man of rape. But juries are more integrated in modern times and prejudices may be somewhat less, so the corroboration requirement may not be necessary for this protection any longer. Another theory is that the corroboration requirement evolved as a method of protecting men. It has been said that to a good woman, being raped is a fate worse than death and she will therefore fight against it with every ounce of her being. Absent evidence of this struggle, though, the theory says that it is more likely than not that the woman enticed the man and the man is therefore blameless in the situation. Such a rationale stems from discrimination against women. Some of these rationales are presumably still valid but some are invalid or at least outdated and no longer true. However, for the present, I feel that the requirement of corroboration is still necessary to a limited degree. Today this court retains a rule that requires independent corroboration of at least some portion of the victim's account. Such evidence will be regarded as sufficient if it permits the jury to decide beyond a reasonable doubt that the victim has not fabricated her story. Corroborating evidence was missing in this case, thus I concur with the court's judgment in reversing the conviction.

Analysis:

There was no common law requirement of corroboration in rape cases, but a significant amount of jurisdictions came to require corroboration over time. Today, however, no state retains a corroboration requirement for forcible rape. The reasons for retaining the requirement, many of which were set out in Judge Bazelon's concurring opinion above, have largely been dismissed by either the state legislatures or the courts. The opinion did not mention another, possibly more compelling reason that has sometimes been advanced in support of the corroboration requirement, however. That is, the nature of the crime is unique because it consists of conduct that under certain circumstances is welcome and invited by the woman. This last reason seems to be focusing on the fact that the woman may or may not have consented to the acts. The courts have dealt with this justification by finding that the matter of consent, or invitation, is primarily a matter of fact for the jury to determine. Because uncertainties are required to be resolved in favor of the defendant in a criminal trial, this last justification for the corroboration requirement has also gone by the wayside. The prosecution must prove *every* element of rape beyond a reasonable doubt in order to obtain a conviction. That being so, the added protection of a corroboration requirement is no longer considered necessary.

State ex rel. Pope v. Superior Court

(State) v. (Court)
113 Ariz. 22, 545 P.2d 946 (Ar. 1976)

M E M O R Y   G R A P H I C

Instant Facts

A County Attorney asked the Arizona Supreme Court to reconsider its existing evidentiary laws, which allowed the introduction of the victim's unchaste character in a rape case where consent was at issue.

Black Letter Rule

Evidence of the victim's unchaste character is generally inadmissible in rape cases.

Case Vocabulary

PREJUDICIAL EFFECT: Occurs when evidence that has some probative value tends to mislead or confuse the finder of fact, or to cause the finder of fact to focus on collateral issues not relevant to the case.

PROBATIVE VALUE: Evidence has probative value when it tends to prove or actually does prove an issue of the case.

Procedural Basis: Certification of a question to the Supreme Court of Arizona relating to the admissibility of evidence in rape cases.

Facts: The County Attorney of Mojave County, acting on behalf of the state of Arizona, asked the Arizona Supreme Court to reconsider the existing evidentiary law, which allowed an accused rapist to introduce evidence of the alleged victim's unchaste character in rape cases where consent was at issue.

Issue: Is a rape defendant generally allowed to introduce evidence of the victim's unchaste character?

Decision and Rationale: (Gordon, J.) No. Evidence of the victim's unchaste character is generally inadmissible in rape cases. Our current law is exemplified by *State v. Wood* [holding that when consent is at issue, evidence of the victim's unchastity is relevant and material]. In *Wood*, we rested our conclusions on logic and the common experience of mankind, both of which we considered would support a conclusion that a woman who has once strayed from virtue is more likely to have done so again. We expressly overrule *Wood*, because such "logic" has been abandoned by our modern society. We no longer think it appropriate to imply that a woman who has once consented to sexual intercourse is more likely to have done so at future dates. Regarding evidence in criminal trials, this court has consistently barred evidence of prior bad acts of a witness because it interjects into the case confusing collateral issues. We find today that the same reasoning applies to bar evidence of a prosecuting witness's prior sexual history in rape cases. We recognize that there will be some limited instances where the evidence of the victim's past sexual history has greater probative value than prejudicial value, but on the whole we believe that the inflammatory nature of such evidence generally outweighs any probative value. In cases where the probative value of such evidence might fairly outweigh it's prejudicial characteristics, a court should hold a hearing outside of the presence of the jury to determine the admissibility of the evidence. Some examples where the probative value may outweigh the prejudicial value are when the victim's prior consensual intercourse with another might account for the presence of semen or other physical evidence, or when the victim is allegedly a prostitute that consented to an act of prostitution. If the defendant can show that the proffered evidence falls into one of these limited exceptions, the court should admit the evidence after a hearing such as the one described above if it is credible.

Concurrence: (Hays, J.) I agree with the holding of the court except for its express exception of prostitution. I do not approve of a policy that admits evidence that the victim is allegedly a prostitute, even on the limited issue of consent. Having properly overruled *Wood*, I think we should take a definitive step toward barring *all* evidence of past sexual history, unless its probative value outweighs its prejudicial effect.

Analysis:

This case is a good example of the early precursors of rape shield laws. Rape shield laws have been enacted by many legislatures in response to outcries from advocates of rape law reform over abusive trial practices. Prior to the enactment of rape shield laws, it was a common trial tactic for the defense counsel to "put the victim on trial" by introducing evidence of her prior sexual history. The idea was that if the woman was sexually active, aggressive or dressed seductively, it might be more likely than not that she actually consented to [or even actively invited] sexual intercourse. Rape shield laws were enacted to protect the victim from such trial tactics. They operate by limiting the admissibility of the prior sexual behavior of the complaining victim in many cases. Still, as noted by the instant case, all rape shield laws recognize that in some instances, evidence of prior sexual history may be admissible if its probative value outweighs its prejudicial effect.

State v. DeLawder

(Government) v. (Convicted Rapist)
28 Md. App. 212, 344 A.2d 446 (1975)

M E M O R Y   G R A P H I C

Instant Facts

A man convicted of having carnal knowledge of a woman under age 14 brought an appeal for post conviction relief because the evidentiary laws in effect at the time of his trial left his counsel unable to effectively cross-examine the victim.

Black Letter Rule

A criminal defendant must be afforded the oppor-tunity to confront the witnesses against him.

Case Vocabulary

CONFRONTATION CLAUSE: A clause in the Sixth Amendment to the Constitution of the United States that guarantees the accused the right to confront the witnesses against him at trial.

Procedural Basis: Writ of habeas corpus for post-conviction review of conviction for having carnal knowledge of a woman under the age of 14.

Facts: DeLawder (D) was found guilty after a jury trial of carnal knowledge of a female under the age of 14. His counsel was not permitted to ask the victim about her past sexual history. He was sentenced to 15 years in prison. His conviction was affirmed by the Maryland Court of Special Appeals on direct appeal. He later sought post-conviction relief from the same court, arguing that the United States Supreme Court decision in *Davis v. Alaska* [holding that the right of confrontation guaranteed by the Sixth Amendment applies to state as well as federal criminal defendants] affected the validity of his conviction.

Issue: Do evidentiary rules that completely prevent a defendant from cross-examining an alleged rape victim violate the Sixth Amendment's right to confrontation?

Decision and Rationale: (Orth, C.J.) Yes. An accused must be permitted to effectively cross-examine the witnesses against him. We affirmed DeLawder's (D) conviction prior to the Supreme Court's holding in *Davis v. Alaska*. At the time, we held that the trial court properly excluded the defense counsel's attempts to cross-examine the victim regarding her prior sexual relations with other men. The general rule is that because consent is not an issue in carnal knowledge prosecution, evidence of the victim's sexual relations with others is immaterial. The trial judge correctly applied the general rule, and we affirmed accordingly. Subsequently, the Supreme Court decided in *Davis* that the right of an accused to confront the witnesses against him is secured in both state and federal criminal proceedings. In *Davis*, the Court held that it was a violation of the defendant's Sixth Amendment rights for the trial court to have prohibited the cross-examination of a witness regarding his record as a juvenile. The trial court had excluded the evidence pursuant to a state rule that preserved the confidentiality of juvenile adjudications of delinquency. Despite the fact that the defense counsel had related his intent to limit the use of the juvenile conviction as a method to show bias, the trial court excluded the line of questioning. The Court held that defense counsel should have been permitted to cross-examine the witness to show his possible bias, and that by preventing him from doing so, the court violated the defendant's right to confrontation guaranteed by the Sixth Amendment. We examine the *Davis* holding to see whether it affects DeLawder's (D) conviction in the instant case. DeLawder's (D) counsel was prohibited from examining the victim regarding her past sexual history. The defense made it clear that its theory was that the victim fabricated the rape charges because she was actually pregnant and did not want to tell her mother that she was engaging in consensual sex. Defense counsel should have been permitted to pursue this line of questioning, as the jury would then have been able to more accurately determine the reliability and credibility of the witness. By denying defense counsel the opportunity to effectively cross-examine the girl, the trial court violated DeLawder's (D) right to confrontation. Reversed.

Analysis:

This case illustrates that rape shield laws and other laws that operate to limit the admissibility of otherwise relevant and probative evidence can occasionally come into conflict with the federal constitution. When they do so, the constitution obviously trumps the shield laws. Several courts have held that highly restrictive rape shield laws violate the constitution when they bar the use of relevant sexual history evidence. So as to avoid a conflict between the need to protect the victim and the defendant's constitutional rights, some shield statutes allow the use of such evidence when it is necessary to preserve the defendant's right to a fair trial under the Sixth Amendment. Absent such language, some courts have avoided striking shield laws by judicially implying a catch all that would operate to preserve the defendant's constitutional rights. In other words, the courts will admit the evidence if its probative value significantly outweighs its prejudicial effect, or if it is otherwise necessary to ensure that the defendant receives a fair trial. On the whole, though, most carefully drafted rape shield statutes will pass constitutional muster. Studies have shown that the use of such laws has improved the treatment of prosecuting victims and that efforts to limit evidence of past sexual history have largely been successful.

Government of the Virgin Islands v. Scuito

(Government) v. (Accused Rapist)
623 F.2d 869 (3d Cir. 1980)

M E M O R Y   G R A P H I C

Instant Facts
A woman accused a man of raping her while he was taking her home from her job as a waitress. The man asked for a psychological evaluation of the woman because he alleged that she was high at the time and in a spaced-out, trance-like state.

Black Letter Rule
It is within the judge's discretion to order a psychological examination of a rape victim if he or she feels that one is necessary.

Case Vocabulary

MANTRA: A sound aid that is repeated over and over again while meditating; a personal creed that is chanted while praying.

Procedural Basis: Appeal to the United States Court of Appeals for the Third Circuit of a conviction for forcible rape.

Facts: The victim worked at a restaurant [the "Drunken Shrimp"] as a waitress. Scuito (D) was a frequent patron of the restaurant and was asked by the owner one night to take the complaining victim home after she'd worked her shift. It was undisputed that Scuito (D) took a detour on the way home and the two had sexual intercourse. The only issue was whether the victim consented. She testified that Scuito (D) turned down a beach road to relieve himself. Afterward, the victim testified that Scuito (D) stopped in a turnaround and began kissing her and making advances. She said she expressed no interest, but that Scuito (D) told her he had a knife and would throw her into the ocean if she did not cooperate. She testified that she did not see a knife but felt something metal cut into her neck in the dark and then she stopped resisting. There was evidence presented at trial that the victim did have a cut on the side of her neck after the alleged incident. She testified that Scuito (D) took off her clothes then raped and sodomized her. During the course of the attack, the victim allegedly recited her "mantra" and prayed. After Scuito (D) dropped her off, she said she kissed him on the forehead because she was praying for him. Scuito (D) testified that he casually knew the woman and her sister and had driven them both home from the restaurant before. He said that on the night in question, the alleged victim was acting really funny, and that she offered him marijuana. He testified that they stopped on the beach road to smoke it and that they later engaged in consensual sexual intercourse. Prior to the first trial the prosecution and defense agreed not to mention that Scuito (D) had previously raped a woman by threatening her with a flare gun. The first trial ended in a mistrial when the prosecutor indirectly referred to the previous rape. Prior to the second trial, the defense moved for a court order compelling the victim to undergo a psychiatric evaluation. Defense counsel contended that he had personally observed the woman in a trance-like state and that he had been told by others that she frequently used mind-altering substances. Defense counsel also contended that the victim's frequent use of LSD and other mind altering drugs was highly indicative of a personality that fantasizes to extremes and one that might therefore be inclined to fabricate a story of rape. The trial court denied the motion and Scuito (D) was convicted of forcible rape. He appealed, contending that the trial court abused its discretion by refusing to order the psychiatric evaluation.

Issue: Is it an abuse of discretion for a trial judge to refuse a defendant's request for a psychiatric evaluation of an alleged rape victim?

Decision and Rationale: (Adams, J.) No. The decision to order a psychiatric evaluation of an alleged rape victim lies within the sound discretion of the trial judge. Scuito (D) does not press the extreme theory endorsed by Wigmore that a psychiatric evaluation should be ordered on *all* alleged victims of sexual offenses. Rather, defense counsel argues that the decision is discretionary on the part of the trial judge, but that in the instant case the trial judge abused that discretion. There are significant considerations that weigh heavily against ordering such an examination. One of the most important is the need to protect the victim's privacy, which is recognized by so called "rape shield laws." A psychological examination may intrude upon the victim's privacy, increase the trauma she experienced or be used as a tool of harassment. It is for these reasons that Federal Rule of Evidence 412 [restricting the use of prior sexual history in sexual offenses] was promulgated. The rationale of the Rule is to "protect rape victims from the degrading and embarrassing disclosure of intimate details about their private lives." We hold that the same rationale applies to a judge's decision not to order a psychiatric evaluation of a rape victim. There was no abuse of discretion in this case. Evidence of the victim's reputation for drug use and propensity to engage in "altered states of mind" could have been introduced by other direct testimony. It did not require expert testimony in the form of a psychiatric examination. Affirmed.

Analysis:

This case presents the exceedingly difficult question of when a woman's alleged frail infirm psychological condition will be relevant and probative enough to outweigh its prejudicial value so as to be admissible in a rape case. Advocates of rape reform applaud decisions such as the one in *Scuito* because they feel that introducing evidence of a victim's psychological instability is really another attempt to put the victim on trial. They also feel that a defendant should be severely restricted in his attempts to gain access to records of prior psychiatric treatment for much the same reasons. But such records are routinely available to defendants accused of other types of crimes, if relevant and otherwise admissible. [There is that nagging matter of confidentiality to overcome, after all.] It does not seem fair to some that the result is different simply because it is rape involved rather than some other crime. Some courts have held that defense counsel should be able to examine records of the victim's prior psychiatric treatment, if it is required to ensure the defendant receives a fair trial. There is no real consensus on the issue, however.

Chapter 5

You are studying the statutory and case law surrounding homicide because it is the best introduction to the theme of punishment in criminal law. Criminal punishments are designed to serve two purposes: They are retributive measures and deterrents. The law reflects society's view that all killings are not the same. Some criminals deserve greater punishments than others, and some crimes are more easily deterred by long prison sentences than others. The statutory and case law surrounding homicide provides an introduction to the ways in which society, lawmakers, and the courts determine which crimes are worse than others, and which punishments best serve society's goals of retribution and deterrence.

In the United States, in most jurisdictions, state statutes provide systems for grading different types of homicides and assign different punishments to each grade. In general, murder is defined as the unlawful killing of another person with malice aforethought. "Malice aforethought" is a term of art that describes a variety of mental states including intent to kill and wanton disregard for human life. Murder is frequently subdivides into classes assigned different punishments. First-degree murder is usually defined as the willful, deliberate, and premeditated killing of another person and is usually punishable by life imprisonment. Capital murder is frequently a first-degree murder with some extra element, for example the victim may have been a police officer. Other killings that involve malice aforethought are usually classified as second-degree murder, and are punishable by a lesser prison sentence.

Manslaughter is the killing of another person without malice aforethought and is generally subdivided into at least two classes. Voluntary manslaughter is the act of killing another person in the heat of passion and is punishable by less prison time than second-degree murder, but more prison time than involuntary manslaughter. Involuntary manslaughter generally describes the situation where an individual's gross negligence or recklessness causes the death of another person. Some states recognize additional classifications for vehicular manslaughter or aiding or causing suicide.

The most severe punishments are reserved for the crime of murder. You might think that because the punishments for murder are so severe, sometimes including the death penalty, the definition of murder would be clear. Clarity might make the severe punishments more effective as deterrents. Unfortunately, the definition of murder is unclear, and involves the kind of fuzzy, court-imposed tests and standards that may seem more at home in the common-law world of torts. First-degree murder is the willful, deliberate, and premeditated killing of another person. But what is "willful, deliberate, and premeditated"? In some states, premeditation is the formation of an intent to kill a particular individual before killing that individual. But how long before? A year? A split second? Some jurisdictions apply the rule that no time is too short. But what about crimes of passion? Surely these crimes involve a split-second decision to kill before the actual killing takes place.

Some states reject the idea that timing is the most important element of premeditation. In these states, premeditation does not involve the formation of an intent to kill at some point before the murder, but rather, it involves careful thought, weighing of considerations, and deliberate planning. Many jurisdictions allow evidence of a defendant's mental impairment at the time of the killing to rebut an inference of premeditation. Still other states have rejected the idea of premeditation altogether. In these states, the belief is that premeditated crimes are not necessarily deserving of the most retributive punishments because a premeditated crime is not necessarily evidence of the defendant's evilness. It may instead be evidence that the defendant acted with a tortured conscience, taking time to wrestle with the moral implications of killing another person.

In the manslaughter area, the standards are more categorical and objective than fuzzy and subjective, but the categories may seem arbitrary and unreasonable to some observers. For example: Voluntary manslaughter is a crime committed in the heat of passion, upon serious provocation. What is serious provocation? Most states have created categories of provocation at common law. In most states, a confession of adultery is not serious provocation, but catching one's spouse in the act of adultery is. In these states, if a man kills his wife after she has confessed to having an affair with another man, he has committed murder, but if he kills her after catching her in bed with another man, he has committed manslaughter and will not receive as great a punishment. To many commentators, this scheme is unreasonable because it seems to sanction domestic violence and it allows juries to determine that a killer is deserving of a lesser punishment because his victim had a bad moral character.

The fuzzy tests come back right where one would think that bright-line rules are the most necessary—with the death penalty. In order for the death penalty to work as a deterrent measure, it might be most helpful to create a system where everyone in society knows exactly what crimes will merit the death penalty and what crimes will not. This is not how the death penalty system works. In fact, the Supreme Court has determined that mandatory death sentences for certain crimes are unconstitutional and only fuzzy tests that allow judges, juries, and prosecutors discretion in deciding when the death penalty will be sought or assigned will do. However, the problem with allowing courts discretion in determining on a case-by-case basis which defendants will receive the death penalty for which aggravated crimes of first-degree murder can have unintended side effects. The death penalty may have a disproportional impact on the poor, who are unable to pay for thorough discovery and adequate legal counsel. The death penalty may also have a disproportionate effect on men, particularly black men.

When studying the statutes and case law surrounding homicide, it is a good idea to keep in mind the retributive and deterrent goals of punishment and whether the tests for determining which punishments apply serve these goals and the wider goal of justice.

Chapter 5

NOTE: THE PURPOSE OF THIS OUTLINE IS TO ORGANIZE THE CASES SO THAT ONE CAN QUICKLY UNDERSTAND THE RELEVANCE OF EACH CASE TO THE COURSE. NO ATTEMPT IS MADE IN THIS OVERVIEW TO ADDRESS EVERY CONCEPT THAT MUST BE STUDIED. BE SURE TO READ THE ENTIRE CASEBOOK AND/OR OTHER MATERIALS TO GAIN A FULL UNDERSTANDING OF ALL CONCEPTS.

I. Introduction
   A. There are two main issues to analyze when considering a category of crime:
      1. Criminality: What distinguishes criminal from non-criminal activity?
      2. Grading of Punishment: What factors within the area of activity defined as criminal warrant greater or lesser punishment?
      3. This chapter deals primarily with the question of punishment grading.
   B. Report of the Royal Commission on Capital Punishment, 1949–1953
      1. The Basic Principles of Murder Law in England
         a. The traditional definition of murder is "unlawful killing with malice aforethought."
         b. "Malice aforethought" is a term of art used as an umbrella term describing a number of different mental states that, if they are found to have been present in the mind of the killer, will render a homicide especially heinous and deserving of greater punishment.
      2. Malice Aforethought
         a. The mental states under the umbrella of "malice aforethought" include:
            (1) An intention to cause death or grievous bodily harm to a particular person.
            (2) Undertaking a course of action that one knows will probably cause death or grievous bodily harm.
            (3) An intention to commit any felony.
            (4) An intention to oppose a police officer by force while the officer is on his way to or on his way from or in the process of lawfully arresting a person, keeping the peace, or dispersing a crowd, as long as the killer had notice that the person he killed was a police officer.
      3. When is a homicide a murder?
         a. When one person intentionally kills another.

b. When a person kills another person through an action intended to kill a third person.
c. When a person kills another through a means intended to kill, but not to kill anyone in particular.
d. When a person kills another through an action intended to cause grievous bodily harm.
e. When a person kills another through an action that he knows is likely to kill or cause grievous bodily harm and when he has recklessly disregarded the risk.
   C. California Penal Code §§187, 188, 189, 192
      1. §187 Murder: the unlawful killing of a human being or fetus with malice aforethought.
      2. §188 Malice: express malice is the deliberate intention to kill; implied malice is killing with no considerable provocation or with an abandoned and malignant heart.
      3. §189 First-Degree Murder: a willful, deliberate, and premeditated killing. A deliberate and premeditated killing is one where the defendant maturely and meaningfully reflected on the action he intended to take. All other killings with malice aforethought are second-degree murders.
      4. §192 Manslaughter:
         a. Voluntary manslaughter is the killing of another person in the heat of passion. Three, six, or eleven years imprisonment.
         b. Involuntary manslaughter is the killing of another while perpetrating a misdemeanor or while performing a lawful action that is likely to cause death if not performed with due caution. Two, three, or four years imprisonment.
         c. Vehicular manslaughter is the killing of another while driving a vehicle and while perpetrating a misdemeanor or committing a lawful action that is likely to cause death. Sentences range from less than one year in county jail to six years imprisonment.
   D. Pennsylvania Penal Code §§2501 to 2505
      1. §2501 Criminal Homicide: the intentional, reckless, knowing, or negligent killing of another person.
      2. §2502 Degrees of Murder:

a. First-Degree Murder: an intentional killing. Intentional killing includes killing by means of poison, lying in wait, and all other willful, deliberate, and premeditated killings. Death or life imprisonment.

b. Second-Degree Murder: criminal homicide committed in the act of perpetrating a felony. Life imprisonment.

c. Third-Degree Murder: all other murders. Maximum of twenty years imprisonment.

3. §2503 Voluntary Manslaughter: killing a person in the heat of passion upon serious provocation. Maximum of ten years imprisonment.

4. §2504 Involuntary Manslaughter: causing the death of another person by engaging in unlawful or lawful activity in a grossly negligent or reckless manner. Maximum of five years imprisonment.

5. §2505 Causing or Aiding Suicide: a defendant may be convicted of criminal homicide when he has intentionally caused a suicide through force, duress, or deception. Maximum of two years imprisonment.

E. New York Penal Law §§125.00, 125.10, 125.15, 125.20, 125.25, 125.27

1. §125.00 Homicide: conduct that causes the death of another person.

2. §125.10 Criminally Negligent Homicide: causing the death of another person through criminal negligence. Maximum of four years imprisonment.

3. §125.15 Second-Degree Manslaughter: recklessly causing the death of another person or intentionally causing the suicide of another person. Maximum of fifteen years imprisonment.

4. §125.20 First-Degree Manslaughter: causing the death of another person with the intention of causing serious physical injury or causing the death of another person *with* the intent to cause death but while under the influence of extreme emotional disturbance. Maximum of twenty-five years imprisonment.

5. §125.25 Second-Degree Murder: intentionally causing death, killing under circumstances that suggest "depraved indifference to human life," or killing another person in furtherance of certain felonies. Fifteen years to life imprisonment.

6. §125.27 First-Degree Murder: second-degree murders are raised to first-degree murders when the victim is a police officer or an employee of a correctional institution, or when the defendant committed the crime while in custody or after escaping from custody. Punishable by death.

F. The Penal Code of Sweden §§1, 2, 7: provides that murder is punishable by ten years to life imprisonment, manslaughter is punishable by six to ten years imprisonment, and negligent homicide is punishable by a maximum of four years imprisonment or by a fine.

II. The Legislative Grading of Intended Killings

A. The Premeditation-Deliberation Formula

1. Before the Model Penal Code, most American jurisdictions applied common-law concepts of murder. The major departure from the common law was the division of murder into degrees. This had the effect of reducing the number of defendants sentenced to death to only those who were found guilty of the most heinous murders. *Model Penal Code and Commentaries, Comment to §210.2.*

2. Many states define a first-degree murder as a premeditated and deliberate killing. *Penn. Penal Code §2502; Cal. Penal Code §189.*

a. Some courts suggest that premeditation and deliberation do not require a lapse of time between the formation of an intent to kill and the actual killing. *Commonwealth v. Carrol.*

b. Other courts have rejected the approach that no time is too short to form the necessary premeditation, holding that premeditation must involve some degree of preexisting reflection. *State v. Guthrie.*

(1) In deciding what kinds of evidence establish premeditation under this stricter standard, one court has held that planning activities, motive and the nature of the killing are all relevant. *People v. Anderson.*

3. Many states follow the Model Penal Code approach and reject premeditation and deliberation as the bases for murders deserving of the greatest punishment because thinking carefully before killing someone may not be evidence of

the defendant's depravity but instead could be evidence of the defendant's tortured conscience over an action that is deeply aberrational. *N.Y. Penal Law §125.27.*

B. Provocation

1. The Rationale Behind the Provocation Defense

   a. Some commentators believe that the provocation defense should be abolished and intentional killers convicted of murder because reasonable people do not kill others no matter how seriously provoked.

   b. Some commentators argue that the provocation defense mitigates murders in cases where the killing is partially justified. This is problematic because it allows defendants to use the victim's bad moral character as an excuse for committing murder, even though the victim's bad behavior did not lead to anyone's death. It also sends society the message that there are circumstances where it is acceptable to take lethal punitive action against others.

2. The Nature of the Required Provocation

   a. Most modern courts follow the approach of finding provocation only in a few narrow circumstances.

      (1) Words as Provocation

         (a) Under Maryland law, words alone are not enough to constitute adequate provocation to mitigate a murder conviction. *Girouard v. State.*

      (2) Sexual Infidelity as Provocation

         (a) The law traditionally regards sexual infidelity as provocation.

         (b) Some commentators object to the idea that sexual infidelity constitutes adequate provocation because most of the people who kill under such provocation are men and allowing this type of mitigation sends a message to society that domestic violence is natural, inevitable, and even acceptable.

      (3) Cooling Time: the common law approach is that too long a time between the act of provocation and the homicide will render the provocation inadequate as a matter of law.

   b. Departures from the Categorical Approach: Words

      (1) Many common law jurisdictions follow the approach of allowing the jury to consider a manslaughter conviction whenever there is evidence of a circumstance that might cause a reasonable person to lose self-control, rather than only in a few narrowly-defined circumstances. *Maher v. People.*

      (2) Cooling time: most modern courts follow the *Maher* approach to cooling time, treating cooling time as a factual issue rather than a matter of law, and allowing the jury to consider all circumstances.

   c. Departures from the Categorical Approach: Extreme Emotional Disturbance

      (1) The test of whether the extreme emotional disturbance of the killer provides a reasonable explanation or excuse depends on an objective evaluation of the external circumstances that the killer believed he was facing and not on the killer's personal point of view. *People v. Casassa.*

      (2) The Model Penal Code Formulation: As many as ten states currently apply the Model Penal Code's "extreme emotional disturbance" formulation.

   d. The Objectivity of the Standard

      (1) Although the Model Penal Code places fewer restrictions on the types of circumstances that can serve to reduce the crime of murder to manslaughter than the common law does, both standards require that the defendant's response to provocation be objectively reasonable.

      (2) When applying the reasonable man standard in manslaughter cases the jury can consider the gender and age of the killer as well as other characteristics which would increase the provocative nature of a particular insult. *Director of the Public Prosecutions v. Camplin.*

      (3) Very few, if any, states apply a subjective standard of provocation. §210.3 of the Model Penal Code inserts an element of subjectivity by providing that reasonableness must be assessed "from the viewpoint of a person in the actor's situation." The actor's situation includes his physical

handicaps and external circumstances but not his moral values.

(d) Some courts have held that a defendant's mental disorder is irrelevant to the determination of whether his act was reasonably provoked. *State v. Klimas.*

III. Legislative Grading of Unintended Killings
   A. Creating the Risk of Homicide
      1. Distinguishing Civil and Criminal Liability
         a. An individual is guilty of involuntary manslaughter when his wanton or reckless breach of a duty of care causes the death of another person. *Commonwealth v. Welansky.*
         b. Defining Unintended Criminal Homicide
            (1) One of the major problems in distinguishing civil and criminal liability is formulating the "extra" quality that criminally liable homicides have that homicides giving rise to civil liability do not.
            (2) The "extra" quality that most state statutes require is gross negligence or recklessness. *State v. Barnett.*
            (3) In order to give rise to criminal liability, the defendant's negligence must show the kind of disregard for human life and safety that amounts to a crime against the state. *Andrews v. Director of Public Prosecutions.*
            (4) Traditional statutes and the common law leave the determination of the "extra" quality to judges. Judges tend to find that the "extra" quality is "willful, wanton negligence." *Model Penal Code and Commentaries, Comment to §2.02*
         c. Contributory Negligence: in criminal law, the homicide victim's contributory negligence is not a defense.
      2. Objective v. Subjective Standards of Liability
         a. Ordinary Negligence: A showing of ordinary negligence may be sufficient to support a conviction of manslaughter. *State v. Williams.*
            (1) Washington, like most states, no longer imposes criminal liability for manslaughter in cases involving ordinary negligence.
         b. Controversy over Standards of Liability
            (1) Objective v. Subjective Liability

(a) The objective standard determines liability by examining the general norms of reasonable behavior. Negligence is an objective standard.

(b) The subjective standard determines liability by examining the defendant's individual characteristics and takes into account the varieties of personality, intellect, and background. Premeditation, deliberation, and diminished capacity are all determined according to a subjective standard.

(2) Defending the Objective Standard
   (a) Arguing that the law was trending toward objective standards, Justice Holmes defended the use of an objective standard in criminal law because it serves to discourage people from engaging in dangerous conduct and requires them to act with common sense in addition to acting within the boundaries of the law.

(3) Criticizing the Objective Standard
   (a) Some commentators argue that the retributive purpose of criminal punishments is not served by applying these punishments to inadvertent acts of negligence as well as to intentional crimes.
   (b) The deterrent purpose of criminal punishment is not served either because applying these punishments to acts of negligence punishes individuals for departing from norms of behavior that they may have been unable to meet.

(4) The Model Penal Code's Approach
   (a) Under the Model Penal Code, an individual is liable for manslaughter when he was aware of the risk in his actions but an individual who was unaware of the risk may be punished only for negligent homicide, a lesser crime.

3. The Line Between Murder and Manslaughter
   a. A killing does not have to be intended in order to constitute second-degree murder. If the killer's actions show a callous disregard for human life and the consequences of his actions, he will have exhibited the malice that distinguishes second-degree murder

from involuntary manslaughter. *Commonwealth v. Malone.*

b. The Common Law Approach vs. The Model Penal Code Approach

(1) The Common Law: *Malone* is an example of a case where the common-law distinction between murder and manslaughter is applied. At common law, an unintentional homicide can be considered murder when the defendant acted with malice. Malice does not have to be aimed at a particular individual, but may be a generally "wicked, depraved and malignant heart."

(2) The Model Penal Code distinguishes murder from manslaughter without using any common-law formulation of "malice." Instead, it treats an unintended homicide as murder when the killer acted recklessly and with an "extreme indifference to the value of human life."

c. Murder by Vehicle

(1) Under federal law, drunk and reckless driving can be evidence of malice when there is evidence that there was a risk of serious harm associated with the defendant's activities and that the defendant knew about the risk and disregarded it. *United States v. Fleming*

(2) The majority of American jurisdictions follow the *Fleming* approach of convicting defendants of murder rather than manslaughter when their recklessness behind the wheel has caused death.

B. The Felony-Murder Rule

1. The Basic Doctrine

a. The felony-murder doctrine provides that a homicide constitutes murder when it was committed while the defendant was perpetrating or was intending to perpetrate a felony, even if the killing was accidental.

(1) Felony murder is homicide caused by an action that is dangerous and probably lethal in and of itself undertaken by a person intending to commit a felony. *Regina v. Serne.*

(2) The felony murder doctrine is not limited to situations where the death was foreseeable. Felons are strictly liable for all killings committed by him, or by his accomplices,

in the perpetration of a felony. *People v. Stamp.*

b. The Causation Requirement

(1) Under the felony-murder doctrine, a defendant can be found guilty of murder without a showing of malice, but the prosecution must still show that the defendant's actions were the proximate cause of the death.

(2) Proximate cause means that the victim's death was the foreseeable or the natural and probable, consequence of the defendant's actions.

c. The Rationale of the Felony-Murder Doctrine

(1) Deterrence: Some commentators believe that the felony-murder rule deters felons from killing people negligently. Others believe that the felony-murder rule has no deterrent effect because no one can act with the certainty that his actions will not cause someone's death.

(2) Retribution: Some commentators argue that allowing the felony-murder rule to elevate an accidental death into first-degree murder renders the punishment disproportionate to the crime, or wrong committed.

(a) Other commentators argue that the felony-murder rule serves proportionality because it reflects society's attitude that an intentionally committed felony that results in someone's death is more serious than an identical felony that does not result in death.

(3) The Model Penal Code: The felony-murder rule is difficult to defend because there is no evidence that accidental homicides occur with more frequency in the perpetration of specified felonies and because it is morally questionable to apply a punishment for murder to someone who has not necessarily shown an indifference to human life.

d. The Misdemeanor-Manslaughter Rule or Unlawful-Act Doctirne

(1) In many states, a misdemeanor that results in death can lead to an involuntary manslaughter conviction without a showing of recklessness.

(2) The Model Penal Code has rejected the unlawful-act doctrine as a form of strict liability. Many states follow the Model Penal Code's approach.

(3) States that apply the unlawful-act doctrine have limited its effects by requiring a proximate cause showing, limiting its application to cases involving *malum in se* misdemeanors rather than *malum prohibitum* misdemeanors or limiting its application to cases where the misdemeanor is inherently dangerous.

   e. Statutory Reform of the Felony-Murder Doctrine

(1) Many states have placed limits on the felony-murder rule by limiting its application to cases involving felonies enumerated in the felony-murder statute or by requiring that the homicide committed during the felony be otherwise culpable because the defendant acted recklessly.

(2) Michigan has abolished the felony-murder rule because it is no longer acceptable to equate the intention to commit murder with the intention to commit a felony. *People v. Aaron.*

   f. Judicial Reform of the Felony-Murder Doctrine: Most courts do not follow the *Aaron* approach. However, some commentators find the felony-murder rule unconstitutional because it presumes malice in contravention of the reasonable doubt requirement or because it eliminates a malice showing in violation of the 8th Amendment.

2. The "Inherently Dangerous Felony" Limitation

   a. If the felony murder rule is to apply, many states require the prosecution to show that the felony is one that is inherently dangerous to human life. *People v. Phillips.*

   b. Question of fact or law?

(1) California courts examine the underlying felony in the abstract, as opposed to the specific facts of the case at hand, in order to determine whether the felony at issue is inherently dangerous. *People v. Satchell.*

(2) Other courts permit the trier of fact to determine whether the felony was one that was inherently dangerous based on

the manner and circumstances in which it was committed. *People v. Stewart.*

3. The Merger Doctrine

   a. Sometimes the killing is so related to the underlying felony that the two are held to "merge," making the felony-murder rule inapplicable

(1) Felony child abuse that results in death is held to merge with the homicide so as to preclude a conviction of second-degree murder on a felony-murder theory. *People v. Smith.*

(2) The merger doctrine and burglary: burglary with intent to commit assault will support a conviction for felony murder, even though the underlying assault would not be enough to sustain a felony murder conviction without the added crime of breaking and entering. *People v. Miller.*

   b. In eschewing the traditional merger doctrine, the California courts have held that all inherently dangerous felonies may serve as the predicate for felony murder, so long as doing so does not elevate all assaults to murder or frustrate the legislative intent. *People v. Hansen.*

4. Killings Not in Furtherance of the Felony

   a. The definition of felony murder will not be extended beyond its requirement that the defendant have acted to cause death to include situations where the felon's actions set off a chain reaction leading to the death of another person. *State v. Canola.*

   b. Should liability for felony murder depend on the identity of the killer or of the victim?

(1) Identity of the killer: Under agency theory, adopted by the *Canola* court, the felony-murder rule will only apply where the homicide was actually committed by a felon or co-felon. Under proximate-cause theory, the issue is whether the homicide was within the foreseeable risk of that particular felony

(2) Identity of the victim: Many statutes and cases have rejected the idea that the death of a co-felon can be considered felony murder. One argument in favor of this rule is that co-felons are usually killed by police officers or the victims of the

felony and that these killings constitute justifiable homicide.

c. Although the felony-murder rule cannot be invoked in a case where a felon is charged with the murder of his accomplice after the accomplice was killed by the victim of the felony, the reckless malice standard can be invoked to convict the felon of murder. *Taylor v. Superior Court.*

IV. The Death Penalty
A. The Current Context
1. Death Row: At the end of 1998, nearly 3,500 prisoners were awaiting execution.
2. Support: Although there have been fluctuations, there remains broad public support for the death penalty.
3. While some states have abolished the death penalty completely, there are a handful of states responsible for more than one-third of all executions.
B. Policy Considerations
1. Deterrence
a. The death penalty has failed as a deterrent because studies have shown that homicide rates follow similar trends in both states that employ the death penalty and states that do not. Sellin, *The Death Penalty*
b. Just because the death penalty has not been proven statistically to be a deterrent does not mean that it is not an effective deterrent. People are not always aware of whether the death penalty is employed in their state and people can remain deterred by the severity of the penalty employed in the past. van den Haag, *On Deterrence and the Death Penalty*
c. The Ehrlich Study: In a 1975 study using complex econometric techniques, Isaac Ehrlich found that there was a significant correlation between the death penalty and the deterrence of homicide.
   (1) Ehrlich's study focuses on the deterrent effects of the death penalty instead of on the deterrent effect presented by the probability of conviction. There is evidence that capital punishment makes convictions harder to come by. Another difficulty with Ehrlich's study is that it fails to measure

the probability of life sentences, and therefore does not allow a comparison between the deterrent effect of the death penalty and the deterrent effect of life imprisonment. Lempert, *Deterrence and Desert: An Assessment of the Moral Bases for Capital Punishment.*

2. Error and Irrevocability
a. The death penalty is an unjust form of punishment because flaws in the criminal justice system ensure that a certain percentage of convicts sentenced to death are actually innocent of the crimes they have been convicted of. Bedau, *Innocence and the Death Penalty.*
b. Errors in the justice system do not justify abolishing the death penalty. Every year innocent people die in car crashes, but no one argues that automobiles should be abolished. The death penalty should only be abolished if the loss of innocent lives outweigh the societal benefits of capital punishment. van den Haag, *Punishing Criminals.*
3. The Sanctity of Human Life
a. The death penalty is barbaric. The state's use of the death penalty and the crime of murder are not moral absolutes that cancel each other out. Clark, *Statement.*
b. The sanctity of human life requires that the state reserve its worst punishment for those who take life. van den Haag, *Punishing Criminals.*
C. Constitutional Limitations
1. Introduction
a. When legislative reform of the death penalty failed in the 1950s, abolitionists turned to constitutional challenges. They based these challenges primarily on procedural due process and cruel and unusual punishment.
2. Procedural Due Process
a. States that applied the death penalty allowed judges and juries discretion in applying it, but provided no standards. *McGautha v. California.*
b. Opponents of the death penalty believed that due process required explicit standards of decision. The Supreme Court rejected this view in the 1971 case. *McGautha v. California.*

3. Cruel and Unusual Punishment
   a. Although the decision rested heavily on the facts, the death penalty has been successfully challenged as an unconstitutional violation of the 8th Amendment's prohibition against cruel and unusual punishment. *Furman v. Georgia.*
   b. In reaction to *Furman*, states enacted legislation making the death penalty mandatory under certain circumstances or else passed legislation that established guidelines for determining when the death penalty should be applied.
      (1) Where the state has established guidelines for determining when the death penalty should be applied, it cannot be held to be a "cruel and unusual punishment" in violation of the 8th and 14th Amendments until society has determined that it is an unacceptably inhumane and disproportionate form of punishment. *Gregg v. Georgia.*
      (2) The mandatory application of the death penalty for any first-degree murder is a violation of the 8th Amendment because mandatory capital punishment is contrary to societal standards of decency and because it undermines the respect for human dignity expressed in the 8th Amendment by prohibiting decision makers from considering the relevant aspects of character and past history of each individual defendant. *Woodson v. North Carolina.*
   c. A death penalty statute cannot be found to be an unconstitutional violation of the 8th Amendment and the Equal Protection Clause on the basis of a study showing that the statute has a disproportionate impact on blacks. *McCleskey v. Kemp.*

Commonwealth v. Carroll

(State of Pennsylvania) v. (Man Who Shot His Wife)
412 Pa. 525, 194 A.2d 911 (1963)

M E M O R Y   G R A P H I C

Instant Facts

A man who shot and killed his wife after a heated argument pled guilty to murder and was held to be guilty of first-degree murder, despite a psychiatrist's testimony that the murder was not premeditated.

Black Letter Rule

In Pennsylvania, when determining whether a murder was premeditated and therefore of the first degree, a court will disregard the length of time it took for the defendant to form the intention to kill and will not treat the testimony of a psychiatrist as conclusive on the issue of premeditation.

Case Vocabulary

MOTION IN ARREST OF JUDGMENT: A request to prevent the rendition of judgment; an arrest of judgment is a judge's staying or withholding judgment after the verdict because of errors in the record that occurred during trial.

Procedural Basis: Appeal to the Supreme Court of Pennsylvania of denial of motions in arrest of judgment and for new trial after a conviction of first degree murder and sentence to life imprisonment.

Facts: Mr. Carroll (D) married Mrs. Carroll in 1955. Mr. Carroll (D) maintained a good reputation as an employee, co-worker, and neighbor. In 1958, Mrs. Carroll fractured her skull while trying to get out of her car during an argument with Mr. Carroll (D). This injury may have contributed to her mental illness—she was later diagnosed as a "schizoid personality type." In January, 1962, Mr. Carroll (D) attended an electronics school in North Carolina for nine days. Mrs. Carroll had been violently opposed to Mr. Carroll's (D) leaving her alone, and at her suggestion Mr. Carroll (D) left a loaded .22 caliber pistol on the windowsill above their bed. When he returned from North Carolina, Mr. Carroll (D) informed his wife that he would be taking a teaching job in Chambersburg and would be required to spend four nights a week out of town. Mr. and Mrs. Carroll argued violently about this until 4 a.m. According to Mr. Carroll (D), Mr. and Mrs. Carroll went to their bedroom at 3 a.m. and continued to argue. Sometime between 3 and 4 a.m., Mr. Carroll (D) remembered the gun on the windowsill. Mr. Carroll (D) picked up the gun and shot Mrs. Carroll twice in the head. Afterward, Mr. Carroll (D) wrapped his wife's body in the bedding and carried her to the cellar. He cleaned up, and that night he hid his wife's body in a desolate spot near a dump. He took his children to his parents' house and was arrested the following Monday at his new job. He pled guilty to an indictment charging him with murder and was tried without a jury. A psychiatrist testified that Mr. Carroll (D) did not premeditate the killing. The court found him guilty of first degree murder and sentenced him to life imprisonment. Mr. Carroll (D) appealed.

Issue: Under Pennsylvania law, does the evidence of a homicide defendant's good character together with the testimony of a psychiatrist that the homicide was not premeditated require the court to fix the degree of the defendant's guilt as no higher than murder in the second degree?

Decision and Rationale: (Bell, C.J.) No. The evidence of a defendant's good character and the testimony of a psychiatrist that the homicide was not premeditated does not require the court to find the defendant guilty of second-degree murder rather than first-degree murder. Under Pennsylvania's murder statute, first degree murder includes killings by poison, lying in wait "or any other kind of willful, deliberate and premeditated killing." In determining whether the defendant had the specific intent to kill necessary to constitute first-degree murder, courts look at factors including the defendant's words and conduct and the circumstances surrounding the homicide. Specific intent to kill will be inferred when the defendant has used a deadly weapon on a vital body part of another person. Even if everything Mr. Carroll (D) alleged was true, his killing of his wife constituted murder in the first degree. Mr. Carroll (D) based his first argument on the axiom that "no time is too short for a wicked man to frame in his mind the scheme of murder." Mr. Carroll (D) tried to persuade the court that this axiom means that a long time is necessary for a good man to form the intent to kill and that because Mr. Carroll (D) was a good person, any intention he might have formed in the seconds before he shot his wife did not happen in enough time to constitute premeditation. However, under Pennsylvania case law whether the defendant formed the intention to kill seconds before the killing or days before is immaterial because courts do not examine length of time in their analyses of whether a killing was willful, deliberate, and premeditated. Mr. Carroll's (D) second argument was that the difficulty he experienced in moving and hiding the body and his lack of an organized escape plan show that there cannot have been any premeditation. This was a "jury argument" with no merit on appeal. Mr. Carroll's (D) final argument was based on a psychiatrist's testimony at trial that because of Mr. Carroll's (D) mental state in the moments leading up to the crime, he could not have been guilty of premeditation. The psychiatrist gave his opinion that "rage," "desperation," and "panic" caused Mr. Carroll (D) to shoot his wife out of an uncontrollable impulse rather than out of intentional premeditation. Mr. Carroll's (D) argument was weakened by the facts that the court is not required to believe the testimony offered by any witness; the psychiatrist's opinion was based on statements made to him by Mr. Carroll (D), which need not be believed and are sometimes contradicted by other facts of the case; and any psychiatrist's opinion of a defendant's state of mind is entitled to little weight in this type of case. Additionally, Mr. Carroll's (D) own statements after his arrest and during the trial strengthen the argument that he should be convicted of first degree murder because he made it clear that during his argument with his wife, he remembered the gun, took it from the windowsill, and deliberately fired two shots into his wife's head. Even if Mr. Carroll (D) had argued that he was insane at the time of the killing, the psychiatrist's opinion that he acted out of an uncontrollable impulse would not be given much weight because a court cannot excuse a murder to reduce a murder from first to second degree simply because the defendant failed to ignore an impulse to kill, an impulse that is fairly common. Psychiatrists cannot be allowed to determine criminal responsibility in the law. Judgment and sentence affirmed.

Analysis:

How long does it take to form a premeditated intention to kill? An intent to kill is inferred when, as in *Carrol*, the defendant uses a deadly weapon against a vital body part of the victim. But when is an intention premeditated? The Carroll court rejects the contention that premeditation constitutes a plan to commit murder, dispose of the body, and escape. Instead, premeditation seems to consist of nothing more than the decision to kill, even if that decision is made in the space of a few seconds and during a heated argument. The problem with this approach is that under it almost any killing could be held to be a first-degree murder because the decision to kill, no matter how impulsive, is enough to constitute premeditation. The Carroll court has blurred the distinction between first and second degree murder by equating the requirement that first degree murder be "willful, deliberate and premeditated" with the requirement for both first and second degree murder that the homicide be committed intentionally.

State v. Guthrie

(Government) v. (Murderer)

194 W.Va. 657, 461 S.E.2d 163 (1995)

M E M O R Y   G R A P H I C

Instant Facts

A man sought to appeal his conviction for premeditated murder on the ground that the evidence established that the stabbing of which he was convicted was the result of teasing and not preexisting intent to kill.

Black Letter Rule

In order to establish that a murder is premeditated and deliberate there must be some proof that the defendant considered and weighed his decision to kill.

Procedural Basis: Appeal from the jury verdict finding the defendant guilty of first-degree murder.

Facts: Dale Guthrie (D) and Steven Farley worked together as dishwashers in a restaurant. One evening, Farley began to tease Guthrie (D), who appeared to be in a bad mood, and snapped Guthrie (D) several times with a dish towel. When Farley snapped Guthrie's (D) nose, Guthrie (D) became enraged and started towards Farley, who persisted with the teasing. Guthrie (D) then took out a pocket knife and stabbed Farley in the neck. Evidence at trial showed that Guthrie (D) suffered from a host of psychiatric problems and panic attacks. The trial court instructed the jury that, to establish that a killing was deliberate and premeditated, it was not necessary to prove that the intent to kill existed for any particular time prior to the killing; it was only necessary to prove that the intent to kill have existed at the time of the killing, or prior thereto.

Issue: In order to obtain a conviction for murder in the first-degree based on a premeditated and deliberate killing, must there be a showing that the defendant weighed his decision to kill?

Decision and Rationale: (Cleckley, J.) Yes. In order to establish that a murder is premeditated and deliberate there must be some proof that the defendant considered and weighed his decision to kill. The most significant problem with the jury instruction given by the trial court is that it fails to inform the jury the distinction between first and second-degree murder. Instead, it equates premeditation with an intent to kill. Premeditation and deliberation should be defined in a manner to give juries both guidance and reasonable discretion. Premeditation and deliberation are not measured by any specific period of time, but there must be some period between the formation of the intent to kill and the actual killing. Such a showing indicates the killing is by prior calculation and design. We do not mean to require that existence of some elaborate plan or scheme. Nevertheless, it is clear that the instruction's notion of instantaneous premeditation and momentary deliberation does not comport with the requirements of a first-degree murder. Reversed and remanded.

Analysis:

This case and *Commonwealth v. Carrol* (a case where a husband was convicted of first-degree murder when he suddenly killed his wife during a heated argument) illustrate the split that exists amongst jurisdictions with respect to the meaning of premeditation and deliberation. The court here expressly rejects the approach taken in *Carrol*, which essentially held that premeditation requires only the formation of an intent to kill prior to the act of killing. As the court noted in this case, the *Carrol* approach blurs the distinction between first- and second-degree murder. Because first-degree murder is a creation of statute, the court here believed it was necessary to give meaning to the distinction between a mere intent to kill and a premeditated killing. Although the holding accomplishes this, it raises the question of what kind of evidence is necessary to prove premeditation. One court has held that evidence regarding planning, motive and the nature of the killing are all relevant to the question of the existence of premeditation and deliberation.

Girouard v. State

(Husband) v. (State of Maryland)

321 Md. 532, 583 A.2d 718 (MD, 1991)

M E M O R Y   G R A P H I C

Instant Facts

A man is convicted of second degree murder when he stabbed his wife 19 times after she insulted his sexual prowess.

Black Letter Rule

Under Maryland law, words alone are not enough to constitute adequate provocation to mitigate a murder conviction.

Case Vocabulary

FIGHTING WORDS: Language that, under community standards, would cause a reasonable person to lose control and react violently.

Procedural Basis: Appeal to the Court of Appeals of Maryland of a conviction of second-degree murder.

Facts: Steven Girouard (D) and his wife, Joyce Girouard, who were both in the Army, had a difficult marital relationship. One night, during an argument, Joyce graphically disparaged Steven's (D) sexual ability, told him that she did not love him, and that she wanted a divorce. She also told him that she had filed charges against him with the Judge Advocate General's Office. Steven (D) then picked up a knife and stabbed Joyce 19 times before slitting his own wrists. His self-inflicted wounds were not life-threatening, and Steven was able to call the police and tell the dispatcher that he had murdered his wife. When the police arrived on the scene, Steven was wandering tearfully outside his apartment building. He talked to the police about how much he had loved his wife and how he could not believe what he had done. Steven was convicted of second-degree murder and sentenced to 22 years imprisonment, 10 of which were suspended.

Issue: Under Maryland law, can words alone constitute adequate provocation to support a finding that a homicide was committed in the heat of passion and thus was manslaughter rather than murder?

Decision and Rationale: (Cole, J.) No. Under Maryland law, words alone cannot constitute adequate provocation to support the mitigation of a homicide from murder to manslaughter. In order to show the kind of provocation that would mitigate a homicide from murder to manslaughter, a defendant ordinarily must show that the provocation falls into one of a few specific categories such as the sudden discovery of a spouse's infidelity. Prior case law in Maryland holds that words alone do not constitute adequate provocation, and this court cannot in good conscience create a new category that would allow a domestic argument to constitute adequate provocation. Public policy would not support a holding that encouraged people to use domestic violence to resolve disputes. The provocation in this case was not enough to cause a reasonable man to stab his provoker 19 times. Judgment affirmed.

Analysis:

The court in this case applies the common-law rule that a murder can only be mitigated if the provocation alleged falls into one of a few narrow categories. These categories are intended to reflect the few cases where all reasonable people agree would cause any person to commit murder. If you discover your husband in bed with another woman and you kill the two of them, it is not because you have the sense of hostility toward them in particular or the reckless disregard for human life in general that constitute malice aforethought, but rather because you have been provoked beyond all reason. While the discovery of one's spouse in the act of committing adultery is the kind of injury that, like false imprisonment or serious assault and battery, could reasonably provoke a violent reaction, fighting words do not cause that kind of injury. It is not clear why an insult to one's sexual prowess is less provoking than catching one's spouse in the act of adultery. It may be that in refusing to extend the number of mitigating circumstances Maryland courts will consider, the court in *Girouard* is serving a policy interest in preventing murder defendants from using the behavior of their victims to excuse their actions. To allow defendants to do this would be to extend tort principles of contributory negligence into criminal law. This would not serve society well as society has an interest in using criminal punishment to deter wrongdoing. If potential murderers know that they will not be punished for killing people they can characterize as "bad" the stiff punishments for murder will not be effective deterrents.

Maher v. People

(Man Who Shot His Wife's Lover) v. (State of Michigan)
10 Mich. 212, 81 Am. Dec. 781 (1862)

M E M O R Y   G R A P H I C

Instant Facts

A man suspected that his wife had been sleeping with another man and when a friend confirmed his suspicions, he shot his wife's lover in a saloon and was charged with assault with intent to murder.

Black Letter Rule

In determining whether an assault was committed with intent to murder, a jury may examine words uttered in the defendant's presence as well as conduct that the defendant witnessed.

Case Vocabulary

ASSAULT AND BATTERY: "Assault" is the use of force or threats that cause the threatened person to have a well-founded fear of physical injury. Battery involves actual physical contact. Firing a gun into the air next to someone's head is assault. Shooting someone in the head and causing injury is battery.

Procedural Basis: Appeal of conviction of assault with intent to murder on the grounds that the trial court erred in granting the prosecution's motion to suppress evidence.

Facts: Maher (D) suspected that his wife had had sexual intercourse with another man, Patrick Hunt. Maher (D) had seen his wife and Hunt disappear into the woods together. When they reappeared, Maher (D) followed Hunt to a saloon. When Maher (D) arrived at the saloon, he entered it through a back door. He was sweaty, excited, and had taken his jacket off. Maher (D) approached Hunt, who was standing with a group of people at the bar. Maher (D) shot Hunt in the head, causing Hunt to lose partial hearing in his left ear and to be confined to bed for a week. Maher (D) was charged with assault with intent to commit murder. At trial, Maher (D) tried to introduce evidence that on his way to the saloon, he had been approached by a friend and told that Hunt and Maher's (D) wife had had sexual intercourse in the woods on the day before the assault as well as on the morning of the assault. The trial court suppressed that evidence and Maher (D) appealed.

Issue: Would evidence that a defendant in an assault case had reason to believe that the victim was engaged in a prolonged sexual relationship with the defendant's wife be enough under Michigan law to constitute evidence of provocation and therefore to reduce an assault with intent to murder charge to an assault and battery charge?

Decision and Rationale: (Christiancy, J.) Yes. Evidence that a defendant in an assault case had reason to believe that the victim was engaged in a prolonged sexual relationship with the defendant's wife would be enough under Michigan law to constitute evidence of provocation. In determining whether Maher (D) is guilty of assault and battery or assault with intent to murder, the court must examine Maher's (D) motivation. The court must treat the case as if Hunt had died as a result of the injuries Maher (D) inflicted in order to determine whether, had Hunt died, Maher (D) would have been guilty of manslaughter or murder. If Maher (D) would have been guilty of manslaughter, he cannot be found guilty of assault with intent to murder. The court must examine the events leading up to the assault to determine whether Maher (D) experienced sufficient provocation to reduce his action from assault with intent to murder to assault and battery. It is the judge's role to determine what the law will consider reasonable or adequate provocation, but it is the jury's role to determine, in each individual case, whether the evidence presented meets the standard of adequate or reasonable provocation. In other words, the question of whether adequate provocation existed is a matter of fact, not of law. A judge can only exclude evidence when no reasonable person could infer provocation from that evidence. The sources of provocation will differ from case to case, and it is the judge's responsibility to allow the jury access to any evidence that could reasonably affect its decision on whether provocation was sufficient to reduce the crime from one of premeditation to one of passion. The jury should likewise be allowed access to evidence of cooling time. The evidence Maher (D) sought to introduce at trial might have shown that when Hunt and Maher's (D) wife disappeared into the woods they were committing adultery. This evidence of provocation was sufficient to go to the jury. The jury, taking this evidence in conjunction with evidence of Maher's (D) appearing in the saloon in a state of extreme agitation, might reasonably have found that had Hunt died from the gunshot wound Maher (D) would have been guilty of manslaughter rather than murder. Judgment reversed and case remanded for new trial.

Dissent: (Manning, J.) The evidence was properly excluded because it would not have shown that Maher (D) was given sufficient provocation. Had this been a case where the court would have to determine whether Maher (D) was guilty of murder or manslaughter, the court would have to decide whether the provocation Maher (D) asserted would have caused a reasonable man to commit the same crime. In order to be found reasonable, the provoking action must have occurred in Maher's (D) presence. Maher (D) did not catch his wife and Hunt in the act of sexual intercourse. To allow juries to find sufficient provocation in cases where defendants merely hear gossip about their spouses' adulterous behavior would undermine society's interest in punishing people who take the lives of others. In a state where the death penalty has been abolished, the public policy reasons for strict scrutiny and the broad interpretation of the law in the defendant's favor are less important than the public policy in favor of preventing defendants from using provocation as an excuse for homicide.

Analysis:

This case stands for the principle that when considering whether a defendant is guilty of manslaughter as opposed to murder, a jury should look at any circumstances leading up to the crime that might lead a reasonable man to lose self-control. Juries should not be forced to consider only conduct witnessed by the defendant, but also words uttered in his presence. This is a flexible approach that may be problematic. Allowing juries too much discretion in deciding whether a defendant was sufficiently provoked so that his crime is reduced to manslaughter causes inconsistency in the law. Some juries may be more lenient than others and cases with similar factual backgrounds may wind up with different results. When punishment is severe and includes long stretches of prison time, the law should perhaps be as unambiguous as possible in order to allow the punishment to serve as an effective deterrent. If everyone knows that killing someone based on a rumor one hears is punishable by prison time in every case, the number of homicides and assaults like the one in *Maher* might decrease.

People v. Casassa

(Prosecutor) v. (Killer)
(1980) 49 N.Y.2d 668, 427 N.Y.S.2d 769, 404 N.E.2d 1310

M E M O R Y G R A P H I C

Instant Facts

After dating Casassa (D) the victim told him that she was not interested. He obsessed about her, stalked her, and killed her. His only defense is that he was acting under extreme emotional disturbance caused by her rejection.

Black Letter Rule

The test of whether the extreme emotional disturbance of the killer had a reasonable explanation or excuse depends on a reasonable evaluation of the external circumstances that the killer believed he was facing and not on the killer's personal point of view.

Case Vocabulary

AFFIRMATIVE DEFENSE: A defense that must be raised by the defendant. Some other affirmative defenses in criminal law include self-defense, insanity, alibi, coercion, and duress.

EXTREME EMOTIONAL DISTURBANCE: The phrase, found in the Model Penal Code, used to describe the state of someone who has temporarily lost their self-control because of something external which had a severe emotional effect on them.

FINDER OF FACT: The party charged with determining, when at least some facts are in contention during a trial, what facts are true. In a jury trial the finder of fact is the jury. In a bench trial the judge combines this role with his role as arbitrator of the law.

Procedural Basis: Appeal of a conviction for murder in the second degree to The Court of Appeals of New York.

Facts: Victor Casassa (D) (Casassa) met Victoria Lo Consolo (Lo Consolo) because they lived in the same apartment complex. They dated a few times casually. Lo Consolo informed Casassa (D) that she was not falling in love with him. Casassa (D) says that this rejection devastated him. After this initial rejection Casassa (D) started doing some odd things. He broke into the apartment below Lo Consolo's so that he could eavesdrop on her while she pursued other relationships. He claims the things he heard further devastated him. He broke into her apartment and lay naked in her bed. He reports having had a knife with him at that time of the break-in. He said he knew he was going to either kill himself or her. Finally on February 28, 1977 he brought several bottles of wine and liquor to her as a gift. When she did not accept this gift he pulled out a steak knife and stabbed her in the throat, after which he pulled her to the bathroom and submerged her body in the tub to make sure she was dead. Casassa (D) does not dispute these facts. He waived a jury trial and had a bench trial before a judge. The defense presented only one witness, a psychiatrist. The psychiatrist testified that Casassa (D) had become obsessed with Lo Consolo and that her rejection combined with his peculiar personality attributes had placed him under the influence of an extreme emotional disturbance at the time of the killing. The state presented several witnesses, among them another psychiatrist. He testified that while Casassa (D) was emotionally disturbed, this should not qualify as an extreme emotional disturbance because his disturbed state was the result of his own twisted mind and not external factors. The trial court found Casassa (D) guilty of murder in the second degree. Casassa (D) appeals arguing that the statute requires the court to examine the case from his point of view and that from his point of view he was suffering from extreme emotional disturbance caused by what he believed was a reasonable explanation or excuse.

Issue: Is the test of whether an extreme emotional disturbance of the killer was caused by a reasonable explanation or excuse determined from the subjective point of view of the killer?

Decision and Rationale: (Jasen) No. This case is to be decided under section 125.25 of the New York Penal Code, which provides that if the killer can show that he acted under the influence of an extreme emotional disturbance for which there was a reasonable explanation or excuse, he qualifies for an affirmative defense reducing murder in the second degree to manslaughter. Section 125.5 was basically adopted from the Model Penal Code. The "extreme emotional disturbance" defense in the Model Penal Code is an outgrowth of the "heat of passion" defense found in the common law, but it is considerably broader. It eliminates entirely the provision which required that there be no cooling off period between the provocation and the actions which caused the death. It also eliminates the rigid rules concerning what is and what is not adequate provocation. Several incidents can be combined to form the reasonable explanation of the killer's extreme emotional disturbance. The arguments presented by individual defendants can be considered on their own merits. However, it is not a wholly subjective test. It has two separate components. The first component, that the act must have actually been done in a state of "extreme emotional disturbance," is considered subjectively from the killer's point of view. The second component, whether there was a reasonable explanation or excuse for that emotional disturbance, is meant to be more objective. It takes the point of view of a person facing the same circumstances, as the killer believed he was facing, but without any of the particular quirks the killer may have had. [Yes, this is another reworking of the "reasonable man" idea; you didn't really think we were going to escape that, did you?] In this case Casassa (D) has no problem meeting the first component. He was acting out of extreme emotional disturbance. However, the judge, acting here as the finder of fact, reached the conclusion that this emotional disturbance was based on factors peculiar to Casassa (D). And that because these factors were peculiar to him, there was no reasonable explanation or excuse. This conclusion is consistent with the correct application of the law. The definition of manslaughter from the Model Penal Code intentionally leaves the finder of fact with the discretion to make judgmental evaluations of what is reasonable. Here the judge, as finder of fact, has made his decision. Overturning his finding in this case would be inconsistent with the intention of the act. We affirm.

Analysis:

In *Giroud* the court, following common law, was very limited in what it could consider as provocation. Certainly words alone could never be enough to mitigate murder down to manslaughter. Then *Camplin* presents a 1957 statute that specifically overturns those limitations, and the debate turns to how to define a "reasonable man." Further on in *Camplin* the definition of a reasonable man is expanded by taking into account at least some of the characteristics of the killer. Now in *Casassa* the Model Penal Code goes even farther by removing the causal nature of the provocation all together. The killer doesn't even have to be provoked, just extremely emotionally disturbed for some acceptable external reason. In this case, there is no justification defense at all; the victim has done nothing of which society disapproves. It seems rather as if the law on manslaughter is sliding down a slippery slope, giving more and more discretion to the jury. What all of these cases have in common is that it is very difficult to define the point where we should have compassion for a person who kills after being pushed too far. It has been argued that manslaughter no longer makes sense. The loss of control is not necessarily a good way to identify someone who should spend less time in prison. The fact that a person can lose control and kill someone because of external circumstances does not tend to lessen a person's dangerousness to society. Feminists have long objected to manslaughter on the basis that it is used as an excuse when abusive men murder their wives. On the other hand is there really anyone who can honestly say that they can't imagine any situation in which he or she might be pushed to kill? What if someone is forced to watch the rape and murder of his mother? What if a person came face to face with some modern-day version of Hitler? If a person kills under those circumstances don't we owe him compassion? Perhaps manslaughter is like pornography, and we have to depend on the jury to "know it when they see it."

Commonwealth v. Welansky

(State of Massachusetts) v. (Nightclub Owner)

316 Mass. 383, 55 N.E.2d 902 (1944)

M E M O R Y   G R A P H I C

Instant Facts

A man who owned a nightclub that burned down is found guilty of involuntary manslaughter because the club's policy of keeping the emergency exit doors locked led to the deaths of several people.

Black Letter Rule

An individual is guilty of involuntary manslaughter when his wanton or reckless breach of a duty of care causes the death of another.

Case Vocabulary

DOMINATION: In the corporate context, the power to control the corporation's activities and dictate its policies and procedures. Domination requires ownership of the largest share of the corporation's stock and influence over the majority of votes on the corporation's board of directors.

Procedural Basis: Appeal to the Massachusetts Supreme Judicial Court of a conviction of numerous counts of involuntary manslaughter through wanton or reckless conduct.

Facts: Barnett Welansky (D) dominated a corporation called New Cocoanut Grove, Inc., which operated a nightclub ("the club") in Boston. The club had one entrance, a single revolving door, and a small number of emergency exits. The various rooms and exits in the club were connected to each other by a series of narrow corridors. Three of the emergency exits were poorly marked and located in obscure areas known only to some of the club's employees. Two other emergency exits were marked with "Exit" lights and equipped with panic bars, but one door was blocked by a screen and the other was kept locked in order to prevent the club's patrons from leaving without paying their bills. On Saturday, November 28, 1942, the club was crowded with patrons. It was one of the busiest nights of the year. At around 10 p.m., a bartender in the Melody Lounge sent a waiter to go change a lightbulb in the corner of the room. The waiter lighted a match so that he could see what he was doing while changing the lightbulb. The flame from the match ignited a nearby palm tree, which in turn ignited a cloth ceiling. The fire spread and the patrons panicked. The door at the head of the stairway to the Melody Lounge was not opened until firefighters broke it down with an ax. It had been locked so that the panic bar could not operate. Firefighters found that two other emergency doors had been locked. A great number of patrons and many employees died inside the building. Welansky (D) had been in the hospital at the time of the fire, but he had closely supervised the club's business before his illness and the club had not changed its procedures while Welansky (D) was in the hospital. Welansky (D) was charged with numerous counts of involuntary manslaughter based on the club's overcrowding, flammable decorations, absence of fire doors, and failure to maintain proper emergency exits. Welansky (D) was found guilty and sentenced to between 12 and 15 years hard labor for each count, sentences to be served concurrently.

Issue: Under Massachusetts law, can a defendant who has committed the tort of breach of the duty of care and caused death be found guilty of the crime of involuntary manslaughter based on his wanton or reckless conduct?

Decision and Rationale: (Lummus, J.) Yes. A defendant who has breached a duty of care and caused the deaths of others through his wanton or reckless conduct can be found guilty of involuntary manslaughter under Massachusetts law. In this case, Welansky (D), as the dominant and controlling party in the New Cocoanut Grove corporation, had a duty of care for the safety of the patrons of the club and his failure to take care and his disregard of the probable consequences of his failure constitute wanton or reckless conduct. Wanton or reckless conduct is different from the negligence or gross negligence required to sustain a tort cause of action. In wanton or reckless conduct cases, it is the conduct that is intentional, not the harm caused by the conduct. The standard for determining wanton or reckless conduct is both subjective and objective. Grave danger to others must have been apparent and the defendant must have chosen to run the risk of causing harm rather than modify his conduct in order to prevent harm. Even if the "reasonable man" would not have realized that a grave danger existed, if the evidence shows that the defendant knew there was a danger, his decision to run the risk will constitute wanton or reckless conduct. If a reasonable man would have realized that a grave danger existed, even a stupid defendant will be liable if his action or failure to act under the circumstances caused harm. "Wanton" and "reckless" are terms that denote a higher degree of risk of liability than "negligence" or "gross negligence." Conduct will not transcend civil liability to become criminally liable unless it meets the high standard of wanton or reckless conduct. In this case, in order to convict Welansky

(D) of involuntary manslaughter, the prosecution did not need to show that he wantonly or recklessly caused the fire. It was enough for the prosecution to show Welansky's (D) disregard of the safety of the club's patrons in the event of fire as evidenced by the club's policy of keeping emergency exits locked and poorly marked. Judgment affirmed.

Analysis:

In spite of Welansky's (D) conviction, this case shows how difficult it is to hold corporate actors criminally liable for conduct that causes people's deaths. In order to convict Welansky (D), the court had to find him guilty of wanton or reckless conduct, a standard higher even than the gross negligence standard applied in tort cases. In order to show wanton or reckless conduct, a prosecutor must show that the defendant knew there was a grave risk and ran the risk. In this case, the corporation that owned the club was completely dominated by one man. Welansky (D) would have been aware of the club's safety policies, and may even have developed them himself. Before his illness, he visited the club regularly and paid close attention to the business. If Welansky (D) had not taken such an interest in New Cocoanut Grove, Inc., he would not have been found guilty of involuntary manslaughter because the prosecutor would not have been able to show that Welansky knew of the risk that patrons would be killed in a fire because the fire doors were locked and intentionally failed to act to ensure the safety of the club's patrons. It is difficult to imagine a situation where a shareholder in a large public corporation could be found guilty of involuntary manslaughter in a case where the corporation's activity has resulted in fatalities. The use of a higher standard than gross negligence in involuntary manslaughter cases has the effect of protecting corporate defendants. This allows corporations, especially corporations that are not dominated by one individual as in *Welansky*, to run the kinds of risks that individuals are not allowed to.

State v. Williams

(Government) v. (Negligent Parents)
(1971) 4 Wash.App. 908, 484 P.2d 1167

M E M O R Y   G R A P H I C

 ### Instant Facts

The Williams (D), parents of a 17-month-old child with an abscessed tooth, did not supply necessary medical care, and the child died as a result.

Black Letter Rule

A showing of ordinary negligence may be sufficient to support a conviction for manslaughter.

Case Vocabulary

ORDINARY NEGLIGENCE: Ordinary or simple negligence is the failure to exercise the caution or care that a reasonably prudent person would have exercised in similar circumstances.

Procedural Basis: Appeal from conviction for manslaughter due to ordinary negligence.

Facts: Walter Williams (D) is a 24-year-old Sheshont Indian with a 6th grade education. His wife, Bernice Williams (D), is a 20-year-old part-Indian with an 11th grade education. At the time of the marriage, Bernice had two children, the younger of whom was a 14-month-old son. Both Walter and Bernice had a great deal of love for the child. The child became ill on September 1. Both defendants were aware that the child was ill. However, Bernice and Walter "were ignorant," and did not realize how sick he was. They thought he had a toothache, which they did not believe to be life-threatening. They gave the child aspirin in hopes of improving his condition. They did not take the child to a doctor for fear that the Welfare Department would take the baby from them. The abscessed tooth developed into an infection of the mouth and cheeks, eventually becoming gangrenous. This condition, accompanied by the child's inability to eat, brought on malnutrition, which lowered the child's resistance and eventually produced pneumonia, causing death on September 12. The infection lasted about two weeks. A pathologist testified that the infection would have to have been treated within the first 5 days in order to save the child. The Williams (D) were convicted of manslaughter due to their negligence in not seeking medical treatment for the child.

Issue: May simple negligence support a conviction for manslaughter?

Decision and Rationale: (Horowitz) Yes. There is a parental duty to provide medical care to a dependent, minor child. To prove involuntary manslaughter, the common law requires that a breach of this duty had to amount to more than mere ordinary or simple negligence—a showing of gross negligence was required. In Washington, however, the statutes defining manslaughter require only a showing of simple or ordinary negligence. The concept of ordinary negligence requires a failure to exercise the "ordinary caution" necessary to make out the defense of excusable homicide. Ordinary caution is the kind of caution that a man of reasonable prudence would exercise under the same or similar conditions. If the conduct of a defendant, regardless of his ignorance, good faith, or good intentions, fails to measure up to this standard, he is guilty of ordinary negligence. If such negligence proximately causes the death of the victim, the defendant is guilty of manslaughter. Timeliness in the furnishing of medical care must be considered in terms of ordinary caution. The law does not require that a parent call a doctor at the first sign of illness. However, testimony from the defendants indicates that they noticed the child was ill 10 to 14 days before the child died. In the five critical days in which it would have been possible to save the child's life, the parents noticed that the child was fussy, could not keep food down, and that his cheek turned a "bluish color like." The defendants thought that dentists would not pull a tooth "when it's all swollen up like that." Also, both parents feared that the child would be taken away from them if they took him to a doctor. Thus, there is sufficient evidence that the defendants were put on notice of the symptoms of the illness, and failed to exercise ordinary caution. Judgment affirmed.

Analysis:

This is a tragic case where the offender "should have known." This standard has troubled some commentators who wonder whether criminal liability should ever be based on an objective standard. Some suggest that the threat of criminal liability does not serve as a deterrent to negligent conduct. The negligent person is unaware of the risk, and cannot be deterred by a thought of possible punishment for taking an unreasonable risk that, in fact, he does not know he is taking. The competing argument contends that the threat of punishment makes people think harder about their conduct generally. When people consider the risks of their conduct, they tend to reduce the risks of their conduct, and thus create a safer society. Another issue that arises in *Williams* is the cultural issue, though the court does not make much of it. There is a great deal of scholarship on the problem of the reasonable person definition, which is primarily informed by a world view that is white, male, and middleclass. To some extent, a trial by jury consisting of one's peers [if this is indeed possible—since many citizens take pride in their ability to avoid jury duty, the choice may be somewhat limited] may counteract some of the potential for injustice in application of the predominant reasonable person standard.

Commonwealth v. Malone

(State of Pennsylvania) v. (Kid Who Shot Friend in "Russian Roulette" Game)
354 Pa. 180, 47 A.2d 445 (1946)

M E M O R Y   G R A P H I C

 Instant Facts

A boy killed his friend in a game of Russian Roulette and was convicted of second-degree murder, in spite of his insistence that he did not intend the gun to go off.

Black Letter Rule

A killing does not have to be intended in order to constitute second-degree murder—if the killer's actions show a callous disregard for human life and the consequences of his actions, he will have exhibited the malice that distinguishes second-degree murder from involuntary manslaughter.

Case Vocabulary

DECEDENT: Deceased.

Procedural Basis: Appeal to the Supreme Court of Pennsylvania of a sentence of five to ten years in prison under a conviction of murder in the second degree.

Facts: On the evening of February 26, 1945, Malone (D), a 17-year-old boy, went to the movies. Malone (D) brought with him a 32-caliber revolver that he had taken from his uncle's house the day before. The gun had been loaded the day before by William Long, a 13-year-old boy, who had taken a cartridge from his father's room. After leaving the theater, Malone (D) met Long at a dairy store. In a corner at the back of the store, Malone (D) took the gun out of his pocket and loaded the chamber to the right of the firing pin. Malone (D) and Long went to sit at the lunch counter and ate. Malone (D) then suggested that they play "Russian Poker" (otherwise known as "Russian Roulette"). Long agreed to play. Malone (D) held the gun against Long's right side and pulled the trigger three times. The third time he pulled the trigger, Malone (D) succeeded in shooting Long. Long died of the gunshot wound two days later. At trial, Malone (D) testified that he had loaded the first chamber to the right of the firing pin and that he did not "expect to have the gun go off." He did not intend to injure Long, who was his friend. Malone (D) was found guilty of murder in the second degree and sentenced to five to ten years in prison. Malone's (D) motion for a new trial was denied and he appealed after sentencing.

Issue: Under Pennsylvania law, if a conviction of murder in the second degree requires a showing of malice on the part of the killer, can a defendant who has killed another in a Russian Roulette game be convicted of murder in the second degree?

Decision and Rationale: (Maxey, J.) Yes. Under Pennsylvania law, a defendant who has killed another in a Russian Roulette game can be found guilty of second-degree murder. A conviction of second-degree murder requires a showing of malice on the part of the killer. "Malice" does not necessarily mean hostility toward the victim, but can include general hostility or a "wicked disposition." When an individual commits an act of gross recklessness and must have reasonably anticipated that another person's death would likely result from his action, he is exhibiting the kind of general "wickedness of disposition, hardness of heart, cruelty, recklessness of consequences" that can constitute "malice." Long's death resulted from an intentional act committed by Malone (D) in reckless and wanton disregard of the consequences. There was at least a 60% chance that Malone's pulling the trigger would result in a fatal shot because he had loaded one bullet into a gun and fired it three times into a vital part of Long's body. Malone's (D) action was intentional, unnecessary, and was committed in the callous disregard of the possible consequences and was therefore evidence of malice in the sense of "a wicked disposition." The fact that Malone (D) had no specific motive for killing Long is irrelevant. Judgment affirmed.

Analysis:

When can an unintentional killing be considered a murder? The Pennsylvania homicide statute at the time of this case divided murder into two degrees. A conviction of murder in the first degree required a showing of "willful, deliberate and premeditated killing." Under Pennsylvania law at the time, "all other kinds of murder shall be deemed murder in the second degree." This case tries to draw a line between the broad statutory category of second-degree murder and involuntary manslaughter. The court is looking for a general hostility, or recklessness and disregard for human life that will have the effect of characterizing an unintentional killing as the result of malice rather than accident. In this case, Malone (D) decided to play with a loaded gun. A loaded gun is a deadly weapon and an obviously dangerous choice for a toy. The court makes a point of mentioning the 60% chance that Malone (D) would end up killing Long in his Russian Roulette game, but the likelihood that the game would result in death, and the factual issue of whether Malone (D) had loaded the bullet in the chamber he thought would fire last, as he testified at trial, or whether he had actually loaded the bullet and then spun the revolver's cylinder as in a traditional game of Russian Roulette, are probably beside the point. The fact that Malone (D) was willing to play Russian Roulette in the first place is what really shows his "wickedness of disposition" rather than the likelihood, or what Malone (D) thought was the likelihood, of Long's being killed.

United States v. Fleming

(United States) v. (Drunk Driver)
739 F.2d 945 (4th Cir. 1984)

M E M O R Y   G R A P H I C

Instant Facts
A drunk driver drove at high speeds and occasionally into oncoming traffic on a busy highway. He crashed into another car and was found guilty of the murder of the driver.

Black Letter Rule
Under federal law, drunk and reckless driving can constitute murder with malice aforethought when there is evidence that there was a risk of serious harm associated with the defendant's activities and that the defendant knew about this risk and disregarded it.

Case Vocabulary

VEHICULAR HOMICIDE: The death of another person caused by the operation of an automobile.

Procedural Basis: Appeal to the 4th Circuit Court of Appeals of a conviction under 18 U.S.C. §1111 of murder in the second degree.

Facts: At 3:00 p.m. on June 15, 1983, David Earl Fleming (D) was driving southbound on the George Washington Memorial Parkway in Virginia (the Parkway is within federal jurisdiction) at speeds estimated by witnesses to be between 70 and 100 miles per hour (the Parkway speed limit was 45 miles per hour). Several times Fleming (D) drove his car into oncoming traffic in order to avoid the heavy congestion on his side of the road. About six miles from where police first observed Fleming (D) driving at excessive speed, Fleming (D) lost control of his vehicle on a sharp curve. His car slid across the northbound lanes and hit the curb on the northbound side of the Parkway. Fleming (D) then straightened out his car and struck a car driven by Mrs. Haley. At the moment of impact, Fleming's (D) car was traveling at between 70 and 80 miles per hour (the speed limit at that point was 30 miles per hour). Mrs. Haley died before she could be pulled from the wreckage of her car. Fleming (D) survived. When he arrived at a Washington, D.C. hospital for treatment, his blood alcohol level was .315 percent. Fleming (D) was convicted of second-degree murder.

Issue: Under federal law, in a case where a vehicular homicide was the unintentional result of the defendant's drunk driving, can the defendant's actions be held to constitute evidence of malice aforethought and therefore support a conviction of second degree murder?

Decision and Rationale: (Winter, C.J.) Yes. Under federal law, a vehicular homicide committed by a drunk driver constitutes murder in the second degree with malice aforethought, rather than involuntary manslaughter. Malice aforethought is the characteristic that serves to distinguish murder from manslaughter. Proof of malice does not have to include proof that the defendant felt any particular hostility toward his victim, nor does it have to include proof that the defendant intended to kill anyone. The government can establish malice by showing conduct that evidences a reckless, wanton, or gross breach of the standard of care in such a way that a jury could reasonably conclude that the defendant was aware that his actions created a risk of death or serious bodily harm. In this case, the government had to show that Fleming (D) intended to drive the way he did and that he acted without regard for the lives and safety of others. Fleming's (D) conduct was sufficient to show that he acted with malice aforethought. Fleming (D), however, has argued that his conviction should be reduced to involuntary manslaughter because he did not intend to kill anyone. If intent to kill or injure is not a requirement for a showing of malice aforethought, all drunk driving homicides and many homicides caused by reckless driving will be held to be murders. This argument is not persuasive. The difference between malice and gross negligence, which is the requirement for a showing of involuntary manslaughter, is one of degree, not kind. In this case, Fleming's (D) actions show a recklessness or wantonness that is different in degree from that found in most vehicular homicide cases. The danger Fleming (D) created did not arise merely from his decision to drive while drunk. In addition to drunk driving, Fleming (D) drove in a manner that showed disregard for human life. His reckless conduct was compounded by his drunkenness. Judgment affirmed.

Analysis:

In this case, the court draws a distinction between dangerous conduct that leads to murder and dangerous conduct that leads to manslaughter. The court states that the difference is one of degree—the difference between murder and manslaughter is found both in the extent to which the defendant is aware of the risk and in the probability of danger that arises from the defendant's action. In other words, Fleming (D) was guilty of murder rather than manslaughter because serious accidents are likely to result when drunk people drive recklessly on congested highways and because he knew that his actions created a probability of serious harm and ignored the risk. The problem with the court's decision here is that Fleming was drunk when he got into his car, and during the period when he was driving recklessly on the highway his mental state may not have been adequate to the task of weighing the risks associated with drunk and reckless driving. The difference between murder and manslaughter usually rests on the mental state of the defendant, and whether there was some degree of forethought—a general hostility toward the victim or a general wantonness and disregard for human life. "Malice aforethought" seems to suggest that the defendant must have a certain amount of awareness of the consequences of his actions, but how "aware" of anything should we expect a drunk person to be? Another difficulty with drunk driving cases is in determining when the wantonness and disregard for human life manifested itself in the defendant's behavior. Was Fleming (D) displaying a wanton disregard for human life when he decided to get drunk? Or was it when, in a weakened mental state, he decided to drive recklessly? The fact that the court in this case does not address these issues may be evidence that the court is acting on a public policy to extend harsh punishments in drunk driving cases in order to create a deterrent that would prevent sober people from deciding to get drunk when there is any possibility that they might have to drive while intoxicated.

Regina v. Serné

(Queen Victoria) v. (Men Accused of Killing Child to Collect Life Insurance)

16 Cox Crim. Cas. 311 (Central Criminal Court 1887)

M E M O R Y   G R A P H I C

Instant Facts

A man, along with his servant, was indicted for the murder of one of his sons when his house and store burned down after he had taken out a life insurance policy on his son.

Black Letter Rule

Felony murder is homicide caused by an action that is dangerous in and of itself and likely to result in the death of another and that is taken by a defendant with the intent to commit a felony.

Case Vocabulary

DOCK: In British criminal procedure, criminal defendants are separated from their defense counsel, witnesses, and the jury in the courtroom during trial. The area where criminal defendants sit is known as "the dock."

INFLAMMABLE: British English for "flammable."

Procedural Basis: Jury instruction in an English murder trial.

Facts: In the summer of 1887, Leon Serné (D1) and his family were in severe debt and living in a house above a store in London. Serné (D1) had taken out a life insurance policy on his 14-year-old son, Sjaak, who was mentally retarded. He had also insured the inventory of his store, his furniture, and his rent. Within a month of Serné's (D1) taking out these insurance policies, the store and house burned down, causing the deaths of both of Serné's (D1) sons. At trial, the prosecution submitted evidence that Serné (D1) and John Henry Goldfinch (D2) had been seen together in the shop shortly before the fire started. Two fires broke out on the lower floor of the building, and two on the second floor. Serné (D1), Goldfinch (D2), and Serné's wife and daughters escaped to the roof of the house and then to the building next door, but Serné's (D1) sons did not. The body of one of the sons was found on the floor near the window through which the others had escaped. The body of the other son was found in the basement. Serné (D1) and Goldfinch (D2) were indicted for the wilful murder of Sjaak Serné.

Issue: Under English law, can any action that causes the death of another person taken by a defendant with the intent to commit a felony be considered felony murder?

Decision and Rationale: (Stephen, J.) No. Under English law, only an action taken with intent to commit a felony that is known to create a danger to human life can constitute felony murder. Murder is an unlawful homicide committed with malice aforethought. "Malice aforethought" is a legal term and must be construed in the light of previous cases, rather than according to the meanings each individual juror is likely to assign to it. One type of murder with malice aforethought is the killing of another person through an action taken with the intention to commit a felony. Another type of murder with malice aforethought is an action taken with the knowledge that that action will probably cause the death of another person. If Serné (D1) and/or Goldfinch (D2) killed Sjaak Serné either through an action undertaken with intent to commit a felony, such as insurance fraud, or through an action undertaken in the knowledge that that action would lead to someone's death, then Serné (D1) and/or Goldfinch (D2) will be guilty of murder. In the past, the definition of "felony murder" was a very broad one, but the law has likely changed and the appellate court would probably apply a narrower definition in a case such as this one. The current definition of felony murder is not any act done in pursuit of an intention to commit a felony that results in the death of another, but rather, any act known to be dangerous to human life and likely to cause death, which is taken for the purpose of committing a felony and that does in fact cause the death of another person. If Serné (D1) and Goldfinch (D2) set fire to the house and store while the family were inside, and the boys died as a result of the fire, then Serné (D1) and Goldfinch (D2) are just as guilty of murder as they would be if they were found to have stabbed the boys. Whether or not Serné (D1) and Goldfinch (D2) intended that all the members of the family would escape from the house is irrelevant if they were the ones who started the fires. However, the seriousness of the crime Serné (D1) and Goldfinch (D2) are accused of means that the jury must take extreme care to weigh the evidence that was presented to it and not impute to Serné (D1) and Goldfinch (D2) anything that was not proved at trial. If the jury finds Serné (D1) and Goldfinch (D2) guilty, it must be with no reasonable doubt. Verdict: not guilty.

Analysis:

In this case, the court asked the jury to apply a new standard for determining whether a felony murder was committed. The standard articulated by the court could not be found in the common law of the time, but was a standard likely to be upheld on appeal. The reason for narrowing the standard of felony murder may have been to lessen the number of defendants found guilty of murder and sentenced to death when their actions would have been found to be evidence of mere manslaughter if the defendant had not also been guilty of a felony. The court in this case may not have wanted the fact that Serné (D1) and Goldfinch (D2) were accused of a felony to unfairly prejudice the jury and encourage it to decide whether the defendants were guilty of murder without also considering whether the defendants had actually started the fires.

People v. Phillips

(State of California) v. (Chiropractor with $700 Cure for Cancer)
64 Cal. 2d 574, 414 P.2d 353 (Ca. 1966)

M E M O R Y   G R A P H I C

Instant Facts

A chiropractor was convicted of felony murder, even though the crime of fraud itself is not a violent one, because his cure for cancer did not save the life of his patient.

Black Letter Rule

Under California law, in order to invoke the felony murder rule, the prosecution must show that the felony the defendant committed is one that is inherently dangerous to human life.

Case Vocabulary

PROXIMATE CAUSE: The foreseeable or probable consequence of an action.

Procedural Basis: Appeal to the Supreme Court of California of a conviction of second-degree murder.

Facts: Linda Epping was an eight-year-old girl who suffered from a fast-growing cancer of the eye. Doctors at a medical center advised her parents to consent to immediate surgery to remove the eye because this was the only means available to save or prolong the child's life. Instead of following the doctors' advice, the Eppings opted to follow the advice of a chiropractor, Phillips, (D). Phillips (D) told the Eppings that he could cure the child without surgery by administering a treatment designed "to build up her resistance." Phillips (D) charged the Eppings $700. Linda died in about six months. Phillips (D) was indicted for murder in the second degree. After the trial, the trial court gave a three-part instruction to the jury, explaining the definition of murder in the second degree. In the third part of the instruction, the trial judge told the jury that the unlawful killing of another person with malice aforethought but without the deliberate and premeditated intent to kill, is murder in the second degree if "the killing is done in the perpetration or attempt to perpetrate a felony such as Grand Theft. If a death occurs in the perpetration of a course of conduct amounting to Grand Theft, which course of conduct is a proximate cause of the unlawful killing of a human being, such course of conduct constitutes murder in the second degree, even though the death was not intended." Phillips (D) appealed on the grounds that this instruction was in error.

Issue: Under California law, can a chiropractor whose cure for cancer did not succeed in saving his patient's life be found guilty of felony murder based on his act of fraud?

Decision and Rationale: (Tobriner, J.) No. Under California law, a homicide committed during the perpetration of a fraud cannot be held to be a felony murder. The trial court erred in giving a felony murder instruction. Phillips (D) argues that the California Penal Code does not set forth any provision for second degree felony murder. The felony murder rule is deeply imbedded in California law. But only felonies that are in themselves "inherently dangerous to human life" fall under the felony murder rule. In order to determine whether a felony is inherently dangerous to human life, California courts do not look to the facts of individual cases, but rather, look to the elements of the felony in the abstract. The felony murder rule is narrowly construed in general and has been widely criticized, and even abandoned in England. No prior case has held that the felony murder rule may be invoked where a death results from the perpetration of a fraud. The prosecution argues that the court should create a new felony, "Grand Theft Medical Fraud," and determine that this felony involves inherent danger to human life. The prosecution's line of reasoning would allow courts to consider a defendant's entire course of conduct in order to determine that the felony he committed was inherently dangerous. This would widen the felony murder rule and cause the rejection of prior cases that have had the effect of narrowing the application of the rule. The felony murder instruction was erroneous. It was also prejudicial because it allowed the jury to convict Phillips (D) without finding malice aforethought. Instead, the jury was able to convict based on their finding that Phillips (D) had committed fraud. The prosecution argues that regardless of the instruction, the jury must have found that Phillips (D) had acted with the conscious disregard for human life necessary for a finding of "malice aforethought." The prosecution's argument is that the jury could not have found Phillips (D) guilty of felony murder without considering evidence that Phillips (D) had recklessly given the parents information that he knew to be false. However, this evidence does not, as a matter of law, establish the existence of the intent to commit, with the conscious disregard for human life, actions likely to result in the death of another. The record could just as easily support a finding that Phillips (D) passed on false information while believing it to be true. Judgment reversed.

Analysis:

This case serves to limit the number of situations in which the prosecution can invoke the felony murder rule. The felony murder rule can only be invoked when the underlying felony is inherently dangerous to human life. It cannot be used any time that a defendant kills someone while committing other types of felonies. The policy behind limiting the application of the rule may be to reduce the number of defendants found guilty of murder in cases where the homicide would have been held to be manslaughter if the defendant had not been committing a crime at the time of the killing. This is an important policy interest when long prison terms are at stake. The requirement that the felony be dangerous to life has been stated in two different ways. Under one approach, the question is whether on the facts of the particular case, including the circumstances under which the felony was committed, there was a foreseeable danger to human life. Thus, while it may be said as an abstract proposition that the theft felonies (larceny, embezzlement and false pretenses) do not involve danger to life, a thief may commit his theft crime in a way which does create a foreseeable danger to life; under this first view it would be felony murder if death did result under these circumstances. The other approach limits the felony-murder doctrine to those felonies which are "inherently dangerous," that is, the peril to human life must be determined from the elements of the felony in the abstract rather than from the facts of the particular case. Under this view, false pretenses is not a dangerous felony even when committed by inducing a person to forego a life-prolonging operation. On principle, the *Phillips* approach is incorrect, for if the purpose of the felony-murder doctrine is to hold felons accountable for unintended deaths caused by their dangerous conduct, then it would seem to make little difference whether the felony committed was dangerous by its very nature or merely dangerous as committed in the particular case. If the armed robber is to be held guilty of felony murder because of a death occurring from the accidental firing of his gun, it seems no more harsh to apply the felony-murder doctrine to the thief whose fraudulent scheme includes inducing the victim to forego a life-prolonging operation. The requirement that the felony be "inherently dangerous" is more understandable, however, if viewed as an attempt by some courts to limit what they believe to be "a highly artificial concept that deserves no extension beyond its required application." It should be noted that the *Phillips* court did not hold that the doctor could not be convicted of murder. Rather, the court only objected to use of the felony-murder concept as a substitute for proof of depraved-heart murder. In the modern criminal codes, the question of what kind of felony will suffice is ordinarily addressed in the felony murder statute. Some of these statutes state without qualification that any felony will do, but it is always possible a court will conclude this language must be construed in light of the history of felony murder rather than literally. Some other of the modern statutes describe a general category of felonies which will suffice; these categories in one way or another relate to the dangerousness of the felony and, depending upon the exact language used, might give rise to the inherent-vs.-in-this-case question herein discussed. But most modern felony murder statutes limit the crime to a list of specific felonies -- usually rape, robbery, kidnapping, arson and burglary -- which involve a significant prospect of violence.

People v. Satchell

(Government) v. (Convicted Felon)
6 Cal. 3d 38, 489 P.2d 1361 (1972)

M E M O R Y G R A P H I C

Instant Facts

An ex-felon was convicted of second-degree felony-murder when he killed a man with a sawed-off shotgun, his possession of which constituted the predicate felony.

Black Letter Rule

Possession of a weapon by a convicted felon is not itself a felony inherently dangerous to human life which will support a felony-murder instruction.

Procedural Basis: Not provided.

Facts: Satchel (D), an ex-felon with four prior convictions, shot and killed a man in a street fight with a sawed-off shotgun Satchel (D) pulled from his car. In California possession of a concealable weapon by an ex-felon constituted a felony. Accordingly, the jury was given an instruction that it could impute to Satchel (D) the intent to kill from his possession of the weapon. Satchel (D) was convicted of second-degree murder.

Issue: Is possession of a weapon by an ex-felon an inherently dangerous felony which will support a felony-murder instruction?

Decision and Rationale: (Not provided) No. Possession of a weapon by a convicted felon is not itself a felony inherently dangerous to human life which will support a felony-murder instruction. The felony-murder rule should not be extended beyond its designated purpose: to deter those engaged in felonies from killing negligently. Instead, the rule should be narrowly applied. In this state, there exist a wide-range of felonies that do not manifest a propensity to endanger human life. Consumer and insurance fraud, elections offenses, and interference with the legislative process are just a few examples. Few would argue that a person who has been convicted of one of these felonies, when armed with a concealable weapon, presents a danger to human life more extreme than by a non-felon similarly armed. Because there are countless situations where it would be illogical to impute an intent to kill from an ex-felon's possession of a weapon, we find that the felony-murder instruction given in this case was unwarranted. Reversed.

Analysis:

This case illustrates the weakness of the "in the abstract" approach illustrated by *People v. Phillips* (case involving the felony-murder conviction of a chiropractor engaged in patient fraud). The court holds that the purpose of the rule – to deter those engaged in felonies from endangering the lives of others – necessitates a narrow application. Is not the stated purpose furthered by the rule's application in the very circumstances presented by this case? After all, Satchell (D) was committing a felony and did so in a manner that threatened the lives of others. The fact that application of the rule would be illogical in certain situations does not mean that the rule should not apply in those circumstances where its stated purpose would clearly be furthered. *Satchell* seems more an attempt at judicial legislation than a narrow construction of the felony-murder rule. The court's holding that possession by an ex-felon of a concealable weapon is not an inherently dangerous felon would seem to frustrate legislative intent. The court justifies its holding on the ground that, because there are some ex-felons who were convicted of crimes not involving any threat to life, it would be illogical to apply the felony-murder rule to possession of a weapon by felons convicted of non-violent crimes. However, the very reason convicted felons are prohibited from possession of such weapons is that the legislature has determined it to pose a threat to the public. Why else would such a law be passed? The legislature was certainly aware that possession of a weapon by a man convicted of insurance fraud is not any more dangerous than possession of a weapon by any other person. Nevertheless, it decided to not exclude these types of ex-felons from the statutory prohibition.

WHETHER A PARTICULAR FELONY IS INHERENTLY DANGEROUS AND MAY SERVE AS
THE PREDICATE FOR FELONY-MURDER IS A QUESTION OF FACT FOR THE JURY

People v. Stewart

(Government) v. (Drug Addict Mother)
663 A.2d. 912 (R.I. 1995)

M E M O R Y G R A P H I C

Instant Facts

A woman was charged with felony-murder when her infant son dies from dehydration, which resulted from the mother's neglect during two to three-day crack binge.

Black Letter Rule

The proper procedure to determine whether a felony is inherently dangerous is to present the facts and circumstances of the particular case to the trier of fact and for the trier of fact to determine if a felony is inherently dangerous in the manner and the circumstances in which it was committed.

Procedural Basis: Appeal to the Supreme Court of Rhode Island challenging the denial of a motion for judgment of acquittal on a felony murder charge.

Facts: Tracey Stewart (D) was charged with second-degree felony murder when her infant son died from dehydration. Stewart (D) went on a crack binge over several days, during which she neither fed nor cared for her son. The prosecution charged Stewart (D) with, essentially, parental neglect, a felony under the Rhode Island statute. The prosecution argued that Stewart (D) could be charged with second-degree murder under the felony murder rule because her acts were the result of neglect, not intentional conduct. Stewart (D) argued that the felony murder rule was inapplicable because her crime was not inherently dangerous in the abstract.

Issue: Must a felony be inherently dangerous in the abstract in order to serve as the predicate for felony-murder?

Decision and Rationale: (Weisenberger, C.J.) No. The proper procedure to determine whether a felony is inherently dangerous is to present the facts and circumstances of the particular case to the trier of fact and for the trier of fact to determine if a felony is inherently dangerous in the manner and the circumstances in which it was committed. We reject the approach adopted by in California, which requires that a court determine whether a particular felony is inherently dangerous "in the abstract," if the felony murder rule is to apply. A number of felonies would appear, at first glance, to not be inherently dangerous, yet they may be committed in such a manner as to be inherently dangerous to life. For example, escape from prison is not inherently dangerous. Nevertheless, we have previously upheld a conviction under the felony murder rule when the escapee's accomplice killed a prison guard. Accordingly, the jury instruction given by the trial court was proper, for it left to the jury the determination of whether the parental neglect was inherently dangerous to human life "in its manner of commission." Affirmed.

Analysis:

In several jurisdictions, application of the felony-murder rule has been limited to the commission of only felonies which are "inherently dangerous to life." In *People v. Phillips* (case involving the felony-murder conviction of a chiropractor engaged in patient fraud) and *People v. Stachell* (case involving the felony murder conviction of an ex-felon in possession of a concealable weapon) you saw that some courts favor application of the felony-murder rule only in those cases where the felony committed was dangerous "in the abstract." The reason for this narrow construction of the inherently dangerous limitation is to limit a rule viewed as artificial and unjust. *Stewart* illustrates a second approach to the determination of what constitutes an "inherently dangerous" felony. The court in *Stewart* adopts a rule under which a felony is inherently dangerous if the jury determines that the felony at issue was committed in an inherently dangerous manner or under inherently dangerous circumstances. This approach clearly broadens application of the felony-murder rule to almost any felony. From a literal point of view, the court's holding seems incorrect. After all, the word "inherently" implies that dangerousness of the felony must be one of its essential characteristics. Linguistics aside however, the rule adopted in this case furthers the purpose of the felony-murder rule: to hold felons accountable for unintended deaths caused by their dangerous conduct. The differing approaches taken toward the inherently dangerous limitation involve contrasting policy considerations. The particular approach adopted by a court depends on how broadly a court wishes to apply the rule. Courts favoring the felony-murder rule will agree with the Rhode Island Court and determine the issue on a case by case basis. On the other hand, courts that desire limited application of the felony-murder rule will likely adopt the approach taken in *Phillips* and *Satchell*.

People v. Smith

(Government) v. (Child Abuser)

(1984) 35 Cal.3d 798, 201 Cal.Rptr. 311, 678 P.2d 886

M E M O R Y   G R A P H I C

Instant Facts

Smith (D) and her boyfriend beat Smith's two-year-old to death; Smith (D) was charged with second-degree felony murder.

Black Letter Rule

Felony child abuse which results in death is held to merge with the homicide so as to preclude a conviction of second degree murder on a felony murder theory.

Procedural Basis: Appeal from conviction of felony child abuse and second-degree murder on the felony murder rule.

Facts: Smith (D) and her two daughters, three-and-a-half-year-old Beth and two-year-old Amy, lived with David Foster. On the day Amy died, she refused to sit on the couch instead of the floor to eat a snack. Smith (D) became angry, and took Amy to her room where she spanked and slapped her. Smith (D) hit her repeatedly, knocking her to the floor. Foster then joined Smith (D) to "assist" in Amy's discipline. Beth testified that Foster and Smith (D) were striking Amy and were also biting her. Beth also testified that Foster put a wastebasket on Amy's head and hit her on the head with his fist. Smith (D) knocked Amy backwards, and Amy hit her head on the closet door. Amy went into respiratory arrest. She was taken to the hospital, but died later that evening. Smith (D) originally took all responsibility for the incident because of concern about the possible effect on Foster's probation status. Later, however, Smith (D) testified that she only spanked Amy, and that Foster had bitten and hit Amy while she was out of the room. Smith (D) testified that she told Foster that she would continue the discipline, and yelled at Amy for 15-20 minutes so that Foster would have time to "cool off." Foster returned to the room and began slapping Amy because she would not look at him. Smith (D) stated that although she realized Amy was being abused she did not think that her life was in danger. Smith (D) finally intervened, at which point Amy stiffened and fainted. Smith (D) was charged with felony child abuse and second-degree murder under the second-degree felony murder doctrine. The second-degree felony murder instruction informed the jury that an unlawful killing is second-degree murder if it occurs during the commission of a felony inherently dangerous to human life, and that felony child abuse is such a crime. Smith (D) contends that the crime of felony child abuse was an integral part of and included with the homicide, and hence it was merged into the homicide.

Issue: May felony child abuse serve as the underlying felony to support a conviction of second-degree murder on a felony-murder theory?

Decision and Rationale: (Mosk) No. Our opinions have repeatedly emphasized that felony murder is a disfavored doctrine. Although felony murder is the law in this state, we have sought to ensure that the doctrine be given the narrowest possible application consistent with its purpose—to deter those engaged in felonies from killing negligently or accidentally. We have restricted the scope of the felony murder rule by holding it inapplicable to felonies that are an integral part of and included in fact with the homicide. However, the felony-murder doctrine may still apply if the underlying offense was committed with an independent felonious purpose. Felony murder jury instructions have the effect of relieving the jury of the necessity of finding one of the elements of the crime of murder—malice aforethought. To allow such use of the felony murder doctrine would effectively preclude the jury from considering the issue of malice in all cases wherein homicide has been committed as a result of a felonious assault—a category which includes the great majority of all homicides. The offenses of assault with a deadly weapon, burglary with intent to assault, and discharging a firearm at an inhabited dwelling [a favorite California pastime] have all been held to merge into a resulting homicide. Cases in which the merger doctrine did not apply include those involving armed robbery, poisoning food, drink, or medicine, kidnapping, and felony child abuse by malnutrition. To violate the felony child abuse statute, the conduct must be willful, and must be committed under circumstances or conditions likely to produce great bodily harm or death. Application of the felony murder rule is barred where "the purpose of the conduct was the very assault which resulted in death." The purpose of the child abuse in this case was plainly the very assault that resulted in death. Thus, the underlying felony was unquestionably an integral part of the homicide. It was therefore error to give a felony-murder instruction in this case. The error must be deemed prejudicial. The judgment is reversed insofar as it convicts Smith (D) of second-degree murder; in all other respects, the judgment is affirmed.

Analysis:

The court claims that "[I]t would be wholly illogical to allow this kind of assaultive child abuse to be bootstrapped into felony murder merely because the victim was a child rather than an adult." Dismissing the propriety of felony child abuse as a basis for felony murder seems somewhat problematic, however. The court seems to be claiming that since the purpose of the conduct was the very assault that resulted in death, it does not matter if the target of the assault is a child or an adult. But the law already distinguishes between assault on an adult and assault on a child, and distinguishes between the two in sentencing. It does not seem wholly illogical [maybe partly illogical, if the idea even makes sense] to argue that this difference supports a finding that felony child abuse may be sufficiently different in seriousness as to support felony-murder. For the court, though, this would represent an expansion of the felony murder doctrine, which they take pains to avoid.

State v. Canola

(State of New Jersey) v. (Jewelry-Store Robber)
73 N.J. 206, 374 A.2d 20 (N.J. 1977)

M E M O R Y   G R A P H I C

Instant Facts

A felon is convicted of the murder of his accomplice when during the armed robbery of a jewelry store, the store's owner shoots the accomplice in self-defense.

Black Letter Rule

The definition of felony murder will not be extended beyond its requirement that the defendant acted to cause the death of another to include situations where the actions of the felon set of a chain reaction leading to the death of another.

Case Vocabulary

CULPABLE: At fault.

Procedural Basis: Certification to the Supreme Court of New Jersey of appeal of conviction of felony murder.

Facts: Canola (D) attempted an armed robbery of a jewelry store with three accomplices. The store owner and his employee resisted the robbery. One of the accomplices fired a weapon, and the store owner returned the gunfire. Both the store owner and the accomplice were fatally wounded. The accomplice was killed by the store owner. Canola (D) and two of his accomplices were indicted on two counts of murder, one count of robbery, and one count of armed robbery. Canola (D) was found guilty on both murder counts and was sentenced to two concurrent terms of life imprisonment. The Appellate Division upheld the trial court's denial of a defense motion to dismiss the count of murder addressed to the killing of the accomplice with one dissent, so the Supreme Court granted certiorari.

Issue: Under New Jersey law, can a defendant be found guilty of felony murder when during his robbery of a store one of the robbery victims shoots one of the defendant's accomplices?

Decision and Rationale: (Conford, J.) No. Under New Jersey law, a defendant cannot be found guilty of the killing of an accomplice by the victim of an armed robbery. The traditional definitions of felony murder do not encompass situations such as the one in this case. Traditionally, the felony murder rule has only been invoked when the defendant himself killed the victim. The general rule throughout the United States is that the felony murder rule may not be applied to homicides not attributable to the defendant. No court currently attaches liability under the felony murder rule to any death proximately caused by the perpetration of the felony, even when the homicide was committed by the victim of the felony. The theory of proximate cause that holds that if a felon sets in motion a chain of events that could foreseeably lead to the death of another he is liable for any death that results was adopted by courts in Pennsylvania and Michigan in cases involving the killing of police officers, but these cases have since been overruled. This theory was also adopted in Illinois in a case involving the killing of an innocent bystander, but that case was later overruled. The so-called "shield" cases can also be distinguished from the present case. The shield cases are those where the victim is fatally shot by police officers after the defendant, trying to escape after committing a felony, uses an innocent bystander as a human shield. In those cases, the defendant is properly found guilty of felony murder because, although he did not pull the trigger, his actions reflect "express malice" in the form of a knowing disregard of the natural and probable consequences of his decision to use a person as a shield. The Appellate Court held that the wording of the New Jersey felony murder statute makes the application of the proximate cause theory necessary. But even if the Appellate Court's reading of the statute is correct, public policy considerations outweigh this reading. Most modern thought rejects the expansion of the felony murder rule, and courts tend to apply it narrowly. The felony murder rule was developed at a time when all felonies were punishable by death. Times have changed, and to classify a homicide as murder simply because the defendant was committing a felony at the time of the homicide is discordant with current views on criminal liability. Judgment modified to strike the conviction and sentencing of Canola (D) for the murder of his accomplice.

Concurrence: (Sullivan, J.) The legislative intent behind the New Jersey felony murder statute compels a different reasoning from that employed by the majority. The statute is designed to hold a criminal liable for any killing that ensues during the commission of a felony, even if the felon or his accomplice did not do the actual killing. The only exception to this rule should be the death of an accomplice. The killing during an armed robbery of an accomplice by the victim of the robbery is a justifiable homicide and does not fall under the statute.

Analysis:

In dissent, Sullivan argues that the felon should not be held liable for killings at the hands of another. Sullivan's statement of the rule is the generally accepted view. The killing of a felon by a non-felon is, he believes, a justifiable homicide. "Justifiable" means simply that the killing was a permissible response to the felony. A justifiable homicide is not imputed to either the store owner or the accomplices. The argument asserts that a felon should not be held liable for the death of his co-felon who willingly participated in a dangerous venture. In contrast, an excusable homicide is one in which a non-felon, in response to the felony, accidentally kills a bystander. The usual example involves a store owner, who, in response to an armed robbery, attempts to shoot the robber but instead hits a store customer. The homicide by the store owner is "excused," and the store owner will not be prosecuted for the death

Taylor v. Superior Court

(Getaway-Car Driver) v. (Trial Court)
3 Cal. 3d 578, 477 P.2d 131 (Cal. 1970)

M E M O R Y   G R A P H I C

 Instant Facts

Getaway-car driver is charged with the murder of his accomplice in a liquor-store robbery although it was the store owner who killed the accomplice and the felony murder doctrine could not be invoked.

Black Letter Rule

Although the felony murder rule cannot be invoked in a case where a felon is charged with the murder of his accomplice after the accomplice was killed by the victim of the felony, the reckless malice standard can be invoked to convict the felon of murder.

Case Vocabulary

INFORMATION: An accusation, sometimes called a complaint or affidavit, that has the effect of bringing the defendant to trial or arraignment.

WRIT OF PROHIBITION: A writ that prevents a court from exercising jurisdiction or exceeding jurisdiction over a case where it does not have jurisdiction.

Procedural Basis: Appeal to the California Supreme Court of trial court's denial of motion set aside the information as to murder in a felony murder case.

Facts: On the evening of January 12, 1969, two men attempted the armed robbery of Jax Liquor Store, which was owned by Linda Lee West and her husband, Jack. James Daniels (D2) entered the store first and asked Mr. West, who was behind the counter, for a pack of cigarettes. Then John Smith entered the store. Mrs. West was standing on a ladder at the back of the store, when she overheard Daniels (D2) order Mr. West to "Put the money in the bag" and observed her husband complying. Daniels (D2) repeatedly told Mr. West that he and Smith were armed and according to Mrs. West, Daniels (D2) "chattered insanely" throughout the robbery. Smith pointed a gun at Mr. West's head throughout the robbery. While Daniels (D2) forced Mr. West to the floor, Mrs. West pulled out a gun and started shooting. She hit Smith in the chest, and Smith returned fire, hitting the wall behind Mrs. West. She also hit Daniels (D2) as he was running to the door, but he kept running. Meanwhile, Mr. West picked up a gun and fired two shots at Smith. Smith died as a result of the gunshot wounds. Taylor (D1) had been sitting outside the store in the getaway car. He was arrested later and connected to the robbery by bills he had been using and by the car, which a witness had observed leaving the scene. Taylor (D1) and Daniels (D2) were charged by information of the murder of John Smith and of robbery and two counts of assault with a deadly weapon. Taylor (D1) moved to set aside the information as to murder and his motion was denied.

Issue: Can the felony murder rule be invoked in a case where a felon is charged with the murder of his accomplice after the accomplice was killed by the victim of the felony?

Decision and Rationale: (Burke, J.) No. The felony murder rule cannot be invoked in a case where a felon is charged with the murder of his accomplice after the accomplice was killed by the victim of the felony. However, the reckless malice standard can be invoked to convict the felon of murder. Under the California Penal Code, an information must be set aside if the defendant has been committed without reasonable or probable cause. The test to determine probable cause is not the same one that is applied during a trial before a jury. A magistrate conducting a preliminary examination, as in this case, need only be convinced of facts that would lead a man of ordinary prudence and caution to believe and conscientiously entertain a strong suspicion of guilt. Under California law, the felony murder doctrine is an exception to the requirement that in order to show that a defendant is guilty of murder the prosecution has to show that he intended to kill or intended to act with a conscious disregard for human life in such a way that the death of another is likely. Taylor (D1) is correct in arguing that he cannot be guilty of felony murder because when a killing is committed by the victim of a robbery, rather than by one of the robbers, malice aforethought is not attributable to the robber as the robber has not killed a person in the perpetration of the robbery. However, although Taylor (D1) cannot be found guilty under the doctrine of felony murder, he could be found guilty of murder under a theory of vicarious liability. Under this theory, adopted in a previous case in California, if Taylor (D1) is found to have been an accomplice to the robbery, he would be vicariously responsible for any homicide caused by the intentional actions of his associates, if these actions were likely to result in homicide and were committed with conscious disregard for human life. The central inquiry in determining whether a felon is criminally liable for a homicide committed by a resisting victim is whether the conduct of the defendant or his accomplice was sufficiently provocative of lethal resistance that it demonstrates implied malice aforethought. In a previous case, the California Supreme Court held that if a defendant initiates a gun battle and his victim resists and kills someone, the defendant may be found guilty of murder. In such a case, the prosecution does not have to show malice by invoking the felony murder rule because the defendant's actions show a disregard for human life. A gun battle is not necessarily initiated by the person who fires the first shot. "Aggressive actions" may be enough to support a finding of malice. In this case, the record shows that Daniels (D2) and Smith committed acts of provocation that suffice to show malice. Daniels' (D2) repeated threats and Smith's pointing a gun at Mr. West were sufficiently provocative to lead an ordinarily prudent man to conclude that a gun battle had been initiated. The evidence supports the magistrate's finding that probable cause exists. Judgment affirmed.

Dissent: (Peters, J.) The Gun-Battle case can be distinguished from the present case. In the Gun-Battle Case, the defendant was an accomplice to a robbery where the victim shot and killed the other robber. The decedent robber had pointed a gun directly at the robbery victim, and yet the court held that the defendant-accomplice could not be convicted of the decedent-robber's murder because the defendant had not initiated a gun battle with the victim. In other words, the defendant was not guilty because his dead accomplice had not fired first. The majority in this case suggests that while pointing a gun at a robbery victim is not sufficient provocation to constitute the initiation of a gun battle, making threats is sufficient provocation. This is an unreasonable evisceration of the principle articulated in the Gun-Battle case.

Analysis:

This case allows felons to be convicted of felony murder without requiring the prosecution to invoke the narrowly applied felony murder rule. The court here actually widens the felony murder rule by extending the doctrine of malice based on reckless conduct to situations involving felons whose accomplices are killed by victims provoked by the robbers' actions. This is a problematic ruling because it makes guilt dependent on the actions of the homicide victim. In other words, under *Taylor*, when a felon is killed by his victim because the felon "asked for it," the victim is not guilty of manslaughter, but the felon's accomplices are. The felon's accomplices are guilty even when they had no control over the provocative actions of the felon. This doctrine allows civil tort theories to be applied in criminal law, bringing with them all the problems of proof and subjectivity associated with tort law. In each case, the jury will be asked to determine what is provocative activity. This is an especially difficult determination to make after the fact, and the difficulty may be compounded by the fact that in cases like *Taylor*, the killer is referred to as the "victim" and the homicide victim referred to as the "decedent accomplice."

Gregg v. Georgia

(Armed Robber) v. (State of Georgia)

428 U.S. 153 (1976)

M E M O R Y   G R A P H I C

Instant Facts

A man convicted of two counts of murder and sentenced to death appeals the sentence to the U.S. Supreme Court on the grounds that the death penalty is a violation of the 8th and 14th Amendments.

Black Letter Rule

The death penalty cannot be held to be a "cruel and unusual punishment" in violation of the 8th and 14th Amendments until society has determined that it is an unacceptably inhumane and disproportionate form of punishment.

Case Vocabulary

PER SE: Latin for "by itself." A "per se" violation is one that can be determined to be a violation in and of itself, with no need to examine other circumstances.

WRIT OF CERTIORARI: A writ directing that a case be remanded to a higher court.

Procedural Basis: Writ of certiorari to the United States Supreme Court of a sentence of death for two counts of murder.

Facts: Gregg (D) was convicted by a jury of two counts of armed robbery and two counts of murder. After the verdicts, a penalty hearing was held before the same jury. The jury imposed the death penalty for all counts of armed robbery and murder. The Georgia Supreme Court set aside the death sentences imposed for the counts of armed robbery because capital punishment had rarely been awarded in that state for armed robbery. The Georgia Supreme Court affirmed the death sentences imposed for the murder counts.

Issue: Does the death penalty violate the 8th and 14th Amendments?

Decision and Rationale: (Justice Stewart) No. The death penalty does not violate the 8th Amendment's prohibition of "cruel and unusual punishment." The meaning of the language of the 8th Amendment changes over time as society's values change. However, the Court must consider other factors besides the public perception of the death penalty. A criminal penalty must be in accordance with the "dignity of man," which means that it cannot be "excessive." In order to decide whether a punishment is excessive the Court must determine whether the punishment involves the unnecessary and wanton infliction of pain. The Court must also determine whether the punishment is grossly out of proportion with the crime. At the same time, it is important that the Court remember that assigning penalties to crimes is primarily a legislature's job and courts must presume that the punishment assigned by a democratically-elected legislature is valid. History and precedent support a finding that the death penalty does not violate the 8th and 14th Amendments. The Framers of the Constitution accepted the existence of capital punishment and throughout its history, the Supreme Court has consistently found that the death penalty is not a per se violation of the 8th Amendment. Gregg (D) argues that the current standards of decency have evolved to the point where society no longer sees death as an acceptable form of punishment. Gregg (D) is mistaken. American society still regards capital punishment as an appropriate and necessary form of punishment. This is demonstrated by the fact that in response to a previous Supreme Court case holding that the death penalty as administered in that case did violate the 8th Amendment, 35 states passed legislation providing for the death penalty in homicide cases. Congress also passed a law extending the death penalty to cases where the hijacking of aircraft leads to homicide. The fact that juries rarely impose the death penalty does not necessarily mean that Americans are opposed to capital punishment. It may just mean that juries wish to reserve the death penalty for the most extreme cases. But in order to be valid under the 8th Amendment, the death penalty must be both acceptable to American society and in accordance with the "dignity of man." This concept of human dignity is the core of the amendment and forbids inhumane punishment that is totally out of proportion with the crime committed. The death penalty serves two major social purposes: retribution and deterrence. Capital punishment is supposed to serve as an outlet for society's outrage at violent crime in order to prevent victims from taking the law into their own hands. In this way, capital punishment adds stability to the legal system by allowing victims to believe that they can obtain through the legal system adequate redress for their injuries. The value of the death penalty as a deterrent is less clear, and it is up to the legislatures to resolve this issue. The final inquiry in the "dignity of man" analysis is whether the death penalty is grossly out of proportion to the crime for which it is imposed. Death is a severe and irrevocable punishment, but when it is imposed for the crime of murder, it does not seem to be out of proportion to the severe and irrevocable crime committed. A final issue is whether the risk that juries could impose the death penalty in an arbitrary and capricious way makes the death penalty unconstitutional. Jury sentencing is important in capital cases because it maintains a link between a community's values and the legal system. But jury sentencing is problematic because information that is relevant to sentencing is often information that would be considered prejudicial for the purposes of the guilt phase of the trial. State legislatures could solve this problem by drafting legislation that would have the effect of separating the guilt phase from the sentencing phase of capital trials and of allowing the state to present to the jury the factors of the crime and of the defendant that the state deems relevant to the sentencing decision. Georgia's capital punishment statute extends the death penalty to anyone convicted of murder. It also provides a limitation that narrows the class of convicted murderers eligible for the death penalty to those who are found guilty beyond reasonable doubt of one of 10 specified aggravating circumstances. A statutory mitigating circumstance must be found before a jury can impose the death penalty. Automatic appeal to the Georgia Supreme Court is allowed as an additional guard against the arbitrariness and caprice of the jury. Gregg (D) argues that the fact that the state allows for several discretionary stages during the pre-trial and trial process, such as plea bargaining and allowing the jury to choose to convict a defendant of a lesser offense, creates arbitrary and capricious outcomes. However, there is no precedent that suggests that it is unconstitutional for an actor in the criminal justice system to make a decision that effectively removes a defendant from consideration as a candidate for the death penalty. The Georgia death penalty statute does not violate the Constitution. Judgment affirmed.

Dissent: (Justice Marshall) The constitutionality of the death penalty depends on the opinion of an informed citizenry. The fact is that the American people are for the most part unaware of the information necessary for a true understanding of the morality of the death penalty. Capital punishment is not an adequate deterrent. There is also no evidence that the death penalty does more that life imprisonment to prevent people from taking the law into their own hands.

Analysis:

This case represents a constitutional challenge to the death penalty in general and to the provisions in the Georgia death penalty statute that allow the jury to consider specific aggravating circumstances in determining whether to sentence a convicted murderer to death. The consideration of these aggravating circumstances has the effect of creating a new degree of murder. There is first-degree murder, which involves killing with malice aforethought, and then there is capital murder, which involves first degree murder plus an aggravating circumstance. Gregg (D) argued first that the death penalty itself is unconstitutional as a "cruel and unusual punishment" and second that the Georgia death penalty statute is unconstitutional because it allows juries too much discretion in deciding whether to impose the sentence. It also allows other actors in the criminal justice system too much discretion. If a crime is so severe that the only way to prevent society from rejecting the rule of law and lapsing into anarchy is to sentence the criminal to death, then why allow a prosecutor to plea bargain with the criminal and let him get away with a lesser sentence? Why allow a jury to choose to convict the criminal of second-degree murder instead of capital murder? Why allow a governor to pardon a convict on death row? The Supreme Court's answer to these arguments is not particularly clear, because instead of addressing these arguments directly the Court merely states that no Supreme Court case has ever held that extending mercy to a defendant is unconstitutional. What the Court is really doing here is refusing to allow its own conception of the "dignity of man" to override those of the individual states. By refusing to invalidate Georgia's death penalty statute, the Court is staying above the fray and allowing the American people to resolve the death penalty debate through the democratic process. When American society decides that the death penalty is an unacceptable form of punishment, we can legislate it out of existence. In the long run, the Court's decision is probably a good one. It allows the definition of "cruel and unusual" to truly change over time as society's views change rather than giving it one, precedential definition developed by nine unelected justices. Georgia's statute can continue to serve Georgia's needs. The discretionary aspects that Gregg (D) sees as inconsistent with the Constitution may actually serve Georgia well. Juries are allowed the flexibility to reserve the death penalty for crimes that especially outrage their communities and prosecutors are allowed to use the penalty as a bargaining chip.

McCleskey v. Kemp

(Black Convict) v. (Prison Superintendent)
481 U.S. 279 (1987)

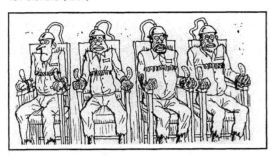

M E M O R Y   G R A P H I C

Instant Facts

A man convicted of murder petitioned for a writ of habeas corpus in federal court, where he used a statistical study to assert that the state's capital sentencing procedure has an unconstitutional disproportionate impact on blacks.

Black Letter Rule

A death penalty statute cannot be found to be an unconstitutional violation of the 8th Amendment and the Equal Protection clause on the basis of a study showing that the statute has a disproportionate impact on blacks.

Case Vocabulary

WRIT OF HABEAS CORPUS: A writ intended to release a person from unjust imprisonment.

Procedural Basis: Challenge in the United States Supreme Court of the denial of a writ of habeas corpus.

Facts: McCleskey (D), a black man, was convicted of two counts of armed robbery and one count of murder in the Superior Court of Fulton County, Georgia on October 12, 1978. McCleskey (D) had planned the armed robbery of a furniture store with three accomplices. During the robbery, a police officer entered the store in response to a silent alarm. The officer was shot twice and killed. The officer was white. At least one of the bullets had been fired by McCleskey (D). McCleskey (D) was convicted of murder and the jury found beyond a reasonable doubt that McCleskey's armed robbery and the fact that he killed a police officer constituted two aggravating circumstances that justified the jury's imposing the death penalty. McCleskey (D) did not offer any evidence that would allow the jury to mitigate the sentence. The Georgia Supreme Court affirmed the convictions and the death sentence. After the state court challenges to the sentence, McCleskey (D) filed a petition for a writ of habeas corpus in the Federal District Court for the Northern District of Georgia. His petition raised several claims, one of which was that the Georgia capital sentencing process has a disproportionate impact on blacks, in violation of the 8th and 14th Amendments. To support his argument, McCleskey (D) produced a study by Professors Baldus, Woodworth, and Pulaski ("Baldus Study") that shows the disparity in the imposition of the death penalty in Georgia on the basis of the race of the murder victim, and to a lesser extent, the race of the defendant. According to the Baldus Study, the death penalty is imposed more often when the victims are white than when the victims are black, and more often when the defendants are black than when the defendants are white. The Baldus Study also demonstrates that the death penalty is imposed more often when the defendant is black and the victim white than when the defendant is white and the victim black. The District Court found that the Baldus Study was flawed in its methodology and dismissed McCleskey's (D) petition for a writ of habeas corpus. The Court of Appeals affirmed.

Issue: Can a statistical study showing that capital punishment has a disproportionate impact on blacks prove that a death sentence is unconstitutional under the Equal Protection Clause of the 14th Amendment or under the 8th Amendment?

Decision and Rationale: (Justice Powell) No. McCleskey's (D) first argument is that the fact that the Georgia death penalty statute has a disproportionate impact on blacks means that he was unconstitutionally discriminated against based on his race and the race of his victim. In order to prevail under the Equal Protection clause, McCleskey (D) must show that he was the victim of purposeful discrimination. He does not offer evidence that shows that he was the particular victim of anyone's purposeful discrimination. Instead, he relies only on the Baldus Study, and argues that the study proves discrimination that would extend to all capital cases involving a white victim and a black defendant in Georgia, including his. The United States Supreme Court requires clear proof that a state court has abused its discretion in order to reverse its decision. The Baldus Study does not constitute clear proof that any of the decision makers in his case acted with purposeful discrimination. McCleskey (D) argues that the state as a whole is guilty of acting with discriminatory purpose in allowing the capital punishment statute to remain in effect in spite of the disproportionate impact it has on black defendants. In order to prevail on this claim, McCleskey (D) must show that the Georgia legislature enacted or maintained the death penalty statute because it anticipated that the statute would have a discriminatory impact. This court found in *Gregg* that the Georgia death penalty statute can operate in a fair manner, and McCleskey (D) has produced no evidence that would lead the Court to change its mind. McCleskey's second argument is that the Baldus Study proves that Georgia's death penalty statute violates the 8th Amendment. This violation is made possible by the fact that the statute allows decision makers too much discretion in choosing whether the death penalty will be imposed in a particular case. However, discretion is an important feature of the American criminal justice system and works to the advantage of defendants as well as the state. The Baldus Study does not evidence the kind of invidious discrimination that would outweigh the advantages of discretion. Two policy concerns influence the Court's decision in this case. One is that to allow McCleskey (D) to prevail on his arguments would be to cast doubt on the principles that underlie the American criminal justice system. The 8th Amendment applies to all punishments, and to allow McCleskey (D) to prevail would open the doors to a flood of litigation on the subject of disproportionate racial impacts in all forms of punishments. This litigation could be extended to cases where punishments have a disproportionate impact on other minorities or on gender, or even on arbitrary variables such as facial characteristics. There is no limiting principle to McCleskey's (D) argument. The second policy concern is that McCleskey's (D) style of argument, reliant on statistical research, is best presented to a state legislature. Legislatures are better qualified than courts to weigh studies against each other and consider an issue from all angles before taking law-making action. Judgment affirmed.

Dissent: (Brennan) The fact that McCleskey (D) cannot prove the influence his race had on the sentencing process in his case is irrelevant to his 8th Amendment claim. This Court, in analyzing an 8th Amendment claim, does not concern itself with whether or not an arbitrary sentence has been imposed, but with the risk that the death penalty might be imposed arbitrarily. The emphasis the Court places on risk suggests that the Court is concerned with the rationality of the capital punishment system as a whole. The Baldus Study shows conclusively that jury discretion leads to racially discriminate outcomes. The study is backed up by Georgia's long history of racism and its historically race-conscious criminal justice system. The majority's policy arguments ignore the particular repugnance the justice system feels for racism and the fact that minorities and convicts have weak voices in state legislatures.

Dissent: (Blackmun) Under past Court decisions, a defendant can establish a prima facie case of discrimination by showing that "the totality of the relevant facts gives rise to an inference of discriminatory purpose." From then on the burden shifts to the prosecution to show that there was no such purpose. McCleskey (D) has shown that he was more likely than not the victim of racial discrimination. The majority's insistence that procedural safeguards protected McCleskey (D) from discrimination ignores the fact that there were no such safeguards.

Dissent: (Stevens) The sort of disparity described in the Baldus Study is constitutionally unacceptable. It violates the Court's usual standard that the death penalty must be imposed fairly and consistently or not at all. The majority's fear that allowing McCleskey (D) to prevail would effectively eliminate the death penalty in Georgia is misplaced. There are according to the Baldus Study serious crimes for which the death penalty is consistently applied in Georgia regardless of the race of the victim or defendant. Georgia should narrow its death penalty statute to cover only these crimes.

Analysis:

In reading this case it is important to take note of the findings of the study and in doing so to understand that race still plays a significant role within the system. If you walk into any criminal court in a major city in the United States you will see that minority groups are seriously over-represented as defendants, while they are seriously under-represented as judges, lawyers, clerks and bailiffs. (Admittedly some progress has been made with court personnel, but the majority remain white.) [If you really want to get honest, take a look at the racial mix of the classroom when you take this class and consider whether race made a difference in getting you here.] All of the justices in this case acknowledge that the system is inevitably imperfect, that discrepancies will exist. This is a tacit admission that race will always play a role. The question thus becomes, is this an acceptable way to administer the death penalty? Some level of imperfection will have to be accepted in the criminal justice system as a whole because we have to have a criminal justice system, and it has to be run by fallible human beings. We do not have to have a death penalty. The court split five-to-four on this case. After his retirement Justice Powell indicated that he regretted his vote and his opinion in this case. If he had changed his vote at the time, what is currently the dissent would have been the law of the land. This is still a very relevant issue.

Chapter 6

This Chapter looks at the significance of resulting harm. There are two areas of study, *causation* and *attempt*.

Causation determines whether the resulting harm to the victim should be attributed to the defendant. If the defendant points a gun at his victim and shoots, there is really no issue whether the defendant *caused* the victim to be shot. Life however is not always that simple! Suppose the defendant flees from the police in a car and drives like a maniac on the highways and byways. He speeds, runs red lights, travels down the wrong side of roads, and runs over anything in his path in an effort to escape from the police cars chasing him. If he causes a collision with another vehicle and persons in that vehicle are injured or killed, there is still no issue whether the defendant *caused* the collision and resulting injury.

However, suppose there are two police helicopters flying above the defendant's car to make sure he doesn't get away. What happens if one of the pilots flies the helicopter *negligently* and causes the two helicopters to crash, killing people in the helicopters? Is the defendant guilty of murder? Would it matter if one of the helicopters crashed because of a mechanical defect? Suppose the defendant is an experienced purse snatcher. He approaches a woman from behind, grabs her purse and runs away. The woman is so scared that she drops dead of a heart attack. Is the defendant guilty of murder?

Suppose the woman survives the heart attack but needs open heart surgery to prevent future heart attacks. The doctor is incompetent and she dies on the operating table. Is the defendant guilty of murder?

Suppose that the woman who was robbed did not have a heart attack, but was so mentally distraught and fearful of being attacked again that she decided to commit suicide. Is the defendant guilty of murder? Suppose the woman tries to get away from the defendant and runs into the street and is hit by a car and killed. Is the defendant guilty of murder?

You must learn the law of causation to find the answers. And, don't just assume common sense will work! The law of attempt is even more mystifying. Issues arise concerning the elements of the underlying crime attempted, and whether the conduct reaches the point where it can be considered a criminal attempt.

Thank goodness bad thoughts do not constitute a crime; otherwise some of you would be in big trouble! For those of you with bad thoughts, you better not "act" on those thoughts since some acts will make you guilty of "attempt."

One of the big issues in attempt cases is whether the defendant's act has gone far enough to constitute criminal attempt. Thank goodness also that that law generally gives one the opportunity to repent, otherwise known as "locus penitentiae." If ever arrested, just say, "But I locus penitentiae."

It's also important to remember that if you ever buy a box of matches with intent to burn a haystack, it is not an attempt to commit arson. But if you take the matches to the haystack, light one, and then blow it out, you are guilty of attempted arson.

Watch out too if you are thinking about robbing a bank. If you drive around and around the bank with guns and handcuffs in your car, you might be in big trouble if the police stop you. If you are really stupid, and are driving around what you think is a bank, but it really is the court house, the law of attempt will determine whether or not you are guilty.

Finally, if you are a big chicken and solicit another to rob the bank, you may be guilty of attempt depending upon what else you do. Then again, your fate may depend upon in what state you committed the acts.

Chapter 6

NOTE: THE PURPOSE OF THIS OUTLINE IS TO ORGANIZE THE CASES SO THAT ONE CAN QUICKLY UNDERSTAND THE RELEVANCE OF EACH CASE TO THE COURSE. NO ATTEMPT IS MADE IN THIS OVERVIEW TO ADDRESS EVERY CONCEPT THAT MUST BE STUDIED. BE SURE TO READ THE ENTIRE CASEBOOK AND/OR OTHER MATERIALS TO GAIN A FULL UNDERSTANDING OF ALL CONCEPTS.

I. Causation
  A. Causation is an element of certain crimes such as homicide. To establish causation, it must be determined whether the defendant's act caused the harm to the victim. Causation becomes an issue when the harm to the victim is not intended and occurs in an unlikely way, or when the harm is intended but occurs in a way not intended.
  B. Foreseeability and Coincidence:
    1. The threshold question in examining causation is: But for the defendant's act would the injury have occurred?
      a. Proximate cause is an artificial line drawn by courts to separate those results for which a defendant is liable from those for which he is not responsible.
      b. Common sense as to the natural order of events is the principle that guides the determination of whether proximate cause exists in any particular case.
    2. Independent Intervening Cause
      a. When the defendant's conduct places the victim in a position which allows some other action to cause the harm, the other action is an independent intervening cause. If the possibility of some harm of the kind that might result from the defendant's conduct was reasonably foreseeable, the independent intervening cause will not supersede the defendant's conduct. *People v. Acosta.*
        (1) In *Acosta*, a fleeing criminal suspect was pursued by police in a 48 mile car chase, and the two police helicopters assisting in the chase collided and killed three people. Acosta was charged with murder. The court held that proximate cause existed, even with intervening negligence and

recklessness on the part of one helicopter pilot, since harm from Acosta's conduct was a possible consequence which reasonably might have been contemplated.
        (2) The court held that the helicopter collision was a possible consequence which might have been contemplated, even though there was no evidence that such a thing had occurred before.
      b. An independent intervening factor that contributes to the harm to the victim does not break the causal link in the chain of events that must exist between the defendant's conduct and the resulting harm. Thus, the defendant's conduct need not be the sole and exclusive factor in the harm to the victim. If a defendant's conduct is a sufficiently direct cause of the harm and if the ultimate harm is something which should have been foreseen as being reasonably related to the acts of the defendant, causation exists. *People v. Arzon.*
        (1) In *Arzon*, a fireman died from fighting fire in a building with two fires, only one of which was set by the accused murderer, Arzon. The court held that it was irrelevant that there was an intervening fire on the second floor which contributed to the conditions that resulted in the death of the fireman.
        (2) The fact that it was foreseeable that firemen would respond to the fire, thereby exposing them and others to life-threatening danger, caused the fire set by Arzon to be an indispensable link in the chain of events that resulted in the death.
      c. The conduct of the defendant must be a sufficiently direct cause of the death and this standard is greater than that required for tort liability; merely exposing the victim to a possible risk of harm is not enough. *People v. Warner-Lambert Co.*
        (1) The court in *Warner-Lambert* set a bright-line rule for determining when a defendant's negligence or recklessness constitutes a "sufficiently direct cause," holding

that the defendant must have foreseen the immediate, triggering cause of the harm.

  (a) When an explosion killed several factory workers, the corporate officers were not held liable for negligent homicide for knowingly exposing employees to a risk of explosion because the precise cause, or "trigger," of the explosion was unknown.

  (b) However, in the "Twilight Zone—The Movie" case the specific causal mechanism of a fatal helicopter crash was not relevant. A helicopter crashed during the filming of a movie killing a famous actor and two children on the ground below. The court held that the precise cause of the crash was irrelevant, and what was determinative was whether the risk of death was reasonably foreseeable.

d. Vulnerability of the Victim

  (1) It is said that the defendant takes his victim as he finds him. Thus, a robber was held guilty of murder where the victim suffered a fatal heart attack triggered by fright during the robbery. *People v. Stamp.*

  (2) A defendant that severely beat an elderly woman was convicted for murder even though the cause of death was choking while eating. The advanced age of the victim caused difficulty in the healing process and she was unable to eat normal food because of pain from the injuries. The choking occurred while eating pureed food. The court held that the defendant takes his victim as he finds him and does not have to foresee death from asphyxiation. *People v. Brackett.*

e. Negligent Medical Treatment

  (1) If a defendant inflicts a serious wound upon another, calculated to destroy or endanger the person's life, there is criminal responsibility even if the victim dies because of improper medical treatment. *Hall v. State.*

  (2) However, if the improper medical treatment is so extraordinary or egregious as to

be regarded as acts independent of the conduct of the defendant, it will break the chain of causation. *Regina v. Cheshire and Regina v. Jordan. Notes on Foreseeability.*

f. When there is failure to act so as to prevent the harm to the victim, an issue of causation by omission exits. The law usually provides that omissions cannot be a basis of criminal liability, unless there is a duty to act. *Note on Omissions As Causes.*

g. The doctrine of transferred intent provides that if one intends to harm another and for some reason harms someone else, the intent to harm the intended victim is transferred to the unintended victim.

  (1) For example, where A fires a gun intending to kill B, but hits C due to poor aim, A's intent to kill B will be "transferred" to the killing of C.

C. Subsequent Human Actions

1. The phrase "Subsequent Human Actions" refers to conduct on the part of another, generally the victim, that follows the defendant's actions and somehow changes what would have been the "natural" result of the defendant's act.

2. Subsequent Actions Intended to Produce the Result

a. As a general rule, intentional subsequent human action breaks the chain of causation, even if such human action was completely foreseeable by the defendant.

  (1) Thus, it was wrong to charge a defendant with murder where he gave his gun to another person, encouraged the person to use it to kill himself, and the person did commit suicide. *People v. Campbell.*

  (2) Because intentional and independent human action suffices to break the causal link, an assisted suicide is not murder unless a statute specifically provides so. *People v. Kevorkian.*

b. If there is intentional subsequent action then Foreseeability is not applicable.

  (1) The reasoning is that human actions are different from those events that happen regularly and necessarily in accordance with the laws of nature, which is the basis of the principle of causation.

(2) Intentional subsequent human actions are not natural results of a chain of events governed by the laws of nature. This is because nothing causes a person to act, rather the person chooses to act on his own free will. *Note On Intervening Human Actions.*

c. Exceptions

(1) Only voluntary or intentional subsequent human actions are outside the laws of causation. Subsequent human action by the victim does not break the chain of causation where the victim is rendered *irresponsible* by the defendant's conduct.

(a) This is so because the actions on the part of the victim are not truly intentional since the victim is rendered irresponsible by being mentally and physically wounded by the defendant.

(b) Where a female victim of sexual assault attempted suicide, but did not immediately die therefrom, causation existed to hold the defendant responsible for her subsequent death from complications. Her state of mind which caused her to ingest poison was the natural and probable consequence of the defendant's horrific conduct.

(2) Thus, causation may exit where the victim's otherwise voluntary or intentional act is rendered *irresponsible* due to the defendant's conduct. *Stephenson v. State.*

(a) However, if a person commits suicide after losing all his money to a criminal swindler, the swindler is not guilty of homicide because the victim was not rendered irresponsible merely from the loss of money. If the intervening actor is insane it will not break the causal connection between the defendant's act and the harm. *Comment on Stephenson.*

3. Subsequent Actions That Recklessly Risk the Result

a. Subsequent human actions that recklessly risk resulting harm break the chain of causation.

(1) Thus, if an actor chooses to engage in subsequent actions that recklessly risk

harm to the actor, the chain of causation will be broken and the defendant will not be criminally responsible for any harm to the actor.

(2) Thus, where two drag racers were racing along a highway and the deceased attempted to pass the defendant's car by driving on the wrong side of the road and was hit by an oncoming truck and died, the defendant was not guilty of manslaughter.

(3) In other words, the actor chose to do what he did and suffered the consequences. *Commonwealth v. Root.*

b. However, where an actor is forced to take action that is a reckless risk to his safety because of fear for his life due to the defendant's assaulting conduct, the defendant is responsible for the actor's death from other intervening forces. *People v. Kern.*

4. Subsequent human actions that recklessly risk resulting harm do not break the chain of causation where the acts of both the defendant and the deceased work concurrently as the cause of the harm.

a. Thus, where one drag racer collided with another non-racing vehicle carrying a child passenger and killing both, the other drag racer was properly convicted of involuntary manslaughter. The deceased drag racer had lost control of his vehicle while racing, resulting in the collision with the vehicle in which the child was a passenger. The deceased and the defendant were acting concurrently, and both of their actions therefore resulted in the fatal collision. *State v. McFadden.*

b. Subsequent human actions that recklessly risk resulting harm do not break the chain of causation where the defendant encourages or cooperates in a joint activity with the victim which results in harm. Thus, where defendant and others played Russian Roulette resulting in the death of the decedent, the defendants were properly charged with involuntary manslaughter. The defendants' concerted action and cooperation brought about the end result. They had a duty not to cooperate or join with the decedent in the deadly game. *Commonwealth v. Atencio.*

c. However, where the defendant leaves the room and is unaware that the decedent is playing Russian Roulette, the defendant is not criminally responsible. *Lewis v. State. Notes and Questions.*

II. Attempt
  A. Introduction
    1. Most states have statutes making it a crime to attempt to commit a crime.
      a. A person is punished much less severely if the intentional attempt to cause harm proves unsuccessful.
    2. Commentators on criminal law have noted that where two people have the same intent to cause harm but for some reason only one actually succeeds in causing harm, the two will be punished differently.
      a. There is a natural "public feeling" to punish the one who actually has caused the harm more severely.
      b. This principle has been criticized since the only difference between the two persons is that one had "bad fortune" and the other "good luck" concerning the outcome of their intended action.
      c. One explanation for the more lenient treatment of attempts at crime is that the public desire for punishment is not aroused to the same degree when serious harm has been averted.
      d. The Model Penal Code's punishment for attempt is a grading system that provides for a reduced factor of the punishment of the crime that was attempted. Others have questioned whether or not in some cases one who attempts to commit a crime should be punished just as severely as one who completed the crime and caused harm.
  B. Mens Rea
    1. Specific intent – the crime of attempt requires a mental state, or mens rea, of an intent to commit the substantive crime, even if a lesser mental state than intent will suffice for conviction of the actual criminal offense attempted. *M.P.C. §5.01.*
      a. For example, attempted murder requires a specific intent to commit murder, even though a murder conviction may be obtained

where the defendant had a lesser mental state – e.g., a reckless disregard for human life.
      b. However, the Model Penal Code permits a defendant to be held liable for attempt for results obtained knowingly, if not intentionally.
      c. Most states have declined to extend attempt liability to reckless crimes on the ground that one cannot intend to commit a crime defined as having an unintended result.
        (1) Thus, because attempt requires a mental state of intent, many states hold that there cannot be an attempt to commit criminal negligence involuntary manslaughter, since involuntary manslaughter requires proof of gross negligence.
        (2) The specific intent to necessary for an attempt conviction may not be inferred where the defendant's conduct simply posed an increased, albeit significant, risk of death. *Smallwood v. State.*
        (a) In *Smallwood* the court held that a rapist infected with *HIV* could not be convicted of attempted murder because the risk of infection did not make death probable or likely.
  C. Preparation versus Attempt
    1. Generally, mere preparation to commit a crime, even if coupled with an intent, is not an attempt if further acts are required to complete the crime.
      a. There is no definite test to determine whether the defendant's act has gone far enough to constitute criminal attempt. It is however established that the first step along the way of criminal intent is not necessarily sufficient and the final step is not necessarily required. *The King v. Barker.*
      b. The law generally desires to preserve for the defendant an opportunity to repent, a "locus penitentiae."
        (1) However that opportunity is lost if a defendant goes too far. At common law, the defense of abandonment was denied.
        (2) However to minimize the potential for unfairness, the court may require the threshold of criminality to be placed very close to the last act, even though this may

result in no criminal responsibility for those defendants who almost certainly would not have repented. *Notes on Abandonment.*

2. The Traditional "Proximity" Approach
   a. Some courts have held that a defendant's conduct suffices for an attempt conviction where the defendant is "dangerously proximate" to the successful commission of the substantive crime. *People v. Rizzo.*
   b. In *Rizzo* the court held that the defendant's could not be found guilty of attempted robbery because they never found their victim, and therefore could not make any advance toward him.
3. Alternatives to the Proximity Approach
   a. Purely innocent conduct may constitute a criminal attempt if an intent to commit the crime is proved. *McQuirter v. State.*
   b. The Equivocality Test
      (1) One alternative to the "proximity" approach is to ask how clearly the defendant's conduct bespeaks of his intent to commit a crime. *King v. Barker.*
      (2) The equivocality test has also been termed the *res ipsa loquitur* test because the act itself is evidence of the defendant's intent.
   c. The Model Penal Code (M.P.C.) Approach or the "Substantial Step" Test
      (1) Conduct which constitutes a substantial step toward commission of the crime and is corroborative of the defendant's intent may suffice for an attempt conviction. *M.P.C. §5.01; United States v. Jackson.*
      (2) Many states use the substantial step test. Some states' statutes have modified or used significant variations on the M.P.C. test. *Note On Statutory Reform.*
      (3) Possible results under the M.P.C.
         (a) If a defendant sets a trap to induce a potential robbery victim, will that constitute an attempt under the Model Penal Code? *United States v. Harper.*
         (b) Under the M.P.C. was it proper for a federal court to uphold a conviction for attempted heroin distribution when all the defendant did was make unsuccessful phone calls at the insistence of an undercover agent? *United States v.*

Mandujano.
         (c) On the ground that the defendant had failed to take a substantial step toward the purchase of cocaine, the federal court reversed an attempt conviction because the defendant left the scene of the "deal" after negotiations were conducted but prior to purchasing the cocaine because the agent was uncooperative. *United States v. Joyce.*
            i. The court held that the defendant's motives for abandoning his effort were immaterial.
4. Preparatory behavior may be made criminal as substantive crimes where burglary and assault are involved.
   a. Although common law burglary required a breaking and entering at night with an intent to commit a felony inside, the offense has been enlarged through statutes and case law.
   b. Often now, the crime occurs when there is an entry, at any time, with intent to commit any crime.
   c. Criminal assault generally requires intent to commit a battery. Some modern statutes expand the crime so that deliberately placing another in fear of a battery is sufficient to convict, even if there is no intent to carry out the attack.
   d. The courts are divided on whether one may be convicted of an attempt to commit an assault.
5. The problem of stalking has developed in recent times. The criminal laws in existence in the past did not adequately protect a person from a stalker, nor was there sufficient punishment for the act. Accordingly, many states have now created anti-stalking legislation to combat the problem. *Notes on Stalking Statutes.*
6. Solicitation or Attempt?
   a. Merely soliciting one to commit a crime does not constitute an attempt; performance of some overt act toward the commission of the crime is required. *State v. Davis.*
      (1) In *Davis* it was held that the acts of having a verbal arrangement with one selected to kill, plus delivery of photographs, drawings and partial payment, are mere acts of

preparation which did not move directly toward the consummation of the crime.

(2) However, a conviction for attempted murder was upheld where the defendant obtained the services of a person to murder his wife, participated in planning the crime, advised the person exactly how he wanted his wife shot, and paid the consideration. *United States v. Church.*

(a) These acts were held to constitute a substantial step toward the commission of the crime because the defendant had done everything in his power, short of pulling to the trigger, to ensure the murder of his wife.

b. Courts differ on whether or not solicitation constitutes attempt. Some hold that a solicitation can constitute a punishable attempt if it represents a substantial step toward the commission of a crime, and others hold that no matter what acts the solicitor commits, there is no attempt because he does not intend to commit the offense personally. Many states have enacted statutes making solicitation a crime. *Notes on Solicitation.*

D. Impossibility

1. Legal impossibility can be a valid defense to the crime of attempt. It occurs in the situation where the defendant did everything he intended to do but yet had not completed the crime.

a. Thus, if he intends to commit a crime and mistakenly believes that his act will be a crime, but in fact it will not, there is no attempt. Therefore, where a person was convicted of attempt to receive stolen goods, believing them to have been stolen, when in fact they were not stolen, the conviction was error and was reversed on appeal. *People v. Jaffe.*

b. Another example of a case applying the legal impossibility defense is where a man has sex with a woman, not his wife, who he believes to be under the age of 18 years. If the woman is over the age of 18 years, there is no crime, even if the defendant believed her to be younger and intended to commit the crime.

2. Factual impossibility is not a defense to the

crime of attempt.

a. It occurs when the defendant intends to accomplish an offense, but is unable to bring about the result because of some circumstances unknown to him when he engaged in the attempt.

b. Examples of such cases include: Pick-pockets are convicted for attempt to commit larceny without the need to prove that there was anything in the pockets; and extortionists are convicted even though they do not know that their intended victim is a decoy for the police, and thus could not be induced with fear to pay money.

3. The Model Penal Code has abolished the defenses of factual and legal impossibility.

a. Many state statutes have also done away with these defenses to the crime of attempt.

b. However, to constitute an attempt, it is still necessary that the result intended by the defendant constitute a crime. It is the defendant's intent that should be the standard for determining criminal liability.

c. For instance, under these statutes and the code, a defendant would be guilty of attempted murder if he believes the intended victim was alive when he shot him, even though the intended victim may have already been dead when the defendant fired the shot. *People v. Dlugash.*

d. The justification for abolishing the defenses is that neither acts nor results alone constitute criminal behavior. *The Case of Lady Eldon.*

(1) Because acts become punishable only when they are committed with a certain intent, it matters not that the defendant would not have succeeded in achieving his intended result; all that matters is that the defendant did something with the requisite intent to commit a crime.

4. Impossibility in Federal Courts

a. The Third Circuit has permitted a defense of impossibility where the defendant intended to commit punishable conduct but the result of his conduct was not punishable due to circumstances unbeknownst to him. *United States v. Berrigan.*

(1) In *Berrigan* the court reversed a conviction

for attempting to smuggle letters in and out of prison with the knowledge and consent of the warden because, unknown to the prisoner, the warden had agreed that the courier should pretend to go along with the prisoner's plan.

b. The Fifth Circuit has taken a different approach to impossibility, focusing on the acts committed and whether they objectively imply an intent to commit a crime. *United States v. Oviedo*.

(1) The *Oviedo* court reversed a conviction for attempting to sell heroin because the substance actually sold was neither heroin or illegal.

(2) There could be no conclusion that the objective acts of the defendant, apart from indirect evidence of intent, marked his conduct as criminal.

People v. Acosta

(Government) v. (Car Chase Murderer)
(1991) 284 Cal.Rptr. 117

M E M O R Y   G R A P H I C

Instant Facts

Fleeing criminal suspect, Acosta (D), was pursued by police in a 48-mile car chase, and the two police helicopters assisting in the chase collided and killed three people.

Black Letter Rule

Proximate cause exists, even with intervening third party negligence and recklessness, if harm from defendant's conduct is a possible consequence which reasonably might have been contemplated.

Case Vocabulary

MALICE: Intending to do the crime without legal justification.
SINE QUA NON: Latin for "without which not."

Procedural Basis: Appeal of judgment following criminal conviction for murder.

Facts: Two police officers saw Acosta (D) in a stolen vehicle parked on the street. The officers approached Acosta (D) and identified themselves. He sped away and led the police on a 48-mile chase. During the chase, Acosta (D) engaged in egregious driving, running stop signs and red lights, and driving on the wrong side of the streets. [He was obviously guilty of something.] Police helicopters from two different cities assisted in tracking Acosta (D) during the chase. During the course of the chase, the helicopters collided with each other and crashed, killing three people in one of the helicopters. Acosta (D) was charged with second degree murder. An aviation expert testified at trial and opined that one of the helicopters violated certain FAA regulations prohibiting careless and reckless operation of an aircraft and operating the aircraft too close to another. Acosta (D) was convicted on three counts of second degree murder. He appeals contending that there was insufficient evidence that he was the proximate cause of the death of the occupants of the helicopter. Acosta (D) argues that it was not foreseeable that two helicopters would crash, and the pilot's own conduct in violation of the FAA regulations was a superseding cause. Acosta (D) also claims that there was insufficient evidence of malice.

Issue: Does proximate cause exist where there is intervening third party negligence and recklessness?

Decision and Rationale: (Wallin) Yes. Proximate cause may exist, even with intervening third party negligence and recklessness, if the harm from the defendant's conduct is a possible consequence which reasonably might have been contemplated. "Proximate cause" requires that an act be the actual cause of the injury. The test is but for the defendant's act would the injury have occurred? If not, it will not be considered a proximate cause. The issue in this case is whether or not the deaths of the helicopter pilots were foreseeable. The standard for determining proximate cause should be to exclude extraordinary results, and allow the trier of fact to determine the issue on the particular facts of the case using common sense. The appellate courts upon review must give due deference to the trier of facts. In this case, but for Acosta's (D) conduct of fleeing the police, the helicopters would never have been in position for the crash. Although a similar occurrence is not known to have occurred, it was a possible consequence which reasonably might have been contemplated. There is an appreciable probability that one may act recklessly or negligently in the heat of the chase. [It's hard to drive or fly within the speed limits when chasing a thief.] On the issue of malice, we find that there was not sufficient evidence to show that Acosta (D) consciously disregarded the risk to the helicopter pilots. Judgment is reversed.

Dissent: (Crosby) I do not believe the risk was foreseeable. The helicopters were not within the range of apprehension of a fleeing criminal on the ground, nor were they in the zone of danger. The manner and circumstances of the collision could not have been foreseen. This was a highly extraordinary result, and beyond the long arm of the criminal law.

Analysis:

This case examines the concept of an independent intervening cause. When the defendant's conduct places the victim in a position which allows some other action to cause the harm, the other action is an independent intervening cause. Often times, the independent intervening cause will supersede the defendant's act so as to preclude a finding of proximate cause. However, if the possibility of some harm of the kind which might result from the defendant's conduct was reasonably foreseeable, the independent intervening cause will not supersede the defendant's conduct. In this case, the majority held that the helicopter collision was a possible consequence which might have been contemplated, even though there was no evidence that such a thing had occurred before. The dissent on the other hand concluded that it was not foreseeable, and relied upon the law of foreseeability as used in civil law. In the Notes section that follows this case, there is a discussion of the "Twilight Zone" case where a helicopter crashed during the filming of a movie killing a famous actor and two children. The court held that the precise cause of the crash was irrelevant, and what was determinative was whether the risk of death was reasonably foreseeable. Similarly, in this case, Acosta (D) should have foreseen that his dangerous driving during the police chase could result in others acting in a negligent or reckless manner and causing injury or death. The collision of the helicopters, although not as possible a consequence as vehicles colliding on the road, was nevertheless something that could be contemplated.

People v. Arzon

(Government) v. (Arsonist)
(1978) 92 Misc.2d 739, 401 N.Y.S.2d 156

M E M O R Y   G R A P H I C

Instant Facts

Fireman died from fighting fire in building with two fires, only one of which was set by the accused murderer, Arzon (D).

Black Letter Rule

A defendant's conduct need not be the sole and exclusive factor in the victim's harm in order to maintain the necessary causal link between the conduct and the resulting harm.

Case Vocabulary

CAUSAL LINK: Connecting a certain chain of events without break or interruption.
INDICTED: Being charged with a crime.
INDICTMENT: Document whereby Grand Jury recommends charging one with a crime.
MOTION TO DISMISS: Challenging the right of the court to entertain the matter on various legal theories.

Procedural Basis: Motion to dismiss grand jury indictment charging criminal conduct.

Facts: Arzon (D) was indicted for two counts of second degree murder after he allegedly intentionally set a fire to a couch on the fifth floor of an abandoned building. A fireman died after sustaining injuries while attempting to control the fire. The fire attributed to Arzon (D) burned the fifth and sixth floors. An independent fire also broke out at the same time on the second floor, but there was no evidence that Arzon (D) was responsible for this arsonist started fire. The charge of murder in the second degree was based upon having, "under circumstances evincing depraved indifference to human life, recklessly engaged in conduct which created a grave risk of death to another person." The smoke from the two fires contributed to the fireman's inability to safely remove himself from the burning building. Arzon (D) [desperately wanting to place blame on the unknown arsonist] argued that there was insufficient evidence to support the charge in that the causal link between the crime and death was missing.

Issue: Must the defendant's conduct be the sole and exclusive factor in the victim's harm in order to maintain the necessary causal link between the conduct and the resulting harm?

Decision and Rationale: (Milonas) No. The defendant's conduct need not be the sole and exclusive factor in the victim's harm. If the conduct of a defendant is a sufficiently direct cause of the victim's death, it is not necessary that the ultimate harm be intended by a defendant. Thus, if an intoxicated robbery victim is abandoned by the side of the road by the thieves and is hit by a truck and dies, there is a causal link in that the ultimate harm is something which should have been foreseen as being reasonably related to the acts of the accused. [In other words, dumping a passed-out person on the side of the road is not a smart thing to do!] However, an obscure or merely probable connection between a defendant's conduct and another person's death is not enough to support a charge of homicide. Thus, if a stabbing victim is operated on for the wound inflicted by the defendant, but the victim dies from an unrelated hernia procedure performed by the surgeon after treating the stab wound, there is no causal link between the crime and the death. [The victim must now sue the doctor.] It is not required that the defendant's conduct be the sole and exclusive factor in the victim's death. If a defendant's conduct was a sufficiently direct cause of the harm and if the ultimate harm is something which should have been foreseen as being reasonably related to the acts of the defendant, this will suffice to establish criminal liability. In this case, it is irrelevant that there was an intervening fire on the second floor which contributed to the conditions that resulted in the death of the fireman. It was certainly foreseeable that firemen would respond to the situation, thereby exposing them and others to life-threatening danger. The fire set by Arzon (D) was an indispensable link in the chain of events that resulted in the death. Motion to dismiss the murder counts of the indictment is denied.

Analysis:

This case examines intervening conduct that contributes to the death of the victim. Two things should be noted about the specific intervening conduct in this case, one, it contributed to the death, and two, it is criminal conduct as opposed to civil conduct. The primary holding of the case is that the defendant's conduct need not be the sole and exclusive factor in the victim's death. Even if intervening conduct contributes to the death, there will still be criminal responsibility if the defendant's conduct was a direct cause of the harm and the ultimate harm is something foreseen as being related to the conduct of the defendant. In the previous case, *People v. Acosta*, the intervening conduct was in the form of civil negligence or recklessness. In this case, the intervening conduct is criminal conduct. The court did not note this fact but it is significant for purposes of establishing causation. Both intervening criminal conduct and civil conduct will not eliminate liability. However, as discussed in *People v. Warner-Lambert Co.* immediately following this case, the conduct of the defendant must be a sufficiently direct cause of the death and this standard is greater than that required for tort liability. Therefore, since smoke from both fires contributed to the resulting harm, this was sufficient to establish that Arzon's (D) conduct was the direct cause of the death, and it was foreseeable that firemen would place themselves in harm's way when battling the fire.

BEFORE CRIMINAL LIABILITY CAN BE IMPOSED, LEGAL CAUSE REQUIRES PROOF THAT THE DEFENDANT'S CONDUCT WAS A SUFFICIENTLY DIRECT CAUSE OF INJURY, A STANDARD OF LEGAL CAUSE GREATER THAN THAT EMPLOYED UNDER TORT PRINCIPLES

People v. Warner-Lambert Co.

(State) v. (Corporate Defendant)

51 N.Y.2d 295, 414 N.E.2d 660 (1980)

M E M O R Y G R A P H I C

Instant Facts

A defendant corporation and several of its officers and employees were indicted for second-degree manslaughter and criminally negligent homicide after several of the company's employees were killed in an explosion, the exact cause of which was unknown.

Black Letter Rule

For a defendant's conduct to be deemed the legal cause of the victim's injury, the immediate, triggering cause of the injury must have been foreseeable to the defendant.

Case Vocabulary

PROXIMATE CAUSE: An event or act which, unbroken by any other cause, produces some injury; the event or act that temporally, spatially and causally precedes some injury; the point at which a defendant's liability should cease due to unforeseeable or bizarre circumstances.

Procedural Basis: Not provided.

Facts: Warner-Lambert Co. (D) and several of its officers and employees were indicted for second degree manslaughter and criminally negligent homicide as a result of an explosion in a Warner-Lambert (D) chewing gum factory. Warner-Lambert (D) used two explosive substances, magnesium stearate and liquid nitrogen, in their manufacturing process. Warner-Lambert's (D) insurance carrier issued a warning concerning the risk of explosion posed by high concentrations of magnesium stearate dust and other conditions, but the company failed to eliminate the hazards prior to the explosion. The evidence presented to the grand jury failed to establish whether the explosion was triggered by a spark in the machines or the liquid nitrogen dripping onto the magnesium stearate and igniting under the impact of moving metal.

Issue: Does the concept of legal cause require that the defendant could have foreseen the immediate, triggering cause of the victim's injury?

Decision and Rationale: (Not provided) Yes. For a defendant's conduct to be deemed the legal cause of the victim's injury, the immediate, triggering cause of the injury must have been foreseeable to the defendant. The People (P) argue that the chain of physical events by which the explosion was set off is irrelevant. In other words, it is enough that a defendant expose his victim to the risk of death and that the victim died. However, we have held as inapplicable to the criminal law the principle of proximate cause, lifted from the civil law of torts. The greater standard for criminal liability requires the defendant's negligence have been a sufficiently direct cause of the injury before there can be any imposition of criminal liability.

Analysis:

Proximate cause is a concept which limits liability when reckless or negligent conduct results in bizarre consequences. Proximate cause is, essentially, an arbitrary line drawn by courts when common sense dictates that it would be unfair to hold the defendant liable. The concept of legal or "proximate" cause is deeply rooted in foreseeability and a common understanding as to the natural sequence of events. The concept is applicable in both the criminal law and the law of torts. However, as this case illustrates, the concept differs in both contexts. Under the law of torts, a defendant may be held liable if his conduct creates a certain risk and the ensuing harm is of the general nature posed by that risk, even though the injury occurs in a freak or unforeseeable manner. For example, in this case the concentration of magnesium stearate combined with other factors posed a risk of explosion. Under the principles of tort law, the company would be held liable if the explosion resulted from the concentration of magnesium stearate, regardless of the igniting agent. In contrast, the court here states that the criminal law requires the defendant's conduct be a "sufficiently direct cause" of the victim's injury before liability can properly attach. Through this articulation the court requires a closer nexus between the risk posed by the defendant's conduct and the manner in which the injury was caused than would be required under the law of torts. In the court's view, this close nexus requires the triggering event to have been foreseeable to the defendant. Thus, Warner-Lambert (D) could not be held liable unless both the risk of harm and the igniting agent were foreseeable, which could not be proved because the exact cause was unknown.

People v. Campbell

(Government) v. (Supplier of Gun to Suicide Victim)
(1983) 124 Mich.App. 333, 335 N.W.2d 27

M E M O R Y   G R A P H I C

Instant Facts

Campbell (D) was charged with murder after giving his gun to another person and encouraging the person to use it to kill himself, which he did.

Black Letter Rule

The doctrine of foreseeability is not applicable to establish causation where intentional subsequent human action exists.

Case Vocabulary

INFORMATION: A document formally accusing one of a crime, issued by public officers other than a grand jury.
MOTION TO QUASH: To void the effect of a legal document.

Procedural Basis: Appeal following denial of motion to quash information and warrant and dismiss criminal proceedings charging murder.

Facts: Campbell (D) was charged with murder in connection with the suicide of Mr. Basnaw. The two had been drinking heavily and Campbell (D), upset at Basnaw for having sex with his wife, encouraged [the no good] Basnaw to kill himself. Basnaw responded that he had no weapon whereupon Campbell (D) [wanting to do everything he could to get Basnaw off the planet] offered to sell him his own gun. Campbell (D) eventually gave Basnaw the gun and ammunition and left. Shortly thereafter, Basnaw shot himself to death with Campbell's (D) gun. Campbell (D) after being formally charged with murder moved to quash the information and warrant and dismiss the proceedings on the ground that providing a weapon to one who uses it to commit suicide does not constitute murder. He asserted that he should not be responsible for Basnaw's subsequent intentional action [i.e., killing himself]. The motion to quash was denied and Campbell (D) appealed.

Issue: Is the doctrine of foreseeability applicable to establish causation where intentional subsequent human action exists?

Decision and Rationale: (Hoehn) No. Where intentional subsequent human action exits, the foreseeability doctrine is not applicable to establish causation. Homicide is defined in the common law as "the killing of one human begin by another". The prosecution (P) urges that inciting one to commit suicide, coupled with furnishing the gun, is willful, deliberate and premeditated killing. We reject this [unfounded and without any statutory basis] argument because the term suicide excludes by definition a homicide and, in this case, Campbell (D) did not kill another person. There was no present intention to kill on the part of Campbell (D), although he certainly hoped that Basnaw would kill himself. We also reject the holding of *People v. Roberts* [husband of wife suffering from multiple sclerosis was convicted of her murder after complying with wife's request to make a lethal potion of poison so that she could reach it and kill herself, which she did, after her past suicide attempts failed.]. We find that this decision does not represent the current law of the state. The matter is reversed and case is remanded with instructions to quash the information and warrant and discharge Campbell (D).

Analysis:

This case involves the doctrine of *subsequent human actions*. If there is intentional subsequent action then foreseeability, as discussed in the previous cases, is not applicable. The reasoning is that human actions are different from those events that happen regularly and necessarily in accordance with the laws of nature, which is the basis of the principle of causation. Intentional subsequent human actions are not natural results of a chain of events governed by the laws of nature. This is because nothing causes a person to act, rather the person chooses to act on his own free will. If there were not a doctrine of subsequent human action, the foreseeability doctrine would have resulted in Campbell's conviction. Note that only voluntary or intentional subsequent human actions are outside the laws of causation. Truly involuntary actions can be caused, as well as actions taken without full knowledge or those that are constrained by factors of compulsion of duty or excusable conditions. These subjects are discussed in the cases in the next section. Note that many states have statutes that make it a criminal offense to assist a suicide.

People v. Kevorkian

(State) v. (Suicide Doctor)
447 Mich. 436, 527 N.W.2d 714 (1994)

MEMORY GRAPHIC

Instant Facts

A doctor was indicted on two counts of murder after he assisted two terminally ill women in committing suicide.

Black Letter Rule

The common law definition of murder does not encompass the act of intentionally providing the means by which a person commits suicide.

Procedural Basis: Appeal to the Supreme Court of Michigan challenging the holding of the court of appeals, which reversed the decision of the trial court quashing an information.

Facts: Two chronically ill women obtained the assistance of Dr. Jack Kevorkian in committing suicide. Both women sought to die by using Kevorkian's (D) "suicide machine," which, essentially injects the "patient" with lethal chemicals when the patient activates the machine. Kevorkian (D) was successful in hooking-up the machine to one of the women, who did as instructed and died shortly thereafter. However, Kevorkian (D) could not place the needle leading to the machine into the other woman. Kevorkian (D) instead strapped a mask connected to a cylinder of carbon monoxide to the woman's face and instructed her on how to open the cylinder using a lever he placed in her had. The woman followed instructions and died of carbon monoxide poisoning. Kevorkian (D) was subsequently indicted on two counts of murder.

Issue: Does the definition of murder encompass assisting in a suicide?

Decision and Rationale: (Cavanagh, C.J.) No. The common law definition of murder does not encompass the act of intentionally providing the means by which a person commits suicide. To convict a defendant of criminal homicide, it must be proven that the death occurred as a direct and natural result of the defendant's act. Unlike the common law, many modern statutes now treat assisted suicide as crime separate from murder. Recent decisions have drawn a distinction between active participation in the suicide and involvement in the events leading up to the suicide. Thus, a defendant may be convicted of murder where he pulls the trigger or holds the gun, but not where he merely furnishes the weapon. Remanded.

Concurrence and Dissent: (Boyle, J.) I disagree that one who provides the means for suicides and participates in the acts leading up to the death may not be charged with murder as long as the final act is that of the decedent. Absent standards to distinguish between those who are terminally ill or in pain and wish to die and those who are not, there exists no means to protect against abuse. The Court's opinion puts at risk those who are the most vulnerable – the sick, the elderly, the depressed and those suffering from stressful situations, such as adolescence, alcoholism and drug addiction. Although Kevorkian did not "pull the trigger," his participation was essential to completing each act.

Analysis:

This case serves as application of the point made in *People v. Campbell* (case where the defendant was indicted for murder in connection with a suicide where the defendant provided the decedent with a gun and encouraged him to kill himself); that an intentional subsequent act breaks the chain of causation, without regard to the foreseeability of the result. The court's holding that active participation in a suicide may support a murder conviction, whereas mere assistance does not, is in line with the modern view held by most courts. How then does one distinguish between active participation and mere assistance? The court here draws a bright-line rule holding that death is the direct and natural result of the defendant's act only where he participates in the *final act* that leads to death. The court provides little rationale for its holding, except stating that many statutes now make it a separate crime to assist in a suicide. There still remains unanswered the question of whether Kevorkian's (D) action crossed the line established by the court. The dissent argues that it did. In Justice Boyle's view, Kevorkian's (D) conduct was analogous to holding the gun while his "victims" pulled the trigger.

Stephenson v. State

(Accused Murderer) v. (Government)

(1932) 205 Ind. 141, 179 N.E. 633

M E M O R Y   G R A P H I C

Instant Facts

Stephenson (D) was charged with murder of a female who died from complications from attempted suicide after being rendered irresponsible due to injuries from his conduct.

Black Letter Rule

Causation exits where subsequent human action occurs as a result of being rendered irresponsible from mental and physical injuries inflicted by the defendant.

Case Vocabulary

APPELLANT: Party who initiates the appeal.

PER CURIAM: An opinion by the whole court, rather than one judge.

PROSECUTRIX: A female prosecutor.

Procedural Basis: Appeal following criminal conviction of second-degree murder.

Facts: The victim was abducted by Stephenson (D) and subjected to sexual perversion and physical wounds over a period of several days. The victim was allowed to go to a store accompanied by Stephenson's (D) chauffeur where she bought poison, and later consumed it alone and unbeknownst to Stephenson (D). Her attempt to commit suicide failed and she became ill. She refused Stephens' (D) suggestion that she be taken to the hospital, and she was eventually taken home where her parents sought medical attention for her. She died ten days later from a combination of shock, loss of food and rest, consumption of the poison, infection, and lack of early treatment. The jury [thankfully] convicted Stephenson (D) of second-degree murder. [It should have been first degree!]

Issue: Does causation exit where subsequent human action occurs as a result of being rendered irresponsible from mental and physical injuries inflicted by the defendant?

Decision and Rationale: (Per Curiam) Yes. Causation exits where subsequent human action occurs as a result of being rendered irresponsible from mental and physical injuries inflicted by the defendant. Stephenson (D) contends that he cannot be guilty of murder since the victim's attempted suicide without his knowledge and of her own free will breaks the chain of causation between his acts and her death. [Stephenson (D) gives "free will" a new meaning.] Stephenson (D) relies on *State v. Preslar* [husband not guilty of wife's murder where, following fight, wife left their home and decided to spend the night outside her father's home till morning, but died later from exposure to the cold] and *Bush v. Com.* [defendant not guilty where he wounded a person who was taken to the hospital and developed scarlet fever from which she died]. The holdings of these cases are not controlling here. We conclude that when suicide follows either a physical or mental wound inflicted by the defendant, his act is homicidal if the victim was rendered irresponsible by such wound and as a natural result of it. In this case, the victim was at all times entrapped by Stephenson (D) and under his custody and control. [His free will argument is laughable.] She had made previous unsuccessful attempts to call for help. At the time she took the poison, she was very ill and weak due to the treatment accorded to her by Stephenson (D). She was at that time still subject to his [sick and perverted] passion, desire and will. It would be a travesty of justice to hold that there was no causal connection between Stephenson's (D) acts and the death of the victim. The evidence is sufficient to show that Stephenson (D) by his acts and conduct rendered the victim distraught and mentally irresponsible, and that such was the natural and probable consequence of such unlawful and criminal treatment. Stephenson (D) is guilty of murder in the second-degree as charged.

Analysis:

This case is an example of a factual scenario where the subsequent human action does not break the chain of causation. Recall that only voluntary or intentional subsequent human actions are outside the laws of causation. Although the victim here intentionally bought and took the poison and refused Stephenson's (D) offer to go to the hospital, her actions were not truly intentional. Why? Because she was rendered irresponsible by being mentally and physically wounded by Stephenson. Moreover, her state of mind was the natural and probable consequence of Stephenson's (D) horrific conduct. Thus, in order to not have a break in the causation chain the subsequent human action must have occurred because the victim was rendered irresponsible from the defendant's infliction of either mental or physical wounds, and the irresponsibility must be the natural and probable consequence of the criminal conduct. Thus, if a person commits suicide after losing all his money to a criminal swindler, the swindler is not guilty of homicide. Why? Because the victim was not rendered irresponsible merely from the loss of money. In addition, this case expands previous case law so that the wound inflicted on the victim which results in her being rendered irresponsible may be mental as well as physical. Here, the victim was rendered irresponsible by the shame and humiliation of having been raped. This case is unique in that the victim, although distraught and upset, was alone when she took the poison. The motive for suicide may not have been to escape further assault, but to escape the shame of what had already been done to her. It is questionable how far reaching this holding will be. It suggests that any unlawful infliction of shame and disgrace may lead naturally to a suicide, thereby holding the defendant responsible for the death. This may not be an appropriate exception to the subsequent human actions doctrine.

Commonwealth v. Root

(Government) v. (Drag Racer)

(1961) 403 Pa. 571, 170 A.2d 310

M E M O R Y   G R A P H I C

Instant Facts

Drag racers were racing along a highway when deceased attempted to pass Root 's (D) car by driving on wrong side of road and was hit by an oncoming truck.

Black Letter Rule

Subsequent human actions that recklessly risk resulting harm break the chain of causation.

Case Vocabulary

DIRECT CAUSE: That which sets in motion the chain of events that produces a result without any new or independent acts.

PROXIMATE CAUSE: That which produces the harm without any break by an intervening cause, and without which the harm would not have occurred.

Procedural Basis: Appeal following criminal conviction for involuntary manslaughter.

Facts: Root (D) was found guilty of involuntary manslaughter for the death of his competitor during an automobile race on a highway. Both were exceeding the speed limit and driving recklessly. The deceased, in an attempt to overtake Root's (D) vehicle, crossed over the dividing line in a no-passing zone and drove on the wrong side of the highway at a high rate of speed. The deceased collided head-on with an oncoming truck and was killed. [This is why no-passing zones exist.] Root (D) appeals his conviction of involuntary manslaughter on the ground that he did not cause the death of the decedent.

Issue: Do subsequent human actions that recklessly risk resulting harm break the chain of causation?

Decision and Rationale: (Jones) Yes. If an actor chooses to engage in subsequent actions that recklessly risk harm to the actor, the chain of causation will be broken and the defendant will not be criminally responsible for any harm to the actor. In so ruling, we believe that the proper standard to be applied in criminal proceedings is the direct causal connection, rather than the more liberalized proximate cause standard used in civil proceedings. In order to prove involuntary manslaughter in this case, there must be evidence that Root (D) was driving in a reckless or unlawful manner. There is clearly sufficient evidence to establish this element. However, another essential element for involuntary manslaughter is that the unlawful or reckless conduct by Root (D) must be the direct cause of the death of the decedent. This second element has not been met. The concept of proximate law, although borrowed from the field of tort law, should not be applied in criminal proceedings in the same liberalized manner as it has been in [those big money] civil cases. To do so would extend criminal liability to persons charged with unlawful or reckless conduct in circumstances not generally considered to present the risk of death or injury. [Isn't drag racing at a high rate of speed on the wrong side of the road generally considered to present the risk of death?] A legal theory which makes guilt or innocence of criminal homicide depend upon such accidental and fortuitous circumstances as are now embraced by the modern day concept of tort law's proximate cause is too harsh to be just. The conduct by the deceased was one by him alone, and was not forced upon him by Root (D). The deceased's reckless conduct in driving his automobile in the manner in which he did is what brought about his death. Root's (D) reckless conduct was not a sufficiently direct cause of the deceased's death to make him criminally responsible. Reversed.

Dissent: (Eagen) If Root (D) had not engaged in the unlawful race, the deceased would not have died in the collision with the truck. Root (D) helped create the event, and the deceased's acts were a natural and normal reaction to the stimulus of the situation. The reaction by the deceased was foreseeable. All of this makes Root's (D) unlawful conduct a direct cause of the collision.

Analysis:

This case, decided by the Supreme Court of Pennsylvania, rejects the civil proximate cause standard and adopts the more stringent direct causal connection standard. However, in the case that follows, *State v. McFadden*, the Supreme Court of Iowa declines to follow the holding in *Root* and applies the proximate cause standard with its foreseeability requirement to criminal matters. These standards, whether direct causal connection or proximate cause, are applied in this section of the text book to cases involving subsequent human actions. The subsequent action in this case involves recklessly risking harm. Note that although the focus of the case in on the deceased's reckless conduct, the underlying principle is the same as in the *Campbell* case, nothing caused the deceased to act in the manner he did, rather the deceased chose to act on his own free will. The difference between those two cases is that in *Campbell* the deceased intended to produce the result of killing himself with the defendant's gun. In *Root*, it is presumed that the deceased did not intend to kill himself, yet he intentionally chose to drive on the wrong side of the road. The court in *Root* held that reckless conduct on the part of the deceased which risked death or injury broke the chain of causation. He chose to do what he did and suffered the consequences.

State v. McFadden

(Government) v. (Drag Racer)

(1982) 320 N.W.2d 608

M E M O R Y   G R A P H I C

Instant Facts

Drag racer collided with vehicle carrying child passenger killing both, and other drag racer, McFadden (D), was convicted of involuntary manslaughter.

Black Letter Rule

Subsequent human actions that recklessly risk resulting harm do not break the chain of causation where the acts of both the defendant and the deceased work concurrently as the cause of the harm.

Case Vocabulary

CAUSAL RELATIONSHIP: Same as "causal link" or "causal connection", connecting a certain chain of events without break or interruption.

Procedural Basis: Appeal following criminal convictions of involuntary manslaughter.

Facts: During a drag race on a city street between McFadden (D) and one Sulgrove, Sulgrove lost control of his car, swerved into oncoming traffic, collided with another vehicle and was killed. A child passenger in the oncoming vehicle was also killed in the collision. McFadden's (D) car did not come in physical contact with either vehicle. [But this did not get him out of trouble.] McFadden (D) was charged with two counts of involuntary manslaughter for the deaths of Sulgrove and the child. He was thereafter convicted. McFadden (D) appealed claiming causation was lacking.

Issue: Do subsequent human actions that recklessly risk resulting harm break the chain of causation where the acts of both the defendant and the deceased work concurrently as the cause of the harm?

Decision and Rationale: (Allbee) No. We first examine the theory of liability that McFadden (D) committed involuntary manslaughter by recklessly engaging in a drag race so as to proximately cause the death of both Sulgrove and the child. By participating in unlawful racing, McFadden(D) initiated a series of events resulting in the death of two others. The fact that Sulgrove voluntary and recklessly participated in the drag race does not of itself absolve McFadden (D) of criminal responsibility for Sulgrove's death. The acts of McFadden (D) were contributing and substantial factors in bringing about the deaths of others [despite his argument that it was all Sulgrove's fault]. Where the acts and omissions of two or more persons work concurrently as the efficient cause of an injury, each act is regarded as a proximate cause. We also reject the contention that the trial judge erred in applying the civil standard of proximate cause to this case, rather than the direct causal connection used in *Commonwealth v. Root* [proximate cause principle rejected in criminal proceedings in favor of more stringent direct causal connection standard so that subsequent human actions that recklessly risk resulting harm break the chain of causation]. As we have said in other cases before us with similar issues [and as we will say again and again and again], the element of proximate cause in criminal prosecutions serves as a requirement that there be a sufficient causal relationship between the defendant's conduct and a proscribed harm to hold him criminally responsible. In the law of torts it requires the same causal relationship between the defendant's conduct and the plaintiff's damage. We do not see a justification for a different standard of proximate causation under criminal and civil matters. The requirement of foreseeability encompassed within proximate cause, together with proof of recklessness, will prevent any unjust results in involuntary manslaughter cases. Affirmed.

Analysis:

This case declines to follow the holding in *Commonwealth v. Root* [subsequent human actions that recklessly risk resulting harm break the chain of causation] and applies the proximate cause standard with its foreseeability requirement to criminal matters. At first blush, it appears that these two cases are identical but reach exactly opposite conclusions. Both involved unlawful car racing, and both defendants were charged with involuntary manslaughter in connection with the deaths of other racers. (McFadden was also charged with the death of the child.) The court in *McFadden* upheld the criminal conviction and the court in *Root* reversed the conviction. How do the cases differ? First, they involve different state supreme courts. Second, the deceased in *Root* intentionally chose to drive on the wrong side of the road and into the oncoming traffic lanes, in an effort to overtake the other race car. By so doing, he recklessly took the risk of injury or death which obviously exists by driving in the wrong way lane. The court in *Root* held that reckless conduct on the part of the deceased which risked death or injury broke the chain of causation. In *McFadden*, however, the deceased lost control of his vehicle while racing, resulting in the collision with the vehicle in which the child was a passenger. The deceased and McFadden were acting concurrently, and both of their actions resulted in the fatal collision. Note that the court said that it was unwilling to hold as a blanket rule of law that proximate cause was inappropriate for criminal trials. By so doing, this allows the court more freedom to apply the law based upon the facts of each case, rather than a hard and inflexible rule.

Commonwealth v. Atencio

(Government) v. (Russian Roulette Player)
(1963) 345 Mass. 627, 189 N.E.2d 223

M E M O R Y   G R A P H I C

Instant Facts
Atencio (D) and others played Russian roulette resulting in the death of the decedent and Atencio (D) and others were charged with involuntary manslaughter.

Black Letter Rule
Subsequent human actions that recklessly risk resulting harm do not break the chain of causation where the defendant encourages or cooperates in a joint activity with the victim which results in harm.

Case Vocabulary

MOTION FOR DIRECTED VERDICT: Requesting judge to enter judgment for one party before return of jury verdict.

Procedural Basis: Appeal from denial of motion for directed verdicts following convictions of manslaughter.

Facts: Atencio (D) and others spent the day drinking in a rooming house. One of the individuals left and returned shortly with a gun, from which he removed one bullet. Later in the evening, the individuals [having nothing better to do] played Russian Roulette [presumably after removing more bullets]. The gun was passed to one of the individuals and he pointed it at his head and pulled the trigger but nothing happened. The gun was given to Atencio (D) and he did the same thing without result. Atencio (D) passed the gun to the [very unlucky] deceased who pulled the trigger resulting in the gun being fired and the deceased being killed. Atencio (D) and others were convicted of manslaughter. They appeal following the denial of their motions for directed verdicts.

Issue: Do subsequent human actions that recklessly risk resulting harm break the chain of causation where the defendant encourages or cooperates in a joint activity with the victim which results in harm?

Decision and Rationale: (Wilkins) No. Subsequent human actions that recklessly risk resulting harm will not break the chain of causation where the defendant encourages or cooperates in a joint activity with the victim which results in harm. We hold that the wanton or reckless conduct of the deceased and others could be found in the concerted action and cooperation of Atencio (D) and the other defendants in helping to bring about the deceased's foolish act. [More like a stupid and crazy act.] It could be found that there was mutual encouragement in a joint enterprise. [This means that the idiots agreed among themselves to play Russian Roulette, a so-called game]. Atencio (D) and the others did not have a duty to prevent the deceased from playing the game. However, there was a duty on their part not to cooperate or join with him in the game. It is not necessary for the decedent to be forced to play or to suggest that he play. It would be incorrect to say that had the deceased been the first one to play, no criminal responsibility would exist. The convicted defendants were much more than merely present at a crime. The result of the game was a certainty, absent misfire. Judgments affirmed.

Analysis:

The court noted in the beginning that if this had been a civil case, the voluntary act of the deceased would bar any claim made by his representatives against Atencio (D). However, the court applied a different rule to the criminal proceedings. The court upheld the convictions because the jury could have found mutual encouragement on the part of Atencio (D) and the rest of the group. The concerted action and cooperation brought about the end result. There was a duty on the part of Atencio (D) and the others not to cooperate or join with the deceased in the certain result of death. In *Lewis v. State* a slightly different Russian Roulette situation existed. The defendant introduced a 15 year old boy to the game and played it on several occasions without incident. The youngster later on played the game by himself and outside the presence of the defendant, and the gun went off killing the boy. Although the court agreed that the youngster would not have died if the defendant had not directed, instructed and influenced him to play, it held that there was no criminal liability because the free will of the youngster was an intervening cause which broke the chain of causation. The difference between the two cases is that the *Atencio* defendants were in the room, participating in the game with the deceased. They had a duty not to cooperate or join with him. In *Lewis*, the defendant had left the room and was unaware the youngster was playing the game alone. If he had been in the room or playing the game at the time, the outcome would have been different. Thus, voluntary actions that recklessly risk resulting harm will not break the chain of causation if the defendant actively encourages, cooperates or participates in the conduct which results in harm.

THE SPECIFIC INTENT NECESSARY FOR A CONVICTION OF ATTEMPTED MURDER MAY NOT BE INFERRED WHERE THE DEFENDANT'S CONDUCT SIMPLY POSED AN INCREASED RISK OF DEATH

Smallwood v. State

(Defendant Rapist Infected With HIV) v. (Government)
343 Md. 97, 680 A.2d 512 (1996)

M E M O R Y   G R A P H I C

Instant Facts

An HIV positive man was convicted of assault with intent to murder after he raped three women without taking precautions to protect his victims from infection..

Black Letter Rule

The specific intent necessary for an attempt conviction may be inferred from the defendant's conduct only if the crime attempted would have been the natural and probable result of such conduct, but for the lack of its successful completion.

Case Vocabulary

SPECIFIC INTENT: The mental purpose of committing criminally prohibited acts combined with the purpose to violate the law.

Procedural Basis: Appeal to the Court of Appeals, Maryland challenging a conviction for attempted murder after a non-jury trial.

Facts: Based on the fact that he knew he was HIV positive and had been warned of the need to practice safe sex, Smallwood (D) was convicted of assault with intent to kill his rape victims. Smallwood (D) challenged his conviction on the ground that the specific intent to kill could not be inferred from his conduct. He argued that the most that could be inferred from his actions was the reckless endangerment of his victims. The State (P) argued that Smallwood's (D) acts were akin to aiming and firing a loaded weapon at his victims.

Issue: May the specific intent to kill be inferred only from conduct which merely poses an significantly increased, though not probable, risk of death?

Decision and Rationale: (Murphy, C.J.) No. The specific intent necessary for an attempt conviction may be inferred from the defendant's conduct only if the crime attempted would have been the natural and probable result of such conduct, but for the lack of its successful completion. We have previously held that the intent in the crimes of assault with intent to murder and attempted murder is the specific intent to murder, i.e., the specific intent to kill under circumstances that would not legally justify, excuse or mitigate the killing. Because it is a subjective matter otherwise requiring the cooperation of the defendant, the intent to kill may inferred from the conduct of the defendant and other circumstantial evidence. Accordingly, the State (P) argues that Smallwood's conviction may stand based on prior cases holding that the intent to kill can be inferred from using a deadly weapon aimed at a vital part of the body. However, this case is different. First, those holdings are based on the notion that death was the "natural and probable result of the defendant's conduct." Because the same inference cannot be made when the defendant risks infecting his victim with HIV (a virus which may or may not lead to death), the State (P) was required to provide additional evidence that death was the natural and probable result of Smallwood's (D) conduct. Smallwood's conduct is consistent with the mere intent to assault and rape, without any intent to kill. In those cases where a defendant has been convicted of attempted murder by knowingly infecting his victims with HIV, the prosecution proved the specific intent with evidence such as the defendants' own statements.

Analysis:

Although various mental states may support a conviction of murder – e.g., reckless disregard for human life or death resulting from the commission of a dangerous felony – a conviction for attempted murder (or the attempt of any other crime) is proper only where the state proves that the defendant possessed the specific intent to commit the particular substantive crime. Several rationales have been forwarded to justify the specific intent requirement. The first of these justifications is that one cannot attempt to produce a result without an intent to do so. For example, it makes no sense to attempt to negligently cause an injury. Another rationale is that one who intends to achieve a criminal result is more morally reprehensible than one who does so recklessly or negligently. This case deals with the issue of how that specific intent may be proved. The court notes that specific intent can be inferred through the defendant's conduct. However, if the prosecution relies solely on the defendant's conduct for proof of intent, that conduct must naturally and probably result in commission of the crime. In certain cases, the inference is a matter of common sense. The example used in this case is the act of firing a gun at a person's vital parts. In the court's view, death is so likely the result of such conduct, that the intent to kill may be inferred from it. However, the court was unconvinced that death was just as likely or probable a result from exposing a victim to the risk of HIV infection. Such an act only increases the risk of death; it does not make death probable.

TO BE GUILTY OF THE CRIME OF ATTEMPT A DEFENDANT MUST BE DANGEROUSLY PROXIMATE TO SUCCESSSFUL COMMISSION OF THE SUBSTANTIVE CRIME

People v. Rizzo

(State) v. (Convicted Robbers)
246 N.Y. 334, 158 N.E. 888 (1927)

M E M O R Y   G R A P H I C

Instant Facts

Four men were convicted of attempted robbery after they were caught driving, searching for their intended victim, who was never found.

Black Letter Rule

An attempt may be found only where the defendants have engaged in an act tending to the commission of the crime which is so near to its accomplishment that in all reasonable probability the crime itself would have been committed, but for timely interference.

Case Vocabulary

ABANDONMENT: The act of deserting a criminal purpose or enterprise; in some jurisdictions abandonment may relieve a defendant of liability for crimes such as attempt and conspiracy.

Procedural Basis: Not provided.

Facts: Charles Rizzo (D), Anthony J. Dorio (D), Thomas Milo (D), and John Thomasello (D) (the Defendants), planned to rob Charles Rao of a payroll which he was to carry from the bank. The Defendants (D), two of whom were armed, searched for Rao while they rode in a car. The Defendants' (D) efforts proved fruitless; they never found Rao or anyone else carrying the payroll. In fact, no payroll had been withdrawn that day. Nevertheless, all four men were arrested when Rizzo (D) jumped out of the car to search the last building the men came to.

Issue: Does every act tending toward commission of a crime constitute a punishable attempt of that crime?

Decision and Rationale: (Crane, J.) No. Only those acts tending to the commission of the crime which are so near to its accomplishment that in all reasonable probability the crime itself would have been committed, but for timely interference, can constitute an attempt. The law recognizes a difference between preparation for the commission of a crime and a punishable attempt to commit a crime. The difference, as stated by Justice Holmes, is a conviction for attempt requires that there be a "dangerous proximity to success." The question then is whether the acts of the Defendants (D) came dangerously close to the commission of a robbery. The intended victim could not have been robbed until he came into sight of the Defendants (D), who never actually found Rao. In fact, an endless search would have proved fruitless because there was no victim who could have been robbed. To analogize, a man cannot be found guilty of attempted murder if he starts out to find his intended victim but is unsuccessful. Here the defendants were not guilty of an attempt to commit robbery when they had not found or reached the presence of the person they intended to rob.

Analysis:

As you read in earlier chapters, a defendant may not be convicted for bad thoughts. Accordingly, the commission of a crime necessarily involves some sort of act. For many crimes there exists little debate as to which acts, when coupled with intent, constitute the offense. The act that effects the prohibited result is usually the *actus reus*. For example, discharge of a gun that winds up killing another is sufficient to constitute murder. However, in the context of crimes of attempt the issue of which acts are punishable becomes more nebulous because an attempt may have no immediate result. The attempt statute at issue in this case made it a crime to commit an "act, done with intent to commit a crime, and tending but failing to effect its commission." Most statutes have similar language, making punishable acts committed "in furtherance of" or "toward the commission of" a crime. However, in one sense every act taken prior to the commission of a crime is in furtherance of its commission. Consequently, there exists the danger of punishing individuals for legal conduct. For example, one should not be convicted of attempted murder for the act of purchasing a gun with the intent to kill someone with it. The purchase of the gun is an act in furtherance of the crime, but it cannot be said to constitute an attempt to commit it. Thus, courts limit liability for attempt to only certain acts. The rationale for limiting liability is to preserve for defendants an opportunity to abandon their efforts before any harm results. It would seem unfair to convict a defendant of attempt if he recants and does everything in his power to prevent the harm from occurring. Because many states do not observe the defense of "abandonment," the "dangerous proximity test" adopted by this court requires that the act in question be sufficiently close to the intended crime. The test is really a question of degree. There is no bright-line or magical point at which legal conduct becomes an attempted crime. It all depends on the facts an circumstances. The outcome of this case may have been all too easy because the Defendants' (D) acts may never have effected their intended result due to the lack of a victim who was present.

PURELY INNOCENT CONDUCT MAY CONSTITUTE CRIMINAL ATTEMPT IF INTENT TO
COMMIT CRIME IS PROVEN, EVEN IF BY INFERENTIAL EVIDENCE

McQuirter v. State

(Attempted Rapist) v. (Government)

(1953) 36 Ala.App. 707, 63 So.2d 388

M E M O R Y   G R A P H I C

Instant Facts

Black man convicted of attempt to commit an assault with intent to rape challenged jury's verdict convicting him of crime.

Black Letter Rule

In order to prove attempt, the intent to commit the underlying crime may be proven by inferential evidence.

Case Vocabulary

GENERAL AFFIRMATIVE CHARGE: Instructing jury that defendant cannot be convicted no matter what the evidence may show.

MOTION FOR NEW TRIAL: Motion made post verdict or post decision by court to have the matter tried again.

Procedural Basis: Appeal from criminal conviction of attempt to commit assault with intent to rape.

Facts: McQuirter (D) was found guilty of attempt to commit an assault with intent to rape. He was sitting in his truck and, when Mrs. Allen and her children walked by, he got out and walked down the street behind them. Mrs. Allen stopped at another house for ten minutes and waited for McQuirter (D) to pass. She proceeded on and he came toward her from behind a telephone pole. She told her children to run to another house and tell the man of the house to come outside. When the man approached, McQuirter (D) went down the street to an area across from Mrs. Allen's house. Mrs. Allen watched him there from the porch of the other house for thirty minuets, after which time he came back down the street and she went home. The police chief testified that McQuirter had confessed while in jail that he intended to rape Mrs. Allen. McQuirter (D) denied making such statements and testified that he had merely been waiting for a friend to return to the truck. The jury [not believing him at all] convicted him and he appealed.

Issue: In order to prove attempt, can the intent to commit the underlying crime be proven by inferential evidence?

Decision and Rationale: (Price) Yes. We hold that the evidence was sufficient to permit the jury to infer from McQuirter's (D) conduct and the surrounding circumstances that intent to commit an assault with intent to rape occurred. An attempt to commit an assault with intent to rape means an attempt to rape which has not proceeded far enough to amount to an assault. In order to convict, there must be proof that the defendant intended to have sexual intercourse with the victim against her will, by force or by putting her in fear. The intent is a question to be determined by the jury. The jury may consider social conditions and customs founded upon racial differences, as exist in this case. [How does this prove intent?] We are of the opinion that the evidence was sufficient to warrant the submission of the defendant's guilt to the jury, and there is ample evidence to sustain the judgment of conviction. Affirmed.

Analysis:

The underlying crime required proof of intent. Thus, in order to prove attempt, the intent to commit the crime was required. Notice that the facts did not disclose that McQuirter (D) lunged at Mrs. Allen or chased her. If such had occurred, it would have been much easier to accept the jury's finding of intent to sexually assault the victim. The jury was faced with conflicting testimony. The police chief testified about McQuirter's (D) statements concerning intent to rape, and McQuirter (D) denied making such statements. The jury was allowed to consider other evidence in order to infer intent. This other evidence was the fact that the victim was white and the defendant was black. Note that had this case been tried today, the results may have been different. The law of the state of Alabama made attempt to commit an assault with intent to rape a crime if it could be proven that the defendant intended to have sexual intercourse with the victim against her will, by force or putting her in fear. In this case, there was no evidence of any attempt to do any act of force or anything against the victim's will. There was evidence that the victim was put in fear. His only conduct was walking up and down the street and standing on corners or next to telephone poles. The conduct was innocent, but the jury was permitted to believe the testimony of the police chief, and consider racial factors, in order to infer intent.

United States v. Jackson

(Government) v. (Bank Robber)
(1977) 560 F.2d 112

M E M O R Y   G R A P H I C

Instant Facts

Jackson (D) and two others were convicted of attempted robbery after driving around bank on two occasions with the necessary paraphernalia to commit a robbery.

Black Letter Rule

Conduct which constitutes a substantial step toward commission of the crime, and is strongly corroborative of the firmness of the defendant's criminal intent may establish attempt.

Case Vocabulary

MEMORANDUM OF DECISION: A written statement by the judge explaining the factual and legal basis for his ruling in the case.

RES IPSA LOQUITUR APPROACH: Also known as the equivocality test—To determine whether the conduct is of such a nature that it is itself, on the face of it, evidence of the criminal intent necessary to constitute criminal attempt.

UNINDICTED CO-CONSPIRATOR: One who is engaged in criminal conspiracy with the defendant but is not formally charged with a crime.

Procedural Basis: Appeal following court trial conviction of attempted robbery.

Facts: Jackson (D), Scott and Allen were convicted, after a court trial, of attempted robbery of a bank, as well as conspiracy. They appealed the convictions of attempted robbery on the ground that their conduct was mere preparation and did not rise to the level of attempt. A female unindicted co-conspirator acted as a government informant and informed law enforcement of the initial plan to rob the bank, which she had organized and participated in, but which was aborted and rescheduled for the following week. The plan was not carried through because they observed a number of bank patrons inside the bank. Before the new date arrived, the female co-conspirator was arrested on unrelated charges and immediately [became a snitch and] began cooperating with the Government. She told the authorities of what had transpired and of the new date planned for the robbery. On the date scheduled for the robbery, the police observed a car and three individuals in it matching the descriptions given to police by the informant. The car was driving up and down the streets near the bank, and stopping for several minutes a few blocks away. The car returned closer to the bank and parked. After thirty minutes, the car began moving toward the bank. However, the occupants of the car detected the police surveillance and the car was then overtaken by the police. The three individuals in the car, including Jackson (D), were arrested. The police discovered in the rear of the car two shotguns, a revolver, a pair of handcuffs, masks, and a license plate lying on the front floor of the car. [Guess what they were going to do.] The judge at trial held that the defendants had engaged in conduct amounting to attempted robbery based upon their conduct and the contents of the car. They were convicted of attempted robbery.

Issue: Can conduct which constitutes a substantial step toward commission of the crime, and is strongly corroborative of the firmness of the defendant's criminal intent establish attempt?

Decision and Rationale: (Frederick van Pelt Bryan) Yes. In reaching the decision to convict, the trial judge applied the following two-tiered inquiry: First, the defendant must have been acting with the kind of culpability otherwise required for the commission of the crime he is charged with attempting; and second, the defendant must have engaged in conduct which constitutes a substantial step toward commission of the crime, and that it be strongly corroborative of the firmness of the defendant's criminal intent. We note that this analysis conforms closely to the definition of an attempt as set forth in the Model Penal Code. The comments to the Model Penal Code state that such an approach shifts the emphasis from what remains to be done—the chief concern of the proximity tests—to what the defendant has already done. There is no finding required as to whether the defendant would probably have desisted prior to completing the crime. This approach is less of a hurdle than the *res ipsa loquitur* approach which requires that the defendant's conduct must itself manifest the criminal purpose. The trial judge in this case concluded that on two [not one, but two] occasions Jackson (D) and the others were seriously dedicated to the commission of a crime. They had passed beyond the stage of preparation, and would have completed the crime had they not been dissuaded by the number of bank patrons inside the bank on the first occasion and detecting the police on the second occasion. They also possessed the necessary weapons and other paraphernalia which served no lawful purpose other than to commit the crimes. Either conduct was sufficient to constitute a substantial step if it strongly corroborated their criminal purpose. Both types of conduct, along with other elements, are strongly corroborative of the firmness of their criminal intents. Affirmed.

Analysis:

This case demonstrates the use of the Model Penal Code's *substantial step* approach to determining attempt. The opinion gives a good comparison of the proximity test—requires that the last proximate act must occur before an attempt can occur, or that the acts must be physically proximate to the intended crime—with the *res ipsa loquitur* test, also known as the equivocality test—an attempt is an act of such a nature that it is itself, on the face of it, evidence of the criminal intent. Note that the Model Penal Code's test draws on the elements of both the proximity and the equivocality tests. It appears that Jackson (D) and his co-conspirators had no chance in succeeding in the appellate court since the court held that the conduct on either of the planned robbery days constitutes a substantial step strongly corroborative of their criminal purpose. The paraphernalia found in the car cemented their convictions. However, there is sometimes a difference of opinion among different courts of appeals in applying the Mode Penal Code test. In a similar attempted bank robbery case referenced in the *Problems* section of the text book following this case, the Ninth Circuit reversed the conviction. It noted that the defendants in that case did not take a single step toward the bank, they displayed no weapons and no indication that they were about to make an entry. The court held that standing alone, their conduct did not constitute the requisite "appreciable fragment" of a bank robbery, nor a substantial step toward the crime. Finally, note that the Model Penal Code contains a section with examples of conduct that may be held to constitute a substantial step. Some examples include, lying in wait, enticing the victim to go to the place contemplated for the commission of the crime, reconnoitering the place contemplated for the commission of the crime, unlawful entry of the place where it is contemplated the crime will occur, possession of materials to be employed in the commission of the crime, and soliciting an innocent agent to engage in the crime.

State v. Davis

(Government) v. (Solicitor for Murder)

(1928) 319 Mo. 1222, 6 S.W.3d 609

M E M O R Y   G R A P H I C

Instant Facts

Davis (D) hired an undercover police officer to kill his lover's husband, and was subsequently tried and convicted of attempted murder.

Black Letter Rule

Mere solicitation of a crime does not constitute attempt.

Procedural Basis: Appeal following criminal conviction for attempted first degree murder.

Facts: Davis (D) was convicted of attempted first degree murder. He and a married woman planned to kill the woman's husband in order to collect life insurance money [and live together happily ever after]. He sought the help of one Earl Leverton in obtaining an ex-convict to kill the husband. Leverton told a police officer of the plot, and the officer decided to pose as the ex-convict. Davis (D) paid the undercover officer money to kill the husband. They had several discussions about arranging a plan for the killing, and Davis (D) provided photographs, drawings and partial payment. When the officer went to the home of the intended victim, he revealed his identity and then went to Davis' (D) home and arrested him. Davis (D) was convicted and appealed. On appeal, Davis (D) argued that there was insufficient evidence to prove that there was performance of some act toward the commission of the crime.

Issue: Does mere solicitation of a crime constitute attempt?

Decision and Rationale: (Davis) No. Something more than solicitation is required before one may be convicted of attempt. The elements of attempt are: 1) The intention to commit the crime; 2) performance of some act toward the commission of the crime; and 3) the failure to consummate its commission. With respect to the second element, the physical overt act required for attempt is distinguishable from solicitation and preparation. There must be an act moving directly toward the commission of the offense. Solicitation is a crime by itself when declared so by law. However, merely soliciting one to commit a crime does not constitute an attempt. The facts of the case do not show overt acts toward the commission of a crime. The acts of having a verbal arrangement with one selected to kill, plus delivery of photographs, drawings and partial payment, are mere acts of preparation. The acts of entering into a contract for hire and payment of money, were not acts moving directly toward the consummation of the crime. [What the heck were they then?] Judgment reversed.

Analysis:

This case shows the difference between the crime of attempt and solicitation. Attempt requires an overt act. Solicitation, on the other hand, exists if one requests another person to commit a crime. In this case, had Davis (D) been charged with solicitation he would have rightly been found guilty. However, the necessary element of an overt act performed toward the commission of the crime did not exist under the facts presented. The court held that they were mere acts of preparation. The court requires for an attempt conviction, acts more proximate in space, time and causation, for example, lunging at the victim or aiming and firing a gun. In the court's view, preparation is not a proximate cause. Not all courts are in agreement with the holding of this case. In *United States v. Church*, which follows this case, the military court of appeals upheld the conviction of attempted murder based upon very similar facts to those in *Davis*.

United States v. Church

(Military) v. (Serviceman Who Sought to Hire a Hit Man)
29 Mil. J. Rptr. 679 (Ct. Milit. Rev. 1989)

M E M O R Y   G R A P H I C

Instant Facts

A serviceman was convicted of attempted pre-meditated murder after he engaged an undercover agent to kill his wife.

Black Letter Rule

Solicitation may be punishable as an attempt if it constitutes a substantial step toward commission of the crime.

Case Vocabulary

SOLICITATION: The hiring of another to commit a crime.

Procedural Basis: Appeal from a conviction in military court.

Facts: When Mr. Church (D), an airman stationed in North Dakota, realized he was unlikely to regain legal custody of his children, he began to talk about hiring a hit man to kill his wife. Church's (D) associates reported his utterances to the authorities, who devised a plan to have Church (D) hire an undercover agent as a hit man. In a meeting, Church provided the agent with a partial payment, expense money, maps, photos and all information necessary to carry out the "hit." After he was officially notified that his wife had been "murdered," Church (D) met with the agent to tender the rest of the payment. Church (D) was then arrested, tried and convicted of attempted premeditated murder.

Issue: May a person be convicted of an attempt to commit a crime when he hires another person to commit the crime?

Decision and Rationale: (Not Provided) Yes. Solicitation may be punishable as an attempt if it constitutes a substantial step toward commission of the crime. That substantial step is taken when the solicitor has done everything possible to effect what he believes will be the commission of a crime. Although many courts have held that the contracting out of a crime is mere preparation which does not lead directly or proximately to consummation of the intended crime, some states have upheld attempt convictions in cases involving crimes for hire. Church's (D) hiring of the agent, his detailed participation in planning the crime, and his payment of the "fee" all constituted a substantial step toward commission of the crime. The was nothing else Church could do to effect the murder of his wife, save for killing her himself.

Analysis:

Courts are divided on the issue of whether solicitation constitutes an attempt to commit a crime. However, those courts that have agreed with the position that a solicitor may be guilty of attempt often require something more than a solicitation. In upholding the attempted murder conviction the military court here relied on the fact that Church (D) had financed the crime, helped plan its commission and gave detailed instructions. The court expressly points out that Church (D) could not have done anything else. Applying the Model Penal Code's approach to the crime of attempt the court held that Church's conduct was a "substantial step toward commission of the crime," because Church (D) had done everything in his power to effectuate the commission of a murder. This test seems broader than the "dangerous proximity test" discussed in *People v. Rizzo* [case involving the attempted robbery conviction of four men riding in a car searching for a victim who they never found; and thus, could not rob]. Under the *Rizzo* test an attempt conviction for solicitation might not be proper because the opportunity to commit the murder may never arise. Notwithstanding, the issue presented here is important only in those states where solicitation is not a separate crime or does not cover a broad range of offenses.

People v. Jaffe

(Government) v. (Buyer of Goods Thought To Be Stolen)
(1906) 185 N.Y. 497, 78 N.E. 169

M E M O R Y   G R A P H I C

Instant Facts

Jaffe (D) attempted to buy cloth thinking it was stolen when it was not, and was convicted of attempted receipt of stolen goods.

Black Letter Rule

A person cannot be convicted of attempt to receive stolen goods, believing them to have been stolen, when in fact they have not been stolen.

Procedural Basis: Appeal following criminal conviction of attempt to buy and receive stolen property.

Facts: Jaffe (D) was convicted of attempting to buy and receive stolen property. Jaffe (D) attempted to buy the property, consisting of 20 yards of cloth, believing it to have been stolen. However, the property no longer had the character of stolen goods when Jaffe (D) attempted to buy it. The property had been returned to the owners, and was being offered to Jaffe (D) through their authority and agency. [Jaffe (D) still was considered a big-time criminal for having the mere intent to commit a crime.] Jaffe (D) appealed the conviction contending that the completed act would not have constituted a crime. He argued that he should not have been convicted of attempting to commit an act which would not have been criminal if completed.

Issue: Can one be convicted of attempt to receive stolen goods, believing them to have been stolen, when in fact they have not been stolen?

Decision and Rationale: (Bartlett) No. If one intends to commit a crime and mistakenly believes that his act will be a crime, but in fact it will not, there is no attempt. This case is distinguishable from those that hold that one may be convicted of an attempt notwithstanding the existence of facts unknown to the defendant which would have rendered the complete perpetration of the crime itself impossible. Examples of such cases include: Pick-pocketers are convicted for attempt to commit larceny without the need to prove that there was anything in the pockets; and extortionists are convicted even though they do not know that their intended victim is a decoy for the police, and thus could not be induced with fear to pay money. In this case, the act would not have been a crime if it had been consummated. Thus, no matter what Jaffe (D) thought, he could not commit the crime since the property was not stolen property. [He sure did luck out!] In the pick-pocket cases, the immediate act, if carried out, would have been criminal. In this case, the act of purchasing the goods would not have been criminal even if carried out and completed. There was no proof that Jaffe (D) possessed knowledge of the actual stolen character of the property since it was not. An example of a case applying the same principle is where a man has sex with a woman, not his wife, who he believes to be under the age of 18 years. If the woman is over the age of 18 years, there is no crime, even if the defendant believed her to be younger and intended to commit the crime. Similarly, Jaffe's (D) conviction cannot stand even though he had intent to commit a crime, but mistakenly believed he was so doing. Judgment reversed.

Analysis:

This case demonstrates the doctrine of legal impossibility as a defense. The criminal code section which Jaffe (D) was convicted of violating required that the person know the property to have been stolen. Jaffe (D) intended to commit a crime, and if the property had been stolen, he would have been able to commit a crime. Thus, Jaffe (D) had done everything he had intended to do, but still had not committed the crime. The pick-pocket and extortion cases referred to by the court in its opinion are examples of factual impossibility cases. They, unlike legal impossibility cases, are not defenses to the crime of attempt. The approach in *Jaffe* has been rejected by many modern day courts. As is discussed in the next case, *People v. Dlugash*, the legislature enacted a statute which prevented the use of both factual and legal impossibility as a defense if the crime could have been committed had the attendant circumstances been as the defendant believed them to be.

People v. Dlugash

(Government) v. (Second Gunman)
(1977) 41 N.Y.2d 725, 363 N.E.2d 1155

M E M O R Y   G R A P H I C

Instant Facts

Dlugash (D) should have been convicted of attempted murder where he shot a person he believed to be alive, although victim had been shot by another moments earlier.

Black Letter Rule

A defendant is guilty of attempted murder if he believes the intended victim was alive, even though the intended victim may have already been dead.

Case Vocabulary

CHARGE THE JURY: Where the judge instructs the jury on the law.

Procedural Basis: Appeal to highest appellate court of state following lower appellate court's reversal of criminal conviction of murder.

Facts: Dlugash (D), Bush and Geller had been out drinking. [You know from previous cases that trouble lies ahead.] On several occasions that evening, Geller had demanded that Bush pay him money because he had been staying at Geller's apartment. After they returned to Geller's apartment, they continued drinking. Geller again demanded money from Bush, whereupon Bush shot Geller three times with his gun. [The guy gets shot over a measly $100 bucks.] Geller fell to the floor. After two to five minutes passed, Dlugash (D) took his own gun and shot Geller in the head and face approximately five times. He contended that by the time he fired shots, it looked as if Geller was already dead. After repeated questioning by the police as to why he did such a thing, Dlugash (D) said that he guessed it must have been because he was afraid of Bush. At trial, the prosecution sought to show that Geller was still alive at the time Dlugash (D) shot him. However, there was conflicting medical testimony and it could not be stated with medical certainty whether or not Geller was alive when shot by Dlugash (D). The jury was instructed to decide whether Dlugash (D) had either intentionally murdered Geller or had attempted to murder him. The jury found Dlugash (D) guilty of murder. The appellate court reversed the conviction of murder. However, it did not modify the judgment to reflect a conviction of attempted murder because the evidence was that Dlugash (D) believed Geller to be dead at the time he shot him. The matter was appealed to the highest court of appeals of the state.

Issue: Is a defendant guilty of attempted murder if he believes the intended victim was alive, although the intended victim may have already been dead?

Decision and Rationale: (Jasen) Yes. The statutory law of this state now makes the defenses of legal and factually impossibility inapplicable to attempt, if the crime could have been committed had the circumstances been as the defendant believed them to be. The statute is patterned after the Model Penal Code, and eliminates the defenses of factual and legal impossibility. Thus, to constitute an attempt, it is still necessary that the result intended by the defendant constitute a crime. However, the defendant's intent should be the standard for determining criminal liability. Under this statute, a person is guilty of an attempt when, with intent to commit a crime, he engages in conduct which tends to effect the commission of the crime. It is no defense that, under the attendant circumstances, the crime was factually or legally impossible of commission, if such crime could have been committed had the attendant circumstances been as the person believed them to be. Therefore, if Dlugash (D) believed Geller to be alive at the time of the shooting, it is no defense that Geller may have been dead. There is sufficient evidence from which the jury could have concluded that Dlugash (D) believed Geller to be alive at the time he shot him. Since the jury convicted Dlugash (D) of murder, they necessarily must have found he intended to kill. Subsumed within this finding is the conclusion that Dlugash (D) believed that Geller was alive. Although it was not established at trial that Geller was alive when shot by Dlugash (D), there is no need for additional fact finding. It is no defense if Geller was alive, since had the circumstances been as Dlugash (D) believed, *i.e.*, that Geller was alive, a murder would have been committed. The Appellate Division erred in not modifying the judgment to reflect a conviction for attempted murder.

Analysis:

This case is an example of a statute patterned after the Model Penal Code which dispenses with the defenses of factual and legal impossibility. Had they been available as defenses, the outcome may have been different. The prosecution was unable to prove if Geller was alive or dead at the time Dlugash (D) fired the gun. If, however, it was shown that he was dead, there could be no crime of attempted murder. Shooting a dead person is not murder, although there may be lesser crimes that could have been charged. The court's opinion noted that after the enactment of the statute at issue, what is of importance is that which is in the defendant's own mind. Thus, liability is measured on the facts as the defendant believes them to be. The court, through its "subsumed" analysis, concluded that since the jury found Dlugash (D) guilty of murder, it must have concluded that he believed Geller was alive. Moreover, the jury must have rejected Dlugash's (D) statement that it looked as if Geller was already dead when he fired his shots. In any event, since the jury must have concluded that Dlugash (D) believed Geller was alive, the court held that the judgment should have been modified to convict for attempted murder.

THE FIFTH CIRCUIT PERMITS A DEFENSE OF LEGAL IMPOSSIBILITY WHERE THE DEFENDANT INTENDS TO COMMIT PUNISHABLE CONDUCT BUT THE RESULT OF HIS CONDUCT WOULD NOT HAVE BEEN PUNISHABLE DUE TO CIRCUMSTANCES UNKNOWN TO THE DEFENDANT

United States v. Berrigan

(Federal Government) v. (Imprisoned Vietnam War Resister)
482 F.2d 171 (3d Cir. 1973)

MEMORY GRAPHIC

Instant Facts

A priest who was in federal prison for resisting the Vietnam War was convicted of attempting to smuggle letters in and out of prison without the knowledge and consent of the warden, even though the warden knew of the arrangement and agreed to let the courier feign cooperation.

Black Letter Rule

The defense of legal impossibility applies where the defendant has intended to commit a criminal act but commits an act that does not amount to a crime.

Procedural Basis: Not provided.

Facts: Father Berrigan (D), an imprisoned Vietnam War resister, was convicted of attempting to violate a federal statute, which in conjunction with regulations promulgated by the Attorney General, made it a crime to take anything in or out of prison "without the knowledge and consent" of the warden. The evidence at trial showed that Berrigan (D) had attempted to smuggle letters into and out of a prison through the use of a courier. Although Berrigan (D) believed that the warden was unaware of his plan, the warden had actually agreed to let the courier pretend to go along with the plan.

Issue: Is legal impossibility a valid defense to a charge of attempt?

Decision and Rationale: (Not Provided) Yes. The defense of legal impossibility applies where the defendant has intended to commit a criminal act but commits an act that does not amount to a crime. The mere intent to commit a crime is, of course, not punishable. Had Berrigan (D) attempted to send the letters through normal channels, somehow believing that it constituted a crime, he could not be punished because the intended consequence was not a crime. If he attempted to send the letter without the knowledge and consent of the warden and the warden was oblivious to the plan, then Berrigan (D) would be guilty of attempt. Here, however, we have a situation where Berrigan (D) intended to send a letter without knowledge or consent of the warden, actually sent the letter, but unknown to him, the letter was sent with the knowledge and consent of the warden. The writing of the letter and its transmittal to the courier constituted the *act* necessary for an attempt conviction. However the government failed to prove the objective situation required by the statute – i.e., the warden's lack of knowledge and failure to give consent. Without this proof, the consequence or result would not have amounted to a violation of the statute. Simply put, attempting to do that which is not a crime is not attempting to commit a crime.

United States v. Oviedo

(Federal Government) v. (Heroin Dealer who Sold a Legal Substance)

525 F.2d 881 (5th Cir. 1976)

M E M O R Y G R A P H I C

Instant Facts

A heroin dealer was arrested when he sold to an undercover police officer what all parties believed to be heroin, but which tests proved was a legal substance.

Black Letter Rule

In order for a defendant to be guilty of a criminal attempt, the objective acts performed, without any reliance on the accompanying *mens rea*, mark the defendant's conduct as criminal in nature.

Procedural Basis: Appeal from conviction for attempt to distribute heroin.

Facts: Oviedo (D) was approached by an undercover agent who asked to purchase heroin. The two arranged a later meeting, at which Oviedo (D) gave the agent a substance he claimed was heroin. The agent performed a field test that came up positive and Oviedo (D) was arrested. When lab tests showed that the substance was not heroin but some other legal substance, Oviedo (D) was charged with attempted distribution of heroin. The jury rejected Oviedo's (D) claim that he knew the substance to be legal and convicted him of the attempt charge.

Issue: May a defendant be convicted of an attempt to distribute what he believes are narcotics, but which in fact are legal substances?

Decision and Rationale: (Not provided) No. In order for a defendant to be guilty of a criminal attempt, the objective acts performed, without any reliance on the accompanying *mens rea*, must mark the defendant's conduct as criminal in nature. We must first note that we reject any distinction between factual and legal impossibility because it often does no service. For example, Oviedo's (D) acts involved factual impossibility in that Oviedo's (D) conduct was not criminal only because of a fact unknown to him – that the substance was not heroin. This case can also be framed as one of legal impossibility because what Oviedo (D) did, transfer a legal substance, was not a crime. We do not believe that we can find an attempt based solely on Oviedo's (D) objectives. When the defendant sells heroin it is reasonable to infer that he knew the physical nature of the substance, and place on him the burden of disproving that inference. However, where the substance is not in fact heroin, a major objective element is eliminated, running the risk of a mistaken conclusion that the defendant believed the substance to be heroin. We cannot conclude that the objective acts of Oviedo (D), apart from any indirect evidence of intent, mark his conduct as criminal in nature. The acts are consistent with a non-criminal enterprise. Therefore, Oviedo's (D) intent cannot form the sole basis of a conviction.

Analysis:

The Fifth Circuit here takes a different approach to the problem of legal impossibility than that announced in *People v. Jaffe* [case where a man believed he was buying stolen goods and was convicted of that crime even though the goods were not in fact stolen] and adopted by the Third Circuit in *United States v. Berrigan* [case involving an imprisoned Vietnam War resistor who was convicted of attempting to smuggle letters in and out of prison]. In *Berrigan* the focus of the inquiry was on whether the results of the defendants' objective acts constituted a crime, regardless of his subjective intent. The rationale (if you can call it a "rationale") behind the *Jaffe/Berrigan* approach to impossibility is that the defendant cannot "intend" to do something which is impossible, he can only hope or desire to do so. Accordingly, a defendant should not be punished for mere desire. This definition of intent is somewhat nonsensical; a person's intent is merely his purpose, which need not make sense. As a result, the *Jaffe/Berrigan* approach has been rejected either by statute or decision in most jurisdictions. For example, the Second Circuit rejected the *Berrigan* concept of legal impossibility and applied the Model Penal Code's approach, which focuses on the facts as viewed by the defendant at the time of his conduct. Both approaches have their faults. The view established by the Model Penal Code and adopted by the Second Circuit carries the danger that a person will be convicted for "bad thoughts." After all, why should someone go to jail because he imagined a certain state of facts? The *Berrigan* approach is too lenient in that it will result in the acquittal of defendants who are deserving of punishment. Here, the Fifth Circuit announced a middle approach to legal impossibility. Like the "test" announced in *Berrigan*, the *Oviedo* approach ignores the subjective intent of the defendant and focuses on his conduct. As the court explained, because it can be inferred that a person intends to do what he actually does, conduct serves as an objective gauge of whether defendant intended to commit a crime. As the court saw it, the problem was really one of the interplay between *mens rea* and *actus reus*. The reason is that no act is criminal without a criminal intent and conduct is the best gauge of what the defendant intended. Thus, if a no crime is actually committed, how can we reasonably be sure the defendant intended to commit a crime? In response to this question, the court recognized that the criminality of the defendant's conduct could be judged objectively by reference to the whole of his acts. In other words, if everything the defendant did leads to the conclusion that he acted criminally, then a conviction is proper; where the defendant's acts are completely consistent with legal conduct, a conviction cannot be had. For example, suppose Oviedo (D) had attempted to bring the same substance across the U.S. border with the belief that he was smuggling heroin. If Oviedo (D) had taken the precautions usually employed by smugglers – i.e., placing the bag in a secret compartment or swallowing the bag whole – the Fifth Circuit might be willing to uphold a conviction because there would be no other reason to so hide a legal substance.

The Case of Lady Eldon's French Lace
(A Hypothetical Decision on a Hypothetical State of Facts)

M E M O R Y   G R A P H I C

Instant Facts
(Hypothetical) A woman attempts to smuggle across the English border what she believes is French lace, but which is actually made in England.

Black Letter Rule
A person cannot escape an attempt conviction based on the fact that her conduct did not constitute a crime under the actual circumstances, if she believed the circumstances to be otherwise, and, had her belief been correct, what she set out to do would constitute a crime.

Procedural Basis: Not applicable.

Facts: (Hypothetical Facts) While on the European continent Lady Eldon (D) bought what she thought was French lace, purchased at an inflated price. In an attempt to smuggle it past English Customs, she hid the lace in a secret pocket. Upon Lady Eldon's (D) arrival at the English port of entry at Dover, a customs agent discovered the package. The lace, however, turned out to be manufactured in England, and as such, not subject to duty.

Issue: May a person who does everything in her power to commit a crime be convicted of attempt even though her conduct under the circumstances did not amount to a crime?

Decision and Rationale: (Not Provided) Yes. A person cannot escape an attempt conviction based on the fact that her conduct did not constitute a crime under the actual circumstances, if she believed the circumstances to be otherwise, and, had her belief been correct, what she set out to do would constitute a crime. Cases such as *People v. Jaffe* [case where a man believed he was buying stolen goods and was convicted of that crime even though the goods were not in fact stolen] and *United States v. Berrigan* [case involving an imprisoned Vietnam War resistor who was convicted of attempting to smuggle letters in and out of prison] stand for the proposition that, under the circumstances at issue here, a conviction is improper. This conclusion is based on the faulty premise that what a person intends to do is what he actually does. Defining intent in this manner is at odds with common sense and common language. After all, a person can mistakenly take someone's umbrella without having the intent to do so. We believe it unsound to conclude that Lady Eldon (D) should not be held criminally liable. In other circumstances, a person's intent is determined by what they thought, not what they did. For example, had Lady Eldon (D) actually purchased French lace believing it to be inexpensive English lace, she could not be found guilty of attempted smuggling because there is the lack of intent to smuggle French lace. Why should not intent be judged in the same manner in this case? The answer, according to some, is that innocent thoughts can exculpate, but a criminal mind should not inculpate because punishing bad thoughts is forbidden. But in this case we are not punishing thoughts. Lady Eldon (D) did everything in her power to and all she thought necessary to commit the crime. Thus Lady Eldon (D) thought *and* acted. Another justification for exculpating Lady Eldon (D) was proffered by the court in *United States v. Oviedo* [case involving a man who sold to an undercover agent what everyone believed was heroin, but turned out to be a legal substance], which held that legal impossibility is a valid defense because a person's conduct is the best evidence of his intent. That may be true, but it does not rule out the possibility that other conduct is evidence of intent. What if Lady Eldon (D) had specially tailored a secret pocket for the lace, made incriminating statements to others, and had a receipt showing she paid a price appropriate for expensive French lace? Such evidence would form a rational basis for concluding she attempted to smuggle what she thought was French lace. Thus, we conclude that Lady Eldon (D) should be found guilty of attempt to smuggle. We do note that there are true cases of legal impossibility which may form the basis of a valid defense. Suppose that Lady Eldon (D) actually purchased French lace and attempted to bring it into the country undetected by Customs, but the day before her arrival the law had changed to make French lace not subject to duties. In this case Lady Eldon (D) cannot be held liable for attempt because what she intended to do was not a violation of criminal law. Her state of mind may be immoral, but it is not criminal.

Analysis:

With this hypothetical the editors attempt to set forth a justification for the Model Penal Code's approach to legal impossibility, while at the same time dispelling the faulty logic upon which the holdings in cases like *Jaffe* and *Berrigan* are reasoned. The basic point is that, absent the requisite *mens rea*, there are no objectively criminal or "bad" acts. Strict liability crimes notwithstanding, the only thing that makes an act criminal is the intent with which it is done. In the view of the editors and the Model Penal Code, it matters not that the acts done were not the one's prescribed by statute because a commission of those acts is not a violation of law if there is no intent to commit them. What matters is that Lady Eldon (D) acted with the intent to commit a crime. This reasoning dispels the logic of *Jaffe* and *Berrigan* because there is no danger of punishing thoughts. Indeed, Lady Eldon (D) did more than think, she acted with intent. As to the fear of a lack of evidence of intent, as expressed in *Oviedo*, the editors state that many acts can be used as objective evidence of intent. They reason that an act is not always evidence of intent. Intent is subjective and can only be determined as such.

Chapter 7

Unlike individual criminality, group criminality poses a different set of concerns that criminal laws have evolved to combat. The crimes involving group conduct grew to encompass not only completed crimes, but also inchoate offenses such as attempt and conspiracy.

One reason to treat group criminality differently than individual criminality is the simple idea that two heads are better than one. Of course, "better" in this context means more likely to succeed, and the goal of the criminal law is to ensure that criminals don't succeed. This not only applies to where two or more persons directly participate in a crime, but also where individuals assist in the encouragement or facilitation of the crime. For example, a bank robber is more likely to succeed if he has someone directly participating in the crime, like a second robber to act as a lookout while the other collects the money. The bank robber is also more likely to succeed if someone facilitates the robbery, like a person who lends the robbers a car for their getaway vehicle.

In addition, group criminal action poses other concerns for criminal law. Not only can group action be more successful, but group action can arguably also be more difficult for law enforcement to detect. If a person plans on robbing a bank, getting a crew of fellow conspirators to do the stakeout, the homework, and research the minutia of the plan may be less likely to raise warning flags than one single person sticking his neck out and doing all the research and planning.

Finally, group action increases the chances of future criminal activity. If a group of conspirators successfully carry out a bank robbery, they may use their combined skills again once the money from the original heist runs out.

Unfortunately, the solution to these problems has proved more complex and often more problematic than courts and defendants would like. The following cases deal with three broad issues.

The first is accomplice liability. While the legal definition of "accomplice" has undergone a number of permutations, the general definition remains the same. An accomplice is essentially a participant in the criminal offense. The cases struggle with the two issues of what level of assistance should merit punishment and what level of culpability is required, if any.

The second is liability within the corporate environment. Because corporations are run by human agents, but are separate legal entities in themselves, courts and lawmakers have developed laws that hold corporations liable for the acts of its agents and vice versa. Like the issues concerning accomplice liability, the debates in this context hinge on the *mens rea* and *actus reus* of the actors involved. In addition, these cases also turn on the degree of responsibility the corporate agents hold over the criminal act in question.

The final issue deals with the inchoate crime of conspiracy. Conspiracy laws deal with the additional issues of determining when parties have actually agreed to engage in a criminal plan and what the scope of the plan should be for the purpose of imposing criminal liability. Conspiracy laws are unique in that the *mens rea* for the crime is, practically speaking, the same as the *actus reus*. This closeness of each element has created a number of additional problems and difficult issues that have made conspiracy laws arguably the most controversial area of criminal law.

As you read the following cases, keep in mind the original reasons why we want to punish group criminal conduct and the traditional requirements of *mens rea* and *actus reus*. When you come across cases that deviate from these concerns, ask yourself if there are additional justifications for expanding the criminal law beyond those norms.

Chapter 7

NOTE: THE PURPOSE OF THIS OUTLINE IS TO ORGANIZE THE CASES SO THAT ONE CAN QUICKLY UNDERSTAND THE RELEVANCE OF EACH CASE TO THE COURSE. NO ATTEMPT IS MADE IN THIS OVERVIEW TO ADDRESS EVERY CONCEPT THAT MUST BE STUDIED. BE SURE TO READ THE ENTIRE CASEBOOK AND/OR OTHER MATERIALS TO GAIN A FULL UNDERSTANDING OF ALL CONCEPTS.

I. Accountability for Participation in Criminal Conduct
  A. Common Law Principles
    1. At common law, criminal acts were categorized based on the perpetrator's level of involvement in the crime.
      a. Principal in the first degree: The person who actually committed the crime.
      b. Principals in the second degree: Those who were present and aided or abetted the crime.
      c. Accessory: Those not present when the crime took place.
        (1) Accessory before the fact: A person who was not present at the time of the crime but assisted the principal in some way.
        (2) Accessory after the fact: A person who assists a principal after the commission of the crime with the knowledge that the principal has committed a felony.
      d. Each of these categories had varying degrees of punishment, and principals in the second degree and accessories could only be tried once the principal was convicted of the crime.
    2. Modern Statutes: The Model Penal Code and State Statutes
      a. Modern statutes have abolished the common law categories, except for accessory after the fact, which entails a less severe punishment.
      b. Further, under most modern statutes anyone who participates in or assists with the commission of a crime with the purpose of facilitating crime is considered a principal.
      c. Also, today the principal need not be convicted in order for other participants to be convicted.
      d. Modern statutes, such as 18 U.S.C. § 2 (the federal complicity statute), permit all partici-

pants in a crime to be punished equally.
      (1) Some have criticized the affixation of equal punishment to all participants in a crime, arguing that a firm application of this approach leaves a judge with too little flexibility in dealing with varying levels of culpable offenders. *Comments of Judge Posner in United States v. Ambrose.*
      (2) Others have suggested that the approach merely permits equal punishment, but does not mandate it, thus preserving the judge's discretion in sentencing.
    3. Theories of Complicity: Kadish, *A Theory of Complicity*
      a. Commentators have suggested that laws regarding complicity are forced to deviate from traditional concepts of *mens rea* and *actus reus* for defining when a crime occurs because it is difficult to find one person guilty of assisting the otherwise volitional acts of others.
      b. Since we conceive of human actions as controlled by free will or choice, it is difficult to prove that one person caused another to commit a crime.
      c. As a result, an alternative doctrine is required to ascertain when the acts of others require criminal sanctions.
  B. The Participant's *Mens Rea*
    1. Conduct of the Principal
      a. When a party intends to promote or facilitate the commission of a crime by a principal, he or she will generally be held responsible for the substantive crime thereafter committed. Prosecutors cannot convict without proof of this specific intent.
      (1) For example, a person cannot be made an accomplice to murder for verbally inciting the killer to action unless the words of encouragement were used with the intention of encouraging the murder. *Hicks v. United States.*
      (2) Some courts have held that because intent to commit the crime is required for conviction, when the accomplice seeks to catch the principal in the act, as in the case of an

undercover law enforcement officer, the accomplice is not guilty of the crime. *Wilson v. People.*

b. On the other end of the spectrum, a defendant clearly cannot be found guilty of aiding or abetting where there is no evidence of any connection or association between the defendant and the principal relating to the commission of a crime. *State v. Gladstone.*

c. There has been some disagreement, however, over whether knowingly facilitating the commission of a crime, in the absence of true intent or purpose to achieve a criminal end, is enough to make one responsible as an accomplice.

(1) Model Penal Code (MPC) § 2.06(3)(a) requires that an accomplice assist the principal with the purpose of facilitating a crime; knowingly facilitating a crime is not enough to establish accomplice liability under the MPC.

(2) New York Penal Code §115 creates a separate offense for those who knowingly facilitate the commission of a crime. In such cases, the proper charge is "criminal facilitation," which carries a sentence less severe than accomplice liability or aiding and abetting does.

(3) And in *United States v. Fountain*, the 7th Circuit held that knowingly facilitating the commission of a crime was enough to make the facilitator guilty of the substantive crime.

d. In some courts, a defendant's intent is sometimes considered to be irrelevant, at least to some extent.

(1) For example, some courts have held that a defendant is liable for the unplanned and unintended acts of co-conspirators that are the natural, probable, and foreseeable consequences of his assistance. *People v. Luparello.*

(a) The District of Columbia Court of Appeals has found that the phrase "natural, probable, and foreseeable consequences" means a consequence reasonably likely to ensue from the planned events without the interference of any intervening factors. *Roy v. United States.*

(2) Other courts have rejected the "natural and probable consequences test," holding that an accomplice is only responsible for those actions which he "procured, counseled, commanded, or encouraged." *State v. Marr.*

(a) The Model Penal Code is in accord with these courts.

2. Attendant Circumstances

a. To be held responsible for aiding and abetting a criminal act, there has to be some knowledge that one's actions are assisting another in the commission of a crime. If a party has no knowledge of the attendant circumstances of a crime, there will be no conviction.

b. For example, a defendant cannot be convicted of aiding and abetting a convicted felon's possession of a firearm if the prosecution has not shown that the defendant had knowledge of the possessor's prior felony. *United States v. Xavier.*

3. The Participant's *Mens Rea* and the End Result

a. A person who encourages or assists another in engaging in dangerous conduct establishes accomplice liability for himself for crimes requiring recklessness or negligence.

(1) For example, a person may be convicted of being an accessory before the fact to the crime of manslaughter arising through criminal negligence when he or she encourages the negligent or reckless behavior. *State v. McVay.*

b. Furthermore, when two or more people intentionally participate in an inherently dangerous and unlawful activity, they share culpability for any crime committed as a part of that activity, even if the crime is committed by only one of the participants. *People v. Russell.*

C. The Participant's *Actus Reus*

1. To be guilty of aiding and abetting, a person must fulfill the *actus reus* element of the crime. This can be done by being present, taking part in, concurring in, or encouraging the act. *Wilcox v. Jeffery.*

2. The accomplice's assistance (his *actus reus*) need not be a "but for" cause of the criminal

conduct. Merely rendering it easier for the principal to accomplish the criminal act is enough, even if the same result would have occurred without the assistance. *State ex rel. Attorney General v. Tally, Judge.*

3. Sometimes the *actus reus* requirement can be satisfied by a failure to act.

   a. Under MPC § 2.06(3)(a)(iii), a person can be an accomplice to a criminal act if that person has a legal duty to prevent the criminal act, but fails to do so with the purpose of facilitating the crime.

      (1) For example, a father who just stands by and watches while his son commits a rape of a family friend is guilty of accomplice liability for facilitating the rape. *State v. Davis.*

   b. In another situation, some states have held that mothers have a legal duty to protect their children from abuse by third parties and are guilty as accomplices where the third party abused the child in the mother's presence. *People v. Stanciel; State v. Walden.*

D. The Relationship Between the Liability of the Parties

   1. Some courts have held that an accomplice cannot be held criminally liable if the principal had no criminal intent. *State v. Hayes.*

      a. Others, however, have disagreed, holding that a party can be held criminally responsible as an accomplice when the crime is committed by an undercover law enforcement officer who, by way of his being a law enforcement officer, did not have the *mens rea* required for the crime. *Vaden v. State.*

   2. In some instances, a principal to a crime has an excuse or justification that makes it so that when he or she commits the normally-criminal act, no crime is recognized.

      a. Courts have held that in some instances, these excuses or justifications are personal to the principal, meaning that they cannot be used by the accomplice as a defense to accomplice liability. *Taylor v. Commonwealth.* Other courts have disagreed.

      b. In this same vein, courts are also split over whether an accomplice can be convicted for the principal's crimes where the principal is immune from prosecution.

3. Innocent Agents and Derivative Criminal Liability

   a. MPC § 2.06(2)(a) recognizes the innocent agent doctrine. Under that section, if the accomplice forces or dupes an innocent agent into committing a criminal act, the accomplice becomes liable as a principal.

   b. Some commentators do not agree with the innocent agent doctrine. *Kadish, Blame and Punishment.*

      (1) The innocent agent doctrine cannot be applied where the innocent agent is the only class of persons who can commit the crime.

      (2) In addition, the innocent agent doctrine cannot be applied where the crime can only be performed by the innocent agent himself.

   c. Some courts have ignored these problems with the innocent agent doctrine and impose liability on the accomplice anyway. *United States v. Walser, United States v. Ruffin.*

4. The acquittal of a principal in a separate trial does not have preclusive effect on the trial of the accomplice. *United States v. Standefer.*

5. Differences in Culpability between the Secondary Party and the Principal

   a. At common law, a secondary party could not be held liable for an offense greater than that carried out by the principal even though the secondary actor intended that a greater offense be committed. *Regina v. Richards.*

      (1) Some commentators have expressed disapproval of this rule. *Williams, Criminal Law: The General Part.*

   b. Courts have held that a secondary party can be held liable for an offense lesser than that carried out by the principal (such as manslaughter instead of murder). *Moore v. Lowe.*

   c. Victims as Accomplices: The Model Penal Code § 2.06(6)

      (1) The MPC and many states prohibit punishment as an accomplice for an offense committed by another if the person is a victim of that offense.

         (a) For example, an underage girl who wilfully has sex with an older man (thereby causing him to commit statutory rape) generally will not be held criminally responsible as his accomplice.

(2) The MPC and many states also prohibit punishment as an accomplice for an offense committed by another if the offense is so defined that his conduct is inevitably incident to its commission.

II. Liability within the Corporate Framework
A. Liability of the Corporate Entity for the Acts of Employees
1. Introduction to the Liability of Corporate Entities
a. A corporation can be held criminally liable for the acts of its employees. *New York Central & Hudson River Railroad Co. v. United States*.
(1) A corporation can also be held liable for the acts of its agents, done within the scope of their employment, even though corporate policy and the agent's specific instructions prohibit such acts. *United States v. Hilton Hotels Corp*.
b. The Commentary to MPC § 2.07 addresses some of the justifications for and problems with the concept of corporate liability:
(1) The imposition of corporate liability may deter criminal corporate conduct by softening pressures on employees to maximize profits.
(2) The imposition of corporate liability may also be necessary where it is difficult to prove who the culpable agent in the corporation is.
(3) However, while the wisdom of imposing corporate liability may be appropriate in these circumstances, juries may impose liability in other less appropriate situations, thereby punishing innocent stockholders without adequate justification.
2. There are two main approaches to the doctrine of corporate liability. The first is the respondeat superior approach followed in *New York Central & Hudson*, and the second is a more restrictive approach adopted by the MPC.
a. Respondeat Superior
(1) The respondeat superior approach is ex-

plained in *Developments in the Law—Corporate Crime: Regulating Corporate Behavior through Criminal Sanctions*.
(a) Under respondeat superior, a corporation can be held liable for the acts of its agents where a corporate agent, acting within the scope of his or her employment, commits a crime with the intent to benefit the corporation.
i. The rule applies even if the act was specifically prohibited by a superior and the corporation made good faith efforts to prevent the crime.
ii. Though the agent must intend to benefit the corporation, the corporation need not actually benefit from the crime to be held responsible.
(b) The requirements of scope of employment and intent to benefit need not be proven if a supervisor subsequently approves the employee's criminal act.
(2) A corporation can be held criminally liable for the acts of its agent if it placed the agent in a position with enough authority and responsibility to act on behalf of the corporation in handling a particular corporate matter and he or she committed the criminal act in furtherance of that particular corporate matter. *Commonwealth v. Beneficial Finance Co.*
(a) In some states, corporate liability attaches under these circumstances only when there exists evidence of a corporate policy (either by action or omission) that authorized, tolerated, or ratified the illegal conduct. *State v. Christy Pontiac-GMC*.
b. The Model Penal Code Approach: MPC § 2.07 imposes three forms of corporate liability.
(1) A corporation is liable for minor infractions and non-code penal offenses whose legislative purpose is to impose corporate liability when those acts are committed by a corporate agent acting within the scope of employment and on behalf of the corporation, except where a high managerial supervisor

having ultimate responsibility over the criminal conduct used due diligence to prevent it.

(2) A corporation is liable for omissions reflecting a failure to discharge specific corporate duties required by law.

(3) A corporation is liable for offenses under the code if the criminal conduct is authorized, commanded, solicited, performed, or recklessly tolerated by the board of directors or a high managerial agent. *Rethinking Corporate Liability Under the Model Penal Code.*

B. Liability of Corporate Agents

1. In addition to corporations being held criminally responsible for the acts of their agents, corporate officers and others can sometimes be held responsible for their own acts performed as corporate agents and for the acts of others in the corporation.

   a. This view is reflected in both the MPC and case law. MPC § 2.07(6)(a) reads: "A person is legally accountable for any conduct he performs or causes to be performed in the name of the corporation . . . or in its behalf to the same extent as if it were performed in his own name or behalf."

   (1) MPC § 2.07(6)(b) states that when the law imposes a duty upon a corporation, the agent in charge of discharging that duty can be held "legally accountable for reckless omission to perform the required act to the same extent as if the duty were imposed by law directly upon himself."

   b. In 1954 in *Gordon v. United States*, the Tenth Circuit held that an unknowing employer can be held criminally liable for an employee's willful criminal acts made while acting in the course of employment. This decision was reversed by the United States Supreme Court on the ground that an employee's knowledge cannot be imputed to an ignorant employer for the purpose of proving the employer's willfulness in violating a statute.

2. In 1975, the Supreme Court announced the "responsible corporate officer doctrine," a doctrine that has since been limited by other courts. Under that doctrine, a corporate officer can be criminally liable without proof of any wrongful action if the officer "had, by reason of his position in the corporation, responsibility and authority either to prevent in the first instance, or promptly to correct, the violation complained of, and . . . he failed to do so." *United States v. Park*

   a. Some courts recognize a defense of impossibility of avoidance of the harm. Under that defense, a corporate officer may offer a defense of impossibility to avoid liability if the officer can prove that he or she used "extraordinary care" in trying to prevent the criminal violations. *United States v. New England Grocers Supply Co.*

   (1) The prosecution may rebut this contention, however, by proving beyond a reasonable doubt that the officer had the power or capacity to correct or prevent the violation.

   b. Some courts have placed limits on the responsible corporate officer doctrine. For example, in *United States v. MacDonald & Watson Waste Oil Co.*, the First Circuit Court of Appeals limited the applicability of the doctrine to strict liability situations and held that in other situations a corporate agent can only be convicted based on the *mens rea* requirement of the applicable statute.

III. Conspiracy

A. Introduction: The Effect of a Conspiracy Charge

1. The Dual Purposes of a Conspiracy Charge: According to the Comment to MPC § 5.03, a charge of conspiracy serves two different functions.

   a. First, the offense of conspiracy seeks to prevent serious criminal conduct by stopping it in the planning stages.

   b. Second, conspiracy seeks to deter the dangers inherent in group criminal activity.

2. Hearsay and Conspiracies

   a. Sometimes special rules apply in conspiracy prosecutions. For example, Federal Rule of Evidence (FRE) 801(d)(2)(E) holds that "a statement by a coconspirator of a party [made] during the course and in furtherance

of the conspiracy" is not hearsay and is therefore admissible in court if relevant. *United States v. Trowery*; *United States v. Gil*.

    (1)   An alleged co-conspirator's statement not made in furtherance of the conspiracy but made to avoid criminal punishment is not admissible under the hearsay rule. *Krulewitch v. United States*.

  b.   Before a co-conspirator's statements can be admitted, however, the judge must determine by a preponderance of evidence that a conspiracy exists and the defendant was involved. *Bourjaily v. United States*.

    (1)   In so doing, federal law allows judges to use the statement itself as evidence of a conspiracy.

    (2)   Some state courts require independent evidence of a conspiracy.

3.   The Duration of the Conspiracy

  a.   Attempts to conceal a conspiracy are not considered part of the original conspiracy unless there is direct evidence that the cover-up was part of an express agreement among the conspirators to act in concert to conceal the crime. *Grunewald v. United States*.

  b.   MPC §5.03(7)(b): A conspiracy terminates (and the statute of limitations begins to run) when the co-conspirators are no longer engaged in any action in furtherance of the conspiratorial objectives.

4.   Abandonment of the Conspiracy

  a.   Most courts hold that a defendant has abandoned a conspiracy where he makes his withdrawal known to all the other conspirators. *Hyde v. United States*; MPC §5.03(7)(c).

  b.   A minority of courts require the abandoning party to engage in some sort of act aimed at thwarting the conspiracy. The federal courts have no such requirement. *United States v. United States Gypsum Co.*

  c.   At common law, withdrawal was not a defense to a charge of conspiracy because the crime of conspiracy was deemed complete at the time the initial agreement was entered into.

    (1)   Today, however, some courts, as well as the MPC, recognize withdrawal as a com-

plete defense to the crime of conspiracy.

5.   Degree of Punishment

  a.   A majority of states fix the level of punishment for conspiracy at some level below that of the object offense.

  b.   Approximately one-third of the states, following the lead of MPC § 5.05(l), punish conspiracies to the same degree as the object crime, except in the case of the most serious felonies.

  c.   A minority of states treat conspiracy as a generic offense with a punishment scale unrelated to the scales for the object crime.

    (1)   18 U.S.C. § 371 follows this approach with respect to conspiracies to commit felonies. Conspiracies to commit misdemeanors, however, are punished in a manner somewhat similar to that advocated by MPC § 5.05(l).

  d.   Consolidation with the Completed Crime

    (1)   Traditionally conspiracy does not merge with the completed underlying crime, and as such can be punished separately. *Callanan v. United States*.

    (2)   Some states and the MPC, however, recognize a merger of the conspiracy with the completed offense when the completed offense is equal to the scope of the original conspiracy.

      (a)   There is no merger where the criminal objectives of the conspiracy exceed the seriousness of the crimes committed in furtherance of the conspiracy.

6.   Some commentators have expressed criticism of conspiracy laws in general. *The Unnecessary Crime of Conspiracy*.

  a.   As an inchoate crime, the doctrine of conspiracy is an abstract concept that eludes traditional concerns of public policy or the interests of the parties.

  b.   The doctrine has created considerable confusion by diverting courts away from these concerns in favor of serving the theory of conspiracy.

  c.   The theory of conspiracy itself has generated several independent procedural and substantive concepts (relating to hearsay, *mens rea*, *actus reus*, punishment, and others) that are each considerably important and complex.

d. These concepts deserve separate consideration and should not be subordinate to a single abstract doctrine.

B. Conspiracy as a Form of Accessorial Liability

1. Under the famous (and to some infamous) *Pinkerton* doctrine, a co-conspirator tried in federal court is criminally liable for all substantive offenses committed by other co-conspirators in furtherance of the conspiracy. *Pinkerton v. United States*.

   a. In some jurisdictions, a co-conspirator may be criminally liable under the *Pinkerton* doctrine for substantive offenses committed by other co-conspirators that are not even within the scope of the conspiracy and were originally unintended so long as they are reasonably foreseeable as the necessary or natural consequences of the conspiracy. *State v. Bridges*; *United States v. Alvarez*.

2. Generally, a newcomer to a particular conspiracy is not liable for the prior substantive offenses committed by co-conspirators before he or she joined the conspiracy. *Pinkerton* is not retroactive. *United States v. Blackmon*.

3. Contrary to *Pinkerton*, the MPC does not equate conspiracy with complicity.

   a. Under the MPC view, conspirators are only liable for substantive offenses that they intend as evidenced by whether or not the conspirator solicited the commission of the offense or aided, or agreed or attempted to aid, in its commission. Comment to MPC § 2.06(3).

   b. According to the MPC, without such limitations there would be no end to the number of additional offenses that could be attributed to a defendant, even though the defendant did not intend or know of the offenses.

C. The *Actus Reus* of Conspiracy

1. Conspiracy is an agreement between two or more people to commit a crime. The *actus reus* of conspiracy is the agreement.

   a. The "agreement [is] the essential element of the crime. *Ianelli v. United States*.

   b. A defendant need not know all of the details or participants of a conspiracy in order to be prosecuted. *United States v. James*.

2. Evidence of a conspiratorial agreement can be based on inferences drawn from the course of conduct of the alleged conspirators. *Interstate Circuit Inc. v. United States*.

   a. "The proof [offered in a conspiracy case], by the very nature of the crime, must be circumstantial and therefore inferential to an extent varying with the conditions under which the crime may be consummated." *Direct Sales Co. v. Untied States*.

   b. Some courts adhere to the Coleridge Instruction, first given in 1837 in England, which states that direct evidence of a conspiratorial agreement is often lacking; as a result, the jury may infer the existence of a conspiracy where persons are pursuing the same object with one person performing part of the act and the other another part so as to complete the act with the object of obtaining a common goal. *Rex v. Murphy*

   (1) Commentators have praised this instruction, but also warned of the danger of it being misinterpreted to mean that a mere concurrence of acts is the equivalence of a conspiracy.

   (2) Some courts feel that it is dangerous to find a conspiracy when the sum total of proof presented finds a mere concurrence of acts without agreement. *United States v. Garcia*.

   (3) Other courts have found a conspiracy when a "mere association" involved knowledge of the crime and a close relationship between the accused conspirator and the principal.

   (a) Specifically, a crew that has knowledge that their captain is illegally shipping contraband on a long voyage can be found guilty of conspiracy to import contraband. *United States v. Freeman*.

3. A defendant's conduct can also be used to infer guilt of participation in a conspiracy. *United States v. Alvarez*.

4. The Requirement of an Overt Act

   a. At common law, the forming of an agreement was enough to make a party guilty of conspiracy. No other overt act was required. *Mulchay v. The Queen*.

   b. Most American statutes now require some

kind of overt act to be made in furtherance of the conspiracy, with some exceptions for conspiracies to commit very serious offenses. States and statutes differ with respect to what type of act is required.

D. The *Mens Rea* of Conspiracy

  1. Courts differ on their view of the *mens rea* required for conspiracy.

    a. Some recognize that intent to enter into a criminal conspiracy is established when a party knows that his goods or services will be put to criminal use and either there is direct evidence of an intent to participate in the crime or an inference that he intends to participate can be drawn from his special interest in the activity or the felonious nature of the crime itself. *People v. Lauria.*

    b. On the other hand, the MPC and most states require purpose for conspiracy liability, as opposed to mere knowledge.

  2. Mistake of Law

    a. Under the *Powell* Doctrine, ignorance that the objective of an agreement is criminal is a defense to the crime of conspiracy. *People v. Powell*; *Commonwealth v. Gormley*.

      (1) The MPC does not follow the *Powell* doctrine.

    b. A defendant who commits a severe offense, which is not based on an "innocent agreement," cannot invoke a mistake of law defense to a conspiracy charge. *United States v. Freed*.

  3. Mistake of Fact

    a. A person cannot be found guilty of conspiring to commit a completed crime based on a mistake of fact. *United States v. Cummins*.

      (1) For example, a person cannot be found guilty of conspiracy to run a red light when he or she does not know of the existence of the light.

    b. However, if the mistake of fact is not relevant to guilt or innocence and merely determines whether a federal court has jurisdiction, then such a mistake is not a defense to the charge of conspiracy (the Jurisdictional Exception). *United States v. Feola*.

E. The Scope of the Agreement- Single or Multiple Conspiracies

  1. When a large and complex criminal network involving many people at various levels of the organization is prosecuted, it is sometimes difficult to determine the number and scope of any conspiracies that might exist therein, and to determine which members of the organization are co-conspirators with one another.

    a. Sometimes courts will find a single conspiracy, and other times the context of the crimes will better lend itself to a finding of multiple conspiracies.

    b. For example, if a court finds a criminal structure in which one person deals with two or more individuals having no connection with each other, and in doing so commits a number of different crimes involving the different persons individually, then it will likely find multiple smaller conspiracies instead of one large conspiracy. *Kotteakos v. United States*.

  2. In making these decisions, courts must look to the facts of a particular case. A number of factors are generally helpful.

    a. Knowledge

      (1) Separate agreements can form a larger conspiracy if the parties to the separate agreements know or must have known that they were participating as part of a larger common plan. *Blumenthal v. United States*.

      (2) Even if none of the defendants ever cooperated or communicated with each other, a conspiracy exists if the defendants are aware of the acts of the other defendants. *United States v. Bruno*.

    b. Joint Objectives

      (1) A joint objective, punishable as a conspiracy, is found where the participants have a joint interest in the success of the activities of the other participants. *United States v. Townsend*.

  3. A mere purchase or sale of contraband does not constitute a basis for inferring an agreement to cooperate with the opposite parties for whatever period they continue to deal in the contraband. *United States v. Borelli*.

  4. Model Penal Code, Comment to §5.03.

    a. The Model Penal Code focuses on the individual's culpability within the conspiracy to determine scope and imposes liability only for crimes that:

(1)   The individual had the purpose of promoting or facilitating;

    (2)   Were committed by parties with whom the individual agreed;

       (a)   Including where the individual agreed with a party to commit a crime but knows that the party has conspired to commit the same crime with another party.

       (b)   In such a circumstance, the individual is guilty of conspiring with the other party to commit that crime, regardless of whether he knows the identity of the other party.

    (3)   In addition, if an individual conspires to commit multiple crimes, he is guilty of only a single conspiracy provided that the crimes are the object of the same agreement or continuous conspiratorial relationship.

  b.   Applying the MPC approach to the facts of *United States v. Bruno* [prosecution of a large drug conspiracy with importers/smugglers, a group of middlemen, and drug retailers in New York and Texas]

    (1)   Under the MPC approach, the smugglers and middlemen would be guilty of conspiracy to import and sell narcotics down to the retail level because they sold to the retailers knowing that the retailers, in turn, would also commit the same crime of selling to addicts.

    (2)   The retailers would be guilty of conspiracy for all sales between themselves and the smugglers and middlemen. However, since the retailers made no agreements as to any activity prior to their receipt of the narcotics, they could not be found guilty of conspiracy to import.

F.   Parties

  1.   A person cannot be convicted of conspiracy to violate a law when it is impossible for him or her to actually violate that law or to commit the substantive crime. *Gebardi v. United States.*

  2.   The Wharton Rule

    a.   According to the Wharton Rule, where a crime requires cooperative action (e.g., bigamy, adultery, dueling, gambling, etc.), participants in the commission of that crime cannot be convicted of conspiracy to commit the crime because the legislature, in such cases, has provided a certain punishment for the offense and it would therefore be improper for a court to allow a prosecutor to go beyond that punishment by charging conspiracy as well. *F. Wharton, Criminal Law § 1604.*

    b.   The MPC does not follow the Wharton rule under the theory that a crime that requires concerted action should still be punishable if preparation is made to commit it.

    (1)   In addition, another rationale for the Wharton Rule, that of avoiding cumulative punishment for the conspiracy and the same completed offense, does not apply under the MPC since it prohibits such cumulative punishment. *Comment to MPC § 5.04.*

    c.   The United States Supreme Court has limited the applicability of Wharton's Rule in certain circumstances, holding that the Rule only creates a presumption against separate punishments in the absence of legislative intent to the contrary, and that legislative intent controls. *Ianelli v. United States.*

  3.   A number of courts have held that a person can be found guilty of conspiracy even if his or her co-conspirator cannot be prosecuted for conspiracy. *Garcia v. State.*

    a.   However, in some jurisdictions, there is no conspiracy if one party is a feigned accomplice. *State v. Grullon; People v. Foster.*

    b.   One reason given by those who adopt this contrary rule is that the societal dangers that arise in collective criminal action are absent where a person unknowingly conspires with a government agent; therefore, liability should not be imposed where the co-conspirator is a government agent.

    c.   Additionally, punishing government-created conspiracies would effectively allow the government to manufacture conspiracies where none would have otherwise existed. *United States v. Escobar De Bright.*

  4.   A person cannot be convicted of "attempted conspiracy." *State v. Kihnel.*

G.   Criminal Enterprises & RICO

1. Introduction
   a. The Racketeer Influenced and Corrupt Organizations Act (RICO) was passed by Congress in response to the perception that traditional conspiracy laws were inadequate tools for dealing with complex criminal endeavors.
   b. The statute has an extremely broad definition of "racketeering activity" and prohibits any person:
      (1) Who has derived income from racketeering activity or collection of illegal debt to use or invest (or conspire to use or invest) such income to acquire an interest in an enterprise that affects interstate or foreign commerce;
      (2) To acquire or maintain (or conspire to acquire or maintain), through a pattern of racketeering or collection of illegal debt, an interest in an enterprise that affects interstate or foreign commerce;
      (3) To be employed or associated (or conspire to be employed or associated) with an enterprise that affects interstate or foreign commerce and to conduct or participate in the enterprise's racketeering activity or collection of illegal debt; or
      (4) From conspiring to commit any of the above violations. 18 U.S.C. § 1962.
   c. The maximum punishment is generally 20 years, though life imprisonment is available if the violation is based on racketeering activity that has life as a maximum punishment.
   d. The RICO statute also allows victims of RICO offenses to sue violators civilly for treble damages.
   e. Definitions
      (1) An "enterprise" for the purposes of RICO may include an exclusively criminal organization, but the separate element of a "pattern of racketeering activity" still must be established independent of the enterprise. *United States v. Turkette.*
      (2) A "pattern" need not involve separate criminal schemes or be indicative of organized criminal activity, but they must be related and pose a threat of continued criminal activity. *H.J. Inc. v. Northwestern Bell Telephone Co.*

   (3) "Conduct or participation" in a prohibited enterprise requires the individual to have some role in directing or managing the enterprise's business. *Reves v. Ernst & Young.*
      (a) Criticism of *Reves. Civil RICO After Reves: An Economic Commentary.*
         i. The *Reves* opinion has contradictory language that seems to indicate that "lower-rung participants" may be subject to liability.
         ii. Such ambiguity undermines the decision and may also create pressure to bend the definition of "enterprise" in order to satisfy the "operation or management" test of *Reves.*
   f. RICO allows the prosecution to charge in a single count what would otherwise constitute multiple, smaller conspiracies. This is because RICO, the violation of which serves as a substantive crime, brings together into a single crime what would otherwise be unrelated and widely-different criminal acts. *United States v. Elliott.*
      (1) Criticism of the *Elliott* Approach. *RICO: The New Darling of the Prosecutor's Nursery.*
         (a) The *Elliott* case is flawed in that it defines the RICO offense or conspiracy by the enterprise in which they arose, as opposed to defining it as a pattern of racketeering activity.
         (b) As a result, completely unrelated offenses can be subject to a RICO prosecution merely because the offenses took place within the same organization and regardless of any actual intent or knowledge of concerted action.
      (2) Multiple offenses or conspiracies can be joined as a single RICO offense or conspiracy if there is direct evidence that the defendants agreed to commit a RICO offense or circumstantial evidence that the nature of the conspiracy is such that each defendant must necessarily have known that the others were also conspiring to violate RICO. *United States v. Sutherland.*
   g. The Controversy over RICO

(1) Some commentators do not like the RICO statute and the results that it produces. *RICO: The Monster that Ate Jurisdiction*

   (a) RICO has "devoured" traditional concepts of federalism, separation of powers, repose of actions, and the basic concept of a government of laws, not of men.

   (b) RICO threatens federalism by encompassing large areas of criminal law that are normally within state law jurisdiction.

   (c) It endangers separation of powers by giving the prosecution (the Executive) and the courts (the Judiciary) considerable law-making discretion normally reserved for the legislature.

   (d) Too much discretion is left in the hands of prosecutors who may be tempted to over extend RICO's reach.

   (e) Finally, the definition of a "pattern of racketeering activity" essentially allows a perpetual cause of action by defining a "pattern" to include two acts of racketeering that occur within 10 years of each other.

(2) Some commentators, however, are not so skeptical. *RICO: The Crime of Being a Criminal*

   (a) RICO allows offenses to be presented in their full context, instead of isolated criminal acts, and allows a jury to understand that these criminal acts may have been committed as part of a larger, more ominous purpose.

   (b) Nevertheless, these benefits of RICO are only viable if we presume that juries can accurately separate different criminal acts committed by different individuals and are not prejudiced by overwhelming and complex evidence.

h. RICO-type Statutes at the State Level

   (1) A number of states have enacted RICO-like statutes pursuant to state law. Many are similar to the federal law, but some are even broader in scope than the RICO Act.

   (2) A number of states have also enacted statutes that make it an offense to participate or conspire to participate in crimes as part of street gangs.

A PERSON CANNOT BE AN ACCOMPLICE TO MURDER UNLESS THE ENCOURAGEMENT WAS MADE WITH THE INTENTION OF ENCOURAGING THE MURDER

Hicks v. United States

(Talkative Bystander) v. (State)
(1893) 150 U.S. 442

M E M O R Y   G R A P H I C

Instant Facts

A Native American man is found guilty of murder for words he uttered that had the effect of encouraging the murderer.

Black Letter Rule

A person cannot be an accomplice of murder unless the words of encouragement were used with the intention of encouraging the murder.

Case Vocabulary

ABET: To assist or encourage.
BILLS OF EXCEPTION: A written statement, signed by the trial court for presentation to the appellate court, of a party's objections made during trial and their foundations.
INCITE: To stir to action or arouse.

Procedural Basis: Appeal of a circuit court decision finding the defendant guilty of murder.

Facts: John Hicks (D) was a Cherokee Indian who was friends with Andrew J. Colvard, a white man who was married to a Cherokee woman and lived in the Cherokee nation. On February 13, 1892, Hicks (D) and Colvard rode on horseback down a road and were confronted by Stand Rowe, another Cherokee Indian. Witnesses saw the three men meet on the road, but they could not hear or understand everything that was said. Colvard and Stand Rowe talked as Hicks (D) listened some 30 or 40 feet away. During the conversation, Stand Rowe pointed his rifle at Colvard twice. The witnesses stated that they saw and heard Hicks (D) laugh aloud each time Stand Rowe raised his rifle and aimed it at Colvard. They also saw Hicks (D) take off his hat, slap his horse with it, and say to Colvard, "take off your hat and die like a man." Stand Rowe then raised his rifle for a third time and shot and killed Colvard. The witnesses then saw Stand Rowe and John Hicks (D) ride off together. Stand Rowe, [who obviously had a troubled childhood], was later killed as officers attempted to arrest him. Hicks (D) was apprehended, tried, and found guilty of the murder of Colvard. At trial, Hicks (D) testified that he did not intend to encourage Stand Rowe to kill Colvard and, in fact, had tried to persuade Stand Rowe not to shoot. Hicks (D) also denied making the statement attributed to him. Hicks (D) also testified that he felt threatened by Stand Rowe and that Stand Rowe demanded Hicks (D) to tell him which road Colvard traveled on. Hicks (D) also testified that, after the murder, he left Stand Rowe on the first opportunity and never met with him again. He further testified that he had never been in the company of Stand Rowe in the weeks before the murder. The trial judge gave the jury an instruction permitting a conviction if they found that Hicks' (D) words had the effect of encouraging Stand Rowe to kill Colvard. Hicks (D) was convicted of murder and appealed to the United States Supreme Court.

Issue: May a person be an accomplice to murder for uttering words that had the effect of encouraging murder, even though the speaker did not intend such a result?

Decision and Rationale: (Shiras) No. The trial judge erred by giving the jury erroneous instructions. First, the judge failed to instruct the jury that any words or acts of Hicks (D) must have been made with the intent of encouraging and abetting Stand Rowe. The effect of Hicks' (D) words is not relevant to the case. To be found guilty of murder, Hicks (D) must have intended the words to have such an effect. In addition, the fact that Hicks (D) intended to utter the words has no bearing on whether he intended encouragement. The statement attributed to Hicks (D) was ambiguous. Hicks (D) made the statement to Colvard, not to Stand Rowe, and Hicks (D) testified that he was fearful for his life and did not know if Stand Rowe would shoot them both. His statement, if made, was "accompanied with the gesture of taking off his own hat," and may have been a statement of desperation made in the belief that both himself and Colvard were about to be killed. Second, the judge also instructed the jury to find guilt if Hicks (D) was "actually present at that place at the time of the firing by Stand Rowe, and he was there for the purpose of either aiding, abetting, advising, or encouraging the shooting of" Colvard, but does not actually aid and abet "because it was not necessary" and "it was done without his assistance." This would have been an otherwise proper instruction if there had been substantial evidence of a prior arrangement or conspiracy between Hicks (D) and Stand Rowe. This instruction assumes that Hicks (D) had a guilty intent; however, the instruction was erroneous because there was insufficient evidence of such an intent. The judgment of the circuit court is reversed and the cause remanded for a new trial.

Analysis:

This opinion illustrates that a criminal intent is required for the criminal liability of the acts of others. In other words, an accomplice should share the same "guilty mind" as the principal. If the principal intends to kill someone and the accomplice shares that intent, then the accomplice can be criminally liable if the principal carries out the act and the accomplice assists. This is different where the alleged accomplice does an intentional act that gives the principal assistance in the crime, but the alleged accomplice did not actually intend to facilitate the crime. For example, a principal could approach a friend to borrow a gun for the stated purpose of target practice, but, in fact, the principal later uses the friend's gun to commit a robbery. Strictly speaking, the friend intentionally committed an act that assists the principal in committing the robbery because she willingly lent her gun to the principal. However, the friend did not intend the principal to use the gun in a robbery. She gave the gun to the principle intending for the principal to use it for target practice. Thus, she cannot be held criminally liable for the robbery. However, if the friend loaned her gun intending for the principal to use it in a robbery, she has a "guilty mind" equivalent to that of the principal and can be held liable for robbery. In this circumstance, she is both intentionally committing an act that assists the principal and intending the end result of that assistance. In the case at hand, the trial court confused the jury by instructing them to hold Hicks (D) liable for murder if his acts were merely intentional.

State v. Gladstone

(State) v. (Drug Peddler)

(1980) 78 Wash. 2d 306, 474 P.2d 274

M E M O R Y   G R A P H I C

Instant Facts

A police informant was hired to buy marijuana from Gladstone (D) who did not sell him any but referred him to a man named Kent who did.

Black Letter Rule

A person cannot be guilty of aiding or abetting where there is no connection or association with the principal to commit the crime.

Case Vocabulary

NEXUS: A connection or link.

Procedural Basis: Appeal of a trial court conviction of the defendant for the sale of marijuana.

Facts: Douglas MacArthur Thompson, Robert Kent, and Bruce Gladstone (D) were all students at the University of Puget Sound. The Tacoma Police Department hired Thompson as an informant to buy marijuana from Gladstone (D). Thompson visited Gladstone (D), but Gladstone (D) did not have any marijuana to sell him. Gladstone (D), instead, gave him the name of Kent as someone who had marijuana to sell. Gladstone (D) gave Thompson Kent's address and drew him a map [they didn't have Yahoo Maps back then] showing him how to get there. Thompson later bought the marijuana from Kent. There was no evidence of any communication between Thompson and Kent concerning the marijuana sale. A jury found Gladstone (D) guilty of aiding and abetting Kent in the sale of marijuana. Gladstone (D) appeals.

Issue: Can a person be guilty of aiding and abetting where there is no connection or association with the principal to accomplish the crime?

Decision and Rationale: (Hale) No. Gladstone's (D) conviction "rests solely" on the conversation between Thompson and Gladstone (D) regarding a possible sale of marijuana. This evidence does not establish that a crime was committed. A crucial element, "a nexus between the accused and the party whom he is charged with aiding and abetting in the commission of a crime," is not present. Gladstone (D) is not charged with aiding or abetting Thompson's purchase of marijuana, but with Kent's sale of marijuana. Gladstone's (D) culpability is determined by R.C.W. 9.01.030 [which "makes a principal of one who aids and abets another in the commission of the crime"]. An accomplice does not need to be physically present at the crime to be found guilty as the principal provided that there is evidence that the accomplice did something "in association or connection with the principal." Similarly, a bystander can be found guilty, even without a prior agreement, if he associates "himself with the venture, that he participated in it as in something that he wishes to bring about, that he seek by his action to make it succeed." There is no evidence of such an association. Gladstone (D) had no communication with Kent before or after the sale in which he expressed any idea that he would aid, encourage, or direct Kent in the sale of marijuana. Gladstone (D) did not benefit from Kent's sale. "It would be a dangerous precedent indeed to hold that mere communications to the effect that another might or probably would commit a criminal offense would amount to an aiding and abetting of the offense should it ultimately be committed." The judgment is reversed and remanded with directions to dismiss.

Dissent: (Hamilton) Yes. The jury was fully warranted in finding that Gladstone's (D) recommendation revealed his intent that his actions would "instigate, induce, procure or encourage" Kent's crime of selling marijuana to Thompson.

Analysis:

This opinion, again, focuses on the issue of intent on the part of the accomplice. An alleged accomplice may carry out all the necessary acts required for the completion of the crime charged, but, if the alleged accomplice does not share the "guilty mind" of the principal, the alleged accomplice has committed no crime. This opinion carries out this principle in full. Gladstone (D) did have the mens rea for the crime of buying marijuana. Gladstone's (D) actions made it clear that he intended to assist Thompson in purchasing marijuana. However, since Thompson was an informant, Thompson cannot be considered a principal culpable of committing the crime of buying marijuana. Therefore, it is legally impossible for Gladstone (D) to be guilty of aiding the purchase of marijuana. As to the issue of aiding and abetting the sale of marijuana, without evidence of any communications between Gladstone (D) and Kent, there is no factual proof to ascertain whether Gladstone (D) intended to assist Kent. Instead, Gladstone (D) merely pointed Thompson in Kent's direction. On the other hand, if Gladstone (D) had telephoned Kent to confirm whether he had marijuana to sell and then directed Thompson to Kent, then there would be evidence that Gladstone (D) intended also to assist Kent in his sale. Some states have dealt with this issue by creating the crime of criminal facilitation. This crime, in general, finds liability where someone provides a person with the means or opportunity to commit a crime. Such statutes usually require that the crime was actually carried out and that the assistance actually had some impact on its success.

People v. Luparello

(State) v. (Heartbroken Mobster)
(1987) 187 Cal. App. 3d 410, 231 Cal. Rptr. 832

MEMORY GRAPHIC

⚡ Instant Facts

Luparello (D), heartbroken over a former lover who ran off and married someone else, sent in his thugs to shake up the husband's friend to discover her whereabouts, but the thugs wound up killing him.

⚖ Black Letter Rule

A person is liable for the unplanned and unintended acts of co-conspirators that are the natural, probable, and foreseeable consequences of his assistance.

📖 Case Vocabulary

AFFIXED: Attached to.
FORTUITY: By chance or luck.
VICARIOUS: An action performed or a harm suffered in substitute for someone else, a surrogate.

Procedural Basis: Appeal of a trial court conviction of the defendant for murder.

Facts: Luparello (D) was heartbroken after his girlfriend left him to marry someone else. Luparello (D) thought he could discover her whereabouts from Mark Martin who was a good friend of her current husband. Luparello (D) called on his "friends" to find Martin and to get the information about his girlfriend's whereabouts "at any cost." Luparello's (D) friends paid Martin a visit, but he refused to [rat out] the former girlfriend. The next evening, Luparello's (D) friends, without Luparello (D) present, ambushed Martin and killed him. Luparello (D) was charged and convicted of murder.

Issue: Can a person be held liable for the unplanned and unintended act of co-conspirators?

Decision and Rationale: (Kremer) Yes. The trial court found Luparello (D) guilty of first-degree murder based on aiding and abetting liability. Luparello (D) argues that the perpetrator and the accomplice must share the exact same intent in order to be charged with the same offense. However, accomplice liability does not require an identical intent, but "an equivalent mens rea." Thus, liability is extended to cover the actual crime committed as opposed to the crime intended. This is done "on the policy [that] aiders and abettors should be responsible for the criminal harms they have naturally, probably and foreseeably put in motion." As a result, Luparello (D) is guilty of any reasonably foreseeable offense committed by anyone he aids and abets in the commission of the offense he intended. The judgment is affirmed.

Concurrence: (Wiener). I concur "under the compulsion of" existing case law; however, I find this principle of law to be logically inconsistent and theoretically unsound. The "foreseeable consequence" doctrine has evolved away from its original definition, "probable and natural consequences," to the current standard of "natural and reasonable consequences." This doctrine creates a problem when assessing the degree of culpability for the accomplice because it depends on the fortuity of the mental state of the perpetrator. Admittedly, Luparello's (D) original conspiracy involved a foreseeable risk of death or serious injury that would normally find Luparello (D) criminally negligent in failing to appreciate the amount of risk. This, usually, would allow a person to be found guilty, at most, of involuntary manslaughter. However, the rule in this case does not base Luparello's (D) mens rea on his individual mental state but instead on the mental state of the perpetrators. Thus, if the perpetrators were drunk and did not have the requisite malice, presumably Luparello (D) would only be guilty of voluntary manslaughter. This result is irrational and inconsistent with the fundamental principles of criminal law because it is not consistent with the "notion that criminal punishment must be proportional to the defendant's culpable mental state." The simple fact that a person had some intent to violate the law does not justify the "artificial imputation of stepped-up intent" based on the actions of others.

Analysis:

This opinion describes how similar the intent of the perpetrator and the alleged accomplice must be to hold the accomplice criminally liable for the perpetrator's acts. The rule laid out essentially states that, as long as the perpetrator and the accomplice share the same mens rea for the crime intended, then the accomplice can be held liable for all foreseeable acts committed by the perpetrator in furtherance of the original crime intended. Thus, as long as the accomplice has a culpable mental state and assists or encourages the perpetrator to act on that mental state, then any further reasonably foreseeable acts committed by the perpetrator can form the basis of liability against the accomplice. This creates the same problems and concerns raised by the felony murder rule. As the concurrence points out, the degree of punishment the accomplice receives is completely based on the fortuity of the actions and mental state of his co-conspirators. It also raises the additional challenge of ascertaining what actions are "reasonably foreseeable." Obviously, in this case, the court found that Luparello's (D) instructions to his "friends" created a recently foreseeable consequence that they would kill Martin. Proponents of this kind of liability argue that it provides a deterrence against crime and criminal conspiracies. Thus, if people know that they can be held entirely liable for the acts of others, they would be more reluctant to enter into criminal conspiracies. However, in most cases, the desire of people to commit criminal acts rests not on the possible degree of punishment, but the likelihood of getting caught in the first place.

TO PROVE ACCOMPLICE LIABILITY IT IS NOT ENOUGH THAT A PROSECUTOR PROVE THAT THE ACCOMPLICE KNEW OR SHOULD HAVE KNOWN THAT THE PRINCIPAL MIGHT COMMIT THE OFFENSE FOR WHICH THE ACCOMPLICE IS CHARGED WITH AIDING AND ABETTING

Roy v. United States

(Defendant Charged with Aiding & Abetting Armed Robbery) v. (United States)

(1995) 652 A.2d 1098

M E M O R Y   G R A P H I C

Instant Facts

Roy (D) was charged with aiding and abetting an armed robbery when an acquaintance of his, Ross, robbed Miller, who Roy (D) had sent to Ross for the purpose of buying a gun.

Black Letter Rule

The phrase "criminal act which in the ordinary course of things was the natural and probable consequence of a crime," as used in an accessory liability context, means a consequence within a reasonably predictable range; it refers to a consequence reasonably likely to ensue from the planned events without the interference of any intervening factors.

Case Vocabulary

NATURAL AND PROBABLE CONSEQUENCE: A consequence that is reasonably likely to result from the commission of an act.

Procedural Basis: Appeal to the District of Columbia Court of Appeals of a jury's finding of guilt in a case for aiding and abetting armed robbery.

Facts: Miller, a paid police informant, approached Roy (D) about the purchase of a handgun. Roy (D) told Miller to return at a later time with $400.00, at which time Roy (D) referred Miller to Ross, who was represented as the one who would sell him the gun. Ross, who had the gun, chose instead to rob Miller. Roy (D) was convicted as an accomplice to the armed robbery. At trial, the judge instructed the jury to find Roy (D) guilty if it concluded that the robbery was the natural and probably consequence of the attempt to sell the gun, even if Roy (D) had not intended that Miller get robbed. The judge also stated, however, that, in his opinion, the case "represented the outer reaches of the permissible use of the doctrine that a person can be criminally liable for an offense which he himself did not intend but which is arguably a natural and probable consequence of an offense which he did intend." The trial judge then explicitly invited the appellate court to review the issue. Roy (D) was convicted and appealed the conviction.

Issue: Can a party to a first crime be found guilty of aiding and abetting a second crime when it was not reasonably predictable that an accomplice would commit the second crime, but it was within the realm of possibility?

Decision and Rationale: (Not Stated) No. By invoking the "natural and probable consequences" theory, the government insists that we sustain Roy's (D) convictions of armed robbery without requiring a showing that he intended to participate in the robbery of Miller. Armed robbery is a felony punishable by life imprisonment; selling a handgun is a misdemeanor. The government's application of the "natural and probable consequences" doctrine would thus dramatically expand Roy's (D) exposure even where he did not intend a crime of violence to be committed. We have stated that "an accessory is liable for any criminal act which in the ordinary course of things was the natural and probable consequence of the crime that he advised or commanded, although such consequence may not have been intended by him." The phrase "in the ordinary course of things" refers to what may reasonably ensue from the planned events, not what might conceivably happen, and in particular suggests the absence of intervening factors. It is not enough for the prosecution to show that the accomplice knew or should have known that the principal might commit the offense which the accomplice is charged with aiding and abetting. The prosecution must prove a good deal more than that. Indeed, a "natural and probable" consequence in the "ordinary course of things" presupposes an outcome within a reasonably predictable range. No impartial jury could rationally conclude, beyond a reasonable doubt, that Roy (D) "cross[ed] a moral divide by setting out on a project involving either the certain or contingent" commission of a robbery. Viewed in the light most favorable to the prosecution, the evidence might support a finding that Roy (D) should have known it was conceivable. The evidence was insufficient, however, to show that a robbery would follow in the "ordinary course of events," or that it was a "natural and probable consequence" of the activities in which Roy (D) was shown to have engaged. Reversed.

Analysis:

When two or more people agree to participate together in the commission of a crime, the general rule is that all are criminally responsible for the unplanned acts of a fellow participant or co-conspirator that are the "natural and probable consequences" of the original crime. The significance of the District of Columbia Court of Appeals' decision in Roy is that the court defines the widely-used phrase "natural and probable consequences." In doing so, it provides a rather narrow definition of those words (at least narrower than the government would have liked to adopt). Specifically, Roy teaches that the "natural and probable consequences" of an act do not include all consequences within the realm of possibility. Certainly the fact that Ross would rob Miller instead of selling him a gun was within the realm of possibility. But because it was not a reasonably predictable result, the court found that it was not a "natural and probable consequence" of the plan to sell Miller an illegal weapon. In sum, it must be reasonably likely that a particular consequence will ensue from a planned criminal act before all participants in the act will be held responsible for one participant's individual actions.

United States v. Xavier

(United States) v. (Ex-Felon Charged with Possessing a Firearm)
(1993) 2 F.3d 1281

NOW... GO SHOOT THE GUY IN THE CAR!

GROCERI

CABBAGE 42¢ LB

FRESH MILK

M E M O R Y   G R A P H I C

Instant Facts

A man was charged with aiding and abetting an ex-felon's illegal possession of a firearm when he helped his ex-felon brother acquire a weapon for the purpose of shooting an enemy.

Black Letter Rule

A defendant cannot be convicted of aiding and abetting a convicted felon's possession of a firearm if the prosecution has not shown that he had knowledge of the possessor's prior felony.

Case Vocabulary

ATTENDANT CIRCUMSTANCES: The circumstances that must be in place for a crime to be committed; any circumstances that are required to accompany a criminal conviction.

Procedural Basis: Appeal to the Third Circuit Court of Appeals of a jury verdict finding a defendant guilty of aiding and abetting an ex-felon's illegal possession of a firearm.

Facts: Franklin and Clement Xavier, two brothers, discovered an enemy sitting in a car outside of a grocery store. Clement (D) instructed Franklin to wait inside the store, left the store, and shortly thereafter returned with an unidentified man. The unidentified man handed Franklin a pistol, which Franklin then used to fire shots at the car. Clement (D) was convicted of, among other things, aiding and abetting an ex-felon's (Franklin) possession of a firearm. Clement (D) claimed he did not know his brother was an ex-felon.

Issue: Can a person be convicted of aiding and abetting an ex-felon's possession of a firearm if the government never proves knowledge of the possessor's prior conviction?

Decision and Rationale: (Scirica, J.) No. Xavier (D) contends he was wrongfully convicted for aiding and abetting possession of a firearm by a convicted felon on the ground that the government never proved his knowledge of his brother's prior conviction. 18 U.S.C. § 922(g) prohibits the possession of a firearm by anyone "(1) who has been convicted . . . of a crime punishable by imprisonment for a term exceeding one year." Section 922(g) is not a specific intent statute. However, criminal liability for aiding and abetting a § 922(g) violation is because it depends on the status of the person possessing the firearm. Congress addressed this exact situation in § 922(d), which reads: "It shall be unlawful for any person to sell or otherwise dispose of any firearm to any person knowing or having cause to believe that such person . . . has been convicted . . . of a crime punishable by imprisonment for a term exceeding one year." As the text of the statute indicates, one cannot be criminally liable under § 922(d) without knowledge or reason to know of the transferee's status. Allowing aider and abettor liability under § 922(g)(1), without requiring proof of knowledge or reason to know of the possessor's status, would effectively circumvent the knowledge element in § 922(d)(1). Therefore, we hold there can be no criminal liability for aiding and abetting a violation of § 922(g)(1) without knowledge or having cause to believe the possessor's status as a felon. Unless there is evidence a defendant knew or had cause to believe he was aiding and abetting possession by a convicted felon, the prosecution has not shown a "guilty mind" under 18 U.S.C. § 2(a). Reversed.

Analysis:

United States v. Xavier addresses the issue of what degree of knowledge of the attendant circumstances of a crime is required to find a person guilty of aiding and abetting that particular crime. In doing so, the court upholds a strict knowledge requirement for at least one crime—aiding and abetting an ex-felon's possession of a firearm. In this case, the statute at issue required knowledge of attendant circumstances. Specifically, § 922(d) required that to be held accountable for aiding and abetting the possession of a weapon by an ex-felon, a person had to know that the person receiving the firearm had been convicted of a felony, and the government had to prove that knowledge beyond a reasonable doubt. But what if § 922(d) did not exist. Would it be fair to hold someone criminally responsible for aiding and abetting an ex-felon's possession of a firearm when the person had neither intent nor knowledge that a crime was being committed? Arguably not. Interestingly, the Model Penal Code takes no position either way, but simply states that the courts should decide the issue. Finally, it should be noted that the court recognized no presumption of knowledge, but was very strict in holding the government to its burden. If anyone would know about a person's conviction for a felony, it would likely be his brother. In this case, however, that relationship alone was not enough to infer knowledge, and Xavier's conviction was reversed.

State v. McVay

(State) v. (Steamship Captain)
(1926) 47 R.I. 292, 132 A. 436

M E M O R Y   G R A P H I C

Instant Facts

Kelley (D3) ordered the captain and engineer of a passenger steamship to depart despite knowing the dangerous condition of the ship's boilers, and the boiler subsequently exploded killing three people.

Black Letter Rule

A person may be convicted of being an accessory before the fact to the crime of manslaughter arising through criminal negligence.

Case Vocabulary

ACCESSORY BEFORE THE FACT: A person who was not present when the crime was committed but encouraged, aided, assisted or commanded the commission of the crime.

Procedural Basis: A question of law was certified to the state supreme court in order to resolve the issue before trial.

Facts: Kelley (D3) instructed the captain, George W. McVay (D1), and engineer, John A. Grant (D2), of a passenger steamship to depart despite knowledge of a dangerous condition with the ship's boilers. The steamship's boilers later exploded killing three people. Grant (D2) and McVay (D1) were indicted for manslaughter and Kelley (D3) [got the heat as well] and was indicted as an accessory before the fact. Specifically, the indictment stated that Kelley (D3) did "feloniously and maliciously aid, assist, abet, counsel, hire, command and procure" the captain and engineer to commit manslaughter. Kelley (D3) [was understandably steamed] and argued that a person could not be an accessory before the fact to manslaughter that arose out of criminal negligence. The issue was brought to the state supreme court for certification before the trial began.

Issue: May a person be convicted of being an accessory before the fact to the crime of manslaughter arising through criminal negligence?

Decision and Rationale: (Barrows) Yes. Kelley (D3) claims that because the captain and engineer were indicted on manslaughter without malice he cannot be said to have incited a sudden and unpremeditated crime that is "inadvertent and unintentional by its very nature." However, not all charges of manslaughter involve unpremeditated acts. Manslaughter also includes intentional unlawful acts that result in unintentional killing. It also may include an unintentional killing as a result of gross negligence stemming from lawful acts. In either case, there are premeditated acts that can be involved in involuntary manslaughter. In this case, the facts allege that Kelley (D3) intentionally directed and counseled the grossly negligent act that resulted in the crime. While Kelley (D3) may not have consciously intended to take life, the facts allege that he was conscious that the boiler was unsafe and negligently chose to use the boiler nevertheless. The defendants "exercised a choice among courses of conduct" and did so with Kelley's (D3) participation. The facts set forth, if true, are sufficient for a jury to find that Kelley (D3) acted with full knowledge that a danger to life existed, but Kelley (D3) still commanded the captain and the engineer to use the ship. Thus, we answer in the affirmative the question certified on each indictment.

Analysis:

This case cites the principle that a person who encourages or assists another to engage in dangerous conduct establishes accomplice liability for crimes requiring recklessness or negligence. This is important because most crimes are defined by specific conduct that are essential elements of the offense (i.e. burglary, kidnapping, larceny, etc.). However, crimes requiring recklessness or negligence usually involve unspecified conduct lacking specific enumerated acts required for the offense. This means that such crimes have the potential of encompassing many different kinds of conduct. This circle is expanded even further if stretched to include those who assist or encourage the conduct. This creates the danger of unsettling results. For example, if a group of friends agree to recklessly ski down a hill and one of them strikes an unwitting skier and kills him, should the skier's friends be accomplices to manslaughter? A better rule would be not to confuse the issue of whether the friends are accessories or not. The issue should be whether the friends' own conduct was itself criminally reckless. This would provide the additional protection of legal causation. In other words, the friends' conduct, while undoubtedly satisfying the requisite culpability of recklessness, would also have to have been a "but for" cause of the unwitting skier's death. Thus, if one of the friends recklessly pushed the other into the unwitting skier, both are the cause of the death and could be held criminally liable. In contrast, an accomplice liability theory would make all the friends culpable regardless of how the accident actually took place. Similarly, in this opinion, the court is essentially arguing that all three defendant's, based on the facts alleged, had the same level of culpability. All three defendants knew of the dangerous condition and that it had a chance of causing injury to human life. The only difference is that the captain and the engineer were the ones who actually turned on the boiler, whereas Kelley (D3) only ordered them to use the boiler. Under the accomplice theory of liability, the inquiry would end there and Kelley (D3) would be guilty. In contrast, under the causation theory, we would ask whether Kelley's (D3) conduct was a "but for" cause of the deaths. Under the facts given, it appears that his order to turn on the boilers was exactly that.

THE FACT THAT A GROUP OF PEOPLE SETS OUT TO INJURE OR KILL ONE ANOTHER
DOES NOT PRECLUDE A FINDING THAT THEY INTENTIONALLY AIDED EACH OTHER
IN CAUSING DANGER TO OTHERS

People v. Russell

(State of New York) v. (Participant in Deadly Shooting)

(1998) 91 N.Y.2d 193, 693 N.E.2d 280

WHICH ONE OF THE THREE DEFENDANTS FIRED THE FATAL SHOT??

WE DON'T KNOW, YOUR HONOR!

M E M O R Y   G R A P H I C

⚡ Instant Facts

Despite the fact that it was unclear as to who fired the fatal shot, Russell (D) was convicted of second degree murder after a gun battle in which he was engaged resulted in the death of an innocent party.

⚖ Black Letter Rule

Two or more people who intentionally participate in an inherently dangerous and unlawful activity share culpability for any crime committed as a result of that activity.

Facts: On December 17, 1992, Russell (D) and two others engaged in a gun battle in a neighborhood in Brooklyn, New York. During the battle, Patrick Daly, an innocent party, was killed. Ballistics were inconclusive in determining which of the three participants fired the bullet that killed Daly. At trial, the prosecution argued that each of the three defendants acted with the mental culpability required for the commission of the crime, and that each intentionally aided the one who fired the fatal shot. All three defendants were convicted of second degree, depraved indifference murder. All three, including Russell (D), appealed on grounds of insufficient evidence.

Issue: Can a group of people who engage in a gun battle each be held individually responsible for the death of an innocent person that results from the battle?

Decision and Rationale: (Kaye, J.) Yes. Although only one bullet killed Patrick Daly and it is uncertain who fired that bullet, the prosecution was not required to prove which defendant fired the fatal shot when the evidence was sufficient to establish that each defendant acted with the mental culpability required for the commission of depraved indifference murder, and each defendant intentionally aided the defendant who fired the fatal shot. Russell (D) argues that the evidence adduced at trial did not support a finding that the defendants—adversaries in a deadly gun battle—shared the community of purpose necessary for accomplice liability. We disagree. The fact that Russell (D) and the others set out to injure or kill one another does not rationally preclude a finding that they intentionally aided each other to engage in the mutual combat that caused Daly's death. This principle is well illustrated by *People v. Abbott* [two drag racers found guilty for criminally negligent homicide when an innocent man was killed by one of them during a race], in which it was held that two people's intentional participation in an inherently dangerous activity requires that they share culpability. After all, both party's participation makes the activity possible. In this case, the jurors were instructed: "If you find that the People have proven beyond a reasonable doubt that defendants took up each other's challenge, shared in the venture and unjustifiably, voluntarily and jointly created a zone of danger, then each is responsible for his own acts and the acts of the others . . . [and] it makes no difference [whose bullet] penetrated Mr. Daly and caused his death." There was adequate proof to justify the finding that the three defendants tacitly agreed to engage in a gun battle that placed the life of any innocent bystander at grave risk and ultimately killed Daly. Indeed, unlike an unanticipated ambush or spontaneous attack that might have taken defendants by surprise, the gunfight in this case only began after defendants acknowledged and accepted each other's challenge to engage in a deadly battle on a public concourse. The evidence adduced at trial was also sufficient for the jury to determine that Russell (D) and the other defendants acted with the mental culpability required for depraved indifference murder, and that they intentionally aided and encouraged each other to create the lethal crossfire that caused the death of Patrick Daly. Affirmed.

Analysis:

Russell stands for the simple proposition that two or more people who intentionally participate in an inherently dangerous and unlawful activity share culpability (responsibility) for any crime that results from that activity. Thus, as in the case of *People v. Abbott*, which is referenced in the opinion, two people who recklessly engage in a drag race that injures or kills a non-participant are both culpable for the injury or death caused. In *Russell*, that principle is applied in the case of a gun battle, and requires that in such a battle all participants, and not just the shooter whose bullet killed the victim, are responsible for the murder. Interestingly, the court did not give any significance to the fact that the participants in the shooting were shooting at one another, or that they were attempting to kill one another (a far cry from a drag race). Despite the intent to kill one another, the court still found that a joint undertaking had occurred, or that the participants had engaged in a common undertaking and as such could be convicted as accomplices of one another. Thus, people need not be friends or even working toward the same goal in order to be found to be accomplices of one another. It should also be noted that *Russell* is a case in which there was no one principal who was aided and abetted by accomplices in the commission of his crime. In this case, the government never proved who fired the fatal shot. This lack of a true principal who was assisted by others did not deter the court, however, which held that the government need not prove whose gun killed Daly because each of the defendants had the requisite reckless mental state necessary to support a charge and conviction of second degree murder.

A PERSON MAY BE GUILTY OF AIDING AND ABETTING A CRIMINAL ACT BY BEING PRESENT, TAKING PART, CONCURRING IN, OR ENCOURAGING THE ACT

Wilcox v. Jeffery

(Magazine Writer) v. (Prosecutor)
(1951) 1 All E.R. 464

M E M O R Y   G R A P H I C

Instant Facts
Wilcox (D) was a music magazine writer who was charged with aiding an alien to illegally take employment.

Black Letter Rule
A person may be guilty of aiding and abetting a criminal act by being present, taking part, concurring in, or encouraging the act.

Case Vocabulary
QUASHED: To end, void, or terminate.
TO WIT: That is to say, namely, in particular.

Procedural Basis: Appeal of a magistrate court conviction.

Facts: Under the law of the United Kingdom, aliens are not permitted to take paid or unpaid employment. Coleman Hawkins was a famous United States saxophone player who was invited to come to the United Kingdom. Herbert William Wilcox (D), who owned a music magazine, greeted Hawkins on his arrival but did not invite him, arrange his visit, or arrange a concert for him. However, Wilcox (D) did have interest in writing an article in his magazine about Hawkins' visit. Wilcox (D) paid for and attended a concert in which Hawkins performed. While there was no evidence that he applauded during the concert, Wilcox (D) did print an article that extolled Hawkins performance. With these facts, the magistrate found Wilcox (D) guilty of aiding and abetting the violation of the alien employment law [we know- we were shocked too]. Wilcox (D) appealed.

Issue: May a person be guilty of aiding and abetting a criminal act by being present, taking part, concurring in, or encouraging the act?

Decision and Rationale: (Goddard) Yes. Anyone can be charged with aiding and abetting no matter what that illegal act is. Had Wilcox's (D) presence at the concert been accidental, there would be no evidence of aiding or abetting. However, in addition to being present, Wilcox (D) actively encouraged the illegal act by paying for the concert and making use of the performance for his own gain by writing about it in his newspaper. Wilcox (D) clearly knew that it was unlawful for Hawkins to play. He was "present, taking part, concurring, or encouraging" the illegal act. The situation may have been different if he had attended the concert and booed Hawkins or made some other protest. However, Wilcox (D) affirmatively encouraged the illegal act. Appeal is dismissed with costs.

Analysis:

This opinion focuses on the actus reus required for accomplice liability. Notice that the actus reus for accomplice liability in this case has nothing to do with causation. An accomplice may still be guilty even if the aid or encouragement, in actuality, provides no assistance or encouragement to the principal. As a result, even a miniscule possibility of assistance or encouragement is sufficient actus reus to establish accomplice liability. Of course, in any case, the illegal act must take place, but the rule does not unequivocally require that the accomplice's aid or encouragement actually have an impact on the illegal act. In this case, Wilcox (D) was undoubtedly not the only person to have attended the concert. In addition, nothing in the evidence suggests that, if Wilcox (D) had not bought a ticket and attended, Hawkins would have cancelled his concert. With or without Wilcox's (D) assistance or encouragement, the concert and the resulting illegal act would still have taken place. The opinion seems somewhat concerned that Wilcox (D) obtained some personal benefit from Hawkins' concert by writing a magazine article. In reality, issues of personal benefit should have no bearing on an accomplice's liability in terms of prohibited conduct. However, Wilcox's (D) magazine article may be relevant in determining an intent to aid or encourage -- in this case, by buying a ticket and writing an article praising the illegal performance.

A DEFENDANT CAN BE CONVICTED OF BEING AN ACCOMPLICE TO A CRIME EVEN THOUGH THE CRIME WOULD HAVE BEEN COMMITTED WITHOUT HIS OR HER ASSISTANCE

State ex. rel. Attorney General v. Tally, Judge

(State of Alabama) v. (Impeached Judge)
(1894) 102 Ala. 25, 69, 15 So. 722, 739

M E M O R Y   G R A P H I C

Instant Facts

Judge Tally (D) was impeached after it was shown that he assisted in the murder of a man by convincing a telegraph operator not to deliver a telegram to the victim warning him of the impending danger.

Black Letter Rule

One who facilitates murder by destroying an opportunity to escape that the victim might otherwise have had is guilty as an accomplice even though it may be found that the victim would not have taken the chance to escape and the death would have resulted anyway.

Procedural Basis: A judge appealed the result of an impeachment proceeding in which he was found to be an accomplice to murder (and therefore impeached).

Facts: Ross seduced Judge Tally's (D) sister-in-law. The victim's brothers decided to go after Ross, who was living in Stevenson, and kill him. While at the local telegraph office, Tally (D) learned that a telegram had been sent to Ross, warning him of the danger. Tally (D) sent his own telegram to the telegraph operator in Stevenson telling him not to deliver the telegram to Ross. The operator did not deliver it and Ross was killed. The court found Tally (D) to be an accomplice to murder. He was impeached from his position of judge and Tally (D) appealed.

Issue: Can a defendant be convicted of being an accomplice to a crime when the crime would have been committed with or without his or her assistance?

Decision and Rationale: (Not Stated) Yes. Before Judge Tally (D) can be found guilty of aiding and abetting the murder of Ross, it must appear that his actions to prevent Ross from being warned aided his brothers-in-law in killing Ross and thereby contributed to his death. The assistance given, however, need not contribute to the criminal result in the sense that but for it the result would not have ensued. It is quite sufficient if it facilitated a result that would have transpired without it. It is quite enough if the aid merely renders it easier for the principal actor to accomplish the end intended by him and the aider and abettor, though the end would have been attained without it. If the aid in homicide can be shown to have put the deceased at a disadvantage, to have deprived him of a single chance of life, he who furnishes such aid is guilty though it cannot be known or shown that the dead man, in the absence thereof, would have availed himself of that chance. One who facilitates murder by destroying an opportunity to escape that the victim might otherwise have had is guilty as an accomplice even though it may be found that the victim would not have taken the chance to escape and the death would have resulted anyway. Affirmed.

Analysis:

Like *Wilcox v. Jeffery*, the case of *State v. Tally* addresses the *actus reus* requirement of an accomplice liability charge. Like *Wilcox*, *Tally* holds that it does not matter that a criminal event would have occurred without the assistance of the person charged with accomplice liability. So long as the person's actions supported the commission of the crime by the principal, accessorial liability attaches (there is no but-for causation requirement). The difference between *Tally* and *Wilcox* is that in *Wilcox*, Wilcox was found guilty because, in attending the music concert of a foreigner without a work permit, he encouraged the commission of a criminal act (a foreigner working without a permit). In *Tally*, however, Judge Tally (D) did more than encourage his brothers-in-law to kill Ross. Judge Tally's (D) actions instead made it easier for the principals to act out their criminal intentions. Taken together, then, these two cases stand for the proposition that a person satisfies the *actus reus* requirement of a charge of accomplice liability by either encouraging the commission of a criminal act or by making it easier for another person to accomplish the desired crime. It should be noted that there is some difference of opinion as to what should happen when a person attempts to encourage the commission of a crime but fails to do so. (This was not the case in either *Wilcox* or *Tally*, but it is related to the principles discussed in those cases.) At common law, there was no liability in such a situation, meaning if Judge Tally's (D) telegram had never gone through, he would not be held criminally responsible for aiding the murder of Ross. Under the Model Penal Code (MPC), however, the view is expressed that "attempted complicity ought to be criminal, and to distinguish it from effective complicity appears unnecessary where the crime has been committed." Comment to MPC § 2.06. In other words, as soon as Judge Tally (D) sent the telegram, he was guilty of aiding the murder of Ross, even if the telegram never arrived or the telegraph operator had disregarded its request.

State v. Hayes

(State) v. (Duped Burglar)
(1891) 105 Mo. 76, 16 S.W. 514

M E M O R Y   G R A P H I C

Instant Facts

Hayes (D) conspired with another man to burglarize a store, but his accomplice set him up to be caught.

Black Letter Rule

An accomplice cannot be held criminally liable if the principal had no criminal intent.

Case Vocabulary

ANTAGONISTIC: Hostile to, opposing.
PETIT LARCENY: Larceny of inexpensive property, usually below a certain value.
VOLITION: Free will, the ability of a person to make a choice or decision.

Procedural Basis: Appeal of a conviction for burglary and larceny.

Facts: Hayes (D) approached Hill to join him in the burglary of a store. Their grand plan was to [quite literally] take home the bacon. Hayes (D) [not exactly a criminal mastermind], did not know that Hill actually happened to be a relative of the store's owners. Hill played along with Hayes (D), but warned the store's owners about the plan. They decided to try to catch Hayes (D) red-handed and have him arrested. On the night of the planned burglary, they arrived at the store, and Hayes (D) opened a window and helped Hill inside the building. Hill picked up a side of bacon and handed it out to Hayes (D). Soon after, they were arrested. Hayes (D) was convicted of burglary and larceny, and he appealed.

Issue: Can an accomplice be held criminally liable if the principal had no criminal intent?

Decision and Rationale: (Thomas) No. The trial court instructed the jury to find Hayes (D) guilty of burglary if he had a felonious intent and assisted and aided Hill to enter the building, regardless of Hill's own intent. This jury instruction was in error. The evidence was clear that Hill did not enter the building with an intent to steal and committed no crime. Yet, the act became criminal when it was imputed to Hayes (D) because of his felonious intent. This may have been appropriate if Hill was a "passive and submissive agent" who was acting under the "control and compulsion" of Hayes (D). However, Hill was working with Hayes (D) on his own free will with the intent to entrap Hayes (D). The intent and acts do not combine to form the elements of the crime. Hayes (D) did not enter the building and, therefore, did not commit the crime of burglary. To make Hayes (D) responsible for Hill's breaking and entry, they must have had a "common motive and common design." But, in fact, "the design and the motives of the two men were not only distinct, that dissimilar, even antagonistic." The court should instruct the jury that if Hill broke into and entered the warehouse with a felonious intent, and Hayes (D) were present, aiding him with the same intent, then he is guilty. However, if he entered the room with no intent to steal, but simply to entrap Hayes (D) and capture him in the commission of a crime and Hayes (D) did not enter the room himself, then he cannot be guilty of burglary and larceny as charged. The judgment is reversed, and the case remanded for a new trial.

Analysis:

This opinion illustrates how entrapment cases can fail under a theory of accomplice liability. If the principal actor committing the criminal act is seeking to entrap the accomplice, the accomplice cannot be held liable unless the accomplice actually commits the acts that constitute the offense. Because the principal actor has no criminal intent, the principal does not have the mens rea for the offense even though she may have completed the actus reus for the offense. Therefore, it would be illogical to transform what could not otherwise be a non-criminal act into a criminal one merely because the principal tricked the accomplice into going along with her plan. Strictly speaking, on a public policy level, we don't want to encourage police and others to entrap people merely for their criminal thoughts. Also, we don't want law enforcement agents committing criminal acts left and right merely to capture people with criminal propensities. The law is designed to prevent criminal acts, not to encourage them. On the other hand, if Hayes (D) had acted as the principal or had actually entered the building, his actions alone would establish a charge of burglary against him. Nevertheless, under the facts of the case, Hayes (D) could still be found guilty of petty larceny or solicitation to commit burglary or attempted burglary (if he actually intended to enter the building).

Vaden v. State

(Illegal Hunter) v. (State of Alaska)
(1989) 768 P.2d 1102

M E M O R Y   G R A P H I C

Instant Facts

A hunter appealed his conviction as an accomplice to illegal hunting, which was obtained after an undercover wildlife agent solicited his assistance in illegally hunting foxes.

Black Letter Rule

The public authority justification defense is personal to law enforcement officers and cannot be used by an accomplice to argue that no crime was committed and that therefore there can be no accomplice liability.

Case Vocabulary

PUBLIC AUTHORITY JUSTIFICATION DEFENSE: A defense against guilt for particular crimes available to law enforcement officers who must break the law in order to enforce it.

Procedural Basis: Appeal to the Supreme Court of Alaska of a hunter's conviction as an accomplice to illegal hunting.

Facts: After hearing a rumor that Vaden (D), a local guide, was promoting illegal hunting to his customers, Fish and Wildlife officers decided to send an undercover officer, John Snell, to Vaden (D). Snell, posing as a hunter, sought Vaden's (D) assistance in illegally hunting foxes. Vaden (D) agreed to help, and in doing so piloted a helicopter from which Snell shot four foxes. Vaden (D) was convicted as an accomplice to the illegal taking of foxes from an aircraft. He was also convicted as an accomplice to the crime of hunting during closed season. Vaden (D) appealed on the ground that he could not be an accomplice because, since Snell was a law enforcement officer, no crime was committed when the foxes were taken.

Issue: Can the public authority justification defense, which justifies the actions of a law enforcement officer who commits a crime, be used by an accomplice to that crime to argue that no criminal action occurred for which he could be convicted of being an accomplice?

Decision and Rationale: (Not Stated) No. The fact that a party's actions are justified in light of the needs of law enforcement (the "public authority justification defense") does not mean that no criminal action occurred to which accomplice liability can attach. In this case we feel that Snell's actions were not, in fact, justified, but even if they were, such would not avail Vaden (D) because the justification would be personal to Snell. Affirmed.

Dissent: (Not Stated) The accomplice liability charges should fail on the ground that the act of a feigned accomplice may never be imputed to the targeted defendant for the purposes of obtaining a conviction, a rule recognized by many courts. This rule is based on sound reason. One who aids and abets another in criminal activity is liable for all of the natural and probable consequences of his accomplice's criminal acts. Thus, the potential for abuse inherent in law enforcement methods such as those employed in this case is substantial. Indeed, once an agent has succeeded in persuading an individual to take some substantial act in furtherance of his general criminal scheme, the ultimate liability of the targeted defendant will depend on which foreseeable crimes the agent chooses to commit in order to secure convictions against his criminal "accomplice." It is clearly inconsistent with due process principles, and manifestly unjust, that a defendant's ultimate criminal liability should be made to depend on the actions (or in this case good aim) of the police officer charged with securing his arrest.

Analysis:

The case of *Vaden v. State* produced a result different from that in the preceding case, *State v. Hayes*. Once again, in *Hayes* the Supreme Court of Missouri held that an accomplice cannot be held criminally liable if the principal had no criminal intent (and the dissent in *Vaden* strongly agreed). In *Vaden*, the principal (Snell, the undercover officer) had no criminal intent. Though he had the *actus reus* (the shooting of the foxes), he did so not with the intent to take them in violation of Alaska's hunting laws, but with the intent to create evidence against Vaden (D). Despite Snell's lack of criminal intent, the majority upheld Vaden's (D) conviction, meaning that they found him, an accomplice, criminally liable despite his principal's lack of criminal intent. One should take note of the fact that the public authority justification defense played a part in the Alaska Supreme Court's decision (and perhaps it was by means of this defense that they got around the rule in *Hayes*). Under that defense, law enforcement is sometimes justified in breaking the law in order to enforce the law (a strange sounding concept). In referencing the justification, the majority stated that the justification was personal to the officer, and could not be used by Vaden (D) in arguing that no crime had been committed. The next case, *Taylor v. Commonwealth*, addresses this issue, that of defenses and justifications belonging to the principal, in greater detail.

Taylor v. Commonwealth

(Accomplice to Child Abduction) v. (Commonwealth of Virginia)

(1999) 31 Va. App. 54, 521 S.E.2d 293

M E M O R Y   G R A P H I C

Instant Facts

A woman was convicted as an accomplice to a child abduction in violation of Virginia law when she assisted her fiancé in forcibly taking his son from its mother's home.

Black Letter Rule

Because excuses to the commission of a crime relate to a condition that is peculiar to a particular actor, such defenses are generally considered to be non-delegable and therefore unavailable to an accomplice.

Case Vocabulary

EXCUSE: A defense to a criminal charge that arises when, under the law, the defendant is not considered blameworthy for acting in an otherwise criminal manner.

JUSTIFICATION: A defense to a criminal charge that arises when a party acts in a manner that the law does not seek to prohibit.

Procedural Basis: Appeal to the Virginia Court of Appeals of a woman's conviction as an accomplice to the abduction of a child.

Facts: Tomika T. Taylor (D) was convicted as an accomplice to child abduction in violation of § 18.2-47 of Virginia's criminal code. Specifically, Taylor (D) assisted her fiancé, Avery Moore, in forcibly taking his ten-month-old son from the child's mother. No custody order was in effect at the time. Section 18.2-47 reads: "Any person who, by force, intimidation or deception, and without legal justification or excuse, seizes, takes, transports, detains or secretes the person of another, with the intent to deprive such other person of his personal liberty or to withhold or conceal him from any person, authority or institution lawfully entitled to his charge, shall be deemed guilty of abduction." Taylor (D) appealed on the ground that Moore's taking of the child did not violate the statute because his conduct was legally justified. She further argued that because Moore's actions did not constitute abduction, she could not be convicted as an accomplice to abduction.

Issue: Is a person charged as an accomplice to child abduction shielded from criminal liability when the principal is the child's parent and thus has a legally recognized excuse for his actions?

Decision and Rationale: (Annunziata, J.) No. Under Virginia law, an accomplice is one "who knowingly, voluntarily, and with common intent with the principal offender unites in the commission of a crime." A principal in the second degree is an accomplice who is "present, aiding and abetting, and intend[s] his or her words, gestures, signals, or actions to in some way encourage, advise, urge, or in some way help the person committing the crime to commit it." Taylor (D) raises the following issue: whether a person charged as an accomplice to abduction, which abduction is effected by a child's parent, is shielded from criminal liability based derivatively on the parent's excuse or justification. A number of jurisdictions have recognized that, in the absence of a court order awarding custody to another, a parent cannot be convicted of abduction and other similar crimes by taking exclusive custody of his or her child. Section 18.2-47 exempts from liability, among others, individuals who are legally excused. While the terms legal justification and excuse are often used interchangeably, they are distinct legal concepts. As to the concept of excuse, there appears to be general agreement with the proposition that "[e]xcuses, in contrast [to justifications], are always personal to the actor." Excuses rest on the presence within the actor of a condition or status that exculpates him or her from culpability for otherwise criminal conduct. Because excuses relate to a condition that is peculiar to the actor, such defenses are generally considered to be non-delegable and thus unavailable to an accomplice. Based on the foregoing principles, even were we to conclude that Moore's abduction of the child was excused by his parental relationship to the child, Taylor's (D) accessorial liability would not be undercut by his personal excuse. In short, the defense of legal excuse is personal to Moore and unavailable to Taylor (D). The evidence adduced at trial was sufficient to establish Taylor's (D) culpability as a principal in the second degree to abduction. Affirmed.

Dissent: (Elder, J.) A split of authority exists regarding whether a person present with and assisting a parent to gain exclusive custody of a child may be found guilty of kidnapping when the parent himself has committed no illegal act. I would hold that the approach adopted by the majority of jurisdictions—and rejected by the majority in this case—is the better approach. In one such case, *State v. Stocksdale*, the New Jersey Superior Court explained the reasoning. It wrote: "An aider or abettor . . . may generally be convicted where the principal has a defense personal to himself which exonerates him from criminal responsibility. There are, however, exceptions to this general rule of accessorial liability. Accomplice liability, for example, is not sustained where the defense of one party not only exonerates himself but also changes the character of the act so that it can no longer be viewed as criminal in nature." The existence of legal justification or excuse for Moore's actions changes the character of his and Taylor's (D) act such that it can no longer be viewed as criminal in nature. I would therefore find that there was no violation of § 18.2-47.

Analysis:

Taylor addresses the issue of excuses and justifications as defenses to charges of criminal conduct. As the court points out, these are distinct legal terms that have different meanings. An excuse is a defense to a criminal charge that arises when the law does not consider the defendant blameworthy for acting in an otherwise criminal manner. For example, when a person burglarizes a store for the sole reason that another is sticking a gun in his back threatening to kill him if he does not commit the burglary, the excuse of duress comes into play. Because the law does not want to make a person blameworthy for committing crimes under duress, the excuse exonerates the unwitting burglar. Other common excuses recognized by the law include infancy, insanity, and intoxication. A justification, on the other hand, is different. A justification is a defense to a criminal charge that arises when a party acts in a manner that the law does not seek to prevent, as opposed to considering a person not blameworthy when he or she acts in a way that the law does seek to prevent. Common justifications to criminal behavior include self-defense, necessity, consent, and the use of force while making an arrest. In *Taylor*, the court's important holding, for the purposes of this chapter, is that excuses are personal to a particular defendant and cannot be used by an accomplice to escape liability. Thus *Taylor* could not use the fact that Moore had a valid excuse as a defense to her giving him assistance. Whether justifications are available only to an individual defendant the court does not say. It merely says that "excuses, in contrast [to justifications], are always personal to the actor." In the last case, however, *Vaden v. State*, the Alaska Supreme Court held that at least one justification—the public authority justification—is personal to individual participants in a criminal activity. Finally, it should be noted, as the dissent points out, that the ultimate holding in this case—that of affirming Taylor's (D) criminal liability—is the minority rule. Had Taylor (D) assisted her fiancé as she did in a different state, she would not have been convicted of the felony of child abduction.

New York Central & Hudson River Railroad Co. v. United States

(Railroad Company) v. (State)
(1909) 212 U.S. 481

M E M O R Y   G R A P H I C

Instant Facts

An employee of a railroad company made a deal with a sugar refining company to pay the sugar company rebates in return for use of the railroad company lines, in violation of a federal statute.

Black Letter Rule

A corporation can be criminally liable for the acts of its employees.

Case Vocabulary

AMENDATORY: Supplemental, adiitional.
WRIT OF ERROR: An order by an appellate court directing the trial court to produce the record of the case it is reviewing.

Procedural Basis: Appeal of a federal circuit court decision finding the railroad company guilty of violating a federal statute against rebates.

Facts: An employee of the New York Central and Hudson River Railroad Company ("railroad company") (D) made a deal to pay rebates to the American Sugar Refining Company if they used the railroad company's (D) lines to ship its sugar. Under this [sweet deal], the railroad company (D) would ship the sugar between New York and Detroit at a rate of $0.18 per 100 lbs. instead of the published rate of $0.23 - $0.21 per 100 lbs. Such rebates were illegal under federal law. The railroad company (D) and its assistant traffic manager were convicted under the statute for the payment of rebates to the sugar company and others. The railroad company (D) appealed the conviction arguing that the statute was unconstitutional because a corporation cannot be held criminally liable for the actions of its employees.

Issue: Can a corporation be held criminally liable for the acts of its employees?

Decision and Rationale: (Day) Yes. The railroad company (D) argues that it is unconstitutional to hold a corporation liable to criminal prosecution because any punishment imposed would actually punish innocent stockholders and deprive them of their property in violation of due process. While earlier common law held that corporations were excluded from criminal liability, the modern rule accepts the capacity of corporations to commit crime. It is an established rule that a corporation can be held responsible in tort for the damages caused by acts of one of its agents acting in the scope of his employment. Since a corporation acts by its officers and agents, their individual "purposes, motives, and intent" are part of the corporation. If a corporation can engage in conduct, it can intend to do such conduct. The officer or agent is acting to benefit the principal, which is, in this case, a corporation. If the conduct is criminal, the corporation must be held accountable for the acts. The payment of rebates by its agents and officers benefited the corporation, and if only the agents and officers may be held liable, the statute against rebates could not be effectively enforced. There is "no valid objection in law, and every reason in public policy," why a corporation cannot be held liable for the actions and intent of its agents to whom the corporation has vested its authority in and whose actions and purposes are otherwise attributable to the corporation for whom they work. In modern times, a great majority of business transactions are conducted through corporations. To afford corporations immunity from all criminal punishment "would virtually take away the only means of effectually controlling the subject matter and correcting the abuses aimed at." Judgment affirmed.

Analysis:

This opinion firmly established the ability of the state to hold a corporation criminally liable for the actions of its employees. As you may note, the underlying theory imposing liability on a corporation is analogous to the doctrine of respondeat superior. Under respondeat superior, an employer can be held liable for the torts committed by an employee during the scope of employment. The rationale behind this theory is similar to the instant case. In both cases, we hold the employer or the corporation liable because we assume that the agent, when acting in the scope of her employment, is committing the wrongdoing for the benefit of the employer or corporation. Thus, it seems logical to hold the superior actor liable for the actions of its subordinates to whom the superior delegates authority to. Of course, a corporation cannot be held liable for some crimes that cannot be committed by corporations in a practical sense. For example, an employee of the corporation may burglarize a competitor's home, but the act of breaking and entering can only be committed by an individual, not the "ether" of the corporation. [It is also very difficult to jail a corporation!]

A CORPORATION CAN BE HELD LIABLE FOR THE ACTS OF ITS AGENTS EVEN IF THE CORPORATION'S POLICY AND SPECIFIC INSTRUCTIONS PROHIBITED SUCH ACTS

United States v. Hilton Hotels Corp.

(State) v. (Hotel)
(1972) 467 F.2d 1000

M E M O R Y   G R A P H I C

Instant Facts

Despite express corporate instructions and policy to the contrary, an agent of a corporation engaged in illegal activity during the scope of his employment.

Black Letter Rule

A corporation can be held liable for the acts of its agents, done within the scope of their employment, even if the corporation's policy and specific instructions prohibited such acts.

Case Vocabulary

BOYCOTT: To join with another in refusing to cooperate with or buy from another in order to punish or coerce.
EXCULPATION: Exoneration, an act freeing someone from blame or responsibility.
PER SE: On its face, without reference to additional evidence.

Procedural Basis: Appeal of a district court conviction under the Sherman Antitrust Act.

Facts: Hilton Hotels Corporation ("Hilton") (D) was one of several hotels, restaurants, and hotel and restaurant supply companies that organized an association in Portland, Oregon to attract conventions to their city. The association was financed by members who made set contributions to the association. To encourage membership, hotel members allegedly agreed to buy their supplies only from suppliers who paid contributions to the association. This agreement was a *per se* violation of the Sherman Antitrust Act. Hilton's (D) purchasing agent admitted that he had been instructed not to participate in a boycott of non-member suppliers. Hilton's (D) president testified that such boycotts were contrary to the policy of the corporation and that supply purchases were made solely on the basis of quality, price, and service. Despite the policy and his instructions, Hilton's (D) purchasing agent threatened a supplier, [in what had to have been an interesting conversation], with a boycott "because of the anger and personal pique toward the individual representing the supplier." The jury was instructed that a corporation can be held liable for the acts and statements of its agents made within the scope of employment on behalf of the corporation regardless, even if the agent's conduct was in violation of specific instructions or of the corporation's stated policies. Hilton (D) was convicted under the Sherman Act, and it now appeals.

Issue: Can a corporation be liable for the acts of its agents who are acting within the scope of their employment even if the corporation's policy and specific instructions prohibited such acts?

Decision and Rationale: (Browning) Yes. Congress has the constitutional power to impose criminal liability on a corporation for the acts of its agents acting within the scope of their employment even though the actions are outside the agent's actual authority or are contrary to express instructions. While the text of the Sherman Act does not expressly address this issue, we believe that this interpretation of the act "best achieves its purpose." It is reasonable for Congress to conclude that exposing a corporation to criminal liability provides a strong incentive for the corporation to prevent illegal actions by employees. Since violations of the Sherman Act are predominantly motivated by the desire to maximize profits, they often involve large and highly decentralized corporate business practices where it is difficult to pinpoint particular corporate agents who acted illegally. At the same time, the complexity of such practices makes it likely that high management officials of the corporation have participated in the policy decisions or have become aware of possible Sherman Act violations. Furthermore, violations of the Sherman Act are usually driven by the desire to increase profits, so directions to comply with the act "are the least likely to be taken seriously." Even where a violation does take place and the responsible agent can be identified, the punishment of the agent may be ineffective since the corporation is the entity that realizes the profits from the illegal activity. For these reasons, we conclude that, despite contrary corporate policy or express instructions to the agent, a corporation can be liable under the Sherman Act for the acts of its agents in the scope of their employment. The corporation's stated policy and the general instructions issued to the corporation's purchasing agent were not sufficient unless proper steps were taken to enforce them. Judgment affirmed.

Analysis:

When compared to the other cases dealing with accomplice liability, this opinion seems like an aberration. A corporation can be held liable for the acts of its agents even though it has instructed the agents not to engage in those acts. Under traditional accomplice liability theory, for the corporation to be held liable, evidence would be required showing that the corporation and the agent had the same or similar intent. In contrast, in this case, it appears that the intent of the corporation is irrelevant. However, the opinion is, in reality, taking into account the corporation's intent, although not quite expressly. The opinion notes that violations under the Sherman Antitrust Act are usually of the type that benefit the corporation, making it very unlikely that a corporation would be anxious to curtail any such illegal activity. In addition, since these activities are often done on a large, complex scale, it is likely that high management has participated in formulating the illegal practices or are at least aware of them. While there was no evidence that Hilton (D) compelled its purchasing agent to engage in the boycott, the opinion seems to imply that Hilton (D) had an affirmative duty to see that its policies dealing with antitrust activity were actually enforced. Thus, in all practicality, the opinion is holding Hilton (D) liable for an omission, a failure to act. The opinion sees this omission as circumstantial evidence that Hilton (D) tacitly endorsed the boycott. The court was skeptical that the corporation was an innocent actor and demanded a higher standard of conduct to prevent Sherman Act violations.

Commonwealth v. Beneficial Finance Co.

(State) v. (Finance Company)
(1971) 360 Mass. 188, 275 N.E.2d 33

M E M O R Y   G R A P H I C

 Instant Facts

A financial company is convicted of bribery for the actions of two of its lower level employees.

 Black Letter Rule

A corporation can be held criminally liable for the acts of its agent if it placed the agent in a position where he has enough authority and responsibility to act for and on behalf of the corporation in handling the particular corporate matter and committed the criminal act in furtherance of that particular corporate matter.

 Case Vocabulary

MALA IN SE: An act that is wrong on its face, inherently evil.

MALA PROHIBITA: An act that is a crime merely by reason of statute, but is not necessarily inherently immoral.

RATIFIED: Confirmed and accepted, often carries a legal obligation.

RESPONDEAT SUPERIOR: A common law doctrine holding that a master is responsible for the actions of her servant committed during the scope of employment.

SUBSIDIARY: A sibling corporation of the large parent corporation.

Procedural Basis: Appeal of a trial court conviction of bribery and conspiracy to bribe.

Facts: Two employees of Beneficial Finance Company ("Beneficial") (D3) bribed state banking officials in order to receive favorable treatment from the State Small Loans Regulatory Board. One of the employees, Farrell (D1), was an officer and director of a wholly owned subsidiary of Beneficial (D3). The other employee, Glynn (D2), was a lower level employee of another wholly owned subsidiary of Beneficial (D3). Beneficial (D3) argued that the corporation should not be held criminally liable for their acts unless their conduct was "performed, authorized, ratified, adopted or tolerated by the corporation's directors, officers or other 'high managerial agents.'" The trial court instructed the jury to find Beneficial (D3) guilty if it had placed the employees in a position where they had enough authority and responsibility to act for and on behalf of the corporation in handling the particular corporate matter and committed the criminal act in furtherance of that particular corporate matter. The employees and Beneficial (D3) were found guilty of bribery and conspiring to bribe. Beneficial (D3) appeals.

Issue: Can a corporation be held criminally liable for the acts of its agent, if the agent has the authority to act for and on behalf of the corporation in handling its business and commits a crime while engaged in that corporate business?

Decision and Rationale: (Spiegel) Yes. Beneficial (D3) argues that corporate criminal liability should be determined under the standard set by the Model Penal Code, where the criminal acts of agents can be imputed to the corporation if the conduct was "performed, authorized, ratified, adopted or tolerated by the corporation's directors, officers or other 'high managerial agents.'" In contrast, the trial court instructed the jury with a different standard with Beneficial (D3) incurring liability where it is found that it placed its employees in a position where they had enough authority and responsibility to act for and on behalf of the corporation in handling the particular corporate matter and committed the criminal act in furtherance of that particular corporate matter. The cases dealing with this issue have reflected the difficulty of imposing theories of vicarious liability on corporate actors since corporate action can only take place through its human agents. Thus, the primary issue is whether the acts and intent of the corporation's agents can be treated as the acts and intent of the corporation itself. There is substantial precedent that corporate liability may attach for intentional crimes committed by a minor employee. While these principles are essentially the same as those expressed under the doctrine of respondeat superior in civil law, the trial court did not directly apply a civil law standard to establish criminal liability. The judge required "a greater quantum of proof," requiring that the authority of the agent be established beyond a reasonable doubt. We think that the Model Penal Code is insufficient in handling the evidentiary problems presented in establishing the culpability of directors or officers. Often evidence of the authorization of criminal activity is easily concealed. Furthermore, the position of an agent should not be determinative in ascertaining criminal responsibility. In large corporations, lower ranking corporate employees are often given considerable authority in dealing with matters they are specialized in, especially as it relates to everyday operations of the corporation. In consideration of these issues, we conclude that a corporation can be held criminally liable for the acts of its agents if it is shown that the corporation "placed the agent in a position where he has enough authority and responsibility to act for and on behalf of the corporation in handling the particular corporate business, operation or project in which he was engaged at the time he committed the criminal act." In addition, a jury can consider additional factors in applying this test such as the following: i) the extent of the agent's control and authority, ii) the extent and matter to which corporate funds were used in the crime, and iii) a repeated pattern of criminal conduct which may reveal a corporate toleration or ratification of the agent's actions. There was sufficient evidence to support a finding that the employees of the corporation had sufficient authority vested in them to act on behalf of Beneficial (D3) in dealing with the state officials who were bribed. Judgment affirmed.

Analysis:

This opinion represents a curtailment of the scope of the previous cases dealing with corporate liability. The opinion describes two possible theories for limiting corporate liability, one based on the Model Penal Code and the other based on the "responsible corporate officer" doctrine. The Model Penal Code theory focuses on the culpability of higher level officials in the corporation in terms of whether these officials authorized or recklessly tolerated the illegal activity. In contrast, the "responsible corporate officer" doctrine focuses on whether the corporation properly delegated its authority to the agent in relation to the business matter, and the agent committed the criminal act in furtherance of that particular corporate matter. These theories of liability differ primarily on how they ascertain a corporation's intent. The Model Penal Code theory looks to the corporation's officers or board as the expression of the corporation's intent. Thus, if a board member authorized or recklessly tolerated the illegal activity, the corporation can be said to be liable. The "responsible corporate officer" doctrine reflects the decentralized nature of corporations. This theory assumes that corporate actions are composed of the actions of all its employees as a whole, and, therefore, cannot be limited to the actions or intentions of only its higher level employees. In addition, corporate responsibilities are delegated to all employees, but each of these employees is granted a narrow "kingdom" of authority. Thus, the corporate mail clerk can't negotiate the next big merger, but he has supreme rule over the mailroom. As a result, under this theory, any action taken by any employee of the corporation is part of that corporation's actions and intentions as well if done within the authority vested in them by the corporation. Criminal liability attaches where the employee commits a criminal act in furtherance of his corporate responsibilities. Thus, a mail clerk that intentionally discards, along with the junk mail, a summons issued for the CEO is acting within his authority and in furtherance of the interests of the corporation; therefore, his actions can be imputed to the corporation. A problem with this approach is determining whether the employee's actions are actually done in furtherance of his or her authority or the actions are done outside the scope of the employee's authority. In the case at hand, the employees had the authority to negotiate with the state regulatory board, but they cannot be said to have the authority to bribe the state regulatory board. The opinion states that the employees were acting within their authority and in furtherance of corporate matters entrusted to them. However, it could also be argued equally strongly that an act of bribery was clearly outside the scope of their authority and responsibility. Is the court implicitly defining "authority" or "responsibility" to include acts that further the interests of the corporation in the business matter? The opinion leaves this unclear.

Gordon v. U.S.

(Appliance Seller) v. (State)

(1954) 203 F.2d 248, rev'd, 347 U.S. 909

M E M O R Y   G R A P H I C

Instant Facts

Without the employer's knowledge, sales-persons of an appliance business violated a federal law by selling machines without collecting down payments.

Black Letter Rule

An unknowing employer can be held criminally liable for an employee's willful criminal acts made while acting in the course of employment.

Procedural Basis: Appeal of a circuit court conviction.

Facts: Gordon (D) was a partner in a sewing machine and appliance business who employed several salespersons. Unknown to Gordon (D), certain salespersons made sewing machine sales without collecting a down payment. [Believe it or not], these sales actually violated a federal law known as the Defense Production Act. Gordon, the other partners, and the salespersons were charged with violating the statute. The jury was instructed to find Gordon (D) and the other partners guilty on the theory that the knowledge of their agents could be imputed to them personally. Gordon (D) and the partners were convicted under this theory. Gordon (D) and the other partners appeal.

Issue: Can an unknowing employer be held criminally liable for an employee's willful criminal acts made while acting in the course of employment?

Decision and Rationale: (Murrah) Yes. The statute at issue requires willfulness as an element of the offense. Willfulness or a guilty mind is "an essential ingredient" of any punishable offense, and is a notion "deeply rooted in our criminal jurisprudence." The trial court instructed the jury that Gordon's (D) intent could be ascertained by circumstantial evidence. The circumstantial evidence was the acts and knowledge of the employees. The trial court did not discard the requirement of willfulness or guilty knowledge. Instead, it charged the employers with "constructive" knowledge of the illegal acts. As partners and employers, the defendants have a responsibility and duty under law to run their business properly. This responsibility extends from the employer to the employees and agents. The action or omission could be construed by a trier of fact as intentional and deliberate or inadvertent and negligent. Since the jury instructions were proper, this is an issue properly left to the jury. Judgment affirmed.

Dissent: (Huxman) Gordon (D) and the other partners did not have the necessary intent unless they had knowledge of the illegal activities or directed them. The majority has erroneously applied corporate liability standards to individual partners. A corporation can be held liable on a constructive knowledge theory because it, as an entity, is a legal fiction. A corporation "has no conscience, will, or power of thought." Thus, a corporation has no knowledge of its own except through its agents. Individual partners should not be subject to such a legal fiction. The only statutes that hold unknowing employers liable for the actions of their employees are public welfare statutes that impose strict liability for violations of food and drug laws. As a result, none of these public welfare statutes required willfulness, intent, or knowledge as an element of the offense. The statute at issue here does have a scienter requirement.

Analysis:

This opinion was later reversed by the U.S. Supreme Court, essentially for the reasons given by the dissent. The court was applying a standard that had evolved in response to the uniqueness of corporate liability. Because a corporation has no free will of its own and is driven by the actions of its agents, a theory of constructive knowledge is essential to subject it to criminal liability. A corporation, like any other individual, must have the requisite mens rea for the crime, albeit a manufactured one. However, individual partners are human beings and should be held to the same mens rea as other individuals. It would be odd to find one person not guilty of being an accomplice, and another guilty under the exact same circumstances solely on the reason that one person is an employer and the other not. The Supreme Court has also treated partnerships as an entity that, like a corporation, can be held criminally liable for the acts of its employees.

United States v. Park

(State) v. (CEO)
(1975) 421 U.S. 658

M E M O R Y   G R A P H I C

Instant Facts

The chief executive officer of a national supermarket chain was convicted under a federal law for unsanitary conditions in the company's regional warehouses.

Black Letter Rule

A corporate officer can be criminally liable without proof of any wrongful action if the officer was in a position of authority and responsibility to prevent or correct the criminal violation.

Case Vocabulary

ALTER EGO: A corporation used by an individual to conduct personal business that can result in the individual being held directly liable for any corporate action.

BYLAW: The internal rules or administrative guidelines of a corporation.

TAUTOLOGY: Needless repetition of an idea.

SEMANTIC: Dealing with the development and evolution of words.

Procedural Basis: Park (D) was convicted in the circuit court, but his conviction was overturned in the court of appeals. The Supreme Court granted the United States' petition for certiorari.

Facts: John Park (D) was the CEO of Acme Markets, Inc., a national supermarket chain. Beginning in April 1970 and over a period of nearly two years, Food and Drug Administration (FDA) inspectors repeatedly found unsanitary conditions at the company's warehouses in Philadelphia and Baltimore. The inspectors found that these warehouses, which were used to hold food for shipment, were accessible to rodents and exposed to contamination by rodents. The inspectors also found evidence of rodent-contaminated food items. Acme pled guilty to various counts of violating the Federal Food, Drug, and Cosmetic Act. Park (D) pled not guilty to these counts. The evidence at trial revealed that Park (D) had the overall responsibility for managing the entire operation of the company. Park, in his testimony, also conceded that he was ultimately responsible for the sanitary conditions at the warehouses in question. Park (D) also admitted that he was aware of the FDA inspections and had received letters from the agency documenting the unsanitary conditions. Park (D) delegated the problem to subordinates, and stated that he did not think "there was anything [he] could have done more constructively than what [he] found was being done." Based on this evidence, the jury convicted him, and Park (D) was [slapped on the wrist] with a $50 fine on each count. The Court of Appeals reversed the conviction arguing that it was based "solely upon a showing that Park (D) was the president of the offending corporation" and lacked any evidence of wrongful action. The United States then petitioned for certiorari in the Supreme Court. Certiorari was granted.

Issue: Can a corporate officer be held criminally liable without proof of any wrongful action if the officer was in a position of authority and responsibility to prevent or correct the criminal violation?

Decision and Rationale: (Burger) Yes. The statute in question does not require proof of "consciousness of wrongdoing," but imposes liability on those who have "responsibility in the business process resulting in" the violation. The statute was drafted for the purpose of protecting public health in the modern industrial age. "In the interest of the larger good," it imposes a duty on those who may be responsible for preventing or causing a public danger. *United States v. Dotterweich*, 320 U.S. 277 (1943) [upholding the conviction of the president of a drug supply company under The Federal Food, Drug, and Cosmetic Act because the president had the responsibility of preventing or correcting the violation]. As Dotterweich points out, the question of responsibility for any individual employee depends on the evidence produced at trial and the judgment of the jury. Dotterweich, and the cases that have followed it, reveal a requirement that corporate agents have "a positive duty to seek out and remedy violations when they occur" and "a duty to implement measures that will insure that violations will not occur." While the statute requires "the highest standard of foresight and vigilance," it does not eliminate any defense against liability. A defendant may still raise the defense of being powerless to prevent or correct the violation. Therefore, we disagree with the Court of Appeals in finding that the statute requires the burden of establishing "wrongful action" in the way it relies on the phrase. The concept of responsibility carries with it "some measure of blameworthiness." Judgment of the court of appeals is reversed.

Dissent: (Stewart) I agree with most of the majority's opinion; however, I believe the jury instructions in this case where inadequate. The jury instructions stated that Park (D) could be found guilty if it found, beyond a reasonable doubt, that Park (D) had a position of authority and responsibility in regards to the violation. However, the jury instructions did not define the meaning of "responsibility" and left it to their "unguided discretion" to define what that term meant. As a result, there were no jury instructions dealing with whether or not Park's (D) actions were wrongful conduct "amounting at least to common law negligence."

Analysis:

This opinion represents a somewhat narrow exception to corporate criminal liability. This rule dispenses with the traditional level of culpability required to hold a corporate agent's conduct criminal. Instead of requiring purpose, knowledge, recklessness, or negligence, cases dealing with public health issues require that the corporate agent share "responsibility" and "authority" over the violation. It also imposes on the corporate agents, with such responsibility and authority, an affirmative duty to protect the public from harm. This is a logical extension of public health statutes that would historically find individuals strictly liable for public health violations, thereby making the individual's state of mind not relevant. Since corporations now largely control the production and sale of products that may pose public health dangers, it would make sense to hold corporations strictly liable for public health violations. However, this opinion stops short of holding corporate officers strictly liable in favor of concepts of authority and responsibility. Nevertheless, as the dissent points out, this standard is not properly defined. No doubt there are degrees of responsibility in which it could be said that one corporate agent has more responsibility than another corporate agent. In the case at hand, Park (D) had delegated the problem of the unsanitary warehouses to his subordinates. Does that mean those subordinates also held authority and responsibility over the violation and could be held criminally liable as well? The opinion gives no such guidance.

United States v. MacDonald & Watson Waste Oil Co.

(State) v. (Waste Disposal Company)
(1991) 933 F.2d 35

M E M O R Y   G R A P H I C

 ## Instant Facts

The president of a waste disposal company was convicted of illegally disposing of solid wastes without the proper permit.

Black Letter Rule

Unless the applicable statute requires strict liability, a corporate agent cannot be held criminally liable under the "responsible corporate officer" doctrine and can only be convicted based on the mens rea requirement of the applicable statute.

Case Vocabulary

SCIENTER: An act done knowingly.
WILLFUL BLINDNESS: The intentional disregard of incriminating knowledge.

Procedural Basis: Appeal of a district court conviction.

Facts: Eugene K. D'Allesandro (D2) was president of a small waste disposal and transportation company named MacDonald & Watson Waste Oil Co. ("MacDonald") (D1) and operated a disposal facility which only had a permit authorizing the disposal of liquid wastes. An employee of MacDonald (D1) contracted and supervised the transportation of solid waste to the disposal facility in violation of the Resource Conservation and Recovery Act [penalizing a person who knowingly transports, or causes to be transported, hazardous waste to a facility that does not have a permit]. The government [figured out that something rotten was amuck] and charged D'Allesandro (D2) and his company with violating the statute. D'Allesandro (D2) argued that he had no knowledge regarding the illegal disposal; however, the prosecution presented evidence that D'Allesandro (D2) was a "hands-on" manager of his small company [(hopefully, he wore gloves)], and his subordinates had contracted for the disposal of the waste at issue. The prosecution argued that D'Allesandro (D2) was guilty of violating the statue regardless of his actual knowledge because, as a "responsible corporate officer," he was in a position to prevent the violation and failed to do so despite the fact that he had been warned on two earlier occasions that shipments of the same type of solid waste had been disposed of without the proper permit. MacDonald (D1) and D'Allesandro (D2) were both convicted of violating the statute. MacDonald (D1) appealed.

Issue: In the absence of an applicable strict liability statute, can a corporate agent be held criminally liable under the "responsible corporate officer" doctrine regardless of the mens rea requirement of the applicable statute?

Decision and Rationale: (Campbell) No. In Dotterweich and Park, the court dispensed with a scienter requirement and established liability under the "responsible corporate officer" doctrine. However, these cases concerned misdemeanor charges and dealt with public welfare statutes in which it was well-established law that no scienter was required to hold a defendant criminally liable. There exists no precedent for ignoring a scienter requirement where Congress has expressly included one in a criminal statue. This is especially true where the crime is a felony carrying the possibility of imprisonment. While the trial court properly instructed the jury to infer knowledge [such as willful blindness] based on circumstantial evidence, it improperly instructed the jury that D'Allesandro's (D2) status as a "responsible corporate officer" was sufficient, conclusive proof that D'Allesandro (D2) had the "knowledge" required for conviction under the statute. The simple knowledge or belief that a prior illegal disposal occurred does not necessarily prove knowledge of the illegal disposal charged in this case. The mere fact that D'Allesandro (D2) is a "responsible corporate officer" does not establish such knowledge and "is not an adequate substitute for direct or circumstantial proof of" that knowledge. The conviction is vacated and remanded for a new trial.

Analysis:

This opinion represents the limits of the "responsible corporate officer" doctrine found in the Park case. The opinion recognizes that the "responsible corporate officer" doctrine arose out of the public welfare statutes and regulations that traditionally held violators to a strict liability standard. It refused to expand corporate agent liability to anything other than the scienter requirement given in the applicable statute. Such an expansion could have potentially exposed individual corporate agents to a flood of criminal indictments with few of the protections criminal law traditionally provides in defining the mens rea of certain crimes. Juries and judges would effectively be re-writing criminal statutes and making their own law if they substituted the scienter requirements of a statute with the vague "responsible corporate officer" doctrine. Hazardous waste disposal may be a public health issue deserving as much attention as regulations dealing with food or medicine; however, absent a specific directive of Congress making illegal waste disposal a strict liability offense, the courts should not be able to substitute the judgment of the legislature with its own judgment.

Krulewitch v. United States

(Pimp) v. (Government)
(1949) 336 U.S. 440, 69 S.Ct. 716, 93 L.Ed. 790

M E M O R Y   G R A P H I C

Instant Facts

The Government (P) introduced hearsay testimony about an effort by Krulewitch's (D) co-conspirators to help Krulewitch (D) avoid punishment.

Black Letter Rule

A statement made in furtherance of an alleged implied but uncharged conspiracy to avoid criminal punishment is inadmissible under the hearsay rule.

Case Vocabulary

HEARSAY: Testimony given by a person relating facts of which he does not have personal knowledge, but has learned or heard from another.

Facts: Krulewitch (D) and a woman defendant were indicted for (1) persuading another woman to go from New York to Miami for the purpose of prostitution; (2) transporting her to Miami for that purpose; and (3) conspiring to commit those offenses in violation of 18 U.S.C. § 371. Krulewitch (D) was convicted on all three counts, and the Court of Appeals affirmed. The Supreme Court granted certiorari to consider the admission of hearsay testimony. The testimony was from the woman who was induced and transported to Miami, and consisted of a narration of a conversation between her and the woman conspirator. Significantly, the conversation took place over one and one-half months after the crime and conspiracy occurred. It took place after arrest. The woman testified, "She asked me, she says, 'You didn't talk yet?' And I says, 'No.' And she says, 'Well don't . . .. It would be better for us two girls to take the blame than Kay [Krulewitch (D)] because he couldn't stand it, he couldn't stand to take it.'" The Government (P) argues for admissibility of the hearsay declaration as one in furtherance of a continuing secondary objective of the conspiracy—the concealment of the conspiracy.

Issue: May hearsay evidence relating to an implied conspiracy to conceal a conspiracy be admitted at trial?

Decision and Rationale: (Black) No. We cannot accept the Government's (P) contention. Out-of-court statements by one conspirator against another are not admissible unless they are made in furtherance of the objectives of a going conspiracy. The Government (P) now asks us to expand this narrow exception to the hearsay rule to allow a statement made not in furtherance of the alleged criminal transportation conspiracy, but in furtherance of an implied conspiracy aimed at preventing detection and punishment. Under this rule, arguments could be made in conspiracy cases that most out-of-court statements admitted into evidence tended to shield co-conspirators. The rule would create a further breach of the general rule against the admission of hearsay evidence.

Concurrence: (Jackson) There is a growing habit of prosecuting for conspiracy in lieu of prosecuting the substantive offense itself. The modern crime of conspiracy is so vague that it almost defies definition. It is "predominantly mental in composition" because it consists of a meeting of minds and intent. The law has its place to prosecute dangerous group criminality, but it may also be trivialized where the conspiracy consists of a pimp and a prostitute going to Miami to ply their trade. At trial, a defendant charged with conspiracy is faced with a hodgepodge of facts and statements by others that he may not have authorized or even knew of, but which help convince the jury that the conspiracy existed. A conspiracy is often proved by evidence that is admissible only upon assumption that conspiracy existed. The naive assumption that prejudicial effects can be overcome by jury instructions is known by all practicing lawyers to be a fiction. A co-defendant may have difficulty in making his own case, especially where co-defendants can be prodded into accusing and contradicting each other. There is a strong temptation to relax rigid standards when they seem the only way to convict wrongdoers. But statutes authorize prosecution for substantive crimes for most wrongdoing, without the dangers to liberty and integrity of the judicial process inherent in conspiracy prosecutions. We should disapprove the doctrine of implied or constructive crime in its entirety.

Analysis:

Hearsay is generally not admitted in a criminal prosecution. An exception to the rule is the co-conspirator exception. An act or statement by one co-conspirator committed during and in furtherance of the conspiracy may be admitted against the other co-conspirators. Although *Krulewitch* indicates some limits on how much courts will allow, the requirement that the act or statement be in furtherance of the conspiracy is applied broadly. And, as Justice Jackson points out, jury instructions may not always temper the prejudicial effects brought on by admission of the evidence. Note that in this case the statements were not admitted to prove conspiracy to commit the original offense (crossing state lines for prostitution). Rather, they were admitted based upon a second conspiracy to hide the facts of the joint conspiracy. The prosecution argued that the latter was merely in furtherance of the original conspiracy.

Pinkerton v. United States

(IRS Scammer) v. (Government)
328 U.S. 640, 66 S.Ct. 1180, 90 L.Ed. 1489 (1946)

M E M O R Y   G R A P H I C

Instant Facts

Two brothers were convicted of both conspiracy and the substantive offense even though only one actually participated in committing the offense.

Black Letter Rule

Participation in the conspiracy is enough to sustain a conviction for the substantive offense in furtherance of the conspiracy.

Case Vocabulary

VICARIOUS LIABILITY: Imputing liability upon one person for the actions of another.

Procedural Basis: Appeal from jury's conviction of the defendant.

Facts: Walter and Daniel Pinkerton (D) are brothers who live a short distance from each other on Daniel's (D) farm. They were indicted for violations of the Internal Revenue Code. The indictment contained ten substantive counts and one conspiracy count. The jury found Walter guilty on nine of the substantive counts and on the conspiracy count. It found Daniel (D) guilty on six of the substantive counts and on the conspiracy count. A single conspiracy was charged and proved. Each of the substantive offenses found was committed pursuant to the conspiracy.

Issue: Is participation in a conspiracy enough to sustain a conviction for the substantive offense?

Decision and Rationale: (Douglas, J.) Yes. It is contended that there was insufficient evidence to implicate Daniel (D) in the conspiracy, but we think there was enough evidence for submission to the jury. There is, however, no evidence to show that Daniel (D) participated directly in the commission of the substantive offenses on which his conviction has been sustained, although there was evidence to show that these substantive offenses were committed by Walter in furtherance of the unlawful agreement or conspiracy existing between brothers. We take the view here that there was a continuous conspiracy which Daniel (D) never took any affirmative action to withdraw from. So long as the partnership in crime continues, the partners act for each other in carrying it forward. It is settled that an overt act of one partner may be the act of all without any new agreement specifically directed to that act. Thus we hold that Daniel's (D) participation in the conspiracy is enough to sustain his conviction for the substantive offense in furtherance of the conspiracy. Affirmed.

Dissent: (Rutledge, J.) The judgment concerning Daniel Pinkerton (D) should be reversed. It is my opinion that it is without precedent here and is a dangerous precedent to establish. The result is a vicarious criminal responsibility as broad as, or broader than, the vicarious civil liability of a partner for acts done by a co-partner in the course of the firm's business.

Defense : withdrawal

Analysis:

The court's decision in this case, taken at face value, appears sound [first clue that something's off]. However, the underlying facts make the judgment a bit harder to swallow. The proof showed that Walter alone committed the substantive crimes, and there was no proof that Daniel (D) even knew that he had done so. In fact, Daniel (D) was in prison for other crimes when some of Walter's crimes were committed [what?]. Walter and Daniel (D) became partners in crime by virtue of their agreement and, without more on his part, Daniel (D) became criminally liable for everything Walter did thereafter so long as there was no proof of a clear withdrawal or revocation from the agreement. The dissent correctly labels Daniel's (D) liability as vicarious, and it seems to be a better argument that vicarious liability should remain in the civil law, and not transferred to the criminal field.

PINKERTON DOES NOT HOLD THAT A MEMBER OF A CONSPIRACY CAN ONLY BE CHARGED WITH A CRIME THAT IS WITHIN THE CONTEMPLATION OF THE CONSPIRACY

State v. Bridges

(State of New Jersey) v. (Convicted Murderer)
(1993) 133 N.J. 447, 628 A.2d 270

M E M O R Y   G R A P H I C

Instant Facts

A teenage boy was found guilty of murder when a plan between the boy and some friends to bring loaded guns to a party resulted in the death of a partygoer.

Black Letter Rule

A co-conspirator may be liable for the commission of substantive criminal acts that are not within the scope of the conspiracy if they are reasonably foreseeable as the necessary or natural consequences of the conspiracy.

Procedural Basis: Appeal to the Supreme Court of New Jersey.

Facts: At a party, Bridges (D) got into an argument with another guest, Andy Strickland. Angry, Bridges (D) left the party to recruit some friends to help him fight Strickland and his friends. He did so, and returned with Bing and Rollie, each of which brought a gun. The plan was that Bing and Rollie would hold the crowd at bay with the guns while Bridges (D) fought Strickland. At the party, Bridges (D) began fighting with one of Strickland's friends. During the fray, Bing was hit in the face. After getting hit, Bing and Rollie fired their guns into the air and then into the crowd. An onlooker was killed as a result. Bridges (D) was tried and convicted of conspiracy to commit aggravated assault and of the substantive crime of murder. He was sentenced to life imprisonment with no possibility of parole for thirty years. Bridges (D) appealed, and the Court of Appeals held that he could not be held responsible for the murder because it was not a planned objective of the conspiracy. The State (D) appealed.

Issue: When a crime not originally contemplated by co-conspirators is committed by one member of the conspiracy during the carrying out of the conspiracy, can other members of the conspiracy be held liable for their co-conspirator's additional crime?

Decision and Rationale: (Handler, J.) Yes. The Court of Appeals determined that the Code of Criminal Justice, which provides that involvement in a conspiracy can be the basis for criminal liability for the commission of substantive crimes, N.J.S.A. 2C:2-6b(4), requires a level of culpability and state of mind that is identical to that required of accomplice liability. It therefore ruled that a conspirator is vicariously liable for the substantive crimes committed by co-conspirators only when the conspirator had the same intent and purpose as the co-conspirator who committed the crimes. In other words, the Court of Appeals concluded that the Code contemplated "complete congruity" between accomplice and vicarious conspirator liability, reasoning that *Pinkerton* mandates that a crime must have been within a co-conspirator's contemplation when he entered into the agreement. This understanding of *Pinkerton* is not supported. *Pinkerton* purported to impose vicarious liability on each conspirator for the acts of others based on an objective standard of reasonable foreseeability. In making that decision, it was understood that the liability of a co-conspirator under the objective standard of reasonable foreseeability would be broader than that of an accomplice, where the defendant must actually foresee and intend the result of his or her acts. We appreciate the concurrence's concern that such a standard of vicarious liability for conspirators differs from that of accomplices. Although conspirator liability is circumscribed by the requirement of a close causal connection between the conspiracy and the substantive crime, that standard concededly is less strict than that defining accomplice accountability. It is, however, evident that the Legislature chose to address the special dangers inherent in group activity and therefore intended to include the crime of conspiracy as a distinctive basis for vicarious criminal liability. N.J. Stat. § 2C:2-6b reads: "A person is legally accountable for the conduct of another person when . . . (3) He is an accomplice of such other person in the commission of an offense; or (4) He is engaged in a conspiracy with such other person." Accordingly, we conclude that a co-conspirator may be liable for the commission of substantive criminal acts that are not within the scope of the conspiracy if they are reasonably foreseeable as the necessary or natural consequences of the conspiracy. The objective of Bridges' (D) conspiracy was not murder. Nevertheless, the evidence discloses that the conspiratorial plan contemplated bringing loaded guns to keep a large contingent of young hostile partygoers back from a beating of one of their friends, and that it could be anticipated that the weapon might be fired at the crowd.

State v. Bridges (Continued)

From that evidence the jury could conclude that a reasonably foreseeable risk and a probable and natural consequence of carrying out a plan to intimidate the crowd by using loaded guns would be that one of the gunslingers would intentionally fire at somebody, and, under the circumstances, that act would be sufficiently connected to the original conspiratorial plan to provide a just basis for a determination of guilt for that substantive offense. Reversed.

Concurrence and Dissent: (O'Hern, J.) This case is an example of the most extreme sort—life in prison with no possibility of parole for thirty years on the basis of a negligent mental state. The most reasonable construction of N.J.S.A. 2C:2-6b(4) is that the Legislature intended that the conspirator to the commission of an offense, like an accomplice to the commission of an offense, be punished as a principal. No liability is foreseen under the statute other than for the crime or crimes that were the object of the conspiracy. As such, to punish Bridges (D) for murder goes beyond the intent of the legislature.

Analysis:

One of the more important aspects of the New Jersey Supreme Court's opinion in *State v. Bridges*, particularly for the purposes of this chapter, is the court's discussion of the difference between conspiratorial liability and accomplice liability (two easily-confused concepts). Once again, *Pinkerton* holds that participation in a conspiracy is enough to sustain a conviction for any substantive offenses committed in furtherance of the conspiracy. Arguably, *Pinkerton* negates any real need for a concept of accomplice liability—at least in a conspiracy context—because participation in the conspiracy is enough for liability for the substantive crimes. In other contexts, however, a clear distinction of the concepts exists. The *Bridges* court makes two observations about this distinction. First, the court states that "the liability of a co-conspirator under the objective standard of reasonable foreseeability [is] broader than that of an accomplice, where the defendant must actually foresee and intend the result of his or her acts." This is true as a co-conspirator, under the rule of both *Pinkerton* and *Bridges*, can be held liable for acts not intended so long as they are "reasonably foreseeable as the necessary or natural consequences of the conspiracy." Second, the court also correctly states that "[a]lthough conspirator liability is circumscribed by the requirement of a close causal connection between the conspiracy and the substantive crime, that standard concededly is less strict than that defining accomplice accountability." These distinctions are important in that they show that complicity and conspiracy are not always coextensive, as the liability and standards for each are different. In this same vein, it is also important to note that a person can act as an accomplice to a crime without having joined a conspiracy to commit it. A perfect example of this principle is the case of *State v. Tally*, found earlier in this chapter, in which Judge Tally was found to be an accomplice to murder without having ever conspired with his brothers-in-law to kill the seducer Ross. In sum, a person need not engage in a conspiracy to be an accomplice. With respect to the reverse proposition, however, *Pinkerton*, a case with which many state courts and legislatures disagree, would argue that a co-conspirator is always punishable as an accomplice.

United States v. Alvarez

(United States) v. (Drug Dealer)
(1985) 755 F.2d 830

M E M O R Y   G R A P H I C

Instant Facts
A number of co-conspirators were held criminally responsible for the death of a federal agent caused when a gun battle erupted during an undercover cocaine buy.

Black Letter Rule
When a co-conspirator is in a position such that it is reasonably foreseeable to him that an unintended crime might occur, he can be held responsible for that crime if it indeed occurs; those not in such a position will be more likely to escape responsibility for the crime.

Case Vocabulary
EVIDENTIALLY: Evidentiary; having to do with evidence.

Procedural Basis: Appeal to the Eleventh Circuit Court of Appeals of three co-conspirator's convictions for the murder of a federal agent that occurred during the effectuation of the object of the conspiracy.

Facts: In Miami, Florida, a group of undercover ATF (Alcohol, Tobacco, and Firearms) agents arranged a $147,000 cocaine buy from Alvarez and some friends of his. When other ATF agents closed in following the buy, a gun battle erupted and an ATF agent was killed. All of the dealers were convicted of conspiracy to commit various drug offenses. Two, including Alvarez, were convicted of first-degree murder, and three others, Portal, Concepcion, and Hernandez (D's) were convicted of second-degree murder. Portal, Concepcion, and Hernandez (D's) played no part in the shooting. However, Portal (D) was armed at the time of the buy. Further, Concepcion (D) was present at the time of the shooting (he introduced the agents to Alvarez), and Hernandez (D) owned the hotel and translated during the meeting that resulted in the shootout. Portal, Concepcion, and Hernandez (D) appealed, contending that their convictions were based on an improper extension of *Pinkerton*. Specifically, they argued that murder was not a reasonably foreseeable consequence of a drug conspiracy, and therefore their convictions should be reversed.

Issue: When a co-conspirator is in a position such that it is reasonably foreseeable to him that an unintended crime might occur in the carrying out of the conspiracy, can he be held responsible for that crime if it indeed occurs?

Decision and Rationale: (Kravitch, J.) Yes. The record contains ample evidence to support the jury's conclusion that the murder was a reasonably foreseeable consequence of the drug conspiracy. In making this determination, we rely on two critical factors. First, the evidence clearly established that the conspiracy was designed to effectuate the sale of a large quantity of cocaine. Second, based on the amount of drugs and money involved, the jury was entitled to infer that at the time the sale was arranged, the conspirators must have been aware of the likelihood (1) that at least some of their number would be armed, and (2) that deadly force would be used, if necessary, to protect the conspirators' interests. These factors provide ample support for the jury's conclusion that murder was a reasonably foreseeable consequence of the conspiracy. Portal (D) and his two cohorts argue that the murder was sufficiently distinct from the intended purposes of the conspiracy, and that their individual roles were sufficiently minor, such that they should not be held responsible for the murder. We disagree. This in not a typical *Pinkerton* case. The murder of Agent Rios was not within the originally intended scope of the conspiracy, and we have found no authority for the proposition that all conspirators, regardless of individual culpability, may be held responsible under *Pinkerton* for reasonably foreseeable but originally unintended substantive crimes. Nevertheless, these considerations do not require us to reverse the murder convictions of Portal, Concepcion, and Hernandez (D). All three were more than minor participants in the conspiracy. Further, each had actual knowledge of at least some of the circumstances and events leading up to the murder. The evidence that Portal (D) was carrying a weapon demonstrated that he anticipated the possible use of deadly force to protect the conspirators' interests. Moreover, both Concepcion and Hernandez (D) were present when Alvarez stated that he would rather die than go back to prison, indicating that they too were aware that deadly force might be used to prevent apprehension of the group. Affirmed.

Analysis:

On the surface, *Alvarez* appears to be and is a reaffirmation of the *Pinkerton* doctrine. Hidden in the opinion (mostly in the footnotes), however, are some statements from the court that express the view that the traditional *Pinkerton* doctrine should be limited in certain situations. Specifically, the *Alvarez* court believes that a distinction should be made between "major" and "minor" participants in a criminal conspiracy when determining whether to apply *Pinkerton*. Further, the court also seems to argue that *Pinkerton* should be applied only to the former, and not to all participants in a conspiracy. (The court was unable to directly implement its views in this opinion because it found that Portal,

Concepcion, and Hernandez (D) were all "major" participants in Alvarez' drug conspiracy.) The court makes the following statements in favor of its limiting position: (1) "We have not found, nor has the government cited, any authority for the proposition that all conspirators, regardless of individual culpability, may be held responsible under *Pinkerton* for reasonably foreseeable but originally unintended substantive crimes." (2) "The imposition of *Pinkerton* liability for [reasonably foreseeable but originally unintended] crimes is not wholly unprecedented." See, e.g., Government of Virgin Islands v. Dowling, 633 F.2d 660, 666 (3d Cir.) (1980) (conspiracy to commit bank robbery; substantive crime of assault with deadly weapons against police officers, committed during escape attempt); Park v. Huff, 506 F.2d 849, 859 (5th Cir.) (1975) (liquor conspiracy; substantive crime of first degree murder of local district attorney, committed in attempt to stop investigation of illegal liquor sales). In each of the aforementioned cases, however, vicarious liability was imposed only on 'major' participants in the conspiracy." (3) "At trial in the instant case, the government's attorney . . . expressed the view that prosecutorial discretion would protect truly 'minor' participants . . . from liability for the far more serious crimes committed by their coconspirators . . . . In our view, the liability of such "minor" participants must rest on a more substantial foundation than the mere whim of the prosecutor." And finally, (4) "Although our decision today extends the *Pinkerton* doctrine to cases involving reasonably foreseeable but originally unintended substantive crimes, we emphasize that we do so only with narrow confines. Our holding is limited to conspirators who played more than a 'minor' role in the conspiracy, or who had actual knowledge of at least some of the circumstances and events culminating in the reasonably foreseeable but originally unintended substantive crime." Is this the proper view? Some state courts and legislatures would agree, as many have rejected *Pinkerton* as applied to both "major" and "minor" participants, adopting instead the view that co-conspirators should only be held liable for the crimes of other co-conspirators when the requirements for accomplice liability have been met. The Model Penal Code agrees with these anti-*Pinkerton* sentiments: "[L]aw would lose all sense of just proportion if simply because of the conspiracy itself each were held accountable for thousands of additional offenses of which he was completely unaware and which he did not influence at all . . . . Conspiracy may prove solicitation, aid or agreement to aid, etc.; it is evidentially important and may be sufficient for that purpose. But whether it suffices ought to be decided by the jurors; they should not be told that it establishes complicity as a matter of law." MPC and Commentaries, Comment to 2.06(3) (1985). Which side is correct?

Interstate Circuit Inc. v. United States

(Theater Chain) v. (State)
(1939) 306 U.S. 208

M E M O R Y   G R A P H I C

Instant Facts
Two theater chains were convicted of entering into a conspiracy with film distributors to violate the Sherman Antitrust Act.

Black Letter Rule
Evidence of a conspiratorial agreement can be based on inferences drawn from the course of conduct of the alleged conspirators.

Case Vocabulary

CREDULITY: Believability
ENJOINED: Prohibited or restrained.

Procedural Basis: Appeal of a district court conviction under the Sherman Antitrust Act.

Facts: Two movie theater chains, Interstate Circuit ("Interstate") (D1) and Texas Consolidated Theaters ("Consolidated") (D2), dominated the market for playing films in the cities where their theaters were located. Interstate (D1) and Consolidated (D2) entered into contractual agreements with eight film distributors. These eight film distributors released 75% of all first run films in the United States. These agreements restricted the distributors from releasing second run films in theaters that charged an admission price of less than $0.25 and restricted the distributors from releasing its first run films on a double bill with another feature film. These agreements were made after an Interstate (D1) manager mailed a letter to each distributor that identified all eight distributors as addressees of the proposal. After this letter was sent out, all eight distributors agreed to accept the restrictions. The government charged Interstate (D1) and Consolidated (D2) with violating the Sherman Antitrust Act. Since each distributor had entered into a separate contract with Interstate (D1) and Consolidated (D2), the letter was the government's only evidence to prove the existence of an unlawful conspiracy. The trial court held that the evidence was sufficient to support a conviction of conspiracy to take uniform action in violation of the Sherman Antitrust Act. Interstate (D1) and Consolidated (D2) appeal.

Issue: Can evidence of a conspiratorial agreement be based on inferences drawn from the course of conduct of the alleged conspirators?

Decision and Rationale: (Stone) Yes. Because of the secretive nature of conspiracies, the government is usually without direct evidence or testimony of a conspiratorial agreement. In order to prove such an agreement, it is proper "to rely on inferences drawn from the course of conduct of the alleged conspirators." The trial court made this inference from the nature of the proposal, the manner in which it was made, from the "substantial unanimity" of the distributor's conduct after the proposal was made, and the fact that the defendants did not call as witnesses any of the superior officials who negotiated the distributor agreements. The letter in question addresses all eight distributors and each distributor knew that those other distributors were considering the proposal. Each distributor also knew that, without group cooperation, there was a risk of a loss of business and that cooperation meant increased profits. In addition, acceptance of the agreement represented a "radical departure from the media's business practices of the industry." It would be impossible to believe that these distributors entered into this agreement without some understanding that all the other distributors would be joining as well. Each knew that the others were asked to participate and understood that cooperation was necessary to make the proposal successful and beneficial to them. In fact, with that knowledge, the agreement was renewed for another two years. A simultaneous action or agreement to join the conspiracy is not necessary to prove an unlawful conspiracy. Judgment affirmed.

Analysis:

This opinion reflects the problems of proving the existence of a conspiracy. Because conspiracies are, by their very nature, clandestine, there is usually little evidence for the prosecution to use to prove the existence of a conspiracy. As a result, courts have allowed the use of circumstantial evidence to infer the existence of a conspiracy. However, these loose standards have often muddled the requirement that conspiracies are generated as a result of an agreement, where the parties manifest and share their intentions. The danger created by using circumstantial evidence is that parallel action may be interpreted as an agreement to engage in common action. Just because different people engage in the same conduct, it does not necessarily mean that they had a prior agreement to work in concert. In this case, the defendants argued that it made individual agreements with each of the distributors separately, not as any concerted, group agreement. As a result, the court did not rely on the letter alone to prove the existence of a conspiratorial agreement. It also looked to the conduct of all the parties and any of the motivations they may have held in entering the agreement. However, other cases may not have such additional evidence. The result is an imperfect rule that may find conspiracies where none existed or fail to recognize conspiracies that actually took place.

United States v. Alvarez

(State) v. (Driver/Underling)
(1981) 625 F.2d 1196

M E M O R Y   G R A P H I C

Instant Facts

A workman, who loaded electrical appliances aboard a plane, was convicted of conspiracy to import marijuana based on his presence, a smile, and a nod.

Black Letter Rule

The conduct of a defendant can be used to infer guilt of participation in a conspiracy.

Case Vocabulary

EN BANC: As a whole, with all judges present.
TRANSGRESSIONS: Violations of the law, regulations, or other orders.

Procedural Basis: Appeal of a district court conviction.

Facts: An undercover Drug Enforcement Agency (DEA) agent made an arrangement with co-conspirators to import marijuana into the United States from Columbia by plane. While in the United States, the undercover agent met the co-conspirators at an airport. The co-conspirators arrived with Alvarez (D) as their driver of a pickup truck loaded with household appliances. The undercover agent asked his co-conspirators who Alvarez (D) was, and they stated that Alvarez (D) "would be at the off-loading site in the United States." The agent also spoke with Alvarez (D) in Spanish and asked him if he planned to be at the unloading site. Alvarez (D) responded by smiling and nodding his head. Alvarez (D) then unloaded the household appliances from the pickup truck. Afterwards, the agent spoke with a co-conspirator to make plans for the arrival of the plane and its unloading. The co-conspirators and Alvarez (D) were then arrested. Alvarez (D) was convicted as a co-conspirator, but, on appeal, a three-judge panel reversed his conviction finding that Alvarez's (D) acts did not prove that he knew of the conspiracy or intended to take part in it. The entire Court of Appeals granted a rehearing.

Issue: Can the conduct of a defendant be used to infer guilt of participation in a conspiracy?

Decision and Rationale: (Reavley) Yes. The government is not required to prove that Alvarez (D) had knowledge of all the details of the conspiracy. In addition, a person can still join a conspiracy after its inception or even if he plays a minor role. We find that the "aggregate of the evidence is sufficient to infer that Alvarez (D) knew that criminal activity was afoot." First, there was evidence showing that Alvarez (D) intended to be at the unloading site. The undercover agent asked Alvarez (D) if he would be present at unloading and Alvarez (D) responded in the affirmative. In addition, even before he asked Alvarez, the co-conspirators told the undercover agent that Alvarez (D) would be present. This suggests that Alvarez (D) had a prior agreement to assist in the unloading. Second, Alvarez's (D) nodded head may be viewed as an assurance to the agent to calm "jittery accomplices." A reasonable jury could have concluded that only a person with knowledge of the scheme to import marijuana would agree "to be on hand at a remote and unlikely area for the unloading of cargo." The conviction is affirmed.

Dissent: (Vance) In this case, a smile and the nod of the head are not sufficient to prove guilt. Alvarez (D) may have been "a humble workman" who was performing a lawful act- loading appliances on to an airplane. His response to the inquiry of whether he would return for the off-loading may simply have been an indication that he would report back to work as previously instructed. While Alvarez (D) was present, there was no contraband in view for Alvarez (D) to infer that any illegal activity was taking place. "The potential for injustice in conspiracy cases is enormous." We should be careful and be sure that the prosecution has actually proved that the defendant was a knowing participant in a conspiracy before he is sentenced to prison. I would reverse.

Analysis:

This opinion, again, illustrates the wide net that conspiracy laws often cast. Because of the difficulty of proving the existence of a conspiracy, courts frequently give the prosecution considerable wiggle room in using circumstantial evidence. This circumstantial evidence can include a person's conduct. However, a person's conduct is not always a clear indicator of a person's intent. In the case at hand, the majority and the dissent had two different interpretations of Alvarez's (D) behavior. Each of these interpretations has validity. Alvarez's (D) true intent may have only become known, for example, if the drugs actually arrived and the undercover agent observed Alvarez (D) unloading dozens of clear plastic bags of marijuana. However, the justification for laws of conspiracy is to prevent crimes from reaching their completion. For better or for worse, Alvarez (D) was trapped in the tangle that these conspiracy laws have created.

A PERSON WHO SUPPLIES A PRODUCT OR SERVICE TO ANOTHER KNOWING THAT IT WILL BE USED AS PART OF A CRIME, MAY BE CONVICTED FOR CONSPIRACY UNLESS ONLY A MISDEMEANOR IS INVOLVED

People v. Lauria

(Government) v. (Telephone Answering Service Provider)
(1967) 251 Cal.App.2d 471, 59 Cal.Rptr. 628

M E M O R Y   G R A P H I C

Instant Facts

Lauria (D) ran a telephone answering service, which he knew was used by several prostitutes in their business ventures; Lauria (D) was indicted with the prostitutes for conspiracy to commit prostitution.

Black Letter Rule

The intent of a supplier who knows his supplies will be put to criminal use may be established by (1) direct evidence that he intends to participate, or (2) through an inference that he intends to participate based on (a) his special interest in the activity, or (b) the felonious nature of the crime itself.

Has to be a serious felony

Procedural Basis: Appeal by prosecution from order setting aside an indictment for conspiracy to commit prostitution.

Facts: In a prostitution investigation, police focused their attention on three prostitutes who used Lauria's (D) telephone service. An undercover policewoman, Stella Weeks, signed up for Lauria's (D) services. Weeks hinted that she was a prostitute, and wanted to conceal that fact from the police. Lauria (D) assured her that his service was discreet and safe. A few weeks later, Weeks called Lauria (D) and complained that because of his operation she had lost two "tricks." Lauria (D) claimed that her tricks probably lied about leaving messages for her. Lauria (D) did not respond to Weeks' hints that she needed more customers, other than to invite her over to become better acquainted. A couple of weeks later Weeks again complained that she had lost two tricks, and the office manager said she would investigate. Two weeks later, Lauria (D) and the three prostitutes were arrested. Lauria (D) testified before the Grand Jury that he only had 9 or 10 prostitutes using his service, and he kept records for known or suspected prostitutes for the convenience of police. However, Lauria (D) did not volunteer the information, but would give it when asked about a specific prostitute. He claimed that he tolerated the prostitutes so long as they paid their bills. Lauria (D) admitted having personal knowledge that some of his customers were prostitutes [use your imagination]. Lauria (D) and the three prostitutes were indicted for conspiracy to commit prostitution. The trial court set aside the indictment as having been brought without a showing of reasonable or probable cause. The Government (P) appeals claiming that a sufficient showing of an unlawful agreement to further prostitution was made. To establish agreement, the Government (P) need show no more than an implied mutual understanding, between co-conspirators, to accomplish an unlawful act.

Issue: Is a person criminally liable for conspiracy if he furnishes goods and services he knows will be used to assist in the operation of an illegal business?

Decision and Rationale: (Fleming) No. *United States v. Falcone* held that a seller's knowledge of the illegal use of the goods was insufficient to make the seller a participant in the conspiracy. In *Direct Sales Co. v. United States*, by contrast, the conviction on federal narcotics laws of a drug wholesaler was affirmed on a showing that the company had actively promoted the sale of morphine. In both cases, however, the element of knowledge of the illegal use of the goods or services and the element of intent to further that use must be present in order to make the supplier a participant in a criminal conspiracy. Proof of knowledge is ordinarily a question of fact. Lauria (D) admitted he knew that some of his customers were prostitutes. He probably knew that some of his customers were subscribing to his service in order to further their trade. The Government argues that this knowledge serves as a basis for concluding that Lauria (D) intended to participate in the criminal activities. We note some characteristic patterns in precedent cases: (1) intent may be inferred from knowledge, when the purveyor of the legal goods for illegal use has acquired a stake in the venture; (2) intent may be inferred from knowledge, when no legitimate use for the goods or services exists; and (3) intent may be inferred from knowledge, when the volume of business with the buyer is grossly disproportionate to any legitimate demand. In response to the first pattern, we note that Lauria (D) had no stake in the venture, and was not charging higher prices to the prostitutes. As to the second pattern, we note that nothing in the furnishing of telephone service implies that it will be used for prostitution, since all sorts of persons might use the service for completely legal activities. Finally, no evidence suggests any unusual volume of Lauria's (D) business was with prostitutes. In all three of these patterns, it can be said that in one way or another a supplier has a special interest in the operation of the criminal enterprise. There are cases in which it cannot be said that the supplier has a stake in the venture, yet still may be held liable based on knowledge alone. Some examples of this would be supplying cutting equipment to be used in a bank robbery, or supplying telephone service to persons involved in the extortion of ransom. Still, we do not believe that an inference of intent drawn from knowledge should apply to misdemeanors. Thus, with respect to misdemeanors, we conclude that positive knowledge of a supplier that his products will be used for illegal activities does not in itself establish intent to participate in the misdemeanor. However, with respect to felonies, we hold that in all felony cases, knowledge of criminal use alone may justify an inference of intent. From this analysis we deduce the following rule: the intent of a supplier who knows of the criminal use to which his supplies are put to participate in the criminal activity connected with the use of his supplies may be established by (1) direct evidence that he intends to participate, or (2) through an inference that he intends to participate based on (a) his special interest in the activity, or (b) the felonious nature of the crime itself. Lauria (D) took no direct action to further the activities of the prostitutes. There is no evidence of a special interest in the prostitutes' activities. The offense with which he has been charged is a misdemeanor. Thus the charges of conspiracy against Lauria (D) fail, and since the conspiracy theory was built around the activities of Lauria's (D) business, the charges against his co-conspirators must also fail. The order is affirmed.

Analysis:

It certainly can be argued that taking account of the seriousness of the criminal objective is appropriate in striking a balance between the conflicting interests of vendors (in regard to their freedom to engage in gainful and otherwise lawful activities without policing their vendees) and that of the community in preventing behavior that facilitates the commitment of crimes. A couple of arguments, offered on whether the specific mental state of conspiracy must be proved, demonstrate that a party has the intent, not just the knowledge, that the object of the conspiracy be achieved. Those who believe that proof of purpose should be required, argue that conspiracy laws should apply to those with criminal goals, rather than "seek to sweep within the dragnet of conspiracy all those who have been associated in any degree whatever with the main offenders." They argue that the law should not be extended to punish "legitimate businessmen" like Lauria (D). On the other hand, some argue that persons should be convicted solely on the basis of their knowledge that they are contributing to a criminal enterprise, even if they do not intend the same goals as the conspiracy. They argue that business people should not be immunized from criminal responsibility under the guise of free enterprise.

Kotteakos v. United States

(Loan Broker) v. (State)

(1946) 328 U.S. 750

M E M O R Y G R A P H I C

 Instant Facts

A loan broker arranged loans for several people knowing that these loans were taken for illegal purposes.

Black Letter Rule

If one person deals with others having no connection with each other, then they are not guilty of one, single conspiracy.

Case Vocabulary

CONFEDERATE: Associate or co-participant.

Procedural Basis: Appeal of a district court conviction and appellate court affirmation.

Facts: Simon Brown (D1) was a loan broker who arranged loans, for a commission, for Kotteakos (D2) and other defendants under the National Housing Act. Brown (D1) knew that these loans were not going to be used for the purposes stated in the applications. This was in violation of the National Housing Act. The other defendants obtained loans from Brown, but none of them were aware of the others and there was no evidence showing any connection between them. Brown (D1) was the only common figure in all the loan transactions. Of the 32 persons indicted for the illegal loans, seven were found guilty. Brown (D1) pled guilty. Kotteakos (D2) and other defendants were brought to trial. The trial court instructed the jury that there was only one conspiracy. The jury found all of them guilty of a single conspiracy. The Court of Appeals found that there was not a single conspiracy, but, at least, eight separate conspiracies between the individual defendants and Brown (D1). The government described the pattern as "separate spokes meeting at a common center." The Court of Appeals found that the trial judge erred in finding a single, common conspiracy, but also found that the error was not prejudicial and harmless. The defendants appealed.

Issue: Can all defendants be guilty of a single conspiracy if one person deals with each of them with no connection with the other defendants?

Decision and Rationale: (Rutledge, J.) No. The jury was misdirected to only find evidence of a single conspiracy. Furthermore, the jury was also instructed that it may use the acts or statements of any of the defendants against all of the defendants. This instruction is only proper if all the defendants are part of a single conspiracy. Since the evidence is clearly otherwise, the jury may have incorrectly imputed the specific acts or statements of unrelated conspirators against the whole group. Judgment is reversed.

Analysis:

This opinion illustrates two important points. First, a conspiracy cannot always occur where, despite a common agent, the defendants have no other connection with one another nor are aware of each other. This goes straight to the simple definition of a conspiratorial agreement. The conspiracy in this case has been called the "hub of the wheel conspiracy." Brown (D1) was the agent that entered into several different, but similar conspiracies. However, none of these conspiracies, besides Brown's (D1) handiwork, had any connection. Second, if there is a common conspiracy, the acts and statements of a single defendant can be used against all other defendants found to be members of the conspiracy. This sometimes has the effect of generating an uneasy feedback loop where the statements of one conspirator are admitted and implicate new, previously unknown conspirators. Can the statement be used against the new conspirator even before there is a finding that the new person was part of the conspiracy at all? Is the statement both admissible as to finding the new person part of the conspiracy and to determine his culpability?

Blumenthal v. United States

(Convicted Conspirator) v. (United States)
(1947) 332 U.S. 539

M E M O R Y G R A P H I C

Instant Facts

Three men found themselves convicted for conspiracy when they each separately agreed to sell whiskey to local taverns at prices above those allowed by law.

Black Letter Rule

When two or more separate agreements are part of a single scheme sharing the same illegal end, there exists one large conspiracy and not two or more smaller conspiracies.

Case Vocabulary

HUB AND SPOKE ARRANGEMENT: An arrangement in which a single party (the hub) engages in the same criminal conduct with a number of other persons (the spokes) who have no connection with one another except for their relationship to the hub.

Procedural Basis: Appeal to the United States Supreme Court of a defendant's conviction for conspiracy to sell whiskey above the maximum price allowed by law.

Facts: Weiss and Goldsmith owned and operated the Francisco Distributing Company, a licensed liquor distributor. Feigenbaum, Abel, and Blumenthal (D) were local businessmen who, before entering into an agreement with Francisco, had no prior connection to the company. The conspiracy began when Weiss and Goldsmith agreed to receive two carloads of whiskey and distribute them under the Francisco name in such a way that the fact that they were selling the whiskey at prices above those permitted by law would be concealed. Weiss and Goldsmith contacted Feigenbaum, Abel, and Blumenthal (D), who each agreed to sell the whiskey to local taverns at an illegal price. Feigenbaum, Abel, and Blumenthal (D) did not know of each other's participation in the conspiracy; nor did they know where Weiss and Goldsmith got the whiskey. Feigenbaum, Abel, and Blumenthal (D) were each convicted of a single conspiracy to sell whiskey at unlawful prices. Each appealed, arguing that there were two distinct conspiracies—one between the original seller of the whiskey and the second between Weiss and Goldsmith and Feigenbaum, Abel, and Blumenthal (D). The appeal was eventually accepted by the Supreme Court.

Issue: When a court finds that two or more separate agreements are part of a single scheme sharing the same illegal end, is it precluded from finding that there exists only one large conspiracy? (Must it find two or more smaller conspiracies?)

Decision and Rationale: (Not Stated) No. (No.) In this case, the two agreements were merely steps in the formation of a single, larger conspiracy. As such, it would be improper to regard Blumenthal's (D) ignorance of the unknown owner's participation as furnishing adequate ground for reversal of his conviction. The scheme was the same scheme; Blumenthal (D) and the other salesmen knew or must have known that others unknown to them were sharing in so large a project; and it hardly can be sufficient to relieve them that they did not know, when they joined the scheme, who those people were or exactly the parts they were playing in carrying out the common design and object of all. By their separate agreement, Blumenthal (D) and the other salesmen became a party to the large common plan, joined together by their knowledge of its essential features and broad scope, though not of its exact limits, and by their common single goal. This case is very different from one such as *Kotteakos* in which two or more agreements are so separate and distinct that they cannot be tied together as stages in the formation of a larger all-inclusive combination, all directed to achieving a single unlawful end result. Where each separate agreement has its own distinct, illegal end, and there is no drawing of all together in a single comprehensive plan, then the outcome is different. Here, in fact, all knew of and joined in the overriding scheme. All intended to aid the owner, whether Francisco or another, to sell the whisky unlawfully, though the two groups of defendants differed on the proof in knowledge and belief concerning the owner's identity. All by reason of their knowledge of the plan's general scope, if not its exact limits, sought a common end. True each salesman aided in selling only his part. But he knew the lot to be sold was larger and thus that he was aiding in a larger plan. He thus became a party to it and not merely to the integrating agreement with Weiss and Goldsmith. Affirmed.

Analysis:

Blumenthal v. United States deals with an issue that is oftentimes difficult and complex—determining the scope of a conspiracy. As the Comment to MPC § 5.03 (1985) states: "Much of the most perplexing litigation in conspiracy has been concerned . . . with the scope to be accorded to a combination, i.e., the singleness or multiplicity of the conspiratorial relationships typical in a large, complex and sprawling network of crime . . . . [I]n most of these cases it is clear that each defendant has committed or conspired to commit one or more crimes; the question now is, to what extent is he a conspirator with each of the persons involved in the larger criminal network to commit the crimes that are its objects . . . The scope of the problem is . . . central to the present concern of courts and commentators about the use of conspiracy, a concern based on the conflict between the need for effective means of prosecuting large criminal organizations, and the dangers of prejudice to individual defendants." *Blumenthal* is a significant case as it gives some insight into determining when a single conspiracy exists, and when a court should instead find multiple smaller conspiracies. In doing so, *Blumenthal* first addresses the reasoning of the prior case, *Kotteakos*, and differentiates the present case from that one. As you will recall, *Kotteakos* involved a single loan broker who arranged loans for several people knowing that the loans were taken for illegal purposes. In finding eight separate conspiracies each involving the defendant and one other person, the court of appeals focused on the fact that the crimes were committed at different times and on behalf of persons who had no connection with or knowledge of one another. In this vein, the *Blumenthal* Supreme Court wrote: "Each loan was an end in itself, separate from all others, although all were alike in having similar illegal objectives. Except for Brown, the common figure, no conspirator was interested in whether any loan except his own went through. And none aided in any way, by agreement or otherwise, in procuring another's loan. The conspiracies therefore were distinct and disconnected, not parts of a larger general scheme, both in the phase of agreement with Brown and also in the absence of any aid given to others as well as in specific object and result. There was no drawing of all together in a single, over-all comprehensive plan." On the surface, *Blumenthal* is arguably similar to *Kotteakos*. In *Blumenthal* there were separate salesman, none of whom knew each other, working for a single hub (Weiss and Goldsmith). Moreover, each entered into separate agreements with the hub (as the defendants in *Kotteakos* did). And yet, contrary to the finding in *Kotteakos*, the *Blumenthal* court found a single conspiracy as opposed to multiple conspiracies. It is this contrary finding which sheds light on what are some of the factors that a court should look at in determining the scope and number of any conspiracies. First, the Supreme Court determined that the scheme at issue in *Blumenthal* was a single scheme with a single goal, and not a bunch of separate and disconnected schemes that just happened to share similar objectives. Second, the Court also concluded that the defendants either knew or should have known that they were sharing in a large project. In *Kotteakos*, there was no such knowledge among the various defendants. Thus, *Blumenthal* teaches that in determining whether single or multiple conspiracies exist, a court should look to whether there is one common scheme with a common goal or distinct individual schemes sharing similar but different objectives. A court should also look to whether various participants, though they may not have personally known other participants in the conspiracy, at least knew of the existence of other participants and their possible roles in a larger plan. Finally, *Blumenthal* also teaches that the existence of a hub and spoke arrangement can sometimes serve as a single conspiracy, depending, of course, on the circumstances.

EVEN IF NONE OF THE DEFENDANTS EVER COOPERATED OR COMMUNICATED WITH EACH OTHER, A CONSPIRACY EXISTS IF THE DEFENDANTS ARE AWARE OF THE ACTS OF THE OTHER DEFENDANTS

United States v. Bruno

(State) v. (Drug Dealers)

(1939) 105 F.2d 921, rev'd on other grounds, 308 U.S. 287

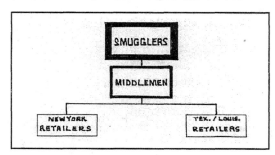

M E M O R Y G R A P H I C

Instant Facts

Eighty-eight different defendants were indicted for a single conspiracy to import, sell, and possess narcotics.

Black Letter Rule

Even if none of the defendants ever co-operated or communicated with each other, a conspiracy exists if the defendants are aware of the acts of the other defendants.

Case Vocabulary

PER CURIAM: An opinion written by the court as a whole.

QUOAD: "As to."

Procedural Basis: Appeal of a conviction of conspiracy.

Facts: Bruno (D1) and Iacono (D2) were indicted along with 86 other defendants for a single conspiracy to import, sell, and possess narcotics [that courtroom must have been standing room only!]. The defendants were alleged smugglers, middlemen who paid the smugglers and distributed to the retailers, and two groups of retailers (one in New York and the other in Texas and Louisiana). The defendants were allegedly involved in smuggling drugs into New York City to distribute them there and in Texas and Louisiana. There was no evidence that any cooperation or communication occurred between the smugglers and the retailers or between the two groups of retailers themselves. However, there was evidence that the smugglers knew that the middlemen sell to retailers and that the retailers knew that smugglers supplied the middlemen. They were found guilty of a single conspiracy, and the defendants appealed.

Issue: Can defendants be guilty of a single conspiracy, even if none of the defendants ever cooperated or communicated with each other, but the defendants are aware of the acts of the other defendants?

Decision and Rationale: (Per Curiam) Yes. While there was no evidence of any direct cooperation or communication among all of the defendants, there is evidence that conspirators "at one end of the chain" knew what the conspirators at the other end of the chain were doing. As a result, a jury may find that a single conspiracy existed. The success of one part "was dependent upon the success of a whole." The argument that two separate conspiracies existed, one including the New York retailers and the other including the Texas and Louisiana retailers, is fallacious. Neither the smugglers nor the retailers had any concern who was feeding who, but each was aware of the link and "were as much parts of a single undertaking or enterprise as two salesmen in the same shop." Judgment affirmed.

Analysis:

This opinion establishes the proposition that a conspiracy can be found where the defendants aid a conspiracy and merely have knowledge of each other's actions. This has the advantage of punishing defendants who aid criminal acts and who arguably exhibit a criminal intent in so doing. However, is this not changing the original definition of what a conspiracy actually is? A conspiracy is supposed to occur where there is an agreement and intent to achieve a criminal objective. Arguably, an agreement cannot take place unless there is some intent to facilitate the other party or parties. This is the purpose of an agreement. Do the smugglers in this case intend to, in any way, help the retailers get rich or are they only interested in making sure that they fill up their own pockets with money? In this case, since the drug smuggling and sales had already been committed, wouldn't it make more intuitive sense to prosecute them as accomplices and not conspirators? These problems were recognized and resulted in the creation of the Racketeer Influenced and Corrupt Organizations (RICO) Act specifically tailored to deal with criminal enterprises. The type of conspiracy addressed in this case is called a "chain" conspiracy, as contrasted with the "wheel" conspiracy described in the previous case.

Gebardi v. United States

(Amorous Mann Act Violator) v. (State)
(1932) 287 U.S. 112

M E M O R Y   G R A P H I C

Instant Facts

Gebardi (D1) and a woman (D2) agreed to go across state lines for the purpose of having sexual intercourse in violation of the Mann Act and were charged with conspiracy to violate the act.

Black Letter Rule

A conspiracy to violate a law cannot take place where it is impossible for the co-conspirator to actually violate that law.

Case Vocabulary

ILLICIT: Illegal, unlawful- usually associated with sexual crimes.

Procedural Basis: Appeal of a conviction of conspiracy to violate the Mann Act. The U.S. Supreme Court granted certiorari.

Facts: Gebardi (D1) and his girlfriend (D2) traveled across state lines to have sexual relations. This was a violation of the Mann Act [it was 1932, after all]. They had made multiple trips, and the evidence showed that Gebardi (D1) purchased at least one of the tickets. In each instance, she consented and voluntarily went with Gebardi (D1). Gebardi (D1) and his girlfriend (D2) [really got screwed when they] were indicted and later convicted for conspiracy to violate the Mann Act. Gebardi (D1) and his girlfriend (D2) appealed all the way to the U.S. Supreme Court.

Issue: Can a conspiracy to violate a law take place where it is impossible for the co-conspirator to actually violate that law?

Decision and Rationale: (Stone) No. When Congress created the Mann Act, it specifically exempted the woman from being charged with the crime if she voluntarily accompanies the man. Since she cannot violate the act, she cannot be convicted of conspiracy to violate the act. Consequently, because a conspiracy requires at least a bilateral agreement to violate the law, neither Gebardi (D1) nor his girlfriend (D2) can be guilty of conspiracy to violate the Mann Act. The convictions are reversed.

Hyp Question w/dangerous proximity: Aarg--- look at what steps remain to be done, Substantial steps.

Analysis:

This opinion proves a simple principle that applies in more ways than one in this case -- it takes two to tango. A person cannot be convicted of conspiracy to violate a law if it is impossible for the person to violate the law in the first place. For example, the underage party cannot be prosecuted for statutory rape, only the older party can. As a result, since Gebardi (D1) did not conspire with anyone else that could be convicted under the act, he was never a part of any conspiracy to violate it. This principle is known as the "Wharton rule." It holds that where a crime requires the consent and voluntary agreement of two parties, the two persons cannot be convicted as conspirators for the offense if it is not possible for one of them to commit the offense if one of them cannot commit the offense. Such crimes include statutory rape, adultery, and has also been applied to gambling, bribes, and drug trafficking. An exception to the Wharton rule exists where the agreement to commit the offense involves more than the minimum number of persons required to carry out the offense. Thus, Gebardi (D1) may have been found guilty if a third person agreed to accompany him and his girlfriend (D2) on their amorous forays.

Garcia v. State

(Murderous Spouse) v. (State)

(1979) 71 Ind. 366, 394 N.E.2d 106

I WANT YOU TO **KILL MY HUSBAND!!**

UNDERCOVER OFFICER

MEMORY GRAPHIC

Instant Facts

A distraught wife asked her friend to hire someone to kill her husband, but the friend called the cops on her.

Black Letter Rule

A person is guilty of conspiracy even if the other co-conspirator cannot be prosecuted for the conspiracy.

Case Vocabulary

FEIGN: To fake or pretend.

[handwritten notes:]
Garcia
bilateral: solicitation
unilateral: conspiracy

Procedural Basis: Appeal of a trial court conviction of conspiracy to commit murder.

Facts: Garcia (D) contacted Allen Young, telling him that her husband constantly beat her and their children and that she wanted him killed. [Instead of calling a marriage counselor] Young called the police. The police then recorded several conversations between Young and Garcia (D) about finding someone to kill her husband. The police then asked Young to set up a meeting between Young, Garcia (D), and a plainclothes detective pretending to be the hitman for hire. Young introduced them, and Garcia (D) gave the detective a $200 down payment [she was on a budget], a picture of her husband, and information about how to find him. Garcia (D) was arrested and convicted of conspiracy to commit murder. Garcia (D) appealed claiming that she cannot be guilty of a conspiracy because she conspired with someone who only "feigned his acquiescence in the scheme."

Issue: Can a person be guilty of conspiracy even if the other co-conspirator cannot be prosecuted for the conspiracy?

Decision and Rationale: (Prentice) Yes. Traditionally, conspiracy was considered a "bilateral" or "multilateral" crime requiring that two or more persons agree to commit a crime with the intent to commit it. As a result, if the other co-conspirators duped the defendant, there was no conspiratorial agreement and a conspiracy conviction was not possible. However, the Model Penal Code adopts a "unilateral" approach in which a defendant's culpability is unaffected by the culpability of the co-conspirators. The reason for this approach is that the existence of a firm purpose to commit a crime, which is the concern of conspiratorial liability, is there regardless of the intentions of the co-conspirators. In 1976, Indiana adopted a statute that follows the unilateral approach. It provides the defendant with no defense if the co-conspirator "cannot be prosecuted for any reason." Despite the prior case law, this new statute is controlling. Judgment is affirmed.

[handwritten notes across lower portion:]
withdrawl (Pinkerton)
renunciation (avoid consp liability)
bi/mutti: 3 party leg exempt
feigning
bi/mutti: if only other person in consp
is leg exempt d feigning
it is a defense (must be 2 people)

Analysis:

This opinion represents yet another troubling mutation of conspiracy laws. Here, the rule requiring a bilateral or multilateral agreement of criminal intent is discarded in favor of holding the defendant liable for her conspiratorial tendencies. It is based on a specific statute. This is intuitive in the sense that the crime of conspiracy seeks to punish those who have the intent to commit a crime and enlist others to assist. Even if the others fake cooperation, the defendant still holds the criminal intent. However, this interpretation creates new problems of a more fundamental concern. Conspiracy laws were created with the recognition that collective, group criminality is a greater social danger than unilateral criminal action. Group criminal actions are more likely to succeed and encourage future criminal activity. Yet, these concerns dissolve where the co-conspirator has no intention of committing the crime. This couldn't be more clear-cut where the co-conspirator is a law enforcement agent trying to entrap the defendant. This creates the danger of the government creating and entrapping conspirators where none would have ever existed.

United States v. Elliott

(Government) v. (RICO Conspirator)
571 F.2d 880 (1978)

M E M O R Y   G R A P H I C

 ### Instant Facts

Elliott (D) and five others were charged with conspiring to violate the RICO statute.

Black Letter Rule

RICO allows a prosecutor to charge, in a single count, what might constitute multiple, smaller conspiracies.

Case Vocabulary

RICO: Racketeer Influenced and Corrupt Organizations Act; federal statute designed to eradicate organized crime.

TRIAL EN MASSE: Group trial.

Procedural Basis: Appeal from the lower court's conviction of the defendant.

Facts: The indictment charged Elliott (D) and five others with conspiring with each other, with 37 unindicted co-conspirators, and with "others to the grand jury known and unknown," to violate Section 1962, subsection (c), of RICO [that's one big party!]. The essence of the conspiracy charge was that Elliott (D) and the others agreed to participate, directly and indirectly, in the conduct of the affairs of an enterprise whose purposes were to commit thefts, fence stolen goods, illegally traffic in narcotics, obstruct justice, and engage in "other criminal activities." The evidence supported the Government's (P) claim that Elliott (D) and the others were involved in one or more of the criminal endeavors. However, at no time did more than three of the defendants participate in any specific criminal endeavor, although one person, J.C. Hawkins, was linked to all of the crimes. The thread tying all of these individuals together was the desire to make money.

Issue: Does RICO allow a prosecutor to charge in a single count what might constitute multiple, smaller conspiracies?

Decision and Rationale: (Simpson, C.J.) Yes. The Court has previously held that proof of multiple conspiracies under an indictment alleging a single conspiracy constituted a material variance requiring reversal where a defendant's substantial rights had been affected. At issue was the right not to be tried en masse for the conglomeration of distinct and separate offenses committed by others. This protects against the transference of guilt from members of one conspiracy to members of another. The impact of that decision was soon limited by the Court in a case where the chain conspiracy rationale was born. The Court reasoned that since the scheme which is the object of the conspiracy must depend on the successful operation of each link in the chain, an individual associating himself with this type of conspiracy knows that for its success it requires an organization wider than may be disclosed by his personal participation. This rationale applies only insofar as the alleged agreement has a common end or single unified purpose. The rationale falls apart, however, where the remote members of the alleged conspiracy are not truly interdependent or where the various activities sought to be tied together cannot reasonably be said to constitute a unified scheme. Applying pre-RICO conspiracy concepts to the facts of this case, we doubt that a single conspiracy could be demonstrated. The activities allegedly embraced by the illegal agreement in this case are simply too diverse to be tied together on the theory that participation in one activity necessarily implied awareness of others. In enacting RICO, Congress found that organized crime continues to grow in part because the sanctions and remedies available to the Government (P) are unnecessarily limited in scope and impact. Thus, one of the express purposes of the Act was to seek "eradication of organized crime by establishing new penal prohibitions, and by providing enhanced sanctions and new remedies to deal with the unlawful activities of those engaged in organized crime." Against this background, we are convinced that, through RICO, Congress intended to authorize the single prosecution of a multi-faceted, diversified conspiracy by replacing the inadequate "wheel" and "chain" rationales with a new statutory concept: the enterprise. The object of a RICO conspiracy is to violate a substantive RICO provision – here, to conduct or participate in the affairs of an enterprise through a pattern of racketeering activity – and not merely to commit each of the predicate crimes necessary to demonstrate a pattern of racketeering activity. Under the statute, it is irrelevant that each defendant participated in the enterprise's affairs through different, even unrelated crimes, so long as we may reasonably infer that each crime was intended to further the enterprise's affairs. To be convicted as a member of an enterprise conspiracy, an individual, by his words or actions, must have objectively manifested an agreement to participate, directly or indirectly, in the affairs of an enterprise through the commission of two or more predicate crimes. In the instant case, it is clear that the essential nature of the plan was to associate for the purpose of making money from repeated criminal activity. Our society disdains mass prosecutions because we abhor the totalitarian doctrine of mass guilt. We nevertheless punish conspiracy as a distinct offense because we recognize that collective action toward an illegal end involves a greater risk to society than individual action toward the same end. That risk is greatly compounded when the conspirators contemplate not a single crime but a career of crime. The evidence could not be taken to support, to the exclusion of all other reasonable hypotheses, a conclusion by the jury that Elliott (D)

agreed to participate, directly or indirectly, in the affairs of an enterprise through a pattern of racketeering activity. At best, the evidence shows he became peripherally involved in a stolen meat deal, which is not enough to prove that he knowingly and intentionally joined the broad conspiracy to violate RICO. Elliott (D) agreed to participate in the affairs of the enterprise, but not through a *pattern* of racketeering activity, hence, not in violation of the Act. The evidence relevant to Elliott (D) as we view the record, was not sufficient to permit the jury to conclude that he conspired with the five other defendants to violate the RICO statute. Accordingly, his conviction must be reversed.

Analysis:

This case holds that a series of agreements that under pre-RICO law would constitute multiple conspiracies could under RICO be tried as a single enterprise conspiracy. What ties these conspiracies together is not the mere fact that they involve the same enterprise, but is instead an agreement on an overall objective. What RICO does is to provide a new criminal objective by defining a new substantive crime. That crime consists of participation in an enterprise through a pattern of racketeering activity. Elliott (D) and the other defendants could not have been tried on a single conspiracy count under pre-RICO law because they had not agreed to commit any particular crime. They were properly tied together under RICO only because the evidence established an agreement to commit a substantive RICO offense. The agreement was an implicit one, but it was an agreement nonetheless.

Chapter 8

We recognize that even people who commit illegal acts should be *exculpated* (exonerated) where some influence overcame their free will, because we recognize that criminal liability requires *mens rea* (guilty mind/criminal intent), and that people who whose free will was overcome cannot be said to have "intended" to do wrong. The difficulty lies in recognizing which influences/circumstances we should deem sufficiently strong to have overcome free will, thus relieving their doer of blame.

First, we generally believe that acts that would otherwise be criminal are *justified* (morally blameless) under extreme circumstances. When innocent people are threatened, we generally allow them to use force to defend themselves. The law of *self-defense* is concerned with how much of a threat must exist before defensive force is justified, and how much force may be use. What complicates the analysis is the psychological fact that, under threat, emotion overrides reason. As Holmes said, "Detached reflection cannot be demanded in the presence of an uplifted knife."

Paradoxically, while the law thus recognizes that people may kill others to prevent harm to themselves, it is traditionally reluctant to grant people the right to kill themselves to prevent themselves from suffering. The law is thus involved in regulating the right to *suicide*, and the right to help others with *assisted suicide*.

Also, we generally recognize that people faced with impending danger may face a *choice of evils*, and may be severely tempted to commit a criminal act to avoid the danger. The law hesitates to punish a person for finding himself in a no-win situation, which most people seek to escape by committing the crime. Further, policy dictates that the law should permit people to commit small crimes/harms if they thereby prevent larger harms. However, the law is concerned with mandating what degree of danger justifies a crime, and limiting the amount of harm that may be inflicted in preventing other harms.

In a different category, we have long recognized that people who commit crimes while unable to think rationally may be *excused* from the *full* punishment for their crimes, because the will they exerted cannot be said to be entirely theirs, or entirely free. For instance, *intoxication* can reduce inhibitions and encourage people to do acts they would not normally choose to do, but we are reluctant to grant them a full pardon, since they were at least "guilty" of becoming intoxicated.

The most difficult excuse is *insanity*. We generally agree that the *truly* insane should not be imprisoned/executed for their crimes, because (i) they cannot be said to have acted out of free will, (ii) we deem them to have acted out of sickness, not malice, and (iii) they are unlikely to be deterred by the threat or imposition of punishment, because they never "chose" to commit crimes at all. At the same time, we are highly suspicious of the insanity defense, because (i) we cannot readily distinguish which claimants are actually "insane" and which are faking or able to control themselves, (ii) we are fearful of spurious and convenient insanity defenses, and (iii) we are afraid that, if we acquit dangerously insane defendants, they will be released to repeat their crimes again and again. Thus, the law must decide what constitutes "insanity," what evidence is sufficiently credible to prove it, and what is be done to punish/treat/control those acquitted because of insanity. Recently, the law has also been asked to decide whether some traditionally criminal/blameworthy behavior, such as alcoholism and drug addiction, should be reclassified as diseases.

Chapter 8

NOTE: THE PURPOSE OF THIS OUTLINE IS TO ORGANIZE THE CASES SO THAT ONE CAN QUICKLY UNDERSTAND THE RELEVANCE OF EACH CASE TO THE COURSE. NO ATTEMPT IS MADE IN THIS OVERVIEW TO ADDRESS EVERY CONCEPT THAT MUST BE STUDIED. BE SURE TO READ THE ENTIRE CASEBOOK AND/OR OTHER MATERIALS TO GAIN A FULL UNDERSTANDING OF ALL CONCEPTS.

I. Justification: Actions, which would otherwise constitute a crime, are *justified* under certain circumstances (self-defense, duress, etc.), meaning that *no* criminal liability attaches, because the action is considered proper under the circumstances.

A. Protection of Life and Person: Self-Defense: The use of force in self-defense is *justified* (permitted) when the defender faces a threat, actual or apparent, from (ii) unlawful and (iii) immediate force, with (iv) no reasonably-available alternative to avoid confrontation, and the defender has (iv) a good faith and (v) reasonable belief that the threat presents (v) imminent risk of (vi) death or serious bodily injury, plus (vii) a belief that the self-defense is necessary to prevent death/injury, and (viii) uses an amount of force proportional to the threat. Deadly force is justified against a threat of deadly force (death or serious injury). *U.S. v. Peterson* (D.C. Cir. 1973).

1. Reasonable Belief

a. Model Penal Code Subjective Test: Under the Model Penal Code, the defender's belief (that the attack is dangerous and self-defense is necessary) may be *subjectively* reasonable (i.e., a good faith belief). *Model Penal Code §§3.04, 3.09, and Comments.*

b. Objective Test: Under many state statutes, the defender's belief must be *objectively* reasonable under the circumstances, but the circumstances may include (reasonable) misperceptions of the attackers' intentions. *People v. Goetz* (N.Y. Ct. App. 1986) [vigilante shoots thugs, believing they intended to rob him].

(1) Unreasonable Self-Defense: In some states requiring reasonability, a defender who kills unreasonably is guilty of intentional murder. In other states, unreasonable

defenders face lesser penalties (e.g., voluntary manslaughter).

(2) Imperfect Self-Defense

(a) In most states, if a defender kills with unreasonable belief *or* unreasonable force, he is guilty of voluntary manslaughter, absent "malice." This doctrine is called "imperfect self-defense," a common law doctrine that is codified in some states.

(b) Some states punish "imperfect self-defense" as *in*voluntary manslaughter. *Shannon v. Commonwealth* (Ky. 1988).

(c) Under the Model Penal Code, killing with an honest but unreasonable need for self-defense is guilty of negligent homicide. *Model Penal Code §3.09.* Few states actually adopted this provision.

c. Battered Woman's Syndrome ("BWS")

(1) When battered women kill their batterers and claim self-defense, expert testimony on BWS is admissible to prove they faced imminent risk of injury, but inadmissible to prove their belief that risk was objectively reasonable. *State v. Kelly* (N.J. 1984).

(2) BWS evidence is admissible on the issue of reasonableness but in a limited way. The jury must decide whether a reasonable *person*, not a reasonable battered woman, would believe in the need to kill to prevent imminent harm. *People v. Humphrey.*

(3) Some courts have moved closer to a completely subjective test by allowing the jury to decide whether the defendant's particular physical and psychological properties created a reasonable belief in the need to use force. *State v. Leidholm.*

(4) BWS testimony is generally accepted as scientifically reliable. Some state statutes explicitly admit BWS evidence. *See, e.g., Cal. Evid. Code. §1107(b), Tex. Pen. Code §19.06.*

(5) Other syndrome evidence, such as battered or abused child who kills abusive

parent, is often admissible. (But see *Werner v. State,* wherein holocaust syndrome evidence was rejected.)

2. Imminent Risk
   a. In most jurisdictions, self-defense (perfect or imperfect) requires an "imminent" ("about to happen") risk of death or serious injury, which does not include perceived threats of later harm. *State v. Norman* (N.C. 1989) [abused wife, who killed sleeping husband whom she believed would eventually kill, not entitled to self-defense].
      (1) A few courts have allowed the jury to determine whether self defense was reasonable even in a sleeping-victim case. *Robinson v. State.*
   b. Defensive Contract Killing: Defenders who suborn/hire others to kill their attackers cannot claim self-defense. *People v. Yaklich* (Colo. App. 1991).
   c. Threats alone may not be sufficient to create an "immediate risk." *State v. Schroeder* (Neb. 1978) [inmate not justified in stabbing violent cellmate who threatened to rob and rape him]. *But see State v. Janes* (Wash. 1993) [battered child justified in killing threatening abuser].
   d. Under the Model Penal Code and some state statutes, it is sufficient *that the defender reasonably believed* defensive force was "immediately necessary ... on the present occasion." *Model Penal Code §3.04(1), see, e.g., N.J. §2C:3-4a; Pa. tit. 18 §505.*
   e. Battered person's syndrome evidence was not permitted in case against battered child who deliberately killed the father who abused him for 14 years. *Jahnke v. State* (Wyo. 1984).

3. Reasonable Force/Deadly Force
   a. Most courts hold that deadly defensive force is only justified against unlawful "deadly force" (force likely to cause death or great bodily harm), but not against non-deadly assault or offensive contact. *State v. Clay* (N.C. 1979).
   b. Under the Model Penal Code, "deadly force" -- which is intended or likely to kill or cause serious harm -- is only permitted when threatened with "death, serious bodily harm,

kidnapping or [sexual assault]." *Model Penal Code §§3.11(2), 3.04(2).*
   c. Accidental Injury to Bystanders
      (1) Under the Model Penal Code, defenders who are justified in using self-defense are still guilty of negligent/reckless homicide if they negligently/recklessly injure or create a risk of injury to innocents. *Model Penal Code §3.09(3).*
      (2) Under some case law, defenders who utilize perfect self-defense are not guilty if they also injure innocent bystanders in the process. *People v. Adams* (Ill. 1972) [defender justified in shooting assailant who fired at him from car, and also justified in accidentally killing assailant's innocent passenger when bullet passed through assailant's body].

4. Burden of Proof
   a. Majority Rule: Most jurisdictions require that, once a defendant presents evidence raising the issue of self-defense, prosecutors must disprove self-defense beyond a reasonable doubt.
   b. Minority Rule: Some jurisdictions require defendants to prove self-defense by a preponderance of evidence. *Martin v. Ohio* (Sup. Ct. 1987) [state statute requiring defendants to prove self-defense is constitutional].

5. Exceptions to Self-Defense: Defensive force is prohibited in certain circumstances, even though the defender faces imminent threat of death or injury.
   a. Duty to Retreat
      (1) In jurisdictions following the duty to retreat rule, persons confronted with force must attempt to retreat before using deadly defensive force, if they know they can retreat with complete safety. *State v. Abbott* (N.J. 1961) [man brawling with armed neighbors had duty to retreat before attacking them with ax].
      (2) Although English common law imposed a strict duty to retreat, American courts began rejecting the doctrine because it did not comport with American values.
      (3) The no-retreat rule is no longer considered the majority rule. About half the states

now require retreat when possible, some treat the possibility of retreat as a factor to be considered, and others permit the person to stand his ground.

    (a) Exception for Defense of Home: Even "retreat" jurisdictions do not normally require retreat when a defender is attacked in his own home. *People v. Tomlins* (N.Y. 1914) [father, attacked in own house by son, was justified in killing son, because no man should be forced to abandon his own home], *see also Model Penal Code.*

    (b) However, if the attacker is a co-habitant, some jurisdictions require the defending co-habitant to retreat from the mutual home. *State v. Shaw* (Conn. 1981) [co-habitants deemed to have a duty to retreat from their homes before using deadly force, because policy should prevent intra-family violence].

  b. Provocateurs

    (1) Majority Rule: In most jurisdictions, the aggressor in a conflict culminating in death cannot claim self-defense, unless he (i) attempted to withdraw from the violent altercation in good faith and (ii) communicated his intent to his adversary by word or deed. *United States v. Peterson* (D.C. Ct. App. 1973) [man who challenged departing aggressor to fight, killing him, cannot claim self-defense].

    (2) Minority Rule: Under *Model Penal Code §3.04 and Comments*, a provocateur cannot use *deadly* defensive force against an "attacker" whom the provocateur attacked with the intent to kill or seriously injure. The provocateur is still justified in using *non-deadly* defensive force.

    (3) Adultery as Provocation: Older cases hold that catching one's wife in the act of adultery constitutes provocation; thus, neither the adulterous spouse nor the lover is justified in using deadly defensive force against the discovering spouse. *Dabney v. State* (So. 1897). Recent cases hold that, if the discovering spouse attacks with the intent to kill/injure, both the adulterous spouse and lover may use

deadly defensive force. *Atkins v. State* (Ga. 1966).

B. Defense of Property

  1. Some courts forbid deadly force against burglary where the defender's life is not endangered. *People v. Ceballos* (Ca. 1974) [homeowner unjustified in setting dangerous trap for non-violent burglars].

  2. Under the Model Penal Code, deadly force against an intruder in the home is strictly limited. However, the use of force other than deadly force to prevent the commission or the consummation of the crime that would expose the actor to substantial danger or serious bodily harm is permitted.

  3. Under New York law, a person in possession of a dwelling may use deadly force against attackers he reasonably believes will commit burglary on their real property. Defenders may use non-deadly force against lesser crimes. *New York Penal Law §35.20(3)*.

  4. Colorado has a statute, referred to as its "Make-My-Day" law, that authorizes deadly force in defense of habitation when another person has made an unlawful entry and when the occupant has a reasonable belief that such other person has committed or intends to commit a crime in the dwelling, and when the occupant reasonably believes that the other person might use physical force against the occupant.

C. Forcible Law Enforcement

  1. Police/peace officers may use deadly force to arrest felony suspects, but may use only non-deadly force to arrest misdemeanor suspects, unless those suspects offer deadly resistance. *Durham v. State* (Ind. 1927) [game warden justified in shooting poacher who attacked him during arrest]. However, suspects arrested with excessive arresting force may use force to defend themselves against the police. *Plummer v. State* (Ind. 1893).

  2. Police officers may not use deadly force to prevent felony suspects from escaping arrest unless (i) they have probable cause to believe the suspect poses a threat of serious harm, to the officer or others, and (ii) they warn the suspect before using deadly force, if feasible. *Tennessee v. Garner* (Sup. Ct. 1985) [police not

justified in killing fleeing unarmed burglar to prevent escape].

3. Model Penal Code: Under Model Penal Code §3.07, peace/police officers making felony arrests may use deadly force if:

   a. They believe the use of force poses no substantial risk of injury to bystanders, and

   b. They believe the suspect poses such danger to life or limb that his immediate apprehension overrides the risks of apprehension.

D. Choice of Evils: Crimes Committed under Necessity and Duress

1. Necessary or Compelled Prison Escapes: Prison escapees may claim the defenses of necessity and duress, [*People v. Unger* (Ill. 1977) prisoner escapes to avoid prison rape], but only if they make a bona fide attempt to surrender or return "as soon as the duress or necessity had lost its coercive force." *United States v. Bailey* (S. Ct. 1980).

2. Poverty as Justification: Poverty is not valid grounds for claiming necessity or duress. *Borough of Southwark v. Williams* (U.K. 1971) [homeless squatters may not claim necessity in occupying houses].

3. Nature of Evil Averted

   a. The danger averted must be clear and immediate. And, persons may not claim necessity when violating statutory laws they find unjust. *Commonwealth v. Leno* (Mass. 1993) [operator of illegal needle-exchange program for addicts may not claim necessity of preventing spread of AIDS].

   b. The use of illegal drugs to treat diseases is not justifiable under necessity. *Commonwealth v. Hutchins* (Mass. 1991) [terminally ill patient cannot claim marijuana use was necessary, despite proof it caused remission].

4. Model Penal Code: Under Model Penal Code §3.02, a person is justified in committing a crime he believes is (absolutely) necessary to avoid a harm to himself or others, if (i) the harm to be avoided is (objectively) greater than that caused by the crime, (ii) no other law defining the offense provides applicable exceptions or defenses, (iii) there was no plain legislative intent to exclude the justification, and (iv) if the crime punishes negligence or recklessness, the person was not negligent or reckless in

bringing about the situation requiring the choice of evils.

5. New York Law: Under New York Penal Law §35.05(2), a person is justified in committing a crime when (i) the crime is necessary to avoid imminent public or private injury, (ii) the emergency developed through no fault of the person, and (iii) the injury is so grave that the desirability and urgency of avoiding the injury clearly outweigh the desirability of avoiding the crime, according to ordinary standards of intelligence and morality. Necessity may not be used to challenge statute's morality or advisability, absent imminent injury. The decision on whether a crime is justified is decided by the court, as a matter of law.

6. Protests/Civil Disobedience: Protesters performing indirect civil disobedience (where they do not challenge the validity of the laws they break) may not claim the necessity defense. *United States v. Schoon* (9 Cir. 1992) [protesters not justified in disrupting IRS office to protest U.S. involvement in El Salvador killings].

7. Killings Necessary to Save Others: If several people face a situation where only some can survive, the law is unclear on how they must act.

   a. The preservation of one's own life is not a justification for killing an innocent person. *Regina v. Dudley and Stephens.*

   b. Some courts hold that each may save his own life and claim the necessity defense, if (i) the choice of who lives is made by lot, and (ii) there is no special relationship between them which would require one to sacrifice himself for another. *United States v. Holmes* (C.C.E.D. Pa. 1842) [sailor who, after shipwreck, threw some passengers off lifeboat to save others is guilty of manslaughter, because crewmen owed special duties to passengers].

   c. Under Model Penal Code §3.02 and Comments, persons are justified in killing to save lives if they save more people than they kill, even if those killed are innocent. However, a person attacked *illegally* may kill all his (not innocent) attackers in self-defense, regardless of their number.

   d. Some cases seem to suggest each may save

oneself, without liability for what happens to the others.

    e.   Some cases suggest that, if no one volunteers to sacrifice himself, then no one may kill any other.

  8. The "necessity" defense may not be used to promulgate rules permitting certain conduct in advance of any criminal activity. *Public Committee Against Torture v. State of Israel.* ["Ticking time bomb" situation does not justify use of necessity defense to authorize in advance interrogation by physical means.]

 E. Euthanasia

  1. Competent adults have a constitutional "due process" right to refuse or discontinue life-preserving treatment. For incompetents (e.g., comatose patients) states may require continued life support continue absent a clear showing the incompetent, while still competent, expressed an intent to die under such circumstances. *Cruzan v. Director, Missouri Dept. of Health* (Sup. Ct. 1989) [comatose patient's parent challenge state restrictions on incompetents' right to die].

  2. Assistance in committing suicide is not a fundamental liberty interest protected by the due process clause. *Washington v. Glucksberg.*

    a.   A New York state task force concluded that legalizing assisted suicide and euthanasia would be dangerous for those who are ill, vulnerable, elderly, poor, socially disadvantaged or without access to good medical care. *New York State Task Force On Life And The law, When Death Is Sought—Assisted Suicide In The Medical Context.*

    b.   Others have asserted that those who argue against the legalization of voluntary euthanasia overlook the merits of the individual cases and favor a blanket prohibition. *Joel Feinberg, Overlooking The Merits Of The Individual Case: An Unpromising Approach To The Right To Die.*

    c.   One of the casebook authors notes that Courts distinguish suicide from refusing medical treatment because suicide requires affirmative action. One who achieves his goal by refusing medical treatment can hardly be a better reason to treat his action differently than one who commits suicide.

Sandfard H. Kadish, Letting Patients Die: Legal And Moral Reflections.

 II. Excuse: Persons committing crimes are *excused* in certain circumstances (insanity, mental defect, provocation, etc.), meaning that, while the action remains a crime, the person's penalty is reduced/waived, because the person is not deemed to have criminal intent. In practice, cases and statutes often confuse justification with excuse.

 A. Involuntary Actions: Persons who commit criminal acts involuntarily, by reflex, or through physical compulsion (e.g., being pushed) are not guilty.

 B. Deficient But Reasonable Actions: The person has the power to choose, but the choice is so constrained than a reasonable person would not so choose. The constraining circumstances may be of two types:

  1. Cognitive Deficiency: The lack of knowledge must be excusable, and not reckless or negligent.

  2. Volitional Deficiency: A lack of will, such as duress.

 C. Irresponsible Actions: The person could not have acted otherwise, because of lack of adequate capacities for making rational judgments, such as legal insanity.

 D. Duress: When a person acts consciously but is forced to act (e.g., by threat of injury), he may be excused from liability for any crimes committed.

  1. Threats of future harm may constitute duress. *State v. Toscano* (N.J. 1977) [chiropractor claims he filed fraudulent insurance claim after racketeer threatened him].

    a.   Common Law Duress: At common law, duress was a valid defense only if the actor committed a crime under threat of *imminent* death/serious physical injury which would reasonably compel a person to comply. A few older decisions held that only a threat of death (not injury) was sufficient. A threat of future harm is insufficient, as is a threat of monetary, reputation, or property loss. Defendants who murder an innocent may not claim duress.

  2. Model Penal Code: Under *Model Penal Code §2.09*, duress is an excuse to any crime, other than murder, if the defendant committed the crime because he was coerced by the use/

threat of unlawful force against himself/another to commit the commanded crime, and the threat is such that a reasonable person in the situation would be unable to resist.

   a. There must have been a command to commit a specific crime; the defendant cannot himself choose to commit an unsolicited crime and then claim duress, though that defendant may be able to claim choice of evils.

   b. The threat need not be imminent, though the "situation" can include the threat's imminence.

   c. The "situation" may include individual consideration of the defendant's size, strength, age, health, etc., but not individual temperament or courage.

3. Immediacy of Harm: Most modern state statutes also require the threatened harm to be "immediate," "imminent," or "instant." *See United States v. Fleming* (Military 1957) [American POW in Korea, forced to prepare anti-American propaganda by threats of unbearable living conditions, may not claim duress, because death was not imminent]. *But see United States v. Contento-Pachon* (9 Cir. 1984) [drug courier, forced by death threats to smuggle drugs, may claim duress despite not attempting to flee or alert police, because threats were credible, Colombian police were corrupt, and escape was practically impossible].

4. Duress Killings: State laws differ on whether defendants who killed innocents under duress are excused. Common law traditionally did not excuse duress killers. A few states following the Model Penal Code may allow duress as an affirmative defense. Most states either do not allow the duress excuse for murder, and possibly other serious crimes, or recognize only a partial excuse, downgrading a duress killing from murder to manslaughter.

5. Contributory Fault: In some cases, a person who placed himself in a position likely to cause duress may not claim duress as a defense.

   a. Gang Membership: Defendants who voluntarily and knowingly join a criminal organization cannot claim duress if they are pressured to commit crimes, *Regina v. Sharp* (U.K. 1987), unless the defendant reasonably

expected to be able to withdraw, *Regina v. Shepherd* (U.K. 1988).

   b. Recklessness: Under *Model Penal Code §2.09(2)*, defendants who recklessly place themselves in situations likely to subject them to duress cannot claim duress as a defense.

E. Intoxication

1. Involuntary Intoxication

   a. Common Law: At common law, involuntary intoxication is no defense to criminal prosecution, though it may allow a lesser sentence. *Regina v. Kingston* (U.K. 1994) [pedophile, charged with molesting boy, claims he molested only because he was drugged by blackmailer].

   b. Model Penal Code: Under *Model Penal Code §2.08*, involuntary intoxication is a defense only if it either negated the required intent or rendered the defendant legally insane (substantially incapable either of appreciating the act's immorality or obeying the law).

2. Voluntary Intoxication

   a. Majority Rule: Voluntary intoxication is a defense to crimes requiring a certain intent if the defendant's intoxication made him unable to understand the following:

     (1) What he was doing,

     (2) Why he was doing it, or

     (3) That it was likely to cause harm.

     (4) Intoxication is *no* defense if it merely made the defendant unable to understand the morality of his acts. *Roberts v. People* (Mich. 1870) [drunken shooter claims intoxication precluded any intent to kill].

   b. Common Law: At common law, voluntary intoxication is no defense, unless either

     (1) The crime charged requires "specific intent" [common law robbery, assault, larceny, burglary, forgery, false pretenses, embezzlement, attempt, solicitation, or conspiracy] and the defendant proves the intoxication negated/kept him from forming the "specific intent" to accomplish the crime's goal, *People v. Hood* (Cal. 1969), *or*

     (2) The defendant's prolonged use of drugs/alcohol caused permanent brain damage or insanity. *State v. Booth* (Iowa 1989).

   c. Some courts have held intoxication evidence

inadmissible to negate specific or general intent crimes (except first-degree murder). *State v. Stasio.*

  d. Model Penal Code: Under *Model Penal Code §2.08*, intoxication is a defense to specific intent (purposeful) crimes, but not to reckless or negligent crimes.

  e. Intoxication as Defense to Recklessness: Most state statutes follow the *Model Penal Code* in disallowing intoxication as a defense to crimes requiring recklessness, even where evidence of intoxication would otherwise be "relevant." Some states allow evidence of intoxication to disprove recklessness.

 F. Mental Disorder. Actors deemed insane are generally entitled to leniency. Criminals who committed crimes while insane may usually offer insanity as a complete defense. Furthermore, defendants who later become insane may not be tried, convicted, sentenced, or executed, and often must be transferred from prison to mental hospitals.

  1. Competence to Stand Trial: In most states, defendants who, as a result of mental disease or defect, cannot understand the proceedings against them or assist in their defense, cannot be tried, convicted, or sentenced for the duration of their insanity. *See also Model Penal Code §4.04.*

  a. The Supreme Court held that, to stand trial, a defendant must be able to

   (1) Consult with his lawyer with a reasonable degree of rational understanding, and

   (2) Understand the proceedings against him, both rationally and factually. *Dusky v. United States* (S. Ct. 1960).

  b. Forced Medication to Stand Trial: Some courts permit normally insane defendants to be medicated forcibly to render them competent to stand trial. *Khiem v. United States* (D.C. 1992). Other courts do not. *State v. Perry* (La. 1992). The Supreme Court permitted this practice, but held that it may violate constitutional due process if other means of rendering the defendant competent were available. *Riggins v. Nevada* (S. Ct. 1992).

  c. Amnesia: Most state courts hold that defendants who suffer total amnesia about the crime's circumstances, but are otherwise sane, are competent to stand trial. *State v.*

Wynn (Del. Super. 1985); *People v. Francobandera* (N.Y. 1974); *but see State v. McClendon* (Ariz. 1966) [trying amnesiac defendant is improper if continuance might enable recollection].

 2. Competence to Be Executed: All states prohibit the execution of condemned prisoners who became insane *after* conviction.

  a. Constitutional Requirements: The Supreme Court held that executing insane convicts would violate the Federal Constitution's Eighth Amendment's proscription of "cruel and unusual punishment." *Ford v. Wainright* (S. Ct. 1986).

   (1) The opinion did not define insanity, but the famous concurrence suggests that execution is inappropriate where the condemned cannot understand the nature of the death penalty and/or why it was imposed.

   (2) The Supreme Court, in a later opinion, suggested this was the correct test of insanity, and also forbade the execution of retarded defendants. *Penry v. Lynaugh* (S. Ct. 1989).

  b. Pennsylvania: Pennsylvania's *Mental Health Act* (1951), which requires mentally ill prisoners to be transferred to mental hospitals, was held to require that condemned inmates' executions be stayed. *Commonwealth v. Moon* (Pa. 1955).

   (1) The *Act* defines "mental illness" as "an illness which so lessens the capacity of a person to use his customary self-control, judgment and discretion in the conduct of his affairs and social relations as to make it necessary or advisable for him to be under care" [meaning that a person's execution should be stayed until the person is able to take care of himself!].

  c. Washington/South Carolina: Washington and South Carolina courts impose a stricter test: prisoners may not be executed unless they both (i) understand the nature of the death penalty and why it was imposed, and (ii) can communicate rationally with defense counsel.

  d. Retardation: The Supreme Court has barred execution of some convicts, and suggested that execution is inappropriate where the retarded prisoner cannot understand the nature of the death penalty and/or why it was imposed. *Penry v. Lynaugh* (S. Ct. 1989). Seven states have enacted legislation barring execution of "seriously mentally retarded" convicts.

e. Forced Medication to Face Execution: Some courts prohibit the state from medicating normally insane convicts involuntarily to render them competent to be executed. *State v. Perry* (La. 1992).

f. Procedure for Determining Sanity: The Supreme Court held that condemned prisoners must be allowed to present evidence of insanity to an impartial officer/tribunal independent of the executive branch. *Ford v. Wainright* (S. Ct. 1985) [Florida statute allowing determination of sanity to be made by governor is unconstitutional]. Under the *California Penal Code*, condemned prisoners may not be executed if found insane by a special jury of 12 non-experts.

G. Insanity Tests

1. Under the (English) *M'Naghten* Rule, a defendant is insane if, at the time of the act, he (i) had a mental disease (ii) which caused a defect of reason (iii) *which made him unable to understand either the act's nature/quality or its wrongness.* *M'Naghten's Case* (U.K. 1843) [delusional man who shot political official, believing his political party persecuted him, is innocent of attempted murder, by reason of insanity].

   a. The insanity must exist at the time the offense was committed. There must be a mental disease, not just being peculiar or abnormal, and the mental condition must prevent him from knowing what he was doing or from knowing that what he was doing was wrong. *The King v. Porter* (U.K. 1933).

   b. People acquitted of a crime by reason of insanity may be automatically committed to a mental hospital for longer than the maximum sentence for that crime, without hearing. *Jones v. United States* (S. Ct. 1983).

   c. Jury Instructions on Insanity Acquittal's Consequences

      (1) A few states provide that, where insanity

acquittals result in *mandatory* commitment at a mental hospital, the jury must be so informed (so jurors won't assume dangerous acquittees will be released).

      (2) Most states' courts have held such instruction improper, because it is irrelevant to the issue of insanity. *See, e.g., People v. Goad* (Mich. 1984). *But see, e.g., Commonwealth v. Mutina* (Mass. 1975) [jury must be informed if insanity acquittal requires mandatory commitment]. For federal prosecutions, the Supreme Court held that juries should not be informed of federal mandatory commitment laws. *Shannon v. United States* (S. Ct. 1994) [jury instructions on mandatory federal commitment is irrelevant and unnecessary]

2. Under the Model Penal Code, one may be found not guilty by reason of insanity if he *lacks "substantial" capacity to appreciate the wrongfulness of the conduct or to conform to the law. Blake v. U.S.*

   a. Under the *Code*, to "appreciate" wrongfulness, a person must personally understand the conduct is wrong, not just realize that society labels it as wrong.

   b. Under the Code, an "irresistible impulse" is one that "substantially" deprives the defendant of free will, even if the deprivation is not total.

3. The Irresistible Impulse Test supplements the *M'Naghten* test so that one may be found not guilty by reason of insanity if he does not have the power to choose between right and wrong because the insane impulse overcame his will. A defendant is deemed insane if "unable to adhere to the right" due to an "irresistible impulse." Typically, an impulse is deemed "irresistible" if it completely deprived the defendant of choice/volition and/or if the defendant would have acted on the impulse even had he known a policeman was present.

   a. The Fifth Circuit rejected the Model Penal Code's irresistible impulse prong of the test of insanity. It held that evidence of drug addiction is admissible to prove defendants suffered from a mental disease or defect that made them unable to appreciate their actions' wrongfulness, but inadmissible to prove they acted under irresistible impulses that made them unable to act legally. *United States v. Lyons* (5 Cir. 1984) [drug addict claims addiction caused mental disease and irresistible impulses].

4. Common Concerns about the Insanity Defense: Public concern about the insanity defense heightened in 1982, when the delusional schizophrenic John Hinckley shot and wounded President Reagan and several aides. At trial, Hinckley pleaded insanity, claiming he shot Reagan to impress actress Jodie Foster. [Surely a case of deific degree.] The defense and prosecution offered psychiatric testimony that differed widely. Hinckley was acquitted under the *Model Penal Code* test, because the jury could not find him sane beyond a reasonable doubt. Many legislators, responding to public outrage, limited the insanity defense in various ways.

a. Return to *M'Naghten*: Several states abandoned the *Model Penal Code* test outright in favor of *M'Naghten*, e.g., California, Texas, Indiana. Some 21 states now use a modified *M'Naghten* rule.

b. Rejection of "Irresistible Impulse" Test: Some courts reject the *Model Penal Code*'s "irresistible impulse" test, e.g., *United States v. Lyons* (5 Cir. 1984).

c. Federal Insanity Test: For federal prosecutions, insanity is an *affirmative* defense requiring:
   (1) "Severe mental disease or defect"
   (2) Which makes the defendant "unable to appreciate the nature and quality or the wrongfulness of his acts." *18 U.S.C. §17(a), see also Comprehensive Crime Control Act of 1984*. This rejects the "irresistible impulse" test.

5. Proof Burden for Insanity
a. All states presume defendants sane; defendants claiming insanity must rebut the presumption. To rebut, defendants must present either "some evidence" of legal insanity, or enough evidence to "raise a reasonable doubt" about their sanity, depending on state law.

b. Once such presumption is rebutted, the defendant's insanity becomes a provable issue. Some states then require the prosecu-

tion to prove the defendant's sanity beyond reasonable doubt, but over 25 states require the defendant to prove insanity by preponderant evidence.

c. In some states, the prosecution has the burden to prove that the defendant's acts were rational, and could not have been the result of insanity. *State v. Green* (Tenn. Ct. App. 1982) [in charging a paranoid schizophrenic with murder, prosecution failed to prove he intentionally fled crime scene or discarded murder weapon].

6. Abolition/Restriction of the Insanity Defense: It is unconstitutional for a state to *completely* abolish the insanity defense. *State v. Strasburg* (Wash. 1910), *State v. Lange* (La. 1929), *Sinclair v. State* (Miss. 1931). However, states may restrict the insanity defense, e.g., allowing evidence of insanity only to disprove the requisite criminal intent. *State v. Korell* (Mont. 1984); *State v. Searcy* (Ida. 1990).

H. Standard of Right and Wrong: Courts are divided on when, under *M'Naghten*, defendants may claim not to have understood that their actions were "wrong."

1. Some courts hold that insane defendants must be unable to understand their acts were *morally* wrong (i.e., immoral, at least by societal standards). *State v. Crenshaw* (Wash. 1983) [husband who butchered wife for presumed infidelity cannot claim insanity as long as he realized the killing was illegal and generally considered wrong].

2. Other courts hold that the defendant must be unable to understand his act was a *legal* wrong (i.e., a crime); in these jurisdictions, knowledge of the law negates an insanity claim. *See, e.g., State v. Hollis* (Kan. 1987); *State v. Hamann* (Iowa 1979).

3. Perceived Deific Decree: Courts generally recognize an insane defendant as unable to distinguish (moral) right from wrong if the defendant believed God instructed him to commit the crime, even if he knew the act was illegal. *See, e.g., People v. Serravo* (Colo. 1992) [schizophrenic believing God told him to kill wife and then build multimillion dollar sport stadium was insane because unable to understand moral wrong]; *State v. Cameron*.

4. The Meaning of Mental Disease or Defect: Under the M'Naghten rule, "mental disease, or defect" includes *any* diagnosed condition, which made the defendant unable to understand his actions or appreciate their immorality. *State v. Guido* (N.J. 1963) [psychiatric witnesses allowed to reverse prior diagnosis of "sane" in mid-trial, without prejudice].

   a. Under *Model Penal Code §4.01(2)*, any condition "manifested only by repeated criminal or otherwise antisocial conduct" is *not* recognized as a "mental disease or defect."

   b. However, some courts will allow evidence of it to support an insanity defense, even under a *Code* jurisdiction *See State v. Werlein* (Wis. Ct. App. 1987) [loner who shot man for no reason may introduce evidence of antisocial personality disorder, because his condition was manifested by more than just repeated crimes]; *Wade v. United States* (9th Cir. 1970) [commenting that almost no mental disease would manifest itself *only* through repeated antisocial conduct]; *United States v. Currens* (3d Cir. 1961) [true psychopaths should be allowed the insanity defense, because they are so seriously ill they have lost touch with reality].

I. Automatism as Insanity: Automatism is a state of unconscious or spasmodic reflex action. Defendants who commit crimes in an automatistic state (e.g., while sleepwalking, because of muscle spasms, etc.) are generally excused. However, jurisdictions that require an insanity plea for an automatism defense raise the issue of whether automatism is "insanity."

   1. Non-insane automatistic conduct may negate the "voluntarily" element of a crime. *McClain v. State.* [evidence of automatism is permissible even though insanity is not claimed as a defense.]

   2. Pleading: Where defendants committed crimes while in an automatistic state due to mental illness, most courts allow them the option of pleading insanity, involuntary action, or both. *See People v. Grant* (Ill. 1977) [automatism is not insanity, but excuses a crime because it negates voluntary action].

   a. An acquittal for involuntary action is prefera-

ble, since it entails no mandatory commitment to mental institutions.

   b. A few jurisdictions allow only an insanity plea where the automatism was caused by mental disease/defect and/or mental retardation.

3. Sleepwalking

   a. Under *Model Penal Code §2.01(2)(b)*, defendants who commit crimes while in a somnambulistic state are entitled to complete acquittal for lack of a voluntary act.

   b. State courts are divided whether somnambulistic criminals may plead involuntary action (thus avoiding commitment) or must plead insanity.

J. Diminished Capacity: Under the "diminished capacity" doctrine, defendants who suffer from a mental illness which falls short of legal "insanity" but prevented their forming the requisite criminal intent charged, are entitled to a lesser charge consistent with the criminal intent they actually formed. (A "diminished capacity" plea does *not* exonerate; the diminished defendant is still *guilty* of the lesser charge.)

   1. Majority Rule: A majority of states recognizes "diminished capacity" as a defense to specific intent crimes. In such states, expert testimony about defendants' mental condition is relevant if it shows they lacked the specific intent, even if their condition fell short of legal insanity. *United States v. Brawner* (D.C. Cir 1972) [mentally ill defendant, deemed sane and convicted of premeditated murder, may present proof that condition prevented premeditation].

   2. Minority Rule: In some states, diminished capacity is no defense. *State v. Wilcox* (Ohio 1982) [Ohio rejects diminished capacity as defense]; *State v. Provost* (Minn. 1992), See also, *Chestnut v. State* (Fla. 1989).

   a. *State v. Brink* (Minn. App. 1993) [man firing at police cannot introduce evidence showing he fired while depressed and suicidal, hoping police would kill him].

   b. Diminished Capacity for General Intent Crimes: Generally, diminished capacity is only allowed as a partial defense to *specific* intent crimes (traditionally, premeditated murder, robbery, assault, larceny, burglary, forgery, false pretenses, embezzlement, attempt, solicitation, conspiracy), or crimes that have a lesser included offense not requiring specific intent.

    (1) *See, e.g., McCarthy v. State* (Del. 1977) [diminished capacity inapplicable to charge of kidnapping and attempted rape],

    (2) Also, *United States v. Busic* [diminished capacity inapplicable to federal charge of forcible aircraft piracy, because piracy is a general intent crime].

  c. Some jurisdictions allow evidence of diminished capacity to prove the accused *did not in fact* form the specific intent, but do not allow it to suggest the defendant was absolutely *incapable* of forming specific intent. *Cal. Penal Code §28(a), see also People v. Saille* (Cal. 1991).

K. New Patterns of Excuse

  1. Drug Addiction: It is unconstitutionally cruel and unusual for states to criminalize drug addiction where the targeted person has not possessed drugs or committed anti-social acts within the state, because narcotics addiction is a disease. *Robinson v. California* (S. Ct. 1962) [addict arrested because track marks indicate addiction].

  2. Alcoholism: It is not unconstitutionally cruel for states to criminalize public drunkenness, because chronic alcoholism is not a disease. *Powell v. Texas* (S. Ct. 1968).

  3. Drug addiction is *no* defense to prosecution for drug possession. *United States v. Moore* (D.C. Cir. 1973).

  4. Justice Clarence Thomas of the United States Supreme Court has written against the use of excuse for not holding someone responsible for his actions. He notes that an "effective criminal justice system—one that holds people accountable for harmful conduct—simply cannot be sustained under conditions where there are boundless excuses for violent behavior and no moral authority for the state to punish. . . . A society that does not hold someone accountable for harmful behavior can be viewed as condoning—or even worse, endorsing—such conduct." *Clarence Thomas, Crime and Punishment—And Personal Responsibility*.

United States v. Peterson

(Federal Prosecution) v. (Self-Defense Killer)

(D.C. Cir 1973) 483 F.2d 1222

M E M O R Y   G R A P H I C

Instant Facts

[Facts omitted from casebook.] Apparently, a man who killed claimed the killing was justified as self-defense under common law.

Black Letter Rule

The use of force in self-defense is justified (permitted) when the defender (i) faces a threat, actual or apparent, from (ii) unlawful and (iii) immediate force, with (iv) no reasonably-available alternative to avoid confrontation, and the defender has (iv) a good faith and (v) reasonable belief that the threat presents (v) imminent risk of (vi) death or serious bodily injury, plus (vii) a belief that the self-defense is necessary to prevent death/injury, and (viii) uses an amount of force proportional to the threat.

Case Vocabulary

SELF-DEFENSE: Doctrine allowing that the use of force, sometimes including deadly force, is justified (permitted) when defending against an unlawful attack under certain circumstances. Generally, deadly self defense is permitted against a deadly attack when there is no alternative.

Procedural Basis: Appeal from criminal conviction for homicide, seeking reversal.

Facts: [Facts omitted from casebook.] Apparently, Peterson (D) killed and claimed he had a common law right to kill justifiably in self-defense, even though no statute specifically authorized it. Peterson (D) was convicted of homicide when the court refused to recognize a common law right to self-defense. Peterson (D) appeals.

Issue: Can a person who kills claim justified self-defense?

Decision and Rationale: (Robinson) Yes. The use of force in self-defense is *justified* (permitted) when the defender (i) faces a threat, actual or apparent, from (ii) unlawful and (iii) immediate force, with (iv) no reasonably-available alternative to avoid confrontation, and the defender has (iv) a good faith and (v) reasonable belief that the threat presents (v) imminent risk of (vi) death or serious bodily injury, plus (vii) a belief that the self-defense is necessary to prevent death/injury, and (viii) uses an amount of force proportional to the threat. Deadly force is justified against a threat of deadly force (death or serious injury). The legal doctrine of self-defense is as viable now as it was in Blackstone's time. But the right of self-defense arises only when the necessity begins and ends when the necessity ends, and deadly defensive force is only justified when no other alternative exists.

Threat of Death or Serious bodily harm
— Must be imminent harm
— Must be unlawful harm
— must be necessary force against harm
— Objectively reasonable & subjectively believed

Analysis:

This case was included in the textbook to demonstrate the traditional common law doctrine of self-defense. Today, all states have superseded the common law with a codified definition of self-defense, but most state statutes retain most elements of the common law. Of course, it is impossible to say if this case was decided properly, since the facts were omitted.

People v. Goetz

(State) v. (Self-Defender)

(N.Y. Ct. App. 1986) 69 N.Y.2d 96, 497 N.E.2d 41

GIMME FI' DOLLAH, MAN.

M E M O R Y   G R A P H I C

Instant Facts

When a white commuter shoots four black men he believed were about to rob him, he contends the shooting was justifiable self-defense because it was subjectively reasonable.

Black Letter Rule

Justifiable self-defense must be objectively reasonable under the circumstances, but the circumstances may include perceptions of the attackers' intentions.

Case Vocabulary

DEADLY FORCE: Force which is known to create a substantial risk of death or serious physical injury (even if it does not actually kill).

JUSTIFICATION: Legal term given to "perfect" (proper) self-defense; justified killings are completely legal.

Procedural Basis: Appeal from order dismissing charges in criminal prosecution for attempted murder, assault, and weapons possession.

Facts: Four [black] youths -- Canty, Cabey, Ramseur, and Allen -- were riding a subway train. When Goetz (D), [a helpless-looking white man] boarded the train, Cabey, and possibly Allen, approached him and said "give me five dollars." Goetz (D), fearing robbery, drew an illegal pistol and shot Canty, Allen, and Ramseur, wounding them. Goetz (D) then shot at Cabey, who had not approached, paralyzing him. Goetz (D) fled, then surrendered. Goetz (D) confessed to police he bought his pistol illegally after being injured in a past robbery which gave him a fear of being "maimed" by robbers. Goetz (D) stated he (i) feared the four youths would rob or hurt him from their expressions, (ii) knew they had no guns,(iii) fired intending to hurt or kill all four, and (iv) would have killed them if he had more bullets. During the grand jury indictment for attempted murder, assault, and weapons possession, Goetz (D) claimed self-defense as a justification. Under New York Penal Law §35.15(1), "a person may ... use physical force ... when and to the extent he reasonably believes such to be necessary to defend himself ... from what he reasonably believes to be the ... imminent use of unlawful physical force." When one juror asked the prosecutor to clarify "reasonably believes," the prosecutor instructed them to consider "whether the defendant's conduct was that of a reasonable man in the defendant's situation" [i.e., objectively reasonable]. The grand jury indicted Goetz (D) on all charges. The trial court dismissed the indictment, holding the prosecutor improperly charged the grand jury to apply "justification" only if Goetz's (D) belief (that he was being robbed) was objectively reasonable, since the statute's language ("he reasonably believes...") suggests the proper standard is whether Goetz (D) [subjectively] reasonably believed it.

Issue: Is self-defense justified if the defender is subjectively reasonable in believing he will be attacked with force?

Decision and Rationale: (Wachtler) No. Justifiable self-defense must be objectively reasonable under the circumstances, but the circumstances may include perceptions of the attackers' intentions. Under New York Penal Law, "justification" is a defense which permits defensive force where the defenders (i) reasonably believe their attackers will use immediate illegal physical force, and (ii) use an amount of force they reasonably believe necessary. *Penal Law §35.15(1)*. Defenders may use deadly physical force only if they (i) reasonably believe their attackers are about to use deadly physical force, *or* (ii) reasonably believe their attackers are attempting to commit certain violent crimes, including robbery. *Penal Law §35.15(2)*. The prosecutor properly instructed the grand jury to consider the defense of justification, since Goetz (D) claimed he reasonably suspected robbery, which, if proven, would constitute justification. The lower court's holding that the proper test is "subjective reasonability" is incorrect, since their test defies the statute's plain meaning and contravenes the legislative intent, which clearly was to require deadly force to be objectively reasonable to be justified. The legislative intent is apparent because (i) the New York Penal Code codifies New York's common law, which requires reasonability, and (ii) the New York statute was modeled on Model Penal Code §3.04 (recognizing unreasonable force as a justification), but the drafters specifically added the reasonability requirement. Also, requiring a subjectively-reasonable belief would require only that a defender genuinely believe; had the drafters intended this, they would not have used the word "reasonably." Public policy should not permit citizens to use deadly force whenever they believe, however irrationally, it is justified. While objective reasonableness is required, the determination of reasonableness must be based on the defender's "circumstances" and "situation," including that defender's prior experience and his knowledge or beliefs about the attacker's intent. The grand jury may consider whether Goetz (D), as a former robbery victim, was reasonable in suspecting an attempted robbery from attackers with appearance similar to the four youths'. Order reversed; all indictment counts reinstated.

Analysis:

At trial, Goetz (D) was acquitted of attempted murder and assault, but convicted of carrying an unlicenced concealed weapon, and sentenced to 1 year in jail (parole-eligible after 60 days). The publicized case came at a time of high subway crime and poor race relations in New York, and quickly became a forum for debates on racism and vigilantism. Technically, the criminal jury disregarded the law in acquitting Goetz (D); he may have been justified in suspecting and shooting those who approached him, but was not justified in then shooting Cabey, who had not approached and was not threatening him. However, the jurors may have felt that, in light of the rate of violent crime by blacks, Goetz (D) was justified in fearing a group of black thugs demanding money would rob him. Compare the *objectively* reasonable belief standard used in this case with the Model Penal code's *subjective* reasonable belief. Thus, under the objective standard, one who honestly though unreasonably believes in the need to use self-defense will loose the defense. In this case, Goetz (D) was allowed to show that his prior experiences in previous muggings provided a reasonable basis for his belief in the need of self defense.

State v. Kelly

(Prosecutor) v. (Battered Wife Who Killed Husband)
91 N.J. 178, 478 A.2d 364 (1984)

M E M O R Y   G R A P H I C

Instant Facts

When a battered wife who stabbed her husband is charged with murder, she contends expert testimony on battered-woman's syndrome would show she acted in self-defense.

Black Letter Rule

When battered women kill their batterers and claim self-defense, expert testimony on battered woman's syndrome is admissible to prove they faced imminent risk of injury, but inadmissible to prove their belief in that risk was objectively reasonable.

Case Vocabulary

BATTERED WOMAN'S SYNDROME: Common psychological pattern which makes battered women unable to escape abusive relationships, because they gradually accept violence as normal, believe the battering will stop, become demoralized, may lack the money to live independently, are afraid to seek help, fear reprisals, etc.

Procedural Basis: Appeal from criminal conviction for reckless manslaughter, seeking reversal, remand, and admission of expert testimony.

Facts: Mrs. Kelly's (D) husband beat her frequently. After one beating, as her husband ran up to her, Kelly (D) stabbed him fatally, possibly by accident, with scissors. Kelly (D) was indicted for murder. At trial, she asserted self-defense, claiming she feared her husband was armed and would hurt her or her daughter, and was only trying to scare him off with the scissors. The prosecution alleged Kelly (D) started the fight and chased her husband before stabbing him. Kelly (D) called an expert witness on battered-woman's syndrome, to show that Kelly (D) lived in constant fear of beating but was unable to leave her husband. The expert testified that battered-woman's syndrome is a psychological pattern which makes battered women unable to escape abusive relationships, because they gradually accept violence as normal, believe the battering will stop, become demoralized, may lack the money to live independently, are afraid to seek help, fear reprisals, etc. The trial court ruled this testimony inadmissible as irrelevant, finding it proved only her subjective belief that self-defense was reasonable, whereas the self-defense statute requires objective reasonability. Conviction, reckless manslaughter.

Issue: When battered women kill their batterers and claim self-defense, is expert testimony on battered woman's syndrome admissible?

Decision and Rationale: (Wilentz) Yes. When battered women kill their batterers and claim self-defense, expert testimony on battered woman's syndrome is admissible to prove they faced imminent risk of injury, but inadmissible to prove their belief in that risk was objectively reasonable. Under the New Jersey criminal statutes, forcible self-defense is justifiable "when the actor reasonably believes that such force is immediately necessary for the purpose of protecting himself against the use of unlawful force by such other person on the present occasion." Deadly force is only justified when the actor "reasonably believes that such force is necessary to protect himself against death or serious bodily harm." Here, Kelly (D) claimed self-defense, contending she believed she was in imminent danger of death. The expert testimony is relevant, since (i) it may support her testimony about the *honesty* of her fear of imminent death, which is a material element, and (ii) it may suggest that Kelly's (D) fear of death or injury was *objectively* reasonable (in light of past abuse and threats to kill her), which is a material element, and (iii) it will answer the question, which will inevitably be raised by jurors, of why Kelly (D) did not simply leave her husband. However, the testimony cannot be used to show that a battered woman might subjectively believe her life in danger where a reasonable person would not, since the self-defense must be objectively reasonable to be justified. "The difficulty with the expert's testimony is that it *sounds* [like testimony] about something the jury knows as well as anyone else, namely, the reasonableness of a person's fear of imminent serious danger. That is not at all, however, what this testimony is *directly* aimed at ... an area where the purported common knowledge of the jury may be very much mistaken, an area where jurors' logic, drawn from their own experience, may lead to a wholly incorrect conclusion ... After hearing the expert ...the jury could conclude that instead of casting doubt on the accuracy of her testimony about the severity and frequency of prior beatings, her failure to leave actually reinforced her credibility" [i.e., that she was battered into submission]. It would not be proper for the expert to suggest Kelly's (D) belief at the time was reasonable, since the expert's knowledge relates only to her failure to leave her husband earlier. The remaining issue is whether, under Evidence Rule 56(2), the expert testimony (i) concerns a subject beyond the ken of the average juror, (ii) the expert's field of study is sufficiently reliable, and (iii) the witness has sufficient expertise to testify. Conviction reversed; remanded for hearing on admissibility of expert's testimony.

Analysis:

The court's holding seems technically correct. Technically, the testimony should be allowed to show Kelly's (D) subjective belief, but the testimony (which concerns her individual psychological state) seems irrelevant to prove/disprove what the objective/reasonable person (who is presumed not to suffer from battered persons' syndrome) would do. However, cases based on the subjective/objective dichotomy usually fail to consider whether a reasonable/average person, thrust into the plaintiff's situation, would not tend to act unreasonably given the situation's psychological stress. It is very feasible that, in psychologically stressful situations, most reasonable people would succumb to irrationality. If the situation is so stressful, it seems unfair for the jury to convict a defendant for doing what most people would be driven to do by the circumstances. But that decision is mandated by the "reasonable person" standard. On remand, the prosecution allowed the expert's testimony, but offered evidence to show Kelly (D) was not battered. Kelly (D) was convicted of murder.

State v. Norman

(Prosecutor) v. (Abused Wife Who Killed Husband)
324 N.C. 253, 378 S.E.2d 8 (1989)

M E M O R Y   G R A P H I C

Instant Facts

An long-abused wife who shot her sleeping husband is charged with murder and claims self-defense on the ground she expected he would kill her eventually.

Black Letter Rule

Self-defense, perfect or imperfect, requires an imminent risk of death or serious injury, which does not include perceived threats of later harm.

Procedural Basis: Appeal from appellate court decision ordering retrial of defendant convicted of voluntary manslaughter.

Facts: Judy Norman (D) was brutally abused for 25 years by her husband, who constantly beat her, threw things at her, burned her with cigarettes, starved her, forced her into prostitution, humiliated her by making her eat pet food and sleep on the floor, threatened to maim or kill her, etc. Norman (D) was afraid to file charges, since her husband inevitably retaliated. She tried suicide, but was rescued despite her husband's instructions. Finally [finally!] Norman (D) shot her husband while he slept. After the first shot, after determining he was still alive, she shot him twice more, killing him. Norman (D) was charged with first degree murder. At trial, she presented evidence she suffered from battered wife syndrome as proof of perfect self-defense (i.e., that her killing of her husband was reasonable self-defense under the circumstances). Her expert witness testified that Norman (D) "believed herself ... doomed ... to a life of the worst ... torture and abuse, ... that it would only get worse, and that death was inevitable." The trail court ruled such evidence inadmissible as irrelevant, reasoning that Norman (D) was not in imminent danger when she shot her sleeping husband. Norman (D) was convicted of voluntary manslaughter, and sentenced to 6 years imprisonment. Norman (D) appealed, contending the evidence was relevant to support a jury finding of justified perfect self-defense. The appellate court held for Norman (D), reasoning that the nature of battered wife syndrome might allow a jury to find Norman (D) killed in self-defense while fearing later injury, and ordered a retrial. The prosecutor (P) appealed.

Issue: Can abused women who kill their abusers while not in immediate danger claim self-defense if they believe their abusers will kill them later?

Decision and Rationale: (Mitchell) No. Self-defense, perfect or imperfect, requires an imminent risk of death or serious injury, which does not include perceived threats of later harm. Under North Carolina criminal law, a defendant is entitled to have the jury consider acquittal by reason of *perfect* self-defense when the evidence suggests the defendant [objectively] reasonably believed the killing necessary to save herself from *imminent* death or great bodily harm, and the defendant was not the aggressor who triggered the fatal confrontation. An "imminent" threat is defined (i) by Black's Law Dictionary as "immediate danger, such as must be instantly met, such as cannot be guarded against by calling for ... assistance" and (ii) by our case law as "about to [happen]." Here, Norman (D) cannot claim perfect self-defense, because the evidence doesn't suggest Norman (D) faced harm from her sleeping husband, and she had ample time to seek help, and the jury had no reason to find she reasonably expected imminent harm. The expert testimony on battered wife syndrome may suggest Norman (D) felt generally threatened by her husband, and subjectively believed she would be harmed at some indefinite future point, but does not suggest she believed herself in "imminent" danger when she shot her husband, as is required to assert perfect self-defense. Public policy supports this finding, because holding otherwise would allow people to kill based merely on subjective predictions of indefinite future assaults and circumstances. Homicidal self-help would then become a lawful solution, and perhaps the easiest and most effective solution, to the problem of domestic abuse, thus legalizing opportune killing by wives. It would also allow the extension of perfect self-defense to any case where the defendant testified she subjectively believed she faced a future threat. The law alternately allows a partial defense -- imperfect self-defense -- which reduces the degree of culpability where the defendant was partially at fault under certain circumstances (ex. provoking a confrontation which escalates, requiring deadly defensive force to escape). Here, however, Norman (D) was not entitled to a jury instruction of imperfect self-defense, which also requires imminent danger. Even if the jury instruction was denied erroneously, it was harmless error, since under imperfect self-defense she would have been guilty of the same voluntary manslaughter for which she was convicted. Order for retrial reversed.

Dissent: (Martin) The evidence presented is sufficient to suggest perfect self-defense under existing law. The expert testified that 20 years of abuse gave Norman (D) the belief, given the circumstances as she saw them, that Norman (D) was in constant danger from her husband, even while he slept. Given evidence of the acute abuse over the last 3 days and the chronic abuse over 20 years, the jury could have reasonably concluded that her husband's threats were viable, that serious harm was imminent, and that it was necessary for Norman (D) to kill to escape that harm.

Analysis:

The majority is correct as a matter of law. Self-defense has traditionally justified a killing while the defender is in the attacker's "zone of danger," but not later, even if the attacker poses a continuing danger. The reasoning is that, once out of the danger zone, the defender has time to go to the police rather than taking the law into his own hands. This case, however, appears to have been chosen by the author as an extreme case where the victim deserved no legal protection. Judy Norman's (D) husband J.T. was, by all accounts, a brutal and merciless sadist who delighted in tormenting and humiliating his helpless wife at will. Judy (D) was utterly helpless to leave; she married at age 14, and was apparently penniless and possibly semi-illiterate, and could not support herself. She may have had no family. She was fully justified in believing no one would ever protect her, since the police had refused to arrest him, the local mental health center would not commit him, and social services allowed him to drag her out of the office, so she could not apply for public assistance to leave him. What realistic choice did she have but to kill him? While her life may not have been in danger, in the sense that a person can continue to survive while being constantly tortured and humiliated, she could look forward to nothing but pain and fear for the rest of her husband's life. The appellate court and dissent apparently thought, not unreasonably, that, after 25 years of punishment, Judy (D) should not lose 6 more years for doing a public service.

State v. Abbott

(New Jersey Prosecution) v. (Self-Defender)
36 N.J. 63, 174 A.2d 881 (1961)

M E M O R Y G R A P H I C

Instant Facts
A man who wounded his neighbors with a hatchet during a brawl is charged with assault for not avoiding the confrontation.

Black Letter Rule
In "retreat" jurisdictions, persons confronted with force must attempt to retreat before using deadly defensive force, if they know they can retreat with complete safety.

Case Vocabulary

RETREAT RULE: Rule in some jurisdictions that a person confronted with imminent unlawful force must attempt to retreat (avoid confrontation) before using deadly defensive force, if retreat is safely possible. If the person cannot safely retreat, she is then justified in killing her assailant.

Procedural Basis: Appeal from criminal conviction for aggravated assault and battery seeking reversal of conviction for improper jury instructions.

Facts: Neighbors Abbott (D) and Nicholas Scarano got into a fistfight, which Abbott (D) allegedly started. Nicholas's parents, Michael and Mary Scarano, allegedly attacked Abbott (D) with a hatchet, knife and fork. [Dinner is served.] In the struggle, the Scaranos were all struck with the hatchet. Abbott (D) claimed their injuries were accidental, but the prosecutor alleged they were intentional, and charged Abbott (D) with atrocious [aggravated] assault and battery against all 3 Scaranos. At trial, the judge gave jury instructions on the duty to retreat, which were allegedly confusing. The jury convicted Abbott (D) of atrocious assault and battery against Nicholas Scarano only. Abbott (D) appealed, alleging the jury instructions improperly explained his duty to retreat.

Issue: May a person confronted with unlawful force use deadly defensive force without first attempting to avoid it?

Decision and Rationale: (Weintraub) No. In "retreat" jurisdictions, persons confronted with force must attempt to retreat before using deadly defensive force, if they know they can retreat with complete safety. The question whether one who is neither the aggressor nor a party to a mutual combat must retreat rather than using defensive force has divided authorities. Critics of the duty-to-retreat rule condemn it as unrealistic, since most reasonable men would not retreat, and society should not demand what smacks of cowardice. Adherents of the retreat rule reply it is better that the assailed retreat than that the life of another be needlessly spent, and a rule so requiring will induce adherence to that worthy standard. While the retreat rule may be the minority rule, it is embraced by both our appellate court and Model Penal Code §3.04(2)(b)(iii), and we will now maintain it, because it preserves lives if reasonably limited to circumstances where retreat may be done safely. In "retreat" jurisdictions, persons confronted with force must attempt to retreat before using deadly defensive force, if they know they can retreat with complete safety. One who is assailed may hold his ground, against either deadly or non-deadly force, while using non-deadly defensive force, but must attempt safe retreat before resorting to deadly defensive force. Here, the jury should have been instructed that Abbott (D) was allowed to stand his ground against the Scaranos, and only had a duty to retreat if he intended to use deadly force. His duty would then be satisfied if he knew at the time that he could not retreat safely, though the jury may consider the total circumstances in determining whether he knew. Here, the judge's instructions to the jury were ambiguous and confusing. Conviction reversed.

Analysis:

The duty to retreat, formely labeled as a minority rule, has been codified in some states under the influence of the Model Penal Code. As the court notes, the main objection is that it is unfair and humiliating to require a man to retreat from wrongful attack, but the law is usually unconcerned with preserving the defendant's dignity, and generally leans toward outlawing private violence. Those jurisdictions that follow the no-retreat rule are no longer the majority. About half the states now require retreat when possible, some treat the possibility of retreat as a factor to be considered, and others permit the person to stand his ground.

United States v. Peterson

(Federal Prosecutor) v. (Aggressive Self-Defender)

(D.C. Cir.) 483 F.2d 1222 (1973)

M E M O R Y   G R A P H I C

Instant Facts

A man who dared another to enter his house, then shot him dead, is charged with murder, but claims self-defense.

Black Letter Rule

The aggressor in a conflict culminating in death cannot invoke the protection of self-defense, unless he (i) attempted to withdraw from the violent altercation in good faith and (ii) communicated his intent to his adversary by word or deed.

Case Vocabulary

LESSER INCLUDED OFFENSE: Crime which involves all but one element of a greater offense. Here, Peterson (D) was charged with (intentional) murder, but convicted of manslaughter, which is basically murder minus the element of specific intent to kill.

Procedural Basis: Appeal from criminal conviction for manslaughter seeking reversal for improper jury instruction.

Facts: When Keitt came to Peterson's (D) house to strip Peterson's (D) wrecked car, the two argued. As Keitt got into his car to leave, Peterson (D) returned to his house, got a pistol, and threatened to kill Keitt if he came in. Keitt got out of his car and approached Peterson (D) with an upraised wrench, and Peterson (D) shot Keitt dead. Peterson (D) was indicted for second degree murder, and claimed self-defense. At trial, the judge instructed the jury that (i) mere words were insufficient to justify self-defense, and (ii) self-defense was not justified if Peterson (D) provoked the conflict, unless Peterson (D) then withdrew from the altercation in good faith and so informed Keitt by words or acts. The jury convicted Peterson (D) of manslaughter, a lesser included offense. Peterson (D) appealed, contending the instructions misled the jury into believing he contributed to the conflict, which he denies.

Issue: Can one who provokes a departing aggressor to attack, then kill the aggressor in self defense?

Decision and Rationale: (Robinson) No. The aggressor in a conflict culminating in death cannot invoke the protection of self-defense, unless he (i) attempted to withdraw from the violent altercation in good faith and (ii) communicated his intent to his adversary by word or deed. It has long been accepted that one cannot support a claim of self-defense by a self-generated necessity to kill. This doctrine is grounded on the principle that defensive killings are unnecessary if the occasion for them can be averted. Here, the uncontroverted evidence shows Peterson (D) was the aggressor, because he threatened Keitt with a pistol as Keitt was about to depart, challenging him to attack. At that point, Keitt was no longer the aggressor. Case law generally holds that issuing an illegal challenge reasonably calculated to provoke a deadly fight nullifies the right to deadly self-defense. *Laney* [man who escaped from violent mob was not justified in returning to confront them], *Rowe v. U.S.* (D.C. Cir. 1966) [man embroiled in argument not justified in returning home to retrieve pistol, then insulting and shooting adversary]. Here, the jury could easily conclude from the facts that Peterson (D) issued such a challenge. While case law holds that self-defense includes the right to arm oneself to proceed upon one's normal activities, it does not allow one to arm oneself and deliberately stir up trouble. Conviction affirmed.

Analysis:

The principle is theoretically semi-sound. To hold otherwise would allow people to intentionally kill with impunity by provoking deadly fights with their intended victims. Note, however, that this principle seemingly applies different standards to the defender's behavior than it does to his adversary's. First, the trial court held that mere words are insufficient to justify violence. However, the appellate court held that defenders may reasonably expect their verbal challenges to provoke a deadly fight, suggesting the court realizes that some words will provoke a reasonable man to violence.

People v. Ceballos

(Government) v. (Garage Gun-Trap Setter)

(1974) 12 Cal.3d 470, 116 Cal.Rptr. 233, 526 P.2d 241

M E M O R Y G R A P H I C

Instant Facts

Ceballos (D) set a gun to shoot at anyone who attempted to enter his garage.

Black Letter Rule

An injury or killing by the use of a deadly mechanical device is not justified where the device injures in response to a non-violent burglary.

Case Vocabulary

DISPOSSESSION: Ejectment or deprivation of a dwelling or other property.

Procedural Basis: Appeal from conviction of assault with a deadly weapon.

Facts: Don Ceballos (D) lived in a small home with the living quarters above the garage, though Ceballos (D) sometimes slept in the garage. In the garage Ceballos (D) had about $2,000 worth of property. In March of 1970, Ceballos (D) noted that some tools had been stolen from his home. In May he noticed that the lock on his garage door was bent and that there were pry marks on the door. The next day he mounted a .22 pistol in the garage. The pistol was aimed at the center of the garage doors and was connected by a wire to one of the doors so that the pistol would discharge if the door were opened several inches. Two boys, Stephen, aged 16, and Robert, aged 15 came to Ceballos' (D) house while he was away. Both were unarmed with a knife or a gun. Stephen removed the lock with a crowbar, and as he pulled the door outward, was hit in the face with a bullet. Stephen testified that he was not sure if he was going to steal anything, but wanted to go in the garage and look. Ceballos (D) testified that he felt he should set some kind of trap to protect himself and his property. When initially questioned by police, Ceballos (D) stated that he did not have much, and wanted to protect what he did have. The jury found Ceballos (D) guilty of assault with a deadly weapon. Ceballos (D) appealed, contending that under Penal Code section 197, had he been present, he would have been justified in shooting Stephen.

Issue: Is the use of a deadly mechanical device justified to protect against a non-violent burglary?

Decision and Rationale: (Burke) No. Courts have concluded that a person may be held criminally liable for injuries or death resulting from a deadly mechanical device that he sets on his premises. However, an exception to the rule is recognized where the defendant would have been justified in taking the life or inflicting the injury with his bare hands. However, allowing persons to employ deadly mechanical devices imperils fireman, police officers, and children. When the actor is present, he may realize that deadly force is not necessary, but deadly mechanical devices are without mercy or discretion. Furthermore, even if the rule justifying the use of deadly mechanical devices were applied here, Ceballos (D) would not be justified in shooting Stephen. A killing in defense of property is justified, inter alia, when committed against one who manifestly intends to commit a felony. Furthermore, the felony intended to be committed must be a forcible and atrocious crime, such as murder, mayhem, rape and robbery. Burglary is sometimes included as a forcible and atrocious crime, but only where the burglary creates a reasonable fear of great bodily harm. The burglary in this case did not threaten death or serious bodily harm. Ceballos (D) also contends that another subsection of Penal Code section 197 justifies the homicide since he committed the homicide while attempting to apprehend a felon. However, his testimony indicates that the purpose of the killing was not to apprehend a felon, but to prevent a burglary. Under the common law, extreme force could be used to prevent dispossession of a dwelling house, or against burning of a dwelling. Here we are not concerned with dispossession or burning, but a burglary that did not justify the use of deadly force. We conclude as a matter of law that the exception to the rule of liability for injuries inflicted by a deadly mechanical device does not apply here. Judgment affirmed.

Analysis:

The common law regarding the use of spring guns or trap guns to protect property is changing. Under the old common law rules, a deadly mechanical device could be used where the intrusion was such that the person, if he were present, would be justified in taking the life or inflicting the harm with his own hands. Now many states hold that a resident may not justifiably use a spring gun to repel an intruder, even if he would be justified in inflicting the same harm with his bare hands. As the court in *Ceballos* noted, spring guns kill indiscriminately. Under the old common law rules, the two kids who entered Ceballos' (D) garage committed larceny, not burglary, since they entered during the daytime, and in a typical common law jurisdiction, Ceballos (D) would not have been allowed to use deadly force [California considers a daytime entry to be burglary]. Had they entered at night, their act likely would have constituted burglary, and Ceballos (D) would have been justified in using deadly force.

Durham v. State

(Game Warden) v. (Indiana Prosecution)
199 Ind. 567, 159 N.E. 145 (1927)

M E M O R Y   G R A P H I C

Instant Facts

When a game warden pursuing a misdemeanor suspect is assaulted and shoots the suspect, the warden is charged with assault for using deadly force in arresting a misdemeanant.

Black Letter Rule

Peace officers may use deadly force to arrest felony suspects, but may use only non-deadly force to arrest misdemeanor suspects, unless those suspects offer deadly resistance.

Case Vocabulary

PEACE OFFICER: Civil officer appointed to maintain public safety. Includes regular police officers and non-police officers, such as game wardens.

Procedural Basis: Appeal from criminal conviction for assault and battery seeking reversal.

Facts: Durham (D), a deputy game warden, arrested Long for illegal fishing. Long fled, with Durham (D) in pursuit. When Durham (D) caught Long, Long resisted arrest, beating Durham (D) with an oar until Durham (D) shot Long, injuring him. Durham (D) was charged with assault and battery for using excessive force in arresting Long. At trial, the judge instructed the jury that, if Long resisted arrest for a misdemeanor, Durham (D) was not authorized to use deadly force to apprehend him. Durham (D) was convicted of assault and battery, but appealed, contending the jury instruction misstated the law, which allows deadly force against suspects offering deadly resistance.

Issue: May a peace officer use deadly force to arrest a misdemeanor suspect?

Decision and Rationale: (Martin) Yes. Peace officers may use deadly force to arrest felony suspects, but may use only non-deadly force to arrest misdemeanor suspects, unless those suspects offer deadly resistance. Under Indiana statutes concerning criminal arrests, "the defendant shall not be subject to any more restraint than is necessary for his arrest," but, if "after notice of the intention to arrest the defendant, he either flees or forcibly resists, the officer may use all necessary means to effect the arrest." Prior case law holds that peace officers may not use more force than is necessary to arrest. Once they use excessive force, suspects are justified in resisting arrest forcibly. However, if a suspect forcibly resists a proper arrest, the arresting officer may use any force necessary to arrest him, including deadly force. *Plummer v. State* (Ind. 1893). However, case law in other jurisdictions often limits the amount of force which may be used to arrest one charged with a misdemeanor, as distinguished from a felony. The general rule deduced from those cases is that an officer making a misdemeanor arrest may not use deadly force to make the arrest, and may not use deadly force against a misdemeanant who is fleeing but not resisting. If the suspect resists, the officer need not retreat, but may use any non-deadly force necessary to make the arrest. The officer may not use deadly force unless the suspect first attempts deadly force in resisting arrest. Here, the jury instruction given was incorrect, since it failed to state that Durham (D) was justified in using deadly force to arrest a misdemeanant who offered deadly resistance. Such a law is necessary to avoid paralyzing the strong arm of the law by enabling misdemeanants to successfully thwart arrest, and to empower the state to use extreme force when extreme resistance is offered. Conviction reversed and remanded for retrial.

Analysis:

This case sets forth the rule concerning the use of deadly force by police/peace officers when making an arrest and facing resistance by the arrestee. This case follows the common law approach that police may use deadly force to arrest a felon, but not a misdemeanant, unless the misdemeanant offers deadly resistance. The officer's use of force is justifiable based upon self-defense, although the rules of retreat do not apply. However, as the next case demonstrates, even where a felony has been committed, police may not shoot non-dangerous fleeing felons. *Tennessee v. Garner.* Just as the common law distinguishes between felony and misdemeanor, the Model Penal Code limits use of extreme force to felony arrests. However, the Code contains additional restrictions such as use of force by those acting as peace officers, restricting use of force if there is a substantial risk to innocent bystanders, and giving consideration to the character of the offender so that force is justified only where he is thought to pose such a danger that immediate apprehension overrides competing considerations. In this case, the court correctly reversed and remanded because the jury was not properly instructed that Durham (D) could have been justified in using deadly force, even though he was arresting a misdemeanant, if there was deadly resistance. In other words, Durham (D) had the right to use self-defense.

Tennessee v. Garner

(Tennessee, Intervening for Tennessee Police Dept.) v. (Slain Burglar's Family)
471 U.S. 1 (1985)

M E M O R Y   G R A P H I C

Instant Facts
When a fleeing unarmed burglar is shot dead by police to prevent his escape, his family sues, contending the police violated his constitutional rights.

Black Letter Rule
Police officers may not use deadly force to prevent felony suspects from escaping arrest unless (i) they have probable cause to believe the suspect poses a threat of serious harm, to the officer or others, and (ii) they warn the suspect before using deadly force, if feasible.

Case Vocabulary

FELONY: Crime punishable by over one year's imprisonment, a.k.a. "major crime."

Procedural Basis: Appeal from judgment for defendants in action for constitutional rights violation seeking damages.

Facts: Officers Hymon (D) and Wright (both police officers) were dispatched to answer a "prowler inside" call. Upon arriving at the scene, a witness told them she heard someone breaking in next door. Hymon (D) confronted the burglar, Garner (P), and saw he was a small unarmed teen. When Hymon (D) yelled "police, halt," Garner (P) fled, attempting to climb a fence. Hymon (D) shot Garner (P) fatally to prevent his escape. Under Tennessee law and Police Department (D) policy, police officers "may use all the necessary means to effect the arrest" of fleeing or resistant suspects. Hymon (D) was acquitted by a police review board and grand jury. Garner's father (P) sued Hymon (D) and the Tennessee Police Dept. (D) in federal court on Garner's (D) behalf, alleging the shooting violated Garner's (D) constitutional rights under 42 U.S.C. §1983. The district court held for the Police Dept. (D). On appeal, the appellate court reversed and remanded, reasoning that the killing, if unreasonable, would constitute an "unreasonable" "seizure" in violation of the Fourth Amendment. Tennessee (D) intervened as defendant, appealing to defend its statute's constitutionality.

Issue: May a police officer use deadly force to prevent a suspected felon from escaping arrest?

Decision and Rationale: (White) No. Police officers may not use deadly force to prevent felony suspects from escaping arrest unless (i) they have probable cause to believe the suspect poses a threat of serious harm to the officer or others, and (ii) they warn the suspect before using deadly force, if feasible. There is no question that police apprehension using deadly force is a seizure subject to the reasonableness requirement of the Fourth Amendment. Police officers may arrest a person if they have probable cause to believe that person committed a crime, but this Court may dictate the reasonableness of that seizure. The use of deadly arresting force is the most intrusive seizure, violating both the suspect's interest in living and the state's interest in keeping defendants alive for trial. But it is sometimes necessary to allow capture. We are not convinced that killing nonviolent suspects is necessary for effective law enforcement. Most police departments have forbidden deadly force against nonviolent suspects, so there is substantial basis for doubting its essentialness. A police officer may not seize an unarmed, nondangerous suspect by shooting him dead, and the Tennessee statute is unconstitutional insofar as it authorizes deadly force against such fleeing suspects, but not unconstitutional on its face. Where the officer has probable cause to believe the suspect poses a threat of serious harm, to the officer or others, it is not constitutionally unreasonable to prevent escape with deadly force after giving a warning, if feasible. Thus, we overturn the common-law rule, which allowed deadly force in arresting fleeing felons, because it is outdated. The common law made sense when virtually all felonies were dangerous crimes punishable by death, but today, most are no longer capital crimes, and many crimes formerly classified as misdemeanors are now felonies, making untenable the assumption that "felons" are more dangerous than "misdemeanants." Here, Hymon (D) was unjustified in shooting, because he could not have believed Garner (D) -- young, slight, and unarmed -- posed any threat, and shot merely to prevent escape. Although burglary is a serious crime, the fact that an unarmed burglar has broken into a building at night does not automatically mean he is physically dangerous; in fact, statistics show burglaries rarely involve violence. Judgment affirmed.

Dissent: (O'Connor) Hindsight cannot provide the standard for judging the reasonableness of police decisions made in uncertain and often dangerous circumstances. Public policy suggests that, since burglary is an especially dangerous and intrusive crime, with "harsh potentialities for violence," police officers should be authorized to use maximum force to prevent it and apprehend suspects. While suspects have substantial interest in their lives, this interest does not encompass a right to flee unimpeded from the scene of a burglary. The suspect is adequately protected by the Tennessee statute's requirement that the police give warning before firing. Furthermore, the majority omits a standard of what kind of threat justifies deadly force and of what constitutes "probable cause" to suspect the suspect "poses a significant threat of death or serious ... injury," which complicates an already hard decision often made under the most trying circumstances.

Analysis:

This landmark case reversed the traditional common law that police may kill fleeing felons to prevent escape, though many jurisdictions had already done away with the traditional rule by this time. Whether this rule is good public policy depends largely on assessing the danger escaped felons pose to innocents, a point on which Justices White and O'Connor disagree sharply. For once, White has the better of the argument, presenting statistical evidence to show that burglary, a felony, rarely involves violence. However, he does not demonstrate statistically that felons of *all* persuasions (not just burglars) pose little risk of violence. However, he mentions the interesting point that the law now classifies many non-violent offenses as felonies, which supports changing the historical rule. O'Connor seems to suggest a common perception that burglary, while perhaps not particularly dangerous, is particularly intrusive and infuriating, since it involves entry into the psychologically significant "man's castle." Still, in a system which has decided not to punish most felonies with death, it would be incongruent to allow police to kill fleeing felony suspects.

People v. Unger

(Illinois Prosecution) v. (Escaped Prisoner)

66 Ill.2d 333, 362 N.E.2d 319 (1977)

M E M O R Y   G R A P H I C

Instant Facts

An escaped prisoner claims his escape was justified to escape inmates' death threats and sexual assaults.

Black Letter Rule

Prison escapees may claim the defenses of necessity and duress.

Case Vocabulary

CHOICE OF EVILS: a.k.a. choice of the lesser evil. The defense of necessity [see NECESSITY].

COMPULSION: a.k.a. duress. Affirmative defense to criminal charge where defendant committed a crime but (i) reasonably believed the crime was necessary to avert a greater injury, to himself or others, than the injury resulting from his crime, and (ii) did not contribute to causing the risk of that greater injury.

NECESSITY: Affirmative defense to criminal charge where defendant committed a crime because he reasonably believed he would be killed or severely injured if he did not commit the crime.

Procedural Basis: Appeal from reversal of criminal conviction for escape, seeking reinstatement.

Facts: Unger (D) was convicted of auto theft and imprisoned. While imprisoned, Unger (D) claims he was sexually threatened and assaulted by inmates, but never reported the incidents because he feared reprisals. When Unger (D) was transferred to the minimum security "honor farm," he escaped, claiming he had received anonymous death threats and escaped to avoid being killed, but planned to return once he got help. Unger (D) was recaptured and charged with escape. At trial, Unger (D) argued his escape was justified to save his life. The judge instructed the jury to disregard any reasons Unger (D) gave for escaping, and refused to instruct the jury on both the affirmative defenses of compulsion and necessity. The jury convicted Unger (D), who appealed, contending the jury instructions erroneously failed to allow the defense of "choice of evils." On appeal, the court held for Unger (D), finding his contentions constituted valid defenses which were erroneously disallowed by the trial court's jury instructions. The prosecution appeals, contending escapees are not entitled to the defenses of compulsion and necessity.

Issue: May a prison escapee claim the defenses of necessity or duress?

Decision and Rationale: (Ryan) Yes. Prison escapees may claim the defenses of necessity and duress. Public policy has traditionally made courts reluctant to permit escapees these defenses, but our recent decisions have recognized their applicability. *People v. Harmon* (Ill. 1974) [escapee raped repeatedly may claim duress as defense to escape], *People v. Lovercamp* [always an unfortunate name to have in prison] [escapees may claim necessity as defense to escaping for fear of rape, under certain conditions]. Here, the defense of necessity, as defined by Illinois statute, is appropriate, because Unger (D) testified he was forced to choose between 2 admitted evils by the situation which arose from actual and threatened homosexual assaults and fear of reprisal. Theoretically, the defense of compulsion would be applicable in the unlikely event a prisoner was coerced by the threat of imminent injury to perform the specific act of escape, though no such situation was alleged here. In the *Lovercamp* decision, the court held that escapees may claim the defense of necessity only if (i) they were faced with the threat of death, rape, or substantial injury in the immediate future, (ii) they either made several complaints to guards which proved futile, or had no time to complain, (iii) they had no time or opportunity to resort to the courts, (iv) they used no force against guards or bystanders, and (v) they surrendered to authorities after attaining a position of safety. These are relevant factors to be used in assessing claims of necessity, but we do not hold that each element is necessary as a matter of law, because the elements are, in our view, matters which tend to prove the defendant's testimony, but the absence of any one does not necessarily disprove necessity. For example, here Unger (D) testified he intended to return to prison upon obtaining legal advice and was attempting to get money from friends to pay for such counsel; regardless of our opinion as to the believability of this tale, that testimony, if accepted, would negate any negative inference arising from Unger's (D) failure to surrender after escape. Under the facts, Unger (D) was entitled to submit his defense of necessity to the jury, and the court committed a reversible error in refusing to so instruct the jury. Judgment affirmed.

Dissent: (Underwood) My dissent stems from an uneasy feeling that unconditional recognition of necessity as a defense to escape carries the seeds of future troubles. Unless narrowly circumscribed, the availability of that defense could encourage escapes, disrupt prison discipline, and cause injury to guards, police, or bystanders. I am not totally insensitive to the sometimes brutal problems faced by inmates and the frequency of sexual assaults. Prisoner complaints to unconcerned or understaffed prison administrations may produce little real help and cause retaliation. I agree a necessity defense should be recognized, but with limitations precluding its wholesale use, such as those in *Lovercamp*. Here, Unger's (D) driving for 9 hours and calling friends in Canada, and his admitted intent to leave to gain publicity for what he saw as an unfair sentence, severely strain the credibility of his intent to return to prison.

Analysis:

The Supreme Court modified *Unger* in *United States v. Bailey* (1980), holding that, for a prison's escape to be defensible under duress or necessity, the prisoner must make a bona fide attempt to return or surrender "as soon as the duress or necessity had lost its coercive force." Here, the majority and dissent both disbelieve Unger's (D) reason for escaping and doubt his intent to return. Perhaps there is some contrary evidence; Unger's original sentence was only 1-3 years, a fairly light sentence to risk increasing by 3-9 years for a failed escape. Of course, non-prisoners are also entitled to the defenses of duress and necessity, without the restrictions imposed by *Lovercamp* or *Bailey*.

Commonwealth v. Leno

(People) v. (Needle Exchange Defendants)

(1993) 415 Mass. 835, 616 N.E.2d 453

M E M O R Y   G R A P H I C

Instant Facts

Operators of needle exchange program, Leno (D), unsuccessful sought to apply necessity defense by asserting that program would reduce the spread of AIDS.

Black Letter Rule

In order to assert the defense of necessity, the danger must be clear and imminent.

Procedural Basis: Appeal from criminal conviction following jury trial for unlawful possession and distribution of instrument to administer controlled substances.

Facts: The State of Massachusetts prohibits the distribution of hypodermic needles without a prescription. Leno (D) and other defendants operated a needle exchange program in order to combat the spread of AIDS. [In spite of their good intentions, the authorities felt that they were breaking the law.] Leno (D) and the others were charged with and convicted of unauthorized possession of instruments to administer controlled substances, and unlawful distribution of an instrument to administer controlled substances. On appeal, Leno (D) contended that the judge erroneously refused to instruct the jury on the defense of necessity.

Issue: In order to assert the defense of necessity, must the danger be clear and imminent?

Decision and Rationale: (Justice's name not given) Yes. Leno (D) and the other defendants did not show that the danger they sought to avoid—the spread of aids through dirty needles—was clear and imminent. Rather, the needle exchange program's success was debatable or speculative. It is a matter of public debate as to the best course to take to avoid the spread of AIDS. Leno (D) argues that the prescription requirement for possession and distribution of hypodermic needles and syringes is both ineffective and dangerous. [He's arguing that the Legislature should not have enacted the law.] However, it is up to the Legislature to determine how it wants to control the distribution of drug-related paraphernalia, and such policy is entitled to deference by courts. Leno's (D) argument that their needle exchange program eventually will result in an over-all reduction in the spread of HIV and the future incidence of AIDS raises the issue of jury nullification, not the defense of necessity. Jurors do not have a right to nullify the law on which they are instructed by the judge. Affirmed.

Analysis:

We learn from this case that the defense of necessity requires a danger that is clear and imminent. Leno's (D) violation of the statute prohibiting the possession and distribution of hypodermic needles in order to prevent the future harm of the spread of AIDS was not done to prevent an "imminent" danger. As the court noted, the needle exchange program's success was debatable or speculative. Similarly, in the case that follows, *Commonwealth v. Hutchins*, the State of Massachusetts again rejected the necessity defense and upheld the conviction of a defendant charged with possession and cultivation of marijuana, even though he suffered from a fatal disease and ingestion of marijuana caused him to be in remission. The court refused to ignore the government's interest in regulating possession of drugs and felt that there was potential harm to the public if they ignored the law. Although both cases are examples of situations where there would be no harm to the public, the court, at least in the State of Massachusetts, was unwilling to permit the defense of necessity to be used because of the failure to show a clear and imminent danger.

United States v. Schoon

(Federal Prosecution) v. (Protesters)
(9 Cir. 1992) 971 F.2d 193

M E M O R Y   G R A P H I C

Instant Facts

Protesters who disrupted an IRS office and disobeyed police orders claim their protest was necessary to stop American involvement with killings in El Salvador.

Black Letter Rule

Protesters performing indirect civil disobedience may not claim the necessity defense.

Case Vocabulary

BENCH TRIAL: Trial without a jury, with the judge acting as trier of fact.

INDIRECT CIVIL DISOBEDIENCE: Violating a law or interfering with a government policy as a political/social protest, where the violated law is not itself the object of protest. For example, here, the protesters opposed American involvement in El Salvador. Rather than protesting *directly* by, say, interfering with CIA operations in El Salvador, they disrupted an IRS office and disobeyed federal police, though their primary aim was not to (directly) challenge their right to disrupt IRS operations or disobey federal officers.

Procedural Basis: Appeal from conviction for federal charges involving obstructing IRS activities and failing to comply with a federal police officer's orders, seeking reversal.

Facts: Schoon (D), Kennon (D), Manning (D), and others protested American involvement in El Salvador by disrupting and vandalizing an IRS office. A federal police officer ordered them to disperse. When they refused, Schoon (D), Kennon (D), and Manning (D) were arrested and charged with the federal crimes of (i) obstructing IRS activities and (ii) failing to comply with orders from a federal officer. At bench trial, they asserted the defense of necessity, contending they acted solely to prevent further bloodshed in El Salvador [by American-supported government death squads]. The judge held that the necessity defense was unavailable as a matter of law to humanitarian protesters, because (i) the harm was not immediate, (ii) the protest would not prevent the harm, and (iii) other legal alternatives existed. They were convicted of obstruction and noncompliance, but appealed, contending necessity was a proper defense.

Issue: May protesters claim the defense of necessity?

Decision and Rationale: (Boochever) No. Protesters performing indirect civil disobedience may not claim the necessity defense. To invoke the necessity defense, defendants colorably must show that (i) they were faced with a choice of evils and chose the lesser evil, (ii) they acted to prevent imminent harm, (iii) they reasonably anticipated their conduct would directly cause the harm to be averted, and (iv) they had no legal alternatives to violating the law. We could affirm the trial court's decision for the reasons cited, but we find a deeper systematic reason for the absence of federal case law recognizing a necessity defense in indirect civil disobedience cases. "Civil disobedience" is the wilful violation of a law for social or political protest. "Direct" civil disobedience involves protesting a law by breaking that law. "Indirect" civil disobedience involves violating a law or interfering with a government policy that is not itself the object of protest. Here, this case involves indirect disobedience, because the defendants were not challenging the laws under which they were charged. For public policy reasons, we conclude that the necessity defense is inapplicable to indirect civil disobedience. Necessity is a utilitarian defense which justifies crimes taken to avert a greater harm, thus maximizing social welfare where the social benefits of the crime outweigh the social costs of failing to commit the crime. The necessity defense allows us to act as individual legislatures, crafting one-time exceptions to criminal statutes, subject to judicial review. Thus, since the necessity defense is utilitarian, strict requirements must restrict its exercise to prevent nonbeneficial crimes. When indirect civil disobediants claim necessity, the "harm" they oppose is merely the existence of a law or policy. This alone cannot constitute a legally cognizable harm, because in a democratic society, a protester cannot simply assert that her view of what is best should trump the decision of the majority of elected representatives. If there is no cognizable harm to prevent, then the harm resulting from the crime necessarily outweighs any possible benefit from the action, making the necessity defense inapplicable. Here, the IRS obstruction and noncompliance were unlikely to abate the killings in El Salvador or immediately change Congress's policy. A final reason why the necessity defense is inapplicable to indirect civil disobedience is that legal alternatives can never be deemed exhausted, as required, when the harm can be mitigated by congressional action. The possibility that Congress will change its mind is sufficient in the context of the democratic process to make lawful political action a reasonable alternative, regardless of the plea's likely success. Conviction affirmed.

Analysis:

This case restates the established principle that illegal protests will not be justified as necessary, but is notable for the breadth of its holding; most jurisdictions allow the possibility of recognizing necessity in indirect civil disobedience cases, though most reject it in practice. This case also attempts to give an economic rationale for the rule. The court is correct in stating that "choice of evils" is essentially a utilitarian doctrine which allows a lesser evil in order to abate greater societal harm. It is probably also correct in suggesting that purely symbolic protests which have no chance of changing law or government policy, should not be permitted, since the nuisance cost outweighs their nonexistent benefit. Interestingly, the court leaves open the possibility of justifying *direct* civil disobedience with the defense of necessity. However, direct disobedience is largely impossible in cases where the government supports tyrannical regimes with money and semi-covert help, since the Supreme Court has held that taxpayers lack standing to challenge how the government spends their money, and the CIA and military are barely accountable to Congress, much less to taxpayers. The real reason why courts usually won't justify civil disobedience is not economic but political; no government wants to allow its appointed officials to permit its laws to be disregarded. But this is justified, as the court notes, because allowing individuals to violate any laws they find unjust would undermine the legislature's ability to govern by majority rule, which is a practical necessity even in democratic governments.

Regina v. Dudley and Stephens

(English Society) v. (Cannibals)
(1884) 14 Q.B.D. 273

M E M O R Y   G R A P H I C

Instant Facts

One of three men faced with starvation kills a teenage boy, and the three men then eat his body parts.

Black Letter Rule

The preservation of one's own life is not a justification for killing an innocent person.

Procedural Basis: Request to Queen's Court to determine if murder was justifiable after lower court rendered a special verdict.

Facts: On July 5, 1884, Mr. Dudley (D1), Mr. Stephens (D2), Mr. Parker, and a teenage English boy set out to sea on a yacht. Subsequently, a storm carried the yacht 1600 miles away from the Cape of Good Hope and forced the men and the teenager to abandon the yacht and board an open boat. For three days, the four individuals subsisted upon two 1-pound cans of turnips. On the fourth day, they caught a small turtle. On the twelfth day in the boat, they had completely consumed the remains of the turtle. From the twelfth day to the twentieth day, the men and the teenager were without food. On the twentieth day, Mr. Dudley (D1), with the assent of Mr. Stephens (D2), approached the teenage boy, who was ill, and fatally cut his throat. The three men then consumed the teenager's body parts. Four days after the incident, a vessel rescued the three men. An English court tried Mr. Dudley (D1) and Mr. Stephens (D2) for murder. The jury returned a special verdict and asked the Queen's Court to tell it if the killing of the teenager was murder under the circumstances.

Issue: Does the need to preserve one's own life justify the killing an innocent person?

Decision and Rationale: (Coleridge) No. The preservation of one's own life is not a justification for killing an innocent person. The issue is whether Mr. Dudley's (D1) and Mr. Stephens's (D2) acts constitute murder. The special verdict states that it is unlikely that the teenager would have survived and that it is likely that he would have died before the men. Whether the men and the teenager were or were not rescued in a timely manner, the killing of the innocent teenager is unnecessary. Some individuals say there are books of authority that state it is lawful to take the life of another to preserve one's own life. However, English legal precedence does not support such a contention. English law regards the private necessity that justifies killing another human being to be self-defense. Therefore, no man has the right to kill an innocent person, even if he faces the peril of death. If the extreme necessity of hunger does not justify larceny, how can it justify murder? To save one's own life is a duty, but the highest duty may be to sacrifice one's own life. The facts in the instant case do not support a finding of a justifiable homicide. Mr. Dudley (D1) and Mr. Stephens (D2) are guilty of murder.

Analysis:

The defense of necessity justifies a criminal offense when the accused acted with the reasonable belief that the commission of the offense would prevent the occurrence of a greater harm. Nonetheless, the law does not justify as a necessity the killing of an innocent human being. When a person kills an aggressor in self-defense, the homicide is justifiable as the aggressor is not innocent. However, the preservation of one's own life does not justify the killing of an innocent person. In the instant case, Mr. Dudley (D1) and Mr. Stephens (D2) faced death by starvation and preserved their own lives by killing and eating the body parts of an innocent teenager. Even though they faced dire circumstances and unimaginable temptation, the killing of the innocent teenager was not justifiable. As the instant opinion states, to save one's own life is a duty, but the highest duty may be to sacrifice it.

"TICKING TIME BOMB" SITUATION DOES NOT JUSTIFY USE OF NECESSITY DEFENSE TO AUTHORIZE, IN ADVANCE, INTERROGATION BY PHYSICAL MEANS

Public Committee Against Torture v. State of Israel

(Criminal Suspects) v. (State of Israel)
(1999) H.C. 5100/94

M E M O R Y   G R A P H I C

Instant Facts

Criminal suspects challenged Israel's methods of interrogation, which permitted physical shaking, etc., and concept of "necessity" was asserted to permit such interrogation.

Black Letter Rule

The "necessity" defense may not be used to promulgate rules permitting certain conduct in advance of any criminal activity.

Case Vocabulary

NISI: Latin for unless. If used following an order or rule, it means the order or rule will stand unless something occurs to revoke it.

Procedural Basis: Petition to Supreme Court of Israel for an order prohibiting the use of physical means during interrogation of criminal suspects.

Facts: Israel's General Security Service (GSS) investigates persons suspected of committing crimes against Israel's security. Administrative directives permit use of physical means during interrogation because they are deemed immediately necessary for saving lives. Examples include extremely forceful shaking, sleep deprivation, and forcing the suspect to wait in painful positions—the Shabach position—all in an effort to thwart bombing attempts or other threatened terrorist attacks. [Read the casebook for details on what shaking can do to one's body.] The Public Committee Against Torture (P), representing suspects arrested and interrogated, sought an order prohibiting the use of these physical means during interrogations. The State of Israel (D) asserted that it should have authority to use physical means based upon the defense of "necessity" in order to thwart attacks upon the State.

Issue: May the "necessity" defense be used to promulgate rules permitting certain conduct in advance of criminal activity?

Decision and Rationale: (Barak) No. We hold that the "necessity" defense may not be used to promulgate rules permitting certain conduct in advance of any criminal activity. Initially, we conclude that the GSS's general mandate to conduct interrogations does not encompass the authority to use physical means based upon both Israeli law and International law. The State (D) asserts that physical interrogation should be permitted in exceptional situations based upon the criminal law defense of "necessity." This defense [or "defence" as they say in Israel] provides that criminal liability will not be imposed upon one who commits any act "immediately necessary for the purpose of saving the life, liberty, body or property, of either himself or his fellow person, from substantial danger of serious harm, imminent from the particular circumstances, at the requisite [time], and absent alternative means for avoiding the harm." The State (D) therefore argues that GSS investigators are authorized to apply physical means during interrogations in the appropriate circumstances, in order to prevent serious harm to human life or body, in the absence of other alternatives. The "ticking time bomb" argument provides that use of physical means during interrogation would be necessary to obtain the information to defuse a ticking bomb that will imminently explode, kill, and injure people. In fact, Israel's Penal Law recognizes the "necessity" defense. We agree that in appropriate circumstances GSS investigators if indicted for criminal wrongdoing during interrogation of suspects may use the necessity defense. However, here we are not dealing with the potential criminal liability of a GSS investigator. We are asked to infer authority to, in advance, establish permanent directives setting out the physical interrogation means that be used under conditions of "necessity." The very nature of the defense does not allow it to serve as a source of a general administrative power. Thus, we cannot authorize the use of physical means during interrogation of suspects. Our decision, however, does not negate the possibility that the "necessity" defense be available to GSS investigators if criminal charges are brought against them. [This should put an end to the Shabach position!]

Concurrence: (J'Kedmi) The State has the right of self-defense in those "ticking time bomb" situations. I propose that the judgment be suspended from coming into force for one year, during which time, the GSS could employ exceptional interrogative methods in those rare "ticking time bomb" cases. During this suspension period, the Legislature will have an opportunity to consider the issue.

Analysis:

By examining the defense of "necessity," the Israel Supreme Court refused to apply the defense as a rule in advance giving government agents the authority to use physical means during interrogations. The court indicated, however, that should physical means be used resulting in criminal charges against the GSS, the necessity defense would be available. The basis for the holding is that although the defense will bar criminal liability where one commits an act that is immediately necessary to prevent imminent harm, it cannot form the basis for an advance directive authorizing certain conduct. The "ticking time bomb" argument was used by the government to argue that threat of injury and danger was imminent. The court was unwilling to allow the defense to be expanded to such a situation, and instead limited its application to those situations where a crime has first been charged.

Cruzan v. Director, Missouri Dept. of Health

(Comatose Patient's Parents) v. (Hospital)
497 U.S. 261 (1989)

M E M O R Y   G R A P H I C

Instant Facts

A comatose patient's parents seek a court order allowing the hospital to discontinue life support.

Black Letter Rule

Competent adults have a constitutional "due process" right to refuse or discontinue life-preserving treatment, but for incompetents, states may require life support to continue absent a clear showing the incompetent, while still competent, expressed an intent to die under such circumstances.

Procedural Basis: Appeal from state supreme court judgment in civil rights case seeking declaratory judgment or injunction to permit hospital to terminate life support.

Facts: Nancy Cruzan (P) was involved in a car crash which left her in a persistent vegetative state (without significant cognitive brain function) with virtually no chance of recovery. Missouri paid her hospital costs. Cruzan's parents (P) asked the hospital to let her die by discontinuing feedings. Missouri law allows an incompetent's surrogates to withdraw life support, but only if the surrogates present clear and convincing evidence that the incompetent, while still competent, expressed a wish to discontinue life support in such circumstances. The hospital refused to honor the request without court approval. The Cruzans (P) petitioned the trail court for an order directing the hospital to let Nancy Cruzan (P) die. The trial court granted the order, holding a person in a persistent vegetative state has a fundamental right to refuse or terminate "death-prolonging procedures," under the Missouri and U.S. Constitutions, and finding Nancy Cruzan's (P) earlier conversations with a roommate suggested her intent to die if unable to live normally. [Someone appealed.] On appeal, the Missouri Supreme Court reversed the order, finding Nancy Cruzan's (P) conversations failed to specify her intent reliably. The Cruzans (P) appealed to the Federal Supreme Court, invoking "federal question" jurisdiction. The Supreme Court granted certiorari to determine whether Nancy Cruzan (D) has a right under the U.S. Constitution to require the hospital to withdraw life-sustaining treatment under these circumstances.

Issue: Is it unconstitutional for a state to require that comatose patients continue receiving life support absent a clear showing the patient expressed an intent to die under such circumstances?

Decision and Rationale: (Rehnquist) No. Competent adults have a constitutional "due process" right to refuse or discontinue life-preserving treatment, but for incompetents, states may require life support continue absent a clear showing the incompetent, while still competent, expressed an intent to die under such circumstances. This Court has long observed that no right is more sacred than an individual's right to the control of his own person, free from interference by others. This notion was embodied in the common-law doctrine that competent adults must make an informed consent to medical treatment. The logical corollary of the "informed consent" doctrine is the patient's right to refuse treatment. Under *In re Quinlan* (N.J. 1976) [comatose girl's parents may disconnect her respirator], the New Jersey Supreme Court held that a person has the right to discontinue life support, under the Federal Constitution's privacy right. After *Quinlan*, most courts based the right to refuse treatment on the common-law right to informed consent and/or the constitutional privacy right. This is the first case where we have been presented with the issue whether the U.S. Constitution's due process clause grants a "right to die." The Fourteenth Amendment provides no State shall "deprive any person of life, liberty, or property, without due process of law." From our prior decisions, we infer the principle that a competent person has a constitutionally protected liberty interest in refusing unwanted medical treatment, but this interest must be balanced against relevant state interests to determine which should prevail. For the purpose of this case, we assume the U.S. Constitution would grant a competent person a constitutionally protected right to refuse lifesaving treatment. The Cruzans (D) assert that an incompetent person should possess the same right, but an incompetent necessarily cannot make an informed decision; it must be made for her by a surrogate. Missouri allows surrogates to withdraw life support, but established the procedural safeguard that this can only be done if the surrogate presents clear and convincing evidence that the incompetent expressed such wishes while competent. Missouri cites as support for this requirement its interest in protecting and preserving human life, which cannot be gainsaid. We now hold that Missouri's demand of such evidence of the incompetent's intent is not unconstitutional, because the state has a strong interest in preserving life. Thus, we cannot say the Missouri Supreme Court committed constitutional error. Judgment affirmed.

Concurrence: (Scalia) Federal courts have no business in this field, because American law has always given the State the power to prevent suicide, by force if necessary, and suicide includes refusing life-preserving treatment. The Due Process Clause does not protect individuals against deprivation of liberty, it only prevents such deprivation "without due process of law." No "substantive due process" claim may be maintained unless the claimant demonstrates the State deprived him of a right historically and traditionally protected against state interference. English common law did not allow suicide under any circumstances, so the right to die is not a protected right. Whether the suicide is accomplished through action or inaction is immaterial, since the effect is the same. Further, preventing suicide is not improper interference with body integrity, because the law permits interference with suicide, a felony. [If suicide was classified under English common law as a felony, and English law punished most attempted or completed felonies by death, does that mean ...?]

Analysis:

The Supreme Court's dicta clearly indicates it would recognize the right of a sane adult to refuse necessary medical treatment. However, it declines to extend this absolute right to an incompetent by allowing the more restrictive Missouri law. Rehnquist's reasoning for doing so is unconvincing. He argues the state has a nebulous abstract interest in preserving life, but surely this should not be taken to mean it must always preserve *every* life. Under economic or public policy analysis, the state *should* preserve productive lives to ensure their productivity continues to enrich society. Cruzan (P), through no fault of her own, was rendered permanently unable to contribute anything further to society. Further, preserving her life requires extraordinary cost. It is therefore highly questionable whether the state has a valid public policy reason to keep her alive, since the costs outweigh any tangible benefits. Alternately, it is argued a compassionate state should allow even unproductive citizens to enjoy life, even severely handicapped citizens to enjoy life as best they can, which is valid. Here, however, Cruzan (P) cannot even derive any appreciable enjoyment from living, since she can no longer think consciously. Further, the Cruzans (P) argue that, while she cannot think pleasant thoughts, her condition still allows her to feel pain. It is difficult to fathom exactly what purpose is served by allowing the state to extend her life where the possibility of enjoyment has been extinguished but the potential for pain remains, at enormous cost, and despite her own intentions.

ASSISTANCE IN COMMITTING SUICIDE IS NOT A FUNDAMENTAL LIBERTY INTEREST PROTECTED BY THE DUE PROCESS CLAUSE

Washington v. Glucksberg

(State) v. (Doctors and Terminal Patients)
(1997) 521 U.S. 702

M E M O R Y   G R A P H I C

Instant Facts

Terminally ill patients and their doctors alleged that state statute banning assisted suicide was an unconstitutional violation of the Due Process Clause.

Black Letter Rule

The Due Process Clause protection of "liberty" does not include a right to commit suicide.

Case Vocabulary

DECLARATORY JUDGMENT: A form of a judgment whereby the court declares the rights of parties or renders its opinion concerning issues of law.

Procedural Basis: Petition to United States Supreme Court from declaratory judgment concerning constitutionality of State statute.

Facts: Glucksberg (P) and other terminally ill patients and their physicians sued the state of Washington for a declaratory judgment that the state's statutory ban on assisted suicide violated the Due Process Clause of the Fourteenth Amendment to the United States Constitution. The district court and the 9th Circuit Court of Appeals held that the statute was unconstitutional. The state of Washington (D) petitioned the United States Supreme Court.

Issue: Does the Due Process Clause protection of "liberty" include a right to commit suicide, which itself includes a right to assistance in so doing?

Decision and Rationale: (Rehnquist) No. The state statute at issue in this case prohibits aiding another person to attempt suicide. For over 700 years, the Anglo-American common-law tradition has punished or otherwise disapproved of both suicide and assisting suicide. In a long line of cases, we have held that the Due Process Clause protects the rights to marry, to have children, to direct the education and upbringing of one's children, to marital privacy, to use contraception, to bodily integrity, and to abortion. We have also assumed that the Due Process Clause protects the traditional right to refuse unwanted lifesaving medical treatment. *Cruzan v. Director, Missouri Department of Health* [competent adults have due process right to refuse or discontinue life support based in part on common law rule that forced medication was a battery]. In *Planned Parenthood v. Casey*, we held that the due process clause protects a woman's right to abortion before the fetus is viable. Such rights and liberties protected by the Due Process Clause sound in personal autonomy; however, the sweeping conclusion that any and all important, intimate, and personal decisions are protected is not warranted. [In other words, there's a limit on the due process protections.] We are thus lead to conclude that the asserted "right" to assistance in committing suicide is not a fundamental liberty interest protected by the Due Process Clause. Moreover, the state's ban on assisted-suicide is rationally related to legitimate government interests such as the "preservation of human life," protecting the "integrity and ethics of the medical profession," protecting "vulnerable groups"—including the poor, the elderly, and disabled persons—from abuse, neglect and mistakes, and from prejudice, negative and inaccurate stereotypes, and societal indifference. We therefore hold that the state's statute banning assisted suicide does not violate the Fourteenth Amendment's Due Process Clause.

Analysis:

Obviously, the subject matter of euthanasia or assisted suicide is a hotly debated topic. [Recall the days of Dr. Kevorkian.] The courts, as this case demonstrates, are hesitant to become involved but are called upon at times to decide the constitutionality of the statutes in question. The court in this case was unwilling to extend the holdings of *Cruzan* and *Casey* to reach the conclusion that any and all important, intimate, and personal decisions are "liberties" protected by the Due Process Clause. This case demonstrates that actions by those who assist in taking the life of another are not legally justified because the suicidal person has consented to or requested such assistance. A distinguishing factor between this case—wherein the Supreme Court rejected the due process argument—and *Cruzan*—wherein the Supreme Court upheld a competent person's due process right to refuse medical treatment—is that the latter is not taking affirmative action to end his life. Rather, by refusing medical treatment, the person is merely letting nature take its course. If the court had struck down the ban on assisted suicide in this case, there would have been an acknowledgment liberty protection of "all basic and intimate exercises of personal autonomy."

State v. Toscano

(New Jersey Prosecution) v. (Fraudulent Insurance Claimant)
(N.J. 1977) 74 N.J. 421, 378 A.2d 755

M E M O R Y   G R A P H I C

Instant Facts

A chiropractor, accused of insurance fraud, claimed the common law duress defense, claiming a co-conspirator forced him to cooperate through threats.

Black Letter Rule

Under New Jersey law [and the Model Penal Code], duress is a defense to any crime, other than murder, if the defendant committed the crime because he was coerced by the use/threat of unlawful force against himself/another, which a reasonable person in the situation would be unable to resist.

Case Vocabulary

DURESS: Excuse to criminal prosecution, allowing actors to avoid criminal liability for most crimes committed under threat of violence.
IMMINENT (THREAT OF HARM): Threatened harm is deemed imminent if the harm is immediate, or if there is not enough time for the threatened person to seek police assistance.

Procedural Basis: Appeal from appellate affirmation of criminal conviction for fraud, seeking reversal because of duress.

Facts: Toscano (D), a chiropractor, and others were charged with conspiring to defraud insurance companies by staging accidents and settling for fictitious injuries. Toscano (D) admitted he fabricated office visits by "victims," but offered the excuse of "duress," contending he feared a co-conspirator, Leonardo, a bookie to whom Toscano (D) owed gambling debts, would hurt him or his wife if he refused to prepare false reports. Toscano (D) testified that Leonardo had threatened him, that Leonardo had not given him any consideration for preparing the reports, and that, to escape Leonardo's threats, Toscano (D) moved, changed his number, applied for a gun permit, and discussed the threats with coworkers. At trial, the judge instructed the jury to disregard Toscano's (D) claims of duress, holding that Toscano (D) was not in imminent danger, as required under the duress doctrine, because he had time to seek police aid. Toscano (D) was convicted and fined $500, but appealed. On appeal, the appellate court affirmed Toscano's (D) conviction. Toscano (D) appeals again.

Issue: Under New Jersey law, may a criminal claim the common law defense of duress if he claims he was coerced with the threat of future violence?

Decision and Rationale: (Pashman) Yes. Under New Jersey law [and the Model Penal Code], duress is a defense to any crime, other than murder, if the defendant committed the crime because he was coerced by the use/threat of unlawful force against himself/another, which a reasonable person in the situation would be unable to resist. We granted certiorari to consider the status of duress as an affirmative defense to a crime. Since New Jersey has no applicable statute defining the defense of duress, we are guided only by common law principles. At common law, duress was recognized only when the coercion is alleged to involve threats of "present, imminent and pending" harm "of such a nature as to induce a well grounded apprehension of death or serious bodily injury if the act is not done." Duress was permitted as a defense to prosecution for serious offenses other than the killing of an innocent. To excuse the crime, the threatened injury must induce "such a fear as a man of ordinary fortitude and courage might justly yield to," which includes a fear of serious but non-deadly physical injury. Duress is also present if the harm is threatened against another person, particularly a near relative of the defendant. Courts have assumed as a matter of law that threats of either slight injury or property damage are insufficient to constitute duress. When the coercion is a threat of "future" harm, courts generally held the defendant had a duty to escape or seek police assistance. The common law's insistence on a danger of immediate force causing death or serious injury is ascribed to judicial fears of perjury and fabricated defenses. We do not discount this concern, but it creates potential for injustice, since minor crimes should be excused if the defendant is coerced with threats of something less than death or serious injury, or with credible threats of future injury. Under the Model Penal Code and a draft New Jersey statute, defendants threatened with future harm would be allowed to assert the duress defense if they could show the threats they received would force a reasonable person to comply. Under the Model Penal Code, duress can be an affirmative defense even to murder, but under the New Jersey draft statute, a murder committed under duress still constitutes manslaughter. Here, Toscano's (D) testimony could allow a jury to find Toscano (D) and his wife were threatened with violence if they did not assist the fraudulent scheme, and that the threats induced a reasonable fear in Toscano (D). Exercising our authority to revise common law, we now adopt this as the law of New Jersey: duress shall be a defense to crimes other than murder if the defendant committed a crime because he was coerced by the use or threat of unlawful force, against himself or another, which a reasonable person in the situation would be unable to resist. Judgment reversed; remanded for retrial.

Analysis:

This case is notable for presenting the law of duress from the perspective of both the common law and the Model Penal Code. At traditional common law, duress was a valid defense only if the person committed a crime under threat of *imminent* death or serious injury, and the threat was so grave that a reasonably courageous person would comply. A threat of future harm was insufficient, because the law held the threatened person responsible for escaping or alerting police. The threat of monetary loss or property damage was also insufficient. At common law, the duress defense was unavailable to defendants who murdered an innocent under duress; they were still deemed guilty of murder. Under the Model Penal Code, the draft New Jersey statute, and this decision, duress is a valid defense against prosecution for crimes other than murder committed under threat of either imminent or future harm, if the threat was so grave a reasonably brave person would have capitulated. If a defendant was forced to kill under duress, the Model Penal Code provides him an affirmative defense if he can prove duress, but the New Jersey draft statute still holds him liable for manslaughter, a lesser charge. New Jersey later codified the draft statute, which is consistent with this opinion.

Regina v. Kingston

(British Prosecution) v. (Drugged Pedophile)

(U.K. 1994) Court of Appeal, Criminal Division, [1993] 4 All E.R. 373, rev'd, House of Lords [1994] 3 All. E.R. 353

M E M O R Y   G R A P H I C

Instant Facts

A pedophile, charged with molesting a boy, claims he did so only because he was drugged by a blackmailer.

Black Letter Rule

Involuntary intoxication is no defense to criminal prosecution, though it may allow a lesser sentence.

Case Vocabulary

INTOXICATION: Diminished physical/mental capacity resulting from using any drug, including but not limited to alcohol.

PEDOPHILE: Adult desiring sex with children, which is illegal in all jurisdictions.

Procedural Basis: Appeal from criminal conviction for sexual assault, seeking reversal on the grounds of involuntary intoxication. This case presents the opinion of both the Court of Appeal and its superior court, the House of Lords.

Facts: Penn, a blackmailer, intended to blackmail Kingston (D), who had pedophilic tendencies. Penn lured a 15-year old boy to his apartment, drugged him, and invited Kingston (D). Penn then drugged Kingston's (D) coffee with an inhibition-reducing drug and invited Kingston (D) to rape the boy. Kingston (D) sexually assaulted the boy, while Penn photographed and audiotaped. Kingston (D) was charged with sexual assault. At trial, Kingston (D) presented the defense/excuse of involuntary intoxication, and requested the court to instruct the jury to find him innocent if the required intent to assault was drug-induced. The trial judge refused, instead instructing the jury that Kingston (D) should be found guilty if he intended to assault the boy. Kingston (D) was convicted of sexual assault. Kingston (D) appeals, contended that the law excuses defendants acting under involuntary intoxication, even if they acted intentionally, as long as they were not responsible for their intoxication.

Issue: Is involuntary intoxication a defense to criminal prosecution?

Decision and Rationale: OF COURT OF APPEAL: (Taylor) Yes. Involuntary intoxication is a defense to criminal prosecution if the intoxication was accomplished by another's trick or fraud, and if the defendant would not have formed the required criminal intent but for the intoxication. Criminal law must inhibit anti-social acts. Having paedophiliac inclinations is not proscribed; practicing them is. The criminal law should not punish people who performed the act solely because their inhibitions were removed by another's clandestine act. A man is not responsible for conditions produced "by stratagem, or the fraud of another." If drink or drug, surreptitiously administered, causes a person to lose his self-control and form an intent which he would not otherwise have formed, the law should exculpate him because the operative fault is not his. The law permits a finding that involuntary intoxication negatives mens rea, and that the intent formed was not criminal. Here, the judge effectively withdrew this defense from consideration, which was a material misdirection. Conviction reversed. [The prosecution then appealed to the House of Lords.]

OF HOUSE OF LORDS: (Mustill) No. Involuntary intoxication is no defense to criminal prosecution, though it may allow a lesser sentence. Here, Kingston's (D) paedophiliac tendencies would ordinarily have been kept under control. The drug (whatever it was) temporarily changed Kingston's (D) mentality, lowering his ability to resist temptation so that his desires overrode his resistance. Thus, the drug is not alleged to have created the desire, but rather enabled it. The appellate court's decision was explicitly founded on the general principle that, if blame is absent, the necessary mens rea must also be absent, but this principle has never been part of the historical common law. "Mens rea" determines the criminality of the act, though, once the crime is proven, the punishment may be reduced by moral judgments of the crime's nature. Here, Kingston (D) contends he is without moral fault, but this is irrelevant to whether he had the mens rea necessary to constitute sexual assault. To adopt involuntary intoxication as a defense would set a dangerous precedent, because (i) it would defend against all offenses except [strict liability], (ii) it is a complete defense, which does not allow prosecution for lesser charges, and (iii) it is subjective, since it turns only on whether the particular defendant's inhibitions were overcome by the drug, and rewards defendants with the lowest inhibitions. Proving this defense is difficult, because the jury would need to be shown the defendant's personality and susceptibilities, which involves psychologist's testimony on unproven and elusive concepts. There would be many opportunities for spurious defenses. Thus, this defense should not be adopted unless necessary. Here, there is no need, since the sentencing judge has sufficient discretion to apply a lesser sentence if he feels the conduct was not blameworthy. Reversed; conviction reaffirmed.

Analysis:

This holding also represents the widespread American doctrine that involuntary intoxication is not defense. Even the Model Penal Code only allows it if the intoxication renders the defendant legally insane. It is difficult to see exactly why this defense is so disfavored. The House of Lords' opinion tries to catalogue some of the dangers of allowing the defense, but its list is rather hollow. The opinion protests that such a subjective standard would open the floodgates of proof, allowing for spurious defenses. Yet we (and they) tolerate the insanity defense, which has the same drawbacks, because we believe criminal law should not punish those who act involuntarily. In truth, it seems involuntary intoxication is a rarely-invoked defense, since the scenario needed to support it rarely occurs, so there does not seem to be a great danger of opening Pandora's box by allowing it. Economic analysis tells us that criminal law punishes anti-social acts with stigma, fines, and imprisonment to deter criminals from repeating these acts, and to deter prospective criminals from attempting them. There is little economic rationale for punishing acts which cannot be prevented in the future, since deterrence is impossible. Hence, we do not punish the insane, or those under duress, because they did not actively choose to commit crimes, and others cannot easily stay sane or duress-free to avoid punishment. In the case of involuntary intoxication, the defendant also did not choose to place himself in a position, cannot realistically strive to evade the situation in the future, and would not have chosen to commit the crime but for the intoxication, which impaired his judgment. Thus, there is little reason, from either policy or retribution, to punish the involuntarily intoxicated.

Roberts v. People

(Drunken Shooter) v. (Michigan Prosecution)
19 Mich. 401 (1870)

M E M O R Y   G R A P H I C

Instant Facts

A drunk who shot at another claims voluntary intoxication prevented him from forming the required intent to kill.

Black Letter Rule

Voluntary intoxication is a defense to crimes requiring intent if the intoxication made the defendant unable to understand (i) what he was doing, (ii) why he was doing it, or (iii) that it was likely to cause harm, but not if it merely made the defendant unable to understand the morality of his acts.

Procedural Basis: Appeal from appellate affirmation of criminal conviction for aggravated assault [with intent to kill], seeking conviction for a lesser included offense and recognition of the defense of voluntary intoxication.

Facts: Roberts (D), while drunk, shot at Greble. Roberts (D) was charged with, aggravated assault with intent to kill. At trial, Roberts presented the defense of voluntary intoxication, and asked the court to instruct the jury that, if he were so intoxicated that he could not form the intent to kill, he should be convicted only of assault without intent to kill. The judge refused, holding as a matter of law that voluntary intoxication cannot disprove the intent to kill, and instructed the jury to judge from Roberts's (D) actions whether he intended to kill. Roberts (D) was convicted, and appealed. On appeal, the Circuit Court affirmed. Roberts (D) again appeals, contending he should be convicted of only the lesser charge, assault [without intent to kill], because his voluntary intoxication rendered him unable to form the required intent to kill.

Issue: Is voluntary intoxication a defense to crimes requiring intent?

Decision and Rationale: (Christiancy) Yes. Voluntary intoxication is a defense to crimes requiring intent if the intoxication made the defendant unable to understand (i) what he was doing, (ii) why he was doing it, or (iii) that it was likely to cause harm, but not if it merely made the defendant unable to understand the morality of his acts. In determining whether the assault was committed with the intent to kill, it was material to inquire whether Roberts's (D) mental faculties were so far overcome by intoxication that he was rendered incapable of entertaining the intent. It was the jury's duty, in gauging Roberts's (D) intent, to consider the nature and circumstances of the assault, Roberts's (D) actions, conduct, demeanor, and his declarations before, at, and after the assault, and especially the nature of the intent and what degree of mental capacity was necessary to enable him to entertain the simple intent to kill. As a matter of law, the jury should have been instructed that, if his mental faculties were so overcome by intoxication, that he was not conscious of either (i) what he was doing, (ii) why he was doing it, or (iii) that he was likely to kill or endanger life, then he had insufficient capacity to entertain the intent to kill. However, the intent to kill need not include the ability to appreciate the morality of the action, so if the intoxication merely renders him unable to judge the action or its intended consequences as right or wrong, he can still be found to have had the intent to kill, because he is deemed to have intended to blind his moral perceptions, which follows from voluntary intoxication. He is not to be held responsible for the intent if he was too drunk to entertain such intent, and did not entertain it in fact. If he did entertain the intent in fact, he is deemed to have acted intentionally, even if he would not have formed the intent but for intoxication. Here, the Circuit Court held as a matter of law that no extent of intoxication could disprove intent, which is material error. Reversed and remanded for retrial.

Analysis:

People v. Hood

(California Prosecution) v. (Drunken Cop-Shooter)
1 Cal. 3d 444, 462 P.2d 370 (1969)

M E M O R Y   G R A P H I C

Instant Facts
A drunk who shot a cop claims voluntary intoxication is a defense to assault.

Black Letter Rule
[Under California law,] voluntary intoxication is no defense to assault.

Case Vocabulary

GENERAL INTENT: Technically, the intent required for most crimes, which is the intent to perform each element of the offense. It includes reckless or negligent crimes, since the theory is that, while the act's final result may have been unintentional, the elemental acts were done intentionally. This case argues that there is no difference between general and specific intent.

SPECIFIC INTENT: Technically, the intent traditionally required for common law robbery, assault, larceny, burglary, forgery, false pretenses, embezzlement, attempt, solicitation, and conspiracy, which is the intent not only to commit the crime's elements, but also the intent to achieve a further result. For example, common law robbery comprises illegally taking property from another's person or presence through violence or intimidation, plus the specific intent to keep the property or deprive the owner of it.

Procedural Basis: Appeal from criminal conviction for (i) assaulting a police officer with a deadly weapon and (ii) assault with intent to kill, seeking reversal and jury instructions to allow voluntary intoxication as a defense.

Facts: Hood (D), a drunk, was arrested by a police officer. Hood (D) resisted, and in struggling with the officer, seized his gun and wounded him. Hood (D) was convicted of assaulting a peace officer with a deadly weapon, and of assault with intent to murder. Hood (D) appeals, contending (i) the conviction for assault with a deadly weapon should be reversed because the jury should have been allowed to consider the lesser included offense of simple assault, and (ii) the conviction for assault with intent to kill should be reversed because the judge's jury instructions on intoxication were confusing.

Issue: Is voluntary intoxication a defense to prosecution for assault?

Decision and Rationale: (Traynor) No. Under California law, voluntary intoxication is no defense to assault. We reverse the conviction for assault, because the trial court failed to instruct the jury on the lesser-included offense of simple assault, and reverse the conviction for assault with intent to kill, because we find the trial court's jury instructions on intoxication "hopelessly conflicting." To guide the retrial, we will now decide whether voluntary intoxication is a defense to assault. California appellate courts are in conflict on whether the crimes of simple assault and assault with a deadly weapon are "specific intent" or "general intent" crimes. This distinction evolved to deal with intoxicated offenders, because while the moral culpability of a drunken criminal is frequently less than that of a sober person inflicting like injury, it is commonly felt that a person who voluntarily gets drunk and commits a crime should not escape the consequences. Formerly, the common law refused to recognize intoxication as a defense, but judges gradually developed the more humane doctrine that evidence of intoxication could be used to negate intent, though to limit the doctrine some judges distinguished "specific" and "general" intent crimes, holding that intoxication was a defense to specific intent crimes but not to general intent crimes. This distinction is illusory; technically, "general" intent is the intent to perform the crime's elements, and "specific" intent is an intent to perform them and also accomplish a further consequence, but there is no real difference between an intent to do an act already performed and an intent to do that same act in the future. California Penal Code §22, drafted in 1872, provides that, "No act committed ... while ... [voluntarily intoxicated] is less criminal by reason of ... such condition. But whenever the actual existence of any particular purpose, motive, or intent is a necessary element ..., the jury may [consider] the fact that the accused was intoxicated at the time ... in determining purpose, motive, or intent with which he committed the act." Yet even this policy is no easier to apply, because we must still characterize the mental element of the crime as either a particular purpose, or something less which would invalidate evidence of intoxication. The difficulty with applying such tests to the crime of assault or assault with a deadly weapon is that the relevant code provisions contain no word which unambiguously denotes a particular mental element. The Penal Code's use of the word "attempt" strongly suggests goal-directed, intentional behavior. This uncertainty accounts for California courts' conflict over whether assault requires intent, or merely recklessness. Our prior case *People v. Carmen* (Cal.) held that assault necessarily involves a [specific] intent to injure, but we need not apply this reasoning, because an assault is equally well characterized by a general intent to do a violent act, and there are countervailing policy considerations. A significant effect of alcohol on human behavior is to distort judgment and relax controls on aggressive and anti-social impulses. Alcohol apparently has less effect on the ability to engage in goal-directed behavior, because even a drunk man is capable of forming an intent to do something simple, such as strike another. What he is rendered incapable of doing is judging the social consequences of his acts or controlling his impulses. It would therefore be anomalous to allow evidence of intoxication to relieve a man of responsibility for simple assault or assault with a deadly weapon, which requires an intent to strike, but does not require recognition of the strike's morality. We note those crimes traditionally characterized as specific intent crimes are unaffected by our holding. Remanded with instructions that trial court instruct jury to disallow intoxication as a defense.

Analysis:

This case is notable for explaining and analyzing the traditional common law of intoxication. At common law, intoxication was a defense to crimes requiring "specific" intent -- robbery, assault, larceny, burglary, forgery, false pretenses, embezzlement, attempt, solicitation, and conspiracy -- to the extent it could be proven that the drunken defendant was capable of performing the proscribed acts, but was rendered incapable of formulating the intent to accomplish the goal, which was usually to steal property or injure/kill the victim. An intoxicated defendant would still be guilty of lesser included offenses not requiring specific intent. Other crimes were classified "general intent" crimes, and courts did not recognize intoxication as a defense to them. This case properly points out that the distinction's theoretical basis is vague. For example, assault, a "general intent" crime, could be characterized as either the general intent to use violence/intimidation or as the specific intent to injure through violence. The other specific intent crimes are similarly characterizeable. However, the court, having noted this arbitrary dichotomy, declines to reverse the common law doctrine, holding instead that assault should be reclassified as a general intent crime, to which intoxication is no defense. This holding may be a correct application of existing law. As noted, California Penal Code §22 provides that, while evidence of voluntary intoxication cannot be presented to show the defendant was absolutely incapable of forming an intent, it is admissible to show the defendant did not actually form a specific intent. The holding merely reclassifies assault as a general intent crime. Traynor bases his opinion on his observation, consistent with that of American and English courts, that alcohol is incapable of creating an intent where none existed, though it may cause a drunken defendant to act on an existing intent where he would otherwise have been restrained by inhibitions and moral judgment. If this characterization of alcohol's effects is scientifically valid, then crimes committed while drunk are still "intentional," and punishable accordingly. This leaves open the possibility that intoxicating drugs other than alcohol may impel the drugged person to commit crimes without forming a conscious intent. However, in reading over an opinion which incorporates doctrine it recognizes as inconsistent, we should consider whether Traynor is not just reluctant to go easy on people who voluntarily got drunk and committed crimes.

M'Naghten's Case

English Judges testifying before House of Lords
(House of Lords 1843) 10 C. & F. 200, 8 Eng. Rep. 718

M E M O R Y   G R A P H I C

Instant Facts

After a delusional man who shot an official was acquitted as insane, the legislature holds hearings on the insanity defense.

Black Letter Rule

[In England], a jury evaluating an insanity defense should be instructed to acquit as insane a defendant who, at the time of the act, (i) had a mental disease (ii) which caused a defect of reason (iii) which made him unable to understand either the act's nature/quality or its wrongness.

Procedural Basis: Legislative hearing before the English House of Lords seeking to prescribe rules for applying the insanity defense.

Facts: M'Naghten (D), who had delusions that the [conservative party] Tories were persecuting him, came to London to kill Prime Minister Robert Peel. M'Naghten (D) instead shot Peel's secretary, Drummond, who he mistook for Peel. M'Naghten (D) was arrested, and explained "the tories [conservatives] in my city follow and persecute me wherever I go, and have entirely destroyed my peace of mind. They do everything in their power to harass and persecute me; in fact they wish to murder me." M'Naghten (D) was charged with attempted murder. At trial, his defense team of 4 lawyers and 9 doctors [!] presented evidence that M'Naghten (D) was acutely insane and delusional. At trial, the judge instructed the jury to acquit M'Naghten (D) as insane if they found he "was not sensible, at the time he committed it, that he was violating the laws both of God and man" and not "in a sound state of mind." The jury found M'Naghten (D) "not guilty, on the ground of insanity." The acquittal attracted public attention and debate about the limits of the insanity defense, so after the trial, the House of Lords invited all English judges to answer questions on the proper application of the insanity defense. [M'Naghten (D) was not affected by these proceedings.] Among these questions were (ii) what is the proper jury instruction for an insanity defense? and (iii) how should the issue of insanity be posed to the jury?

Issue: What is the proper jury instruction for an insanity defense?

Decision and Rationale: (Tindal) [In England], a jury evaluating an insanity defense should be instructed to acquit as insane a defendant who, at the time of the act, (i) had a mental disease (ii) which caused a defect or reason (iii) which made him unable to understand either the act's nature/quality or its wrongness. We submit that jurors ought to be told that every man is presumed sane, possessing sufficient reason to be responsible for his crimes, until the contrary be proved. To establish an insanity defense, it must be clearly proved that, at the time of the act, the accused was laboring under such a defect of reason, from disease of the mind, as not to know the nature and quality of the act, or that the act was wrong. Customarily, the question presented to the jury was whether the accused knew the very act he did was wrong [i.e., illegal], but this is confusing, since it may lead the jury to believe the accused must have had actual knowledge of the law to be convicted, which is not required.

Analysis:

This legislative hearing produced the traditional English common law on insanity, the M'Naghten Rule. The common law test of insanity is fairly strict. To qualify for the insanity defense, the defendant must have a *mental defect* which prevented him from appreciating his actions' "nature and quality" *or* immorality. The meaning of "mental defect" is unclear; it may mean (i) only verifiable brain damage or deformity, or (ii) that and recognized forms of insanity, or something broader. The words seem to suggest a permanent or chronic impairment is required; poor impulse control is insufficient, and isolated acts/feelings may not be. The act's "nature and quality" presumably means the crime's circumstances; e.g., presumably, M'Naghten (D) would have been acquitted if he had thought the secretary he shot was a deer, or if he thought the shot would improve the secretary's health. As the court explains, "immorality" does not mean that the defendant must understand the act he committed is punishable as a crime, only that it was morally wrong, or at least deemed wrong by the British judiciary; it is necessarily an "objective" standard of morality. A later English case, *The King v. Porter*, recounted the policy reasons for the strictness of the insanity defense, saying "The purpose of the law is to prevent others from committing ... like ... crimes. Now, it is perfectly useless for the law to attempt [to deter people with punishments they are incapable of understanding]. What is the utility of punishing people if they are beyond the control of the law ...? [You may have noticed] that a great number of people who come into a Criminal Court are abnormal. They would not be there if they were the normal type of everyday person. Many of them are very peculiar in their dispositions and peculiarly tempered. Nevertheless, they are mentally quite able to ... appreciate the threatened punishment. It would be very absurd if the law were to withdraw that check on the ground that they were somewhat different from their fellow creatures in mental make-up ... at the very moment when the check is most needed."

King v. Porter

(People) v. (Insane Criminal)
(1933) 55 Commw. L.R. 182

M E M O R Y   G R A P H I C

Instant Facts

Facts not stated; judge is reading jury instructions regarding insanity.

Black Letter Rule

The elements of the insanity defense are: (1) insanity at the time the crime occurred; (2) the state of mind must have been one of disease, disorder or disturbance; and, (3) it must have been of such a character as to prevent the defendant from knowing the physical nature of the act he was doing or of knowing that what he was doing was wrong.

Procedural Basis: Trial court instructing the jury on the law of not guilty by reason of insanity.

Facts: Trial court instruction to jury regarding the law of insanity.

Issue: Can a person who is abnormal and peculiar but understands the wrongfulness of their act successfully assert insanity as a defense?

Decision and Rationale: (Dixon) No. The purpose of the law in declaring one not guilty by reason of insanity is to deter people from committing offenses. This is its primary purpose. It is useless for the law to attempt, by threatening punishment, to deter people from committing crimes if their mental condition is such that they cannot be in the least influenced by the possibility of later punishment, if they cannot understand what they are doing or cannot understand the ground upon which the law proceeds. Many people who come into a Criminal Court are not your average, normal, everyday people. Many are very peculiar in their dispositions and temperament. Nevertheless, they are mentally quite able to appreciate what they are doing and quite able to appreciate the threatened punishment of the law and the wrongness of their acts, and they are held in check by the prospect of punishment. It would be absurd to find these people not guilty on the ground that they were somewhat different from others in mental make-up. [Abnormality defense rejected!] It is a difficult task to determine if one has a mental disorder sufficient to justify a finding of not guilty on the ground of insanity. First, you must consider the condition of the mind at the time the act complained of was done. Second, the state of mind must have been one of disease, disorder or disturbance. Mere excitability of a normal man, passion, even stupidity, obtuseness, lack of self-control, and impulsiveness, are quite different from a state of disease or disorder or mental disturbance arising from some infirmity. If that existed it must then have been of such a character as to prevent him from knowing the physical nature of the act he was doing or of knowing that what he was doing was wrong.

Analysis:

The court instructs the jury on the necessary elements for the defense of insanity, using the elements laid down in *M'Naghten*. The insanity must exist at the time the offense was committed. There must be a mental disease, not just being peculiar or abnormal, and the mental condition must prevent him from knowing what he was doing or from knowing that what he was doing was wrong. The court explains that because the main purpose for punishing criminals is to deter crime, it would serve no valid purpose to punish one who is insane and not influenced by the possibility of punishment. The case demonstrates that to qualify as a mental disease, there must be more than just abnormality or peculiarity.

Blake v. U.S.

(Schizophrenic/Psychotic) v. (United States)

(1969) 407 F.2d 908

M E M O R Y   G R A P H I C

Instant Facts

Blake (D), suffering from schizophrenia for many years, robbed a bank and challenged the definition of "insanity" given to the jury requiring complete lack of capacity.

Black Letter Rule

Under the Model Penal Code, one may be found not guilty by reason of insanity if he lacks "substantial" capacity to appreciate the wrongfulness of the conduct or to conform to the law.

Case Vocabulary

VEL NON: Or not.

WRIT OF HABEAS CORPUS: A writ procedure seeking release from custody, alleging that being in custody violates the law or the Constitution.

Procedural Basis: Appeal following criminal conviction for robbery.

Facts: Blake (D) robbed a bank and was charged with bank robbery. At trial, Blake (D) raised insanity as a defense. Blake (D) was convicted and thereafter appealed, urging that the definition of insanity given to the jury for determining whether he was not guiltily by reason of insanity was outmoded and prejudicial. Blake (D) attended college, served in the Navy and was given a medical discharge after suffering an epileptic seizure. Thereafter, he had mental difficulties and received electro-shock treatment, and was hospitalized for two to three months a year later. He taught school, married, had children, and worked with his father in construction. He became a heavy drinker. He was hospitalized again for two months, spent time in psychiatric institutions and received further electro-shock treatment. He began to use stimulants and drugs, and had yet additional shock treatment. He was eventually adjudged incompetent and placed under his father's guardianship and housed in a private institution. After discharge, he continued psychiatric treatment, divorced, and married again. He was arrested for shooting his second wife. He was thereafter placed in a mental hospital for several months, and then was released on probation. He was sentenced to prison after violating probation. While in prison, he was hospitalized a number of times and saw the prison psychiatrist. He divorced his third wife, and married a fourth wife. [This guy has problems!] Blake (D) committed the bank robbery while attempting to obtain a court order that would allow him to go to Miami without violating his prison release restrictions. [At least he was attempting to go to Miami without breaking the law.] He even told a bar waitress that it was possible that he planned to rob a bank. He robbed the bank in question because of his quarrel and bitterness with it over the handling of a trust over a number of years. At trial, there was psychiatric testimony that Blake (D) was suffering from schizophrenia, marked with psychotic episodes, and that his behavior during the robbery indicated that he was in a psychotic episode. This was described as a form of severe mental illness. There was testimony that during a psychotic episode he would not be subject to his will. On the other hand, there was psychiatric testimony that he had a sociopathic personality and was not suffering from a mental disease.

Issue: Must there be a complete lack of mental capacity in order to find a person not guilty by reason of insanity?

Decision and Rationale: (Bell) No. There need not be a complete lack of mental capacity in order for one to be found not guilty by reason of insanity. Blake (D) contends that the Model Penal Code's standard of lack of "substantial" capacity to appreciate the wrongfulness of the conduct or to conform to the law should be used. The government (P) asserts that there must be a "complete" lack of mental capacity as set forth in *Davis v. United States* in order for insanity to be a defense. The facts of this case show that Blake (D) would not be considered insane under the *Davis* standard, but might be if the Model Penal Code's standard were applied. In light of the current knowledge regarding mental illness, we think that the "substantiality" type standard under the Model Penal Code is called for. A person, as Blake (D) here, may be a schizophrenic or may merely have a sociopathic personality. He may or may not have been in a psychotic episode at the time of the robbery. But, he was not unconscious, incapable of distinguishing right and wrong nor was his will completely destroyed in terms of the *Davis* definition. Modifying the lack of mental capacity by applying "substantial," still leaves the matter for the jury to determine mental defect vel non and its relationship to the conduct in question. [There's hope for Blake—but will more hospitalization and shock treatment do him any good?] We therefore adopt the Model Penal Code standard, but substitute the term "wrongfulness" for "criminality" with respect to the conduct that he is unable to appreciate.

Analysis:

This case shows why some courts have chosen to adopt the Model Penal Code's definition of "insanity." The Government (P) obviously did not want to the court to adopt the Model Pena Code standard because it would allow Blake (D) an opportunity to show that he might have been insane at the time of the robbery because he lacked "substantial" capacity either to appreciate the wrongfulness of his conduct or to conform his conduct to that required by the law. If the *M'Naghten* type standard urged by the Government (P) had been adopted, Blake (D) would not have been able to prove that he suffered from complete mental disorientation. The facts of the case show the limitation of the *M'Naghten* type standard. It could be proven that Blake (D) was aware of the wrongfulness of his conduct, but yet, his mental disease prevented him from restraining his action thereby destroying his power of self-control. Under the Model Penal Code standard, however, Blake (D) would not be criminally responsible if, because of his mental disease or defect, he lacked substantial capacity to appreciate the wrongfulness of his conduct or, he lacked substantial capacity to conform his conduct to the requirements of the law. This standard rejects any test that calls for complete impairment of ability to know or to control.

United States v. Lyons

(Federal Prosecution) v. (Drug Addict)
(5 Cir.) 731 F.2d 243, 739 F.2d 994 (1984) (en banc)

OKAY... NOW, THE OPIUM PIPE, PLEASE!

LUDES

M E M O R Y   G R A P H I C

Instant Facts
A drug addict, convicted of possessing drugs, claims the trial court improperly excluded evidence of drug-induced insanity.

Black Letter Rule
[In the 5th Circuit,] evidence of drug addiction is admissible to prove defendants suffered from a mental disease or defect which made them unable to appreciate their actions' wrongfulness, but inadmissible to prove they acted under irresistible impulses which made them unable to act legally.

Case Vocabulary

EN BANC: "On the bench," meaning that all judges/members participate in the decision.

Procedural Basis: Appeal from criminal conviction for knowingly and intentionally securing controlled narcotics, seeking reversal because evidence was excluded improperly.

Facts: Lyons (D) was caught carrying drugs and was indicted for knowingly and intentionally securing controlled narcotics. At trial, Lyons (D) offered an insanity defense, contending he had become addicted to painkillers taken to treat painful ailments, and presented witnesses who would testify that Lyons's (D) addiction caused physiological (brain) damage and psychological (behavior) changes, which left Lyons (D) substantially incapable of conforming to law. The trial court excluded this evidence, holding evidence of narcotics addiction cannot support an insanity defense, since it does not prove the required element of "mental disease or defect." Lyons (D) was convicted of securing narcotics. Lyons (D) appealed, contending his evidence showed a "mental disease or defect" was caused by drug use.

Issue: Is evidence of drug addiction admissible to support an insanity defense?

Decision and Rationale: (Gee) Yes. Evidence of drug addiction is admissible to prove defendants suffered from a mental disease or defect which made them unable to appreciate their actions' wrongfulness, but inadmissible to prove they acted under irresistible impulses which made them unable to act legally. Most legal authorities hold that mere evidence of narcotics addition, standing alone without evidence of other physiological or psychological effects, raises no issue of mental defect or disease, and thus cannot support an insanity defense. The Fifth Circuit adopted the *Model Penal Code*'s definition of insanity in *Blake v. United States* (5 Cir. 1969), because then-current knowledge of behavioral science supported that standard. We now overrule the *Model Penal Code* test, because the insanity defense's volitional prong -- incapacity to conform one's conduct to legal requirements -- does not comport with current scientific knowledge. Most psychiatrists now believe they lack sufficient scientific basis to measure a person's capacity for self-control, and are thus unable to opine whether defendants' impulses were irresistible and whether they could conform their conduct to legal requirements. Also, such testimony confuses jurors. We now hold that a person is deemed not guilty by reason of insanity only if, at the time of his conduct, he was unable to appreciate the wrongfulness of that conduct as a result of mental disease or defect. This test is more accurate because (i) psychiatrists can more easily opine on whether defendants understood the morality of their acts, (ii) there is considerable overlap between the inability to understand and the inability to control, (iii) evidence of understanding is more comprehensible to jurors, and (iv) federal prosecutors cannot prove beyond a reasonable doubt that defendants were unable to control themselves, as required by case law, because of the present murky state of psychiatric knowledge about the controllability of impulses. We see no prudent legal course but to treat all criminal impulses as resistible; to do otherwise would cast the insanity defense adrift upon a sea of unfounded scientific speculation about the unknown and unknowable. Here, Lyons's (D) proposed evidence suggests he suffered from a mental disease or defect, which might have rendered him unable to understand his actions' wrongfulness, so fairness demands that Lyons be allowed to present that evidence to support his insanity defense. Conviction reversed and remanded.

Dissent: (Rubin) Our criminal law should punish wilful blameworthy choices. This ideal requires a free agent confronted with a choice between right and wrong, and freely choosing to do wrong. Defendants who, because of their medical condition, are unable to make that choice, should get the benefit of the insanity acquittal. The majority opinion accepts this ideal, but incorrectly restricts the insanity defense on incorrect public policy decisions. The majority opinion suggests that the public is endangered by allowing violent criminals to escape punishment by fraudulently pleading insanity, but empirical data suggests little harm to public safety, because the insanity defense is rarely made and even more rarely successful. Also, the majority opinion assumes that defendants pleading insanity are quickly released, which is empirically false. Further, the majority assumes that juries are easily manipulated by vague standards of insanity and misleading experts, but this is not a widespread problem, because (i) most cases are settled by plea bargain without reaching the jury, (ii) the remaining cases usually present psychiatric evidence by deposition transcripts, without misleading debate by experts and lawyers, and (iii) where a dispute develops, defendants are usually convicted. The majority opinion does not assert that the insanity defense doesn't work in practice; it contents that the defense *can't* work, without presenting any empirical justification. The absence of useful expert evidence does not obviate the need for deciding whether defendants should be held accountable for criminal acts. The relevant inquiry under the insanity test is the defendant's mental state, since this determines his blameworthiness. The availability of expert testimony and its probative value are just evidentiary problems which can be accommodated within the existing 2-prong test. The majority's fear that the present test invites mistakes results in a rule certain to convict some who are not morally responsible or deferrable. Judges should not allow uninformed and irrational public opinion to serve as the basis for judicial decision making.

Analysis:

This opinion is noteworthy as a policy decision by the 5th Circuit to disallow the Model Penal Code's "irresistible impulse" test of insanity. It was superceded by statute in 1984. It is also included in the casebook as a debate between the majority and dissent on concerns jurors and judges share on allowing the insanity defense. The majority clearly believes that current psychiatric evidence on what constitutes an "irresistible impulse" is so vague and inconsistent that admitting it is more likely to confuse and manipulate the jury than to guide it. The majority suggests that what constitutes an "irresistible impulse" may be absolutely unknowable. However, the majority retains the Model Penal Code insanity test's second prong of the inability to understand morality, due to mental disease/defect, without examining whether psychiatrists and jurors are better at determining these criteria than they are at identifying irresistible impulses. The dissent cites compelling statistics showing that lay people (jurors) often reject the insanity plea impulsively because they irrationally believe that plea is an effective sham which endangers them by frequently releasing violent criminals, which is empirically false. Specifically, the studies cited show that people believe the insanity plea is entered in 13% to 57% of cases, and succeeds in 19% to 44% of those cases. In reality, it was used in one half of 1% of cases, and succeeded in less than 1% of those.

State v. Green

(Tennessee Prosecution) v. (Insane Cop-Killer)
(Tenn. Ct. App. 1982) 643 S.W.2d 902

M E M O R Y   G R A P H I C

 ## Instant Facts

A paranoid schizophrenic, convicted of murdering a policeman, claims the jury ignored overwhelming evidence of his insanity.

Black Letter Rule

In a jurisdiction adopting the *Model Penal Code* insanity test, if the proof burden is on the prosecution, the prosecution must prove that the defendant's acts were sane, and could not have been the result of insanity.

Case Vocabulary

PARANOID SCHIZOPHRENIA: Mental disease under which various situations can trigger paranoia, irrational thoughts, delusions, and strong impulses. Sufferers often think rationally and appear normal when not confronted with these situations.

Procedural Basis: Appeal from criminal conviction for murder in the first degree, seeking reversal because of jury error in rejecting "overwhelming evidence" of insanity.

Facts: Green (D), apparently insane, came to an FBI office and told FBI agent Hanrahan that people were "directing" with mind control, but that a doctor had invented an "ousiograph" which could detect these matters [whew! what a relief!]. Green (D) asked Hanrahan to find him an "ousiograph." Hanrahan [, noticing he had more pressing problems,] suggested Green (D) seek psychiatric help. Later, a police officer was found shot dead, with a note, addressed to Hanrahan, containing meaningless phrases and references to said "ousiograph." Green (D) was arrested for murder. Initially, Green (D) was adjudged incompetent to stand trial, because he would only speak gibberish. After therapy, Green's (D) condition improved, and he was charged with murder in the first degree. Green (D) explained he killed the officer because voices told him that, if he killed, he would be Hitler. Green (D) raised an inanity defense under the *Model Penal Code* test. Green (D) presented testimony, medical and lay, showing he was a paranoid schizophrenic with a lifelong history of bizarre behavior, psychiatric treatment, and random violence. The jury convicted Green (D) of murder in the first. Green (D) appealed, contending the jury erred in rejecting his insanity defense despite "overwhelming proof" of insanity, and presented further evidence from psychiatrists that Green (D) was genuinely insane when apprehended after the killing. The prosecution offered rebuttal evidence by police officers, who testified Green (D) seemed coherent when arrested and during prior police encounters, and suggested Green (D) was faking insanity, or alternately that his psychosis arose after the murder.

Issue: In a criminal trial raising the insanity defense, has the prosecution met its burden of proof if it shows some of the defendant's acts were rational?

Decision and Rationale: (Daughtrey) No. In a jurisdiction adopting the *Model Penal Code* insanity test, if the proof burden is on the prosecution, the prosecution must prove that the defendant's acts were sane, and could not have been the result of insanity. Under *Graham v. State*, once a Tennessee defendant presents evidence of insanity, the prosecution bears the proof burden of establishing his sanity beyond reasonable doubt. Applied to the *Model Penal Code* insanity test, this means the prosecution must prove that either (i) the defendant had no mental disease or defect at the time of the offense, or (ii) if the defendant had a mental disease or defect, it did not prevent him from knowing the wrongfulness of his conduct *and* conforming his conduct to the requirements of law. Here, the prosecution could not have met that burden, because, at trial, there was overwhelming evidence of Green's (D) insanity. The record clearly refutes the prosecution's theory that Green (D) faked insanity, because it is difficult to believe Green (D) could fool the trained and experienced psychiatrists who treated him. Also, the extensive history of Green's (D) mental illness, as evidenced by testimony from psychiatrists and family, refutes the theory that Green (D) dropped into a sudden psychotic condition upon shooting the officer. The prosecution argued that Green understood his act was wrong, because he fled the scene and hid the murder weapon. Yet the evidence only shows that Green (D) left at some point, and that the weapon was never recovered, which does not establish beyond reasonable doubt that Green (D) was attempting to evade capture or understood what he had done. Also, the record is devoid of evidence that Green (D) was able to conform his conduct to the law's dictates at the time he shot the officer. The prosecution suggests that, since Green (D) was later able to refrain from attacking police officers, he must have been able to keep from killing the police officer. This argument begs the question, since it suggests that the initial violent impulse is always controllable. This argument also ignores the nature of paranoid schizophrenia; psychiatric testimony suggests that paranoid schizophrenics may think and act normally most of the time, but be driven to irrational thoughts and impulsive violence by specific situations. The prosecution correctly points out that juries are not required to accept expert testimony, but the Tennessee Supreme Court has held that the state, to meet its proof burden, must present expert or lay testimony that the defendant's acts were both consistent with sanity *and* inconsistent with insanity. Here, the prosecution merely proved that Green (D) acted in some ways which could be considered sane, but failed to prove that Green (D) could not have taken those same steps out of insanity. Conviction reversed.

Analysis:

This case's holding is unexceptional, and seems largely influenced by Tennessee-specific case law. The case was apparently included to showcase defendant Green's (D) bizarre behavior, and to show the latent nature of paranoid schizophrenia, which makes it difficult to classify under the *Model Penal Code* insanity test and conventional understanding of insanity. Psychiatrists testified that paranoid schizophrenics seem normal -- and indeed do think normally -- most of the time. However, certain unpredictable situations can trigger paranoid delusional episodes which can become violent, though violence is rare. During these episodes, the schizophrenic may lose touch with reality, misunderstand the circumstances/consequences of his actions, believe his actions are morally correct or commanded by God(s), or have strong impulses, which are the types of behavior excused by the *Model Penal Code* insanity test. However, as the *Green* trial showed, jurors are reluctant to acquit a defendant who is/was capable of rational thought, because they often believe the defendant is faking insanity.

State v. Crenshaw

(Washington Prosecution) v. (Wife-Killer)

98 Wash. 2d 789, 659 P.2d 488 (1983)

M E M O R Y G R A P H I C

Instant Facts

A husband who butchered his wife for presumed infidelity claims insanity, contending insanity and religious belief convinced him the killing was moral.

Black Letter Rule

Under the M'Naghten test, a defendant is deemed to know his act was "wrong" if he understands that society considers his act wrong, though he is excused if, because of mental defect, he believed God commanded him to perform the act.

Procedural Basis: Appeal from criminal conviction for murder, 1st degree, seeking reversal because of erroneous jury instruction.

Facts: Newlywed Crenshaw (D) honeymooned with his wife in Canada until he was involved in a brawl and deported back to Washington. When his wife rejoined him two days later, Crenshaw (D) suspected his wife had been unfaithful [without apparent reason]. Crenshaw (D) beat his wife unconscious at a hotel, then went to a store, stole a knife, and returned to fatally stab his wife 24 times. Crenshaw (D) then drove to the farm where he worked, borrowed an ax, and returned to decapitate his wife. Crenshaw (D) tried to conceal the crime, cleaning the hotel room of blood and fingerprints and hiding the body. Crenshaw (D) then picked up two hitchhikers and attempted to enlist their help in dumping his wife's car into a river. The hitchhikers contacted the police, who apprehended Crenshaw (D). [Hence the saying that you shouldn't trust hitchhikers.] Crenshaw (D) confessed voluntarily. Crenshaw (D) was tried for murder, 1st degree. At trial, Crenshaw (D) pleaded the insanity defense. Crenshaw (D) testified he followed the Muscovite religious faith, which requires husbands to kill adulterous wives. Crenshaw (D) gave as his reason for killing his wife his sense that "it wasn't the same Karen ... she'd been with someone else." Crenshaw (D) also presented evidence of his past hospitalization for mental problems. The court instructed the jury that, under the M'Naghten rule as codified by Washington statutes, to acquit by reason of insanity, the jury must find that, "as a result of mental disease or defect, the defendant's mind was affected to such an extent that the defendant was unable to perceive the nature and quality of the acts ... or was unable to tell right from wrong. The court also added that "right and wrong" [means] knowledge of a person at the time of committing an act that he was acting contrary to the law." The jury found Crenshaw (D) sane and guilty of first degree murder. Crenshaw (D) appealed, contending the jury instruction erroneously misstated the law in defining "[right and] wrong" as a legal wrong rather than a moral one. [I.e., Crenshaw (D)'s defense was that, while he obviously knew it was illegal to kill his "adulterous" wife and took steps to avoid detection, he did not believe it was immoral, because of insanity and/or religious belief.]

Issue: Under the M'Naghten test, can a defendant claim insanity if he knew his act was illegal but did not believe it was immoral?

Decision and Rationale: (Brachtenbach) No. Under the M'Naghten test, a defendant is deemed to know his act was "wrong" if he understands that society considers his act wrong, though he is excused if, because of mental defect, he believed God commanded him to perform the act. The definition of "wrong" under the M'Naghten test is disputed by scholars, and other jurisdictions are divided on the issue. This court has held that, "when M'Naghten is used, all who might possibly be deterred from [committing] criminal acts are included within the sanctions of the criminal law." State v. White (Wash. 1962). "Only those ... "who have lost contact with reality so completely that they are beyond ... the influences of the criminal law," may have the benefit of the insanity defense...." State v. McDonald (Wash. 1977). Under this holding, the trial court should assume that one who knew the illegality of his act was not beyond influence of criminal law. Thus, the court's jury instruction here was correct. Alternately, the court's jury instruction here is correct because, in this case, legal wrong is synonymous with moral wrong. Under M'Naghten, "moral wrong" must be judged by society's morals, not the individual's, because holding otherwise would allow criminals to escape punishment solely because they believed their acts were not morally wrong. Here, there was medical evidence that Crenshaw (D) knew his actions were wrong by society's standards, including Dr. Belden's testimony ("I think Mr. Crenshaw is quite aware on one level that he is in conflict with the law *and with people*. However, this is not something that he personally invests his emotions in."). We conclude Crenshaw (D) understood his acts were both illegal and considered morally wrong by society. A narrow exception to the societal standard of moral wrong has been drawn for instances where a party performs a criminal act, knowing it is morally and legally wrong, but believing, because of mental defect, that the act was ordained by God, because the party's free will has been subsumed by the belief in the deific decree. Here, Crenshaw (D) cannot claim this exception, because he argued only that Muscovites believe it is their duty to kill unfaithful wives, and this does not constitute a perceived deific command. We follow most courts in holding that, where a religious group's rituals encourage illegal acts, a member is still criminally liable for performing those acts [as long as he does not believe, because of mental defect, that God so commanded]. *People v. Schmidt* (N.Y. 1915) [cultist criminally liable for animal sacrifice].

Analysis:

This decision is notable for affirming a broad pragmatic application of the *M'Naghten* test. The Washington courts' prior decisions have held that anyone who comprehends enough to be deterred by the threat of prosecution should be deemed sane, which accomplishes the law's goal of punishing and deterring crime, but stops short of punishing those who cannot be deterred by punishment. Thus, the law deems sane/punishable those who can understand their acts are either illegal or considered by society to be immoral. As the court notes, the test of immorality must be deemed objective rather than subjective, otherwise unrepentant criminals would escape punishment. In this sense, the court's decision furthers correct public policy, and should be considered "correct." However, Crenshaw (D) was correct in contending that the trial court misstated the M'Naghten doctrine in its jury instruction. The trial court said that, when the M'Naghten test excuses a defendant who is unable to tell right from "wrong," this excuses a defendant who is unaware his act constitutes a crime. This is incorrect; in the English legislative hearings which produced the M'Naghten test, Justice Tindal, who expounded the rule, expressly said the rule excuses a defendant so insane he is unaware his act is immoral, but not a defendant who is unaware his act is punishable as a crime. Ignorance of the law is, again, no defense, though ignorance of the crime's immorality is a defense when caused by mental defect. Had Tindal addressed the definition of "immoral," he would doubtless have defined it as objective, as this court did, since holding otherwise would excuse immoral criminals.

State v. Guido

(New Jersey Prosecution) v. (Abused Wife Who Killed Husband)
40 N.J. 191, 191 A.2d 45 (1963)

M E M O R Y   G R A P H I C

Instant Facts

A killer claiming insanity was convicted after psychiatrists re-classified her "insane" in mid-trial.

Black Letter Rule

At a criminal trial incorporating an insanity defense, expert witnesses may change their conclusions of sanity or insanity without prejudice, if they do so in good faith, even without diagnosing a change in the defendant's condition.

Case Vocabulary

NEUROSIS: Generally, a "mild" mental disorder or cognitive trait, such as anxiety, panic, phobia, etc.
PSYCHOSIS: Generally, a "serious" mental disorder, such as one involving delusions, multiple personalities, violence, etc. It is often difficult to distinguish psychoses from (mere) neuroses on principled grounds.

Facts: Adele Guido (D) shot and killed her husband, who was unfaithful, possessive, threatening, and occasionally abusive, and would not let Guido (D) divorce him. Guido (D) claimed she had taken a pistol from her suitcase intending to kill herself, but then reconsidered. As she put the pistol back, she saw her sleeping husband and killed him. Guido (D) was charged with murder, 2nd degree. At trial, Guido (D) claimed "temporary insanity." Guido (D) was examined by 2 court-appointed psychiatrists, whose report found Guido (D) had "anxiety neurosis," but pronounced her "legally" sane. However, the psychiatrists changed their ruling to "legal" insanity after discussions with Guido's (D) attorney, though their medical findings were unchanged. At trial, the prosecutor accused the doctors of collaborating with Guido's (D) attorney in defrauding the court. The psychiatrists explained they changed their conclusions because Guido's (D) attorney convinced them that "anxiety neurosis" qualifies under M'Naghten as a "mental disease." Apparently, the trial judge was unconvinced, and may have suggested to the jury that Guido's (D) defense was dishonest. Guido (D) was convicted of murder, 2nd degree, and sentenced to 27-27 years' imprisonment. Guido (D) appealed, contending the psychiatrists should be allowed to change their conclusions without prejudice.

Issue: At a criminal trial incorporating an insanity defense, may expert witnesses change their conclusions of sanity or insanity without finding a change in the underlying condition?

Decision and Rationale: (Weintraub) Yes. At a criminal trial incorporating an insanity defense, expert witnesses may change their conclusions of sanity or insanity without prejudice, if they do so in good faith, even without diagnosing a change in the defendant's condition. During Guido's (D) trial, defense counsel and psychiatrists were subject to unwarranted humiliation, because their change in the report was honest, if mistaken. The doctors explained they changed their report based on Guido's (D) attorney's explanation of M'Naghten. Previously, the doctors diagnosed Guido (D) with "anxiety neurosis," which caused severe panic and anxiety and kept Guido (D) from knowing the killing was wrong. The doctors had pronounced her legally sane because they believed M'Naghten's requisite "disease of the mind" could mean only psychosis qualified as insanity, and anxiety neurosis is a lesser illness than "psychosis." They changed their report when Guido's (D) attorney convinced them M'Naghten's rule included any condition preventing the defendant from appreciating wrong, including neurosis. Under M'Naghten, insanity is defined as a "disease of the mind," but the hard question is, What constitutes "disease"? The theory is that some wrongdoers are bad while others are sick, and it is immoral to stigmatize the sick. The question is ethical, not medical, because psychiatrists do not yet know which illnesses are morally blameworthy. M'Naghten's rule does not identify the exact diseases excused, but specifies the requisite effect the disease must create -- at the time of the act, the accused must have labored under a defect of reason such that he did not know the nature and quality of the act he was doing, or did not know the act was wrong. Though the emphasis is on the state of mind, it is nonetheless required that that state be due to "disease," not something else, so our cases do not excuse "emotional insanity" or "moral insanity" which is attributable to moral depravity or weakness, even if the offender's rage is so blinding he really cannot appreciate what he is doing. We cannot resolve the problem, but we recognize the unfairness of charging the defense with fraud for changing their report based on a good faith change in their understanding of the legal meaning of "disease." Judgment reversed.

Analysis:

Guido illustrates the principle that the *M'Naghten* insanity test does not require a diagnosis of any particular mental disease, but only some recognized condition which renders the defendant unable to appreciate the nature or morality of his actions. Thus, a defendant need not be diagnosed "psychotic" to claim the insanity defense; a "neurotic" is eligible. Any condition which causes those results should qualify as a mental disease or defect. However, the diagnosis must be of *something* generally recognized as a mental disease or defect, otherwise the condition is likely to be ascribed to "emotional" or "moral" lapse, which is not excused. More generally, this case illustrates just how much confusion exists in both the legal and psychiatric communities about what constitutes a disease and how much blame to ascribe to irrational actions.

McClain v. State

(Sleep-Deprived Criminal) v. (State)
(1997) 678 N.E.2d 104

M E M O R Y   G R A P H I C

Instant Facts

McClain (D) sought to introduce expert testimony concerning automatistic behavior, not as part of an insanity defense, but to show lack of voluntariness.

Black Letter Rule

Evidence of automatism is permissible as a separate defense from the defense of insanity.

Case Vocabulary

AUTOMATISM: A state of unconscious or spasmodic reflex actions such as sleepwalking or muscle spasms.
INTERLOCUTORY APPEAL: An appeal of a matter which does not resolve the entire controversy, but which relates to an intervening matter.
MOTION IN LIMINE: Asking the court either before or during trial to exclude certain evidence.

Procedural Basis: Interlocutory appeal to state's Supreme Court from court of appeal's affirming of trial court's granting of motion in limine to exclude expert evidence during criminal battery trial.

Facts: During McClain's (D) trial on charges of aggravated assault and resisting arrest, he sought to introduce expert testimony concerning sleep disorders and dissociative states. McClain (D) contends that but for a lack of sleep over the course of several days, he would not have been in a sleep deprived, sleep violence, or sleepwalking state at the time that he allegedly involuntarily struck police officers. [Is this the best defense he could come up with?] He sought to show at trial that his automatistic behavior precluded him from voluntarily committing the crimes. Indiana law provides that a person commits an offense only if he voluntarily engages in the criminal conduct. The trial judge excluded the testimony because McClain (D) had withdrawn his insanity defense, and the court of appeals agreed holding that the testimony was a species of the insanity defense. Indiana law also provides that defendants may not introduce evidence of legal insanity if they have not given notice to the court of their intention to interpose the defense.

Issue: May automatism be asserted as a separate defense from the defense of insanity?

Decision and Rationale: (Boehm) Yes. We hold that the under Indiana law, automatism should be distinguished from insanity, and thus McClain's evidence should be presented as bearing on the voluntariness of his actions. While automatistic behavior could be caused by insanity, evidence of automatism does not need to be presented under the insanity defense. To hold otherwise would require a sane but automatistic defendant to be forced to plead the insanity defense and face a choice of possible commitment, or effectively plead no defense to the crime. Automatism testimony in this case is simply a denial of one element—voluntary action—that the Legislature has required for most crimes. It is not a disease or defect within the meaning of Indiana's insanity statute. The case is remanded for proceedings in the trial court consistent with this opinion. [Do you suppose the jury bought the sleepwalking defense?]

Analysis:

McClain (D) withdrew his insanity defense but wanted to introduce testimony concerning his automatistic condition as a separate defense. The crimes he was charged with required voluntary action, and if the jury believed that he acted while in an automatistic state, i.e., with lack of voluntariness, he would be found not guilty. The court was therefore faced with the issue of whether automatism is part of the insanity defense. If it was, McClain (D) could not introduce his evidence because there was a state statute that provided that if you were not asserting insanity as a defense, you could not introduce evidence concerning being insane at the time the crime occurred. The court, by allowing the evidence to be admitted, is using a "voluntary" test concerning McClain's (D) conduct. Remember that under M'Naghten, a defendant would be found not guilty only if he totally lacks the capacity to know the nature of his act or whether it was right or wrong. Under this court's "voluntary" approach, if McClain's (D) automatistic condition prevented him from engaging in a voluntary act, he will be found not guilty. Why? Because he lacked the capacity to choose to act as he did. Courts are divided on whether a defendant claiming some form of sleep disorder is entitled to an acquittal due to lack of a volitional act, or whether he must plead insanity and face commitment. An English case, Regian v. Burgess, held the opposite of this case. The court would not allow the defendant to raise a defense of non-insane automatism. Under the Model Penal Code, a defendant would be entitled to an acquittal if conduct during a somnambulistic state would result in a lack of a voluntary act.

United States v. Brawner

(Federal Prosecution) v. (Criminal Defendant Pleading Insanity)

(D.C. Cir 1972) 471 F.2d 969

M E M O R Y   G R A P H I C

Instant Facts

Not Stated. Apparently, a mentally ill defendant convicted of premeditated murder contends his condition prevented his forming the requisite specific intent.

Black Letter Rule

Expert testimony about defendants' mental condition is relevant if it shows the defendant lacked the requisite intent, even if his condition fell short of legal insanity.

Case Vocabulary

DIMINISHED CAPACITY: Doctrine whereby defendants with a mental illness which falls short of legal insanity, but prevented their forming the criminal intent charged, are entitled to a lesser charge, but not acquittal.

Procedural Basis: Not Stated. Apparently, appeal from criminal conviction for first degree (premeditated) murder, seeking introduction of evidence of mental condition to support conviction for lesser included offense.

Facts: [Facts Not Stated. Apparently, a mentally ill defendant was charged with first degree (premeditated) murder, a specific intent crime. The defendant's mental condition did not qualify as legal insanity, because he was able to understand the nature of his crime and control it. However, the defendant argued his condition prevented him from forming a specific deliberate intent to kill, and introduced psychiatric testimony to that effect (i.e., the defendant argued he was guilty of only the lesser offense, voluntary manslaughter, because he lacked the specific intent required for first-degree murder.) At trial, the judge refused to allow the testimony, and the defendant was convicted of first degree murder. Defendant appeals.]

Issue: Can defendants who are legally sane introduce evidence of mental illness to disprove the requisite criminal intent?

Decision and Rationale: (Leventhal) Yes. Expert testimony about defendants' mental condition is relevant if it shows they lacked the requisite intent, even if their condition fell short of legal insanity. Earlier cases call this doctrine "diminished responsibility," though we find this term misleading. Procedurally, the issue of abnormal mental condition which negates intent may arise in different ways. For example, the defendant may offer evidence of (i) a mental condition which does not qualify as a "disease," (ii) a mental disease in which he was still aware his act was wrongful and was able to control it. This issue often arises when defendants charged with first degree premeditated murder offer proof of a mental condition which prevented premeditation. Conviction for offenses like deliberate and premeditated murder requires a subjective specific intent; the mere act does not prove premeditation. If the defendant's mental condition prevented the formation of specific intent, the defendant may present expert testimony to that effect, and may be entitled to a lesser charge. The judge must then determine whether such testimony has sufficient scientific support and probative value in deciding whether to admit it. Since case law recognizes that murderers who voluntarily became intoxicated are entitled to a lesser charge than premeditated murder if their intoxication prevented their forming specific intent, it would be unfair to deny a similar defense to mentally ill defendants who, through no fault, were unable to form specific intent.

Analysis:

This case presents the doctrine commonly called "diminished capacity." When a defendant has a mental illness which falls short of legal insanity (i.e., the illness did not prevent him from understanding or controlling his actions), but which may have prevented his forming the criminal intent charged, he is entitled to a lesser charge consistent with the criminal intent he actually formed. A "diminished capacity" plea does *not* exonerate; the diminished defendant is still guilty of a lesser charge, and punished accordingly.

State v. Wilcox

(Ohio Prosecution) v. (Mentally Impaired Burglar)
70 Ohio St. 182, 436 N.E.2d 523 (1982)

M E M O R Y   G R A P H I C

Instant Facts

A mentally impaired burglar, convicted for felony murder and burglary, argues mental defects kept him from forming the specific intent to kill or steal.

Black Letter Rule

In Ohio, diminished capacity is no defense, and defendants may not offer psychiatric testimony showing they lacked the mental capacity to form the requisite mental state, unless such testimony supports an insanity defense.

Procedural Basis: Appeal from appellate reversal of criminal conviction for aggravated felony murder and aggravated burglary, seeking reinstatement of conviction.

Facts: Wilcox (D), who suffered from various mental conditions, aided a burglary in which the victim was killed. Wilcox (D) was charged with aggravated felony murder (which requires a purpose to kill) and aggravated burglary (which requires a purpose to commit a felony). Before trial, the court-appointed psychiatrist diagnosed Wilcox (D) as borderline retarded, schizophrenic, dyslexic, and brain damaged. At trial, Wilcox (D) pleaded insanity and diminished capacity. The judge allowed Wilcox (D) to introduce psychiatric testimony to prove insanity, but excluded testimony suggesting diminished capacity, and refused to instruct the jury that Wilcox's (D) mental condition could negate the (specific) intent required for aggravated murder and aggravated burglary. Wilcox (D) was convicted on both counts and sentenced to life imprisonment. Wilcox (D) appealed, and the appellate court reversed. The prosecution (P) appeals.

Issue: Does Ohio recognize diminished capacity as a partial defense?

Decision and Rationale: (Sweeney) No. In Ohio, diminished capacity is no defense, and defendants may not offer psychiatric testimony showing they lacked the mental capacity to form the requisite mental state, unless such testimony supports an insanity defense. If the *Brawner* (diminished capacity) rule were applied, Wilcox (D) would be allowed to present psychiatric testimony showing he lacked the requisite mental state -- in this instance, the purpose -- to kill and commit a felony. However, we decline to adopt the diminished capacity defense in Ohio, based on public policy considerations. The diminished capacity defense developed as a covert judicial response which supposedly (i) ameliorated defects in the insanity test, (ii) permitted mentally disabled killers to be punished, but not executed, and (iii) permitted the jury to make more accurate individualized culpability judgments. However, we find the diminished capacity doctrine does none of these. (i) While the doctrine ameliorated the traditional *M'Naghten* rule, Ohio has abandoned *M'Naghten*; Ohio's test is now whether the accused lacked the capacity to know the wrongfulness of his act or conform his conduct to law as a result of mental disease or defect. Since this standard is considerably more flexible than *M'Naghten*, we see no need for "diminished capacity" as a halfway measure. Further, the availability of a diminished capacity defense tends to supersede the insanity defense, allowing defendants to opt for reduced sentences rather than indefinite commitment and treatment. (ii) In Ohio, diminished capacity is not necessary to prevent executing the mentally ill, because under Ohio law mental capacity is already a formal mitigating factor against capital punishment. (iii) We are not at all confident that evidence of diminished capacity is easier for juries to comprehend than evidence of insanity. *Brawner* reached its decision based on the analogy that voluntarily intoxicated defendants receive a reduced charge upon showing their intoxication negated specific intent, but the analogy is inapplicable here. Juries can easily determine whether an defendant was so intoxicated he was able to intend anything (i.e., unconscious), but they cannot easily determine an allegedly diminished defendant's degree of diminution. Also, we are concerned that the doctrine's open-endedness may require allowing psychiatrists to present evidence that defendants lacked the capacity for not just specific intent, but any requisite intent. Therefore, we hold that the partial defense of diminished capacity is not recognized in Ohio. Consequently, a defendant may not offer psychiatric testimony showing he lacked the mental capacity to form the requisite mental state, unless such testimony supports an insanity defense.

Analysis:

Wilcox demonstrates that state courts are split on whether to accept diminished capacity as a defense. It is also notable for outlining the policy reasons behind its adoption in some jurisdictions, and for listing policy factors against recognizing that defense. As Judge Sweeney notes, the diminished capacity was more necessary under earlier law, when mentally impaired defendants -- who could not always claim their mental defects constituted excusable "insanity" under *M'Naghten* -- were likely to be convicted, and could face execution. Sweeney correctly notes that mentally impaired defendants may no longer be executed in any state. However, while Ohio has liberalized its insanity test, adopting the *Model Penal Code* test instead of *M'Naghten*, presumably some states which do not recognize diminished capacity still use *M'Naghten*. Sweeney is also correct in noting that jurors cannot readily discern whether a defendant's mental defect prevented his forming the specific intent to commit a crime, though of course they are asked to do the same when considering an insanity defense.

Robinson v. California

(Drug Addict) v. (State Prosecution)

370 U.S. 660 (1962)

M E M O R Y   G R A P H I C

Instant Facts

A drug addict, arrested for narcotics addiction, challenges the state's right to criminalize the "status" of addiction.

Black Letter Rule

It is unconstitutionally cruel and unusual for states to criminalize drug addiction where the targeted person has not possessed drugs or committed anti-social acts within the state, because narcotics addiction is a disease.

Procedural Basis: Appeal from criminal conviction for narcotics addiction, challenging constitutionality of statute criminalizing addiction.

Facts: A California statute made it illegal for a person to "be addicted to … narcotics." Robinson (D) was arrested by policemen who noticed he had scars and track marks caused by drug use, and was charged with being an addict. At trial, the judge instructed the jury that the defendant was guilty if either he committed the denounced "act" (i.e., used narcotics in California) or was of the proscribed "status" (i.e., was addicted to narcotics while in California). Robinson (D) was convicted (presumably because of "status," since no one had seen him use drugs in California) and sentenced to 90 days' imprisonment. Robinson (D) challenged the statute's constitutionality, contending it is cruel and unusual for a state to criminalize a drug addiction not involving any affirmative act within the state.

Issue: May a state criminalize drug addiction (independent of actual drug use) within the state?

Decision and Rationale: (Stewart) No. It is unconstitutionally cruel and unusual for states to criminalize drug addiction where the targeted person has not possessed drugs or committed anti-social acts within the state, because narcotics addiction is a disease. The issue here is not the State's broad power to regulate drug traffic within its borders, but rather the power to criminalize the "status" of drug addiction. This statute does not punish drug use, purchase, sale, or possession, or behavior resulting from drug use, and does not provide or require medical treatment, but merely punishes the "status" of drug addiction. Further, California courts have interpreted it to mean a person can be found continuously guilty of addiction "at any time before he reforms," even if he never uses or possesses narcotics within the state or performs any antisocial behavior there. It would be unconstitutionally cruel and unusual, in violation of the Eighth and Fourteenth Amendments, for any state to criminalize being mentally or physically ill, and we cannot but consider this statute to be of the same category. The prosecution (P) recognizes that narcotics addiction is an illness, which may even be contracted innocently or involuntarily (e.g., from birth). The state may require treatment and even confine addicts. However, we hold it cruel and unusual for a state to criminalize drug addiction where the person has not possessed drugs or committed anti-social acts within the state. Reversed.

Concurrence: (Douglas) The addict is a sick person who may be confined for treatment for society's protection. Cruel and unusual punishment results not from such confinement, but from convicting the addict of a crime. A prosecution for addiction, with its resulting stigma and irreparable reputational damage, cannot be justified to protect society, since civil confinement would do as well. To convict and punish people for sickness violates the Eighth Amendment. The age of enlightenment cannot tolerate such barbarous action.

Concurrence: (Harlan) It is not clear that a state which concludes that narcotics addiction is not an illness has acted irrationally, and thus unconstitutionally, because medical knowledge is incomplete. However, this statute is unconstitutional because it allows addicts to be punished for nothing more than a bare desire to commit the crime of drug use while in the state, without any act.

Dissent: (White) The majority opinion frustrates public policy. It effectively removes California's policy to deal with addiction where there is ample evidence of past use, but it is unclear where the use occurred. This decision also leaves unclear the precise limits on state's powers to institute drug control policies.

Analysis:

While this landmark opinion is known for its holding that states may not constitutionally outlaw drug addiction without evidence of an affirmative act within the state, it is included in the casebook to highlight the Supreme Court's recognition that drug addiction is a "disease" rather than an offense. This view presents the interesting contradiction that drug possession or use may be criminalized, while drug addiction (which is manifested by past or attempted drug use/possession) may not be criminalized.

Powell v. Texas

(Publically Intoxicated Alcoholic) v. (Texas)
(1968) 392 U.S. 514, 88 S. Ct. 2145, 20 L. Ed.2d 1254

M E M O R Y G R A P H I C

Instant Facts

Powell's (D) conviction for being drunk in public upheld by the Supreme Court.

Black Letter Rule

The Eighth Amendment prohibition against cruel and unusual punishment is not violated when a state imposes sanctions for public behavior (public intoxication) which violates its law.

Procedural Basis: On appeal to the United State Supreme Court affirming conviction.

Facts: Leroy Powell (D) (Powell) was arrested, charged, convicted, and fined $50.00 for being found in a state of intoxication in a public place. A psychiatrist (Dr. Wade), after examining Powell (D), testified that Powell (D) is a "chronic alcoholic," who by the time he is intoxicated is not able to control his behavior, and who has reached this point because he has an uncontrollable compulsion to drink. When asked, on cross-examination, whether Powell's (D) act in taking the first drink when he was sober was a "voluntary exercise of his will," Dr. Wade answered yes. He qualified his answer, however, by stating that "these individuals have a compulsion, and this compulsion, while not completely overpowering, is a very strong influence, an exceedingly strong influence, and this compulsion coupled with the firm belief in their mind that they are going to be able to handle it from now on causes their judgment to be somewhat clouded." He admitted that when Powell (D) is sober he knows the difference between right and wrong. Powell (D) testified regarding the history of his drinking problem, his many arrests for drunkenness, that he was unable to stop drinking, that when he was intoxicated he could not control his behavior, and that he did not remember his arrest on the occasion for which he was being tried. He admitted, on cross-examination, that he had one drink on the morning of the trial and had been able to discontinue drinking. Texas (P) made no attempt to obtain expert psychiatric testimony of its own. It did nothing to examine the scope of Dr. Wade's reference to "compulsion" which was "not completely overpowering," but which was "an exceedingly strong influence," or to inquire into the question of the proper role of such a "compulsion" in constitutional adjudication. The trial judge disallowed the claimed defense, finding as a matter of law that chronic alcoholism was not a defense to the charge. Powell's (D) counsel submitted, and the trial court entered, the following "findings of fact": (1) That chronic alcoholism is a disease which destroys a person's will power to resist the constant, excessive consumption of alcohol; (2) That a chronic alcoholic does not appear in public by his own volition but under a compulsion symptomatic of the disease; (3) That Powell (D) is a chronic alcoholic.

Issue: May a state court interpreting a state law find as a matter of law that chronic alcoholism (even if it is a disease) is not a defense to the crime of public intoxication?

Decision and Rationale: (Marshall) Yes. The "findings of fact" are not findings of fact in any recognizable, traditional sense in which that term has been used in a court of law. They are nothing more than disguised premises designed to bring this case within the scope of this court's decision in *Robinson v. California*. There is no agreement in the medical community for a definition of alcoholism. We will not extend our decision in *Robinson* which only dealt with the addiction or sickness of a person, to this situation where the conviction is for the act of being in public while intoxicated. In *Robinson*, this court held as unconstitutional a state law which imposed jail time on a defendant solely based upon his "status" of being a drug addict. On its face the present case does not fall within that holding, since Powell (D) was convicted, not for being a chronic alcoholic, but for being in public while drunk on a particular occasion. The criminal sanction is imposed on public behavior which may create substantial health and safety hazards, both for Powell (D) and the public, and which offends the moral and esthetic sensibilities of a large segment of the community. The dissent suggests that *Robinson* stands for the principle that "criminal penalties may not be inflicted upon a person for being in a condition he is powerless to change." However, the entire point of *Robinson* is that criminal penalties may be inflicted only if the defendant has committed some act, has engaged in some behavior, which society has an interest in preventing. It does not deal with the question of whether certain conduct cannot constitutionally be punished because it is, in some sense, "involuntary" or "occasioned by compulsion." The record from below is woefully inadequate to support the contention that Powell (D) was unable at the time of the incident to control either his drinking or his being in public when drunk. It is easily admitted that a system which provided for the adequate treatment of alcoholics would be good for society, not to mention the alcoholic, however, such a system does not exist on the necessary scale. The criminal system of jail time and/or fines for petty offenses such as public drunkenness is minimal. The criminal system in place, although an unpleasant reality, cannot be said to be irrational. Without a better rehabilitation system in place, it is difficult to say that the criminal process is utterly lacking in social value. The doctrines of criminal law that are utilized to assess the moral accountability of an individual for his antisocial needs cannot be set aside here. The elements of a crime, (e.g., the intent, the act) and the defenses (e.g., insanity, mistake, justification, duress) work together and are adjusted over time to reflect the evolving goals of criminal law and the changing religious, moral, philosophical, and medical views of the nature of man. This process has always been thought to be the province of the States. Conviction affirmed.

Concurrence: (Black) Texas (P) law serves many state purposes, e.g., it gets alcoholics off the street and into a jail where they are provide food, clothing, and shelter long enough to sober up, thus keeping the public and themselves safe. A State should not be held constitutionally required to make the inquiry as to what part of a defendant's personality is responsible for his actions and to excuse anyone whose action was, in some complex, psychologic sense, the result of "compulsion." We are asked to apply *Robinson*, but it is not applicable here because it involved punishment for the mere propensity, or the desire to commit an offense, evidence of which is considered relatively unreliable and difficult for a defendant to rebut. Laws which require the State to prove that the defendant actually committed some proscribed act involve none of the problems encountered in *Robinson*, and the requirement of a specific act

provides some protection against false charges. The question of whether an act is "involuntary" is an inherently elusive question, and one which Texas (P) may treat as irrelevant.

Concurrence: (White) The chronic alcoholic with an irresistible urge to consume alcohol should not be punished for drinking or for being drunk. Powell's (D) conviction was for the different crime of being drunk in a public place. Many alcoholics do make it a point to begin and end their drinking binges in private. It is possible that such an alcoholic will lose his power to control his movement and appear in public. The Eighth Amendment might forbid conviction in such a circumstance, but only on a record satisfactorily showing that is was not feasible for him to have made arrangements to prevent him being in public when drunk and that his extreme drunkenness sufficiently deprived him of his faculties on that occasion. Alcoholics without homes [sounds like a support group, doesn't it] are not only unable to resist drinking, but are then necessarily drunk in public. If such facts were sufficiently proved, punishment would be for the single act of unresistible drunkenness for which punishment would violate the Eighth Amendment.

Dissent: (Fortas) Criminal penalties may not be inflicted upon a person for being in a condition he is powerless to change. In this case, Powell (D) is charged with a crime composed of two elements — being intoxicated and being found in a public place while in that condition. The crime, so defined, differs from that in *Robinson*. The statute covers more than a mere status. But the essential constitutional defect here is the same as in *Robinson*, for in both cases the particular defendant was accused of being in a condition which he had no capacity to change or avoid. A person may not be punished if the condition essential to constitute the defined crime is part of the pattern of his disease and is brought about by a compulsion symptomatic of the disease. Such punishment violates the Eighth Amendment prohibition against cruel and unusual punishment.

Analysis:

Powell (D) was asking the court to apply the rule in *Robinson*, that is, to find the sanctions for being intoxicated in public inflicted cruel and unusual punishment. The Court refused to extend the rule to the facts presented here. It did not consider the "status" of "being addicted" to be the same thing as the "act" of "being drunk in public." It had no [none, nada] problem finding that Texas (P) had the right to determine the extent to which it would define and penalize a person's offensive actions. Justice White, although attempting to provide constitutional protection to at least some chronic alcoholics also seems to think that while they are drunk they should be more responsible. This simply doesn't seem to be a practical possibility. Justice Stewart who penned *Robinson* joined the dissent. There are various views on the usefulness of punishing alcoholics/addicts. One view is that to punish alcoholics deters others from drinking in the first place. It also brings to the individual alcoholics attention that society considers his drinking and resulting behavior to be unacceptable. Another view is that once a person is addicted and out-of-control that the desire for vengeance (retribution) does not justify treating such a person as a criminal.

United States v. Moore

(Federal Prosecution) v. (Heroin Addict/Possessor)
486 F.2d 1139 (D.C. Cir. 1973)

M E M O R Y G R A P H I C

Instant Facts

Heroin addict, convicted of possession and trafficking, contends addiction is a defense to prosecution for possessing drugs.

Black Letter Rule

Drug addiction is no defense to prosecution for drug possession.

Procedural Basis: Appeal from federal conviction for drug possession and trafficking, seeking reversal on basis of drug addiction.

Facts: Moore (D), a heroin addict, was caught possessing heroin and charged with drug possession and trafficking. At trial, Moore (D) testified that he was an addict and possessed heroin for personal use, but did not sell it. Moore (D) argued he, as an addict, had a disease/overpowering need for heroin which overcame his "free will" and compelled him to possess it, for which he should not be held responsible. The judge excluded expert testimony about Moore's (D) addiction, and declined to instruct the jury that nontrafficking addicts could not be convicted of possession. Moore (D) was convicted, and now appeals.

Issue: Is drug addiction a defense to a charge of drug possession?

Decision and Rationale: (Wilkey) No. Drug addiction is no defense to prosecution for drug possession. We believe it clear from the evidence that Moore was not merely an addict, but engaged in the drug trade. Yet even if he were a nontrafficking addict, his conviction must be sustained. Moore (D) contends that common law requires the capacity for control a prerequisite for conviction, and that he, as an addict, has lost the power of self-control. We believe heroin addicts may be able to control themselves in some cases. Further, holding that addicts are never responsible for addiction-compelled acts would violate public policy, since it would tend to excuse every crime committed for drug money. This would frustrate necessary anti-heroin programs. Our holding is consistent with *Robinson*, which prohibits criminalizing addiction, but does not prohibit criminalizing addiction-compelled acts. *Powell* also does not prohibit such a holding. Conviction affirmed.

Concurrence: (Leventhal) Addiction does not qualify as insanity, and does not warrant similar treatment. Moore (D) contends that, since the insanity defense excuses irresistible impulses caused by mental disease or defect, then addicts should be excused because addiction negates free will, much like an irresistible impulse, without creating mental disease. Traditionally, criminal law excuses actions which are completely involuntary or forcibly compelled, or lack a guilty mental state. This is inapplicable to drug possession, which involves voluntary acts and guilty mental state. For policy reasons, criminal law must be allowed to reach the vast bulk of the population, even those of admitted limited mental capacity or high susceptibility to impulses. The criminal law sometimes recognizes a condition deserving exculpation, such as insanity. However, insanity was recognized as such only after systematic research and a consensus on its effects. For drug use, however, there is no consensus on whether addicts can refrain, and on whether excusing addiction will help the problem. Thus, we decline to excuse addiction, for policy reasons.

Dissent: (Wright) The developing common law of mens rea should now embrace the principle that a drug addict who, by reason of drug use, lacks substantial capacity to stop using drugs should not be held criminally liable for mere possession of drugs for personal use. Historically, our jurisprudence has held men criminally liable when their acts manifest "free will," with exceptions for mental impairment/incapacity and duress. Today, there is a consensus that at least some addicts cannot overcome drug addiction by "free will." Allowing a defense for addiction would encourage rehabilitation. Criminalizing possession does not deter addicts, because any threat of punishment is overcome by addiction's psychological and physiological compulsions. Punishment only furthers revenge, which is inappropriate because addicts, once addicted, are no longer making a conscious decision to use drugs. Civil confinement and treatment would better resolve the problem. However, I would limit the addiction defense to crimes which harm only the addict, such as possession.

Dissent: (Bazelon) I agree with Judge Wright's dissent that addicts are not "guilty," because they act under a compulsion which negates free will. However,

I would expand the addiction defense to other offenses motivated by addiction, such as robbery or trafficking, [!!!] where the defendant's addiction caused sufficient duress or compulsion to render him unable to conform his conduct to legal requirements.

Analysis:

This case is important for indicating that courts will not read *Robinson* to prohibit the criminalization of possession. This holding is legally correct, since *Robinson* made it unconstitutional to criminalize addiction *absent possession or any other antisocial act*, but specifically left possession as a proscribable offense. However, this case, with its many dissenting opinions, is perhaps more valuable to highlight judge's widely divergent views on drug addiction's psychological effects and the best drug control policy.

Chapter 9

Larceny is the oldest common law theft crime. Larceny means stealing. Under early common law, larceny was the only type of theft punishable as a crime. Its elements were carefully construed. Many actions that we consider theft today were not included under larceny. Such deceptions were left to the civil, not the criminal law. Under the English common law, larceny was divided into grand larceny and petit larceny, with the difference being the value of the goods stolen. By statute, England later abolished the distinction between grand and petit larceny. Until recently, most United States jurisdictions distinguished between grand and petit larceny, although the amounts involved varied considerably. Determining the value of property is often a problem, however, because the real value may exceed the actual cost. Market value generally is used as a measure of the property's value. Other jurisdictions which have abandoned the grand versus petit larceny approach, have also abolished the use of the term larceny, and organized their codes around a consolidated theft statute. This approach follows that of the Model Penal Code. However, jurisdictions that take this approach may use the common law as a basis for defining theft. Thus it is important to understand the common law of larceny.

Acts that today are defined as embezzlement and fraud were not included in common-law larceny, because a person already in lawful possession of property could not be charged with larceny. Statutory requirements were necessary to bring under the criminal law the acquisition of another's property by misappropriation or misapplication when the actor already had legal control of the property. Although embezzlement is considered larceny (or part of a general theft statute) in some jurisdictions, others define it as a separate crime.

Similar to fraud is the crime of false pretenses. False pretense is a statutory crime, so the definition will vary from jurisdiction to jurisdiction. Generally, the crime refers to obtaining title to property by falsely representing facts to the owner with the intent to defraud that person. The crime of false pretenses was necessary to cover a loophole in the common law of larceny; for if by false pretense a person obtained title to property but did not get possession of that property, a larceny had not been committed. The crime of false pretenses covers this act, and most U.S. jurisdictions have followed the English precedent.

Property rights were extremely important in the common law. The emergence and development of crimes to protect property has been closely related to those rights. Some of the restrictions on the crimes or requirements for the crimes do not make sense in modern times. Some of those have changed, while others remain. It is therefore important to understand the common law of property crimes.

Chapter 9

I. The Means of Acquisition
 A. Distinctions among the different theft offenses are explicable in terms of a long history of expansion of the role of the criminal law in protecting property. *Model Penal Code and Commentaries, Comment to Sec. 223.1.*
 B. Trespassory Takings
  1. One who is in lawful possession of goods or money of another cannot commit larceny by feloniously converting them to his own use, for the reason that larceny, being a criminal trespass on the right of possession, cannot be committed by one who, being invested with that right, is consequently incapable of trespassing on it. *Commonwealth v. Tluchak.*
  2. The asportation requirement for a theft reflects a concern that the crucial elements of possession and control were established. Many codes have eliminated the requirement of an asportation and substitute the requirement that the defendant "exercise unlawful control" over the movable property. *People v. Alamo.*
  3. A defendant can be convicted of larceny for concealing merchandise, even though he was apprehended before leaving the store. *People v. Olivo.*
  4. If the property taken was delivered by a servant to the defendant by the master's direction, the offense cannot be larceny, regardless of the purpose of the defendant. *Topolewski v. State.*
  5. The law of aggravated theft developed to protect not only against misappropriation, but also against injuries that may result from peculiarly dangerous means devised for accomplishing misappropriation. *A Rationale of the Law of Aggravated Theft.*
 C. Misappropriation
  1. Goods that have reached their destination are constructively in the owner's possession al-

though he may not yet have touched them and, hence, after such termination of transit, the servant who converts them is guilty of larceny, not of embezzlement. *Nolan v. State.*
  2. A person who recovers another's property which has been lost or irresponsibly cast away is a bailee, and if he gives the property to another, that person assumes the duties of a bailee, and may be guilty of larceny by bailee. *Burns v. State.*
   a. Some state statutes abolish the distinction between conversion by a bailee who does or does not break bale or break bulk.
  3. A collection agent receiving money in a fiduciary capacity for a client is within the purview of the Illinois embezzlement statute. *State v. Riggins.*
 D. Fraud
  1. The obtaining of property by trick or fraud, even with the consent of the owner, may constitute larceny. *Hufstetler v. State.*
  2. One who obtains money from another upon the representation that he will perform certain service therewith for the latter, intending at the time to convert the money, and actually converting it, to his own use, is guilty of larceny. *Graham v. United States.*
  3. A defendant cannot be convicted of larceny if his deceit induces the owner to transfer his entire interest in the property, whereas he can be if it induces consent merely to his possession or use of the property. *Theft by False Promises.*
  4. To support a conviction of theft for obtaining property by false pretenses, it must be shown that the defendant made a false pretense or representation with intent to defraud the owner of his property, and that the owner was in fact defrauded. *People v. Ashley.*
  5. The intent to injure or defraud is presumed when the unlawful act, which results in loss or injury, is proved to have been knowingly committed. *Nelson v. United States.*
 E. Blackmail (Extortion)
  1. A demand for settlement of a civil action, accompanied by a malicious threat to expose the wrongdoer's criminal conduct, if made with

intent to extort payment, against his will, constitutes the crime of blackmail. *State v. Harrington*.

    a. Examples of threats include threats of injury to person or property, threats to accuse of crime, threats to make defamatory disclosures and, in some states, threats to disclose secrets or private matters.

  2. The extortion statutes were intended to prevent the collection of money by the use of fear induced by means of threats to accuse a debtor of a crime. *People v. Fichtner*.

  3. In blackmail, the heart of the problem is that two separate acts, each of which is a moral and legal right, can combine to make a moral and legal wrong. *Unraveling the Paradox of Blackmail*.

  4. In order to counteract the power of the criminal over the victim, the state must intervene by exercising power over the criminal. *Blackmail: The Paradigmatic Crime*.

  5. The illegality of blackmail is an economically rational rule. If such threats were lawful, there would be an incentive for people to expend resources to develop embarrassing information about others in the hope of then selling their silence. *Blackmail: An Economic Analysis of the Law*.

  6. Policymakers prohibit blackmail less because of economic waste or inefficiency than because they perceive the act of blackmail to be wrong in itself. *Truth and Consequences: The Force of Blackmail's Central Case*.

  F. Consolidation: The principal means of reform, which has gained widespread acceptance, is to consolidate the variety of common law forms of wrongful acquisition of another's property into one single crime, which might be called "theft" or "larceny" and to deprive the differences in modes of acquisition of any legal significance.

II. Property That Will Qualify For Theft

  A. Traditional Theft

    1. In order to be convicted of obtaining property by false pretenses, the "property" must be something capable of being possessed and the title to which can be transferred. *State v. Miller*.

    2. The Government has a property interest in certain of its private records, which it may protect by statute as a thing of value. *United States v. Girard*.

    3. Confidential information is not "property" for the purposes of the law of theft. *Regina v. Stewart*.

    4. If property was owned by two or more persons, none of the owners could commit larceny from the others. *People v. Zinke*.

  B. Mail and Wire Fraud

    1. The mail fraud statute is violated when a fiduciary fails to disclose material information, which he is under a duty to disclose to another, under circumstances where the non-disclosure could or does result in harm to the other. *United States v. Siegel*.

    2. There is no requirement that the government prove that the misappropriated funds were used by the defendant for his own enrichment. *United States v. Weiss*.

    3. The expansion of judicial doctrine in mail fraud cases has at times ignored the restraints of the nulla poena principle in the area of its most basic application: that of requiring the criminal law to give fair notice to potential offenders of the threat of criminal punishment. *The Erosion of Legality in American Criminal Justice: Some Latter-Day Adventures of the Nulla Poena Principle*.

  C. Mens Rea

    1. To be guilty of larceny, the felonious intent must be to deprive the owner of the property permanently. *People v. Brown*.

    2. The mens rea of larceny is simply not satisfied by an intent temporarily to use property without the owner's permission, or even an intent to appropriate outright the benefits of the property's short-term use. *People v. Jennings*.

    3. In a trial for theft, the issue of whether the defendant acted dishonestly is a matter for the jury to decide, not the judge. *Regina v. Feely*.

    4. A good-faith claim of right does not negate the intent to commit robbery by a defendant who uses force to recover cash allegedly owed him. *People v. Reid*.

Commonwealth v. Tluchak

(State) v. (Home Sellers)
166 Pa. Super. 16, 70 A.2d 657 (1950)

M E M O R Y   G R A P H I C

Instant Facts
Tluchak (D) and his wife were convicted of larceny for retaining possession of property which was sold along with their farm.

Black Letter Rule
One who is in lawful possession of the goods or money of another cannot commit larceny by feloniously converting them to his own use, for the reason that larceny, being a criminal trespass on the right of the possession, cannot be committed by one who, being invested with that right, is consequently incapable of trespassing on it.

Case Vocabulary
CONVERSION: The deprivation of another's property without his authorization or justification.
LARCENY: The unlawful taking of another's property with the intention of depriving the owner of its use.

Procedural Basis: Appeal from the lower court's denial of the defendant's motion for a new trial and arrest of judgment following his conviction and sentence for larceny.

Facts: Tluchak (D) and his wife entered into a written contract to sell their farm to the prosecutor and his wife. The agreement did not include any personal property but it did cover "All buildings, plumbing, heating, lighting fixtures, screens, storm sash, shades, blinds, awnings, shrubbery and plants." When the purchasers took possession of the farm, they discovered that certain articles which had been on the premises at the time the agreement was executed were missing. These articles were charged in the indictment as subjects of the larceny. Tluchak (D) and his wife were found guilty of larceny. The court below overruled their motions for new trials and arrest of judgment. Tluchak (D) was sentenced to pay a fine of $50 and to make restitution. This appeal followed.

Issue: Are sellers who refuse or fail to deliver goods sold to their purchasers guilty of larceny?

Decision and Rationale: (Reno, J.) No. While Tluchak (D) contends that the evidence is not sufficient in law to sustain a conviction, we shall assume, for the purposes of this decision, that the testimony established a *sale* of the personal property by Tluchak (D) and his wife to the prosecutor and his wife. That is, Tluchak (D) and his wife sold but failed or refused to deliver the goods to the purchasers. Tluchak (D) and his wife had possession of the goods, not mere custody of them. The evidence indicates that they were allowed to retain possession without trick or artifice and without fraudulent intent to convert them. Presumably title passed upon payment of the purchase price; nevertheless Tluchak (D) and his wife had lawful possession thereafter. One who is in lawful possession of the goods or money of another cannot commit larceny by feloniously converting them to his own use, for the reason that larceny, being a criminal trespass on the right of possession, cannot be committed by one who, being invested with that right, is consequently incapable of trespassing on it. Judgments and sentences reversed.

--- **Analysis:** ---

A person may come into possession of someone else's property in a legal way. If he then converts that property to his own use, or withholds it from the owner so that the owner is deprived of its use, he may be guilty of fraudulent conversion. Thus, although the defendant could not be guilty of larceny because he received the property legally, he can be found guilty of fraudulent conversion because after having received the property, he has deprived the rightful owner of its use. Tluchak (D) and his wife were indicted for larceny only, and of that, the Court was correct in ruling they were clearly not guilty. The Court also leaves open the question that the Tluchaks (D) could possibly have been found guilty of fraudulent conversion, if only they had been charged with that crime. They weren't, however, so the Court was bound to reverse the convictions and discharge the Tluchaks (D).

Topolewski v. State

(Meat Stealer) v. (State)
130 Wis. 244, 109 N.W. 1037 (1906)

M E M O R Y   G R A P H I C

Instant Facts

Topolewski's (D) friend, Dolan, allowed him to steal barrels of meat from Dolan's employer to repay a debt that Dolan owed Topolewski (D).

Black Letter Rule

If property taken was delivered by a servant to the defendant by the master's direction, the offense cannot be larceny, regardless of the purpose of the defendant.

Case Vocabulary

MASTER AND SERVANT: Terms to describe an employer/employee relationship.

Procedural Basis: Appeal from the defendant's conviction for larceny.

Facts: Dolan, an employee of the Plankinton Packing Company, owed Topolewski (D) money. In lieu of payment, Topolewski (D) arranged for Dolan to place three barrels of the company's meat on the loading platform. The plan was for Topolewski (D) to then load the meat barrels on his wagon and drive away as if he were a customer [what a deal!]. Dolan reported the plan to the company's representatives, who instructed him to feign cooperation and carry out his end of the plan. Topolewski (D) took the barrels as planned and was arrested, charged and convicted of stealing the barrels of meat.

Issue: Can a person be convicted of larceny where the property taken was delivered by a servant to the defendant by the master's direction?

Decision and Rationale: (Marshall, J.) No. The case is very near the borderline, if not across it, between consent and nonconsent to the taking of the property. It has been held that if the property was delivered by a servant to the defendant by the master's direction, the offense cannot be larceny, regardless of the purpose of the defendant. In this case the property was not only placed on the loading platform, as was usual in delivering such goods to customers, with knowledge that Topolewski (D) would soon arrive, having a formed design to take it, but the packing company's employee in charge of the platform, Ernst Klotz, was instructed that the property was placed there for a man who would call for it. Klotz had every reason to infer from such a statement that when Topolewski (D) arrived and claimed the right to take the property, that he was the one to which the management referred. He had every right to believe that it was proper to make delivery to Topolewski (D), and he acted accordingly. While Klotz did not physically place the property, or assist in doing do, in the wagon, he stood by, witnessing such placing by Topolewski (D). The evidence showed that Klotz then assisted him in arranging the wagon, and taking the order, in the usual way, from Topolewski (D) as to the disposition of the fourth barrel. Thus Klotz's conduct thereto amounted, practically, to a delivery of the three barrels to Topolewski (D). We cannot well escape the conclusion that this case falls under the condemnation of the rule that where the owner of property by himself or his agent, actually or constructively, aids in the commission of the offense, as intended by the wrongdoer, by performing or rendering unnecessary some act in the transaction essential to the offense, the would-be criminal is not guilty of all the elements of the offense. The judgment is reversed, and the cause remanded for a new trial.

Analysis:

The logical basis for the doctrine relied upon by the Court is that there can be no larceny without a trespass [makes sense]. So, if one procures his property to be taken by another intending to commit larceny, or delivers his property to such other, the latter intending to commit such crime, the element of trespass is lacking and the crime not fully consummated, however plain may be the guilty purpose of the one possessing himself of such property. That does not militate against a person's being free to set a trap to catch one whom he suspects of an intention to commit the crime of larceny, but the setting of such trap must not go further than to afford the would-be thief the amplest opportunity to carry out his purpose. This must occur without such inducement on the part of the owner of the property so as to put him in the position of having consented to the taking. There is a great deal of criticism for practicing deception to facilitate and encourage the commission of a crime. Some believe that the owner's deception is sufficient reason to excuse the would-be criminal, or to preclude his being prosecuted. That criticism is wrong, however. It is the removal of the element of *trespass* or *nonconsent*, from the standpoint of the property owner, that makes this not larceny. (Even though from the standpoint of the would-be criminal, the act may have all the ingredients of larceny.)

Nolan v. State

(Money Thief) v. (State)
213 Md. 298, 131 A.2d 851 (1957)

M E M O R Y   G R A P H I C

Instant Facts

Nolan (D), who worked for a loan company, appropriated the payments customers made to the company while he was working.

Black Letter Rule

Goods which have reached their destination are constructively in the owner's possession although he may not yet have touched them and, hence, after such termination of transit, the servant who converts them is guilty of larceny, not of embezzlement.

Case Vocabulary

APPROPRIATE: Steal.
EMBEZZLEMENT: The fraudulent appropriation to one's own use of property lawfully in his possession.

Procedural Basis: Appeal from the defendant's conviction for embezzlement.

Facts: Nolan (D) was the office manager of the Federal Discount Corporation, a finance company engaged in the business of making loans and collections. The evidence showed that he appropriated money from his employer with the help of a co-worker. As payments were received from customers, the payments would be placed in the cash drawer. At the end of the day, the co-worker would prepare a report showing the daily cash receipts. Nolan (D) would then appropriate some of the cash from the drawer, and his co-worker would recompute the adding tapes to equal the remaining cash [what masterminds!].

Issue: Is an employee who unlawfully appropriates goods from his place of employment, after delivering them to his employer, guilty of embezzlement?

Decision and Rationale: (Collins, J.) No. The law holds that if the case is larceny at common law because the money was taken from the prosecutor's possession, the charge for embezzlement fails. The embezzlement statutes were passed, not to cover any cause within the common law range of larceny, but to cover new cases outside of that range. If the goods were taken from the owner's possession, the crime is larceny, not embezzlement. Goods which have reached their destination are constructively in the owner's possession although he may not yet have touched them and, hence, after such termination of transit, the servant who converts them is guilty of larceny, not of embezzlement. The money was not taken by Nolan (D) until it had been placed in the cash drawer and balanced at the end of the day. When it was taken, the cash was in the possession of the Federal Discount Corporation. We must therefore conclude that there was not sufficient evidence in this case to find Nolan (D) guilty of embezzlement. The case will be remanded for further proceedings in order that the State, if it deems proper, may try Nolan (D) on an indictment for embezzlement and larceny, if such an indictment is returned against Nolan (D).

Concurrence: (Prescott, J.) Courts sometimes indulge in an ethereal refinement between larceny and embezzlement that in practical operation very often results in the criminal escaping his just punishment.

Analysis:

The opinion of Judge Prescott is listed as a concurrence in the opinion, but rather reads as a dissent. This would seem to be a better opinion, as the logic holds better than that of the majority. The majority's opinion gets caught up in dealing with semantics, and the import of the law is pushed to the side. The majority holds that, simply, because the money went into the drawers before its fraudulent conversion, the offense was larceny and not embezzlement. This seems to put the law in a somewhat indefensible position. Does it make any sense to say that if you steal your employer's money *before* it is placed in a drawer you are guilty of embezzlement, but if you steal that same money after it has *first* been placed in that drawer it is larceny, and larceny alone? This is simply too subtle a distinction to make good law [although that doesn't always seem to matter]. A better solution would be to provide that under an indictment for larceny, or for larceny in one count and embezzlement in another, there may be a conviction of either offense.

Burns v. State

(Constable) v. (State)
145 Wis. 373, 128 N.W. 987 (1911)

M E M O R Y   G R A P H I C

Instant Facts

A constable unlawfully kept a roll of money he recovered from a man he arrested.

Black Letter Rule

A person who recovers another's property, which has been lost or irresponsibly cast away, is a bailee, and if he gives the property to another, that person assumes the duties of a bailee, and may be guilty of "larceny by bailee."

Case Vocabulary

BAILEE: Party holding goods of another for a specific purpose.
BONA FIDE: Without fraud or deceit.
INTER PARTES: Between two or more parties.

Procedural Basis: Appeal from the defendant's conviction of larceny by bailee.

Facts: Burns (D), a constable, arrested an insane man after pursuit. Another of the pursuers gave to Burns (D) a roll of money which the insane man had thrown away during his flight [he must be insane!]. Evidence was presented that Burns (D) (the constable) misappropriated the funds, and a jury convicted him of larceny by bailee.

Issue: Did the court err by instructing the jury to the effect that if Burns (D) converted to his own use any of the insane man's money he did so as bailee?

Decision and Rationale: (Marshall, J.) No. Error is assigned because the court instructed the jury to the effect that, if Burns (D) converted to his own use any of the insane man's money he did so as bailee. It is suggested that the court should have defined the term "bailee," as used in the statute, and left it to the jury to find the fact as to whether the circumstances satisfied such statute or not. A court may properly instruct a jury in a criminal case, as well as any other, respecting any fact, or facts, established by the evidence beyond any room for reasonable controversy. An essential of any ultimate conclusion sought, it is not harmful error, if error at all, to treat such essential as having been proven, as the court here did in saying that Burns (D) was a bailee of whatever of the insane man's money came into his possession. Taking possession without present intent to appropriate raises all the contractual elements essential to a bailment. So the person who bona fide recovers the property of another which has been lost, or irresponsibly cast away by an insane man, as in this case, is a bailee as much as if the same property were intrusted to such person by contract *inter partes*. In the latter case the contract creates the duty. In the former the law creates it. The finder of property who voluntarily bona fide takes it into his possession, has immediately imposed upon him by law the duties of a depository, the mildest type as regards degree of duty of bailee. So the finder here of the cast-away money was clearly a bailee, and when his duties were voluntarily assumed by Burns (D) he became such. As there was no controversy in respect to such finding and assumption, the court's reference to the matter was proper. Burns (D) also argues that if he is guilty of any offense, it was that of having broken the package and appropriating only a part of it, thus committing the offense of larceny, not conversion by bailee. It is sufficient to answer that the purpose of the statute was to abolish the distinction between conversion by a bailee of an entire thing, and conversion of part of the contents. Thus Burns' (D) conviction is proper, and as such, is affirmed.

Analysis:

It seems that Burns' (D) flawed argument [though a worthy effort] was that a bailment was not established by the evidence because some sort of contract between the parties was essential. However, no particular ceremony or actual meeting of the minds is necessary to the creation of a bailment. If one, without the trespass which characterizes ordinary larceny, comes into possession of any personalty of another and is duty bound to exercise some degree of care to preserve and restore the thing to such other, or to some person for that other, or otherwise account for the property as that of such other, according to circumstances, he is a bailee. It is the element of lawful possession, however created, and the duty to account for the thing as the property of another, that creates the bailment, regardless of whether such possession is based on contract in the ordinary sense or not. It is said generally that a bailment is created by delivery of the personalty to one person by another to be dealt with as the property of such other person under a contract, express or implied, but the word "contract" is used in a broad sense. The mutuality essential to the contractual feature may be created by operation of law as well as by the acts of the parties with intention to contract, such as in this case. Thus, it makes no difference whether the thing is given to a person by the owner, or another, or by someone for the owner or by the law to the same end. Note that Burns (D) could not be found guilty of larceny because he had the right to possession of the money. Thus, he could only be found guilty if there were a special statute for larceny by bailee (as there was). Some state statutes, as in this case, abolish the distinction between conversion by a bailee who does or does not break bale or break bulk.

State v. Riggins

(State) v. (Collections Agent)
8 Ill. 2d 78, 132 N.E.2d 519 (1956)

I SWEAR THEY HAVEN'T PAID THE ACCOUNT, YET!

M E M O R Y   G R A P H I C

Instant Facts

Riggins (D), a collection agent, misappropriated money he collected for accounts due to his employer, Tarrant.

Black Letter Rule

A collection agent receiving money in a fiduciary capacity for a client is within the purview of the Illinois embezzlement statute.

Case Vocabulary

AGENT: One authorized by a party to act on that party's behalf.

FIDUCIARY: A person having a legal duty, created by his undertaking, to act for the benefit of another.

Procedural Basis: Appeal from appellate court's reversal of the defendant's indictment and conviction for embezzlement.

Facts: Riggins (D) was the owner and operator of a collection agency, maintaining an office, full- and part-time employees, and a clientele of 500 persons and firms for whom he collected delinquent accounts. He approached Dorothy Tarrant, operator of Cooper's Music and Jewelry, and asked her if he could collect her firm's delinquent accounts. As a result, they reached and oral agreement whereby Riggins (D) was to undertake the collections. Riggins (D) was to receive one third on city accounts and one half on out-of-city accounts [not a bad payoff]. It was further agreed that he need not account for the amounts collected until a bill was paid in full, at which time he was to remit by check. The parties operated under this agreement for almost two years. During that time, Tarrant exercised no control over Riggins (D) as to the time or manner of collecting the accounts, and with her knowledge he commingled funds collected for all his clients in a single bank account. He also used this as a personal account, from which he drew for business, family and personal expenses [hmmm]. Tarrant eventually became aware that Riggins (D) had collected several accounts for her in full, but had not accounted to her [send a collections agent after him!].

Issue: Can a collection agent be convicted of embezzlement in Illinois?

Decision and Rationale: (Hershey, J.) Yes. To decide whether Riggins (D), a collection agent, can be guilty of embezzlement in Illinois, it is helpful to consider our embezzlement statutes in the historical context of this crime. Embezzlement, unknown at common law, is established by statute, and its scope, therefore, is limited to those persons designated therein. Viewed in their entirety, our laws relating to embezzlement are broad and comprehensive. In this instance, we are particularly interested in the general embezzlement statute, and the special statute under which Riggins (D) was indicted. In significant part, the statute provides that "any clerk, agent, servant, . . . receiving any money, . . . in his fiduciary capacity . . . shall be punished . . . [for] larceny . . . irrespective of . . . any commission or interest in such money." It can hardly be disputed but that Riggins (D) acted as agent for Tarrant in collecting her accounts. He undertook the collections on her behalf by virtue of authority which she delegated to him. He had no right to collect from anyone except as authorized by her and was required to render a full account of all matters entrusted to him, the same as any agent. We conclude that Riggins (D) was an "agent" of Tarrant, receiving money in a "fiduciary capacity" and, therefore, within the purview of said embezzlement statute.

Dissent: (Schaefer, J.) The conclusion of the majority that Riggins (D) was an agent rests upon the assertion that the term "agent" as used in the embezzlement statutes is construed in its popular sense. That generalization runs counter to the basic rule that criminal statutes are strictly construed. If "agent" has the broad meaning which the majority gives it, each of the other terms is superfluous because all are embraced within the single term "agent." Many of the specific enumerations in the statute referred to by the majority likewise become largely, if not entirely, meaningless, for the particular relationships they seek to reach are also swallowed up in the expanded definition of the term "agent."

Analysis:

The critical question in this case is whether Riggins (D) was the agent of Tarrant. The majority has no difficulty in ruling that indeed Riggins (D) was Tarrant's agent. The question does not truly seem to be as easy as the majority makes it. Riggins (D) maintained his own office, had his own employees, and collected accounts for approximately 500 other individuals and firms. He was subject to no control whatsoever by any of his clients in making his collections. His clients knew that he kept all of his collections in a single account. It seems that the picture would be quite different, and Riggins (D) would not be labeled Tarrant's agent, if vicarious liability was sought to be asserted against Tarrant on account of Riggins' (D) conduct in the course of his collection activities. Thus, the majority may have oversimplified this case, and arrived at a less than ideal conclusion. That is not to say that Riggins' (D) conduct in this situation should not be made criminal, however the Court's justification seems to be lacking.

Hufstetler v. State

(Gas Thief) v. (State)
37 Ala. App. 71, 63 So. 2d 730 (1953)

M E M O R Y   G R A P H I C

Instant Facts
Hufstetler (D) drove away from a service station without paying for 6½ gallons of gas.

Black Letter Rule
The obtaining of property by trick or fraud, even with the consent of the owner, may constitute larceny.

Case Vocabulary

FALSE PRETENSES: Obtaining property as a result of misrepresentations.
PETIT LARCENY: Theft of low value; exact amount is set by statute.
TRESPASS: A wrongful interference with the possession of property.

Procedural Basis: Appeal from the defendant's conviction by the court on a charge of petit larceny.

Facts: Hufstetler (D) drove an automobile up to the gasoline tanks at a service station. There were two or three other men in the car with him, and a man in the back seat got out, went into the store and asked if there was a telephone. Whorton told him there was no telephone [a plan is beginning to form], and the man said he wanted some gasoline. He then went back and got in the car. Whorton asked the man how much gas he wanted, and he was told to "fill it up." Whorton put 6½ gallons of gasoline in the car and the man in the back seat then told him to get a quart of oil [can't ya just see it coming?]. When Whorton went for the oil, Hufstetler (D) drove off with all the men in the car without paying for the gasoline. The gasoline was valued at $1.94 [wow, what a score!].

Issue: Does driving away without paying for gas constitute petit larceny?

Decision and Rationale: (Carr, J.) Yes. The only question of critical concern is whether, on the basis of the evidence presented, the judgment of conviction can be sustained. Hufstetler's (D) attorney urges that Whorton voluntarily parted with the possession and ownership of the gasoline [yeah, sure!]. In this case, the circumstances clearly show that by the application of the well known doctrine of aid and abet, Hufstetler (D) secured the possession of the gasoline by trick or fraud. The obtaining of the property by the consent of the owner under such conditions will not necessarily prevent the taking from being larceny. In other words, an actual trespass is not always required to be proven. The trick or fraud vitiates the transaction, and it will be deemed that the owner still retained the constructive possession. Additionally, it is certainly a logical conclusion that Whorton had no intention of parting with the ownership of the property until he had received pay therefor. The element of Hufstetler's (D) intent is inferable from the factual background. Affirmed.

Analysis:

The evidence in this case is so clear-cut, it seems that the Court could not have arrived at any other conclusion. Hufstetler's (D) argument that the store owner voluntarily parted with the gasoline without payment is simply laughable. The Court probably had to work harder to answer with a straight face. The Court also embarks upon a means to distinguish between the offenses of larceny, false pretenses, and embezzlement [probably to fill up space in the opinion]. If a person honestly receives the possession of goods and then fraudulently converts them to his own use, that is embezzlement. If possession is obtained by fraud, and the owner intends to part with his title as well as his possession, that is the offense of obtaining property by false pretenses. Finally, if the possession is fraudulently obtained, with the owner's intent to part with merely his possession and not his title, the offense is larceny. Since it was ruled that Hufstetler (D) secured the possession of the gasoline by fraud, it is clear that larceny is the correct offense.

Graham v. United States

(Attorney) v. (Government)
187 F. 2d 87 (1950)

M E M O R Y   G R A P H I C

Instant Facts

Graham (D), an attorney, was charged with having stolen $2,000 from his client Gal, an immigrant who did not speak English well.

Black Letter Rule

One who obtains money from another upon the representation that he will perform certain service therewith for the latter, intending at the time to convert the money, and actually converting it, to his own use, is guilty of larceny.

Case Vocabulary

CHATTEL: Any tangible, movable, personal property.
GRAND LARCENY: Theft of a high value; required amount set by statute.

Procedural Basis: Appeal from the defendant's judgment and conviction for grand larceny.

Facts: Graham (D), an attorney [uh oh], was consulted in his professional capacity by Francisco Gal. Gal had been arrested and charged with disorderly conduct. He was seeking American citizenship and was concerned that the arrest would impede or bar his attainment of that goal. Gal's command of the English language was far from complete, and his testimony was that Graham (D) told him he would have to "talk to the policeman" because "money was talk." He further testified that Graham (D) told him he would charge him $200 for a fee; that he would have to pay an additional $2,000 for the police; and that Graham (D) told him "don't mention the money for nobody and the police either." As a result, Gal testified that he paid Graham (D) a total of $2,100 (of which he said $200 was paid as a legal fee). The police officer who originally had arrested Gal testified that he went to Graham's (D) office, and after talking with Graham (D), told Gal that he wasn't in any trouble. The officer testified that Graham (D) did not then or at any time offer or give him money. Graham (D) testified that the entire payment was intended as a fee for legal services [and what a fair price it was!]; that he had never mentioned money for the police; and that no part of the money was in fact paid to the police or anyone else, but was kept by Graham (D).

Issue: Did the trial court err in not sufficiently distinguishing between the situation where one obtains complete title to another's property by fraud or trick and the case where possession only is obtained?

Decision and Rationale: (Washington, J.) No. Graham's (D) principal contentions are, first, that the evidence supports the proposition that Gal voluntarily gave Graham (D) complete title to the money and therefore Graham (D) is entitled to a directed verdict. We think this contention without merit. If the jury believed Gal's testimony and did not believe Graham (D), we think it possible for the jury to conclude beyond a reasonable doubt that Graham (D) fraudulently induced Gal to give him the $2,000 to be used to bribe the police, that Graham (D) did not intent so to use the money, and converted it to his own use. This would be larceny by trick. Graham (D) also contends that the trial court's charge to the jury was erroneous in not sufficiently distinguishing between the situation where one obtains complete title to another's property by fraud or trick and the case where possession only is obtained. The appropriate Code section provides: "Whoever shall feloniously take and carry away anything of value of the amount or value of $50 or upward, . . . shall suffer imprisonment of not less than one nor more than ten years." Interpreting this statute, this court has held that one who obtains money from another upon the representation that he will perform certain service therewith for the latter, intending at the time to convert the money, and actually converting it, to his own use, is guilty of larceny. In classic terminology, the distinction drawn by the common law is between the case of one who gives up possession of a chattel for a special purpose to another who by converting it to his own use is held to have committed a trespass, and the case of one who, although induced by fraud or trick, nevertheless actually intends that title to the chattel shall pass to the wrongdoer. Thus, under the circumstances in this case, Graham (D) can be found guilty of larceny, for title to the money remained in Gal until the accomplishment of the purpose for which he gave Graham (D) the money. The judgment of the District Court is affirmed.

Analysis:

Larceny by trick is theft by stealth. It punishes misappropriation effected by unauthorized disposition of the owner's property. The focus is upon the defendant's behavior behind the owner's back, that is, did it amount to an unauthorized misappropriation? One cause of confusion is that larceny by trick requires some deceit in addition to the unauthorized disposition of property which is its gravamen. It is thus thought of as a type of theft by fraud. However, the requirement of deceit in larceny by trick stems from its history rather than its function and plays a minor role. It permits a circumvention of the requirement of a "trespassory taking" in order to reach a misappropriation by a person in possession as common law larceny. Fraud for this highly technical purpose need not be subjected to close scrutiny or held to an exacting standard, for there is adequate external evidence of Graham's (D) antisocial bent in his subsequent misappropriation. Indeed it is true generally that the only substantial evidence of the initial fraud is found in the subsequent unauthorized appropriation. Thus it can be said that larceny by trick does not punish deceit, it punishes the subsequent unauthorized misappropriation.

People v. Ashley

(State) v. (Business Manager)
42 Cal. 2d 246, 267 P.2d 271 (1954)

M E M O R Y   G R A P H I C

Instant Facts

Ashley (D), a business manager, conned two old women out of over $25,000 by deceiving them and threatening them.

Black Letter Rule

To support a conviction of theft for obtaining property by false pretenses, it must be shown that the defendant made a false pretense or representation with intent to defraud the owner of his property, and that the owner was in fact defrauded.

Case Vocabulary

FALSE PROMISE: Misstatement as to a future fact; modern statutes include false promises in the definition of false pretenses.

Procedural Basis: Appeal from the defendant's conviction and the court's order denying the defendant's motion for a new trial.

Facts: Ashley (D), the business manager of a corporation chartered for the purpose of "introducing people," obtained a loan of $7,200 from Mrs. Russ, a 70 year-old woman [now that's dirty]. He promised Mrs. Russ that the loan would be secured by a first mortgage on certain improved property of the corporation, and that the money would be used to build a theater on other property owned by the corporation. In fact, the corporation leased but did not own the improved property, and no theater was ever built. The money was used instead to meet Ashley's (D) corporation's operating expenses. After Ashley (D) received the money, Mrs. Russ frequently quarreled with him over his failure to deliver the promised first mortgage. She finally received a note of the corporation secured by a second trust deed on some unimproved property owned by the corporation. She testified that she accepted this security because Ashley (D) told her to "take that or nothing." She subsequently received four postdated checks in payment of the loan. After it became apparent that these checks would not be paid, Ashley (D) requested an extension. Mrs. Russ granted the extension after Ashley (D) threatened to kill himself if she refused so that she might be paid from the proceeds of his life insurance policies [take the insurance!]. Ashley (D) also obtained $13,590 from a Mrs. Neal, representing that the corporation intended to use the money to buy a theater. She was initially told that the loan would be secured by a trust deed on the theater building and that she would have good security for her loan because the corporation was worth half a million dollars. However, after obtaining the money, Ashley (D) issued Mrs. Neal a note of the corporation for $13,500. Subsequently, she loaned the corporation an additional $4,470, receiving a note for $17,500 in exchange for the previous note. Mrs. Neal testified that when she hesitated in making the additional loan, Ashley (D) placed a gun on his desk and threatened her [ooh, big man with a gun!]. The corporation did not buy the theater, Mrs. Neal never received the trust deed, and the money was deposited to the corporation's account. The case went to the jury with instructions relating to larceny by trick and device and obtaining property by false pretenses.

Issue: Did Ashley (D) knowingly and with intent to deceive make false promises to obtain property in violation of California statute?

Decision and Rationale: (Traynor, J.) Yes. Ashley's (D) defense was not based on distinctions between title and possession, but rather he contends that there was no unlawful taking of any sort. To support a conviction of theft for obtaining property by false pretenses, it must be shown that Ashley (D) made a false pretense or representation with intent to defraud the owners of their property, and that the owners were in fact defrauded. It is unnecessary to prove that Ashley (D) benefitted personally from the fraudulent acquisition. The false pretense or representation must have materially influenced the owners to part with their property, but the false pretense need not be the sole inducing cause. If the conviction rests primarily on the testimony of a single witness that the false pretense was made, the making of the pretense must be corroborated. In this state, false promises can provide the foundation of a civil action for deceit. In such actions, something more than nonperformance is required to prove the defendant's intent not to perform his promise. Nor is proof of nonperformance alone sufficient in criminal prosecutions based on false promises. In such prosecutions the People must, as in all criminal prosecutions, prove their case beyond a reasonable doubt. Any danger, through the instigation of criminal proceedings by disgruntled creditors, to those who have blamelessly encountered "commercial defaults" must, therefore, be predicated upon the idea that trial juries are incapable of weighing the defendant's fraudulent intent beyond a reasonable doubt, or that appellate courts will be derelict in discharging their duty to ascertain that there is sufficient evidence to support a conviction. Moreover, in cases of obtaining property by false pretenses, it must be proved that any misrepresentations of fact alleged by the People were made knowingly and with intent to deceive. If such misrepresentations are made innocently or inadvertently, they can no more form the basis for a prosecution for obtaining property by false pretenses than can an innocent breach of contract. If false promises were not false pretenses, the legally sophisticated, without fear of punishment, could perpetrate on the unwary fraudulent schemes like that divulged by the record in this case. The inclusion of false promises within the statutory sections will not materially encumber business affairs. The judgment and order denying the motion for a new trial are affirmed.

Concurrence: (Schauer, J.) I concur in the judgment solely on the ground that the evidence establishes, with ample corroboration, the making by Ashley (D) of false representations as to existing facts. On that evidence the convictions should be sustained pursuant to long accepted theories of law.

Analysis:

In a prosecution for obtaining property by the making of a false promise, knowingly and with intent to deceive, the matter to be proved is purely subjective. It is not, like the specific intent in such a crime as burglary, a mere element of the crime; it is, in any significant sense, all of the crime. The proof will necessarily be of objective acts, entirely legal in themselves, from which inferences as to the ultimate illegal subjective fact will be drawn. But, whereas in burglary the proof of the subjective element is normally as strong and reliable as the proof of any objective element, in this type of activity the proof of such vital element can almost never be reliable; it must inevitably depend on inferences drawn by creditors, prosecutors, jurors, and judges from facts and circumstances which by reason of their nature cannot possibly exclude innocence with any certainty. Such inferences as proof of the alleged crime have long been recognized as so unreliable that they have been excluded from the category of acceptable proof. The suggestion the majority makes that it is inconceivable "that trial juries are incapable of weighing the defendant's fraudulent intent beyond a reasonable doubt, or that appellate courts will be derelict in discharging their duty" affords no substantial basis for striking down a rule of proof. With the rule the majority now enunciates, no man, no matter how innocent his intention, can sign a promise to pay in the future, or to perform an act at a future date, without subjecting himself to the risk that at some later date others, in the light of differing perspectives and subsequent events, may conclude that the accused should have known that he could not perform as he promised. And, if he as a reasonable man should have known, then it may be inferred that he did know, and convictions will be affirmed regardless of true intent.

Nelson v. United States

(Appliance Salesman) v. (Government)
227 F.2d 21 (1955)

M E M O R Y   G R A P H I C

Instant Facts

Nelson (D) lied to his supplier regarding a security interest he offered in return for more credit, and then he defaulted on his account.

Black Letter Rule

The intent to injure or defraud is presumed when the unlawful act, which results in loss or injury, is proved to have been knowingly committed.

Case Vocabulary

CHATTEL MORTGAGE: A conveyance of some present legal or equitable right in personal property as security.
DEMAND NOTE: A note which is payable immediately upon presentation.

Procedural Basis: Appeal from the defendant's conviction for obtaining goods by false pretenses.

Facts: Nelson (D) purchased merchandise for resale over a period of months from Potomac Distributors. His account was in arrears more than thirty days when he sought immediate possession of two television sets and a washing machine, which he had already sold and received payment for. Schneider, the secretary-treasurer for Potomac Distributors, told Nelson (D) that no further credit could be extended to him because of his overdue indebtedness. Nelson (D) offered to give security for the desired items as well as for the delinquent account. He represented himself as the owner of a Packard car for which he paid $4,260.50, but failed to disclose an outstanding prior indebtedness on the car of $3028.08 secured by a chattel mortgage in favor of City Bank [sucker!]. Instead, he represented that he owed only one payment of $55, not then due. Relying on such representations, Potomac Distributors delivered two televisions worth $136 each to Nelson (D), taking in return a demand note for the entire indebtedness, past and present, secured by the chattel mortgage on the Packard and the television sets. When Nelson's (D) promised payment was not forthcoming, Schneider attempted to locate him but learned he had left town [oops!]. The Packard about that time was in a collision, incurring damage of about $1,000, and was thereupon repossessed on behalf of the bank which held the prior lien for Nelson's (D) car purchase indebtedness [oops again!].

Issue: Were Nelson's (D) misrepresentations material enough to constitute fraud?

Decision and Rationale: (Danaher, J.) Yes. Nelson (D) argues that Potomac Distributors could not have been defrauded, for the car had an equity of between $900 and $1,000 when he offered it as security, which was roughly five times the value of the two television sets. That fact is immaterial. Nelson (D) has sold two television sets, and apparently had taken payment therefor although he had no television sets to deliver to his customers. He could not get the sets from Potomac Distributors without offering security for his past due account as well as for his present purchase. In order to get them he lied. He now complains because his victim believed him when he lied. He argues that the misrepresentations were not material although the victim, Potomac Distributors testified, and the jury could properly find, that it would not have parted with its goods except in reliance upon Nelson's (D) statements. He argues that there was no proof of an intent upon his part to defraud his victim, however wrongful acts knowingly or intentionally committed can neither be justified nor excused on the ground of innocent intent. The intent to injure or defraud is presumed when the unlawful act, which results in loss or injury, is proved to have been knowingly committed. Affirmed.

Dissent: (Miller, J.) The majority is wrong in permitting the jury to infer that Nelson (D) intended to defraud, and to conclude that he then did fraudulently obtain from Potomac Distributors the three articles purchased. I suggest it is wholly irrational to presume or infer that one intends to defraud when he buys goods on credit and safeguards that credit by giving more than triple security for it – no matter if he does falsely pretend that the security is even greater. It is equally illogical to conclude that the creditor was thereby defrauded.

Analysis:

The difference in opinion between the majority and the dissent is really quite remarkable, however it seems the dissent was snowed by Nelson (D). The dissent believes, and heartily argues, that Nelson was merely guilty of a moral wrong in falsely and grossly misrepresenting his debt to the bank, but that in the circumstances he should not have been indicted and convicted of it. The dissent strongly believes that a grave injustice has been done in this case, as even a liar is entitled to the full protection of the law. While this is a nice sentiment, the dissent is blindly setting aside the facts presented. Nelson (D) purposely misled his supplier, Potomac Distributors, in order to get merchandise from it. He would not have been able to obtain the goods any other way, and so he lied. The fact that the car had a value in excess of the value of the television sets does not relieve him of this falsehood, for if he truly believed that was enough he wouldn't have needed to lie in the first place. Additionally, Nelson (D) promised to make a cash payment on the note within a few days. Again he defaulted, and even left town! The evidence could not be more indicative of an intent to defraud Potomac Distributors. The majority was correct in its decision upholding the lower court's conviction of Nelson (D).

A THREAT OF ANY PUBLIC ACCUSATION IS AS MUCH WITHIN THE REASON OF THE BLACKMAIL STATUTE AS A THREAT OF A FORMAL COMPLAINT

State v. Harrington

(State) v. (Blackmailing Attorney)
128 Vt. 242, 260 A.2d 692 (1969)

M E M O R Y   G R A P H I C

Instant Facts

Mrs. Morin's attorney wrote a letter to her husband threatening exposure of his adultery and other improprieties if he didn't agree to her divorce settlement.

Black Letter Rule

A demand for settlement of a civil action, accompanied by a malicious threat to expose the wrongdoer's criminal conduct, if made with intent to extort payment, against his will, constitutes the crime of blackmail.

Case Vocabulary

CONTINGENT FEE: Charge for attorney's services which are dependent upon a successful outcome in the case.
BLACKMAIL: Malicious threatening of a person to compel him to do an act against his will.
EXTORTION: Used interchangeably with blackmail.
STIPULATION: An agreement made by the parties relating to the business before the court.

Procedural Basis: Appeal from the defendant's conviction for extortion.

Facts: John Harrington (D) was an attorney [another one!?] retained by Mrs. Morin to obtain a divorce from her husband. As Mrs. Morin was without funds, Harrington (D) agreed to work on a contingent fee basis. The couple owned assets worth approximately $50,000, including a motel where the two had previously lived. Harrington (D) and Mrs. Morin arranged to obtain evidence of Mr. Morin's infidelity by hiring a woman, armed with a tape recorder, to entice him into having sex with her in one of his motel rooms [very clever]. She succeeded, and at the appropriate moment, Harrington (D) and his associates entered the room and took pictures of Mr. Morin and the woman naked in bed [caught with his pants down -- literally!]. Several days later, Harrington (D), in the presence of Mrs. Morin, dictated a latter to Mr. Morin proposing a settlement of the divorce action in which she would receive her divorce, give up her interest in the marital assets, waive alimony, and receive a lump sum of $175,000. The letter also provided that Mr. Morin would also receive all recordings and photos from the incident in the hotel room. The letter ended by saying that if Mr. Morin did not accept the offer, divorce proceedings would be brought, alleging adultery, and would require the disclosing of the infidelity, as well as other improprieties Mr. Morin was involved in with respect to the IRS and Customs Service. A photograph from the hotel room was included in the letter to Mr. Morin.

Issue: Did the letter constitute a threat towards Mr. Morin in support of a demand for a cash settlement in violation of the state's extortion statute?

Decision and Rationale: (Holden, C.J.) Yes. A Vermont statute provides: "A person who maliciously threatens to accuse another of a crime or offense, or with an injury to his person or property, with intent to extort money or other pecuniary advantage, or with intent to compel the person so threatened to do an act against his will, shall be imprisoned in the state prison not more than two years or fined not more than $500. Harrington (D) maintains that his letter does not constitute a threat to accuse Mr. Morin of the crime of adultery, but merely to bring an embarrassing, reputation-ruining divorce proceeding unless a stipulation could be negotiated. We believe that the statute is aimed at blackmailing, and a threat of any public accusation is as much within the reason of the statute as a threat of formal complaint, and is much easier made, and may be quite as likely to accomplish its purpose. There is nothing in the statute that requires such a restricted meaning of the word "accuse," and to restrict it thus would destroy the efficacy of the act. Harrington (D) also urges that the totality of the evidence does not exclude the inference that he acted merely as an attorney, attempting to secure a divorce for his client on the most favorable terms possible. This, of course, was the theory of the defense. However, quite clearly, the veiled threats in Harrington's (D) letter exceeded the limits of his representation of Mrs. Morin in the divorce action. A demand for settlement of a civil action, accompanied by a malicious threat to expose the wrongdoer's criminal conduct, if made with intent to extort payment, against his will, constitutes the crime alleged in the indictment. Judgment affirmed.

Analysis:

The Court once again deals with a smooth-talking lawyer. The letter that Harrington (D) wrote and marked "personal and confidential," makes a private accusation of adultery in support of a demand for a cash settlement. An incriminating photo was enclosed for the avowed purpose of demonstrating that Harrington and Mrs. Morin "have all of the proof necessary to prove adultery beyond a reasonable doubt." According to the writing itself, cost of refusal would be public exposure of incriminating conduct in court. The evidence at hand establishes beyond dispute that Harrington's (D) participation was done with preconceived design. The incriminating evidence which his letter threatens to expose was willfully contrived and procured by a woman hired for that purpose. These factors in the proof are sufficient to sustain a finding that Harrington (D) acted maliciously and without just cause, within the meaning of the criminal statutes. The sum of the evidence supports the further inference that the act was done with intent to extort a substantial contingent fee to Harrington's (D) personal advantage. Thus the evidence of guilt is ample to support Harrington's conviction for blackmail.

People v. Fichtner

(State) v. (Supermarket Manager)

281 A.D. 159, 118 N.Y.S.2d 392, aff'd without opinion, 305 N.Y. 864, 114 N.E.2d 212 (1952)

M E M O R Y   G R A P H I C

Instant Facts

Fichtner (D), a supermarket manager, threatened to accuse Smith publicly of petit larceny unless he signed an admission and paid him $50.

Black Letter Rule

The extortion statutes were intended to prevent the collection of money by the use of fear induced by means of threats to accuse a debtor of a crime.

Case Vocabulary

AIDING AND ABETTING: Active assistance in the commission of a crime.

GOOD FAITH: Total absence of any intention to defraud another party.

MALICE: Intent to cause harm.

Procedural Basis: Appeal from the defendant's conviction for extortion.

Facts: Fichtner (D) is the manager of the Hill Supermarket. He was charged with two counts of extortion due to the fact that he and another, aiding and abetting each other, obtained money from Smith, with his consent, which consent was induced by a wrongful use of fear. The facts are as follows: One day, Smith purchased several items in the store amounting to $12, but left without paying for a $0.53 jar of coffee, which he had concealed in his pocket [just couldn't afford that last 53 cents]. Fichtner (D) asked Smith to return to the store, and then threatened to call the police to have Smith arrested for petit larceny, with resulting publicity in the newspapers and over the radio, unless he paid $75 and signed a paper admitting that during the course of several months he had unlawfully taken merchandise from the store in that amount [hope that's good coffee!]. Smith insisted that the only merchandise he had ever stolen was the jar of coffee that evening, and a $0.65 roll of bologna one week previously. However, he finally signed the paper admitting that he had taken $50 worth of merchandise from the store during a period of four months [pushover!]. That evening Smith paid $25 in cash and promised to pay the balance in weekly installments of $5. Smith testified that he was induced to sign the paper and make the payment because Fichtner (D) threatened to accuse him of petit larceny and to expose him to the disgrace of the criminal charge and the resulting publicity. It is undisputed that the $25 was "rung up" on the store register, went into the company funds, and Fichtner (D) received no part of the money. During the following week, Smith reported the incident to the police, and Fichtner (D) was arrested when Smith, accompanied by a detective, returned to the store and paid the first $5 installment. Fichtner (D) testified that over the course of several weeks he saw Smith steal merchandise in the amount of $5.61, and he honestly believed that during the several months Smith had been shopping there that he had stolen merchandise in the amount of $75. Fichtner (D) also admitted that the Smith incident was not an isolated incident, but rather part of a continuing course of conduct pursued even after warning by the police to discontinue the practice.

Issue: Was the evidence presented sufficient to sustain Fichtner's (D) conviction for extortion?

Decision and Rationale: (Johnston, J.) Yes. Fichtner requested the court to charge that if the jury found that Fichtner (D) honestly believed that the amount which Smith paid or agreed to pay represented the amount of the merchandise he had previously stolen then Fichtner must be acquitted. The court refused this request "except as already charged." Although two members of the court are of the opinion that the trial court was justified in refusing to charge as requested, four members of the court are of the further opinion that the request was legally incorrect and, therefore, should have been refused. In other words, we believe that the portion of the main charge to the effect that, under the circumstances of this case, extortion is committed only when one obtains property from another by inducing fear in that other by threatening to accuse him of crime unless he pays an amount over and above what was rightfully due was more favorable to Fichtner (D) than that which he was entitled to receive. In our opinion, the extortion statutes were intended to prevent the collection of money by the use of fear induced by means of threats to accuse a debtor of a crime, and it makes no difference whether the debtor stole any goods, nor how much he stole, and that Fichtner (D) may properly be convicted even though he believed Smith was guilty of the theft of the supermarket's goods in an amount either equal to or less, or greater than any sum of money obtained from Smith. Nor is Fichtner's (D) good faith in thus enforcing payment of the money alleged to be due to the supermarket a defense. Conviction affirmed.

Dissent: (Wenzel, J.) In my opinion, although the question is one as to which there is a conflict of authority, if Fichtner (D), cting without malice and in good faith, made an honest mistake, he was not guilty of the crime charged. There was no criminal intent.

Analysis:

The jury was permitted to convict Fichtner (D) of the crime of extortion on proof that he had induced Smith, by the threats alleged, to pay to Fichtner (D) more than he rightfully owed for goods which he had stolen, even though Fichtner (D) might have honestly believed that the amount demanded from Smith was the amount which he rightfully owed. Fichtner (D) was not acting in his own behalf, but in that of his employer, in recovering what he believed to be rightfully due it. The law does not authorize the collection of just debts by threatening to accuse the debtor of crime, even though the debtor is in fact guilty of the crime. It makes no difference whether the indebtedness for which a defendant demands repayment is one arising out of the crime for the prosecution of which he threatens the debtor, or is entirely independent and having no connection with the crime which forms the basis of the accusation. The result in both cases is the concealment and compounding of a felony to the injury of the State. It is that result which the extortion statutes were intended to prevent.

State v. Miller

(State) v. (Debtor)
192 Or. 188, 233 P.2d 786 (1951)

MEMORY GRAPHIC

Instant Facts

Miller (D) was convicted of obtaining property by false pretenses for inducing a company to guarantee his indebtedness based upon a false representation.

Black Letter Rule

In order to be convicted of obtaining property by false pretenses, the "property" must be something capable of being possessed and the title to which can be transferred.

 ## Case Vocabulary

CHOSE IN ACTION: A claim or debt upon which a recovery may be made in a lawsuit.
FORGERY: Fraudulent making or altering of a writing with the intent to prejudice the rights of another.
PRIVITY: A relationship between parties which raises some mutuality of interest.

Procedural Basis: Appeal from the defendant's conviction for obtaining property by false pretenses.

Facts: Miller (D) induced the Hub Lumber Company to agree to guarantee his indebtedness to the Howard Cooper Corporation on the false representation that he owned a tractor free of encumbrance and on his executing a chattel mortgage thereto as security. In fact, Miller (D) was purchasing the tractor under a conditional sales contract. He was convicted of obtaining property from Hub Lumber by false pretenses.

Issue: Does obtaining an agreement to pay an indebtedness induced by false pretenses constitute a crime under the Oregon statute?

Decision and Rationale: (Lusk, J.) No. The statute under which this prosecution is attempted to be maintained reads: "If any person shall, by any false pretenses or by any privity or false token, and with intent to defraud, obtain or attempt to obtain, from any other person any money or property whatsoever, or shall obtain or attempt to obtain with the like intent the signature of any person to any writing, the false making whereof would be punishable as forgery, such person, upon conviction thereof, shall be punished by imprisonment." Reduced to its simplest terms, this indictment means that by false pretenses Miller (D) induced the Hub Lumber Company to agree to pay his indebtedness to the Howard Cooper Corporation if he should fail to pay it. The question is whether this amounts to an allegation that, in the sense of the statute, Miller (D) obtained "any property" from the Hub Lumber Company. If not, then the indictment does not charge a crime. This court has recognized that "property" under the statute must be something capable of being possessed and the title to which can be transferred. It need hardly be said that the thing which Miller (D) is charged with obtaining in the present indictment, the guaranty, or, to be more accurate, the benefit of the guaranty which the Hub Lumber Company gave to the Howard Cooper Corporation, could not be possessed, and that there could be no such thing as holding title to it. Had the indictment alleged that Miller (D) obtained the signature of the Hub Lumber Company or its agent to a guaranty of Miller's (D) indebtedness, we would have had an entirely different question. The failure so to allege was not due to an oversight of the pleader but to the facts themselves, for the proof is that no written guaranty was ever executed but merely an oral one. The indictment, in our opinion, does not allege a crime, and the judgment must therefore be reversed and the action dismissed.

Analysis:

The English courts hold that the thing obtained must be the subject of larceny at common law, and accordingly a conviction for obtaining two dogs by false pretenses was quashed because at common law dog stealing is not larceny. Similarly, an indictment for obtaining food and lodging by false pretenses was quashed. Under statutes like the one in this case, many of the American courts take the same view of the law; only certain "things" may be the subject of the crime of false pretenses. The offense of false pretenses, under the English statutes, has always been construed as largely analogous to, and closely bordering upon, that of larceny, and as applying only to personal property, which was capable of manual delivery. Real property under the English law was never the subject of the offense either of cheating or of false pretenses. Even though the statute included "a thing in action," it did not help the prosecution, because the guaranty was not, so far as Miller (D) was concerned, a "thing in action." It is doubtless true that a guaranty is a chose in action, a right to indemnity from the guarantor, but it is the right of the creditor who extends credit on the faith of the guaranty, not of the debtor to whom credit is given. Accordingly, Miller (D) did not receive even a chose in action from the Hub Lumber Company. Similarly, obtaining a loan by fraud is a violation of the statute, however Miller (D) obtained credit not from the victim of his false representations, but from another. Thus the legislature has not undertaken to make every fraud a crime.

United States v. Girard

(Government) v. (Former DEA Agent)
601 F.2d 69 (1969)

M E M O R Y   G R A P H I C

Instant Facts
Girard (D) was a former DEA agent who illegally sold government information and was then double-crossed by his partner in crime.

Black Letter Rule
The Government (P) has a property interest in certain of its private records which it may protect by statute as a thing of value.

 ### Case Vocabulary

OVERBREADTH: A statute which proscribes both improper conduct as well as constitutionally protected conduct.

VAGUENESS: Persons of common intelligence must necessarily guess at a statute's meaning and differ as to its application.

Procedural Basis: Appeal from the defendant's conviction for the unauthorized sale of government property and of conspiring to accomplish the sale.

Facts: Girard (D), a former DEA agent, began discussions with James Bond regarding a proposed illegal venture that involved smuggling a planeload of marijuana from Mexico into the United States [didn't know 007 was one of the bad guys!]. Girard (D) told Bond that for $500 per name he could, through an inside source, secure reports from the DEA files that would show whether any participant in the proposed operation was a government informant. Unfortunately for Girard (D), Bond himself became an informant and disclosed his conversations with Girard (D) to the DEA [ooh, the double-cross!]. Thereafter, dealings between Bond and Girard (D) were conducted under the watchful eye of the DEA. Bond asked Girard (D) to secure reports on four men whose names were furnished to him by DEA agents. DEA records are kept in computerized files, and the DEA hoped to identify the inside source by monitoring access to the four names in the computer bank. In this manner, the DEA learned that Girard's (D) informant was Lambert, a DEA agent who obtained the reports through a computer terminal located in his office.

Issue: Does government information constitute "property" as contemplated by the statute forbidding the unauthorized sale of government property?

Decision and Rationale: (van Graafeiland, J.) Yes. Section 641, so far as pertinent, provides that whoever without authority sells any "record . . . or thing of value" of the United States or who "receives . . . the same with intent to convert it to his use or gain, knowing it to have been embezzled, stolen, purloined or converted," shall be guilty of a crime. Girard (D) contends that the statute covers only tangible property or documents and therefore is not violated by the sale of information. This contention was rejected by the District Judge, and we agree with that decision. Like the District Judge, we are impressed by Congress' repeated use of the phrase "thing of value" in section 641 and its predecessors. These words are found in so many criminal statutes throughout the United States that they have in a sense become words of art. The word "thing" notwithstanding, the phrase is generally construed to cover tangibles as well as intangibles. Although the content of a writing is an intangible, it is nonetheless a thing of value. The existence of a property in the contents of unpublished writings was judicially recognized long before the advent of copyright laws. Although we are not concerned here with the laws of copyright, we are satisfied, nonetheless, that the Government (P) has a property interest in certain of its private records which it may protect by statute as a thing of value. The District Judge also rejected Girard's constitutional challenge to section 641 based upon alleged vagueness and overbreadth, and again we agree with his ruling. Where we are not dealing with Girard's (D) exercise of a First Amendment freedom, we should not search for statutory vagueness that did not exist for Girard (D) himself. Neither should we find a constitutional infirmity simply because the statute might conceivably trespass upon the First Amendment rights of others. In view of the statute's plainly legitimate sweep in regulating conduct, it is not so substantially overbroad that any overbreadth that may exist cannot be cured on a case by case basis. The judgments are affirmed.

Analysis:

The Court made a good decision in determining that the phrase "thing of value" should be construed to cover intangibles as well as tangibles. There are many instances in which this premise holds true. For example, amusement is held to be a thing of value under gambling statutes. Sexual intercourse, or the promise to have sexual intercourse, is a thing of value under a bribery statute. So also are a promise to reinstate an employee, and an agreement not to run in a primary election. The testimony of a witness is a thing of value under 18 U.S.C. section 876, which prohibits threats made through the mails with the intent to extort money or any other "thing of value." Conversion has been held to be the misuse or abuse of property or its use in an unauthorized manner, thus Girard (D) was properly found to have converted DEA's computerized records. Girard (D), a former employee of the DEA, must have known that the sale of DEA confidential law enforcement records was prohibited. The DEA's own rules and regulations forbidding such disclosure may be considered as both a delimitation and clarification of the conduct proscribed by the statute. Thus Girard's (D) conviction was proper.

Regina v. Stewart

(Government) v. (Hired Snoop)
50 D.L.R.4th 1, 41 C.C.C.3d 481 (1988)

M E M O R Y   G R A P H I C

Instant Facts

Stewart (D) was hired to obtain confidential information regarding hotel employees and tried to pay a security guard to snoop in the records.

Black Letter Rule

Confidential information is not "property" for the purposes of the law of theft.

Case Vocabulary

INTER ALIA: Among other things.
PER SE: By means of itself.

Procedural Basis: The accused was acquitted by a single judge court, but on appeal (In Canada, a prosecutor may appeal an acquittal) the Ontario Court of Appeal reversed and entered a verdict of conviction, and the defendant appealed.

Facts: A union attempting to organize the approximately 600 employees of a hotel was unable to obtain the names, addresses and telephone numbers of the employees because of a hotel policy that such information be treated as confidential [how rude!]. Stewart (D), a self-employed consultant, was hired by someone he assumed to be acting for the union to obtain the names and addresses of the employees. Stewart (D) offered a security guard at the hotel, Hart, a fee to obtain this information. Hart reported the offer to his security chief and the police [tattle-tale]. As a result, a subsequent telephone conversation between Hart and Stewart (D) was recorded, and Stewart (D) was indicted for, inter alia, counseling the offense of theft.

Issue: Is confidential information considered "property" for the purposes of the law of theft?

Decision and Rationale: (Lamer, J.) No. We are here dealing not with the theft of a list or any other tangible object containing confidential information, but with the theft of confidential information per se, a pure intangible. The assumption that no tangible object would have been taken was part of the agreed statement of facts, and the case was argued throughout on that basis. The word "anything" is not in itself a bar to including any intangible, whatever its nature. It is clear that to be the object of theft, "anything" must be property in the sense that to be stolen, it has to belong in some way to someone. For instance, no conviction for theft would arise out of a taking or converting of the air that we breathe, because air is not property. It is possible that, with time, confidential information will come to be considered as property in the civil law or even be granted special legal protection by statutory enactment. Even if confidential information were to be considered property under civil law, it does not, however, automatically follow that it qualifies as property for the purposes of criminal law. Conversely, the fact that something is not property under civil law is likewise not conclusive for the purpose of criminal law. Whether or not confidential information is property under the Criminal Code should be decided in the perspective of the criminal law. Indeed, the realm of information must be approached in a comprehensive way, taking into account the competing interests in the free flow of information and in one's right to confidentiality or again, one's economic interests in certain kinds of information. The choices to be made rest upon political judgments that, in my view, are matters of legislative action and not of judicial decision. Appeal allowed; acquittal restored.

Analysis:

The qualification of confidential information as property must be done in each case by examination the purposes and context of the civil and criminal law. It is understandable that one who possesses valuable information would want to protect it from unauthorized use and reproduction. In civil litigation, this protection can be afforded by the courts because they simply have to balance the interests of the parties involved. However, criminal law is designed to prevent wrongs against society as a whole. From a social point of view, whether confidential information should be protected requires a weighing of interests much broader than those of the parties involved. As opposed to the alleged owner of the information, society's best advantage may well be to favor the free flow of information and greater accessibility to all. The criminalization of certain types of conduct should not be done lightly. If the unauthorized appropriation of confidential information becomes a criminal offense, there would be far-reaching consequences that the courts are not in a position to contemplate. Moreover, because of the inherent nature of information, treating confidential information as property simply for the purposes of the law of theft would create a host of practical problems. For instance, what is the precise definition of "confidential information"? Is confidentiality based on the alleged owner's intent or on some objective criteria? At what point does information cease to be confidential and would it therefore fall outside the scope of the criminal law? And should only confidential information be protected under the criminal law, or any type of information deemed to be of some commercial value? It seems that these questions are best left to be determined by Congress rather than by the courts.

United States v. Siegel

(Government) v. (Toy Store Officer)
717 F.2d 9 (1983)

M E M O R Y G R A P H I C

Instant Facts
Siegel (D) was involved in creating a hidden cash fund from the sales of "off the books" merchandise at the store where he was an officer.

Black Letter Rule
The mail fraud statute is violated when a fiduciary fails to disclose material information which he is under a duty to disclose to another under circumstances where the non-disclosure could or does result in harm the other.

Case Vocabulary

BRIBERY: Giving something of value to influence performance of an official duty.
PRIMA FACIE: Not requiring further support to establish credibility.
WIRE FRAUD: A scheme to defraud by means of the use of wire, radio, or television communication in interstate commerce.

Procedural Basis: Appeal from the defendant's conviction for wire fraud.

Facts: Abrams and Siegel (D) were officers and directors of Mego International, a publicly held manufacturer and distributor of toys and games. They were charged with and convicted of violating the wire fraud statute by engaging in a scheme to defraud Mego and its stockholders by violating their fiduciary duties to act honestly and faithfully in the best interest of the corporation and to account for the sale of all Mego property entrusted to them. The fraudulent scheme involved the creation of a hidden cash fund derived from cash sales of merchandise that had been closed out, marked down for clearance, or returned as damaged [oh, so clever]. These "off the books" sales all together generated sales of $100,000 in cash [that's a lot of Legos!]. The indictment charged that Abrams and Siegel (D) used the cash for pay-offs to union officials and to other persons dealing with the corporation.

Issue: Was evidence of self-enrichment sufficient to prove violations of the wire fraud statute?

Decision and Rationale: (Pratt, J.) Yes. While we have described the mail fraud and wire fraud statutes as seemingly limitless, we have also recognized that a mere breach of fiduciary duty, standing alone, may not necessarily constitute a mail fraud. However, we have held that the statute is violated when a fiduciary fails to disclose material information which he is under a duty to disclose to another under circumstances where the non-disclosure could or does result in harm the other. There was testimony which showed that Abrams and Siegel (D) personally received the proceeds from the cash sales and either pocketed them or placed them in the corporate safe deposit box. Further, although the cash sales generated in excess of $100,000, the testimony concerning the use to which the money was put accounted for approximately $31,000, used mainly for illicit payoffs. The reasonable mind can think of several destinations for the more than $69,000 that was missing, and, since we have rejected the view that a jury may not rely upon an inference to support an essential allegation unless no opposite inference may be drawn from the proof, we conclude that the jury could have inferred that Abrams and Siegel (D) used some or all of the remainder of the proceeds for their own benefit, and could have fairly concluded beyond a reasonable doubt that theirs was a scheme to misappropriate the proceeds from the sale of Mego assets for self-enrichment. In affirming Abrams' and Siegel's (D) convictions on the wire fraud counts, we in no way wish to encourage the type of indictment prosecuted here. Twenty counts were brought against five defendants, all but two of whom were acquitted of all charges. Siegel (D) and Abrams, although convicted of the wire fraud charges, were acquitted on several other counts. While we applaud the government's (P) concentration on unrecorded cash sales, a particularly common form of criminal activity, we nevertheless urge the government (P) to think carefully before instituting other massive prosecutions having such slender foundations as this one. Affirmed.

Dissent: (Winter, J.) Once again sailing against the wind in mail or wire fraud cases (or so they are called), I dissent. There is no evidence – *none* – that any of the money was diverted to the personal use of either Siegel (D) or Abrams. The government's (P) prima facie case is thus made out solely by a showing of improper corporate record keeping. Moreover, there is no evidence – again, *none* – that the transactions in question harmed the corporation. Now we are eliminating the need to show fraud. In effect, a new crime – corporate improprieties – which entails neither fraud nor even a victim, has been created.

Analysis:

While the prosecution must show that some harm or injury was contemplated by the scheme, it need not show that direct, tangible economic loss resulted to the scheme's intended victims. In this record there was sufficient evidence from which the jury could reasonably have concluded that Abrams and Siegel (D) received the cash proceeds and used them for non-corporate purposes in breach of their fiduciary duties to act in the best interest of the corporation and to disclose material information to Mego and its stockholders. Abrams and Siegel (D) did not seriously contend that the wire fraud statute is not violated when a corporate officer or employee breaches his fiduciary duty to the corporation by taking the proceeds from unrecorded cash sales and using them for his own benefit. Rather, they argued that even if they did participate in the unrecorded cash sales, the record is devoid of any evidence that the money was used for other than corporate purposes and thus fails to support a finding of a breach of fiduciary duty. Abrams and Siegel (D) claimed that at best the evidence merely shows that they received the proceeds from the cash sales and that Siegel (D) periodically placed the money in the corporate safe deposit box. While neither Abrams nor Siegel (D) testified, they argue that they received none of it for personal use and that any use of the proceeds for labor payoffs served a legitimate corporate purpose and was not in violation of any fiduciary duty. While there is little, if any, direct evidence to show that Siegel (D) and Abrams used the cash proceeds for other than corporate purposes, the court correctly concluded that the record as a whole does support the determination that Abrams and Siegel (D) used the money for their own enrichment, and the jury was proper in so finding.

People v. Brown

(State) v. (Bicycle Thief)
105 Cal. 66, 38 P. 518 (1894)

M E M O R Y   G R A P H I C

Instant Facts

Brown (D), with the intent to eventually return it, took an acquaintance's bicycle to get even with him for throwing oranges at Brown (D).

Black Letter Rule

To be guilty of larceny, the felonious intent must be to deprive the owner of the property permanently.

Case Vocabulary

MENS REA: The mental state accompanying a criminal act.

Procedural Basis: Appeal from the defendant's conviction of burglary.

Facts: Brown (D), a seventeen-year-old boy, entered an acquaintance's house and took a bicycle. He testified that he intended to return the bicycle, but that he just took it temporarily to get even with the other boy. The other boy had thrown oranges at Brown (D), and Brown (D) was angry with him. Before Brown (D) could return the bicycle, he was arrested. He was convicted of burglary on an information charging that he entered a house with intent to commit larceny.

Issue: Can a defendant be convicted of larceny if his intent was to merely deprive the owner of his property temporarily?

Decision and Rationale: (Garoute, J.) No. The court told the jury that larceny may be committed even though it was only the intent of the party taking the property to deprive the owner of it temporarily. This instruction is erroneous. We think the authorities form an unbroken line to the effect that the felonious intent must be to deprive the owner of the property permanently. If the boy's story is true, he is not guilty of larceny in taking the bicycle; yet under the instruction of the court, the words from his own mouth convicted him. For the foregoing reasons, it is ordered that the judgment and order be reversed, and the cause remanded for a new trial.

Analysis:

Why isn't it larceny when someone steals a car and then returns it to its owner? Because, as in this case, there is no intention to permanently deprive. That is why most states have enacted joyriding statutes. Such statutes made it a crime to temporarily deprive the owner of possession. While the mens rea of the taking party need not necessarily be an intention to convert the property to one's own use, still it must in all cases be an intent to wholly and permanently deprive the owner thereof. However, there have been some limited exceptions made judicially and by statute to this requirement. The early courts found that, where the thing taken was abandoned or recklessly exposed to loss by the taker, this fact was not only evidence of an intent to effect a permanent deprivation, but would sustain larceny even if a permanent taking was not the object of the defendant's acts.

Regina v. Feely

(Government) v. (Bookmaker Till Dipper)
2 W.L.R. 201 (1973)

M E M O R Y   G R A P H I C

 Instant Facts

Feely (D) was arrested for borrowing, with the intent to repay, money from the till at his place of employment.

Black Letter Rule

In a trial for theft, the issue of whether the defendant acted dishonestly is a matter for the jury to decide, not the judge.

Case Vocabulary

THEFT: Dishonestly appropriating property belonging to another.

Procedural Basis: Appeal from the defendant's conviction for theft.

Facts: Feely (D) was a branch manager for a firm of bookmakers [an honest trade]. The firm sent a circular to all branch managers that the practice of borrowing money from tills was to stop. Nevertheless, Feely (D) took about £30 from a branch safe the next month [naughty, naughty!]. Four days later, Feely was transferred to another branch. His successor discovered a cash shortage of £40, for which Feely (D) gave him an IOU. Though his successor did not report the deficiency, a member of the firm's security staff did and asked Feely (D) for an explanation. Feely (D) accounted for about £10 by reference to some bets he had paid out, but as to the balance he said that he had taken it because he was "stuck for cash." Feely (D) stated he borrowed the £30 intending to pay it back and that his employers owed him about £70 from which he wanted them to deduct the money. Trial testimony showed that the firm did owe him that amount. He was convicted of the theft of the £30.

Issue: Can it be a defense in law for a man charged with theft, and proved to have taken money, to say that when he took the money he intended to repay it, and had reasonable grounds for believing, and did believe, that he would be able to do so?

Decision and Rationale: (Lawton, L.J.) Yes. The trial judge directed the jury that if Feely (D) had taken the money from either the safe or the till (which was already admitted) it was no defense for him to say that he had intended to repay it and that his employers owed him more than enough to cover what he had taken. At no stage of his summation did the judge leave the jury to decide whether the prosecution had proved that Feely (D) had taken the money dishonestly. This was because the judge seems to have thought that he had to decide as a matter of law what amounted to dishonesty and he expressed his concept of dishonesty as follows: ". . . if someone does something deliberately knowing that his employers are not prepared to tolerate it, is that not dishonest?" We do not agree that judges should define what "dishonestly" means. This word is in common use whereas the word "fraudulently" has acquired as a result of case law a special meaning. Jurors, when deciding whether an appropriation was dishonest can be reasonably expected to, and should, apply the current standards of ordinary decent people. The jury should have been left to decide whether Feely's (D) alleged taking of the money had been dishonest. They were not, with the result that a verdict of guilty was returned without their having given thought to what was probably the most important issue in the case. For this reason we allow the appeal.

Analysis:

There were two decisions the lower court mistakenly relied upon when deciding to take the issue of defining "dishonestly" away from the jury. The first case involved a man who took money from his place of employment without the honest belief that the money could be repaid. That case, however, can easily be distinguished from the facts in this case as a strong inference of fraud was raised by the facts there. In the second case, a man took money from a till without any present intent to replace the money. Such intent was not raised until after he had been charged with the offense of larceny. Again, the facts are significantly different in this case, where Feely (D) made his intention of repayment known immediately. On appeal, this Court was astute enough to distinguish these facts from the prior case law to arrive at a just conclusion. While people who take money from tills without permission are usually thieves, if they do not admit that by pleading guilty however, it is for the jury, not the judge, to decide whether they have acted dishonestly.

People v. Reid

(State) v. (Robber)
69 N.Y.2d 469, 508 N.E.2d 661 (1987)

M E M O R Y   G R A P H I C

Instant Facts
Reid (D) and a friend were convicted of armed robbery for using force to try to recover money allegedly owed to them.

Black Letter Rule
A good-faith claim of right does not negate the intent to commit robbery by a defendant who uses force to recover cash allegedly owed him.

Case Vocabulary
CLAIM OF RIGHT: Doctrine holding that a person is entitled to the property in issue.
ROBBERY: Forcible stealing.

Procedural Basis: Appeal from the Appellate Division's affirmance of the defendant's conviction for armed robbery.

Facts: Reid (D) and Riddles were convicted of armed robberies of money from their victims, despite evidence that they were only trying to recover money owed to them [now that's how to collect a debt!]. The trial court, conducting a trial without a jury, stated that it credited the testimony of Reid (D) that he had taken the money to satisfy a debt, but the court denied him the defense of claim of right because he used force.

Issue: Does a good-faith claim of right negate the intent to commit robbery by a defendant who uses force to recover cash allegedly owed him?

Decision and Rationale: (Simons, J.) No. The issue presented here is whether a good-faith claim of right, which negates larcenous intent in certain thefts, negate the intent to commit robbery by a defendant who uses force to recover cash allegedly owed him. We hold that it does not. We have not had occasion to address the issue, but the Appellate Divisions to which it has been presented have uniformly ruled that claim of right is not a defense to robbery. Their determinations have been based upon the interpretation of the applicable statutes and a policy decision to discourage self-help, and they are consistent with what appears to be the emerging trend of similar appellate court decisions from other jurisdictions. For similar reasons, we conclude that the claim of right defense is not available in this case. We need not decide the quite different question of whether an individual who uses force to recover a specific chattel which he owns may be convicted of robbery. It should be noted, however, that because taking property "from another owner thereof" is an element of robbery, a person who recovers property which is his own (as compared to fungible cash taken to satisfy a claimed debt in the cases before us) may not be guilty of robbery. Consequently, we find the courts in this case correctly denied Reid's (D) request to assert claim of right defenses.

Analysis:

A person commits robbery when, in the course of committing a larceny, he uses or threatens the immediate use of physical force. The larceny statute, in turn, provides that an assertion that property was appropriated under a claim of right made in good faith is a defense to larceny. Since a good-faith claim of right is a defense to larceny, and because robbery is defined as forcible larceny, Reid (D) claimed that claim of right is also a defense to robbery. He conceded the culpability of his forcible conduct, but maintained that because he acted under a claim of right to recover his own property, he was not guilty of robbery, but only of some lesser crime, such as assault or unlawful possession of a weapon. This contention is not without support, as several jurisdictions have held that one who acts under a claim of right lacks the intent to steal and should not be convicted of robbery. That logic is tenable when a person seeks to recover a specific chattel; it is less so when asserted under the circumstances presented in this case. Since such forcible conduct is not merely a transgression against property, but also entails the risk of physical or mental injury to individuals, the Court was correct in determining that it should be subjected to criminal sanctions.